MW01598334

FRESH CITRUS FRUITS

Second Edition

Edited by

Wilfred F. Wardowski

William M. Miller

David J. Hall

William Grierson

Florida Science Source, Inc.
Longboat Key, Florida

The cover photograph was taken at Winter Garden Citrus Growers Association, Winter Garden, Florida. Two of three packinghouse labor intensive areas can be seen with graders in the background and packers in the foreground. The third labor intensive area, hand palletizing, has been replaced in many packinghouses by mechanical palletizing.

FRESH CITRUS FRUITS, Second Edition

Library of Congress Cataloguing-in-Publication Data

Fresh citrus fruits / edited by Wilfred F. Wardowski ... [et al.]. – 2nd ed.
  p. cm.
Includes bibliographical references and index.
ISBN 0-944961-08-8 (hardcover: alk. paper)
1. Citrus fruit industry. 2. Citrus fruits. I. Wardowski, Wilfred F.
HD9259.C52F74 2006
338.1'74304-dc22
                                  2006018765

Current printing (last digit): 10 9 8 7 6 5 4 3 2 1
Published in the United States of America
E. O. Painter Printing Co., DeLeon Springs, Florida

Contents

Contributors

Agustí, Manuel (213). Instituto Agroforestal Mediterráneo, Universidad Politécnica de Valencia (U.P.V.), Camino de Vera s/n, 46022, Valencia, SPAIN; magusti@prv.upv.es

Barry, Graham H. (159). Citrus Research International, Department of Horticultural Science, Stellenbosch University, P. Bag X1, Matieland, 7602 SOUTH AFRICA; gbarry@sun.ac.za

Bocardo, Arturo (135). Department of Economics, University of Veracruz, Xalapa, Veracruz, MEXICO; abocardo@uv.mx

Brown, G. Eldon (339). 501 Hillcrest Drive, Winter Haven, FL 33884, USA; gbrown012 @sprintmail.com

Brown, Galen K.[1] (223). Former Harvesting Director, Florida Department of Citrus, Lake Alfred, FL, USA

Chin, Teung F. (513). USDA, Office of Pest Management Policy, USDA APHIS, 4700 River Road, (Unit 149 Room 3D-06.8), Riverdale, MD 20737-1237, USA; teung.f.chin@usda.gov

Cope, Hugh (175). c/-GPO Box 2216 Adelaide SA, 5001 AUSTRALIA; citrusboard@ adelaide.on.net

Davidson, Mena (153). Agro-Marketing and Consulting. Former General Manager of the Citrus Marketing Board of Israel and former President of CLAM - Comite de Liaison de L'Agrumiculture Mediterraneenne; mena@jaffa.co.il

Eckert, Joseph W. (339). 5539 Malvern Way, Riverside, CA 92056, USA; profeckert@earthlink.net

El-Otmani, Mohamed (67). Professor of Horticulture, Department of Horticulture, Complexe Horticole d'Agadir, Institut Agronomique et Vétérinaire Hassan II, B.P. 728, Agadir 80.000, MOROCCO; melotmani@iavcha.ac.ma

Emond, Jean-Pierre (451). Packaging Science, ABE Co-Director, Center for Food Distribution and Retailing, 229 Frazier Rogers Hall, Museum Road, University of Florida, Gainesville, FL 32611-0570, USA; jpemond@ufl.edu

Forsyth, John (175). Citrus Consultant, 7 Leigh Place, Raymond Terrace NSW 2324 AUSTRALIA; jb.forsyth@bigpond.com

Grierson, William (1, 23, 251, 267, 277, 299, 307, 397, 547). 18 Golf View Circle NE, Winter Haven, FL 33881, USA

Halbert, Susan E. (471). Division of Plant Industry, Florida Department of Agriculture and Consumer Services, P.O. Box 147100, Gainesville, FL 32614-7100, USA; halbers@doacs.state.fl.us

Hall, David J. (421, 513, 527). Agri-Chem Consulting, Inc., 420 North Street, Clermont, FL 34711, USA; agrichem@iag.net

Iwagaki, Isao (143). Emeritus, Faculty of Agriculture, Shizuoka University, 426-1001 348-15 Kamata, Suruga-ku, Shizuoka-shi 421-0133 JAPAN; iwagaki@s9.dion.ne.jp

Kelsey, D. Frank (105, 397). Highland Fresh Technologies, 300 NW Phosphate Blvd., Mulberry, FL 33860, USA; fkelsey@highcor.com

Miller, William M. (277, 299, 307, 547, 583). University of Florida, Citrus Research and Education Center, 700 Experiment Station Road, Lake Alfred, FL 33850, USA; wmmiller@ufl.edu

Muraro, Ronald P. (135). University of Florida, Citrus Research and Education Center, 700 Experiment Station Road, Lake Alfred, FL 33850, USA; rpm@ufl.edu

---

[1]Deceased

Nunes, Maria Cecília do Nascimento (451). Food Science and Human Nutrition Department, Center for Food Distribution and Retailing, University of Florida, IFAS, P.O. Box 110370, Gainesville, FL 32611-0370, USA; cnunes@ifas.ufl.edu

Ortiz de Taranco, José (205). Plaza Cagancha 1329 Ap. 801, Código Postal 12000, Montevideo URUGUAY; tarankez@adinet.com.uy

Pao, Steven (105). Agricultural Research Station, Virginia State University, P.O. Box 9061, Petersburg, VA 23806, USA; spao@vsu.edu

Petracek, Peter (397). Valent BioSciences Corporation, 6131 Oakwood Road, Long Grove, IL 60047, USA; peter.petracek@valent.com

Porat, Ron (153). Department of Postharvest Science of Fresh Produce, ARO, The Volcani Center, P.O. Box 6, Bet Dagan 50250 ISRAEL; rporat@volcani.agri.gov.il

Rabe, Etienne (159). Department of Horticultural Science, Stellenbosch University, P. Bag X1, Matieland, 7602 SOUTH AFRICA; ahort2000@yahoo.com

Reilly, John (513). International Trade Specialist, USDA, FAS, Food Safety and Technical Services, 1400 Independence Ave., SW, Washington, DC 20250-1000, USA; John.Reilly@fas.usda.gov

Ritenour, Mark A. (251). University of Florida, Indian River Research and Education Center, 2199 S. Rock Road, Ft. Pierce, FL 34945, USA; mritenour@ifas.ufl.edu

Rouse, Robert E. (49). University of Florida, Southwest Florida Research and Education Center, 2686 Hwy. 29N, Immokalee, FL 34142-9515, USA; rer@ifas.ufl.edu

Schubert, Timothy S. (471). Division of Plant Industry, Florida Department of Agriculture and Consumer Services, P.O. Box 147100, Gainesville, FL 32614-7100, USA; schubet@doacs.state.fl.us

Singh, R. Paul (583). University of California-Davis, Department of Biological & Agricultural Engineering, Davis, CA 95616, USA; rpsingh@ucdavis.edu

Smilanick, Joseph L. (339). Research Plant Pathologist, USDA ARS, San Joaquin Valley Agricultural Sciences Center, 9611 S. Riverbend Ave., Parlier, CA 93648, USA; Jsmilanick@fresno.ars.usda.gov

Sorenson, David (421). Fruit Growers Supply, Company, 674 East Myer Ave., Exeter, CA 93221, USA; david.sorenson@fruitgrowers.com

Spreen, Thomas H. (135). Professor and Chair, University of Florida, Food and Resource Economics Department, P.O. Box 110240, Gainesville, FL 32611-0240, USA; tspreen@ufl.edu

Steck, Gary (471). Division of Plant Industry, Florida Department of Agriculture and Consumer Services, P.O. Box 147100, Gainesville, FL 32614-7100, USA; steckg@doacs.state.fl.us

Sun, Xiaon (471). Division of Plant Industry, Florida Department of Agriculture and Consumer Services, P.O. Box 147100, Gainesville, FL 32614-7100, USA; sunx@doacs.state.fl.us

Varela, Roberto A. (129). Facultad de Ciencias de la Alimentación, Departamento de Industrias, Mons. Rosch 1450, Concordia - 3200 - Entre Ríos - ARGENTINA; varelar@fcal.uner.edu.ar

Wardowski, Wilfred F. (251, 267, 277, 299, 307). Florida Science Source, Inc., P.O. Box 8217, Longboat Key, FL 34228-8217, USA; fssource@aol.com

Xiuxin, Deng (195). Citrus Research Institute, Huazhong Agricultural University, Shizhishan Street No. 1, Wuhan, Hubei 430070 P. R. CHINA; xxdeng@mail.hzau.edu.cn

Zaragoza, Salvador (213). Departamento de Citricultura y otros Frutales, Instituto Valenciano de Investigaciones Agrarias (I.V.I.A.), Carretera de Moncada a Náquera km 4.5, 46113, Moncada (Valencia) SPAIN; szarago@ivia.es

Zekri, Mongi (49). Multi-County Citrus Agent, University of Florida, IFAS, Hendry County Extension Office, P.O. Box 68, LaBelle, FL 33975, USA; maz@ifas.ufl.edu

Preface

The First Edition of this book was published 20 years ago. On an international level, it is still well used by both citrus packers, growers and students. It gained the nickname, The Green Bible, throughout the citrus packing industry. The many changes in citrus industries around the world are found in this book. New subjects are included in this second edition of *Fresh Citrus Fruits*, such as Food Safety Programs, and Organic Fresh Fruit. Likewise, much of the material under old chapter headings has been updated or is completely new.

Color plates have been added to the book for the identification of postharvest diseases, physiological disorders, citrus canker and Mediterranean Fruit Fly. Also, a fruit color-add test is illustrated as a color plate. Having these color illustrations in the book will aid readers in identifying problems.

The presence of Citrus Canker in Florida and Australia made the Plant Pest Regulations a difficult chapter to complete. Likewise, the Pesticide Tolerances chapter addresses a constantly changing subject. In these and other chapters the reader will find Internet addresses which can provide continually updated information.

Fresh Citrus Fruits, Second Edition, is a comprehensive treatise on citrus fruits destined for fresh markets. From grove-to-packinghouse-to-market may appear as a simple path of delivery of citrus fruits to consumers, but there are many obstacles and important problems which are discussed here in depth. *Fresh Citrus Fruits*, Second Edition should be of considerable interest to growers, handlers, packinghouse workers, exporters, produce buyers, students, citrus scientists and consumers.

The many authors are to be commended for their contributions, which made this book possible. They put their talents to work and their faith in the editors that the work would be published. Also, the editors give a special thanks to Karla Flynn and Barbara Thompson, University of Florida, Citrus Research and Education Center, for their word processing and computer skills which were important to develop and update several chapters in this volume.

Wilfred F. Wardowski
William M. Miller
David J. Hall
William Grierson

1

Anatomy and Physiology

William Grierson

The growth and development of a citrus flower's ovary into a fruit ready to harvest takes 6-18 months or more, depending upon the type of fruit and particular cultivar. The developing fruit is subjected to a host of internal and external influences that may modify its inherent (hereditary) anatomical, chemical, and physical characteristics and physiological behavior to a greater or lesser extent. This is to say, a citrus fruit reflects both its ancestry and its particular history when examined at any stage. The particular rootstock-scion combination, type of fruit set (i.e., parthenogenesis, adequate pollination followed by seed abortion, or pollination plus fertilization for proper seed development), availability of essential nutrients, hormone growth regulator levels, water supply, position on the tree (exposure to light, wind, and other environmental factors), and crop load are among the factors that determine or modify fruit size and external and internal qualities. An orange remains an orange and a grapefruit, a grapefruit barring an unlikely mutation; however, each of these and all of the other kinds of citrus (species, cultivars, and hybrids) still exhibit substantial variations among individual fruit. Knowledge of anatomical and physiological aspects of citrus fruits is necessary for predicting probable postharvest behavior (and consequent palatability) when the fruit are harvested, prepared in the packinghouse, and transported to the consumer's table (Soule and Grierson 1978).

ANATOMY AND MORPHOLOGY

A citrus fruit is botanically a *hesperidium*, a particular kind of berry with a leathery rind and divided internally into segments. This type of fruit is unique to six genera-*Citrus*, *Fortunella*, *Poncirus*, *Microcitrus*, *Eremocitrus*, and *Clymenia*-that compose the True Citrus Fruit Group of the Citrus subfamily (*Aurantioideae*) in the Rue family (*Rutaceae*); it is not found in other genera of the *Aurantioideae* nor in any other plants (Swingle 1943). The structure of a hesperidium is incredibly complex compared to that of a typical berry,

1

such as grape (*Vitis* spp.) or blueberry (*Vaccinium*), or to that of a drupe (e.g., peach, *Prunus persica*; coconut, *Cocos nucifera*; or mango, *Mangifera indica*), all of which are also derived from the ovary proper, as is citrus.

Citrus fruits range from less than 2.5 cm for calamondin (*Citrus madurensis*) or kumquats (*Fortunella* spp.) to more than 12 to 18 cm in diameter for grapefruit (*C. paradisi*) or pummelo (*C. grandis*). Shape is variable: oblate in grapefruit, mandarins (tangerines, *C. reticulata*), and mandarin hybrids; globose (spherical or nearly so) in sweet orange (*C. sinensis*) and sour orange (*C. aurantium*); prolate in lemon (*C. limon*), citron (*C. medica*), and lime (*C. aurantifolia*); distinctly pyriform (sheepnosed) in some pummelo cultivars, Ponderosa lemon, off-bloom grapefruit, etc.; and obovoid in some limes. The rind is often roughened from numerous small indentations or, infrequently, small protrusions, and the degree of roughness influences the brightness or dullness of perceived colors. Citrus fruits typically have 8-15 segments (Fig. 1.1A) or occasionally 17 or 18 in the case of grapefruit or pummelo; kumquats have 3-5, and trifoliate orange (*Poncirus*), 6-8 segments. Seeds vary in number from zero in a few cultivars, such as Tahiti lime and navel oranges, to 40-50 in seeded forms of grapefruit or pummelo. Seed size and shape also vary among species but are relatively uniform within any given species (Hume 1926; Hodgson 1967).

Developmental Morphology

The citrus fruit develops from a superior ovary (i.e., one lacking nonovarian tissues) with axile placentation (ovules attached to a central column; Fig. 1.1B). Several distinct tissues are readily apparent (flavedo, albedo, segments, seeds, central axis, and vascular bundles) when the fruit is cut transversely or longitudinally (Fig. 1.1). The usually five-pointed or -lobed calyx and buttonlike receptacle (distal end of the peduncle) at the stem end of the fruit has an abscission zone at its base, so that the calyx will remain attached to the branch if this zone is mature enough for natural separation to occur. Natural abscission is quite irregular, however, being dependent upon numerous endogenous and exogenous factors. See Schneider (1968) and Bain (1958) and Chapter 7 for details.

External Layers

The outer layers of a citrus fruit, collectively denoted as rind or peel, include the *flavedo*, the outer, colored portion, and the *albedo*, the inner, colorless or sometimes tinted (as in red grapefruit) portion. The *flavedo* (Fig. 1.1A, top left) consists of the epicarp proper, hypodermis, outer mesocarp, and oil glands. There is a multilayered protective skin or *cuticle* (Fig. 1.1A, bottom left) of complex origin, structure, and development overlying

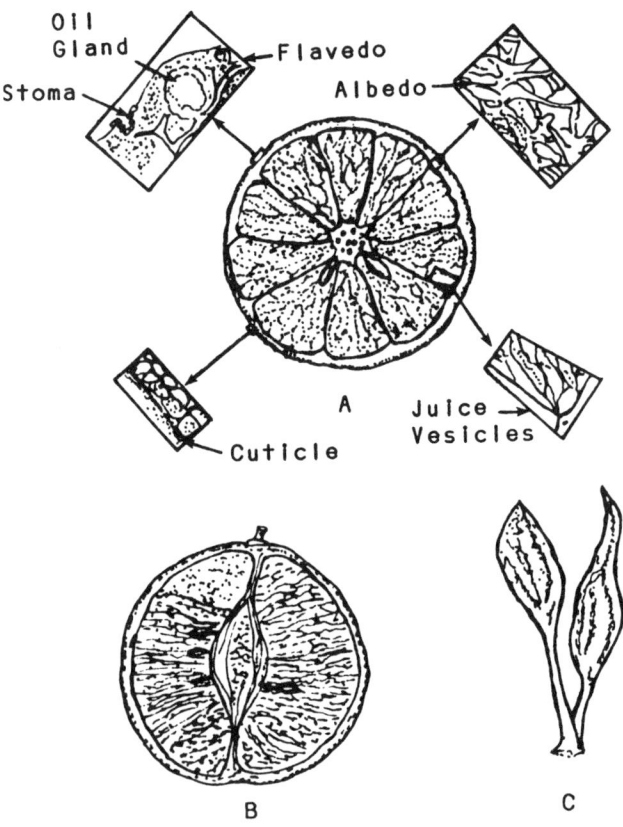

Fig. 1.1. A citrus fruit. A—transverse section with enlarged views of the flavedo and cuticle on the left and the albedo and juice vesicles attached to the outer tangential and radial locule walls on the right. B—longitudinal section showing the lunate locules with seeds attached to the inner tangential wall next to the central axis. C-separate juice vesicles. *From Grierson (1964); Soule and Grierson (1978). (C) Courtesy K. E. Koch.*

the epicarp and usually separated from the latter by a pectin layer. The cuticle proper consists of an inner layer of cutin (a heterogeneous polymer of fatty acids) and cellulose and an outer layer consisting entirely or mainly of cutin (Baker *et al.* 1975), with waxy materials as platelets, rods, and other shapes embedded within and over the cuticular surface (Albrigo 1972; Freeman 1978). *Epicuticular waxes* are a complex of primary alcohols, secondary alcohols, paraffins, aldehydes, diketones, etc., with the composition changing and compounds continually being renewed as the fruit develops (Freeman 1978). This outer surface is dull and easily washed, polished, or abraded away. Numerous *stomata* are scattered over the surface of the epicarp and remain functional throughout the life of the fruit unless plugged by epicuticular wax. The single-layered *epicarp* also has cells with plastids initially containing chlorophyll (i.e., chloroplasts) which are gradually metamorphosed into chromoplasts as the fruit degreens (Thompson 1969) and sometimes back to chloroplasts again if regreening occurs late in the spring (Thompson *et al.* 1967). Such changes are obviously due to the weather, the internal control mechanism being endogenous growth regulators of the tree (Eilati *et al.* 1969; Rasmussen 1973). Layers of colorless cells, called *hypodermis* and *outer mesocarp*, lie immediately below the epicarp and contain *oil glands*. The latter are formed through a combination of the splitting apart and dissolution of cells. Oil glands range in size from 10 to 100 μm or more, many large and some small ones being located below one or two layers of epicarpal cells, which may be essentially level, sunken slightly below the surrounding surface, or bulged out. The number, distribution and aromatic (volatile) constituents, largely terpenes and sesquiterpenes, of oil glands are characteristic for a given citrus species. The oil is highly phytotoxic, causing necrosis of epicarpal cells if the glands are ruptured from abrasion or a blow, the characteristic lesion being called oleocellosis (Wardowski *et al.* 1976).

The albedo (Fig. 1.1A, top right) consists of a loose anastomosed network of parenchymatous cells with numerous large air spaces as part of the *inner mesocarp*. Albedo cells originate as tightly packed spheres. As the fruit enlarges, these cells stretch at the eight contact points with surrounding cells, resulting in a web of very thin-walled cells and connecting strands with a high proportion of air-filled intercellular space (Scott and Baker 1947). This is an extremely effective cushioning mechanism against pressure, but a fertile culture medium if the flavedo is pierced and fungal spores penetrate into the albedo. The albedo is 1 to 2 mm thick in some fruit, such as Honey tangerine (Murcott), and a centimeter or more thick in grapefruit (particularly in off-bloom specimens), pummelos, and citrons. It merges imperceptibly into the flavedo towards the outside and cannot be separated from it but is clearly bounded on the inside, although it may adhere tightly, to the tangential segment membranes.

The rind of most citrus fruits is generally considered inedible, largely because of the oil; however, that of kumquats is sweet and can be eaten along with the pulp.

Internal Structures

A series of more or less broadly triangular lunate segments surrounding the central axis forms the largest (edible) proportion of a mature citrus fruit. Each segment is surrounded by a rather tough, continuous membrane, the *endocarp* proper, with an easily torn membrane of mesocarp tissue extending radially between adjacent segments. The interior of a segment has two major components, the *juice* (or pulp) *vesicles* (Fig. 1.1A, bottom right; 1.1C) and *seeds.*

Juice vesicles are multicellular sacs each enclosed in a membrane and consisting of a multicellular threadlike stalk and enlarged spindle-shaped multicellular body with a minute oil gland in the center. These are attached by the stalk to vascular bundles adjacent to the tangential and outer third to half of the radial segment walls. These extrusions, denoted botanically as pulpa, fill the whole segment exclusive of the space taken up by seeds.

The shape and size of seeds are characteristic for a given species. Seeds are attached to axial vascular bundles and extend into the segments from the inner tangential segment wall in two rows, with four to six superposed per row. Some, or occasionally all, of the seeds are aborted. A few cultivars possess no seeds; however, some such as Hamlin or Valencia sweet oranges, although commercially called seedless, may contain up to about six seeds. A better term would be few seeded or sparsely seeded, since most of these fruit have at least one or two seeds.

The *central axis* is composed of the same type of colorless or tinted, loose spongy network of cells as the albedo and, as mentioned earlier, is connected with the latter by membranes between each segment. The central axis of all citrus fruits is solid in the immature stages of development. That of sweet oranges, grapefruit, lemon, lime, and citron remains solid, but may develop a cavity as the fruit become senescent. The central axis of mandarins and their hybrids and of pummelo is normally open, with an air space in the center, which has the interesting consequence of slowing down heat transfer markedly during cooling or warming.

Vascular System

Vascular bundles in a citrus fruit (Fig. 1.2) form a highly ramified network of main and subsidiary traces whereby every cell in the various tissues is connected directly, or is adjacent to, a cell in contact with a particular sector of the vascular system. The vascular system of the proximal portion of the peduncle (fruiting stem) is similar to that of other young stems on the tree, consisting of concentric cylinders of phloem, lateral meristem or cambium, and xylem surrounding a central core of pith. This arrangement changes to a series of discrete bundles containing phloem and xylem tissues within an enveloping sheath as they enter the distal portion of the peduncle. Vascular bundles in the receptacle (button) form three concentric circles (Fig. 1.2B), the innermost of which emerge as *axial bundles*, the middle ones as *dorsal bundles*, and the outermost as *septal bundles*. The first form a ring in the central axis, with branches designated as *ovular bundles* (Fig. 1.2A) leading to the ovules attached to the inner tangential wall of the locules (segments). The ovular bundles continue through the funiculus (ovule or seed stem) and around the periphery to the opposite, chalazal end of the ovule, this portion being termed the *seed bundle* (or seed trace). The axial bundles then gradually diverge outward to positions opposite the septa between locules; these *marginal bundles* then merge with the septal and dorsal bundles near the stylar scar.

The outer portion of the fruit has two separate sets of *vascular bundles* (Fig. 1.2C, D). Individual *dorsal bundles* diverge from the receptacle to a position in the inner albedo midway along the outer tangential wall of each locule. Numerous branches feed the hypodermis in the flavedo and also the juice vesicles attached to the outer tangential wall of the locules. Juice vesicles proper, however, apparently do not have a vascular trace as a seed does. *Septal bundles* are located opposite and at the outer ends of the septa in the upper (stem end) portion of the fruit, with numerous branches to furnish nutrients and photosynthates to juice vesicles attached to the radial walls of the locules. The main septal bundles gradually move inward radially and develop numerous large and small lateral branches in the lower (stylar) portion of the fruit.

Studies of the movement of photosynthates in mature fruit utilizing ^{14}C treatment of leaves attached to the stem immediately proximal to the peduncle have shown that there is little tangential diffusion of nutrients. Each vascular bundle or group of them is essentially a separate system for a particular longitudinal sector. Furthermore, photosynthates accumulate in the peel rather than in the seeds, meaning that the primary movement of nutrients at this stage is via the network of dorsal and septal vascular bundles (Koch 1982).

Anomalous Structures

The tendency of citrus, fruit (and vegetative organs) to exhibit mutations appearing as periclinal, sectorial, or mericlinal chimeras or other aberrations is well known and several cultivars have been selected from these. Secondary fruitlets or navels are found in many mandarin hybrids (e.g., Temple, a reputed tangor, and tangelos), some grapefruit, and other citrus; however, they are most prominent and commercially important in the navel-type sweet orange. Secondary (and occasionally even tertiary) structures are clearly evident in the navel orange flower (Fig. 1.3).

Navel oranges produced in dry Mediterranean-type climates with cool winters (e.g., California, Israel, and South Australia) generally have a small fruitlet and navel mark at the stylar end. Those produced in warm, humid subtropical areas (e.g., Florida, the Caribbean, and much of South America) typically have much more pronounced development of the fruitlet and a correspondingly larger opening (Fig. 1.4), both of which may limit salability of the fruit (i.e., may be grade-lowering factors). The larger stylar opening often seen on Florida navels also provides an entry and harboring place for

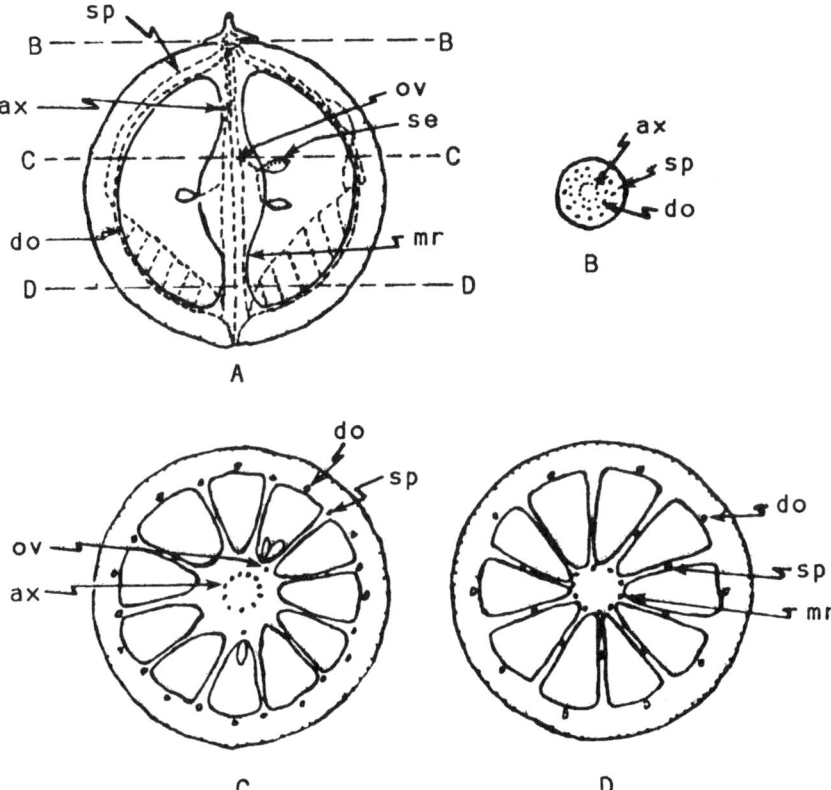

Fig. 1.2. Arrangement and different types of vascular bundles in a citrus fruit. A-longitudinal section; B, C, D-transverse sections at levels indicated in A. ax = axial bunles; ov = ovular bundles; se = seed trace; mr = marginal bundles; do = dorsal bundles; and sp = septal bundles (branches and ramification not shown).
Adapted from Schneider (1968) and Koch (1982).

insects, mites, and/or fungi that can cause sufficient damage in nearly mature fruit to induce development of the abscission layer located immediately below the secondary fruitlet. This in turn triggers the same response in the abscission of the primary fruit, even though the latter may be sound (Lima and Davies 1982). This is an important factor contributing to the very low fruit set of navels in climates such as Florida's (Southwick *et al.* 1982).

Other anomalous structures include those in which segments are united only at the stem end although all surfaces have an apparently normal exocarp—e.g., the Buddha's Hand citron (*C. medica* var. *sarcodaciylis*)-and those with a persistent style (which in most fruit abscises soon after petal fall)— e.g., Etrog citron (*C. medica* var. ethrog) used in Jewish religious ceremonies (Swingle 1943; Grierson 1970).

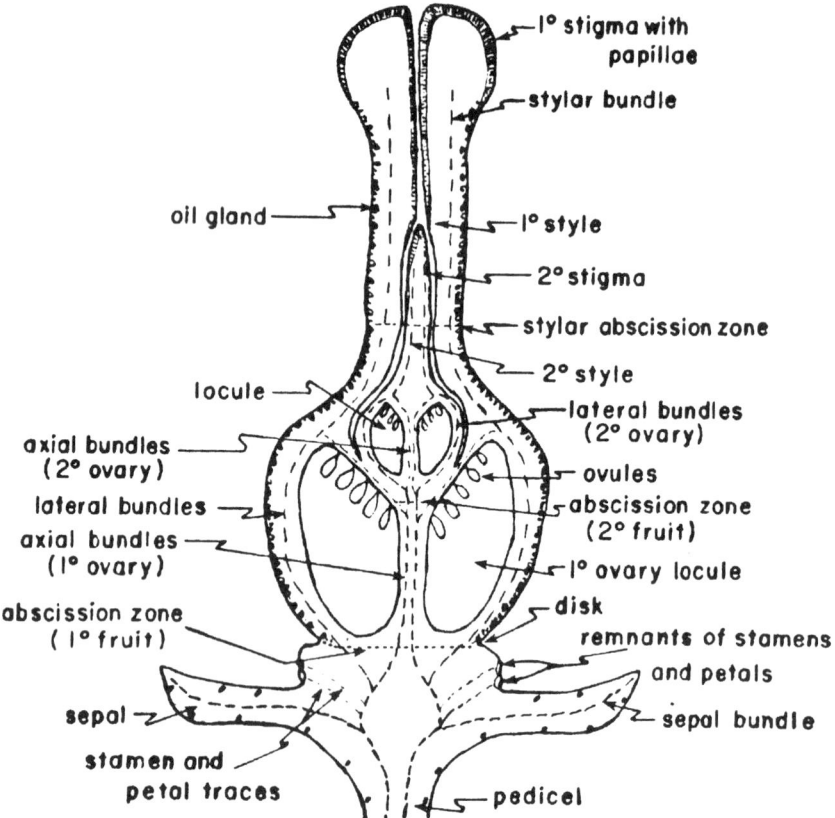

Fig. 1.3. Navel orange flower at petal fall (median longitudinal section). 1° = primary; 2° = secondary. Lateral bundles include dorsal and septal (see Fig. 1.2). Stylar abscission normally occurs postpetal fall; 2° fruit abscission zone formation, if it occurs, will induce the 1° one.
Courtesy Jose Lima.

Other Characteristics

Miscellaneous characteristics include weight, size, form (shape), firmness, and age. Seasonal trends in *weight* among the various kinds of citrus are similar to those for juice. Each species and its cultivars and hybrids have a characteristic range in *size*, which is influenced by crop load, rootstock, and other factors. Large fruit always have lower total soluble solids, titratable acidity, and juice content (% by weight) than small fruit of the same cultivar and tree (Harding and Lewis 1941). *Form (shape)* is also a varietal characteristic but is subject to appreciable variation as a consequence of off-bloom, orchard location, tree age, weather conditions, and various cultural

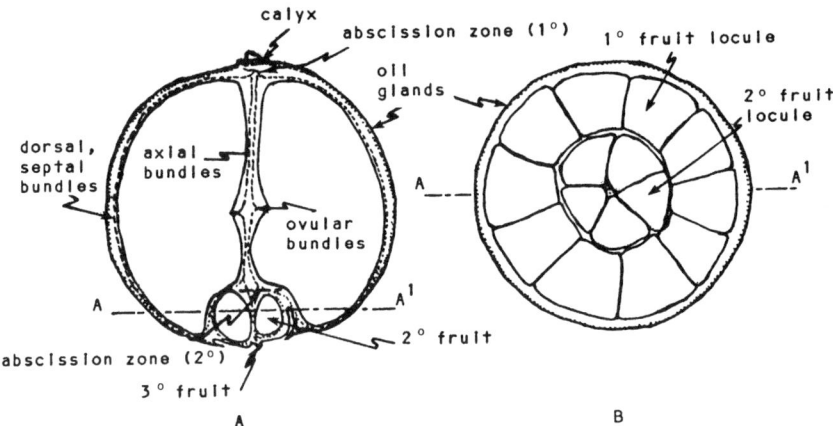

Fig. 1.4. Immature navel orange fruit (70 mm in diameter). A-Median longitudinal section; B-Transverse section at dashed line on A. 1° = primary fruit; 2° = secondary fruit; 3° = tertirary fruit.
Courtesy Jose Lima.

practices. All citrus fruits show variation in form; however, the tendency toward deviations from the cultivar norm seems more pronounced for tangerines and other specialty fruits, grapefruit, and limes, particularly among fruit on young trees and in warm, wet seasons. The shape of grapefruit (an important marketing factor) is related to winter night temperatures. Mild winter nights are necessary for thin skinned oblate fruit. Cold winter nights result in sheepnosed, thick skinned, undesirable grapefruit (Wutscher 1976). *Firmness* is associated with fruit turgidity and peel thickness. Fruit become less firm as the segments shrink and tend to pull away from the peel late in the season (most noticeably in mandarins and their hybrids) and with the excessive development of the albedo typical of late-bloom fruit.

Two physical characteristics that are of particular importance for citrus fruits are the volume of extractable juice and number of seeds. Lemons and limes have always been valued for their juice content, 30% and 40% juice by weight or volume being typical minimum levels for these two fruits, respectively (Grierson and Ting 1978). Because oranges are increasingly used for juice, rather than for eating out of hand, the percentage of extractable juice (commonly 50% or more for the thin-skinned juice oranges of Brazil and Florida) is increasingly important. The nonjuice portions of a citrus fruit include seeds (the presence or absence of which is largely a varietal characteristic), central axis, vascular bundles, segment walls, and parts of the albedo adhering to the segments, which are collectively called rag. The proportion of juice to nonjuice components is generally a cultivar characteristic but is subject to seasonal variations influenced by numerous factors, including the stage of edibility at the time of harvest. Seedless fruit (e.g., Marsh grapefruit) are desired for fresh consumption even though seeded cultivars (e.g., Duncan grapefruit) generally have higher sugar, flavor, and vitamin C than their seedless counterparts. Nevertheless, cultivars of mediocre quality are increasingly grown for fresh use because of consumer preference for citrus fruits with few or no seeds.

PHYSIOLOGY AND MATURATION

Preharvest

The life of a citrus fruit begins with bloom and ends when it is consumed fresh or processed into juice and other products, several to many months later. Its general pattern of growth and development on the tree is sigmoidal with three fairly well-defined periods, as is common with many other tree fruits. Citrus has, however, several distinctive characteristics related to how fruit are set, the influence of seed presence (or absence) and numbers upon development, seasonal changes in constituents, and physical parameters as modified by environmental factors. The picture as a whole is complicated, the literature on preharvest and postharvest physiology is vast, and experimental results obtained from different cultivars and/or locations frequently are contradictory. Nevertheless, there are discernible general patterns.

Fruit Set. Frost and Soost (1968) give a good overall discussion of seed reproduction in citrus. Mature trees of most citrus cultivars produce sufficient bloom to give an adequate crop if only a few percent of the flowers develop into fruit. Pollination, fertilization, and development of zygotic embryos is ordinarily not an absolute requirement for fruit set, as it is for most other tree fruit crops. Adventitious embryony is widespread; that is, seeds are formed whether fertilization has taken place and the zygotic embryo persists or not. Only a few species or cultivars are monoembryonic (e.g., pummelo and Temple tangor). Certain cultivars such as Clementine mandarin, tangelos (tangerine-grapefruit hybrids), tangerine-tangelo crosses, and some pummelos are self-incompatible and thus require cross-pollination.

Several cultivars or groups, including ordinary cultivars of navel orange, satsuma, Tahiti lime, and certain others, regularly set fruit parthenocarpically; that is, they do not require pollination, although the crop load may be increased if they are pollinated by another cultivar. Many kinds of citrus, including navel oranges, satsumas, Tahiti lime, and others, have nonviable pollen, or none whatever; some, like Tahiti lime and many satsumas, regularly have degenerate ovules. Navel oranges in Florida, many lemon cultivars, and Marsh grapefruit are weakly parthenocarpic, requiring pollination but not fertilization, which is impossible in some cultivars (e.g., Marsh grapefruit) because of degenerate ovules (Ali-Dinar 1980).

It has been shown through experiments utilizing known numbers of pollen grains per flower in hand-pollinations that there is also a significant correlation between seed number and fruit size in Orlando tangelo (Adigun 1972). Valencia orange will set a good crop of essentially seedless fruit with a small amount of pollen (Erickson 1968), but the fruit will be larger and have more seeds if a larger amount of pollen is used (i.e., enough viable pollen grains to pollinate all of the ovules present in the ovary). See also comments in the preceding paragraph regarding navel oranges.

Growth and Development. A citrus flower ordinarily abscises within a few days if it has not been pollinated or a pollinationlike stimulus has not begun. A second wave of dropping occurs after another week or two if fertilization has not been consummated or a fertilizationlike stimulus has not developed. A third period of drop, called in the Northern Hemisphere the June drop, occurs two or three months later, or about the time that cell division (Stage I, Fig. 1.5) ceases, when stress conditions induce a burst of ethylene and consequent abscission of abortive fruitlets. Subsequent fruit drop is usually attributable to pest damage, faulty cultural practices, or adverse environmental conditions (e.g., dry weather, wet weather, high winds) but most of the fruit remaining after the June drop generally is retained.

There are three fairly well-defined periods of growth and development in citrus (Fig. 1.5). The first is much the shortest (little over a month), but during this period cell division in all but the outer peel takes place and a surprising amount of cell differentiation occurs even before there is any considerable enlargement of the small fruitlet (Bain 1958). Cell division can continue in the peel until close to fruit maturation (Scott and Baker 1947).

The tiny fruitlet, when during Stage I it is no longer protected by the calyx, is virtually devoid of cuticle and extremely susceptible to surface injury; the latter may be caused by brushing against a leaf. These small injuries enlarge as the fruit grows to form the characteristic wind scars typical of areas in which windy weather typically follows fruit set (Dodson 1966; Broderick 1970; Freeman 1976A, B, 1977; Albrigo 1976). Wind scarring is particularly troublesome in humid areas (such as Florida) where waterborne spores of the fungus melanose [*Diaporthe citri* (Faw.) Wolf] germinate in the newly formed wind scar lesions, greatly exacerbating the surface blemish.

Stage II is the period of cell (and hence fruit) enlargement. The fruit expands rapidly, and so does respiration per fruit (Fig. 1.5B). However, the rate per unit weight of tissue, which is the usual way of expressing respiration (Fig. 1.5A), continues to decline from its peak early in Stage I. This decline continues in Stage II as the various tissues begin to assume the size and form that they will attain in Stage III.

The growth rate of the fruit slows down in Stage III compared with that in Stage II. This final stage is also characterized by a reduced rate of fruit en-

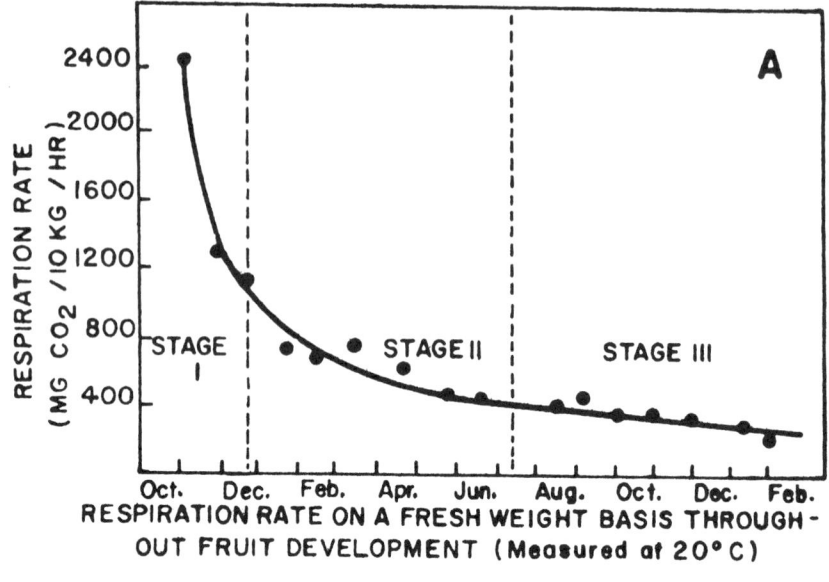

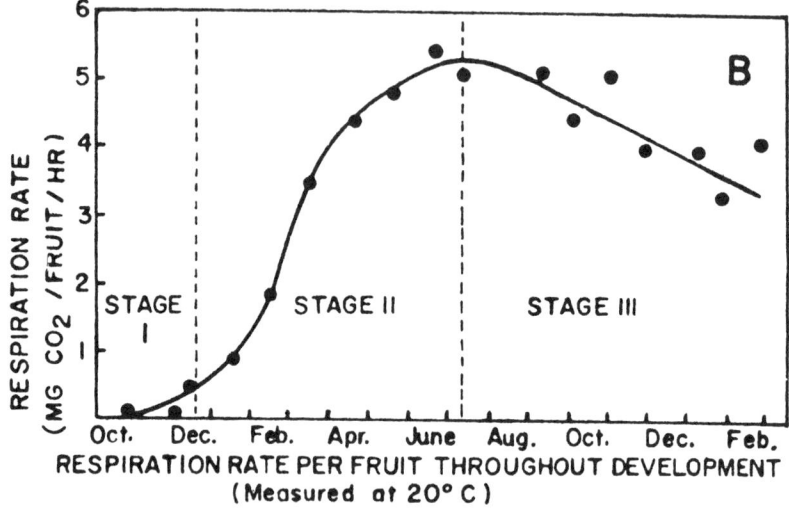

Fig. 1.5. Respiration during fruit development. A-Expressed in the usual manner as CO_2 evolution per unit fresh weight. B-Expressed in the usual manner as CO_2 evolution per fruit, a form that much more clearly defines the stages of fruit development. *From Bain (1958).*

largement and by numerous compositional changes, mainly increases in sugars and nitrogenous compounds and a continued decrease in the concentration of organic acids from the peak attained earlier (Bain 1958).

Chemical Composition. Over 400 different constituents have been iso-lated from fruit of various citrus species. The principal components of a nonacid fruit are carbohydrates, which include mainly sucrose, glucose, and fructose, plus trace amounts of several other sugars (Table 1.1). These constitute about three-fourths of the total soluble solids (TSS) in orange juice (USDA-ARS 1960; Ting and Attaway 1971; Nagy *et al.* 1977; Nagy and Attaway 1980). Organic acids, mainly citric and malic with traces of others, constitute somewhat less than 10% of the TSS, and free amino acids plus ni-trogenous bases and glutathione, about 6%. The remaining components include inorganic ions (about 3%), vitamins (2.5%), flavonoids and vola-tiles (1.2%), and lipids (1.2%); see Table 1.1.

Analysis of the composition of TSS in juice from mature navel oranges, Valencia oranges, and lemons in California (Erickson 1968) show typical differences among cultivars and species (Table 1.2). In comparison with lemons, navel and Valencia oranges have somewhat higher protein content, much higher sugar levels (with total sugars divided almost equally between sucrose and reducing sugars), and much lower acid content. Examination of Tables 1.1 and 1.2 reveals further differences among orange cultivars (e.g., higher fat and P-carotene levels in Valencia oranges than in navel oranges.

Erickson (1968) also pointed out that the free amino acid content of cit-rus juice varies both quantitatively and qualitatively during fruit development; proline is the most abundant in mature Valencia (up to 2.67% of the soluble solids) and also in Washington navel oranges, Dancy tangerines, and Eureka and Lisbon lemons. The proportion of citric and malic acids is about 9:1 in the juice but just the reverse in the peel; in fact, the principal acid in the latter may actually be oxalic (Clements 1964,

TABLE 1.1. Average Composition of Soluble Solids in Orange

Constituents	No. of compounds	Percentage of TSS
Carbohydrates	10	76.00
Organic acids	13	9.60
Free amino acids	19	5.40
Nitrogenous bases as glutathione	6	0.40
Inorganic ions	67	3.20
Vitamins	14	2.50
Flavonoids	24	0.81
Volatiles	192	0.38
Carotenoids	21	0.01
Enzymes	49	—
Lipids	26	1.20

Source: USDA-ARS (1960); Ting and Attaway (1971); Nagy *et al.* (1977); Nagy and Attaway (1980).

TABLE 1.2. Average Composition of Soluble Solids in Juice of California Navel and Valencia Oranges and Lemons

	Percentage of TSS		
Constituent	Navel	Valencia	Lemons
Protein	7.7	7.8	5.7
Amino nitrogen	0.4	0.5	0.5
Fat	0.8	2.2	2.2
Total sugar	80.0	76.2	13.1
Sucrose	(40.0)	(37.1)	(1.1)
Reducing sugars	(39.8)	(39.1)	(13.0)
Acid (as citric)	7.4	8.0	72.0
Ascorbic acid	0.5	0.34	0.53
β-Carotene	0.01	0.22	—
Inositol	1.2	1.2	0.8
Potassium	1.4	1.3	1.2
Calcium	0.08	0.07	0.07
Total soluble solids (%) in juice	12.96	12.76	8.3

Source: Adapted from Erickson (1968).

quoted by Erickson 1968). Also, ascorbic acid is highest in immature fruit and there is a strong concentration gradient from the peel (highest) to the center of a fruit (lowest).

Citrus fruits derive their unique qualities from about 20 principal factors, which are conveniently grouped as internal, external, and miscellaneous. Several of these, notably sugars (measured as total soluble solids, TSS), organic acids (measured as titratable acidity, TA), sugar:acid ratio (total soluble solids:titratable acidity ratio, TSS:TA), juice content, and color, are of vital concern in consumer acceptance and preference. Knowledge of the changes in internal composition that take place in oranges, grapefruit, and other citrus is based mainly upon the studies of Collison (1913), Harding and his associates (Harding *et al.* 1940, 1959; Harding and Lewis 1941; Harding and Fisher 1945; Harding and Sunday 1949, 1953; Long *et al.* 1962), and several others including Rasmussen *et al.* (1966) in Florida; Wood and Reed (1938). Krezdorn and Cain (1952), and Krezdorn and Maxwell (1959) in Texas; Bartholomew and Sinclair (1941, 1943), Sinclair (1961, 1972), and Rygg and Getty (1955) in California; and Hilgeman (1941) in Arizona (cited by Rose *et al.* 1951).

Maturation. Harding *et al.* (1940, 1959) and other writers applied the same terminology to citrus with respect to maturity and ripening as for apples. The term ripening appears repeatedly in the citrus literature, yet it is erroneous because there is no starch, oil, etc., present in citrus fruit during maturation capable of being converted to sugars or other soluble products. *Citrus fruits, being nonclimatic, do not possess a well-defined ripening mechanism* as do apple, pear, banana, mango, avocado, etc. (Grierson 1973). Instead they gradually become edible and remain so on the tree over a more or less extended period, which may last 1-2 months for tangerines or tangerine hybrids and up to 7 or 8 months for grapefruit (Fig. 1.6). The dates and duration of citrus cropping periods are related to the time of onset of rapid physiological changes, principally increases in sugar, decreases in acid, and changes in the amount of extractable juice (Fig. 1.7D). These changes are expressed most sharply in the ratio of total soluble solids (mainly sugars) to titratable acid, which is commonly called *maturity index* in Europe (Fig. 1.7C). Because these physiological changes occur very slowly in grapefruit, its harvesting season in Florida can extend over 8 months for a single cultivar. Conversely, the very rapid changes in such factors explain the short cropping season of Dancy tangerine.

An additional complication is that the various fruit quality factors (TSS, TA, TSS:TA, and juice content) vary with the position of the fruit on the tree, as shown in Table 1.3 (Sites and Reitz 1949, 1950A, B). Quality improves up to a peak for any given cultivar then declines gradually *while the fruit remain on the tree.* It is true that lemons are generally harvested immature and develop their edible qualifies off the tree during the curing process, but this is a special situation dictated by market requirements (Bartholomew and Sinclair 1951).

Citrus fruits are nonclimacteric (Fig. 1.6); that is, they lack both a ripening cycle and a well-defined abscission period. Thus, just when they are harvested is a matter of human discretion rather than a naturally imposed physiological necessity. There has to be some generally acceptable agreement about what constitutes maturity, but this can depend on both external appearance and internal quality; moreover, wide differences in maturity standards may exist among growing and marketing districts even for the same cultivar (Grierson and Ting 1978; Chapter 2). Climate is not under the control of the grower, but cultural practices are, and these can affect both internal and external quality and maturity factors (Chapter 3). Additionally, standards that are optimum for the fresh fruit market may not be optimum for cannery utilization (Chapter 9).

Many citrus fruits, notably navel oranges, tangerines, and tangerine hybrids have short periods of peak edibility, before or after which the fruit are noticeably deficient in flavor and aroma. Fruit harvested very early or very late in the season (season here referring to the period when they become edible and later) generally have poorer keeping quality and greater susceptibility to postharvest disorders (see Chapter 14) than those picked near peak edibility. Optimum palatability for grapefruit, which has an unusually long harvest season, tends to coincide with the onset of the next bloom, after which keeping quality deteriorates. Overripe (senescent) fruit generally have a stale, aged, or dull taste and little aroma.

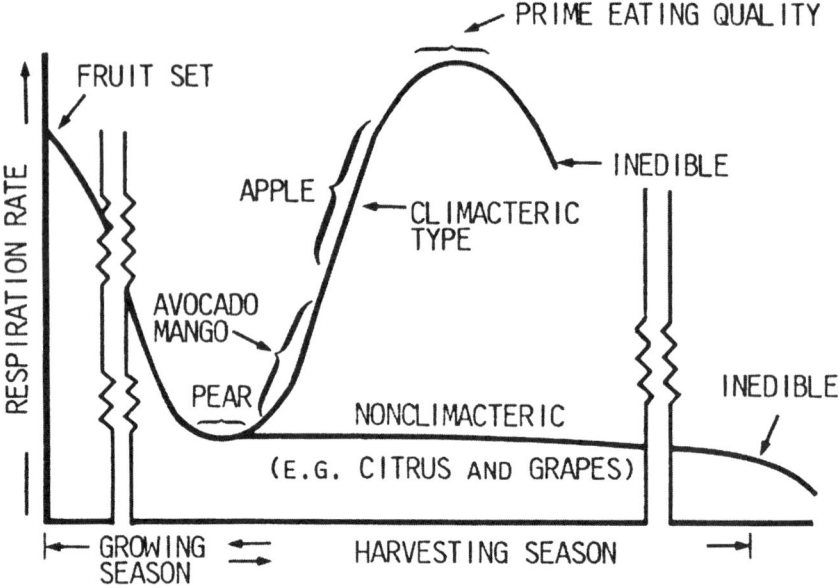

Fig. 1.6. Climacteric and nonclimacteric life cycles for fruits.
From Grierson (1973).

Something that is often misunderstood, particularly by the buying public, is the development of so-called typical varietal colors. Citrus fruits evolved in the humid tropics and warm subtropics, hence all types of citrus fruits are green when mature under such conditions. Low night temperatures in Mediterranean-type climates (e.g., the Mediterranean basin, California, South Australia), or at high, cooler altitudes in the tropics, stress citrus fruits sufficiently for them to produce internal ethylene in quantities large enough to destroy chlorophyll in the flavedo and promote the further development of yellow, orange, or red carotenoid pigments, some of which are already present and others produced *de novo* (Grierson and Ting 1978; Grierson *et al.* 1982). Chloroplasts change to chromoplasts, which may change back to chloroplasts again (regreening) with the advent of warm night temperatures (Caprio 1955; Thompson 1969; Thompson *et al.* 1967; Rasmussen 1973).

Postharvest

Respiration. Citrus fruits are nonclimacteric, hence postharvest ripening cannot occur. However, the total absence of a respiratory climacteric has occasionally been challenged in the literature. For example, a respira-

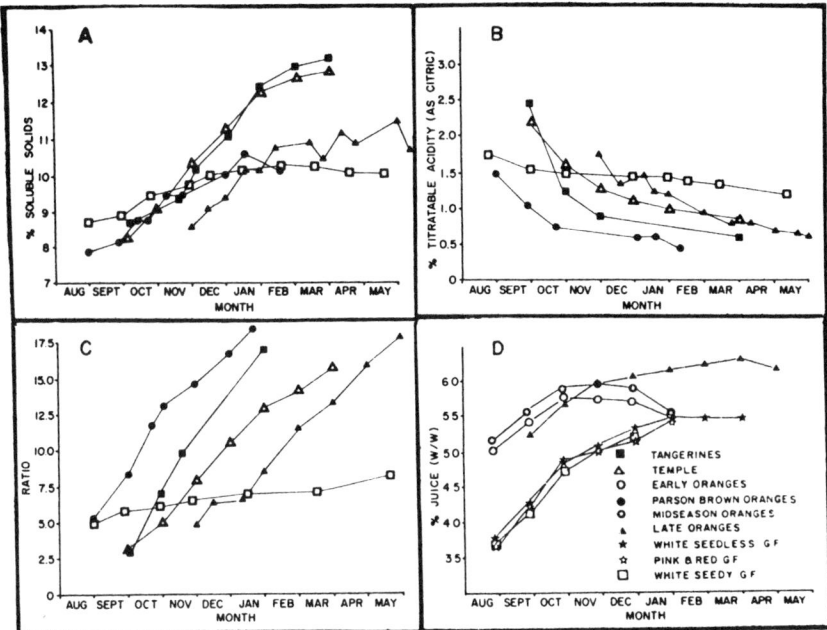

Fig. 1.7. Changes in the composition of Florida citrus fruits during development. A—
Total soluble solids (as % sucrose); B—Titratable acidity (as % anhydrous citric acid);
C—Total soluble solids: titratable acidity ratio; D—Juice content (% by weight).
Graphs A, B, and C based on four-season averages.
*From Harding and Lewis (1941); Harding and Fisher (1945); Harding and Sunday
(1949, 1953); and Grierson and Ting (1978).*

tory climacteric can be detected if fruit are picked early enough (well prior
to normal harvest) (Aharoni 1968), and a concealed climacteric manifests
itself if fruit are placed in pure oxygen (Biale and Young 1947). Such observations do not support a necessary climacteric rise in respiration in citrus.

A true respiratory climacteric, does occur in avocado, apple, or pear,
and is completely irreversible once started. Such a climacteric rise is usually
associated with a physiologically potent evolution of ethylene, and always
with conversion of starch to sugar and/or other biochemical changes. It
may be depressed by lowered temperature or by modified-atmosphere storage, but the preclimacteric condition is never restored. Eaks (1970) showed
that the response to exogenous ethylene of citrus fruits was reversible and
so not a climacteric. Vines *et al.* (1968), using multiple respiration lines,
raised triplicate samples of oranges, lemons, grapefruit, and tangerines
from 10°C to 35°C in stages over several days, and respiration of each of
these fruits rose with a steady Q_{10} ratio. They then reversed the process, lowering the temperature in stages back to 10°C, at which temperature all four

TABLE 1.3. Average Total Soluble Solids (TSS), Total Acid (TA), Solids:Acid Ratio (TSS:TA), and Juice Content of Valencia Oranges from Different Positions on Tree

Position on tree	TSS (%)	TA (%)	TSS:TA ratio	Juice content (% w/w)
Outside	11.08	0.88	12.56:1	49.6
	(500)[a]	(509)	(509)	(510)
Canopy	11.01	0.91	10.99:1	49.6
	(580)	(582)	(582)	(579)
Inside	8.7	0.86	10.14:1	47.7
	(321)	(323)	(323)	(323)
Top outside	11.21	0.88	12.78:1	49.3
	(250)	(254)	(254)	(254)
Top inside	9.93	0.86	11.56:1	48.7
	(137)	(135)	(135)	(135)
All	10.24	0.885	11.56:1	49.15
	(1788)	(1803)	(1803)	(1801)

Source: Adapted from Sites and Reitz (1949; 1950A, B).
[a]Values in parentheses are number of fruit sampled.

types of citrus fruits resumed their original respiration rate with no evidence whatever of a climacteric. Respiration of the peel of grapefruit (measured both as O_2 uptake and as CO_2 evolution) is considerably higher than that of the pulp, but tends to decrease after harvest while that of the rest of the fruit remains constant (Vakis et al. 1970).

The evolution of physiologically potent quantities of ethylene is typical of fruits undergoing a true respiratory climacteric. Endogenous ethylene was not detected in citrus fruits until the advent of gas chromatography (Biale et al. 1954). Minute amounts of internal ethylene are normally detectable with modern instruments, but not usually in physiologically potent concentrations (i.e., below threshold) concentrations. The small amounts of ethylene found in healthy, nonstressed citrus fruits are counteracted by the considerably larger amounts of endogenous CO_2 (Burg and Burg 1967). Various forms of stress such as excessive waxing (Vines et al. 1968), rough handling (Grierson et al. 1971), freezing (Vines et al. 1968), fungal invasion (Biale 1950), or senescence (S. P. Burg, personal communication) can cause an increase in ethylene evolution and consequent marked rises in respiration.

Postharvest respiration of a healthy, nonstressed citrus fruit is essentially stable under constant conditions, more like a potato or a turnip than an avocado or apple.

Transpiration. Water loss is usually of more consequence than is respiration when citrus fruit are held for considerable periods (see Chapter 20 for detailed discussion of storage). An outstanding example of long-term storage of a citrus fruit has been the traditional practice of harvesting lemons in the coastal districts of California in mid- to late winter and storing them until mid-summer. Such lemons are green, thick skinned, and deficient in extractable juice when harvested, but yellow, thin skinned, and juicy after several months storage. The traditional explanation of this phenomenon was that water migrated from the peel into the juice vesicles. This was disproved by Eaks (1961), who showed that the thinning of the peel is due to transpiration losses and the increase in juice yield is due to physiological changes in which water in the juice vesicles changes from gel to liquid form.

Biochemical Components. Studies of citrus fruit biochemistry have concentrated on the amounts and proportions of nutritional and flavor constituents, rather than on the limited postharvest changes (Ting and Attaway 1971). The irregular distribution of such components within the fruit is notable and rather consistent (Ting 1969). In general, the blossom (distal) end is higher in total sugars than the stem (proximal) end, and the sugar:acid ratio is higher in the periphery than in the center of the pulp in oranges and grapefruit. The intrafruit differential in ascorbic acid (vitamin C) is pronounced: In oranges the vitamin C content is three to five times higher in the peel than in the juice, and in grapefruit it is five to seven times higher in the peel. Normally this high concentration of vitamin C, or what is left of it after processing, is used only in cattle feed. However, when unlimited amounts of unprepared grapefruit were made available to destitute Florida children during the worst of the 1930s depression, they ate the grapefruit like apples, peel and all, as long as blood tests showed them to be deficient in vitamin C. They ate only the grapefruit pulp prepared for them in the usual manner when their blood vitamin C reached normal levels. (Ouida Abbott, formerly Head, Dept. of Home Economics, University of Florida, personal communication).

Biochemical changes in citrus fruits after harvest are very gradual, but the sugar:acid ratio tends to rise under suitable storage conditions since acids tend to decrease faster than do sugars. Thus, palatability tends to increase as long as decay and desiccation are controlled, although volatile flavor components will be lost during prolonged storage (Ting and Attaway 1971).

REFERENCES

ADIGUN, O. O. 1972. The influence of seed, gibberellic acid and girdling on the development of Orlando tangelo fruit. Ph.D. Dissertation. University of Florida, Gainesville.

AHARONI, Y. 1968. Respiration of oranges and grapefruit harvested at different stages of development. Plant Physiol. 43, 99-102.

ALBRIGO, L. G. 1972. Distribution of stomata and epicuticular wax on oranges as related to stem end rind breakdown and water loss. J. Amer. Soc. Hort. Sci. 97, 220-223.

ALBRIGO, L. G. 1976. Influence of prevailing winds and hedging on citrus fruit and wind scar. Proc. Fla. State Hort. Soc. 89, 55-59.

ALI-DINAR, H. M. 1980. Levels of endogenous growth regulators of grapefruit (*Citrus paradisi* Macf.) during fruit set. Ph.D. Dissertation. University of Florida, Gainesville.

BAIN, J. M. 1958. Morphological, anatomical, and physiological changes in the developing fruit of the Valencia orange, *Citrus sinensis* (L.) Osbeck. Aust. J. Bot. 6 (1), 1-25.

BAKER, E. A., PROCOPIOU, J. and HUNT, G. M. 1975. The cuticles of *Citrus* species: Composition of leaf and fruit waxes. J. Sci. Food Agr. 26, 1093-1101.

BARTHOLOMEW, E. T. and SINCLAIR, W. B. 1941. Unequal distribution of soluble solids in the pulp of citrus fruits. Plant Physiol. 16, 293-312.

BARTHOLOMEW, E. T. and SINCLAIR, W. B. 1943. Soluble constituents and buffer properties of orange juice. Plant Physiol. 18, 185-206.

BARTHOLOMEW, E. T. and SINCLAIR, W. B. 1951. The Lemon Fruit: Its Composition, Physiology, and Products. University of California Press, Berkeley.

BIALE, J. B. 1950. Postharvest physiology and biochemistry of fruits. Annu. Rev. Plant Physiol. 1. 183-206.

BIALE, J. B. and YOUNG, R. E. 1947. Critical oxygen concentrations for the respiration of lemons. Am. J. Bot. 34, 301-309.

BIALE, J. B., YOUNG, R. E. and OLMSTEAD, A. J. 1954. Fruit respiration and ethylene production. Plant Physiol. 29, 168-174.

BRODERICK, H. T. 1970. Investigations into blemishes on citrus fruits. S. Afr. Citrus J. 441 (Sept.), 7-31.

BURG, S. P. and BURG, E. A. 1967. Molecular requirements for the biological activity of ethylene. Plant Physiol. 42, 144-152.

CAPRIO, J. M. 1955. Regreening of Valencia oranges. Calif. Citrogr. 40, 287-288.

COLLISON, S. E. 1913. Sugar and acid in oranges and grapefruit. Fla. Agr. Exp. Stn. Bull. 115.

DODSON, P. G. C. 1966. Damage to citrus fruit by wind. S. Afr. Citrus J. 393 (Sept.) 4-5, 7, 11.

EAKS, I. L. 1961. Effect of temperature and holding period on some physical and chemical characteristics of lemon fruits. J. Food Sci. 26, 593-599.

EAKS, I. L. 1970. Respiratory response, ethylene production, and response to ethylene of citrus fruit during ontogeny. Plant Physiol. 45, 334-338.

EILATI, S. K., GOLDSCHMIDT, E. E. and MONSELISE, S. P. 1969. Hormonal control of colour changes in orange peel. Experienta 25, 209-210.

ERICKSON, L. C. 1968. The general physiology of citrus. *In* The Citrus Industry, Vol. II, rev. ed. W. Reuther, L. D. Batchelor, and H. J. Webber (Editors). Div. Agr. Sci., University of California, Berkeley.

FREEMAN, B. 1976A. Artificial windbreaks and the reduction of wind scar of citrus, Proc. Fla. State Hort. Soc. 89, 52-54.

FREEMAN, B. 1976B. Rind blemish of citrus. I. Initiation and development. II. Structure and ultrastructure. Scientia Hort. 4, 317-327, 329-336.

FREEMAN, B. 1977. Effects of wind and wind protection on rind blemish and production of `Valencia' oranges. pp. 81-93. Int. Proc. Int. Soc. Citriculture, Vol. 3.

FREEMAN, B. 1978. Cuticular waxes of developing leaves and fruits of citrus and blueberry: Ultrastructure and chemistry. Ph.D. Dissertation. University of Florida, Gainesville.

FROST, H. B. and SOOST, R. K. 1968. Seed reproduction: Development of gametes and embryos. *In* The Citrus Industry, Vol. II, rev. ed. W. Reuther, L. P. Batchelor, and H. J. Webber (Editors). Div. Agr. Sci., University of California, Berkeley

GRIERSON, W. 1964. Fruit quality in relation to the agricultural engineer. Citrus Ind. 45 (8), 5-7, 10.

GRIERSON, W. 1970. About our cover: The Etrog. HortScience 5 (5), 374.

GRIERSON, W. 1973. Quality of produce as influenced by prestorage treatment and packaging. Int. Inst. Refrig. Comm. C-2, 51-65.

GRIERSON, W. and TING, S. V. 1978. Quality standards for citrus fruits, juices and beverages, pp. 21-27. Proc. Int. Soc. Citriculture.

GRIERSON. W., WARDOWSKI, W. F. and EDWARDS, G. J. 1971. Postharvest rind disorders of Persian limes. Proc. Fla. State Hort. Soc. 84, 294-298.

GRIERSON, W., SOULE, J. and KAWADA, K. 1982. Beneficial aspects of physiological stress. Hort. Rev. 4, 247-271.

HARDING, P. L. and FISHER, D. F. 1945. Seasonal changes in Florida grapefruit. USDA Tech. Bull. 886.

HARDING, P. L. and LEWIS, W. E. 1941. The relation of size of fruit to solids, acid and volume of juice in the principal varieties of Florida oranges. Proc. Fla. State Hort. Soc. 54, 52-66.

HARDING, P. L. and SUNDAY, M. B. 1949. Seasonal changes in Florida tangerines. USDA Tech. Bull. 988.

HARDING, P. L. and SUNDAY, M. B. 1953. Seasonal changes in Florida Temple oranges. USDA Tech. Bull. 1072.

HARDING, P. L., WINSTON, J. R. and FISHER, D. F. 1940. Seasonal changes in Florida oranges. USDA Tech. Bull. 753.

HARDING, P. L., SUNDAY, M. B. and DAMS, P. L. 1959. Seasonal changes in Florida tangelos. USDA Tech. Bull. 1205.

HODGSON, R. W. 1967. Horticultural varieties of citrus fruit. In The Citrus Industry, Vol. I, rev. ed. W. Reuther, H. J. Webber, and L. D. Batchelor (Editors). Div. Agr. Sci. University of California, Berkeley.

HUME, H. H. 1926. The Cultivation of Citrus Fruits. Macmillan, New York.

KOCH, K. E. 1982. Distribution of ^{14}C photosynthates translocated into citrus fruits. HortScience 17 (3), 45. (Abstract)

KREZDORN, A. H. and CAIN, R. F. 1952. Internal quality of Texas grapefruit. Proc. Rio Grande Valley Hort. Inst. 6, 48-52.

KREZDORN, A. H. and MAXWELL, N. P. 1959. Fruit quality studies of eight strains of red fleshed grapefruit on two rootstocks. J. Rio Grande Valley Hort. Soc. 13. 54-58.

LIMA, J. E. O. and DAVIES, F. S. 1982. Secondary fruit ontogeny in navel oranges. HortScience 17 (3), 45. (Abstract)

LONG, W. G., SUNDAY, M. B. and HARDING, P. L. 1962. Seasonal changes in Florida Murcott Honey oranges. USDA Tech. Bull. 1271.

NAGY, S. and ATTAWAY, J. A. (Editors). 1980. Citrus Nutrition and Quality. Am. Chem. Soc., Washington, DC.

NAGY, S., SHAW, P. E. and VELDHUIS, M. K. (Editors). 1977. Citrus Science and Technology. Vol. I. AVI Publishing Co., Westport, CT.

RASMUSSEN, G. K. 1973. The effect of growth regulators on degreening and regreening of citrus fruit. Acta Hort. 34, 47378.

RASMUSSEN, G. K., REECE, P. C. and HENRY, W. H. 1966. Seasonal changes in fruit quality factors of Robinson, Osceola, Lee and Dancy tangerines. Proc. Fla. State Hort. Soc. 78, 51-55.

ROSE, D. H., COOK, H. T. and REDIT, W. H. 1951. Harvesting, handling and transportation of citrus fruits. USDA Bibliogr. Bull. 13, 53-106.

RYGG, G. S. and GETTY, M. R. 1955. Seasonal changes in Arizona and California grapefruit. USDA Tech. Bull. 1130.

SCHNEIDER, H. 1968. The anatomy of citrus. In The Citrus Industry, Vol. II, rev. ed. W. Reuther, L. D. Batchelor, and H. J. Webber (Editors). Div. Agr. Sci., University of California, Berkeley.

SCOTT, F. M. and BAKER, K. C. 1947. Anatomy of Washington navel orange rind in relation to water spot. Bot. Gaz. 108, 45975.

SINCLAIR, W. B. (Editor). 1961. The Orange. Its Biochemistry and Physiology. University of California Press, Berkeley.

SINCLAIR, W. B. 1972. The Grapefruit. Its Composition, Physiology and Products. Div. Agr. Sci., University of California, Berkeley.

SITES, J. W. and REITZ, H. J. 1949. The variation in individual Valencia oranges from different locations of the tree as a guide to sampling methods and spot-picking for quality. I. Soluble solids in the juice. Proc. Am. Soc. Hort. Sci. 54, 1-10.

SITES, J. W. and REITZ, H. J. 1950A. The variation in individual Valencia oranges from different locations of the tree as a guide to sampling methods and spot-picking for quality. II. Titratable acid and the soluble solids/titratable acid ratio of the juice. Proc. Am. Soc. Hort. Sci. 55, 73-80.

SITES, J. W. and REITZ, H. J. 1950B. The variation in individual Valencia oranges from different locations on the tree as a guide to sampling methods and spot-picking for quality. III. Vitamin C and juice content of the fruit. Proc. Am. Soc. Hort. Sci. 56, 103-110.

SOULE, J. and GRIERSON, W. 1978. Citrus maturity and packinghouse procedures. Hort. Sci. Dept., University of Florida, Gainesville.

SOUTHWICK, S. M., DAMES, F. S., EL-GHOLL, N. E. and SCHOULTIES, C. L. 1982. Ethylene, fungi, and summer fruit drop of navel orange. J. Am. Soc. Hort. Sci. 107, 800-804.

SWINGLE, W. T. 1943. The botany of citrus and its wild relatives of the orange subfamily: Group C. The true citrus fruit trees. *In* The Citrus Industry, Vol. I. W. Reuther, H. J. Webber, and L. D. Batchelor (Editors). Div. Agr. Sci., University of California, Berkeley.

THOMPSON, W. W. 1969. Ultrastructural studies on the epicarp of ripening oranges, pp. 1163-1169. Proc. Int. Soc. Citriculture, Vol. 3.

THOMPSON, W. W., LEWIS, L. N. and COGGINS, C. W. 1967. The reversion of chromoplasts to chloroplasts in 'Valencia' orange. Cytologia 32, 117-124.

TING, S. V. 1969. Distribution of soluble components and quality factors in the edible portion of citrus fruits. J. Am. Soc. Hort. Sci. 94, 515-519.

TING, S. V. and ATTAWAY, J. A. 1971. Citrus fruits. *In* The Biochemistry of Fruits and Their Products. A. C. Hulme (Editor). Academic Press, New York.

USDA-ARS. 1960. Chemistry and technology of citrus, citrus products and by-products. USDA. Handbk. 98.

VAKIS, N., SOULE, J., BIGGS, R. H. and GRIERSON, W. 1970. Biochemical changes in grapefruit and 'Murcott' citrus fruits as related to storage temperature. Proc. Fla. State Hort. Soc. 83, 304-310.

VINES, H. M., GRIERSON, W. and EDWARDS, G. J. 1968. Respiration, internal atmosphere and ethylene evolution of citrus fruit. Proc. Am. Soc. Hort. Sci. 92, 227-234.

WARDOWSKI, W. F., McCORNACK, A. A. and GRIERSON, W. 1976. Oil spotting (oleocellosis) of citrus fruit. Fla. Ext. Circ. 410.

WOOD, J. F. and REED, H. M. 1938. Maturity studies of Marsh seedless grapefruit in the Lower Rio Grande Valley. Texas Agr. Exp. Stn. Bull. 562.

WUTSCHER, H. 1976. Influence of night temperatures and day length on fruit shape of grapefruit. J. Am. Soc. Hort. Sci. 101, 573-575.

2

Maturity and Grade Standards

William Grierson

The global citrus industry furnishes a wide spectrum of markets. Sweet orange, lemon, mandarin, lime, pummelo, countless natural hybrids, and sour orange originated in southeastern Asia from southern China and possibly India to Indochina (Kampuchea, Laos, and Vietnam), Malaysia, and various islands in the Malay Archipelago. Citrus has been cultivated in this region since ancient times so that it is now impossible to ascertain the true centers of origin or to determine which ones are strictly cultigens. Grapefruit, Ortanique, and Temple orange all originated in the West Indies, yet none of the *Aurantioideae* (Citrus subfamily of *Rutaceae)* is native to the western hemisphere. Citrus, like other major tropical and subtropical crops (e.g., banana, pineapple, coconut, coffee, cacao, and tea) is broadly adapted to a wide range of environmental conditions. Fruit of its numerous species and cultivars are able to withstand shipment to distant markets and there is widespread acceptance of the crop for its nutritive qualities. The trees flourish in a broad belt around the globe, limited only by their inability to survive temperatures much below freezing.

Citrus represents a group of closely related species whose undoubted affinity is clearly expressed in their propensity to hybridize when given an opportunity, as shown by numerous natural hybrids and the success of many man-made crosses. Most of the species are more or less highly nucellar; their seedlings or budded trees also mutate readily. Indeed, the historical pattern in all of the major citrus-growing regions has been one of continual trial and selection of cultivars to find those best suited for local areas plus constant vigilance to maintain varietal integrity in successive generations of propagules.

Geographical influences, seasonal weather conditions, rootstocks, cultural practices, and tree age all have profound effects on external and internal fruit qualities wherever citrus is grown. Lack of a well-defined ripening mechanism results in a more or less prolonged period of edibility during which the fruit of a given cultivar may be marketed. Appearance, palatability, and keeping quality have special importance in consumer acceptance of fresh fruit.

Orderly marketing requires legal standards for maturity (internal qualities) and grade (external qualities) of fruit in the various citrus production areas of the world. These standards represent compromises among several disparate interests. Standards are obviously necessary to delay harvest of immature fruit and prevent shipment of unwholesome fruit. Maturity and grade standards are arbitrary from a legal standpoint: In theory, they can be set at any point. In practice, however, they must: (1) be formulated within the natural limits of the fruit involved; (2) take into account the right of growers to sell their fruit at some time during the crop season; and (3) meet the various, often conflicting, economic strictures of production and market requirements and consumer preferences. Test procedures for these standards must not only represent the true situation for a given lot of fruit but also be quick, simple, and objective. It is thus inevitable that there is a conspicuous lack of uniformity in standards among citrus-growing areas, given the hundreds of cultivars, innumerable microclimates, differing consumer preferences, etc., involved. The only real basis for fresh fruit maturity and grade standards, however, is *economics* and what may be justifiable in one situation may not be in another.

HISTORICAL BACKGROUND

Unfortunately, there are few records of how maturity or grade standards evolved in the several states of the United States or in numerous other regions where citrus is now grown commercially. Florida is an exception: The accounts of Hume (1907, 1926), Pierce (1956), and other writers, plus numerous statutes (Soule and Grierson 1978), provide an overview of maturity requirements and the genesis of grade standards. Hume's Florida reports also afford a comparison with California's grade standards.

Florida and California have sharply contrasting climates, the former being warm and humid with rains mainly in the summer and the latter being semiarid with cool nights and winter rains. Sweet oranges were brought from Spain to Florida in the 1500s, grapefruit from the West Indies about 1810, mandarins (and some hybrids) from the Far East in the 1840s and later, navel oranges from Brazil, about 1835 and again in the 1870s, and Valencia orange from Europe (mainly Spain) and England in the mid- to late 1800s. Present commercial production in Florida includes six or eight major orange cultivars, five types of grapefruit, several tangerines, Temple orange, tangelos, and other mandarin hybrids. These span a harvest season of about 8-9 months. By contrast, California's citrus industry is based on two main oranges, navels (introduced in 1871) and Valencia (late 1700s to early 1800s), with numerous strains of each. Lemons, principally Eureka and Lisbon, from stock brought by the Spanish during the founding of the missions in the late 1700s and from later European importations, are also a major crop. Marsh seedless grapefruit was brought to California from Florida in the early 1900s. A few mandarins and mandarin hybrids also are cultivated in California (Webber *et al.* 1967)

Evolution of Maturity Standards

Florida's modem citrus industry began in 1875 with the adoption of the 1³/₅-bu. (56.6-liter) box, devised by E. Bean, as the standard shipping container in which sized fruit were place-packed in an orderly arrangement. The most comprehensive and complicated standards for citrus fruit anywhere in the world have evolved in Florida since then. Highlights of their development are given in Table 2.1.

The accumulation of essential background information on a large number of fruit characteristics and taste tests for the major cultivars began with Collison's (1913) study of seasonal changes in oranges and grapefruit in 1912-1913. Quick, accurate, simple procedures were developed in 1915 for total soluble solids (TSS) as % sucrose equivalent using a hydrometer and for total (titratable) acid (TA) as % anhydrous citric acid in juice. TSS:TA ratios of 8:1 and 7:1 were then also stipulated for oranges and grapefruit, respectively, in interstate commerce. Harding and coworkers (Harding and Fisher 1945; Harding and Sunday 1949, 1953; Harding *et al.* 1940, 1959; Long *et al.* 1962) reported multiyear studies of seasonal changes in oranges, grapefruit, tangerines, Temple orange, tangelos, and Murcott (now Honey tangerine) from 1936 to 1962. Deszyck and Ting (1956) made a similar study of pink and red grapefruit in 1955-1956. This work provided the basis for recommendations for changes in maturity standards in the Florida Citrus Code of 1949 and subsequent amendments (Wardowski *et al.* 1995). The studies of Sites and Reitz (1949, 1950A, B) of individual fruit on a Valencia orange tree contributed vital information as to how to obtain a representative sample. The long-term evolution of Florida's maturity laws and regulations has been fostered by continuous support from all segments of the industry for *higher* internal requirements and legislative recognition in 1957 that these were minimum quality standards (Florida Dept. of Citrus 1996).

The evolution of maturity standards for citrus in California, Arizona, and Texas is less well documented. California and Arizona adopted the, TSS:TA ratio of 8:1, as recommended in 1915 by the USDA Bureau of Chemistry, plus a color break requirement, for oranges. The initial juice standard for lemons of 25% by volume, adopted in the 1930s, was raised later to 30% (Calif. Dept. of Food and Agriculture 1975: AFVSS 1945) in conformity with the federal standard (USDA 1964). Two TSS:TA ratios, 5.5:1 and 6:1, were adopted as standards for coastal and desert grapefruit, respectively, in California, with the higher ratio also applying to Arizona (USDA 1950). Texas standards parallel those of Florida, except the former

TABLE 2.1. Chronological Summary of Florida's Citrus Maturity Standards through 1977.

Year	Description
1911	Immature Fruit Law: unlawful to ship green, immature fruit (upheld by U.S. Supreme Court).
1913	Maturity Law: fruit inspection Sept. 1-Nov. 15; maximum 1.3% crystalline citric acid for oranges, 1.75% for grapefruit or half color on 12-fruit sample.
1925	Maturity Law: first comprehensive standards for TSS, TA, and TSS:TA ratio (minimum 8:1) with sliding scale (ratio dependent upon TSS of juice); inspection fees.
1927	Arsenic Law: arsenic banned on bearing trees.
1933	Maturity Law: minimum juice requirement for grapefruit; color break for oranges. Permanent injunction prohibited enforcement of Arsenic Law on grapefruit.
1935	Maturity Law: higher standards Color Add Law: color add legal on oranges, with higher standards.
1941	Creation of Indian River Citrus Area.
1949	Florida Citrus Code: consolidation of existing statutes and changes; higher maturity requirements (e.g., 9:1 minimum TSS:TA ratio for oranges) on all fruit, including Temple; mandatory year-round fruit inspection.
1951 1953	Code Amendments: separate requirements for seeded, white seedless, and pink and red seedless grapefruit.
1955	Code Amendments: Tangelo Act established requirements for tangelos; early-season juice requirement for grapefruit increased.
1957	Code Amendments: revision of grapefruit juice requirements; limes dropped from Code; changes in test procedures.
1959	Code Amendments: grapefruit requirements revised; Murcott requirements established.
1961	Code Amendments: Temple orange color added under permit; grapefruit requirements revised.
1967	Code Amendments: grapefruit requirements revised.
1970 1971	Code Amendments: definitions for tangerines and hybrids revised; requirements of hybrids established by Florida Citrus Commission Regulations (changed in 1975 to Official Rules); test procedures revised.
1977	Code Amendments: grapefruit requirements revised (standards for seeded and seedless only).

Source: Soule and Grierson (1978).

has requirements only for oranges and grapefruit (Texas Dept. of Agriculture 1956), the major citrus grown in that state. Studies of seasonal changes in grapefruit were carried out by Wood and Read (1938), Krezdorn and Cain (1952) and Krezdorn and Maxwell (1959) in Texas and by Rygg and Getty (1955) in Arizona and California.

Evolution of Grade Standards

Florida and California growers who shipped fruit to distant markets were acutely aware even in the late 1800s of the necessity for meticulous grading and sizing if they were to market their fruit profitably. Florida packinghouses were small then, with little coordination or organization among growers and shippers. This was a very different situation from that in California where the California Citrus Exchange (now Sunkist) and other smaller cooperatives marketed citrus going to eastern destinations.

Florida oranges, grapefruit (then called pomelos), and tangerines were held for several days after harvest to allow the fruit to soften and allow detection of bruise injuries and thorn damage. They were then sized and sorted into three grades of *brights* and two of *russets* (fruit with rust mite discoloration), each of which was shipped under different brands. Lemons, which are customarily picked at an immature, more-or-less fully green stage, were cured for a few weeks, to allow the internal tissues to soften and thus release more juice, prior to sizing and grading. California oranges and lemons were handled in similar fashion, except lemons were cured for a much longer period (i.e., were harvested at an earlier stage of maturity) and they and other fruit were stored before their long cross-country journey in railcars. Criteria for grades in Florida and California about 1900 are summarized in Table 2.2 (Hume 1907).

The first, tentative U.S. standards for grades of Florida and California citrus were established in 1924 (Hume 1926). The marked disparity in external qualities of fruit from the two states is clearly evident in these early standards, which include nine grades and subclasses for Florida but only five for California Table 2.3). Standards for Florida fruit applied to all citrus, but were written primarily for oranges, grapefruit, and tangerines. Lemon plantings in Florida had largely disappeared following the devastating freezes of 1894-1895, and limes were then only a minor crop on the keys below Miami at the southern tip of the state. Standards for California applied mainly to oranges. The greater complexity of the grade requirements for Florida citrus compared with those for California is necessitated by the presence of rust mite, occurrence of a far broader assortment of blemishes, and the generally lighter, less uniform color of Florida fruit. California standards have always placed primary emphasis upon color, whereas those for Florida have stressed superior internal qualities, as will be discussed in later sections.

U.S. standards for grades of citrus fruits have undergone numerous alterations since 1924. Separate standards have been adopted for the major production areas-Florida, California-Arizona, and Texas (plus other states)-and species as their industries evolved (Table 2.4). Periodic amendments have also been adopted to reflect inclusion of additional cultivars or hybrids and changes in inspection procedures. U.S. standards apply primarily to fruit in interstate commerce, with sales to Canada and Mexico classed as "domestic" for grade purposes. Standards for export shipment elsewhere are often less restrictive. Individual states also have grade standards that apply to fruit shipped within their boundaries. These may be identical to their

TABLE 2.2. Criteria for Grades of Florida and California Citrus 1875 to about 1900

Class	Grade	Criteria
		FLORIDA
Bright (no rust mite)	Fancy	Bright, smooth, thin skinned, without specks, spots or injuries: quality and appearance fancy.
	No. 1	Smooth, thin-skinned, with a few small spots or specks; quality equal to Fancy grade.
	No. 2	Large spots or marks, slight indentures[a], and discolorations.
Russet (rust mite discoloration)	Fancy	Same as Bright Fancy.
	No. 1	Same as Bright No. 1 plus No. 2
	Culls	Fruit with large unsightly marks, thorn punctures, bruises, dieback (ammoniation), creasing, etc.
		CALIFORNIA
Fancy		Extra bright, very smooth, thin skin.
Choice Bright		Strictly bright, fairly smooth skin, desirable size.
Bright		Bright, free from smut.

Source: Hume (1907).
[a]Equivalent to "indentations" in modern usage.

U.S. counterparts but may also stipulate additional, usually more stringent, requirements on allowable discoloration and color for Florida fruit.

MEASUREMENT OF FRUIT CHARACTERISTICS

The accurate measurement of fruit characteristics requires samples that are truly representative of the lot, trees, or grove (orchard) and tests for each quality factor that are precise, may be run quickly and easily, and are as objective as possible. Chemical and physical procedures for determining internal qualities are inherently more precise and objective than the visual and tactile ones for determining external factors. Measurement of fruit characteristics involves two quite different situations: (1) The grower, packinghouse manager, or fruit buyer who must ascertain the status of the fruit with respect to certain internal (i.e., the stage of maturity) and external (i.e., range in sizes and grade) qualities before harvest of the crop; and (2) the inspector who checks harvested fruit for compliance with legal standards. Samples in either case normally consist of fruit of a given size for test purposes.

Internal Qualities (Maturity)

Five characteristics are commonly utilized worldwide as indicators of maturity: TSS, TA, TSS:TA ratio, juice content, and color break. The first four are internal factors, the last is an external one.

TABLE 2.3. Summary of Tentative U.S. Standards for Grades of Florida and California Citrus Fruits in 1924

	FLORIDA
Grades and subclasses	U.S. Fancy, U.S. Fancy Bright, U.S. Fancy Golden, U.S. No. 1 Bright, U.S. No. 1 Golden, U.S. No. 1 Russet, U.S. No. 2 (Choice) Bright, U.S. No. 2 (Choice) Golden, U.S. No. 3.
Criteria:	Similar varietal characteristics: firm; mature; free from decay (with none at point of origin and not greater than 3% at destination), cuts, and bruises; limitations as to smoothness, skin thickness, percentage of light discoloration (principally rust mite but including some scars and melanose), and degree of damage (slight in Fancy and No. 1; serious damage in No. 2) caused by dirt and other foreign materials, dryness, limb rubs, thorn scratches, scars, scale, insects, or mechanical or other means.[a]
	CALIFORNIA
Grades:	Fancy, Extra-Choice (Fancy and Choice), Choice, Standard, Orchard Run.
Criteria:	Mature, hand-picked oranges of one variety; limitations on color, form, texture, shape, cleanliness, scarring, sunburn, puffiness, thrips marks, and scales; free of splits, cuts, or bruises (practically free in Standard); compliance with state requirements on color, sugar content, and frost damage.[a]

Source: Hume (1926).
[a] 10% lot tolerance included to allow for variations in grading and handling.

About 75-80% of the TSS in the juice of nonacid citrus is sugar, principally sucrose and glucose plus fructose in roughly equal amounts. This proportion is high enough and sufficiently consistent that TSS or °Brix (a processing term now widely adopted for fresh fruit) can be expressed in terms of percentage pure sucrose. This test may be substituted for the much more laborious and time-consuming procedures used to determine disaccharides (sucrose) and monosaccharides (glucose and fructose) separately. There are two methods for determining TSS: Measuring the specific gravity with a hydrometer, or the refractive index with a refractometer. The former is the official method in most, if not all, parts of the world. A hydrometer calibrated in percentage TSS (or °Brix) is placed in a cylinder containing about 500 ml of strained juice, is allowed to float for a few minutes, and then is read. Temperature of the juice is determined at the same time so that the hydrometer reading can be calibrated to a standard temperature, usually 20°C. The alternative, nonofficial method is to determine TSS with an Abbe or hand refractometer, both of which have a juice scale calibrated at either 20° or 25°C, or rarely 28°C. This measurement is much faster, utilizes only one or two drops of juice and is ideal for field use. Values, however, tend to be a little higher than those obtained with a hydrometer. Juice samples containing more than about 2% acid must have an acid correction applied to the °Brix reading.

TABLE 2.4. Summary of Changes in U.S. Standards for Grades of Citrus Fruits since 1924

Year	Fruit/grades for which standards adopted
1941	Sweet oranges, grapefruit, and mandarins, except tangerines.
1947	Florida oranges and mandarins, except tangerines: U.S. Fancy, No. 1 Bright, No. 1, No. 1 Golden, No. 1 Bronze, No. 1 Russet, No. 2 Bright, No. 2, No. 2 Russet, No. 3.[a] Florida grapefruit: (Same grades as for oranges). California and Arizona oranges: U.S. Fancy, No. 1, No. 2, Combination (40% No.[a] 1, 60% No. 2), No. 3.
1948	Tangerines: U.S. Fancy, No. 1, No. 1 Bronze, No. 2, No. 2 Russet, No. 3.[a]
1950	California and Arizona grapefruit: (Same grades as for oranges).
1955	Grapefruit in Texas and states other than Florida, California, and Arizona: U.S. Fancy, No. 1 Bright, No. 1 Bronze, Combination, No. 2. Russet, No. 3.
1959	Oranges in Texas and states other than Florida, California and Arizona: (Same grades as for grapefruit).
1976	Florida oranges and tangelos (and mandarins except tangerines): (Same grades as in 1947).

Sources: USDA (1948, 1950, 1957, 1969A, B, 1980A, B, C).
[a]With the considerable development of citrus processed products since World War II, these multiple grades are seldom, if ever, used. Florida packers typically ship only No. 1, the rest of the crop going to processing. An exception is after a natural disaster such as a major freeze or hurricane. Then No. 2 grade is often used.

Organic acids, of which citric acid is the major component, are equal to roughly a tenth or somewhat less of the TSS in the juice of nonacid fruits and up to about 80% in that of acid fruits. TA is measured by titrating a known volume of juice, typically 10 or 25 ml, with standard NaOH to the phenolphthalein (indicator) endpoint of pH 8.3, then converting the quantity (ml) of alkali consumed to percentage anhydrous citric acid. (True TA involves a double titration to free tightly bound acid groups, hence is seldom measured as such.) TSS:TA (°Brix:acid) ratio is a calculated value.

Juice content is determined by cutting individual sized fruit of a sample transversely at the equator, extracting the juice with a hand-operated or motor-driven reamer (whose speed should not exceed 400 rpm unless the juice is to be deaerated prior to testing), and squeezing it through a fine-mesh screen to remove seeds and pulp. Juice content is expressed in at least four different units: U.S. gallons per box (e.g., Florida and Texas oranges); cubic centimeters per fruit (e.g., Florida and Texas grapefruit); percentage by volume (e.g., lemons and limes); and percentage by weight [e.g., in Mediterranean countries (OECD 1971), Australia (Australian Citrus News 1976), and a number of others]. The first two are double units, since the standard weight of a Florida box (56.4 liters) is 90 lb (40.8 kg) for oranges and juice volume is dependent upon fruit size (maximum equatorial diameter) in grapefruit. The last two are single units, with both juice and fruit measured either as volume or weight, and they are interconvertible provided the specific gravity is known. Percentage of juice by volume and by weight, however, is influenced by specific gravity, which varies among individual fruit of a given cultivar, that of sound larger fruit always being lower than smaller ones. It should also be pointed out that specific gravity is the most convenient means of separating freeze-damaged or otherwise dry fruit from sound ones (Wardowski and Grierson 1972).

Color break is defined as follows: "A break in color caused solely by nature shall mean that the change produced by nature converting the dark green color to the yellow or orange color has progressed to the extent that a tinge of yellow or orange is apparent" (Florida Dept. of Citrus 2006). It is measured by reference of every fruit in a sample (50 or 100) toting 2978 a standard color, e.g., a Maerz and Paul color (Maerz and Paul 1930) for Florida or a Munsell color (Munsell 1970) for California (and Arizona) fruit, which must be matched or exceeded. Color break at harvest is seldom enforced rigorously (especially in Florida), since fruit have to meet far more stringent color requirements when they are graded before shipment.

Most maturity standards stipulate that fruit may be inspected on the tree, during transport, or at the packinghouse. In practice, fruit are inspected immediately upon arrival at the packinghouse before it is run over the packingline; sized fruit are inspected again, as they are packed, if there is a question of maturity. Packinghouse personnel customarily run unofficial maturity and grade tests before a picking crew is sent out to the grove.

Maturity standards may include any or all of the characteristics discussed here. They are "tailor made" in terms of which factors are included and the values of individual standards for cultivars grown in a given state, country, or region. They tend to be rather simple in cool, dry areas with relatively few kinds of fruit and more complex in warm, humid climates with a broad spectrum of species and hybrids, as may be seen in the examples summarized in Table 2.5. Obvious problems may arise from this lack of uniformity, especially for different areas shipping fruit to the same market, as discussed later in this chapter.

External Qualities (Grade)

Standards for grade of fresh citrus fruit basically relate to external factors, such as color, texture, discoloration (especially in warm, humid areas), blemishes, similar varietal characteristics, form, and firmness, as well as maturity and uniformity of fruit size and pack. Color is, of course, the single most important factor because of its vital role in consumer acceptance. Definitions for certain factors and individual blemishes for each grade and subclass (if listed), with allowable limits, are expressed as a percentage of the surface or an accumulative circle of specified diameter. Tolerances allow for variations incidental to proper grading, sizing, and packing. Measurement of external factors is, however, much more subjective than that of internal

TABLE 2.5. Summary of Maturity Standards for Fresh Citrus Fruit in the United States, New South Wales (Australia) and OECD Countries

State/Country	Fruit	No. fruit in sample[a]	Periods during year	Color break (% surface)	Juice content	Acid (%)	TSS[b] (%)	TSS:TA ratio, min.[b,c]
Florida	Oranges	20/50	3	25/50[d]	5.0 gal./box	0.5	8.0	9.0:1
	Grapefruit[e]	10/50	3	25	cc/fruit[f]	—	7.0	6.0:1
	Tangerines[e]	20/50	2	50	—	—	9.0, 8.75	7.5:1
	Honey Tang[c]	20/50	1	—	—	1.0 (max)	—	12.0:1[g]
	Tangelos	20/50	5	50	—	—	9.5-8.5	8.0:1
	K-Early							
	Temple	20/50	1	50	—	—	9.0	8.5:1
Texas	Oranges	10	1	—	4.5 gal./box	—	8.5	9.0:1
	Grapefruit[e]	5	1	—	cc/fruit[f]	—	9.0	7.2:1
California	Oranges[e]	100	1	25	—	—	—	8.0:1
Arizona	Grapefruit[e]	30	1	66⅔	—	—	—	5.5:1[i]
	Lemons[e,g,h]	25	1	—	30% by vol.	—	—	6.0:1[j]
								—

[a]First number (and single number) refers to sample size for maturity tests; second number, to color break sample.
[b]Note that °Brix = %TSS (total soluble solids).
[c]Also required ratio according to actual TSS in juice; higher for CA fruit.
[d]Parson Brown 8/1 through 10/31.
[e]Cannot be color added.
[f]Varies according to fruit size.
[g]No required ratio.
[h]Must not have greater than 20% dryness.
[i]North and west of San Gorgonio pass.
[j]South and east of San Gorgonio pass.
[k]Additional standards may be imposed by individual countries.

TABLE 2.5. (Continued) Summary of Maturity Standards for Fresh Citrus Fruit in the United States, New South Wales (Australia) and OECD Countries

State/Country	Fruit	No. fruit in sample[a]	Periods during year	Color break (% surface)	Juice content	Acid (%)	TSS[b] (%)	TSS:TA ratio, min.[b,c]
Australia	Oranges[e]							
	Navels	10	—	—	33% by wt	1.92 (max)	8.0	7.0:1
	Other	10	—	—	33% by wt	2.24 (max)	8.0	5.5:1
	Grapefruit[e,g]	10	—	—	33% by wt	—	—	—
	Ellendale							
	Tangor[e]	10	—	—	25% by wt		8.0	7.0:1
	Other	10	—	—	25% by wt	—	—	—
OECD[k] countries	Oranges[e]	—	—	—	—	—	—	8.0:1
	Lemons[e,g]	—	—	—	20% by wt	—	—	—
	Mandarins[e,g]	—	—	—	40% by wt	—	—	—

[a]First number (and single number) refers to sample size for maturity tests; second number, to color break sample.
[b]Note that °Brix = %TSS (total soluble solids).
[c]Also required ratio according to actual TSS in juice; higher for CA fruit.
[d]Parson Brown 8/1 through 10/31.
[e]Cannot be color added.
[f]Varies according to fruit size.
[g]No required ratio.
[h]Must not have greater than 20% dryness.
[i]North and west of San Gorgonio pass.
[j]South and east of San Gorgonio pass.
[k]Additional standards may be imposed by individual countries.

qualities, because the former are judged mainly by visual observation (e.g., color, discoloration, blemishes, form) or by feel (e.g., texture and firmness) rather than by chemical or physical measurements. The summary of standards for grades (and subclasses) for California-Arizona, Florida, Texas, and Australia given in Table 2.6 provides examples of those found worldwide.

Grading is one of the few hand operations left in modern-day packinghouses, sizing being fully automated and packing largely so. Electronic color machines, developed about 50 years ago, are most practical for lemons and other citrus in areas where the fruit have comparatively few blemishes and no rust mite discoloration (e.g., in California and Arizona). In Florida packinghouses, electronic grading is increasingly replacing manual grading (see Chapter 12).

Citrus fruit are inspected twice, once as they are run over the grade table in the packingline to sort out *eliminations* (those with external qualities unsuitable for shipment as fresh fruit) and *culls*, and again during official inspection. Sorting on the grade table entails inspection of *every* fruit in a lot, except for those removed earlier as undersized or oversized in the presizing operation. A great deal of attention has been given to overall improvement of grading, especially during the last decade. A discussion of the conditions and machinery needed for efficient grading is presented in Chapter 12.

Official inspection for grade is typically carried out on samples of about 50 oranges, mandarins, etc., and two-thirds as many grapefruit. Samples are obtained at random from sized fruit in packing bins or from packed boxes, cartons or bags at the rate of about one sample per 50 boxes in a lot (fruit of a single grade). Current practice in the United States is to inspect each size separately on its own merits with a system of cumulative allowances for defects in a given grade (or subclass in the case of Florida or Texas fruit) on sequential samples from a given lot. The advantage of this procedure is that an entire lot is not rejected if a single size is out of grade, as was formerly the case.

FACTORS INFLUENCING LOCAL STANDARDS

The unstable nature of citrus fruits in general is clearly evident in the marked variation among internal and external fruit qualities of any cultivar in response to location, seasonal weather conditions, rootstocks, cultural practices, and tree age. Climate, broadly speaking, is the major determinant as to whether internal or external qualities are emphasized in marketing fruit from a given region.

Climate and Cultivars

In general, the nearer oranges are grown to their climatic limit in terms of low night temperatures, the more brilliant is their "typical color." This is es-

TABLE 2.6. Summary of Standards for Grades (and Subclasses) of Oranges from California-Arizona, Florida, Texas, and New South Wales

---

A. CALIFORNIA AND ARIZONA

Grades

U.S. Fancy, No. 1, Combination (at least 40% No. 1), No. 2.

Factors

a. Similar varietal characteristics, mature (all).

b. Well colored (Fancy. No. 1, except Valencia orange fairly well), fairly well colored (No. 2).

c. Firm (Fancy, No. 1), fairly firm (No. 2).

d. Well formed (Fancy, No. 1, fairly well formed (No. 2).

e. Smooth (Fancy), fairly smooth (No. 1), slightly rough (No. 2).

f. Free from decay, broken skins not healed, hard or dry skin, exanthema, growth cracks (all grades).

g. Free from bruises (Fancy, No. 1).

h. Free from dryness or mushiness (Fancy).

i. Free from injury (Fancy); free from damage (No. l); or free from serious damage (No. 2) caused by split, tough protruding navels, creasing, scars, oil spots, scale, sunburn, dirt or other foreign material, disease, or insects or mechanical or other means.

B. FLORIDA

Grades

U.S. Fancy, No. 1, No. 2, No. 3.

Subclasses of grades

No. 1 Bright, No. 1 Golden, No. 1 Bronze, No. 1 Russet, No. 2 Bronze, No. 2 Russet.

Discoloration (% surface in the aggregate)

a. Fancy 10%.

b. No. 1 Bright 20%, No. 1 33⅓%, No. 1 Golden (approx. 45% fruit >33%), No. 1 Bronze (all fruit discolored with at least approx. 22% fruit >331/s%, predominantly rust mite). No. 1 Russet (same as No. l Bronze except scars and speck melanose allowed).

c. No. 2 Bright 20%, No. 2 Russet (same as No. 1 Russet except >50%).

Factors

a. Firm (Fancy, No. 1, fairly firm (No. 2), slightly spongy (No. 3).

b. Mature and similar varietal characteristics fall grades).

c. Well formed (Fancy, No. 1), slightly misshapen (No. 2, misshapen (No. 3).

d. Well colored (Fancy), fairly well colored (No. 1, early and midseason cultivars, at least 50% for late cultivars), reasonably well colored (No. 2), poorly colored (No. 3).

e. Smooth texture (Fancy), fairly smooth (No. 1), slightly rough (No. 2), rough (No. 3).

f. Free from cuts not healed, decay, wormy fruit (all grades).

g. Free from ammoniation, buckskin, caked melanose, creasing, scab, split navels, sprayburn, undeveloped segments (Fancy).

h. Free from bruises, growth cracks (Fancy, No. 1, No. 2).

i. Free from caked melanose, spray bum, undeveloped segments (Fancy).

j. Free from injury by green spots, oil spots, rough, wide or protruding navels, scale, scars, skin, breakdown, thorn scratches (Fancy).

k. Free from damage by dirt or other foreign material, disease, dryness or mushiness, hail, insects, riciness or woodiness, sunburn, other means (Fancy).

Source: U.SDA (1957, 1969B, 1980B); Australian Citrus News (1976).

TABLE 2.6. (Continued) Summary of Standards for Grades (and Subclasses) of Oranges from California-Arizona, Florida, Texas, and New South Wales

l. Free from damage specified for Fancy plus ammoniation, buckskin, caked melanose, creasing, scab, split navels, sprayburn, undeveloped segments, oil spots, rough, wide or protruding navels, scale, scars, rind breakdown, thorn scratches (No. 1).

m. Free from very serious damage: All factors listed under f-h-free from, i-free from injury plus j-k-free from damage (No. 2).

n. Free from very serious damage: All factors listed under f, l and m, damage or serious damage (No. 3).

C. TEXAS (and states other than Florida, California and Arizona)

Grades

U.S. Fancy, No. 1, U.S. Combination, No. 2 Russet (up to approx. 58% No. 2's permitted), U.S. No. 3.

Discoloration (% surface) in aggregate

a. Fancy 10%.

b. No. 2 Bright 10%, No. 1 33⅓%, No. 1 Bronze (all fruit with some, predominantly rust mite), Combination (up to approx. 20% fruit with 50%).

c. No. 2, 50%, No. 2 Russet (at least approx. 2% fruit with 50%).

Factors

a. Firm (Fancy, No. 1), fairly firm (No. 2), slightly spongy (No. 3).

b. Mature and similar varietal characteristics (all grades).

c. Well colored (Fancy), fairly well colored (No. 1, early and midseason and at least 50°C for late cultivars), reasonably well colored (No. 2), not more than 25% of surface dark green (No. 3).

d. Well formed (Fancy, No. 1), slightly misshapen (No. 2), misshapen (No. 3).

e. Smooth texture (Fancy), fairly smooth (No. 1), slightly rough (No. 2), rough (No. 3).

f. Free from cuts not healed, decay, wormy fruit (all grades).

g. Free from ammoniation, buckskin, creasing, scab, skin breakdown (Fancy).

h. Free from bruises, growth cracks (Fancy, No. 1, No. 2).

i. Free from caked melanose, spray burn, undeveloped segments (Fancy, No. 1).

j. Free from injury by green spots, oil spots, split navels, rough, wide or protruding navels, scale, scars, thorn scratches (Fancy).

k. Free from damage by anything else not listed under free from or free from injury (Fancy).

l. Free from damage by everything not listed under f-i-free from, plus anything else (No. 1).

m. Free from serious damage by anything else not listed under free from (No. 2).

n. Free from very serious damage by anything else not listed under free from (No. 3).

D. NEW SOUTH WALES (AUSTRALIA)

Grades

No. 1, No. 2, Bulk No. 1-2 (must contain at least 50% No. 1), Bulk No. 2 (all No. 2 but not a single size).

Factors

Shape: Normal (No. 1, No. 2).

Similar varietal characteristics (if of a variety): No. 1, No. 2.

Rind thickness: Medium (No. 1, No. 2).

Color: Even (No. 1), reasonably even (No. 2).

Source: U.SDA (1957, 1969B, 1980B); Australian Citrus News (1976).

TABLE 2.6. (Continued) Summary of Standards for Grades (and Subclasses) of Oranges from California-Arizona, Florida, Texas, and New South Wales

Sound: No. 1, No. 2.
Mature: No. 1, No. 2 (see Table 2.5).
Blemishes: Less than 15% (No. 1), less than 25% of surface in the aggregate (No. 2).
Diameter of oranges: At least 60 mm (No. 1, No. 2).
[Diameter of grapefruit: At least 80 mm (No. 1, No. 2).]

Source: U.SDA (1957, 1969B, 1980B); Australian Citrus News (1976).

pecially true when a near-freezing condition is accompanied by low atmospheric humidity, as occurs in semiarid regions. Such fruit also tend to have higher acidity with lower sugar and juice content than fruit from other climatic regions. However, when winter temperatures are not as low, fruit have conspicuously higher sugar content than those in cool-night areas in arid areas with a Mediterranean-type climate (e.g., the California-Arizona desert region) (Tucker and Reuther 1967). Oranges remain more-or-less completely green when edible in lowland tropical areas, and they also have comparatively low sugar content if rainfall is fairly evenly distributed throughout the year (i.e., no months with less than about 100 mm). Acceptable color and sugar are obtained in the lower latitudes only where there are alternating wet and dry seasons and then usually above an altitude of about 1000 m. By contrast, grapefruit, mandarins, and mandarin hybrids attain better color and internal qualities in areas with warmer nights, higher soil temperatures, and higher atmospheric humidity. These generalizations also apply to the innumerable local microclimates found within any large citrus region.

Orange growers and shippers in districts with low rainfall (especially during winter, i.e., dormant-season rains) and consistently low night temperatures inevitably seek to capitalize on the "consumer appeal" of good, bright, uniform external color. Those in consistently warm, humid areas emphasize high sugar content and juice yield while minimizing color as a grade standard.

Not all cultivars produce well in all districts. Trees of Washington and other navel orange cultivars typically bear good yields of medium-sized, well-colored smooth fruit in California. The same orange grown in Florida has irregular, often scant, crops of large, coarse-textured, poorly colored fruit, valued only for its earliness and size (mainly as a gift fruit) when fruit of other cultivars are immature and/or too small. Attempts to apply California's external (grade) standards to Florida navel oranges, or Florida's internal (maturity) standards to California navel oranges, would be quite unrealistic. Similarly, Temple orange (a presumed tangor that originated in Jamaica) is a superlative dessert and breakfast fruit in Florida but coarse and sour when grown in California. The famous Shamouti orange is a mainstay of the Israeli citrus industry; nevertheless, it has performed poorly elsewhere, moreover it produces export-quality fruit only within a limited area of Israel (Monselise 1977). Internal quality of grapefruit is closely related to minimum night temperature. High quality, low acid grapefruit come from areas with few, if any, cold winter nights (Grierson and Ting 1978).

The foregoing examples illustrate the basic complexity of relationships among production area climate and soil, cultivar, and fruit quality (see Chapter 3). Why should Shamouti orange have so limited a cultural range when growing conditions around the entire Mediterranean Basin are uniform enough that fruit from all of the citrus areas can meet Organization for Economic Cooperation and Development (OECD) grade standards (Grierson and Ting 1978)? OECD requirements are also quite similar to those for other arid summer, cool-rainy winter regions such as California or New South Wales in Australia. Standards for external qualities in such regions may be too rigorous, thus essentially unattainable, for fruit grown in humid, warm subtropical to tropical areas, such as Florida, the West Indies, Brazil, or Queensland (Australia), whereas the OECD standards for internal qualities may actually be unrealistically low.

Internal vs. External Standards

The principal impact of internal standards is at the beginning of the harvest season of each cultivar when fruit will often barely meet maturity requirements. What is considered suitable for harvesting fruit in one area may be completely unacceptable in another. For example, coastal and desert-grown Marsh grapefruit in California may be shipped when TSS:TA ratios are 5.5:1 and 6.0:1, respectively (Calif. Dept. of Food and Agriculture 1975), whereas a ratio of 7.0:1 (with minimum TSS of 7.5%) is required for the same cultivar in Florida (Wardowski et al. 1995). Moreover, different criteria (e.g., juice content, TSS, TA, TSS:TA ratio, and color break) are used quite arbitrarily in different citrus-growing areas, as pointed out earlier. Statements in International Organization for Standardization (1973) sum up the situation nicely, with reference to acid, TSS, and the ratio between them: ". . . values depend on . . . variety and on ecological conditions. They should, therefore, be considered only in relation to the variety and to a well-defined area of production."

Internal standards applied to fresh citrus fruits have special importance to the consumer because fresh fruit are eaten individually or juiced a few at a time. Blending, which is customary with processed products, can greatly dilute the quality-lowering effects of a small proportion of off-bloom fruit or those otherwise legally mature from a palatability standpoint. It is logical to expect that internal maturity standards would be applied equally to fresh and processed fruit, and this is the case in most states or regions. However, some areas, such as New South Wales, have no internal standards whatever for fruit going to a cannery (Australian Citrus News 1976).

External standards, except for color break applied as a maturity standard (Calif. Dept. of Food and Agriculture 1975; Florida Dept. of Citrus 1996, 2006), apply consistently throughout the year. They have little relationship to *edibility*, but contribute enormously to *salability*. Brilliantly colored, blemish-free fruit invariably outsell drab, scarred fruit of greater palatability, demonstrating that consumers select fruit primarily on the basis of *appearance*. Certain cosmetic treatments, particularly ethylene degreening (an acceleration of the natural process) are commonly used to improve appearance. Some areas (e.g., Texas and Florida) also permit the external application of a dye (color adding) to pale-colored oranges and to Florida Temple oranges and tangelos (Florida Dept. of Agriculture and Consumer Services 1983; Florida Dept. of Citrus 1996, 2006; Texas Dept. of Agriculture 1956). External grade factors affect cannery quality when packinghouse eliminations (i.e., fruit rejected for fresh shipment) go to a processing plant. This can militate for or against juice quality, depending upon the time of year, delays in handling, packingline treatments (e.g., use of fungicides, waxes, or dyes) before rejection, etc. (Grierson and Wardowski 1977). Economic considerations and increasing concern over residue problems with eliminations are excellent reasons for placing the grading operation ahead of such treatments on a packingline (Grierson and Wardowski 1977 and Chapter 12).

MARKETS AND FRUIT MARKETABILITY

The only real basis for fresh fruit maturity and grade standards is economics. Certainly, quite different approaches are required to meet the disparate needs of widely differing citrus production areas. The ultimate source of revenue in a wide spectrum of fresh citrus markets is the consumer. As noted already, appearance is the chief quality influencing consumers' initial selection of fruits; palatability is important in determining subsequent sales. Certain fruit, notably oranges grown in warm, humid climates, have internal characteristics (e.g., high juice content and sugar) that enhance their value for processing into high-quality products like frozen concentrate or chilled (pasteurized) juice. This provides a viable alternative outlet for profitable disposal of blemished or surplus fruit that may be lacking in cool, arid climates where fruit is produced almost exclusively for the fresh fruit market.

A basic premise of maturity and grade standards is that growers must be allowed to dispose of their fruit sometime during the season, but the levels of such standards must also be consistent with the requirements of the market or markets that the area serves. The ultimate criterion for internal fruit qualities is taste, yet consumer acceptance varies over a surprisingly wide range from one person to another. Taste can not, however, be used as a maturity standard. All of these factors concerning markets and fruit marketability are interrelated in complex fashion. Their application relative to different growing areas necessitates compromises among many disparate, often conflicting, interests.

Types of Markets

The simplest marketing of all involves a locally grown crop without outside competition, such as might be found in a village market or a small roadside stand next to a grove. Orderly marketing begins with rudimentary sizing, while ignoring maturity and decay control (Grierson 1961, 1975). The first step toward required standards is the selection of a premium grade for which a higher price can be obtained. A market whose clientele demands blemish-free fruit, i.e., buys sound mature fruit on the basis of appearance rather than internal quality, is much more costly to supply because fruit must be sorted and blemished fruit offered separately or diverted to another outlet (e.g., a cannery), if one is available. The real problem is that blemished fruit are discriminated against and soon discounted price-wise in such a market, rather than the far better solution of paying a premium for good appearance. That both blemished and blemish-free fruit may have identical internal quality is usually completely ignored.

More sophisticated, complex grade standards become necessary when fruit from a developing area (e.g., one that follows the general pattern just described) are shipped to a market that is also supplied with fruit from established regions. This situation occurs in export trade to Western Europe or Japan from the United States. Here, the supplier can either meet the generally accepted standards of the consuming market area or persuade this market to accept standards more attuned to the conditions of the production area. The latter approach can be so difficult and expensive that it would be possible only for high-volume shipping areas, given the fact both custom and legal standards are generally so ingrained that changes in either are made slowly and with great reluctance.

Packout

The proportion of fruit shipped fresh compared to that harvested can be the major factor in determining profit or loss for the entire operation from grove to market (Grierson 1958). Market acceptance, however, sharply limits the extent to which grades can accommodate existing exterior blemishes. One solution is to have multiple grades from premium down to variously discounted inferior ones. The feasibility of this approach often depends upon the availability of alternative outlets. Florida oranges and grapefruit provide an interesting contrast in this respect. Superb frozen concentrated orange juice (FCOJ) or chilled (pasteurized) juice (POJ), for which there are excellent markets, can be made from oranges; thus fruit eliminated in the course of grading can be used profitably at a cannery. Grapefruit, on the other hand, yield far less juice per box and the yield of equivalent °Brix is much less when the juice is concentrated. Frozen concentrated grapefruit juice (FCGJ) sells, therefore, at a lower price and eliminations seldom return a profit, though since ca. 1990, Florida has developed a modestly profitable market for high Brix single strength grapefruit juice for the health food market. Packinghouses specializing in grapefruit may pack a whole series of grades (USDA 1980A) rather than send the fruit to a processing plant if this can be avoided.

The whole concept of packout has, however, been given comparatively little attention. Disfiguring scars, blemishes, etc., originate in the grove (orchard), yet a grower often cares little about what happens to the fruit after it is harvested, so long as he receives what he considers a fair return on his investment. Careful cost accounting of all of the expenses involved in growing, harvesting, handling, packing, shipping, and marketing generally show that a grower receives a lower net return in direct proportion to the percentage of fruit diverted into outlets other than fresh fruit. A grower may, however, actually make a higher net profit on *oranges* of concentrate quality sent to a processing plant depending upon the relative prices obtained for fresh and cannery fruit. The situation is quite different in the case of grapefruit, mandarins, and other specialty fruit, where the profit on fresh plus cannery fruit depends primarily upon how *few* boxes of the latter are involved. Alternative outlets are generally available in warm, humid areas, thus processors can capitalize on the superior internal qualities of fruit grown there. This may not be true in other regions where citrus is produced strictly for the fresh market and growers try to keep packout as high as possible.

Legal Constraints

The gradual improvement of internal characteristics (i.e., TSS, TA, TSS:TA ratio, and juice content) throughout the season without a well-defined period of maturity (as for deciduous fruits) allows citrus fruit to be stored on the tree for a long time. This provides considerable flexibility in marketing, since fruit may be harvested over a period of from several weeks to as much as 7 or 8 months, depending upon the species or hybrid. In the absence of regulations, however, there will always be shippers who "rush the season" to the detriment of the majority who wait until fruit have attained acceptable edibility and ship later to the same market.

State, federal, and/or regional agencies who set maturity standards for a controlled market tread a narrow path: Early-season standards must be low enough to accommodate the lower internal quality fruit at that time so that the later marketing period is not too brief to sell the remainder of the crop; yet standards must always be set high enough to ensure shipment only of high quality fruit and to avoid antagonizing buyers of the earliest shipped fruit. Florida's complex standards provide a solution to this dilemma: Requirements are higher early in the season and stepped down in two to six periods throughout the crop year (Florida Dept. of Citrus 1996). Fruit shipped early in the season may have inferior internal quality (i.e., may actually be physiologically immature). There is particularly a danger with respect to early season shipments when only a single internal standard, such as °Brix:acid ratio or percentage juice, is applied uniformly throughout the year.

Palatability in Relation to Maturity Standards

Taste is the only reliable index of fruit quality, despite the fact that consumers make their purchases largely on the basis of external appearance. Numerous internal characteristics influence palatability, including levels of aromatic constituents, TSS, TA, TSS:TA ratio, fruit age, and juice content. All vary from one year to another, and there are substantial variations during a crop season. The most important factor of all, as noted earlier, is the likes and dislikes of the individual who eats the fresh fruit or drinks its juice.

Taste correlates best with TSS or TSS:TA ratio. A tarter fruit (i.e., one with higher acid content) may be more acceptable than a sweeter one if the former also has higher °Brix. This occurs because of the buffering action of potassium and other salts in the juice. Both rind color and juice content are also correlated to some extent with palatability of fruit from the same tree or stage of maturity (Sites and Reitz 1949, 1950A, B). The variability of individual tastes is plainly evident in Fig. 2.1 in which the results of taste tests vs. TSS and TSS:TA ratio for several hundred samples of California orange juice are plotted as a scatter diagram and a line drawn around the points indicative of acceptable taste (Baier 1954). This "Pritchett tongue" also shows that the lower limit for acceptability of °Brix:acid ratio was 8:1, the legal standard in California. Similar tests conducted in Florida revealed essentially the same pattern, although the limit for °Brix:acid ratio in an acceptable sample was higher and less precisely defined.

The primary purpose of maturity standards is to provide an objective measure of palatability. Methods are restricted, however, to those that can be carried out in the field and packinghouse with simple equipment and give results that can be expressed objectively and preferably in numerical form. This rules out taste and aroma, both of which are utilized routinely in coffee and tea testing but cannot be used for a perishable product like citrus fruits

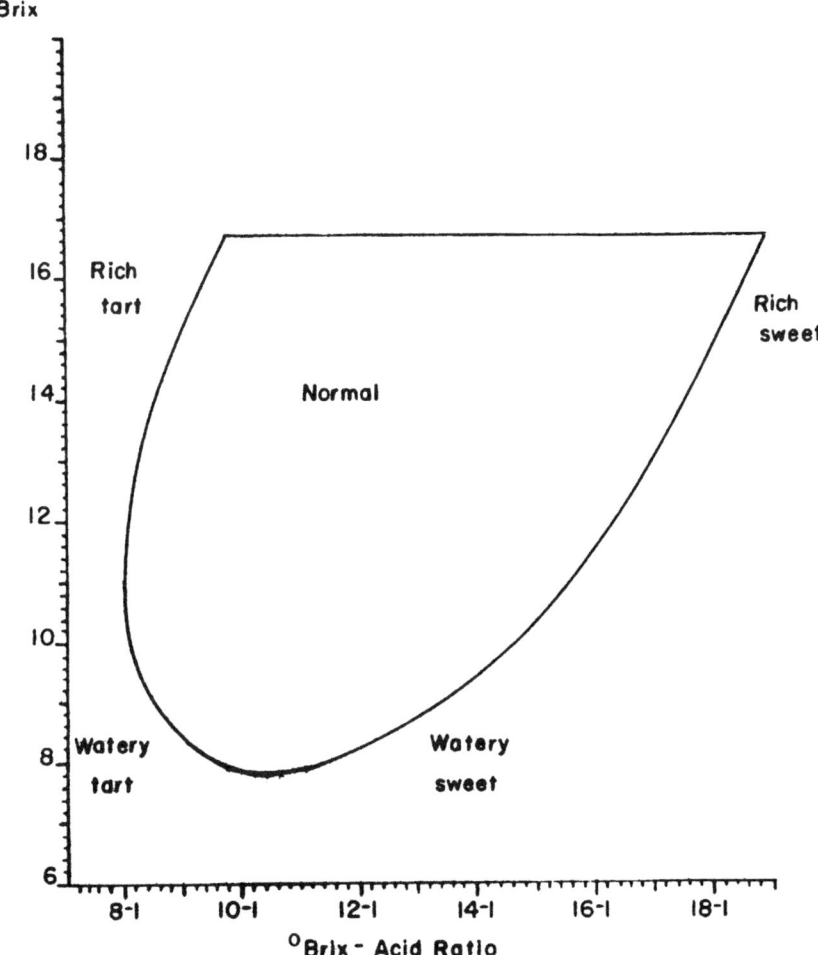

Fig. 2.1. Pritchett tongue diagram outlines limits of TSS (_Brix) and TSS:TA (°Brix:acid) ratio that correspond to acceptable taste in orange juice as determined by taste tests. From Baier (1954).

with their numerous species, cultivars, and hybrids. Furthermore, all maturity tests (except surface color) are destructive. Accurate sampling is thus of crucial importance since only a minute fraction of a lot can be tested.

The TSS:TA ratio, a calculated value from two different tests, probably approximates taste more closely than any other criterion. It can be deceptive, however, since an 8:1 ratio can mean 8 °Brix and 1% acid, 12 °Brix and 1.5% acid, or 4 °Brix and 0.5% acid. California circumvents this problem by also requiring a color break.

Because juice is the substrate for taste components, it has value as an index of maturity. Juice content (percentage by weight) is the only internal requirement in OECD (1971) standards. However, "In the case of juice quality, it is recommended that exporting countries should prohibit exports of insufficiently ripe fruit, using their own methods of determination on the varieties concerned" (Grierson and Ting 1978). Juice content (percentage by volume) is the sole internal standard for lemons (Calif. Dept. of Food and Agriculture 1975; USDA 1964) and limes (USDA 1958). Percentage of extractable juice is also useful as an index of early-season maturity for Florida grapefruit (Fig. 2.2), for early and midseason oranges and as a measure of senescence in lemons (Fig. 2.3). Juice yield is a good criterion for various types of citrus, but its application has been sadly lacking in standardization. As noted in a previous section, there are four separate methods for expressing juice content and they are not readily interconvertible. Florida's standards in particular are clumsy, but they and the others work reasonably well. The real problem with different methods arises when fruit from different regions are shipped to the same export market.

SUMMARY

The present legal standards for maturity and grade of citrus fruits in the various production areas around the world have evolved in response to several major influences, notably climate, market requirements, and the adaptability of species and individual cultivars to local conditions. Regions with a Mediterranean-type climate (i.e., semiarid to arid with winter rains, cool nights. high light intensity, and low atmospheric humidity) grow relatively few species. These conditions result in fruit with excellent external color and few blemishes but low in sugar and juice content, and high in acid. Grade standards in such regions emphasize color and freedom from blemishes, while maturity standards are simple, usually only a single TSS:TA ratio or a specified juice content. Regions with a warm, humid climate (i.e., predominantly summer rains, generally warm nights, and high atmospheric humidity, hence lower average light intensity from cloud cover) grow numerous species, often with many cultivars. These conditions result in rather poorly colored fruit with rust mite discoloration and numerous blemishes. Standards for grades include subclasses for discoloration and those for maturity are generally based on several factors.

The standards developed for each production area seek to maximize its advantages and minimize its disadvantages to as great an extent as the market will permit. Consumer reliance upon external appearance handicaps fruit from warm, humid regions with respect to initial acceptance. Higher standards for internal quality in such areas, however, provide a considerable advantage in terms of palatability not only for fresh fruit but also for pro-

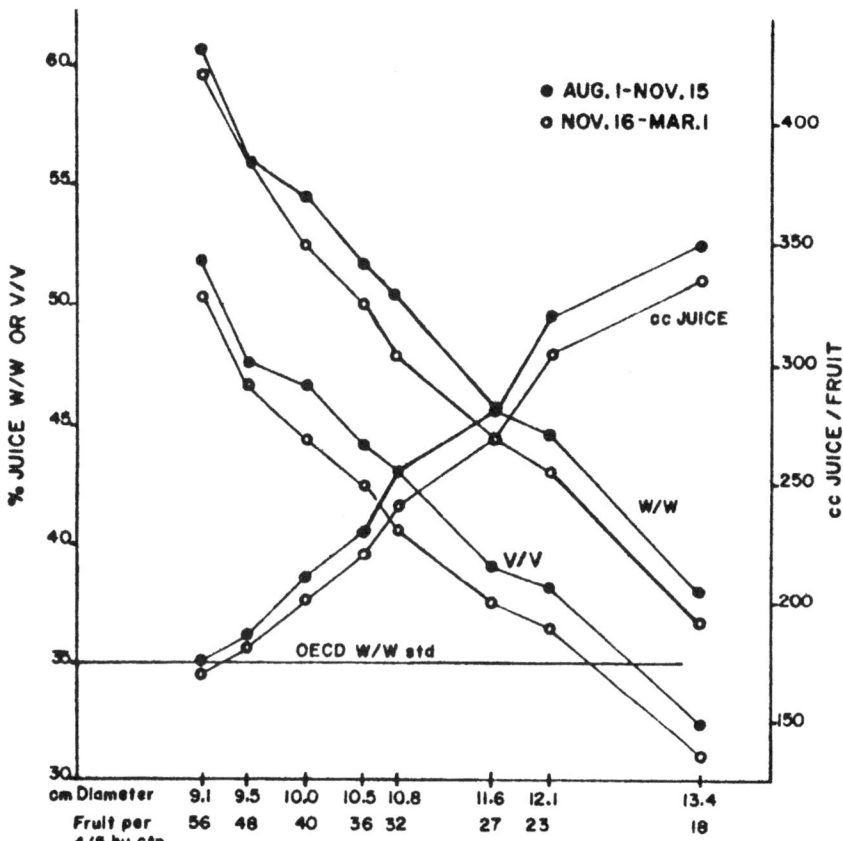

Fig. 2.2. Minimum juice requirements for Florida grapefruit for Aug. 1-Nov. 16-Mar. 1, expressed as cc juice/fruit, % by weight (w/w), and % by volume (v/v), for fruit of different size. Values are calculated based on oblate fruit with height:diameter ratio of 0.85; specific gravity of the fruit 0.88; and specific gravity of juice 1.04 (Nov. 16-Mar. 1) to reflect changes in the total soluble solids; fruit diameters and sizes are from Florida Dept. of Citrus Official Rules 20-34.06(2). From Grierson and Ting (1978); Turrell (1946).

cessed products, especially those of oranges. All attempts to devise uniform international standards have failed in the past. There is little likelihood of success in the future either, largely because of the overriding influences of environmental factors, particularly climate, on fruit qualities and the widely differing views among people who purchase citrus fruits as to what constitutes acceptable taste.

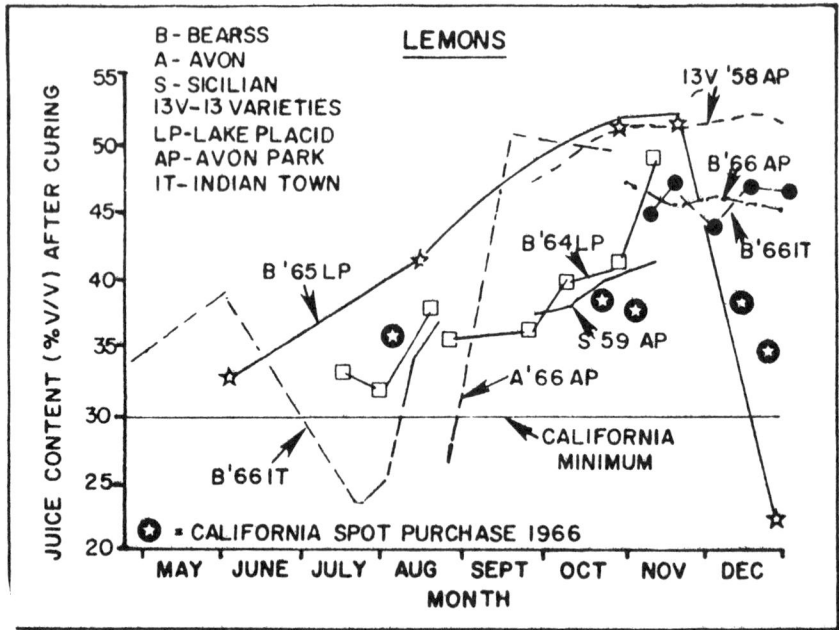

Fig. 2.3. Juice content of lemon cultivars at three locations during the 1958, 1959, 1964, 1965, and 1966 crop seasons. From Grierson and Ting (1978).

REFERENCES

AFVSS (Arizona Fruit and Vegetable Standardization Service). 1948. Extracts from the Arizona fruit and vegetable standardization laws.

AUSTRALIAN CITRUS NEWS. 1976. N.S.W. regulations, Plant Disease Act., 1924—Grading of citrus fruit. Aust. Citrus News (March), 8-9.

BAIER, W. E. 1954. The "Pritchett tongue." Calif. Citrogr. 39 (12), 442.

CALIF. DEPT. OF FOOD AND AGRICULTURE. 1975. Food and agricultural code, Title 3, Article 22, Sections 1430.22,.23,.53,.54,.81,.83,.85,.89.

COLLISON, S. E. 1913. Sugar and acid in oranges and grapefruit. Fl. Agr. Exp. Stn. Bull. 115.

DESZYCK, E. I. and TING, S. V. 1956. Seasonal changes in the juice content of pink and red grapefruit during 1955-1956. Proc. Fla. State Hort. Soc. 69, 68-72.

FLORIDA DEPT. OF AGRICULTURE AND CONSUMER SERVICES. 1983. 1982-83 season annual report. Div. of Fruit and Vegetable Inspection.

FLORIDA DEPT. OF CITRUS. 1996. Florida citrus fruit laws. Chapt. 601, Florida Statutes.

FLORIDA DEPT. OF CITRUS. 2006. Official rules affecting the Florida citrus industry: Pursuant to Chapt. 601, Florida Statutes, as amended.

GRIERSON, W. 1958. Causes of low pack-outs in Florida packinghouses. Proc. Fla. State Hort. Soc. 71, 166-170.

GRIERSON, W. 1961. Establishment of orderly citrus marketing in Latin America. Ceiba 9 (1), 3-12.

GRIERSON, W. 1975. Market preparation of tropical and subtropical fruits, pp. 504-513. *In* Postharvest Physiology, Handling and Utilization of Tropical and Subtropical Fruits and Vegetables. E. B. Pantastico (Editor). AVI Publishing Co., Westport, CT.

GRIERSON, W. and TING, S. V. 1978. Quality standards for citrus fruits, juices and beverages. Proc. Int. Soc. Citriculture 1978, 21-27.

GRIERSON, W. and WARDOWSKI, W. F. 1977. Packinghouse procedures relating to citrus processing, pp. 128-140. *In* Citrus Science and Technology, Vol. 2. S. Nagy, P. E. Shaw, and M. K. Veldhuis (Editors). AVI Publishing Co., Westport, CT.

HARDING, P. L. and FISHER, D. F. 1945. Seasonal changes in Florida grapefruit. Tech. Bull. 886. U.S. Dept. Agr.

HARDING, P. L. and SUNDAY, M. B. 1949. Seasonal changes in Florida tangerines. Tech. Bull. 988. U.S. Dept. Agr.

HARDING, P. L. and SUNDAY, M. B. 1953. Seasonal changes in Florida Temple oranges. Tech. Bull. 1072. U.S. Dept. Agr.

HARDING, P. L., WINSTON, J. R. and FISHER, D. F. 1940. Seasonal changes in Florida oranges. Tech. Bull. 753. U.S. Dept. Agr.

HARDING. P. L., SUNDAY, M. B. and DAVIS, P. L. 1959. Seasonal changes in Florida tangelos. Tech. Bull. 1205. U.S. Dept. Agr.

HUME, H. H. 1907. Citrus Fruits and Their Culture. Orange Judd Co., New York.

HUME. H. H. 1926. The Cultivation of Citrus Fruits. The Macmillan Co., New York.

INTERNATIONAL ORGANIZATION FOR STANDARDIZATION. 1973. Citrus fruits: Guide to storage and transport. Sub-committee LSO/TC 34/3C 3: Fruits and Vegetable "Working Group 8" Storage and Transport. Assn. Francaise de Normalisation, Tour Europe, Cedex 7, 92080 Paris. La Defense, France.

KREZDORN. A. H. and CAIN, R. F. 1952. Internal quality of Texas grapefruit. Proc. Rio Grande Valley Hort. Inst. 6, 48-52.

KREZDORN. A. H. and MAXWELL, N. P. 1959. Fruit quality studies of eight strains of red fleshed grapefruit on two rootstocks. J. Rio Grande Valley Hort. Soc. 13, 54-58.

LONG, W. G., SUNDAY, M. B. and HARDING, P. L. 1962. Seasonal changes in Florida Murcott Honey oranges. Tech. Bull. 1271. U.S. Dept. Agr.

MAERZ, A. and PAUL, M. R. 1930. Dictionary of Color. McGraw-Hill Book Company, New York.

MONSELISE, S. P. 1977. Citrus fruit development: Endogenous systems and external regulation, pp. 664-668. Proc. Int. Soc. Citriculture, Vol. 2.

MUNSELL, A. H. 1970. Munsell Book of Color. Munsell Color Company, Inc., Baltimore.

OECD. 1971. International standardization of fruit and vegetables: Standard No. 7, citrus fruit. Organization for Economic Cooperation and Development, Paris.

PIERCE, W. C. 1956. Citrus. Section 3-18, 29-34. *In* Florida Law and Practice. Harrison Publishing Co., Atlanta.

RYGG, G. S. and GETTY, M. R. 1955. Seasonal changes in Arizona and California grapefruit. Tech. Bull. 1130. U.S. Dept. Agr.

SITES, J. W. and REITZ, H. J. 1949. The variation in individual Valencia oranges from different locations of the tree as a guide to sampling methods and spot-picking for quality. I. Soluble solids in the juice. Proc. Am. Soc. Hort. Sci. 54, 1-10.

SITES, J. W. and REITZ, H. J. 1950A. The variation in individual Valencia oranges from different locations of the tree as a guide to sampling methods and spat-picking for quality. II. Titratable acid and the soluble solids/titratable acid ratio of the juice. Proc. Am. Soc. Hort. Sci. 55, 75-80.

SITES, J. W. and REITZ, H. J. 1950B. The variation in individual Valencia oranges from different locations of the tree as a guide to sampling methods and spot-picking for quality. III. Vitamin C and juice content of the fruit. Proc. Am. Soc. Hort. Sci. 56, 103-1 10.

SOULE. J. and GRIERSON, W. 1978. Citrus maturity and packinghouse procedures. Dept. of Fruit Crops (now Horticultural Sciences), IFAS. University of Florida, Gainesville.

TEXAS DEPT. OF AGRICULTURE. 1956. Citrus laws.

TUCKER, D. P. H. and REUTHER, W. 1967. Seasonal trends in composition of processed Valencia and navel oranges from major climatic zones of California and Arizona. Proc. Am. Soc. Hort. Sci. 90, 529-540.

TURRELL, F. M. 1946. Tables of surfaces and volumes of spheres and prolate and oblate spheroids, and spheroidal coefficients. University of California Press, Berkeley.

USDA. 1948. U.S. standards for tangerines. U.S. Dept. Agr., Consumer and Marketing Serv., Washington, DC.

USDA. 1950. U.S. standards for grapefruit (California and Arizona). U.S. Dept. Agr., Agr. Marketing Serv., Washington, DC.

USDA. 1957. U.S. standards for oranges (California and Arizona). U.S. Dept. Agr., Agr. Marketing Serv., Washington, DC.

USDA. 1958. U.S. standards for grades of limes. U.S. Dept. Agr., Agr. Marketing Serv., Washington, DC.

USDA. 1964. U.S. standards for grades of lemons. U.S. Dept. Agr., Agr. Marketing Serv., Washington, DC.

USDA. 1969A. U.S. standards for grades of grapefruit (Texas and states other than Florida, California and Arizona). U.S. Dept. Agr., Consumer and Marketing Serv., Washington, DC.

USDA. 1969B. U.S. standards for grades of oranges (Texas and states other than Florida, California and Arizona). U.S. Dept. Agr., Agr. Marketing Serv., Washington, DC.

USDA. 1980A. U.S. standards for grades of Florida grapefruit. U.S. Dept. Agr., Food Safety and Quality Serv., Washington, DC.

USDA. 1980B. U.S. standards for grades of Florida oranges and tangelos. U.S. Dept. Agr., Food Safety and Quality Serv., Washington, DC.

USDA, 1980C. U.S. standards for grades of Florida tangerines. U.S. Dept. Agr., Food Safety and Quality Serv., Washington, DC.

WARDOWSKI, W. F. and GRIERSON, W. 1972. Separation and grading of freeze damaged citrus fruits. Fla. Agr. Ext. Serv. Circ. 372.

WARDOWSKI, W. F., WHIGHAM, J., GRIERSON, W. and SOULE, J. 1995. Quality tests for Florida citrus. University of Florida, IFAS, SP 99.

WEBBER, H. J., REUTHER, W. and LAWTON, H. W. 1967. History and development of the citrus industry, pp. 1-39. In Citrus Industry, rev. ed. W. Reuther, H. J. Webber, and L. D. Batchelor (Editors). Div. Agr. Sci., University of California, Berkeley.

WOOD, J. F. and READ, H. M. 1938. Maturity studies of Marsh seedless grapefruit in the Lower Rio Grande Valley. Texas Agr. Exp. Stn. Bull. 562.

3

Preharvest Factors that Influence Fresh Fruit Quality

Robert E. Rouse and Mongi Zekri

It has long been recognized that there are large differences among citrus growing regions, not only in growth and yield of trees, but also in physical and chemical characteristics of the fruit. Most commercial citrus is grown between 20 to 40 degrees north latitude and 20 to 40 degrees south latitude. Within this zone, Mediterranean climatic areas are best suited for fresh fruit because of high external appearance with low peel blemish and lower juice quality. Subtropical areas have high juice content and juice quality, and high external blemish. In the tropical climatic area near the equator it is difficult to produce quality fruit because of external blemishes and poor juice quality due to multiple blooms that produce several age fruit on the trees each year at various stages of maturity. There are marked differences in the time lapse between anthesis (bloom) and market maturity and in the period of time that mature fruit may be stored on the tree and remain marketable. These factors determine the adaptability of a specific variety for commercial use in a particular citrus growing region.

Quality in citrus fruit involves good taste or juice flavor as well as good physical appearance. Other determinants of fresh fruit quality are peel thickness, firmness or texture. Both extremes in peel thickness are not desirable. Fruit with thick peel are usually low in juice, while those with thin peel are prone to splitting and are sensitive to postharvest problems that can occur during shipping and storage. The juicier the fruit, the better is its acceptance not only for the juice market but also as a fresh fruit. The flavor and palatability of citrus fruits is a function of relative levels of soluble solids, acids, and presence or absence of various aromatic or bitter juice constituents. Fruit quality standards, which determine minimum levels of acceptability, have been established in several citrus producing countries. Total soluble solids (TSS) and titratable acidity (TA) of the juice are important parameters for fresh fruit and important factors in overall juice quality and in determining time of harvest. The most important factors that may influence the physical (exterior) and chemical (interior) characteristics associated with fruit quality are discussed in this chapter.

Other than production practices, fruit quality is influenced by many factors that have complex interrelationships. Applying a particular cultural practice may result in a mixture of desirable and undesirable effects on fruit quality. To take advantage of the relationships between cultural practices and quality, one must know the specific quality factors preferred, the specific fruit quality problems existing in the grove in question, and the effects of cultural practices on those quality factors. The most important determinant of fruit quality under the control of the grower is the cultivar planted. Selection of appropriate cultivars and the quality factors associated with several cultivars are briefly discussed. The amount of fruit that is set has a very significant effect on fruit quality. Researchers have commonly observed a positive correlation between the number of fruit per tree and fruit quality (Cary and Weerts 1977; Finch and McGeorge 1939; Marloth 1950). When the number of fruit per tree is low, the peel texture, shape of fruit, and often fruit color are poor.

Quality of individual fruit varies significantly, even on the same tree. Studies of the juice composition comparing fruit borne in various positions on the tree canopy show clearly that inside heavily shaded fruit have less total soluble solids than outside exposed fruit. Insufficient light contributes to reduced total soluble solids concentration of inside fruit nourished by heavily shaded leaves. The highest TSS concentrations and TSS:TA ratios occur in fruit from the upper outside portion of the tree. The more desirable colors occur on fruit from the outside of the canopy and from the upper parts of the tree (Sites and Reitz 1949, 1950A, B). Generally, the largest fruit are found in the lower and north sides of the tree in northern latitudes (Wallace *et al.* 1955). In most cases, small fruit contain higher TSS and TA in the juice (Harding and Lewis 1941; Wallace *et al.* 1955). Other reports are in general agreement with these observations (Iwagaki and Kudo 1977; Kunte and Deshpandi 1969-1970; Suzuki *et al.* 1969; Tominaga and Daito 1982).

CLIMATE

Research data gathered over the last two decades showed that climate has the dominant effect on fruit quality in commercial citrus producing areas. All the fruit produced in a specific regional climatic area share a common set of quality characteristics. Areas with hot, dry summers and cool, more humid or wet winters (Mediterranean climate) generally produce fruit with better peel color but thicker coarser peel than areas having more humid growing seasons and warmer winter nights (Reuther 1980; Reuther and Rios-Casttaffo 1969; Reuther *et al.* 1969). Cultural practices cannot completely overcome these differences. For example, there is no known cultural practice that will allow California (with Mediterranean climate) to produce low-acid, thin-peel Florida-type grapefruit. Nor is it possible to achieve California's navel quality in south Florida's warm to hot fall months.

Among all the elements of climate, temperature or energy regime during fruit development is probably the dominant one influencing fruit quality. It has been recognized that there are large differences among citrus growing regions, not only in growth and yield of trees, but also in physical and chemical characteristics of the fruits. To further complicate matters, the several tissues making up citrus fruit tend to respond independently to climatic diversity during the course of development and maturation. Under certain climatic conditions, the internal fruit quality of early maturing varieties reach maturity standards while the peel is still green. On the other hand, under certain other climatic conditions, some varieties obtain optimum peel color and other characteristics suitable for marketing before juice characteristics reach market quality. In those areas, fruit peel enters the senescent stage while the internal juice characteristics are still of good market quality.

It is clear that climatic conditions, year to year and even season to season variations, can influence time and amount of bloom and subsequently fruit quality and production. In subtropical areas, spring bloom fruit is of better quality than summer bloom fruit. The latter is likely to be of coarser texture and thicker rind and develop faster from bloom to market maturity than the former.

Climatic factors have an influence on the vigor of vegetative growth and consequently fruit development and quality. Vegetative growth is competitive with fruit growth for available nutrients such as sugar and minerals. Flushes of heavy vegetative growth will reduce the solids available to developing fruit, while a period of dormancy will increase the solids available. This competition between vegetative growth and fruit development for nutrients is one reason for the relatively low solids concentrations often found in tropical oranges as compared to subtropical oranges. Also tending to reduce solids is the relatively high rates of respiratory loss of carbon during the warm nights typical of the tropics. In the subtropics, the cooler fall months check growth somewhat but favor high rates of photosynthesis. This points out that climatic factors tend to interact in complex ways with growth, flowering, and metabolic factors to influence fruit growth and maturity, and ultimately, market quality of the fruit.

Physical Characteristics and Size

Climate affects rate of fruit maturation, fruit morphology, rind texture, color, thickness, and shape. Such effects may be moderated by non-climatic factors, such as crop load, rootstock, and certain cultural practices. Nevertheless, the temperature regime during fruit growth and development plays a dominant role influencing fruit morphology. Larger fruit size is generally associated with high temperatures. However, Fucik and Norwine (1979) reported that ultimate fruit size of Ruby Red grapefruit in the Rio Grande Valley of Texas was positively correlated with spring temperatures but negatively correlated with August-September temperatures. Data of Hilgeman *et al.* (1959) on Valencia orange in Arizona are in agreement with the Texas data; that is, summer temperatures in excess of 38°C depressed fruit growth rate. Their studies showed that 96% of the variation in fruit enlargement was accounted for by number of fruit per tree, bloom date, and summation of degree days above 38°C. Hilgeman *et al.* (1959) also reported a significant negative correlation between fruit growth rate and degree days below 0°C in the November 21-February 28 period. When the relative humidity (RH) in the Yuma area of Arizona remained low through the night, the growth rate of Valencia orange fruit was reduced; 37% RH appeared to be the critical level (Hales *et al.* 1968).

Juice Composition

Even though production practices may modify climatic effects, smooth thin peel and high juice content were associated with hot, humid climates during the fruit development period (Cooper *et al.* 1963; Hilgeman 1966; Reuther 1973; Webber and Batchelor 1943). Haury *et al.* (1978) observed in tropical climates a reduction in TSS and TA in mandarin, orange, grapefruit, tangelo, and tangor, but not in lemon and lime. Pehrson (1976) associated advanced maturity, based on TA in the juice, of navel orange with a greater number of degree-days above 13°C in the spring.

There is a fairly consistent broad qualitative relationship between the prevailing temperature level and the rate of decrease of acid concentration in the juice, especially during the latter half of the fruit growth and maturation period. The inverse relation of temperature and acid is generally true, under orchard conditions, for oranges, grapefruit, mandarins, pummelos and their hybrids. Lemons and limes, however, mostly appear to have as high acid content in juice in a hot as in a cool climate, but there are exceptions.

The genetic level of acidity in the juice of a cultivar, together with its rate of decline as maturation progresses in relation to the seasonal temperature regime, are important factors determining the ultimate quality of fruit, as well as earliness or lateness of maturity. Thus the rapid decrease is acidity of navel cultivars and its slower decrease in Valencia types are important factors, among others, determining their ranges of climatic adaptations, as well as their seasons of maturity and ultimate market quality.

Sunburned fruit is a problem in some citrus-growing areas of the world. Fruit grown under full exposure to the sun are smaller, weigh less, and have less juice, higher TSS concentrations, and more granulated carpels than fruit grown in the shade (Ketchie and Ballard 1968). The incidence of granulation in sweet orange is positively and significantly related to the heat units received throughout the year, and the extent of granulation is significantly related to heat units and maximum and minimum temperatures during the early part of fruit growth (Awastii and Nauriyal 1971). Numerous reports suggest that TSS, the TSS:TA ratio, and ascorbic acid are positively correlated with solar radiation (Iwagaki 1981; Randahawa and Dinsa 1947; Syvertsen and Albrigo 1980; Winston and Miller 1947).

Color

Many facets of climate interact with each other and with production practices to influence ultimate fruit quality. Climatic effects vary with the stage of development of the fruit. There are some striking effects of the seasonal temperature regimes on rind color, especially with oranges and mandarins. Low air temperatures (below 13°C) were associated with initial color break of oranges in the fall (Stearns and Young 1942), while regreening of Valencia orange in California was strongly influenced by shoot temperature (Coggins et al. 1981). These effects were related to influences upon chlorophyll and carotenoid pigments. Temperature effects upon exterior fruit color are dependent upon the particular pigments in the peel. Stewart and Wheaton (1971) showed that the quantity of β-citraurin, one of the main sources of red color of mandarin-type fruit, was reduced at high temperatures. They speculated that high temperatures in the tropics limit the accumulation of the pigment and prevent the peel from obtaining deep color.

The deeper orange color of the peel (greater carotenoid content) of mature oranges such as navel and Valencia varieties in California and Arizona is due mostly to the greater incidence of chilling temperatures (below 15°C) in the west than in Florida. Especially significant in this regard are the much cooler night temperatures during the fall months in the drier climates prevailing in the western U.S. citrus growing states like California and Arizona citrus. The effect of chilling temperatures on the flesh or juice color is less striking than the effect on the peel.

It has been suggested that the commonly observed relation between the onset of chilly nights in subtropical climates and the beginning of yellow or orange coloration (color break) of the peel of most commercial citrus varieties is a chilling injury reaction causing increased ethylene production associated with a stimulation of chlorophyll breakdown and synthesis of carotenoids. In hot, tropical climates having an almost complete absence of chilling temperatures, oranges characteristically have a green to pale yellow pigmentation of the peel at maturity.

The so-called blood oranges contain the pigment anthocyanin in the flesh. They tend to be heavily pigmented in climates with a great frequency of cool nights and less heavily pigmented in climates with warmer nights. Under very hot, tropical conditions, such pigmentation may be reduced to a few flecks or even be completely absent. In grapefruit and pummelos in particular, some varieties have a pink or red flesh color due to another pigment, lycopene. In contrast to the pigment of blood orange, hot climates tend to increase lycopene concentration in the flesh, and cool climates to reduce it.

Varietal Interactions

There is considerable diversity among cultivars and species of citrus in their response to climate, especially as regards to market quality of the fruit. For example, the navel group of cultivars develops its best eating and eye-appeal qualities in a Mediterranean type climate with cool, wet winters and hot, dry summers. In wet, tropical regions, it tends to be large, with poorly colored rinds, and low total soluble solids and acid in juice. On the other hand, cultivars of the Valencia type are adapted to a broad range of climates, producing excellent to acceptable fruit quality in most of the important citrus regions of the world. Most cultivars of the Satsuma group produce high market quality fruit in humid climates, having abundant chilling temperatures in winter. Unlike the navel cultivars, most grapefruit cultivars develop optimum internal quality in warm climates with little winter chilling.

The warmer climates of tropical and semi-topical regions produce orange, mandarin, and grapefruit cultivars of earlier maturity and lower acid content than in cooler, cold winter subtropical climates. The peel color of oranges and mandarins is more intense and of greater eye-appeal at maturity in the cold-winter subtropical climates. Most citrus cultivars may tend to have somewhat lower soluble solids in juice in tropical climates having no cool temperature or drought-induced dormant periods, as compared to subtropical climates with distinct cool temperature-induced dormant periods (Davies and Albrigo 1994).

Even though citrus trees develop largely in response to their genetic endowment and the climate, production practices can have some favorable influences upon fruit quality. Cultural practices that attempt to cope with climatic or weather problems include irrigation and nutrition.

IRRIGATION AND PLANT NUTRITION

The effects of irrigation and nutrition on fruit quality are very important and should be understood by producers to increase profitability. These effects should also be and taken into consideration to enhance sustainability and competitiveness. In general, excessive irrigation and nutrition reduce fruit quality. Therefore, balanced nutrition with sound irrigation scheduling should be a high priority management practice for every grower. Citrus trees require a properly designed, operated, and maintained water management system and a balanced nutrition program formulated to provide specific needs for maintenance and for expected yield and fruit quality performance. Irrigation contributes to the efficiency of fertilizer programs. Adequately watered and nourished trees grow stronger, have better tolerance to pests and stresses, yield more consistently, and produce good quality fruit. On the other hand, excessive or deficient levels of watering or fertilization will result in poor fruit quality.

The most important management practices influencing fruit quality are irrigation and nitrogen, phosphorus, potassium, and magnesium nutrition. The effect of other macronutrients and most micronutrients on fruit quality is not significant or not known. However, when any nutrient element is severely deficient, fruit yield and fruit quality will be negatively altered. Trends in fruit quality response to high nutrition and irrigation are described and summarized below and in Table 3.1.

Irrigation

❑ Increases juice content and soluble solids-acid ratio.

❑ Reduces soluble solids and acid contents. Soluble solids per box will decrease, but soluble solids per acre may increase due to yield increase.

❑ Increases fruit size and weight, increases green fruit at harvest but decreases rind thickness.

❑ Increases incidence of blemish from wind scar, scab and *Alternaria* brown spot, but reduces rind plugging.

❑ Reduces stem-end rot incidence but increases incidence of green mold in storage.

Specific effects on juice and external fruit qualities are summarized in Table 3.1. This summary is based on numerous field experiments conducted over many years, mostly on responses of oranges to irrigation and fertilizer practices. Most of these effects were consistently observed, but some of them appear to depend on local conditions and growing regions. These observations are useful in developing a strategy to improve fruit quality for a particular variety or location.

Plant Nutrition

Nitrogen (N)

❑ Increases juice content and color, total soluble solids (TSS), and acid content.

TABLE 3.1. Effects of Mineral Nutrition and Irrigation on Fruit Quality

Variable	N	P	K	Mg	Irrigation
Juice quality					
Juice content	+	0	–	0	+
Soluble solids (SS)	+	0	–	+	–
Acid (A)	+	–	+	0	–
SS/A ratio	–	+	–	+	+
Juice color	+	0	–	?	0
Solids/box	+	0	–	+	–
Solids/acre	+	+	+	+	+
External fruit quality					
Size	–	0	+	+	+
Weight	–	0	+	+	+
Green fruit	+	+	+	0	+
Peel thickness	+	–	+	–	–

Increase (+), Decrease (–), No change (0), No information (?).
Source: Koo 1988.

❑ Increases soluble solids per box and per acre. However, excessive N, particularly with inadequate irrigation, can result in lower yields with lower TSS per acre.

❑ Decreases fruit size and weight.

❑ Increases peel thickness and green fruit at harvest.

❑ Increases incidence of creasing and scab but decreases incidence of peel blemishes such as wind scar, mite russeting, and rind plugging.

❑ Reduces stem-end rot incidence and green mold of fruit in storage.

Phosphorus (P)

❑ Reduces acid content, which increases soluble solids-acid ratio. Phosphorus rates have no effect on soluble solids per box but may increase soluble solids per acre due to increase in fruit production in soils that are low in P.

❑ Increases number of green fruit but reduces peel thickness.

❑ Increases expression of wind scar but reduces that of russeted fruit.

Potassium (K)

❑ Potassium produces mostly negative effects on juice quality except soluble solids per acre. Potassium increases fruit production therefore producing more soluble solids per acre.

❑ Decreases juice content, soluble solids, ratio, and juice color.

❑ Increases acid content.

❑ Increases fruit size, weight, green fruit and peel thickness.

❑ Reduces incidence of creasing and fruit plugging. In storage, reduces stem-end rot.

Magnesium (Mg)

❑ Slightly increases soluble solids, soluble solids-acid ratio, soluble solids per box and soluble solids per acre.

❑ Slightly increases fruit size and weight but decreases rind thickness.

GROWTH REGULATORS

Application of plant growth regulators (Chapter 4) can provide significant economic advantages to citrus growers when used appropriately. Depending on cultivar and timing, plant growth regulators may improve fruit set, increase fruit size by reducing cropload, extend the harvest season by delaying rind aging, and reduce preharvest fruit drop (Davies and Albrigo 1994).

Gibberellic acid (GA) is recommended to be used on citrus hybrids that are weakly parthenocarpic and without sufficient cross-pollination to improve fruit set. Applied from full bloom to two-third petal fall, GA can effectively set and produce an excellent crop of seedless Robinson, Nova, Orlando, Minneola, or other self-incompatible mandarin hybrids. Application of GA to citrus fruit approaching maturity enhances peel firmness and delay peel senescence (Stover 2000).

Application of GA in the fall often increases juice extraction from sweet oranges. It is likely that GA enhances juice extraction efficiency because increased peel firmness provides better mechanical support for fruit within extraction cups (Stover and Davies 2000).

Applied in winter during floral induction to cultivars that routinely flower heavily but set poor crops such as navel, Ambersweet, and Ortanique, GA reduces flowering and often results in increased fruit set. A combination of GA and 2,4-D has been used in many fresh fruit growing regions to enhance peel strength and extend the harvest seasons for grapefruit and oranges.

Naphthaline acetic acid (NAA) is used to reduce the number of fruit with excessive set. The advantage of NAA thinning in heavily cropping trees is increased fruit size (Stover et al. 2000). The greatest response has been shown when the average fruit diameter is around half an inch, which typically occurs 6 to 8 weeks postbloom. Thinning of Murcott (Honey tangerine) and Sunburst tangerine with NAA was found to increase fruit size, mean fruit weight, and percentage packout through improved fruit appearance (Stover *et al.* 2002).

CULTIVAR/ROOTSTOCK

The most important determinant of fruit quality under the control of the grower is the selected cultivar. Under comparable conditions, Hamlin orange always has poorer juice color and lower soluble solids than Pineapple or Valencia orange. Valencia is worldwide known to produce premium quality fruit. Its internal quality is excellent (Wutscher 1988). The fruit has high sugars, superior flavor, and deep orange juice color at maturity.

Many horticultural characteristics including tree vigor and size, fruit yield, fruit size, maturity date, and fruit quality are influenced by the rootstock (Castle *et al.* 1993; Krezdorn 1979) (Table 3.2). Rootstock effects are usually dramatic and can be easily seen even without taking measurements. One of the best-known examples is the small fruit size of Valencia budded on Cleopatra mandarin rootstock (Wutscher 1988).

Cleopatra mandarin is well suited for use with tangerines, Temple, and tangerine hybrids. Cleo is not widely used for grapefruit and Valencia. Sweet orange and grapefruit cultivars on Cleo generally produce small fruit and are not precocious. Low yield results from poor fruit set and size and fruit splitting.

TABLE 3.2. Rootstock Influence on Citrus Fruit Quality, Tree Longevity, and Fruit Size

	Rootstock influence on fruit quality and size				
Rootstock	Brix	Acid	Ratio	Life of tree	Fruit size
Rough lemon group					
Rough Lemon	Lowers	Lowers	Raises	Decreases	Increases
Macrophylla	Lowers	Lowers	Raises	Decreases	Increases
Volkamer lemon	Lowers	Lowers	Raises	Decreases	Increases
Milan Lemon	Lowers	Lowers	Raises	Decreases	Increases
Rangpur lime	Lowers	Lowers	Raises	Decreases	Increases
Sweet lime	Lowers	Lowers	Raises	Decreases	Increases
Sour orange and trifoliate group					
Sour orange	Raises	Raises	Lowers	Increases	Standard
Cleopatra mandarin	Raises	Raises	Lowers	Increases	Decreases
Sweet orange	Raises	Raises	Lowers	Increases	Standard
Carrizo citrange	Raises	Raises	Lowers	Increases	Standard
Troyer citrange	Raises	Raises	Lowers	Increases	Standard
Swingle citrumelo	Raises	Raises	Lowers	Increases	Standard
Trifoliate orange	Raises	Raises	Lowers	Increases	Variable

Source: Krezdorn 1979.

Larger fruit with thicker, rougher peel, and lower concentrations of soluble solids and acids in the juice are generally associated with cultivars budded on fast-growing vigorous rootstocks such as rough lemon, Volkamer lemon, *Citrus macrophylla*, and Rangpur lime. However, these rootstocks impart high vigor to the scion and induce high yield. Tangerine fruit from trees grown on vigorous rootstocks tends to be puffy, hold poorly on the tree, and have high incidence of granulation (Castle *et al.* 1993; Wutscher 1988).

Cultivars budded on slower-growing rootstocks, generally do not produce vigorous vegetative growth, but tend to produce small to medium size fruit with smooth peel texture and good quality fruit with high soluble solids and acid contents in the juice. This latter group of rootstocks includes trifoliate orange and some of its hybrids (citranges and citrumelos).

SUNLIGHT AND PRUNING

Even though citrus trees can tolerate shade and still flower and fruit, maximum flowering occurs when leaves are fully exposed to the sun. Therefore, pruning including topping and hedging to avoid crowding is extremely important for optimum flowering and fruit quality. The amount of fruit that is set has a very significant effect on fruit quality. There is a positive correlation between the number of fruit per tree and fruit quality. When the number of fruit per tree is low, the peel texture, shape of fruit, and often fruit color are poor (Tucker *et al.* 1991). Quality of individual fruit varies significantly, even on the same tree. Inside heavily shaded fruit have lower total soluble solid than outside exposed fruit. Insufficient light contributes to reduced total soluble solid concentration of inside fruit nourished by heavily shaded leaves.

It is well established that shoots with fruit do not flower the following year. A heavy fruit crop tends to deplete carbohydrates and results in a small crop and increased vegetative growth the following year. Pruning after a heavy crop additionally stimulates vegetative growth and reduces fruit yield and quality the following year. Pruning after a light crop and before an expected heavy crop can increase fruit size and help reduce alternate bearing. Pruning or topping and hedging usually increase fruit size and packout of fresh-market fruit by reducing crop load, thus increasing net cash returns to growers (Tucker *et al.* 1991).

PESTS AND DISEASES

Leaves produce the food and the energy source for trees. Excessive leaf loss will noticeably reduce flowering. The primary causes of leaf loss are freeze injury, salt and water stress problems including drought stress and flooding injuries, herbicides and pesticide phytotoxicities. Loss of leaves

TABLE 3.3. Factors Affecting Citrus Production and Fruit Quality

Influencing factors	Fruit yield	Time to maturity	Fruit size	Fruit shape and texture	Peel thickness	Peel color (A); Regreening (B)	Peel disorders[a]	Granu-lation	Juice content	Brix	Acid	Ratio	Soluble solids pro-duction per acre	Juice color	Postharvest handling (A)[b]; Overall quality defects (B)
Climate[c]															
Humid tropical	L-I	short	large	flat & smooth	thinner	A: g-y; B: yes	A, B, C, D, E: ↑	H	H-I	L-I	L	H	L	L	A: H; B: GFT-L
Dry tropical	L-I	med-short	smaller	round & pebbly	I	A: g-y; B: some	A, B, D: ↓	I	I	I	I-L	H	I-L	L	A: H; B: H
Humid subtropical	H	med-long	medium	I	I	A: y-o; B: yes		I	H	H	I	I	H	H	A: I; B: I
Dry subtropical	I-H	longer	smaller	pyriform & coarse	thicker	A: y-o; B: some	A, B, C, D, E: ↓	L	L	I-H	H	L	I-H	H	A: L; B: L, GFT-H
Rootstock[d]															
Lemon-types	H	later	young: lg old: med	coarser	thicker	A: greener; B: yes	A, B, D: ↓	H	L	L	L	I-L	I-H	L	A: L; B: H
Sour orange	I ORG: L-I MAN: H	earlier	med	smoother	thinner	A: orange; B: no	A, B, D: ↓	L ORG: I MAN: L	H	H	H	I	I-H	H	A: I; B: L
Mandarin-types[e]		med	med-lg	smooth	I	A: orange; B: some	A, B, D: ↓		I	H	I	I	I-L	I	A: I; B: I
Trifoliate orange	L-I	later	med-sm	smooth	thinner	A: orange; B: no	A, B, D: ↑	L	H-I	H	H	H	L	H	A: I; B: L
Citrumelos	I-H	later	med	slightly coarse	I	A: y-o; B: no	A, B, D: ↑	L	I	I	H-I	I	I	H	A: I; B: L
Citranges	I-H	med	med	I	I	A: o-y; B: no	A, B, D: ↑	L	I	I	I	I	I	H	A: I; B: L
Water[f]															
Rainfall and irrigation	↑	↑	↑	slightly coarse	thinner	B: ↑	D: ↑g		↑	↓	↓	↓	↑	I	A: H; B: H

TABLE 3.3. (Continued) Factors Affecting Citrus Production and Fruit Quality

Influencing factors	Fruit yield	Time to maturity	Fruit size	Fruit shape and texture	Peel thickness	Peel color (A); Regreening (B)	Peel disorders[a]	Granulation	Juice content	Brix	Acid	Ratio	Soluble solids production per acre	Juice color	Postharvest handling (A)[b]; Overall quality defects (B)
Nutrition[h]															
N	←	later	smaller	coarser	thicker	A: greener; B:↑	A:↑	←	→	→	→	→	←	←	A: H
P				smoother	thinner		A:↑		←		→←	←→	←←		
K	←		larger	coarse	thicker	A: greener	A, D:↓			→		→←		→	A: L; B: H
Tree spacing and pruning															
Spacing[j]	L-H[j]	later	[k]			A: greener	C:↓	←	→	→	higher	→	—	→	
Hedging	→	earlier	←	coarser	thicker	A: improved			←	—	—	—	→→		
Topping	→	earlier	←			A: improved				—	—	—	→→		
Tree age															
Young bearing	→	later	larger	coarser	thicker	A: greener; B:↑	A, B, D:↓		→	→	→	→	←	→	A: H; B: H
Mature bearing	←	earlier	smaller	smoother	thinner	A: improved; B:↑	→		←	←	←	←	←	←	A: L; B: L
PGRs[m]															
GA	n	later color		o		later color break	A, B:↓		p	—	—	—	—	↓	A:↓
2,4-D	←		←							—	—	—	—		A:→
Bloom															
Early[q]	←	shorter		flatter & smoother	thinner	A: greener			←	←	→	←	←	←	A: H; B: H
Late	L	longer	r	longer & coarser	thicker	A: y-o			→	→	←	→	→	→	A: L; B: L
Leafless	lower set		smaller						←→	←→	←→	→←	→←	—	—
Leafy	higher set	earlier	larger			A: earlier			←→	←→	←→	→←	→←	—	—

TABLE 3.3. (Continued) Factors Affecting Citrus Production and Fruit Quality

Influencing factors	Fruit yield	Time to maturity	Fruit size	Fruit shape and texture	Peel thickness	Peel color (A); Regreening (B)	Peel disorders[a]	Granu-lation	Juice content	Brix	Acid	Ratio	Soluble solids pro-duction per acre	Juice color	Postharvest handling (A)[b]; Overall quality defects (B)
Pests and diseases															
Insects and mites	↓ by high pop.		↓ by high pop.				E: ↑	—	RM: ↓	RM: ↑		RM: ↑			B: H
Melanose	little effect		—	rough			E: ↑	—							A: ↑ B: H
Scab	—		—	rough			E: ↑	—							A: ↑ B: H
Greasy spot	L-I		—	—		greener	E: GFT ↑	—					—		A: ↑ B: H
Alternaria	L-I		—	rough			E: MAN ↑	—					→	→	A: ↑ B: H
PDF	L-I		—	—			—	—					→	→	—
Virus/ viroid	L-I		—	—			—	—							—

Abbreviations: ORG = oranges, GFT = grapefruit, MAN = mandarins, H = high, I = intermediate, L = low, g-y = green to yellow, o-y = orange to yellow, ↑ = increases, ↓ = decreases, — = no effect.

[a]A) Creasing; B) Breakdown; C) Wind-scar; D) Splitting; E) Blemish.

[b]Refers to susceptibility of fruit to post-harvest handling. Poor spraying practices can adversely affect external appearance. Freeze damage can have major effects on fruit production, juice yield, and juice quality.

[c]Not all production regions adequately fit into the four categories listed: humid tropical, e.g., Central America and Caribbean; dry tropical, e.g., parts of Mexico and north South Africa; humid subtropical, e.g., Brazil, Florida, eastern South Africa; dry subtropical, e.g., Mediterranean-type climates—Mediterranean Basin, California Central Valley, western Cape of South Africa.

[d]Fruit production is relative to canopy volume.

[e]Cleopatra mandarin is not-precocious.

[f]Increasing levels of water within recommended range results in the shown responses.

[g]Increased splitting incidence associated with fluctuating moisture conditions.

[h]Increasing levels of nutrients within recommended ranges results in shown responses, whereas excess nutrition can reduce yield and fruit quality.

[i]Responses to closer spacing.

[j]Low density: production is initially low, increasing with canopy volume; High density production is initially high, decreasing with overcrowding.

[k]Dependent on crop load; smaller fruit size with high densities.

TABLE 3.3. (Continued) Factors Affecting Citrus Production and Fruit Quality

[l]High initially, decreases with overcrowding.

[m]GA - fruit set, 2-4-D - stop drop, NAA - fruit thinning (refer to Florida Citrus Pest Management Guide).

[n]Crop load management: effect dependent on timing of application. Winter application to reduce flowering in "on" year of alternate bearing trees; post-bloom application on seedless cultivars to increase fruit set.

[o]Response to GA application is time-dependent; fruit set spray results in coarser peel texture, whereas pre-harvest spray results in smoother peel texture.

[p]GA maintains juice yield via maintained fruit integrity.

[q]Applies to relative time of spring bloom.

[r]June bloom produces larger fruit.

Source: Compiled from Tucker *et al.* 2000.

can reduce flowering the following spring and fruit quality and production. Excessive leaf loss in late summer, fall, and early winter is the worst thing that can happen to citrus trees. Leaf loss in the fall from mite damage can be harmful, and greasy spot can cause devastating leaf loss and reduced flowering and fruiting (Davies and Albrigo 1994).

The improvement in fruit quality that a grower can achieve through choice of rootstocks, irrigation/nutrition management, and other grove practices may easily be overwhelmed by pests, diseases, and other injuries. Pests, which seriously affect the external appearance of fresh fruit, include citrus rust mites, thrips, scales, and other insects. Fruit quality may also be reduced by melanose, alternaria, scab, and other diseases or disorders.

SUMMARY

Many factors associated with the environment and cultural practices influence the quality of citrus fruit produced. Much of the data discussed have been summarized in chart form (Table 3.3) (Tucker et al. 2000). No one factor determines the fruit quality of citrus. Fruit quality in a given year is most influenced by climatic factors, and then management of cultural factors can be manipulated to avoid swings to the extremes and provide some consistency from year to year.

REFERENCES

AWASTHI, R. P. and NAURIYAL, J. P. 1971. Studies on granulation in sweet orange (*C. sinensis* Osbeck). I. Effect of climate on granulation. Punjab Hort. J. 11 (1/2), 6-14.

CARY, P. R. and WEERTS, P. G. J. 1977. Crop management factors affecting growth, yield and fruit composition of citrus, pp. 39-43. *In* Proc. Int. Soc. Citriculture, Vol. 1.

CASTLE, W. S., TUCKER, D. P. H., KREZDORN, A. H. and YOUTSEY C. O. 1993. Rootstocks for Florida citrus. Fla. Coop. Ext. Serv. Bull. SP 42.

COGGINS, C. W., JR., HALL, A. E. and JONES, W. W. 1981. The influence of temperature on regreening and carotenoid content of the 'Valencia' orange rind. J. Am. Soc. Hort. Sci. 106, 251-254.

COOPER, W. C., PEYNADO, A., FURR, J. R., HILGEMAN, R. H., CAHOON, G. A. and BOSWELL, S. B. 1963. Tree growth and fruit quality of Valencia oranges in relation to climate. Proc. Am. Soc. Hort. Sci. 82, 180-192.

DAVIES, F. and ALBRIGO, L. G. 1994. Citrus: Crop Production Science and Technology. CAB International, Oxon, United Kingdom.

FINCH, A. H. and McGEORGE, W. T. 1939. Studies of grapefruit fertilization in Arizona. Proc. Am. Soc. Hort. Sci. 37, 62-67.

FUCIK, J. E. and NORWINE, J. 1979. Climatological parameters and grapefruit size relationships in Rio Grande Valley of Texas. J. Rio Grande Valley Hort. Soc. 33, 83-89.

HALES, T. A., MOBAYEN, R. G. and RODNEY, D. R. 1968. Effects of climatic factors on daily Valencia fruit volume increases. Proc. Am. Soc. Hort. Sci. 92, 185-190.

HARDING, P. L. and LEWIS, W. E. 1941. The relation of size of fruit to solids, acid and volume of juice in the principal varieties of Florida oranges. Proc. Fla. State Hort. Soc. 54, 52-56.

HAURY, A., FOUQUE, A., MOREUIL, C. and SOULEZ, P. 1978. Variety studies of citrus overseas. Fruits 33 (11), 763-766. [Hort. Abstr. 49 (1979), 7921.]

HILGEMAN, R. H. 1966. Effect of climate of Florida and Arizona on grapefruit enlargement and quality: Apparent transpiration and internal water stress. Proc. Fla. State Hort. Soc. 79, 99-106.

HILGEMAN, R. H., TUCKER, H. and HALES, T. A. 1959. The effect of temperature, precipitation, blossom date and yield upon the enlargement of Valencia oranges. Proc. Am. Soc. Hort. Sci. 74, 266-279.

IWAGAKI, I. 1981. Tree configuration and pruning of satsuma mandarin in Japan, pp. 169-172. In Proc. Int. Soc. Citriculture, Vol. 1.

IWAGAKI, I. and KUDO, K. 1977. Fruit quality relating to the location of fruit in a canopy of satsuma mandarin tree. Bull. Shikoku Agr. Exp. Stn. 30, 17-23.

KETCHIE, D. O. and BALLARD, A. L. 1968. Environments which cause heat injury to Valencia oranges. Proc. Am. Soc. Hort. Sci. 93, 166-172.

KOO, R. C. J. 1988. Fertilization and irrigation effects on fruit quality, pp. 35-42. In J. J. Ferguson and W. F. Wardowski (Editors). Factors Affecting Fruit Quality. Citrus Short Course Proceedings. University of Florida, Lake Alfred.

KREZDORN, A. H. 1979. Selecting citrus rootstock for fruit size and quality. Fla. Grower & Rancher Mag. 72, 16-17.

KUNTE, Y. N. and DESHPANDE, V. B. 1969-70. Quality of santra fruit (Citrus reticulata, Blanco) as affected by aspect (direction) and height on the tree. Nagpur ic. Coll. Mag. 42, 33-39.

MARLOTH, R. H. 1950. Citrus growth studies. II. Fruit growth and fruit internal quality changes. J. Hort. Sci. 25, 235-248.

PEHRSON, J. 1976. Delayed maturity in navels. Citrograph 61, 200.

RANDAHAWA, G. S. and DINSA, H. S. 1947. Quality of Valencia oranges as affected by aspect, exposure, and height on the tree. Proc. Am. Soc. Hort. Sci. 50, 161-164.

REUTHER, W. 1973. Climate and citrus behavior, pp. 280-377. In W. Reuther, L. D. Batchelor and H. J. Webber (Editors). The Citrus Industry, Vol. 3. Div. Hort. Sci., University of California, Berkeley.

REUTHER, W. 1980. Climatic effects on quality of citrus in the tropics. Proc. Amer. Soc. Hort. Sci., Trop. Reg. 24:15-28.

REUTHER, W., RASSMUSSEN, G. K., HILGEMAN, R. H., CAHOON, G. A. and COOPER, W. C. 1969. A comparison of maturation and composition of Valencia oranges in some major subtropical zones of the United States. Jour. Amer. Soc. Hort. Sci. 94, 144-157.

REUTHER, W. and RIOS-CASTAFFO, D. 1969. Comparison of growth, maturation, and composition of citrus fruits in subtropical California and tropical Colombia, pp. 277-300. In H. D. Chapman (Editor). Proc. First Intern. Citrus Symp. 1. University of California, Riverside.

SITES, J. W. and REITZ, H. J. 1949. The variation in individual Valencia oranges from different locations of the tree as a guide to sampling methods and spot-picking for quality. I. Soluble solids in the juice. Proc. Am. Soc. Hort. Sci. 54, 1-10.

SITES, J. W. and REITZ, H. J. 1950A. The variation in individual Valencia oranges from different locations of the tree as a guide to sampling methods and spot-picking for quality. II. Titratable acid and the soluble solids/titratable acid ratio of the juice. Proc. Am. Soc. Hort, Sci. 55, 73-80.

SITES, J. W. and REITZ, H. J. 1950B. The variation in individual Valencia oranges from different locations on the tree as a guide to sampling methods and spot-picking for quality, III. Vitamin C and juice content of the fruit. Proc. Am. Soc. Hort. Sci. 56, 103-110.

STEARNS, C. R., JR. and YOUNG, G. T. 1942. The relation of climatic conditions to color development in citrus fruit. Proc. Fla. State Hort. Soc. 55, 59-61.

STEWART, I. and WHEATON, T. A. 1971. Effects of ethylene and temperature on carotenoid pigmentation of citrus peel. Proc. Fla. State Hort. Soc. 84, 264-266.

STOVER, E. W. 2000. Relationship of intensity of flowering and cropping in fruit species. HortTechnology 10, 729-732.

STOVER, E., CILIENTO, S., RITENOUR, M. and COUNTER, C. 2002. NAA thinning of 'Murcott': comparison of small plot and commercial harvest data. Proc. Fla. State Hort. Soc. 115, 287-291.

STOVER, E. and DAVIES, F. 2000. Gibberellic acid to enhance juice yield and late-season quality of processing oranges. Fla. Coop. Ext. Serv. Fact Sheet HS-794.

STOVER, E., WHEATON, A. and ALBRIGO, L. G. 2000. Chemical thinning of citrus with NAA for bigger fruit, less branch breakage, and more regular cropping. Fla. Coop. Ext. Serv. Fact Sheet HS-800.

SUZUKI, T., KANEKO, M. and TANAKA, M. 1969. Effects of soil moisture supplied at various stages on the growth and fruiting of young citrus trees. J. Jap. Soc. Hort. Sci. 38, 287-294.

SYVERTSEN, J. P. and ALBRIGO, L. G. 1980. Some effects of grapefruit tree canopy position on microclimate, water relations, fruit yield, and juice quality. J. Am. Soc. Hort. Sci. 105, 454-459.

TOMINAGA, S. and DAITO, H. 1982. Fruit quality of satsuma mandarins at various locations on differently trained trees in a cool and cloudy summer. J. Jap. Soc. Hort. Sci. 51, 9-18.

TUCKER, D. P. H., BARRY, G. H. and GOODRICH, R. M. 2000. Factors affecting citrus production and fruit quality. University of Florida, IFAS Printing, Gainesville.

TUCKER, D. P. H., WHEATON, T. A. and MURARO, R. P. 1991. Citrus tree spacing and pruning. SP-74. University of Florida, IFAS Printing, Gainesville.

WALLACE, A., CAMERON, S. H. and WIELAND, P. A. T. 1955. Variability in citrus fruit characteristics, including the influences of position on the tree and nitrogen fertilization. Proc. Am. Soc. Hort. Sci. 65, 99-108.

WEBBER, J. H. and L. D. BATCHELOR. 1943. History, Botany, and Breeding. *In* The Citrus Industry Volume I. University of California Press, Berkeley.

WINSTON, J. R. and MILLER, E. V. 1947. Vitamin C content and juice quality of exposed and shaded citrus fruits. Proc. Fla. State Hort. Soc. 60, 63-67.

WUTSCHER, H. K. 1988. Rootstock effects on fruit quality, pp. 24-32. *In* J. J. Ferguson and W. F. Wardowski (Editors). Factors Affecting Fruit Quality. Citrus Short Course Proceedings. University of Florida, Lake Alfred.

4

Growth Regulator Improvement of Postharvest Quality

Mohamed El-Otmani

In citrus species, growth and development are complex processes governed by plant internal factors (plant genes, endogenous hormonal balance), the environment of the plant (climate, soil factors) and production practices (irrigation, fertilization, pruning, planting density, pest control, planting density, plant growth regulators, etc.).

Since their discovery and availability in the market, plant growth regulators (PGRs) have been used by growers and researchers to manipulate plant growth and development of citrus to meet the challenge of increased demand for fruit of high quality. The oldest work suggesting that PGRs can be produced by citrus and used on citrus to bring about a specific biological response is that of Cousins (1910) who observed that when bananas and oranges were stored together during commercial shipments, gas produced by wounded and by decaying orange fruits caused bananas to ripen. In 1924, Ethylene was identified as the component in combustion fumes from kerosene heaters used for protection in orchards in California that caused lemon degreening (Denny 1924). Consequently, ethylene was referred to as the fruit ripening hormone and is nowadays commercially used to elicit this biological effect on various species (see below). Since then several naturally occurring plant hormones were identified in various citrus organs and tissues and their concentrations were quantified (see review by El-Otmani *et al.* 1995). In addition, a lot is known about variation of their species distribution and relative abundance among organs and about the plant/organ factors and environmental parameters affecting their endogenous levels. However, although significant progress has been made in the understanding of their implication in different growth and development processes, most of the existing knowledge and its use in the world of citrus production and evaluation has heavily relied on observed response of the tree/organ to exogenous applications of theses substances. These compounds are mainly used in propagation, control of flowering and manipulation of yield partitioning to optimize orchard productivity, enhancement and preservation of fruit quality, manipulation of harvest date and facilitation of the harvest itself.

Consumers of fresh citrus fruit are increasingly demanding fruit of excellent eating qualities with good appearance (in terms of size, color, shape), free of blemishes, with adequate firmness, and devoid of pests and pesticide residues.

Postharvest losses can be due to rough handing in the field and postharvest but can also occur during storage, transport and shelf-life. They can be total in the case of disease invasion of the fruit (e.g., *Penicillium, Phytophthora*) or partial in the case of respiration (i.e., loss of sugars and acids, etc.) and transpiration (i.e., water loss), both of the latter causing weight loss, shrivelling and loss of shine. Inadequate or sub-optimal cultural practices during the production cycle in the orchard as well as inadequate postharvest conditions can cause rind breakdown, discoloration and softening thus causing significant loss in fruit shelf-life.

Growth regulators have been used on citrus with the objective of reducing postharvest losses, maximizing (i.e., improving and/or preserving) postharvest quality and extending shelf-life of the fruit.

In this article, we reviewed existing literature related to the use of PGRs on citrus, pre- and postharvest with the objective of maximizing quality and fulfilling consumers demand in this respect with the aim of giving the reader an up-to-date review of recent developments and published information. The physiology of these substances and limitations of their use are also discussed. The reader can also find additional information in reviews by Davies (1986), El-Otmani and Ait-Oubahou (1996, 1999) and El-Otmani *et al.* (2000).

FRUIT SIZE: AN IMPORTANT COMPONENT OF POSTHARVEST QUALITY

Introduction

Although it has nothing to do with compositional quality or with cosmetics of the fruit, fruit size (either fruit too small or too large depending on the destined market) is often a limiting parameter in sales of fruit for fresh consumption. This is particularly true for the small-size fruit since in clementine mandarins, an alternate-bearing cultivar, the proportion of discarded fruit due to this defect can be as high as 30% or more of total yield in years of high yields. In fact, the results of citrus growing as an economic activity are best expressed in monetary terms. Large yields do not always mean high profits. Considerable revenues are lost every year in the main citrus areas of the world because of the production of small-sized fruit (Monselise 1973; Gilfillan 1987). Consumer preference worldwide is for medium or slightly large for oranges and large-sized fruit for mandarins (Gilfillan 1987; Miller and Hofman 1988). Moreover, the current demand for larger fruit by the international fresh fruit market has resulted in an increase in the proportion of fruit that go to juice which, in some years, results in a net loss of revenue to the grower (Robison 1987). It is important to note that, in addition to its importance for the fresh market, fruit size is the only attribute which can be correlated directly with all juice quality constituents (Hutton 1989). Fruit juice acidity (percent citric acid) and juice volume are very much affected by fruit size. Small fruit have a substantially higher percent acid than larger fruit and total soluble solids per fruit is considerably lower in small fruit. If the proportion of small fruit rejected from the packinghouse lines could be reduced, returns would be greater both for fresh fruit (because there would be more fruit of commercially valuable export size) and for juice (because of increased total soluble solids).

Factors Affecting Fruit Size

Fruit size is determined by a large number of factors (e.g., plant genes, climate, soil, diseases, cultural practices) all of which interact to influence final size. The common denominator between these factors is that they all impact absolute concentrations and relative amounts of endogenous plant growth regulators and source sink relationships and availability of photosynthate and nutrients. In citrus, development of the ovary into a mature fruit proceeds through three stages: cell division, cell enlargement, and cell maturation (Bain 1958; Fig. 1.5). During Stage I, growth by cell division dominates. Cell division is essential for the formation of the ovary during flower initiation and continues past petal fall to approximately mid-June in northern hemisphere (i.e., time of maximum peel thickness). At this time, cell division, which occurred in all tissues, is completed except in the flavedo. Thus, during the period encompassing fruit set and June drop (northern hemisphere), fruit growth is dominated by cell division. The number of cell divisions occurring before *versus* after anthesis to produce the final size of the ovary at the end of Stage I is not known. Despite this, it is generally accepted that final fruit size is determined at, or even before, anthesis both in oranges and mandarins. Stage II is the period of maximum fruit growth occurring from mid-June (northern hemisphere) over the next 5 to 7 months, depending upon the cultivar. This stage of fruit development is dominated by cell enlargement and cell differentiation. The juice vesicles and locules increase in size, the flavedo continues cell division. Stage III is the period of fruit maturation. Fruit continue to increase in size predominantly by cell expansion, but at a slower rate. For citrus, the relative contribution of cell number (growth by cell division) *vs.* cell size (growth by cell expansion) in the flavedo, albedo, and endocarp to final fruit size is not known. Strategically increasing cell number first followed by increasing cell size provides two time frames and two means to increase final fruit size, whereas attempting to increase cell size alone reduces one's options. Second, less is known about Stage I of citrus fruit development with regard to its effect on final fruit size. The goal of most investigations of this stage of citrus fruit development has been to reduce fruit abscission in order to enhance fruit set and yield. The potential for increasing fruit size by enhancing cell division is a relatively undeveloped approach.

For a given crop load, there is an optimal leaf-to-fruit ratio essential for maximum fruit size. The research of Lovatt and others have demonstrated that the leaf-to-fruit ratio of the flowering shoot is an important determinant of fruit size. They reported that flowers (ovaries) borne on inflorescences with more than one leaf per flower were faster growing, produced faster-growing ovaries, and eventually larger fruit than flowers borne on inflorescences with less than one leaf per flower (Lovatt *et al.* 1984, 1992A, B; Hofman 1988; Erner 1989). This establishes that, final fruit size is significantly influenced during the very early development of the ovary.

In citrus production, it is well known that there is an inverse relationship between fruit number and fruit size (Goldschmidt and Monselise 1977; Guardiola *et al.* 1982; Agustí and Almela 1984; Guardiola 1988). Increases in yield above the optimum for a specific cultivar result in a decrease in fruit size. Fruit must draw on the supply of photosynthetic products (carbohydrates, organic acids, and amino acids) manufactured in the leaves, mineral nutrients mobilized to and stored in the leaves, and PGRs produced or stored in the leaves for the energy, building blocks, and chemical signals necessary for their growth and maturation. Thus, fruit growth is dependent on both the sink strength of developing fruit, which has been shown to be regulated by endogenous levels and exogenous supply of PGRs at all stages of fruit development (Goldschmidt 1976; Powell and Krezdorn 1977; Wilson 1983; Davenport 1990) and on the number of leaves (source) supplying photosynthate to the fruit. The effect of competition exerts its influence on final fruit size early in ovary development (Guardiola and García-Luis 2000). Several researches have documented an inverse relationship between the number of flowers initially produced per tree and final fruit size at harvest (Guardiola *et al.* 1982; Guardiola 1988; Marioka and Yahata 1989). It is interesting to note that the larger size of fruit from trees of low floral intensity was due to an increase in both cell number and cell size compared to smaller fruit from trees of high floral intensity (Guardiola *et al.* 1982). Greater floral intensity is always linked to a lower number of leafy inflorescences. It is well established that fruit borne on leafy inflorescences grow faster than those borne or leafless inflorescences (Lenz 1966; Lovatt *et al.* 1984, 1992A).

Fruitlet growth rate may be determined by the sink strength of the fruit tissues, the capacity of the transport system, and/or the supply of metabolites from the leaves. All three processes may be affected by hormones. Evidence for hormone involvement in differentiation of xylem and phloem is overwhelming (Goodwin 1978; Aloni 1987). In mandarins, auxins, gibberellins, and cytokinins enhanced vascularization of the pedicel (Guardiola *et al.* 1993) and auxins increased fruit peduncle diameter (El-Otmani *et al.* 1993) and cell size of the vascular tissues (Agustí *et al.* 1996)

Mesocarp as well as endocarp explants from persisting fruitlets grew faster than those from abscising fruitlets when cultured *in vitro* using basal medium (Ruiz and Guardiola 1994). When auxin alone or in combination with gibberellin or cytokinin were added to the basal medium, explants from abscising fruitlets grew faster than those from persisting fruitlets but the final weight was identical for explants from abscising and from persisting fruitlets. These results indicate that maximum growth required the presence of hormones at an optimal concentration identical for both fruit classes, and that the particularly more vigorous growth of the endocarp explants from persisting fruitlets in the absence of added hormones indicates that differences in hormone concentrations or their ratios in tissues determine the sink strength of the persisting fruitlets (Ruiz and Guardiola 1994). In particular, auxins appear to play a major role in increasing sink capacity of endocarp and thus of fruit resulting in greater mobilization activity of carbohydrates and mineral elements to the fruit leading to faster growth and fruit persistence.

Ovaries as well as fruitlets borne on leafy inflorescences had more polyamines than those borne on leafless inflorescences (Lovatt *et al.* 1992A, B). The former had a faster growth rate and, therefore, a better chance to set and persist until harvest (Zucconi *et al.* 1978; Ruiz and Guardiola 1994). Winter application of urea to Washington navel trees resulted in increased yield without any significant effect on fruit size or its relative distribution according to commercial size-classes (Lovatt *et al.* 1992A, B; Ali and Lovatt 1994B), but had more fruits per tree than control trees at harvest (Ali and Lovatt 1994B) indicating a direct effect of treatment on fruit set. These results are consistent with the hypothesis that urea application to the foliage of citrus trees provides sufficient ammonia to drive the *de novo* arginine biosynthesis and lead to an increase in polyamine titers (Sagee and Lovatt, 1991) that promotes flower initiation and development (Ali and Lovatt 1994A) and ovary growth resulting in increased fruit set and yield (Ali and Lovatt 1994B).

Hormonal Regulation

Auxins are used to increase fruit size of sweet oranges, grapefruit, and mandarins (Monselise 1979). In Israel, 20 ppm 2,4-D is applied with 5% KNO_3 at the end of May-to-beginning of June. Because fruit size is a major problem in mandarins and particularly Clementines, which are grown essentially in the Mediterranean Basin significant research efforts are devoted to solving the problem and published results indicate that new compounds of the auxin type such as 2,4-dichlorophenoxypropionic acid (2,4-DP) (El-Otmani *et al.* 1993; Agustí *et al.* 1994A) and 3,5,6-trichloro-2-pyridyloxiacetic acid (3,5,6-TPA) (Agustí *et al.* 1994B) can yield a significant fruit size increase if used at the right timing and concentration. Moreover, the auxin 2,4-D is applied to control the drop of mature navel, grapefruit and Valencia oranges, but provides the secondary benefit of increasing fruit size of the new crop of the latter varieties. Valencia orange is more responsive than grapefruit to fruit-sizing sprays (Hield *et al.* 1965; Erner *et al.* 1993).

Auxins have been demonstrated to increase fruit stem transport capacity (Stewart *et al.* 1952A; Guardiola and Lazaro 1987); the increase in the size of the fruit peduncle was demonstrated to parallel the increase in fruit size (El-Otmani *et al.* 1993). Auxins also increase vesicle size, but not vesicle number, resulting in increased locule size (Agustí *et al.* 1992; El-Otmani *et al.* 1993). Increased locule size was a result of enhanced enlargement rather than cell division in the juice vesicles (El-Otmani *et al.* 1993; Aznar *et al.* 1995). Recently, 3,5,6-TPA has been reported to promotes sink strength *via* an induction of carbohydrate accumulation, thus stimulating fruit growth (Agustí *et al.* 2002). Auxin effect is dependent upon the timing of its application, the concentration used, the formulation applied and the cultivar (Agustí *et al.* 1992, 1995, 1996). For example, on most citrus, 2,4-DP enhanced fruit size better than NAA or 2,3,4-T (Agustí and Almela 1991). It stimulates fruit growth but not thinning, and best results are obtained if it is applied at the end of physiological drop at a concentration of 50 ppm (Agustí *et al.* 1994A). When 3,5,6-TPA was used on clementine, thinning was greater if applied during June drop but was much reduced if applied at the end of the June drop (Agustí *et al.* 1995). The early application resulted in a transient arrest in fruit growth, whereas the later application had no depressive effect on early fruit growth. Thinning was severe when treatments were applied during June drop and resulted in the reduction of fruit number, with a significant increase in fruit size, which was not sufficient to compensate for the reduction in fruit number, so yield was significantly reduced. Treatment application at the end of the June drop did not thin the fruit if the concentrations were lower than 25 mg l^{-1} but at this concentration, fruit number at harvest was reduced by 40%, which resulted also in reduced yield, although fruit size was improved. These results indicate that final fruit size is only partially related to fruit competition; only when fruit thinning was very heavy (>4%) did it affect fruit size. In addition, treated fruit accumulated significantly greater amounts of dry matter in the juice sacs as a result of increased sink strength. The determinant of the final effect is the balance between the early depressive and the subsequent stimulatory effects elicited by most auxins (Guardiola *et al.* 1988; Agustí *et al.* 1995). Currently, best results are obtained when 2,4-DP or 3,5,6-TPA was used as a foliar spray at respectively 50 ppm and 10 ppm at the end of June drop when clementine fruits have a diameter of 15-20 mm mandarin fruits are 20-25 mm in diameter and oranges are 25-30 mm in diameter (Agustí 2000).

The uncertainty of the future use of some or all auxins makes it essential to understand the roles of auxin in regulating both cell division and cell expansion during citrus fruit development in order to develop practical methods to mimic the effect of auxin application or to increase endogenous levels of IAA in the ovary without applying a commercial auxin.

Ethephon has been used effectively to thin tangerine crops. Galliani *et al.* (1975) applied 200 ppm ethephon to Wilking mandarin when fruit were approximately 1 cm in diameter. This application increased fruit size by thinning the crop and reduced titratable acidity so that fruit attained a minimum TSS:TA ratio earlier. Ethephon applied at 200-300 ppm also effectively increased fruit size of Imperial mandarin in Australia, again by thinning the crop by about 25% (El-Zeftawi 1976). The tendency toward alternate bearing was also reduced. Ethephon increased carotenoid and decreased chlorophyll *a* and *b* levels in the peel. Chapman (1980), also working with Imperial mandarin, found that fruit diameter was increased from an average of 58.9 mm for untreated fruit to 62.6 mm for fruit treated with 500 ppm ethephon; however, ethephon at this concentration also caused defoliation. Wheaton (1981) successfully thinned Dancy tangerine using 150-250 ppm ethephon, although these concentrations tended to overthin Honey tangerine. Similarly, 250 ppm ethephon applied in April and May to Dancy tangerines increased the percentage of large fruit and more importantly increased dollar returns per tree (Jahn 1981). Combination sprays of ethephon (100 ppm) and cycloheximide (5 ppm) applied to Robinson tangerines in Florida during September had no effect on fruit size, packout, or internal quality when harvested in November (F. S. Davies unpublished data).

Gibberellic acid applied prior to bloom rather than during June drop has proven effective in reducing blossom number of Satsuma mandarin in Japan (Iwahori 1978). Potassium gibberellate at 100 or 500 ppm increased set and yields of Clementine mandarin but also reduced fruit size and delayed color development and maturity (Soost and Burnett 1961). Krezdorn and Cohen (1962) noted that GA_3 increased fruit set and delayed color development and maturity of Orlando and Minneola tangelos.

There is a very strong and significant correlation between ovary weight, ovary volume, and the gibberellin content of the ovary during Stage I of fruit development of navel oranges (Wiltbank and Krezdorn 1969). In addition, paclobutrazol, an anti-gibberellin, has been found to decrease vegetative shoot and fruit growth of citrus (Monselise 1986; Greenberg *et al.* 1993). It is of interest that: (i) $NH_4{}^+$ increases the endogenous GA_3 content of citrus fruit (Bar-Akiva 1975); (ii) GA_3 is known to increase polyamine synthesis and content (Smith *et al.* 1985); (iii) polyamines have been proposed to regulate the GA_3 response that results from cell division (Evans and Malmberg 1989); and (iv) faster-growing fruit, i.e., those borne on leafy inflorescences have higher concentrations and total amounts of GA_3 and polyamines than slower-growing fruit on leafless inflorescences (Erner and Bravdo 1983; Sagee and Erner 1991; Lovatt *et al.* 1992A). Applications of GA_3 sprays to Clementine trees have yielded positive, reproducible results; however, erratic results were obtained when navel and Valencia trees were sprayed with GA_3 (Wiltbank and Krezdorn 1969). Early bloom GA_3 sprays increased fruit size during early fruit development, but that additional sprays were needed to sustain the initial increase in fruit size (M. El-Otmani and C. J. Lovatt unpublished data). Foliar spray of GA_3 or benzyladenin on Satsuma mandarin at flower opening caused a transient increase in cell division in the ovary wall but had no significant effect on final fruit size (Guardiola *et al.* 1993). Fruitlet sensitivity to these hormones decreased with fruitlet growth and no growth enhancement was obtained 11 days after anthesis. Conversely, 2,4,5-T resulted in a transient reduction in growth due to a reduction in cell size when applied at early fruit development, but when applied later than 30 days post anthesis, an increase in fruit size at harvest was observed (Guardiola *et al.* 1993). *In vitro* culture of the fruit tissues confirmed *in vivo* results and the authors concluded that a direct effect of the growth regulators on the fruit tissues was the primary cause for the final effect on size, and that treatment affecting peel growth (cytokinins and gibberellins) had a transient effect on fruit size whereas treatments affecting endocarp growth (i.e., auxins) increased final fruit size.

Citrus cultivars undergo a period of flower and fruit abscission continuing through the end of June drop. This critical period of fruit retention/fruit drop spans the entire cell division phase of ovary development (Stage I). The newest contribution to our understanding of fruit retention in citrus comes from studies which compared changes in the concentrations of endogenous PGRs in developing fruit borne on leafy *versus* leafless inflorescences of Valencia (Hofman 1988) and Shamouti oranges (Erner 1989; Sagee and Erner 1991). Fruit borne on leafy inflorescences are faster-growing, have a high potential to set and survive to harvest, and are larger at harvest. Fruit borne on leafless inflorescences are slower-growing, tend to abscise early in their development and are smaller at harvest (Lovatt *et al.* 1984; Hofman 1988; Erner 1989; Lovatt *et al.* 1992A, B). No differences in concentrations of gibberellic acid (GA_3) or abscisic acid (ABA) (ng/g dry wt) were observed for Shamouti (Sagee and Erner 1991) and Valencia (Hofman 1988) fruit borne on leafy *versus* leafless inflorescences. However, because fruit borne on leafy inflorescences were larger in mass than fruit of the same age borne on leafless inflorescences, fruit on leafy inflorescences had more GA_3 and ABA per fruit. High temperatures 40 to 55 days after full bloom of Valencia were associated with a large decrease in GA_3 concentration in the fruit, but there was a lesser effect on ABA (Hofman 1988). Thus, a shift toward a greater ratio of growth inhibitor to growth promoter occurred during the stress. The increased ratio of growth inhibitor to growth promoter may be the cause of reduced growth by cell division and increased abscission. Abscission would be greater for fruit borne on leafless inflorescences because these fruit had less GA_3 than fruit on leafy inflorescences even before the stress. These differences in endogenous PGRs may be the basis for differences in fruit size.

Cytokinin content is greater in fruitlets from leafy inflorescence than in those from leafless inflorescences (Saidha *et al.* 1985) and has been suggested as directly affecting initial fruit growth and development (Hernandez-Miñana *et al.* 1989; Hernandez-Miñana and Primo-Millo 1990). This is in agreement with the greater fruit set (Agustí *et al.* 1990) and early fruit growth (Lovatt *et al.* 1992A, B) on leafy inflorescence shoots but does not guarantee fruit survival until maturity, the latter being markedly dependent upon subsequent growth which is dependent upon fruit nutrition and sink capacity, and environmental factors. Fruit sink strength has been linked to fruit content in plant growth substances (Erner and Bravdo 1983). Fruit borne on leafy inflorescences have greater amino acid content, necessary for sustained faster growth rate, particularly polypeptides of a relatively high molecular weight which are significantly increased as a result of cytokinin application (Primo-Millo *et al.* 1984).

An additional but indirect proof of the implication of hormonal nutritional interactions on fruit enlargement is the stimulatory effect obtained by girdling of branches (Hochberg *et al.* 1977; Cohen 1984A, B; Agustí *et al.* 1990). Greater concentrations of gibberellins (Wallerstein *et al.* 1974) and auxins (Dann *et al.* 1985) above the girdle have been observed along with increased carbohydrates (Wallerstein *et al.* 1974, 1978; Fishler *et al.* 1983) and mineral elements (Kurtzman 1966).

Erner (1989) has proposed that fruit borne on leafy inflorescences have a greater ability to withdraw water from the transpiration stream than those borne on leafless inflorescences. Since the transpiration stream (xylem sap) of citrus contains high levels of cytokinins, fruit borne on leafy inflorescences would be expected to have a higher ratio of this class of growth promoting PGRs to growth inhibiting PGRs than fruit borne on leafless inflorescences. In addition, it would be expected that fruit borne on leafless inflorescences would accumulate more ABA than fruit borne on leafy inflorescences (Sagee and Erner 1991). Since fruit on leafless inflorescences have lower levels of growth promoting cytokinins, the ratio would be shifted significantly toward growth inhibition and fruit abscission. Of interest is also the fact that GA_3 and cytokinins are well documented to increase polyamine synthesis and content, while ABA inhibits polyamine synthesis with a concomitant decrease in polyamine content (Smith *et al.* 1985; Evans and Malmberg 1989).

It is unknown whether PGRs regulate cell division directly or indirectly through second messengers like polyamines (Evans and Malmberg 1989) or by increasing sink strength in a manner as of yet unknown. For example, application of GA_3 to small fruit increased importation of [14C]assimilates (Powell and Krezdorn 1977; Mauk *et al.* 1986) and macronutrients (García-Martinez and García-Papi 1979).

Fruit size in mandarins has been correlated with seed number per fruit (Feinstein *et al.* 1975; Monselise 1977). Not only auxin-like and gibberellin-like substances have been obtained from mandarin seeds (García-Papi and García-Martínez 1984) but cytokinins have been isolated as well from lemon seeds (Khalifah and Lewis 1966). Growth and development of fruit have also been related to production of hormones by seeds in many other plant species (Barendse *et al.* 1991; Luckwill 1953; Powell and Pratt 1966). However, results of Turnbull (1989) and Barendse *et al.* (1991) lead to the conclusion that presence of seed is not essential for fruit growth suggesting that hormones are also produced by other tissues such as ovary wall (Monselise 1977, 1978).

In conclusion, it appears that fruit size is controlled by a complex balance between promoters and inhibitors with the balance progressively shifting toward the inhibitors as fruit development reached maturity (Goren and Goldschmidt 1970; Goldschmidt 1976; Monselise 1986). However, more evidence points to the specific auxin effect on increasing fruit size through a direct effect on endocarp growth enhancement (Ruiz and Guardiola 1994; Guardiola *et al.* 1993; El-Otmani *et al.* 1993). Any factor that would cause the ratio promoters/inhibitors to shift towards the inhibitors (high temperature for example) would result in reduced fruit growth (Hofman 1988) which may be irrecoverable (Erickson and Richards 1955) or may even cause abscission (Zucconi *et al.* 1978). The effect of hormones on fruit growth has been related to sink strength of the fruit and its capacity to mobilize water (Erner 1989), carbohydrates (Mauk *et al.* 1986; Kriedmann 1968) and minerals (Ruiz and Guardiola 1994). However, because several GAs as well as several cytokinins have been found in the fruitlets and other tree organs during the critical phase of fruit growth (see review by El-Otmani *et al.* 1995) the most critical and effective molecules to growth processes and final size remain to be determined. Similarly, the optimum concentration for growth per species and per variety need be determined to better manage cultural practices such as growth regulator sprays to supplement the deficit of a growth regulator in the tree or just to change the balance to favor one over the others.

FRUIT PEEL QUALITY

Much of the available information on the physiological and biological influence of plant growth substances on citrus fruit rind quality has come from studies using exogenous applications of these regulators.

Fruit Peel Resistance/Softening

Gibberellic acid has been the most studied, and its effect on delaying fruit peel aging and color and the subsequent reduction in peel disorders has been demonstrated (see review by Coggins 1981). This effect has been consistent over the years and across most citrus cultivars (Coggins 1981; El-Otmani et al. 1990; El-Otmani and Coggins 1985A, 1991; Agustí et al. 1988). Treatment application calls for use of GA_3 at 10 ppm at, or just prior to, fruit color break.

Histological studies showed that GA_3-treated fruit had peel with a structure similar to that of a younger fruit (Coggins and Hield 1968; Coggins 1969). In particular, senescing peel had an albedo with larger intercellular spaces and weakened cell walls, which break easily to result in a tissue with a low amount of cytoplasm, suggesting tissue with low metabolic activity (Coggins 1969). Senescing fruit also had greater epicuticular wax accumulation, with significant structural changes (El-Otmani and Coggins 1985A), with the subsequent development of many disorders (Coggins 1969, 1981). Gibberellic acid has been shown to delay these rind structural changes. GA_3-treated fruit had firmer rinds, with epicuticular wax morphology and composition of a physiologically young fruit (El-Otmani et al. 1985A, 1985B).

Biochemical changes associated with natural and GA_3-delayed senescence in the navel fruit rind were studied (Lewis et al. 1967). GA_3 effects were observable in the form of a higher rate of O_2 uptake, higher rate of respiration, a lag in sugar accumulation, a lower $K/Ca + Mg$ ratio and a higher level of P. These results imply that GA action is through preservation of more functional mitochondrial and plasma membranes. This was confirmed using tests on membrane permeability and electrolyte leakage and protoplast viability as affected by GA_3 in the albedo tissue (Nolte et al. 1990).

Ben-Arie et al. (1996) found that GA_3 either delays or inhibits all of the cell wall changes that were found to accompany fruit softening.

Preharvest applied auxins such as 2,4-D at 16 ppm have been reported to relatively delay rind softening of fruit on the tree and in cold room storage, but their effect is very small compared with that of GA_3 (El-Otmani et al. 1990). Some improvement of fruit firmness of mature fruit was also observed as a result of 2,4-DP treatment to enhance fruit growth (Agustí et al. 1994A).

Fruit Rind Color

Fruit pigment changes are usually associated with maturation and have been reported to be under hormonal control (Coggins and Jones 1977; Goldschmidt 1980). Growth regulators have been shown to affect citrus fruit peel color in two ways. They can 1) enhance or accelerate color change from green to orange or 2) delay this process. Enhancement of color change can be a direct result from use of ethylene as a degreening agent either as a preharvest spray of ethephon (200 to 500 ppm), an ethylene-generating compound (El-Zeftawi 1978; El-Zeftawi and Garrett 1978) or as a postharvest ethylene treatment in gas chambers at 5-10 ppm (Chapter 10; Eaks 1977). Earliness in color development can also be an indirect result from an enhancement of fruit growth using auxins (see above) so that fruit reaches maturity earlier and colors earlier compared to untreated fruit.

Delay in color change can be obtained using gibberellic acid at 10 ppm or more (Coggins 1981; Coggins and Henning 1988A; El-Otmani et al. 1990) and allows for prolonging harvest and shelf-life of the fruit.

Peel color development results from changes in carotenoid (Eilati et al. 1969B; Stewart and Wheaton, 1972; El-Zeftawi, 1978) and chlorophyll concentrations (El-Zeftawi; 1978). Concomitant changes in plastids have also been reported (Thomson et al. 1967; El-Zeftawi and Garrett 1978) and factors influencing chloro-chromoplast interconversions were reviewed by Goldschmidt (1988).

Ethylene and ethylene-releasing compounds such as ethephon cause carotenoid accumulation (Stewart and Wheaton 1972; El-Zeftawi 1978) and a reduction in chlorophyll content (El-Zeftawi 1978). Ethephon also increased carotenoid content of the rind of regreened Valencia fruit (El-Zeftawi and Garrett 1978). Preharvest applications of ethephon to Bearss lemon had little effect on peel chlorophyll, but postharvest applications caused significant loss in this pigment, suggesting the presence of an influencing tree factor on ethephon (John and Young 1972). Regreened fruit are more resistant to ethylene effect than ordinary mature fruit (Eaks 1977).

The role of endogenous ethylene in the degreening process of citrus fruit has been controversial until recently. Because ethylene evolution by mature citrus fruit is very low, a direct correlation between color development and ethylene evolution has been difficult to establish. Purvis (1980) indicated that changes in flavedo chloroplast ultrastructure of natural and ethylene-degreened fruit were similar and suggested that low levels of physiologically active ethylene may be bound in the tissue and not be evolved as ethylene. This idea was later tested (Goldschmidt et al. 1993) using 2,5-norbornadiene (NBD) and silver nitrate which are known to interfere with ethylene action (Beyer 1976; Sisler and Yang 1984). The results indicated that, under natural conditions, silver nitrate and NBD inhibited the loss of chlorophyll and that, NBD antagonized the degreening induced by exogenous ethylene which supports the suggestion of Purvis (1980).

Auxins have been reported to have no direct significant effect on citrus fruit peel coloration (Coggins and Hield 1968; El-Zeftawi 1978) whereas benzyladenine delayed loss of chlorophyll bud did not effect carotenoid accumulation (Eilati et al. 1969A). Cytokinins were also reported to enhance the regreening process (Cooper and Henry 1968; Rasmussen 1973). While the loss of chlorophyll during natural coloring Satsuma mandarin fruit peel was regarded by GA_3 but not by cytokinins, carotenoid accumulation was reduced by both growth hormone classes (García-Luís et al. 1986).

Gibberellins delay the senescence pigment change (Coggins 1981) and oppose the ethylene-induced chlorophyll loss (El-Zeftawi 1978). In addition, consistent with their effect, gibberellins antagonized ethylene effect on chlorophyll loss from senescing Shamouti orange peel (Goldschmidt and Galily 1974) and detached Bearss lemon (Jahn and Young 1972).

When applied in the spring-summer months to Valencia orange (i.e., when 2 crops are present on the tree, mature fruits of last spring and fruits set the spring of year of the study) GA_3 enhanced the regreening process of the mature fruit and decreased orange rind color of the following crop (Coggins et al. 1960). The enhancement of the regreening process was shown to be the result of an inhibitory effect on carotenoid accumulation and an increase in chlorophyll concentration (Coggins and Lewis 1962; El-Zeftawi and Garrett 1978). Similarly, when applied during, or just prior to color change, GA_3 delays the net loss of chlorophyll (Lewis et al. 1967) and retards the accumulation of carotenoids in navel orange fruit (Lewis and Coggins 1964) or even increased green color in Valencia fruit (Embleton et al. 1973). When used in August-September on fruitlet to reduce creasing GA_3 was shown to delay color development of Valencia fruit with a strong linear dependence on GA_3 concentration applied (Coggins and Henning 1988A). GA_3 also delayed the chloroplast to chromoplast conversion when applied to the orange peel (Thomson et al. 1967).

The combination of 10 ppm GA_3 and 20 ppm 2,4-D has effectively prolonged storage life of Marsh grapefruit both on-tree and in cold storage. Maintenance of a firmer peel and yellowish color with less fruit drop is the most consistent benefit resulting from application of these growth regulators. Occasionally, however, these materials have been ineffective (F. S. Davies and M. A. Ismail unpublished data). Variable results could result from various factors including improper application (rate or timing), or variations in temperature, rainfall, or irrigation during harvest. Insufficient or excessive irrigation decreased the effectiveness of GA_3 in South Africa (Gilfillan et al. 1973), whereas soil moisture content had little effect on GA_3 efficacy for mature Marsh trees in Florida (Ferguson et al. 1983). Complete fruit coverage appears necessary for GA_3 to be effective in improving peel quality (Gilfillan et al. 1973), while 2,4-D appears to be effective as a stop drop spray even when applied at very low volumes (Stewart et al. 1952A). Recommendations from Florida (Knapp 1982) and California (Coggins and Hield 1978) caution against low-volume application of GA_3 or 2,4-D because of potential phytotoxicity particularly leaf distortion from 2,4-D and excessive leaf drop from GA_3 treatments. Recently, Anthony and Coggins (2001) have demonstrated that NAA and 3,5,6-TPA can potentially substitute for 2,4-D in controlling fruit drop.

Mature fruit were reported to contain significant amounts of ABA (Goldschmidt *et al.* 1972; García-Luís *et al.* 1985; Rhodes 1980). Ethylene was shown to increase endogenous ABA in fruit peel (Goldschmidt *et al.* 1973) whereas benzyladenine retarded color change and inhibited ethylene-induced ABA formation (Brisker *et al.* 1976; Goldschmidt *et al.* 1972) indicating that there might be a relationship between ABA levels and carotenoid content of the fruit peel. This question was examined in the leaves by Norman *et al.* (1990) who found no direct relationship between carotenoids and ABA. In addition, inconsistency in fruit coloration as a response to exogenous ABA (Cooper and Henry 1968; Goldschmidt 1974) is another reason ruling out a direct link between these 2 parameters.

Coggins *et al.* (1970) and Yokoyama *et al.* (1971, 1972) reported on the significant effect of the compound 2-(4-chlorophenylthio)-triethylamine hydrochloride (CPTA) on the formation of carotenoids in citrus fruit peel. Lycopene increased in the flavedo of Marsh grapefruit when CPTA was applied either pre-or postharvest (Coggins *et al.* 1970). When CPTA was applied to immature Sinton citrangequat, at maturity fruit colored normally and lycopene accumulated as the main pigment and was responsible for the rich color in the flavedo (Yokoyama *et al.* 1971). In addition, synthesis of methylketone carotenoids. Application of CPTA to nearly mature fruit (i.e., when lycopene has already accumulated as a major pigment) no effect on methylketone carotenoids which are responsible for the production of the red color-commercially unacceptable was observed (Yokoyama *et al.* 1971). Moreover, when treated with CPTA, fully mature coloring fruit of Marsh seedless grapefruit and Washington navel orange which do not normally accumulate lycopene accumulated significant amounts of this pigment (Yokoyama *et al.* 1972). John and Young (1975) applied CPTA to fruit of Bearss lemon, Hamlin orange, Marsh grapefruit and Robinson Tangerine at harvest or at several weeks of storage. CPTA had little effect on lycopene concentration in the peel when applied at harvest but increased levels with increasing time in storage.

Chlorophyllase is the color-regulating enzyme most studied in citrus fruit peels. Its involvement in chlorophyll catabolism of senescing citrus peel has been demonstrated (Shimokawa *et al.*1978). The activity of this enzyme increased several-folds in citrus peel in response to ethylene (Barmore 1975; Shimokawa *et al.* 1978; Purvis and Barmore 1981; Amir-Shapira *et al.* 1987). Trebitsh *et al.* (1993) demonstrated that during the degreening process, ethylene enhanced *de novo* synthesis of chlorophyllase and that this synthesis is inhibited by the senescence-delaying compound GA_3 and to a lesser extent by benzyladenine (BA). Although BA reduced the ethylene-induced loss of chlorophyll, it did not reduce chlorophyllase activity since chlorophyllase was detected in BA-treated fruit. Differences in pigment changes to GA_3 and BA were also previously reported by Goldschmidt *et al.*

(1977) and García- Luís *et al.* (1986) when they observed that both GA_3 and cytokinins apposed ethylene-induced chlorophyll destruction, while the loss of chlorophyll during natural color-change was retarded by gibberellin but not by cytokinins. However, the basic mechanisms underlying these differences are unknown. Recently, a number of cDNAs corresponding to mRNAs inducible by ethylene were isolated by differential screening of a cDNA library from ethylene-treated orange fruit (Alonso *et al.* 1996). Northern analysis of RNA extracted from flavedo of ethylene-treated fruit and from fruits at different maturation stages showed that some of the mRNAs corresponding to these cDNAs were regulated both by ethylene treatment and during fruit maturation.

The possible role of ethylene in specific gene induction, the nature of the gene products and their possible function during maturation of citrus needs further research to determine the ethylene-dependent step in the molecular control of chlorophyll degradation. In addition, a citrus cDNA clone encoding phytoene synthase, which is an enzyme catalyzing the synthesis of phytoene, a carotenoid synthesized during citrus fruit maturation, has recently been isolated and characterized (Yano *et al.* 1996).

Fruit Rind Creasing

Creasing (Chapter 14) is an important problem in citrus production particularly in oranges and mandarins. Losses due to creasing can reach 50% of the total production (Gilfillan *et al.* 1981; Monselise *et al.* 1976). This disorder was thoroughly described by Jones *et al.* (1976) and its probable inducing factors were summarized by Hortzhausen (1981). It is characterized by cracks in the albedo of the fruit peel, weakening the fruit and rendering it valueless. Its incidence changes from year to year for a given grove and increase with delaying the harvest.

Anatomical studies showed that creasing is a result of cell segregation taking place in the albedo due to pectolytic activity which was shown to be higher in creased peel than in healthy fruit (Monselise *et al.* 1976; Jona *et al.* 1989). Monselise *et al.* (1976) suggested that creasing might be determined during the early 2 months of fruit development although it becomes evident only at or near fruit maturity. Jona *et al.* (1989) showed microscopically that it takes place early in fruit development and Storey and Treeby (1994) demonstrated that the cracks of albedo tissue were due to the separation of adjacent cells rather than the cleavage of individual cells and suggested that biochemical changes in the middle lamella of adjoining cells predispose fruit to albedo breakdown.

When fruits were treated with ethylene, creasing or pectolysis activity were not affected but internal atmospheres of creased fruit contained twice the ethylene (0.09 ppm) found in sound fruit (Monselise *et al.* 1976).

Jona *et al.* (1989) found a more rapid solubilisation of cell wall constituents in the creased fruit which could be a result of an activation of cell wall degrading enzymes such as pectinemethyl esterase and polygalacturonase (Pressey and Avants 1982).

In Israel, Gibberellic acid (at 10-20 ppm) reduced creasing of Valencia orange with the highest efficacy when sprays were applied from mid-June to mid-July (i.e. fruit has 3-4 cm in diameter) (Monselise *et al.* 1976). Nov.-Dec. (fruits about 6.5 cm in diameter) sprays were also efficacious but with less intensity. Similar results were observed for Washington navel orange in South Africa with GA_3 applications made 70-100 days after anthesis when fruit were 3-5 cm in diameter (Gilfillan *et al.* 1981). Narr *et al.* (1973) confirmed a reduction in creasing of Washington navel when sprayed before fruit color break using 20 ppm GA_3 and showed that other cultivars of the navel group require 30 ppm. Monselise *et al.* (1976) suggested that GA_3 effects at both dates were due to growth activity of tissues peaking in June-July and resuming in Nov. A report from Australia (Moulds *et al.* 1995) also indicated that GA_3 sprays to trees with 3-5 cm diameter navel oranges reduced the incidence of albedo break down late in the harvest season. Recently, research from California showed that October GA_3 treatments were better than those of September which were in turn better than those made in July or August (Coggins *et al.* 1997). The fact that GA_3-treated fruit had higher protein content than nontreated fruit indicated a larger protein turnover in creased than in the treated tissue (Monselise *et al.* 1976). This led Jona *et al.* (1989) to conclude that GA_3 effect was *via* a decrease in pectinemethyl esterase activity.

Application of GA_3 (50 ppm) to Nova mandarin trees at full bloom resulted in improved fruit set which was accompanied by an increase in creasing incidence (Goren *et al.* 1992) in agreement with earlier reports (see Holzhausen 1981). The physiological explanation of this is unknown. On the contrary, NAA application on Valencia orange significantly thinned fruit and reduced creasing incidence (Greenberg *et al.* 1996).

Fruit Rind Puffing

Puffing is a physiological disorder of citrus fruits usually affecting mandarins. Depending on the growing area and the yearly environmental conditions, it can affect all mature fruits, although with different degrees of severity. Puffy fruits are very sensitive to damage during postharvest handling and transport. They are also very susceptible to decay, thus giving rise to important economic losses. To avoid its appearance, early harvesting and commercialization are necessary. In mandarin-exporting countries, puffing is of such an importance that figures of exported fruit greatly depend on its yearly extent and severity (Almela *et al.* 1987; El-Otmani 1990).

In Satsuma mandarin, puffing is originated by the appearance of great intercellular spaces in the deeper layers of the albedo when the fruit had completed the cell division stage (Kuraoka 1962; Kuraoka *et al.* 1966). The development of these air spaces gives rise to broken cells and subsequently to a cracked albedo with little resistance. Similar initial symptoms have been detected in some other mandarin varieties, but puffing does not appear except if a high loss of juice takes place after full maturity (Agustí *et al.* 1988). In Satsuma mandarin, however, puffing appears irrespective of juice loss because, in contrast to other mandarins, peel resumes growth at maturity (Kawase and Hirai 1983). As a consequence of that, peel separates from the endocarp and fruit becomes puffy (Kuraoka 1962).

Growth regulators also seem to play a role in the appearance and control of puffing. The disorder can be controlled by applying gibberellic acid (Kuraoka *et al.* 1967), although with different efficiencies according to date of treatment. Thus, sprays of gibberellic acid (at 10 ppm) at fruit color-break delayed peel senescence and coloration, and enhanced peel resistance (Agustí *et al.* 1981); however, puffing was not avoided but was commercially reduced; albedo cracks were evident and fruit behavior postharvest did not differ from that of untreated controls. Best results were obtained when applying gibberellic acid 2 weeks to 1 month approximately before color break, coinciding with the initial steps of chlorophyll degradation (Kawase *et al.* 1981; Agustí *et al.* 1981, 1986; García-Luís *et al.* 1985). At this stage, 20 ppm concentration gave rise to a saturating effect, but 10 ppm were enough for on-tree storage of the fruit for an additional 2 months (Agustí and Almela 1984). The loss of chlorophyll in the flavedo was delayed more than 1 month and puffy fruit was reduced by 80% (Agustí *et al.* 1981). Earlier treatments were not effective in reducing fruit puffiness or delaying in color change of the rind (García-Luís *et al.* 1985).

The mechanism through which gibberellic acid controls puffing has been related to the role of gibberellins in delaying peel aging. Accumulation of gibberellin in peel after gibberellic acid treatment has been shown and the gibberellin/abscisic acid antagonism in senescing peel was demonstrated (Kuraoka *et al.* 1977). This gives rise to an inhibitory effect on the later peel growth of mature fruit (Agustí *et al.* 1981; García-Luís *et al.* 1985), which is responsible for puffing appearance (see above). However, this contradicts the accepted role of the endogenous fruit gibberellins enhancing peel growth (Erner *et al.* 1976A) and with their higher fruit content when chlorophylls begin degradating (García-Luís *et al.* 1985), all of which coincide with the dates of higher fruit sensitivity to treatments. Exogenous hormones are not any more efficacious than endogenous ones (Goldschmidt and Eilati 1970) but probably compartmentation phenomena and conjugation can suppress action of the latter and render them inactive (Leopold and Noodén 1984) or that they do not reach activity centers which are probably more easily accessible to exogenous hormones (García-Luís *et al.* 1985).

The addition of inorganic nitrogen compounds improved the gibberellic acid efficacy, but did not modify its concentration dependence. Optimum concentration was 10 ppm (Agustí *et al.* 1981, 1986; Agustí and Almela 1984; García-Luís *et al.* 1985).

Auxins have also been reported to be efficacious in the control of puffing. Treatments at early fruit development stages (i.e., at the end of June drop) were most effective (Kawase *et al.* 1981; Guardiola and Lazaro 1987), especially in the case of 2,4-dichorophenoxypropionic acid (2,4-DP), which reduced commercial puffiness by more that 70%, probably as a result of increased firmness due to treatment (Agustí and Almela 1991; Kawase *et al.* 1981). Undesirable effects such as thick rinds and hard rinds have been reported to be associated with these treatments, especially if used at high concentrations (Kawase *et al.* 1981).

Ethylene has been shown to have a significant enhancing effect on puffing of Satsuma mandarin (Maotani *et al.* 1983). Puffing was enhanced when fruit was sprayed with ethephon (an ethylene-releasing compound) at fruit color break. Dipping fruit in an ethylene biosynthesis inhibitor, ethylene evolution by fruit was suppressed and puffing incidence reduced. In addition, when fruit was stored in a container with an ethylene absorbent, ethylene concentration in the container was lower and puffing was reduced. Both the ethylene biosynthesis inhibitor and the ethylene absorbent decreased the peel content of water-soluble pectins and increased the insoluble fraction. The reverse was observed for ethylene-treated fruit. These results indicate a possible relationship between ethylene and pectin enzymes in the regulation of peel puffing.

Fruit Rind Splitting

Splitting is a physiological disorder consisting of fruit peel fissures, variable in length, which originate often but not always in the stylar-end and usually reaching the equatorial fruit zone or, inclusive, the complete fruit height (Cook 1913; Del Rivero 1968; Erickson 1968). It represents a worldwide problem to the oranges (Lima *et al.* 1980; Erickson 1957; de Cicco *et al.* 1988; Ruiz and Primo-Millo 1989; Bar Akiva 1975; Monselise *et al.* 1986) and mandarins (Monselise and Costo 1985; Ruiz and Primo-Millo 1989; Almela *et al.* 1990; Monselise *et al.* 1986). Its incidence varies from year to year.

Although the exact factors causing splitting are not well defined (see Holtzhausen 1981), environmental conditions have often been suspected to cause this disorder (Cook 1913; Del Rivero 1968; Cohen *et al.* 1972). Nutritional unbalances (Chapman 1968; Erickson 1957) and some pathogens (Fawcett 1936) have been suggested as promoters, as well. Peel strength and its capacity to accommodate sudden changes in internal pressures have been suggested among other factors involved in controlling this disorder (Goldschmidt *et al.* 1992; de Cicco *et al.* 1988; Kaufman 1970), and this is in concordance with the fact that the thinner the peel, the greater the percentage of split fruit (Cohen *et al.* 1972; Almela *et al.* 1992). On the other hand, in mandarins, splitting begins in late August and reaches the maximum incidence during late September and early October (Almela *et al.* 1990), coinciding with the fruit development stage of pulp expansion and thinning of the peel (Bain 1958). Rabe *et al.* (1989) showed that split in Ellendale mandarin was initiated during the early cell division of fruit growth.

A hormonal unbalance in the fruit, caused by some adverse climatic conditions or inappropriate cultural practices, as an origin of this physiological disorder, may be involved since fruit growth and development are under hormonal control (Monselise 1977, 1978). Citrus fruit peels have low auxin content throughout development with relatively high gibberellin activity (see review by El-Otmani *et al.* 1995). A shifting balance in the peel between growth promoters (gibberellins + cytokinins) and inhibitors (abscisic acid) has been reported (Goren and Goldschmidt 1970). In general, promoters are high in early fruit development stages and inhibitors are high at fruit maturity.

High endogenous levels of gibberellins and cytokinins cause rough and thick rinds (Erner *et al.* 1976A, B). Therefore, it must be possible to promote peel growth to obtain a more split-resistant peel by means of hormonal treatments.

Results to this effect are not consistent, and it has been reported that gibberellic acid and 2,4-D not only did not control splitting but they promoted it in some cases (Krezdorn and Cohen 1962; Lima and Davies 1981, 1984). However, Coggins and Hield (1968) pointed out a positive effect of 2,4-D in the control of splitting in Washington navel orange. Borroto *et al.* (1981) reported a significant reduction in splitting of Valencia orange by applying 2,4-D (10 and 20 ppm) once at approximately mid-June. Almela *et al.* (1992) obtained a reduction in splitting of Nova mandarin (more than 50%, reaching even a 70% of reduction) with foliar application of the mixture 2,4-D (20 ppm) + gibberellic acid (20 ppm) twice, in late-June and late-July. Goren *et al.* (1992) reduced the disorder in this variety through an application of gibberellic acid (50 ppm) at mid-anthesis.

Although low tree levels of potassium (Erickson 1957), calcium and nitrogen (Almela *et al.* 1992) have been well correlated with increasing splitting, their addition as nitrates did not improve the plant growth regulator effect (Almela *et al.* 1992).

Because of the possible implications of the rind cell pectic components in the development of splitting, Bower *et al.* (1992) showed that splitting was most closely correlated with pectin methylesterase (PME) activity during the fruit cell division stage, followed by the ratio of water-soluble to calcium pectate and then total pectin content. Possible regulation of PME is not ruled out. In fact, a cDNA for a fruit pectin esterase has been identified in tomato and used to construct an antisense gene. Expression of this antisense gene in transgenic tomatoes inhibited PME activity in fruit (see review by Gray *et al.* 1992). Transgenic fruit had a delayed ripening and a better resistance to splitting. Opposite effects of GA and ABA on á-amylase regulation is well documented (Jacobsen and Beach 1985). Ca^{2+} ion has been shown to play a role in mediating the effects of these growth regulators on the synthesis and secretion of the enzyme (Gilroy and Jones 1992). Regulation of PME by hormones is not known. Two major pectinesterases were purified from citrus fruit tissues, one located in the peel, the other in the endocarp MacDonald *et al.* 1993A). The peel pectineasterase requires a higher concentration of cations than the endocarp enzyme, for optimal activity. MacDonald *et al.* (1993A) suggested that these enzymes may differ in their mode of action. Application of GA_3 to barley aleurone increased the influx of Ca^{2+} into protoplasts (Gilroy and Jones 1992). It has also been reported that lack of Ca^{2+} in the fruit as compared to its levels in the leaves accompanied creasing (Cutuli 1968/1969), which is also a disorder related to the pectin status of the tree. In addition, spraying the tree with GA_3 reduced creasing (Cutuli 1968/1969; Embleton *et al.* 1973) or splitting (García-Luís *et al.* 1994; Almela *et al.* 1994). Similarly, potassium spray on developing fruit reduced creasing (Embleton *et al.* 1973) and calcium foliar supply also reduced splitting in orchards prone to this disorder (Almela *et al.* 1994; Monselise *et al.* 1986). Whether GA_3 transforms the fruit into a strong sink for cations, thus reducing splitting, is unknown. GA_3 has a variable affect on splitting of Nova mandarin, depending upon timing of treatment (García- Luís *et al.* 1994). It increases it when applied at flowering and reduces it when applied shortly after the June drop.

In cultivars presenting a secondary fruit at the stylar end of the primary fruit (Lima and Davies 1984; García-Luís *et al.* 1994) splitting was reported to be associated with senescence of the navel tissue. This senescence is accompanied by an increase in ethylene evolution (Lima and Davies 1984) a cessation of cell division and loss of chlorophyll in the epidermal tissue around the stylar scar, making it prone to splitting.

The increase in splitting observed when GA_3 was applied at full bloom was explained by the fact that there was a significant increase in the size of the secondary fruit as a response to GA_3 subsequently resulting in splitting of the primary fruit at the stylar end (García-Luís *et al.* 1994). The reduction in the severity of the disorder, obtained when GA_3 was applied 12 weeks post-bloom (July) was probably due to the inhibitory effect of GA_3 on ethylene-induced senescence of the rind (Goldschmidt *et al.* 1977; García-Luís *et al.* 1986).

Conclusion

These rind problems appear to have some common denominator. Although not with certainty, they all appear to be related to changes taking place at the cell wall of albedo cells primarily than probably extending to the flavedo tissue in the case of splitting, for example. Dissolution of the middle lamella, increased solubilisation of pectic polymers and loss of membrane integrity all contribute to loss of firmness and tissue strength and have been reported to be delayed or inhibited by GA_3 in fruit tissues (Ben-Arie et al. 1996; Lewis et al. 1967). However, the response of the fruit to GA_3 is dependent upon the timing of application in relation to fruit development. Although these disorders have some similarities, the enzymatic complex involved in each process may be different (C. Lovatt personal communication).

CHILLING INJURY

Chilling injury (CI) is a postharvest physiological disorder of citrus fruit in storage or transit (Grierson 1981; Chapter 14). A malady showing similar symptoms has also been described as a preharvest problem of some cultivars such as Fortune mandarin (Agustí and Almela 1989; Almela et al. 1992). Strong cold winds and both low temperature and relative humidity are reported to be involved in the development of pitting of Fortune fruits before harvesting (Almela et al. 1992). The common storage disorder starts with pitting, with collapsing of discrete areas of the peel, forming sunken brown-reddish areas that tend to coalesce producing larger affected areas. CI symptoms may not actually appear during cold storage. Rather, their expression may occur once fruit are brought to ambient temperature. The incidence of this disorder varies from year to year and also with fruit position on the tree (Almela et al. 1992; Purvis 1980), fruit exposure (Purvis 1984; McDonald et al. 1993) and cultivar (Chalutz et al. 1985).

Growth regulators have been reported to influence CI development (Grierson 1981; Ismail and Grierson 1977). Arpaia and Eaks (1990) demonstrated that GA_3 applied as a foliar spray on navels at fruit color-break reduced CI of fruit stored at 1°C to 5°C and prolonged storage life of fruit held at 20°C. ABA applications reduced CI of grapefruit (Kawada et al. 1979) while ethylene pre-treatment or its presence during storage significantly increased CI in lemons (McDonald 1986; Wild et al. 1976).

POSTHARVEST FRUIT DECAY

The flavedo of the fruit is the first line of resistance to invasion by decay pathogens. Mechanical injuries to the peel inflicted during harvesting and handling are the principal sites of infection by the wound-invading pathogens *Penicillium* and *Geotrichum*.

Storage at low temperature and high humidity is beneficial to the maintenance of the natural resistance of both the peel and the button of the fruit to infection (Eckert and Eaks 1989). Peel and button senescence and drying are delayed. Similarly, removal of ethylene in the storage room reduced decay incidence of citrus fruit (Testoni *et al.* 1992).

The fruit button (receptacle + sepals) constitutes a major barrier and is also a sign of freshness. Hence, chemical treatments and environmental conditions that maintain its vitality will also delay decay development. Low temperature and high humidity delays button abscission. Stewart (1949) reported that field sprays of 2,4-D increased the storage life of citrus by delaying the abscission and senescence of the fruit button. Fresh lemons are particularly susceptible to decay around the nectary disk, or button, of the fruit. Application of 2,4-D reduced black button from 26 to 2% and decay from 4.9 to 0.7% (Erickson 1952). Use of 2,4-D also retarded color development, delayed increases in juice content, and intensified rind injuries. Application of 2,4-D at 100 to 1000 ppm in a water wax formulation to lemons before storage delayed button deterioration, rate of coloration, and water loss by fruit during storage (Stewart *et al.* 1952B). Today virtually all California lemons are treated with a water wax containing 250 to 500 ppm 2,4-D (Eckert and Eaks 1989). 2,4-D has also been recommended in South Africa (Pelser 1975) and Israel (Schiffmann-Nadel *et al.* 1972) to control stem-end rots during long-distance shipment, and prolonged storage of oranges and grapefruit. In Morocco, it is a general practice that during the degreening season, clementine fruits are harvested into buckets containing water plus 2,4-D at 4-8 ppm to maintain fruit button vitality and prevent its abscission during the degreening process.

Preharvest application of gibberellic acid maintains fruit peel quality on the tree and in storage, and reduced postharvest fruit decay (El-Otmani and Coggins 1991). Coggins *et al.* (1992) demonstrated that postharvest application of gibberellic acid (50 ppm) in storage wax reduced the incidence of *Geotrichum* decay.

INTERNAL QUALITY

Variable effects of growth regulators on citrus fruit quality are reported in the literature. Pre-harvest sprays of either 2,4-D or GA_3 increased juice °Brix (a measure of juice soluble solids) of grapefruit at harvest (El-Zeftawi 1980A). GA_3 applied pre-harvest to navel oranges had no effect on fruit juice content and acid and soluble solids content at harvest (Coggins 1969), but when applied to cultivar Valencia orange, it increased solids and acid in juice (Embleton *et al.* 1973). In cultivar Joppa oranges, a pre-harvest spray of 2,4-D reduced juice content, increased titratable acidity, reduced total soluble solids and therefore reduced the TSS/TA ratio (Randhawa *et al.*

1961). On cultivar Satsuma mandarin GA_3 had no effect on juice soluble solids and acids, but depressed fruit juice content (Kuroaka *et al.* 1977). 2,4-D was reported to increase fruit juice content, but had no significant effect on soluble solids, acidity or the solids/acids ratio (Singh and Randhawa 1961). Kokkalos (1981) found that 2,4-D had no influence on juice content, TSS, TA or Brix/acidity ratio of on-tree-stored grapefruit. In an experiment using preharvest application of 2,4-D (16 ppm) and GA_3 (10 ppm) on clementine mandarin and Valencia orange to delay peel ageing and lengthen the harvest season, El-Otmani *et al.* (1991) found no effect of these PGRs, used either separately or in combination, on fruit weight loss in storage, extractable juice, juice titratable acidity (TA) and total soluble solids (TSS) or the ratio TSS/TA. Recently, Fidelibus and Davies (2000) indicated possible reduction of °Brix associated with delay coloring of oranges treated with GA_3 preharvest and destined for processing.

Potassium gibberellate applied to Lisbon lemons in April during full bloom produced greener fruit which also were slower to develop yellow color in storage (Coggins *et al.* 1960A). Additionally, KGA increased stem thickness, percentage of button loss, and percentage of black button; KGA also delayed maturation and consequently juice content was less (43.9% compared with 54%), but TSS and vitamin C were greater in treated fruit. Titratable acidity levels, however, were unchanged. GA_3 is applied commercially in California at 5-10 ppm prior to yellow color development (October to December) to delay maturity and shift the production peak in the following season. Jahn and Young (1972) found preharvest ethephon sprays to have little effect on degreening of Bearss lemons, even at concentrations as high as 750 ppm. In contrast, El-Zeftawi (1980) sprayed 10 ppm GA_3 alone and in combination with 1000 ppm CCC on Lisbon lemon trees development and reducing juice content 4-6 weeks after application. The combination treatment reduced fruit circumference by 6% compared with untreated fruit, resulting in a greater percentage of marketable fruit late in the season when fruit usually became too large for the commercial market.

Gibberellic acid also has promise for maintaining juice color of Red-blush grapefruit (M. A. Ismail unpublished data). Fruit treated with 20 ppm GA_3 and 10 ppm 2,4-D in late June had significantly redder juice color than untreated fruit by March when internal color generally is poor.

Seed sprouting (vivipary) can be a major problem for late-harvested grapefruit in some years (Albrigo *et al.* 1980). A single germinated seed causes a reduction in grade and may result in off-flavor. Ali-Dinar *et al.* (1976) reduced vivipary of Marsh grapefruit from 38.8 to 15.1% using 15 ppm GA_3; however, subsequent studies in Florida have shown no effect of GA_3 or 2,4-D on vivipary (Albrigo *et al.* 1980; Ferguson *et al.* 1982; F. S. Davies and M. A. Ismail unpublished data). Nevertheless, vivipary in untreated fruit was much less severe or extensive in these seasons (Davies 1986).

Granulation is also severe in certain years. As much as 76% of Marsh grapefruit harvested in May and stored until July contained dry sections during the 1980 season in Florida (Albrigo *et al.* 1980); F. S. Davies (unpublished data) noticed a reduction in granulation from 32.3 to 13.0% for Marsh grapefruit sprayed with 10 ppm GA_3 and 20 ppm 2,4-D in 1980; however, this effect has not been consistently reproduced. In contrast, Gilfillan *et al.* (1973) found a slight increase in granulation with 10 ppm GA after 3 weeks storage; however, granulation was much less severe in this study.

FRUIT WEIGHT LOSS

Weight loss is an important factor in citrus deterioration in storage and/ or on the supermarket shelves. It is essentially due to water loss by transpiration as this accounts for 90% of total weight loss (Ben-Yehoshua 1969). It is high immediately after picking and declines afterwards. The decline in both respiration and transpiration during storage is due to shriveling and drying of the peel. Peel shrinkage resulted in a significant increase in resistance of the rind to gas diffusion. Shrivelling is immediately visible on the peel, and affected fruit loses its shiny appearance, softens and senesces.

The peel (McDonald *et al.* 1993) and particularly the flavedo portion (Ben-Yehoshua 1969) is the primary site of resistance to gas diffusion from and into the fruit. This resistance increased with fruit maturation and storage and was reduced by gibberellic acid treatment during color-break (El-Otmani *et al.* 1986). Loss of water vapor from fruit is a passive process with the driving force provided by the vapor pressure gradient between the peel inside and the outer atmosphere (Ben-Yehoshua *et al.* 1994). The outermost cell layer of the flavedo is covered by a cuticular membrane covered by a waxy layer whose thickness, chemical composition and structure varies with species, fruit age, environmental conditions, preharvest cultural practices and postharvest conditions (see review by El-Otmani 1985; El-Otmani and Coggins 1985A; El-Otmani *et al.* 1989). It is noteworthy that gibberellic acid, used to delay fruit senescence, reduced wax accumulation on fruit but this reduction did not have any significant and consistent effect on weight loss (El-Otmani *et al.* 1986). This indicates that wax quantity may not be the only parameter involved in restricting water vapor loss, but morphology and composition of the wax layer may also play a role. In fact, gibberellic acid maintained the peel of mature fruit at a physiologically young stage, with wax characteristics of younger fruit (El-Otmani and Coggins 1985A, B).

SEEDINESS

Seediness can be an undesirable characteristic of many commercially important mandarins and mandarin hybrids. Feinstein *et al.* (1975) found that application of GA_3 at midbloom or NAA to 10 mm diameter fruits decreased seed number in Dancy tangerine and Temple orange. Unfortunately, these treatments only reduced seed number from an average of 12.5 to 9.2 in Dancy and 22.8 to 18.6 in Temple. Complete or nearly complete reduction in seed number is necessary to be commercially important. Seedless fruit are preferred for the European market; however, this characteristic is less important to consumers in the United States.

EFFICACY OF PLANT GROWTH REGULATORS

This subject has been thoroughly reviewed in another publication (El-Otmani et al. 2000); however, it is important to note that:

1. Inclusion of surfactants in the PGR spray mix improves wetting of the target organs by lowering the surface tension and thus reducing the contact angle between the liquid and the target organ (Henning and Coggins 1988). Consequently, effectiveness of the PGR is significantly increased. Greenberg and Goldschmidt (1988) reported that enhanced effectiveness of GA_3 in retarding rind chlorophyll degradation resulted from better uptake of GA_3 due to changes occurring in the epicuticular wax when Silwet ® L-77, an organosilicone surfactant, was used in the spray solution.

2. Not all surfactants are equally effective (Henning and Coggins 1988; Greenberg et al. 1987) and some of them can even cause rind injury and blemish to the fruit (Coggins and Henning 1988B; Gilfillan et al. 1973) or phytotoxicity and excessive leaf drop (Wilson et al. 1981). It is therefore advisable to test these compounds and assess their interaction with the PGR and their reaction under specific local environmental conditions and with the cultivars or strains of citrus considered.

3. Highly alkaline (pH >8) conditions (Coggins 1981) and pH lower than 4 (Plant Protection Ltd. 1969) can cause decomposition and loss of activity of certain PGRs like GA_3 for example. Acidification of the spray solution is a common practice in Israel (Greenberg et al. 1993) and South Africa (Gilfillan 1986).

4. Uptake of PGRs is proportional to the concentration (within saturation limits) of the compound in the spray mix and to the duration of uptake (Greenberg and Goldschmidt 1988).

5. Uptake is greater at high relative humidity (>60%) and increased with temperature in the range of 5 to 35°C (Greenberg and Goldschmidt 1988). Therefore, it appears that the best time of day for field spray applications is early morning and late afternoon when

the humidity is high and the temperature is not too warm (for summer) or too cold (for winter) and the nightly increase in relative humidity in the field may induce renewed uptake of the active ingredient from the dry residue on the leaf or fruit (Greenberg and Goldschmidt 1988) and increase its physiological effect provided the PGR is stable on the plant surfaces. In addition, optimum temperature and humidity not only enhances uptake but also reduces phytotoxicity and leaf and fruit drop for compounds such as ethephon and NAA for example.

6. Light and low humidity caused GA_3 decomposition (Goldschmidt and Greenberg 1989) and rain within hours following a field spray application may eliminate treatment effect (Biggs and Kossuth 1981; Wilson *et al.* 1977).

7. Optimum cultural practices in the field (irrigation, fertilization, pruning) and tree health ensures consistent optimum results in the grove and postharvest (Gilfillan *et al.* 1973; Gallasch 1984; Monselise and Sasson 1977).

8. Compatibility of the PGR with other foliar or postharvest treatments should be considered since combining treatments will reduce the number of sprays and thus reduce cost of production (Gallasch 1984).

9. Timing of application is critical since the physiological stage of the target organ plays an important role in the type of response observed as a result of treatment. It is also critical since it allows avoidance of product residues in the fruit (Erner and Coggins 1989; El-Otmani *et al.* 1998).

REFERENCES

AGUSTÍ, M. 2000. Citricultura. Ed. Mundi Prensa, Barcelone.

AGUSTÍ, M. and ALMELA, V. 1984. Mejora de la calidad del fruto de la mandarina Satsuma. Bco. de Santander, Madrid.

AGUSTÍ, M. and ALMELA, V. 1989. El cultivo de la mandarina Fortune en España. Problemas y perspectivas. Frutic. Prof. 25, 39-48.

AGUSTÍ, M. and ALMELA, V. 1991. Aplicación de fitorreguladores en Citricultura. Ed. AEDOS, Barcelona.

AGUSTÍ, M., ALMELA, V. and GUARDIOLA, J. L. 1981. The regulation of fruit cropping in mandarins through the use of growth regulators. Proc. Int. Soc. Citriculture 1, 216-220.

AGUSTÍ, M., ALMELA, V. and GUARDIOLA, J. L. 1986. Recolección tardía del fruto en el mandarino Satsuma. Efecto del ácido giberélico. Actas II Cong. Nal. SECH, I, 352-361.

AGUSTÍ, M., ALMELA, V. and GUARDIOLA, J. L. 1988. Aplicaciones de ácido giberélico para el control de alteraciones de la corteza de las mandarinas asociadas a su maduración. Invest. Agr. Prod. Prot. Veg. 3, 125-137.

AGUSTÍ, M., ALMELA, V., AZWAR, M., EL-OTMANI, M. and PONS, J. 1994A. Satsuma mandarin fruit size increased by 2,4-DP. HortScience 29, 279-281.

AGUSTÍ, M., ALMELA, V., AZNAR, M., PONS, J. and EL-OTMANI, M. 1992. The use of 2,4-D P to improve fruit size in citrus. Proc. Int. Soc. Citriculture 1, 423-427.

AGUSTÍ, M., ALMELA, V., JUAN, M., PRIMO-MILLO, E., TRENOR, I. and ZARAGOZA, S. 1994B. Effect of 3,5,6-trichloro-2-pyridyl-oxyacetic acid on fruit size and yield of "Clausellina" mandarin (*Citrus unshiu* Marc.). J. Hort. Sci. 69, 219-223.

AGUSTÍ, M., EL-OTMANI, M., AZNAR, M., JUAN, M. and ALMELA, V. 1995. Effect of 3,4,5-trichloro-2-pyridyloxyacetic acid on Clementine early fruitlet development and on fruit size at maturity. J. Hort. Sci. 70, 955-962.

AGUSTÍ, M., MINGO-CASTEL, A. M. and ALMELA, V. 1990. Efecto de la quinetina y el rayado sobre el cuajado en la variedad de naranjo Navelate (*Citrus sinensis* (L.) Osbeck). Invest. Agr. Prod. Prot. Veg. 5, 69-76.

AGUSTÍ, M., ZARAGOZA, S., EL-OTMANI, M., ALMELA, V. and PRIMO-MILLO, E. 1996. Recent findings in the mechanism of action of the synthetic auxins used to improve fruit size. Proc. Int. Soc. Citriculture 2, 922-928.

AGUSTÍ, M., ZARAGOZA, S., IGLESIAS, D. J., ALMELA, V., PRIMO-MILLO, E. and Talón, M. 2002. The synthetic auxin 3,5,6-TPA stimulates carbohydrate accumulation and growth in citrus fruit. Plant Growth Regul. 36, 141-147.

ALBRIGO, L. G., KAWADA, K. HALE, P. W., SMOOT, J. J. and HATTON, T. T., JR. 1980. Effect of harvest date and preharvest and postharvest treatments on Florida grapefruit condition in export to Japan. Proc. Fla. State Hort. Soc. 93, 323-327.

ALI, A. G. and LOVATT, C. J. 1994A. Low-temperature stress-induced flowering of the "Washington" navel orange (*Citrus sinensis* [L.] Osbeck) was increased by application of putrescine or spermidine to the foliage. HortScience 29, 516 (Abstr. #590).

ALI, A. G. and LOVATT, C. J. 1994B. Winter application of low buret urea to the foliage of the "Washington" navel orange increased yield. J. Amer. Soc. Hort. Sci. 119, 1144-1150.

ALI-DINAR, H. M., KREZDORN, A. H. and ROSE, A. J. 1976. Extending the grapefruit harvest season with growth regulators. Proc. Fla. State Hort. Soc. 89, 4-6.

ALMELA, V., AGUSTÍ, M. and AZNAR, M. 1990. El "splitting" o rajado del fruto de la mandarina Nova. Su control. Acta Hort. 6, 142-147.

ALMELA, V., AGUSTÍ, M. and GUARDIOLA, J. L. 1987. El bufado del fruto en la mandarina Satsuma. Importancia de la alteración y vías de control. Frutic. Prof. 10, 12-18.

ALMELA, V., M. AGUSTÍ and PONS, J. 1992A. Rindspots in Fortune mandarin. Origin and control. Physiol. Plant. 85, A60 (Abstr.).

ALMELA, V., ZARAGOZA, S., PRIMO-MILLO, E. and AGUSTÍ, M. 1994. Hormonal control of splitting in "Nova" mandarin fruit. J. Hort. Sci. 69, 969-973.

ALMELA, V., ZARAGOZA, S., AGUSTÍ, M. and PRIMO-MILLO, E. 1992. Estudio del rajado del fruto de la mandarina Nova y su control. Levante Agrícola 320, 144-150.

ALONI, R. 1987. Differentiation of vascular tissues. Annu. Rev. Plant Physiol. 38, 179-204.

ALONSO, J. M., CUBELLS, X., CHAMARRO, J. and GRANELL, A. 1996. Ethylene-induced genes are also expressed during fruit ripening in orange fruits. Programme and Abstracts, VIII Congress Int. Soc. Citriculture, Sun City Resort, South Africa, 12-17, 1996 105, (Abstr. #P072).

AMIR-SHAPHIRA, D., GOLDSCHMIDT, E. E. and ALTMAN, A. 1987. Chlorophyll catabolism in senescing plant tissues: in vivo breakdown intermediates suggest different degradative pathways for citrus fruit and parsley leaves. Proc. Natl. Acad. Sci. 84, 1901-1905.

ANTHONY, M. F. and COGGINS, C. W., JR. 2001. NAA and 3,5,6-TPA control mature fruit drop in California citrus. HortScience. 36, 1296-1299.

ARPAIA, M. L. and EAKS, I. L. 1990. The effect of cultural practices on the postharvest responses of navel oranges. XXIII Int'l. Hort. Congr., Florence, Italy. Abstr. N-2494.

AZNAR, M., ALMELA, V., JUAN, M., EL-OTÙMANI, M. and AGUSTÍ, M. 1995. Effect of the synthetic auxin phenothiol on fruit development of 'Fortune' mandarin. J. Hort. Sci. 70, 617-621.

BAIN, J. M. 1958. Morphological, anatomical and physiological changes in the developing fruit of the Valencia orange, *Citrus sinensis* (L.) Osbeck. Austr. J. Bot. 6, 1-25.

BAR-AKIVA, A. 1975. Effect of potassium nutrition on fruit in Valencia orange. J. Hort. Sci. 50, 85-89.

BARENDSE, G. W. M., KARSSEN, C. M. and KOORNNEEF, M. 1991. Role of endogenous gibberellins during fruit and seed development, pp. 179-187. *In* Gibberellins, N. Takahashi, B. O. Phinney, and J. Macmillan (Editors). Springer Verlag, New York.

BARMORE, C. R. 1975. Effect of ethylene on chlorophyllase activity and chlorophyll content in calamondin rind tissue. HortScience. 10, 595-596.

BEN-ARIE, R., SAKS, Y., SONEGO, L. and FRANK, A. 1996. Cell wall metabolism in gibberellin-treated persimmon fruits. Plant Growth Regul. 19, 25-33.

BEN-YEHOSHUA, S. 1969. Gas exchange, transpiration and the commercial deterioration in storage of orange fruit. J. Amer. Soc. Hort. Sci. 94, 524-528.

BEN-YEHOSHUA, S., GOLDSCHMIDT, E. E. and BAR-JOSEPH, M. 1994. Citrus fruits. Encyclopedia Agr. Sci. 1, 357-378.

BEYER, E. M., Jr. 1976. A potent inhibitor of ethylene action in plants. Plant Physiol. 58, 268-271.

BIGGS, R. H. and KOSSUTH, S. V. 1981. Physiological model-A Citrus harvest aid for 'Valencia' fruits. Acta Hort. 120, 71-76.

BORROTO, C. G., LÓPEZ, V. M., GONZÁLEZ, A. and PYLA., L. 1981. Orange drop under tropical conditions and measures of control. Proc. Int. Soc. Citriculture 1, 268-271.

BOWER, J., GILFILLAN, I. M. and SKINNER, H. 1992. Fruit splitting in "Valencia" and its relationships to the pectin status of the rind. Proc. Int. Soc. Citriculture 1, 511-514.

BRISKER, H. E., GOLDSHMIDT, E. E. and GOREN, R. 1976. Ethylene-induced formation of ABA in citrus peel as related to chloroplast transformations. Plant Physiol. 58, 377-379.

CHALUTZ, E., WAKS, J. and SCHIFFMAN-NADEL. 1985. A comparison of the response of different citrus fruit cultivars to storage temperature. Scientia Hort. 25, 271-277.

CHAPMAN, H. D. 1968. The mineral nutrition of citrus. *In* The Citrus Industry, Vol. II, W. Reuther, L. D. Batchelor, and H. J. Webber (Editors). Div. Agr. Sci., University of California, Berkeley.

CHAPMAN, J. C. 1980. Ethephon for fruit thinning of imperial and beauty of Glen Retreat mandarins in the Central Burnett district, Queensland. Austr. J. Exp. Agr. Anim. Husto. 20, 508-512.

COGGINS, C. W., JR. 1969. Gibberellin research in citrus ring aging problems. Proc. 1st. Int. Citrus Symp. 3, 1177-1185.

COGGINS, C. W., JR. 1981. The influence of exogenous growth regulators on rind quality and interval quality of citrus fruits. Proc. Int. Soc. Citriculture. 1, 214-216.

COGGINS, C. W., JR. and HENNING, G. L. 1988A. A comprehensive California field study of the influence of preharvest applications of gibberellic acid on the rind quality of Valencia oranges. Israel J. Bot. 37, 145-154.

COGGINS, C. W., JR. and HENNING, G. L. 1988B. Grapefruit rind blemish caused by interaction of gibberellic acid wetting agents. Proc. 6th Int. Citrus Congress 1, 333-338.

COGGINS, C. W., JR. and HIELD, H. Z. 1968. Plant growth regulators, pp. 371-389. *In* The Citrus Industry, Vol. II., W. Reuther, L. D. Batchelor, and H. J. Webber (Editors). Div. Agr. Sci., University of California, Berkeley.

COGGINS, C. W., JR. and HIELD, H. Z. 1978. Plant growth regulators for citrus University of California Publ. 4047.

COGGINS, C. W., JR. and JONES, W. W. 1977. Growth regulators and coloring of citrus fruits. Proc. Int. Soc. Citriculture 2, 686-688.

COGGINS, C.W., JR., ANTHONY, M.F. and FRITTS, R., Jr. 1992. The postharvest use of gibberellic acid on lemons. Proc. Int. Soc. Citriculture 1, 478-481.

COGGINS, C. W., JR., ANTHONY, M. F., HALL, M. O. and ATKIN, D. R. 1997. A new look at gibberellic acid spray timing for navel orange. Proc. Western Plant Growth Regul. Soc. 9, 31-35.

COGGINS, C. W., JR., HENNING, G. L. and YOKOYAMA, H. 1970. Lycopene accumulation induced by 2,(4-chlorophenylthio)-triethylamine hydrochloride. Science 168, 1589-1590.

COGGINS, C. W., JR., HIELD, H. Z. and GARBER, M. J. 1960. The influence of potassium gibberellate on Valencia orange trees and fruit. Proc. Amer. Soc. Hort. Sci. 76, 193-198.

COHEN, A. 1984A. Citrus fruit enlargement by means of summer girdling. J. Hort. Sci. 59, 119-125.

COHEN, A. 1984B. Effect of girdling date on fruit size of Marsh seedless grapefruit. J. Hort. Sci. 59, 567-573.

COHEN, A., LOMAS, J. and RASSIS, A. 1972. Climatics effects on fruit shape and peel thickness in "Marsh seedless" grapefruit. J. Amer. Soc. Hort. Sci. 97, 768-771.

COOK, A. I. 1913. California Citrus Culture. California Stat, Printing Office, Sacramento.

COOPER, W. C. and HENRY, W. H. 1968. Effect of growth regulators on the coloring and abscission of citrus fruit. Israel J. Agr. Res. 18, 161-174.

COUSINS, H. H. 1910. III: Agricultural Experiment, Citrus. Annual Report. Dpt. Agr., Jamaica, 7.

CUTULI, G. 1968/1969. Il "creasing" delle arance. Ann. Inst. Sperim. Agrumicoltura. Vol. 1-2.

DANN, I. R., JERIE, P. H. and CHALMERS, D. J. 1985. Short-term changes in cambial growth and endogenous IAA concentration in relation to phloem girdling of peach (*Prunus persica*). Aust. J. Plant Physiol. 12, 395-402.

DAVENPORT, T. L. 1990. Citrus flowering. Hort. Rev. 12, 349-408.

DAVIES, F. S. 1986. Growth regulator improvement of postharvest quality, pp. 79-99. *In* Fresh Citrus Fruits, W. F. Wardowski, S. Nagy, and W. Grierson (Editors). AVI Pub. Co., Inc., Westport, CT.

de CICCO, V., INTRIGLIOLO, F., IPPOLITO, A., VANADIA, S. and GUIFFRIDA, A. 1988. Proc. 6th Int. Citrus Congress 1, 535-540.

DEL RIVERO, J. M. 1968. Los estados de carencia en los Agrios. Ed. Mundi Prensa, Madrid.

DENNY, F. E. 1924. Hastening the coloration of lemons. J. Agr. Res. 27, 753-769.

EAKS, I. L. 1977. Physiology of degreening—summary and discussion of related topics. Proc. Int. Soc. Citriculture 1, 223-226.

ECKERT, J. W. and EAKS, I. L. 1989. Postharvest disorders and diseases of citrus fruits. *In* The Citrus Industry, W. Reuther, E. C. Calavan, and G. E. Carman (Editors). Vol. V, University of California, Div. Agr. Nat. Res., Oakland.

EILATI, S. K., GOLDSCHMIDT, E. E. and MONSELISE, S. P. 1969A. Hormonal control of color changes in orange peel. Experientia. 25, 209-210.

EILATI, S. K., MONSELISE, S. P. and BUDONSKI, P. 1969B. Seasonal development of external color and carotenoid content in the peel of ripening "Shamouti" oranges. J. Amer. Soc. Hort. Sci. 94, 346-348.

EL-OTMANI, M. 1985. Ontogeny of *Citrus sinensis* (L.) Osbeck fruit epicuticular wax. Ph.D. Dissertation. University of California, Riverside.

EL-OTMANI, M. 1990. Causes of low packouts in citrus packinghouses of southern Morocco. VIII Congress Mediterranean Phytopathol. Union, Agadir, Morocco (Abstr.).

EL-OTMANI, M. and AIT-OUBAHOU, A. 1996. Prolonging citrus fruit shelf-life: recent development and future prospects. Proc. Intl. Soc. Citriculture 1, 59-69.

EL-OTMANI, M. and AIT-OUBAHOU, A. 1999. Improving and/or maintaining quality of citrus fruit by pre- and postharvest application on plant growth regulators, pp. 35-55. *In* Recent advances in Postharvest Diseases and Disorder Control of Citrus Fruit, M. Schirra (Editor). Research, Singpost, Trivandrum, India.

EL-OTMANI, M. and COGGINS, C. W., JR. 1985A. Fruit age and growth regulator effects on the quantity and structure of the epicuticular wax of "Washington" navel orange fruit. J. Amer. Soc. Hort. Sci. 110, 371-378.

EL-OTMANI, M. and COGGINS, C. W., JR. 1985B. Fruit development and growth regulator effects on normal alkanos of "Washington" navel orange fruit agricultural wax. J. Food Agr. Food Chem. 33, 656-663.

EL-OTMANI, M. and COGGINS, C. W., JR. 1991. Growth regulator effects on retention of quality of stored citrus fruits. Sci. Hort. 45, 261-272.

EL-OTMANI, M., AGUSTÍ, M., AZNAR, M. and ALMELA, V. 1993. Improving the size of "Fortune" mandarin fruits by the auxin 2,4-DP. Sci. Hort. 55, 283-290.

EL-OTMANI, M., AIT-M'BAREK, A. and COGGINS,. C. W., JR. 1990. GA₃ and 2,4-D prolong on-tree storage of citrus in Morocco. Sci. Hort. 44, 241-249.

EL-OTMANI, M., ARPAIA, M. L., COGGINS, C. W., JR., PEHERSON, J. E., JR. and O'CONNELL, N. V. 1989. Development charges in 'Valencia' orange fruit epicuticular wax in relation to fruit position on the tree. Scientia Hort. 41, 69-81.

EL-OTMANI, M., COGGINS, C. W., JR., AGUSTÍ, M. and LOVATT, C. J. 2000. Plant growth regulators in citriculture: world current uses. Critical Rev. Pl. Sci. 19, 395-447.

EL-OTMANI, M. COGGINS, C. W., JR. and EAKS, I. L. 1986. Fruit age gibberellic acid effect on epicuticular wax accumulation, respiration and internal atmosphere of navel orange fruit. J. Amer. Soc. Hort. Sci. 111, 228-232.

EL-OTMANI, M., LOVATT, C. J., COGGINS, C. W., JR. and AGUSTÍ, M. 1995. Plant growth regulators in citriculture: factors regulating endogenous levels in citrus tissues. Crit. Rev. Plant Sci. 14, 367-412.

EL-OTMANI, M., ZOUGGARH, E., AIT-OUBAHOU, A., SEBBATA, A. and LEKCHIRI, A. 1998. Evaluation de la persistance du 2,4-D dans les fruits d'agrumes: cas du clémentinier, pp. 356-360. In Nouveaux Acquis de la Recherche en Agrumiculture, M. El-Otmani and A Ait-Oubahou (Editors). Institut Agronomique et Vétérinaire Hassan II, Agadir, Morocco.

EL-ZEFTAWI, B. M. 1976. Effects of ethephon and 2,4,5-T on fruit size, rind pigments and alternate bearing of 'Imperial' mandarin. Scientia Hort. 5, 315-320.

EL-ZEFTAWI, B. M. 1978. Chemical and temperature control of rind pigment of citrus fruits. Proc. Int. Soc. Citriculture 33-36.

EL-ZEFTAWI, B. M. 1980A. Effects of gibberellic acid and cycocelon on coloring and sizing of lemon. Scientia Hort. 12, 177-181.

EL-ZEFTAWI, B. M. 1980B. Regulating pre-harvest fruit drop and the duration of the harvest season of grapefruit with 2,4-D and GA. J. Hort. Sci. 55, 211-217.

EL-ZEFTAWI, B. M. and GARRETT, R. C. 1978. Effects of ethephon, GA, and light exclusion on rind pigments, plastid ultrastructure and juice quality of Valencia oranges. J. Hort. Sci. 53, 215-223.

EMBLETON, T. W., JONES, W. W. and Coggins, C. W., Jr. 1973. Aggregate effects on nutrients and gibberellic acid on "Valencia" orange crop value. J. Amer. Soc. Hort. Sci. 98, 281-285.

ERICKSON, L.C. 1952. Growth regulators and lemon storage. Calif. Citragr. 37, 321.

ERICKSON, L.C. 1957. Compositional differences between normal and splitting Washington navel oranges. J. Amer. Soc. Hort. Sci. 70, 257-260.

ERICKSON, L. C. 1968. The general physiology of citrus. In The Citrus Industry, Vol. II, W. Reuther, L. D. Batchelor, and H. J. Webber (Editors). Div. Agr. Sci., University of California, Berkeley.

ERICKSON, L.C. and RICHARDS, S. J. 1955. Influence of 2,4-D and soil moisture on size and quality of Valencia orange. Proc. Amer. Soc. Hort. Sci. 65, 109-112.

ERNER, Y. 1989. Citrus fruit set: carbohydrate, hormone and leaf mineral relationships, pp. 233-242. In Manipulation of Fruiting, C. Wright (Editor). Butterworths.

ERNER, Y and BRAVDO, B. 1983. The importance of inflorescence leaves in fruit setting of Shamouti orange. Acta Hort. 139, 107-112.

ERNER, Y. and COGGINS, C. W., JR. 1989. Free and bound residues of 2,4-D in 'Marsh' grapefruit and 'Washington' navel orange fruit. J. Amer. Soc. Hort. Sci. 114, 846-850.

ERNER, Y., GOREN, R. and MONSELISE, S. P. 1976A. The rough fruit condition of the Shamouti orange-connections with the endogenous hormonal balance. J. Hort. Sci. 51, 367-374.

ERNER, Y., GOREN, R. and MONSELISE, S. P. 1976B. Reduction of peel roughness of Shamouti orange with growth regulators. J. Amer. Soc. Hort. Sci. 101, 513-515.

ERNER, Y., KAPLAN, Y., ARTZI, B. and HAMOU, M. 1993. Increasing fruit size using auxins end potassium. Acta Hort. 329, 112-119.

EVANS, P. T. and MALMBERG, R. L. 1989. Do polyamines have roles in plant development? Annu. Rev. Plant Physiol Plant Mol. Biol. 40, 235-269.

FAWCETT, H. S. 1936. Citrus Diseases and Their Control. 2nd ed., McGraw Hill Book Co., New York.

FEINSTEIN, B., MONSELISE, S. P. and GOREN, R. 1975. Studies on the reduction of seed number in mandarin. HortScience 10, 385-386.

FERGUSON, L., DAVIES, F. S., ISMAIL, M. A. and WHEATON, T. A. 1983. Growth regulator and nutritional effects on grapefruit color and storage quality. Proc. Plant Growth Regul. Soc. Amer. 10, 175-181.

FERGUSON, L., ISMAIL, M. A., DAVIES, F. S. and WHEATON, T. A. 1982. Pre- and postharvest gibberellic acid and 2,4-dichlorophenoxyacetic acid applications for increasing storage life of grapefruit. Proc. Fla. State Hort. Soc. 95, 242-245.

FIDELIBUS, M. W. and DAVIES, F. S. 2000. Gibberellic acid application timing effects on °Brix and peel color of processing oranges. Int. Soc. Citriculture IX Congress, Orlando, Florida, Program and Abstracts: Abstract #P352.

FISHLER, M., GOLDSCHMIDT, E. E. and MONSELISE, S. P. 1983. Leaf area and fruit size in girdled grapefruit branches. J. Amer. Soc. Hort. Sci. 108, 218-221.

GALLASCH, P. T. 1984. Practical aspects of the use of ethephon to control alternate cropping of Valencia orange. Proc. Intl. Soc. Citriculture 1, 285-288.

GALLIANI, S., MONSELISE, S. P. and GOREN, R. 1975. Improving fruit size and breaking alternate bearing in 'Wilking' mandarins by ethephon and other agents. HortScience 10, 68-69.

GARCÍA-LUÍS, A., AGUSTÍ, M., ALMELA, V., ROMERO, E. and GUARDIOLA, J. L. 1985. Effect of gibberellic acid on ripening and peel puffing in "Satsuma" mandarin. Sci. Hort. 27, 75-86.

GARCÍA-LUÍS, A., DUARTE, H. M. M., PORRAS, I., GARCÍA-LIDON, A. and GUARDIOLA, J. L. 1994. Fruit splitting in "Nova" hybrid mandarin in relation to the anatomy of the fruit and fruit set treatments. Sci. Hort. 57, 215-231.

GARCÍA-LUÍS, A., FORNES, F. and GUARDIOLA, J. L. 1986. Effects of gibberellin A3 and cytokinins on natural and post-harvest, ethylene induced pigmentation of Satsuma mandarin peel. Physiol. Plant 68, 271-274.

GARCÍA-MARTINEZ, J. L. and GARCÍA-PAPÍ, M. A. 1979. Influence of gibberellic acid on early fruit development, diffusible growth substances and content of macronutrients in seedless Clementine mandarin. Sci. Hort. 11, 265-274.

GARCÍA-PAPÍ, M. A. and GARCÍA-MARTINEZ, J. L. 1984. Endogenous plant growth substances content in young fruits of seeded and seedless Clementine mandarin as related to fruit set and development. Sci. Hort. 22, 265-274.

GILFILLAN, I. M. 1986. Acidification of gibberellic acid sprays on citrus trees. Citrus Subtrop. Fruit J. 628, 8-10.

GILFILLAN, I. M. 1987. Factors affecting fruit size in 'Tomango' and 'Valencia' oranges and practical measures for its improvement. Citrus Subtrop. Fruit J. 638, 7-13.

GILFILLAN, I. M., KOEKEMOER, W. and STEVENSON, J. 1973. Extension of the grapefruit harvest season with gibberellic acid. I Cong. Mundial Citricultura 3, 335-341.

98   Mohamed El-Otmani

GILFILLAN, I. M., STEVENSON, J. A., WAHL, J. P. and HOLMDEN, E. A. 1981. Control of creasing in navels with gibberellins acid. Proc. Int. Soc. Citriculture 1, 224-226.

GILROY, S. and JONES, R. L. 1992. Gibberellic acid and abscisic acid coordinately regulate cytoplasmic calcium and secretory activity in barley aleurone protoplasts. Proc. Nat. Acad. Sci. 89, 3591-3595.

GOLDSCHMIDT, E. E. 1974. Hormonal and molecular regulation of chloroplast senescence in citrus peel, pp. 1027-1033. *In* Plant Growth Substances, The Hirokawa Press, Tokyo.

GOLDSCHMIDT, E. E. 1976. Endogenous growth substances of citrus tissues. HortScience. 11, 95-99.

GOLDSCHMIDT, E. E. 1980. Pigment changes associated with fruit maturation and their control, pp. 207-217. *In* Senescence in Plants, K. V. Thimann (Editor). CRC Press, Boca Raton, FL.

GOLDSCHMIDT, E. E. 1988. Regulatory aspects of chloro-chromoplast interconversions in senescing citrus fruit peel. Israel J. Bot. 37, 123-130.

GOLDSCHMIDT, E. E. and EILATI, S. K. 1970. Gibberellin-treated Shamouti oranges: effects on coloration and translocation within peels of fruits attached to or detached from the tree. Bot. Gaz. 131, 116-122.

GOLDSCHMIDT, E. E. and GALILY, D. 1974. The fate of endogenous gibberellins and applied radioactive gibberellin A3 during natural and ethylene-induced senescence in citrus peel. Plant Cell Physiol. 15, 485-491.

GOLDSCHMIDT, E. E. and GREENBERG, J. 1989. GA_3 on citrus fruit surface: uptake and persistence. Acta Hort. 239, 55-61.

GOLDSCHMIDT, E. E. and MONSELISE, S. P. 1977. Physiological assumptions toward the development of a citrus fruiting model. Proc. Int. Soc. Citriculture. 2, 668-672.

GOLDSCHMIDT, E. E., AHARONI, V., EILATI, S. K., RIOV, J. W. and MONSELISE, S. P. 1977. Differential counteraction of ethylene effects by gibberellin A_3 and N_6-benzyladenine in senescing citrus peel. Plant Physiol. 59, 193-195.

GOLDSCHMIDT, E. E., EILATI, S. K. and GOREN, R. 1972. Increase in ABA-like growth inhibitors and decrease in gibberellin-like substances during ripening and senescence of citrus fruits, pp. 611-617. *In* Plant Growth Substances, D. J. Carr (Editor). Springer-Verlag, Berlin.

GOLDSCHMIDT, E. E., GALILI, D. and RABBER, D. 1992. Fruit splitting in "Murcott" tangerines: control by reduced water supply. Proc. Int. Soc. Citriculture 1, 657-660.

GOLDSCHMIDT, E. E., GOREN, R., EVEN-CHEN, Z. and BITTNER, S. 1973. Increase in free and bound abscisic acid during natural and ethylene-induced senescence of citrus fruit peel. Plant Physiol. 51, 879-882.

GOLDSCHMIDT, E. E., HUBERMAN, M. and GOREN, R. 1993. Probing the role of endogenous ethylene in the degreening of citrus fruit with ethylene antagonists. Plant Growth Regul. 12, 325-329.

GOODWIN, P. B. 1978. Phytohormones and growth and development of organs of the vegetative plant, pp. 31-173. *In* Phytohormones and Related Compounds. A Comprehensive Treatise, Vol. II, D. S. Letham, P. B. Goodwin, and T. V. J. Higgins (Editors). Elsevier, Amsterdam.

GOREN, R. and GOLDSCHMIDT, E. E. 1970. Regulative systems in the developing citrus fruit. I. The hormonal balance in orange fruit tissues. Physiol. Plant. 29, 937-947.

GOREN, R., HUBERMAN, M. and RIOV, J. 1992. Effects of gibberellin and girdling on the yield of "Nova" (Clementine × "Orlando" tangelo and "Niva" ("Valencia" × "Wilking"). Proc. Int. Soc. Citriculture 1, 493-499.

GRAY, J., PICTON, S., SHABBEER, J., SCHUCH, W. and GRIERSON, D. 1992. Molecular biology of fruit ripening and its manipulation with antisense genes. Plant Mol. Biol. 19, 69-87.

GREENBERG, J. and GOLDSCHMIDT, E. E. 1988. The effectiveness of GA_3 application to citrus fruit. Proc. 6th Int. Citrus Congr. 1, 339-342.

GREENBERG, J., GOLDSCHMIDT, E. E. and GOREN, R. 1993. Potential and limitation of the use of paclobutrazol in citrus orchards in Israel. Acta Hort. 329, 58-61.

GREENBERG, J., ESHEL, G. and GOTFREED, A. 1996. Effects of NAA, 2,4-D and 2,4-DP on yield, fruit size and creasing of "Valencia" orange. Programme and Abstracts, VIII Congress Int. Soc. Citriculture, Sun City Resort, South Africa. 21 (Abstr. #008).

GREENBERG, J., MONSELISE, S. P. and GOLDSCHMIDT, E. E. 1987. Improvement of gibberellin efficiency in prolonging the citrus harvest season by the surfactant L-77. J. Amer. Soc. Hort. Sci. 112, 625-629.

GRIERSON, W. 1981. Physiological disorders of citrus fruits. Proc. Int. Soc. Citriculture 2, 764-767.

GUARDIOLA, J. L. 1988. Factors limiting productivity in citrus. A physiological approach. Proc. 6th Intern. Citrus Congr. 1, 381-394.

GUARDIOLA, J. L. and GARCÍA-LUIS, A. 2000. Increasing fruit size in citrus. Thinning and stimulation of fruit growth. Plant Growth Regul. 31, 121-132.

GUARDIOLA, J. L. and LÁZARO, E. 1987. The effect of synthetic auxins on fruit growth and anatomical development in Satsuma mandarin. Sci. Hort. 31, 119-130.

GUARDIOLA, J. L., ALMELA, V. and BARRÉS, M. T. 1988. Dual effect of auxins on fruit growth in 'Satsuma' mandarin. Scientia Hort. 34, 229-237.

GUARDIOLA, J. L., BARRES, M.T., ALBERT, C. and GARCÍA-LUIS, A. 1993. effect of exogenous growth regulators on fruit development in *Citrus unshiu*. Ann. Bot. 71, 169-176.

GUARDIOLA, J. L., MONERRI, C. and AGUSTÍ, M. 1982. The inhibitory effect of gibberellic acid on flowering in citrus. Physiol. Plant 55, 136-142.

HENNING, G. L. and COGGINS, C. W., Jr. 1988. Bioassay used to determine the impact of surfactants on the biological effectiveness of exogenous gibberellic acid. Proc. 6th Int. Citrus Congr. 1, 325-331.

HERNANDEZ-MIÑANA, F. M. and PRIMO-MILLO, E. 1990. Studies on endogenous cytokinins in Citrus. J. Hort. Sci. 65, 595-601.

HERNANDEZ-MIÑANA, F. M., PRIMO-MILLO, E. and PRIMO-MILLO, J. 1989. Endogenous cytokinins in developing fruits of seeded and seedless citrus cultivars. J. Exp. Bot. 40, 1127-1134.

HIELD, H. Z., COGGINS, C. W., JR. and GARBER, M. J. 1965. Effect of gibberellin sprays on fruit set of Washington navel trees. Hilgardia 36, 297-311.

HOCHBERG, R., MONSELISE, S. P. and COST, J. 1977. Summer girdling and 2,4-D effects on grapefruit size. HortScience 12, 228.

HOFMAN, P. J. 1988. Abscisic acid and gibberellins in the fruitlets and leaves of the Valencia orange in relation to fruit growth and retention. Proc. 6th Int. Citrus Congress 1, 355-362.

HOLTZHAUSEN, K. C. 1981. Creasing: formulating a hypothesis. Proc. Int. Soc. Citriculture 1, 201-204.

HUTTON, R. 1989. Crop regulation and its relationship to fruit size and juice quality. Austr. Citrus News 65 (Dec.) 6-8.

ISMAIL, M. A. and GRIERSON, W. 1977. Seasonal susceptibility of grapefruit to chilling injury as modified by certain growth regulators. HortScience 12, 118-120.

IWAHORI, S. 1978. Use of growth regulators in the control of cropping of mandarin varieties. Proc. Int. Soc. Citriculture 1, 263-270.

JACOBSEN, J. V. and BEACH, L. R. 1985. Control of transcription of a-amylase and rRNA genes in barley aleurone protoplasts by gibberellin and abscisic acid. Nature 316, 275-277.

JAHN, O. L. 1981. Effects of ethephon, gibberellin and BA on fruiting of 'Dancy' tangerines. J. Amer. Soc. Hort. Sci. 106, 597-600.

JAHN, O. L. and YOUNG, R. 1972. Influence of the tree on the response of citrus fruits to preharvest applications of (2-chloroethyl) phosphoric acid. J. Amer.Soc. Hort. Sci. 97, 544-549.

JAHN, O. L. and YOUNG, R. 1975. Effects of maturity, storage, and ethylene on the induction of carotenoid synthesis in citrus fruits by 2-(4-chlorophenylthio)-triethylamine (CPTA). J. Amer. Soc. Hort. Sci. 100, 244-246.

JONA, R., GOREN, R. and MAMORA, M. 1989. Effect of gibberellin on cell-wall components of creasing peel in mature "Valencia" orange. Sci. Hort. 39, 105-115.

JONES, T. W. A. and THOMA, A. M. 1993. Flowering and gibberellins in a mutant red clover (*Trifolium partense* L.). Plant Growth Regul. 12, 11-16.

JONES, W. W., COGGINS, C. W., JR. and EMBLETON, T. W. 1976. Endogenous abscisic acid in relation to bud growth in alternate bearing "Valencia" orange. Plant Physiol. 58, 681-682.

KAUFMAN, M. R. 1970. Extensibility of pericarp tissue in growing citrus fruits. Plant Physiol. 46, 778-781.

KAWADA, K., WHEATON, J. A., PURVIS, A. C. and GRIERSON, W. 1979. Levels of growth regulators and reducing sugars of 'Marsh' grapefruit peel as related to seasonal resistance to chilling injury. HortScience 14, 446.

KAWASE, K. and HIRAI, M. 1983. Growth, sugar accumulation and puffiness of the mandarin peel during colouring. J. Jap. Soc. Hort. Sci. 52, 231-237.

KAWASE, K., SUZUKI, K. and HIROSE, K. 1981. Use of growth regulators to control rind puffing of Satsuma mandarin fruit. Proc. Int. Soc. Citriculture 1, 237-239.

KHALIFAH, R. A. and LEWIS, L. N. 1966. Cytokinins in citrus: isolation of a cell division factor from lemon seeds. Nature 212, 1472-1473.

KNAPP, J. L. 1982. Florida spray and dust schedule. Fla. Coop. Ext. Serv. Circ. 393-H.

KOKKALOS, T.I. 1981. Effect of 2,4-dichlorophenoxyacetic acid on grapefruit. Hort. Res. 21, 1-9.

KREZDORN, A. H. and COHEN, M. 1962. The influence of chemical fruit-set sprays on yield and quality of citrus. Proc. Fla. State Hort. Soc. 75, 53-60.

KRIEDEMANN, P. E. 1968. An effect of kinetin on the translocation of ^{14}C labelled photosyntate in citrus. Aust. J. Biol. Sci. 21, 569-571.

KURAOKA, T. 1962. Histological studies on the fruit development of the Satsuma orange with special reference to peel-puffing. Men. Ehime Univ., Sect. VI, 8, 106-154.

KURAOKA, T., IWASAKI, K. and DAITO, H. 1967. Studies on the control of peel- puffing of Satsuma mandarin. VI. On the time of gibberellic acid application. Proc. Spring Meet. Jap. Soc. Hort. Sci. XX, 36-37 (Abstr.).

KURAOKA, T., IWASAKI, K. and ISHII, T. 1977. Effects of GA_3 on puffing and levels of GA-like substances and ABA in the peel of Satsuma mandarin (Citrus unshiu Marc.). J. Amer. Soc. Hort. Sci. 102, 651-654.

KURAOKA, T., IWASAKI, K. and KADOYA, K. 1966. Studies on peel puffing of Satsuma mandarin. V. On the application of gibberellic acid. Proc. Spring Meet. Jap. Soc. Hort. Sci. XX, 43-44 (abstr.).

KURTZMAN, R. H., JR. 1966. Xylem sap flow as affected by metabolic inhibitors and girdling. Plant Physiol. 41, 641-646.

LENZ, F. 1966. Flower and fruit development in 'Valencia late' orange as affected by type of inflorescence and nutritional status. Hort. Res. 6, 65-78.

LEOPOLD, A.C. and NOODÉN, L.C. 1984. Hormonal regulatory systems in plants. In Hormonal Regulation of Development, II. The function of hormones from the level of the cell to the whole plant, T. K. Scott (Editor). Springer Verlag, Berlin.

LEWIS, L. N. and COGGINS, C. W., JR. 1964. The inhibition of carotenoid accumulation in navel oranges by gibberellin A_3, as measured by thin layer chromatography. Plant Cell Physiol. 5, 457-463.

LEWIS, L. N., COGGINS, C. W., JR., LABANAUSKAS, C. K. and DUGGER, W. M. 1967. Biochemical changes associated with natural and gibberellin A_3 delayed senescence in the navel orange rind. Plant Cell Physiol. 8, 151-160.

LIMA, J. E. O. and DAVIES, F. S. 1981. Fruit set and drop of Florida Navel orange. Proc. Fla. State Hort. Soc. 94, 11-14.

LIMA, J. E. O. and DAVIES, F. S. 1984. Growth regulators, fruit drop, yield and quality of Navel orange in Florida. J. Amer. Soc. Hort. Sci. 109, 81- 84.

LIMA, J. E. O., DAVIES, F. S. and KREZDORN, A. H. 1980. Factors associated with excessive fruit drop of Navel orange. J. Amer. Soc. Hort. Sci. 105, 902-906.

LOVATT, C. J., SAGEE, O. and ALI, A. G. 1992A. Ammonia and/or its metabolites influence flowering, fruit set, and yield of the "Washington" navel orange. Proc. Int. Soc. Citriculture 1, 412-416.

LOVATT, C. J., SAGEE, O., ALI, A. G., ZHENG, Y. and PROTACIO, C. M. 1992B. Influence of nitrogen, carbohydrate, and plant growth regulators on flowering, fruit set, and yield of citrus. Proc. 2nd Int. Sem. Citrus Physiol. Bebedouro, S. P., Brazil. 31-53.

LOVATT, C. J., STREETER, S. M., MINTER, T. C., O'CONNELL, N. V., FLAHERTY, D. L., FREEMAN, M. W. and GOODWILL, P. B. 1984. Phenology of flowering in *Citrus sinensis* (L.) Osbeck cv. "Washington" navel orange. Proc. Int. Soc. Citriculture 1, 186-190.

LUCKWILL, L. C. 1953. Studies on fruit development in relation to plant hormones. I. Hormone production in the developing seed in relation to fruit drop. J. Hort. Sci. 28, 4-24.

MAOTANI, T., KAWASE, K., KAMURO, Y. and HIRAI, K. 1983. Effects of ethylene on peel puffing of Satsuma mandarin. J. Japan. Soc. Hort. Sci. 52, 238-242.

MARIOKA, S. and YAHATA, S. 1989. Influence of fruit load just before fruit thinning on fruit size, yield and flower bud formation in Satsuma mandarin. J. Japn. Soc. Hort. Sci. 58, 97-103.

MAUK, C. S., BAUSHER, M. G. and YELENOSKY, G. 1986. Influence of growth regulator treatments on dry matter production, fruit abscission, and 14C assimilate partitioning in citrus. J. Plant Growth Regul. 5, 111-120.

McDONALD, R. E. 1986. effects of vegetable oils, CO_2 and film wrapping on chilling injury and decay of lemons. HortScience 21, 476-477.

McDONALD, R. E., McCOLLUM, T. G. and NORDBY, H. E. 1993. Temperature conditioning and surface treatments of grapefruit affect expression of chilling injury and gas diffusion. J. Amer. Soc. Hort. Sci. 118, 490-496.

MILLER, J. E. and HOFMAN, P. J. 1988. Physiology and nutrition of citrus fruit growth with special reference to the 'Valencia'—A mini review. Proc. Int. Soc. Citriculture. 2, 393-398.

MONSELISE, S. P. 1973. Recent advances in the understanding of flower formation in fruit trees and its hormonal control. Acta Hort. 34, 157-166.

MONSELISE, S. P. 1977. Citrus fruit development: endogenous systems and external regulation. Proc. Int. Soc. Citriculture. 2, 664-668.

MONSELISE, S. P. 1978. Understanding of plant processes as a basis for successful growth regulation in Citrus. Proc. Int. Soc. Citriculture, pp. 250-255.

MONSELISE, S. P. 1979. The use of growth regulators in citriculture; a review. Sci. Hort. 11, 151-162.

MONSELISE, S. P. 1986. Citrus, pp. 87-108. *In* Handbook of Fruit Set and Development. CRC Press, Inc., Boca Raton, FL.

MONSELISE, S. P. and COSTO, J. 1985. Decreasing splitting incidence in Murcott by 2,4-D and calcium nitrate. Alon Hanotea 39, 731-733.

MONSELISE, S.P. and SASSON, A. 1977. Effects of orchard treatments on orange fruit quality and storage ability. Proc. Intl. Soc. Citriculture 1, 232-237.

MONSELISE, S. P., COSTO, J. and GALILI, D. 1986. Additional experiments to reduce the incidence of citrus fruit splitting by 2,4-D and calcium. Alon Hanotea 40, 1237-1238 (Abstr.).

MONSELISE, S. P., WEISER, M., SHAFIR, M., GOREN, R. and GOLDSCHMIDT, E. E. 1976. Creasing of orange peel - physiology and control. J. Hort. Sci. 51, 341-351.

MOULDS, G., TREEBY, M., SKOREY, R., TUGWELL, B. and BEVINGTON, K. 1995. Managing albedo breakdown. Aust. Citrus News 75 (Dec.), 9-10.

NASR, T. A., EL-AZAB, E. M. and EL-ABD, A. S. 1973. Effect of gibberellic acid on fruit creasing, time of flower-bud differentiation, mineral content, vegetative growth and flowering in citrus. Int. Citrus Congress, Murcia, Spain 2, 409-413.

NOLTE, K. D., NOTHNAGEL, E. A. and COGGINS, C. W., JR 1990. Electrolyte leakage and protoplast viability of pummelo mesocarp tissue as influenced by exogenous GA_3. J. Amer. Soc. Hort. Sci. 115, 592-597.

NORMAN, S. M., MAIER, V. P. and PON, D. L. 1990. Abscisic acid and carotenoid and chlorophyll content in relation to water stress and leaf age of different types of citrus. J. Agr. Food. Chem. 38, 1326-1334.

PELSER, P. du T. 1975. Recommendations for the control of postharvest decay of citrus fruits. South Afr. Co-op. citrus Exchange, Pretoria.

PLANT PROTECTION LTD. 1969. Berelex for Promoting Natural Plant Growth. Information booklet prepared by Plant Protection Ltd., Imperial Chemical Industries, Fernhurst, Halsmere, Surrey, England.

POWELL, A. A. and KREZDORN, H. A. 1977. Influence of fruit setting treatment on 14C-metabolites in citrus during flowering and fruiting. J. Amer. Soc. Hort. Sci. 102, 709-714.

POWELL, L. E. and PRATT, C. 1966. Growth promoting substances in the developing fruit of peach (*Prunus persica* L.). J. Hort. Sci. 41, 331-348.

PRESSEY, R. and AVANTS, J. K. 1982. Solubilization of cell walls by tomato polygalacturonaes: effects of pectinases. J. Food Biochem. 6, 57-74.

PRIMO-MILLO, E., GUERRI, J., CULIAÑEZ, F., TADEO, J. L. and HERNÁNDEZ, F. M. 1984. Metabolic changes induced by kinetin in sweet orange fruits during the fruit period. Proc. Int. Soc. Citriculture 1, 202-207.

PURVIS, A. C. 1980. Sequence of chloroplast degreening in calamondin fruit as influenced by ethylene and $AgNO_3$. Plant Physiol. 66, 624-627.

PURVIS, A.C. 1984. Importance of water loss in the chilling injury of grapefruit stored at low temperature. Scientia Hort. 23:261-267.

PURVIS, A. C. and BARMORE, C. R. 1981. Involvement of ethylene in chlorophyll degradation in peel of citrus fruits. Plant Physiol. 68, 854-856.

RABE, E., VAN DER WALT, J., and KLEYNHANS, S. 1989. Ann. Rept. S.A. Co-Op. Citrus Exchange Ltd., Nelspruit.

RANDHAWA, G. S., JAIN, N. L and SHARMA, B. B. 1961. Pre-harvest drop, size and quality of Joppa oranges (*Citrus sinensis* Osbeck) as affected by dipping in aqueous solutions of plant regulators. Indian J. Hort. 18, 277-284.

RASMUSSEN, G. K. 1973. The effect of growth regulators on degreening and regreening of citrus fruit. Acta Hort. 34, 473-478.

RHODES, M. J. C. 1980. The maturation and ripening of fruits, pp. 157-205. *In* Senescence in Plants, K. V. Thimann (Editor). CRC Press, Boca Raton, FL.

ROBISON, L. 1987. Mountain of marbles a challenge in 'Valencia'. Calif. Citrograph. 72, 108-109.

RUIZ, L. I. and PRIMO-MILLO, E. 1989. El rajado, agrietado o "splitting" de los frutos cítricos. Levante Agrícola. 291, 98-102.

RUIZ, R. and GUARDIOLA, J. L. 1994. Carbohydrate and mineral nutrition of orange fruitlets in relation to growth and abscission. Physiol. Plant. 90, 27-36.

SAGEE, O. and ERNER, Y. 1991. Gibberellins and abscisic acid contents during flowering and fruit set of 'Shamouti' orange. Scientia Hort. 48, 29-39.

SAGEE, O. and LOVATT, C. J. 1991. Putrescine content parallels ammonia and arginine metabolism in developing flowers of the "Washington" navel orange. J. Amer. Soc. Hort. Sci. 116, 280-285.

SAIDHA, T., GOLDSCHMIDT, E. E. and MONSELISE, S. P. 1985. Endogenous cytokinins from developing "Shamouti" orange fruits derived from leafy and leafless inflorescences. Sci. Hort. 26, 35-41.

SCHIFFMAN-NADEL, M., LATTAR, F.S. and WAKES, J. 1972. The effects of 2,4-D applied in waxes on the preservation of 'Marsh Seedless' grapefruit and 'Valencia' orange during prolonged storage. HortScience. 7, 120-121.

SHIMOKAWA, K., SHIMADA, S. and YAEO, K. 1978. Ethylene-enhanced chlorophyllase activity during degreening of Citrus unshiu Marc. Sci. Hort. 8, 129-135.

SINGH, J.P. and. RANDHAWA. S. S. 1961. Effect of plant regulators on fruit drop, size and quality in mandarin (Citrus sinensis Blanco) var. Nagpuri and Lahore Local. Indian J. Hort. 18, 285-294.

SISLER, E. C. and YANG, S. F. 1984. Anti-ethylene effects of cis-2-butane and cyclic defines. Phytochemistry 23, 2765-2768.

SMITH, M. A., DAVIES, P. J. and REID, B. J. 1985. Role of polyamines in gibberellin-induced internode induced growth in peas. Plant Physiol. 78, 92-99.

SOOST, R. K. and BURNETT, R. H. 1961. Effects of gibberellin on yield and fruit characteristics of Clementine mandarin. Proc. Amer. Soc. Hort. Sci. 77, 194-201.

STEWART, I. and WHEATON, T. A. 1972. Carotenoids in citrus: their accumulation induced by ethylene. J. Agr. Food Chem. 20, 448-449.

STEWART, W. S. 1949. effects of 2,4-dichlorophenoxyacetic acid and 2,4,5-trichlorophenoxyacetic acid on citrus fruit storage. Proc. Amer. Soc. Hort. Sci. 54, 109:117.

STEWART, W. S., HIELD, H. Z. and BRANNAMAN, B. L. 1952A Effects of 2,4-D and related substances on fruit drop, yield, size and quality of Valencia oranges. Hilgardia 21, 301-329.

STEWART, W. S., PALMER, J. E. and HIELD, H. 1952B. Packinghouse experiments on the use of 2,4-dichlorophenoxyacetic acid and 2,4,5-trichlorophenoxyacetic acid to-increase storage life of lemons. Proc. Amer. Soc. Hort. 59, 327-334.

STOREY, R. and TREEBY, M. T. 1994. The morphology of epicuticular wax and albedo cells of orange fruit in relation to albedo breakdown. J. Hort. Sci. 69, 329-338.

TESTONI, A. CAZZOLA, R. RAGGOZZA, L. and LANZA, G. 1992. Storage behaviour of orange 'Valencia' late in rooms with ethylene removal. Proc. Int. Soc. Citriculture 3, 1092-1094.

THOMSON, W. W., LEWIS, L. N. and COGGINS, C. W. JR. 1967. The reversion of chromoplasts to chloroplasts in Valencia oranges. Cytologia 32, 117-124.

TREBITSH, T., GOLDSCHMIDT, E. E. and RIOV, J. 1993. Ethylene induces de novo synthesis of chlorophyllase, a chlorophyll degrading enzyme in citrus fruit peel. Proc. Natl. Acad. Sci. 90, 9441-9445.

TURNBULL, C. G. N. 1989. Gibberellins and control of fruit retention and seedlessness in Valencia orange. Acta Hort. 239, 335-339.

WALLERSTEIN, I., GOREN, R. and MONSELISE, S. P. 1974. The effect of girdling on starch accumulation in some orange seedlings. Can. J. Bot. 52, 935-937.

WALLERSTEIN, I., GOREN, R. and BEN-TAL, Y. 1978. Effects of ringing on root starvation in sour orange seedlings. J. Hort. Sci. 53, 109-113.

WALLERSTEIN, I., GOREN, R. and MONSELISE, S. P. 1973. Seasonal changes in gibberellin-like substances of Shamouti orange (Citrus sinensis [L.] Osbeck) trees in relation to ringing. J. Hort. Sci. 48, 75-82.

WHEATON, T. A. 1981. Fruit thinning if Florida mandarins using plant growth regulators. Proc. Int. Soc. Citriculture 1, 263-268.

WILD, B. L., McGLASSON, W. B. and LEE, T. H. 1976. Effects of reduced ethylene levels in storage atmosphere on lemon keeping quality. HortScience 11, 114.

WILSON, W. C. 1983. The use of exogenous plant growth regulators on citrus, pp. 207-232. In Plant Growth Regulating Chemicals, Vol. 1, L. G. Nickell (Editor). CRC Press, Inc., Boca Raton, FL.

WILSON, W. C., COPPOCK, G. E. and ATTAWAY, J. A. 1981. Growth regulators facilitate harvesting of oranges. Proc. Int. Soc. Citriculture 1, 278-281.

WILSON, W. C., HOLM, R. E. and CLARK, R. K. 1977. Abscission chemicals-Aid to citrus fruit removal. Proc. Intl. Soc. Citriculture 2, 404-406.

WILTBANK, E. J. and KREZDORN, A. H. 1969. Determination of gibberellins in ovaries and young fruits of Navel oranges and their correlation with fruit growth. J. Amer. Soc. Hort. Sci. 94, 195-201.

YANO, M., OGAWA, K. and IKOMA, Y. 1996. Isolation and characterization of a citrus cDNA clone encoding phytoene synthase. VIII Congress Int. Soc. Citriculture, South Africa. Programme and Abstracts. 109 (Abstr. #P087)

YOKOYAMA, H., COGGINS, C. W., Jr. and HENNING, G. L. 1971. The effect of 2-(4-chloro-phenylthio)-triethylamine hydrochloride on the formation of carotenoids in citrus. Phytochemistry 10, 1831-1834.

YOKOYAMA, H., DEBENEDICT, C., COGGINS, C. W., JR. and HENNING, G. L. 1972. Induced color changes in grapefruit and orange. Phytochemistry 11, 1721-1724.

ZUCCONI, F., MONSELISE, S. P. and GOREN, R. 1978. Growth abscission relationships in developing orange fruit. Sci. Hort. 9, 137-146.

Food Safety Programs

Steven Pao and D. Frank Kelsey

Food safety is a major public health issue. In the United States, unsafe food causes as many as 76 million illnesses, 325,000 hospitalizations, and 5,000 deaths each year (Mead *et al.* 2001). Driven by regulatory and market demands, food safety has become an increasingly significant topic of concern to food producers. The produce industry has not been spared from this attention. Many new guidelines and regulations have been issued in recent years to raise sanitation standards in produce production and handling. Citrus fruit has many natural features that help protect against food safety hazards, and has always been regarded as a very safe item for consumption. The fruit has a thick, leathery, oil-gland bearing rind with physical strength and chemical resilience to help avoid interior damage and contamination from the environment. The thick peel also allows the fruit to be treated with rigorous washing, brushing, and sanitizing processes in the packinghouse and processing plant. Citrus is distinct in that no well-documented outbreak report has ever been linked to the direct consumption of fresh citrus fruit. This record is an indication of the superiority of citrus fruit safety in comparison to other fruits that have been involved in multiple human disease outbreaks. In addition, researchers have reported anti-microbial potential among citrus fruit and their derivatives. These include anti-cholera activity of lemon juice (d'Aquino and Teves 1994; de Castillo *et al.* 2000), anti-malarial activity of sweet orange (Bhat and Surolia 2001), and anti-microbial activity of citrus oil (Dabbah *et al.* 1970; Vargas *et al.* 1999).

One important basis for the safe use of citrus is that the fruit peel serves as a natural protective barrier that helps prevent the internalization of human pathogens into the fruit under normal processing conditions. Thus, unadulterated fresh fruit and juice could be produced after adequate fruit surface sanitizing treatments. This basis is affirmed by a recent bacterial in-filtration study where fresh orange fruit was treated at the stem end area with dye and either *Salmonella* Rubislaw or *Escherichia coli* strains expressing green fluorescent protein (Pao *et al.* 2001). Microscopic images developed from this study revealed that bacterial contaminants tend to localize at the surface or near surface areas that may be accessible to sanitizing treatments. Unlike pome fruit, the citrus fruit is derived from a superior ovary that is completely separate from the calyx (Weier *et al.* 1974). This anatomical distinction, along with peel thickness, makes citrus fruit less vulnerable to infiltration and provides greater opportunities for effective decontamination in comparison to fruit with a cavity at the blossom end (Buchanan *et al.* 1999; Pao *et al.* 2001). Since citrus does not require water flume systems in fruit handling, potential infiltration related to fruit immersion in contaminated water can be easily avoided (Wei *et al.* 1995; Zhuang *et al.* 1995; Pao *et al.* 2001).

Food safety is an increasingly important challenge that encompasses many interrelated biological, chemical, and physical issues from the farm to the dinner table. The attention to food safety programs at all stages of production is needed. Equipped with modern detection tools, a current outbreak investigation is capable of tracing product contamination back to its originating point(s), thus keeping the entire fruit production and handling system liable to the negative consequences of the event. Food safety is particularly challenging when fresh fruit is to be used for preparing fresh or minimally processed products such as fresh-squeezed juice or fresh-cut fruit. The process of preparing these items consists of removing inedible protective barriers as well as transforming the interior portions of fruit to a ready-to-serve product. Both the preparation process and the resulting product are more vulnerable to contamination.

PRINCIPLES OF FOOD SAFETY PROGRAMS

Food safety programs in the food industry are often developed with the influences of multiple scientific, social, and economic factors. One can expect that different citrus production regions have different emphases in their program design and implementation. However, all food protection guidelines and programs are generated using some combination of the principles of prevention, intervention, and verification (Fig. 5.1).

Prevention

It is generally accepted that prevention is the most effective approach for food safety (USFDA 1998). The goal of prevention is to minimize the risk of fruit contamination by identifying potential sources of contamination and then implementing preventive measures to control them. Fresh citrus fruit are frequently in contact with dust, rain, insects, and animals during growing and harvesting. Consequently, their surfaces are not free

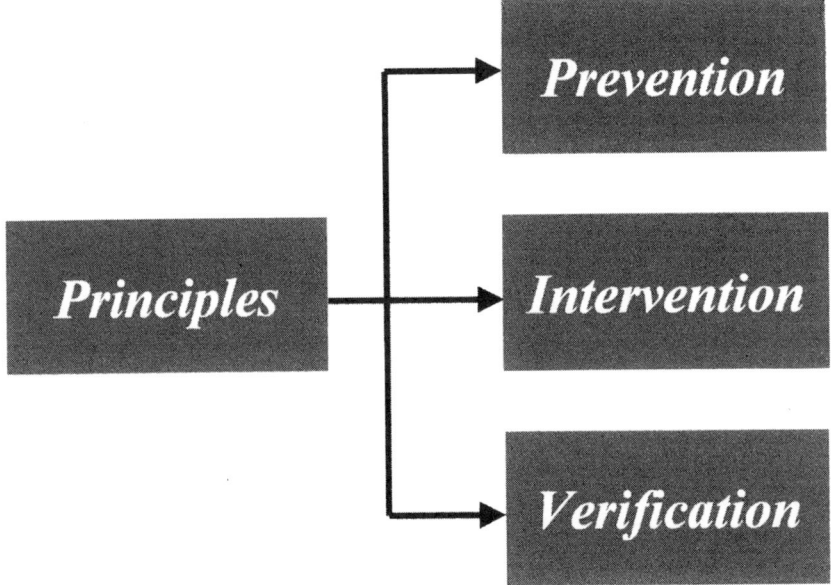

Fig. 5.1. Major food protection principles.

from natural contaminants. The realistic goal of prevention is to make con-tamination less likely to occur. It is impossible to guarantee a zero-defect rate for all fruit through prevention alone.

Contamination agents can be grouped into three categories: biological, chemical, and physical hazards (Fig. 5.2). Potential biological hazards in-clude viruses, bacteria, fungi, insects, etc. Potential chemical hazards may include agricultural and processing chemicals such as insecticides, fungi-cides, herbicides, waxes, dyes, cleaners, sanitizers, lubricants, paint, etc. In addition, environmental pollutants from tainted water and soil may also lead to a chemical contamination. Potential physical hazards include bro-ken pieces of wood, equipment, glass, nails, rocks, rust, etc.

Some biological contaminants are visible on fruit, but most of them are too tiny to be observed by the naked eye. The term microorganism (or mi-crobe) is used to describe these organisms since their presence at an individual level can only be seen under a microscope. It is clear that a fruit is considered as unwholesome and not suitable for human consumption when it is highly infected with microorganisms or insects. In addition to the visible quality degradation caused by such contaminants, the surface dam-age may lead to internal microbiological contamination. Concern with the potential for microbial contamination has been emphasized on all types of raw produce due to its linkage to numerous disease outbreaks worldwide

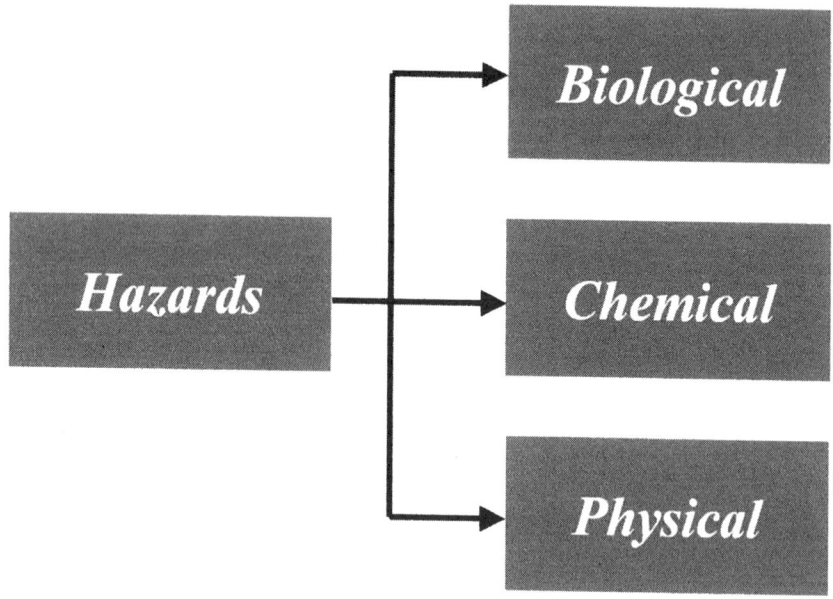

Fig. 5.2. Major groups of food safety hazards.

(European Commission 2002). Within the citrus industry, potential food safety problems associated with fresh-squeezed juice were previously thought to be prevented by the acidity of the juice (Kimball 1999). However, outbreaks caused by *Salmonella* spp. and *Escherichia coli* O157:H7 involving unpasteurized fruit juice has changed this traditional view and increased industry awareness on the potential consequences of fruit surface contamination and its impact on fresh juice safety (Parish 1997, 1998A; US-FDA 2001). Surface contamination may affect the safety of peeled or fresh-cut citrus fruit as well. Removing the peel of citrus subjects the interior portion of fruit to microbial contamination and growth. A report by Pao and Petracek (1997) showed that the microbial spoilage of peeled oranges can be caused by microorganisms such as bacteria (such as *Enterobacter agglomerans* and *Pseudomonas* sp.) and yeasts (such as *Cryptococcus albidus*, *Rhodotorula glutinis*, and *Saccharomyces cerevisiae*). To assess the potential influence of microbial contaminants on the safety of fresh-cut fruit, the fates of *Salmonella* spp., *E. coli* O157:H7, *Listeria monocytogenes*, and *Staphylococcus aureus* on peeled orange fruit were studied (Pao et al. 1998). In this investigation, growth was observed with all the inoculated pathogens at the abusive storage temperature (24°C), while refrigeration (4 or 8°C) effectively inhibited the growth of all pathogens and caused population reduction of *Salmonella* spp. and *S. aureus.* These studies illustrated the importance of fruit clean-ing, processing sanitation, and product refrigeration.

Evidence of chemical contamination may be visible on the fruit surface. Ritenour *et al.* (2000, 2001) reported that residual quaternary ammonia san-itizer contacting fruit in harvest bins could cause a visible chemical burn on the intact citrus peel. Fruit sensitivity was not dependent upon time of sea-son or variety. Since quaternary ammonia is not approved for direct food contact, it is fortunate that exposed fruit can easily be graded out of com-mercial processing lines due to the obvious physical defects. However, many potential chemical contaminants may not be evident at harvest, packing or retail handling stages. The United States Department of Agriculture (USDA) reported that from a period of 1998-2000, up to 3.7% of food crops and their products sampled in the retail market had pesticide residues that exceeded the established legal tolerance (USDA 1999, 2000, 2001). During the same period, the number of samples containing pesticides that were not registered for use on the tested commodity ranged from 0.15-0.30%. While this potential exists in citrus, there were no such cases observed on fresh cit-rus fruit sampled as a part of the USDA pesticide data program. Concern of residue levels in fruit juice is legitimate and a continuous monitoring effort is deemed necessary. However, reported residue levels in citrus juice sold in the U.S. market were below legal limits (Hankin and Pylypiw 1991; Bolles *et al.* 1999). Alternatively, some potential chemical contamination issues can be avoided by organic farming practices (Kilcher 2001).

There are many approaches that can be used to reduce contamination risk. A preferred approach is to prevent the existence of potential contam-inants in the production and handling environment. This may be accomplished by barring their entry or actively removing them or their sup-porting surroundings from the environment. In addition, chemical hazards should be contained within restricted and secure locations. For instance, registered pesticides should be stored only in designated areas, away from raw or finished products. Access to pesticides should be restricted. Mea-sures to reduce the risks of accidental cross contamination should also be employed. For example, washing fruit bins between uses is a way to reduce microbiological or chemical cross-contamination from one load of fruit to another. Finally, containing or packaging product in a closed or protected environment is particularly important for preventing a re-contamination of product after it has been cleaned or decontaminated.

Intervention

In the citrus grove, not all causes of contamination are preventable. Re-search reports show that the surfaces of freshly harvested citrus fruit often retain populations of about 10,000 microorganisms/cm^2 (Pao and Brown

1998; Chun and McDonald 1987; Murdock and Brokaw 1957; Murdock *et al.* 1953). Although most of these microbes are not considered harmful to humans, low levels of fecal coliforms were observed among them. The presence of these fecal bacteria, including *E. coli*, is indicative to prior fecal contamination. In addition to biological contamination, unwashed fruit may also contain chemical or physical contaminants such as pre-harvest pesticides or fertilizers. Therefore, intervention treatments applied to fruit are needed to reduce the severity of potential field contamination.

In citrus packing and processing facilities, field contaminants of fruit can be reduced via sorting, washing, and waxing. Initial fruit sorting removes a bulk volume of field debris and damaged fruits, and is the preparatory step for thorough fruit washing and decontamination. Decayed or damaged fruit may not become apparent before the fruit are cleaned on the packing or processing lines; therefore, additional manual or automatic sorting steps are often used to complete the sorting task.

Most of the visible field contaminants are loosely attached on the fruit surfaces and can be easily removed by washing and brushing. Microbiological contaminants can also be removed by washing. However, the efficacy may be influenced by the washing system. A recent study indicates that high pH washing solution is relatively effective in reducing fruit surface and initial juice microbial loads (Pao *et al.* 2000). Washing fruit on roller brushes with high pH cleaners (such as SOPP cleaner and NaOH solution formulated to pH 11.8) followed by a potable water rinse reduced surface inoculated *E. coli* by about 3.5 log cycles. The same pilot-plant study reported that adequate spraying volume is necessary to achieve the maximum reduction. Physical or biological contaminants such as sand, scale insects and sooty mold can be effectively removed by utilizing high pressure washing systems (Petracek *et al.* 1998; Kelsey 1997). This approach is capable of stripping surface contaminants and natural wax platelets that are not easily removed by conventional washing, and may be a useful tool to reduce pesticide residues after harvest.

Information on commercial-scale washing operations is also available. Pao and Brown (1998) evaluated surface microbial populations of citrus fruit following various packing-line procedures of seven Florida commercial citrus packing facilities. Results of this survey indicated that washing and waxing procedures used in commercial packinghouses are capable of reducing surface microbial contaminants. Waxing alone reduced the average fruit surface total and fecal coliform counts from 35.2 and 5.0 MPN (most probable number)/cm^2, respectively, to 1.4 and 0.1 MPN/cm^2. Isolated fecal coliforms were identified as *Klebsiella pneumoniae*, *Enterobacter* spp., *Citrobacter freundii*, and *E. coli*. *E. coli*, which was occasionally found on unwashed fruit samples, were not recovered from fruit at the end of the surveyed packinghouse operations, and no salmonellae were found on fruit during the entire survey.

Waxes that are applied to fresh citrus are generally alkaline in nature and are dried after application at elevated temperatures (see Chapter 15). One laboratory study demonstrated that mildly heated ($\geq 50°C$), high pH waxes ($\geq pH$ 10) had the ability to reduce fruit surface microbial contaminants (Pao et al. 1999) although most citrus waxes are pH 9.5 and lower. This may be a reason for the previously reported microbial reduction caused by citrus waxing in commercial packing facilities. Further research is needed to develop wax formulations with greater sanitizing potency.

The initial microbial loads of fresh citrus products (such as fresh-squeezed juice, fresh-cut fruit) are influenced by the fruit surface microbial loads. Commercial juice extraction, while apparently separating the peel from the juice, does not completely exclude surface microflora from the juice. The transfer of natural and inoculated microorganisms from fruit to fresh orange juice during juice extraction was quantified by a recent study (Pao and Davis 2001A). The results suggested that microbial levels detected in fresh juice were about 1-2 log (equivalent to 90-99%) lower than levels found on fruit. Several citrus peeling studies also indicate the peeling processing will not eliminate surface contaminants. Therefore, an effective fruit surface sanitizing treatment prior to fruit extraction, peeling, or cutting must be incorporated in processing protocols to protect end product safety. Current regulations by the U.S. Food and Drug Administration require fresh juice processors to use HACCP (Hazard Analysis Critical Control Point) programs that meet the criteria of 5-log (equivalent to 99.999%) microbial pathogen reduction for juice safety (USFAD 2001).

Research data shows that 5-log reduction can be achieved using fruit surface thermal treatment (Pao and Davis 1999; Pao et al. 2001). The efficacy of thermal sanitizing treatments was validated by inoculated challenge studies. The study demonstrated that hot water immersion of oranges at about 70°C for 2 min or 80°C for 1 min can achieve a 5-log reduction of fruit-surface or initial juice E. coli loads. Hot water increased fruit peel temperatures rapidly. However, the slow rate of heat transfer and the short exposure time prevents pulp temperature from rising to excessive levels and thereby retains original sensory quality of fresh products. This finding has promoted the use of thermal sanitizing treatments in fresh juice operations by some juice processors. Such extreme surface treatment temperatures are not recommended for fruit destined for the fresh fruit market, as peel injury and discoloration can develop soon after treatment. Another approach to enhance juice safety is to inactivate pathogens in fresh juice with advanced minimal- or non-thermal treatments (Wei et al. 1991; Takahashi et al. 1993; Shomer et al. 1994; Soffer and Manheim 1996; Parish 1998B; Linton et al. 1999; Liang et al. 2002). Post-extraction treatments hold great potential for commercial production of safe, fresh-like fruit juices; however, treated juice may no longer be categorized as fresh citrus juice (Pao et al. 2000; USFDA 2003).

Verification

Verification is complementary to prevention and intervention and is implemented to validate and monitor process efficacy, operation normalcy, and product conformity. If a significant deviation is identified, it offers critical information for appropriate corrective actions, such as equipment adjustment, staff retraining, operation suspension, or product recall.

Generally speaking, process validation is to be conducted when a new or modified system is established for production. For example, a decontamination process designed for achieving a required level of microbial reduction of fruit or juice can be validated by a inoculation or challenge study (Pao *et al.* 2001; Notermans *et al.* 1993). In the study, high levels of targeted microorganisms or their surrogates are artificially inoculated to the surface of fruit prior to the process of decontamination (Pao and Davis 2001B). The level of microbial reduction can then be measured and used for process validation. On the other hand, the tests of operation normalcy and product adequacy are more likely to be performed on a routine basis. For instance, the concentration of chlorine solution can be monitored by either in-line or manual testing systems to ensure operation normalcy. Similarly, the absence of *E. coli* in bottled fresh juice can be detected by either rapid or conventional microbial detection methods (Pao *et al.* 2002). In all circumstances, sound scientific investigation and sampling techniques are essential for getting reliable results.

Many user-friendly kits and systems for chemical and microbiological detections have been developed in recent years allowing verification tasks to be accomplished with minimal cost and effort. For example, there are convenient pH, chlorine, quaternary ammonia and peracetic acid tests available that require simple dipping of a test strip into a treatment solution and the resulting color change on the reactive portion of the strip is then compared to a color chart indicating concentration. These test methods can be used to verify that treatment solutions are in the desired concentration range for optimal performance, and are quick and convenient ways to find deviations. For more quantitative results, there are dilution, titration, and even some biotechnology based test kits that are becoming available for on-site testing. Rapid test kits for detecting microbial contamination are also used. Some of these tests can be performed by sampling the surface of interest with a pre-wetted swab followed by an incubation step for rapid chemical or microbial reaction for developing a measurable result. For setting an effective and economical verification work plan, the following questions should be answered: 1) what is the verification purpose and minimal requirement? 2) what is the most adequate sampling and testing time, frequency, and location? 3) would a qualitative test, instead of a more expensive quantitative test, provide sufficient information? 4) who is qualified and available to operate the verification system or test? 5) how should the verification results be interpreted and who will manage the consequences of that information? 6) what are adequate record keeping and reporting methods? Private consultants, service laboratories, equipment and chemical suppliers, university extension specialists, and government regulatory agencies can assist in answering these questions.

Verification is an effective approach to increase confidence in product safety. However, even the best auditing or testing is only capable of monitoring a fraction of the overall process or product. Therefore, verification is not an alternative to proper sanitation. Product produced under an unsanitary environment should automatically be considered as unfit for human consumption regardless of its verification results.

IMPLEMENTATION OF FOOD SAFETY PROGRAMS

Food safety programs should be implemented at each step of production for building a farm-to-fork food protection net. Although all types of food safety programs are implemented with the same food protection goal in mind, variations in program practices are necessary to reflect existing environmental and operational differences. In general, Good Agricultural Practices (GAP), Good Manufacturing Practices (GMP), and Hazard Analysis Critical Control Points (HACCP) are the most recognized programs (Fig. 5.3).

Good Agricultural Practices (GAP)

In response to several widely reported outbreaks of foodborne illness associated with produce (NACMCF 1999), the United States Food and Drug Administration (FDA) released a set of Good Agricultural Practices (GAP) guidelines for the produce industry in 1998 (USFDA 1998). These guidelines were intended to educate the industry on the primary microbial risk factors associated with growing, packing, and handling fresh produce. Since then, many other countries have adopted similar guidelines focused on reducing the likelihood of contamination from either microbial or chemical sources. In addition to government driven programs, several retail chain driven food safety programs have been developed. For example, the British Retail Consortium sets standards for its members and trains qualified personnel to audit suppliers for adherence to food safety guidelines. EUREPGAP is a consortium of European retailers that have developed a set of guidelines for the produce industry that emphasizes control of chemical hazards more so than microorganisms. The Codex Alimentarus Commission also has a produce guidance document under development that is expected to be finalized in 2003 (see Chapter 13).

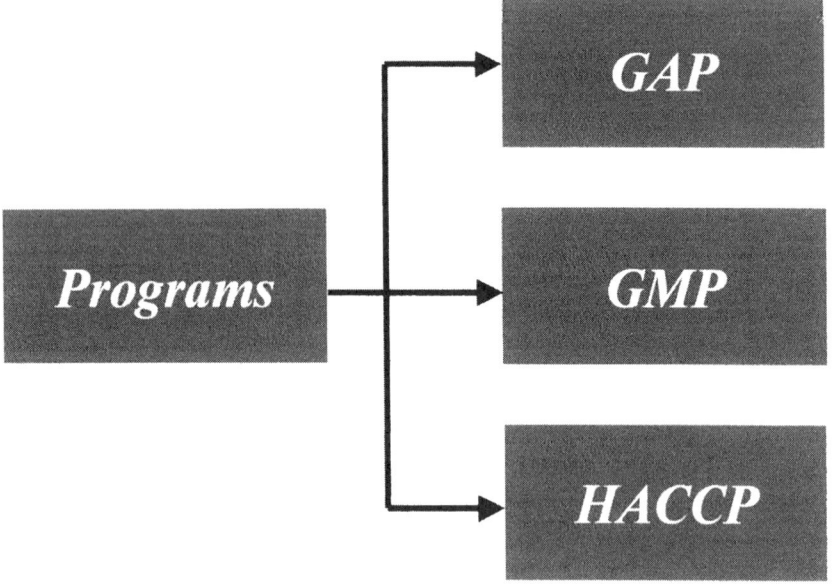

Fig. 5.3. Most recognized food safety programs.

The focal point of Good Agricultural Practices (GAP) is to avoid contamination, rather than relying solely on intervention strategies to eradicate contaminants. The key components of GAP guidance cover water quality, manure and bio-solids applications, worker health and hygiene, field and facility sanitation, and product transportation and trace-back (USFDA 1998; Rangarajan *et al.* 2001; JIFSAN 2002). At the grove, sources of potential contamination include soil, dust, wild and domestic animals, irrigation water, inadequately composted manure, agricultural chemicals, inadequate field worker hygiene, harvesting and transport equipment (Beuchat 1996; Rangarajan *et al.* 2001). In untreated manure, disease causing bacteria such as *Salmonella* spp. and *E. coli* O157:H7 can persist for months in the field. To minimize the risk of fruit contamination domestic animals should be excluded from the grove and manure should be used in accordance with GAP guidelines. Water quality also can have an impact on the potential microbial contamination of fresh fruit. Overhead irrigation should not be drawn from a water source of unknown quality. Periodic testing of water for microbes and potential chemical contaminants is advisable to reduce the likelihood of such contamination. Since dropped fruits and other field wastes can attract animals and insects that could transmit disease pathogens, good grove-keeping and pest management programs should be employed. In addition, it is advisable for the fresh fruit and juice operations to avoid using fruit that had direct contact with the ground during harvesting, storage, and transportation. Fruit dropped to and then picked up from the ground may carry significantly greater amounts of soil and microorganisms than the fruit picked directly from trees (Seeman *et al.* 2002).

To prevent illegal pesticide residues, use only registered pesticides applied in accordance with the label. Proper mixing and application rates must be followed and the material must be applied far enough ahead of harvest to ensure that pesticide residues will not exceed established legal tolerances at the time of harvest. Specific records should be kept to indicate what materials have been applied, at what rate, and on what days. Many USA states require that such operations be conducted by a certified pesticide applicator or under the supervision of such an individual. There are many worker protection standards in place in the United States that require extensive record keeping for pesticide application. These rules also require sanitary facilities for workers, reducing the likelihood of fruit contamination during the harvest process.

The creation of a functional GAP program requires analysis of the growing and handling practices and the implementation of strategies to address any chemical or microbial risk factors that are identified. Employee training should focus on personal hygiene, proper hand-washing techniques, segregation of food and drink from fruit handling areas, and the need for reporting illnesses, cuts and open sores to supervisors so that employees with such conditions are excluded from fruit handling and food contact surface exposure. Training should be refreshed at least annually for continuing employees and all employees should be trained on food safety principles prior to beginning work. The goal of repeated training is to create a culture of food safety awareness and action within the organization.

One of the principle focal points in any food safety program is that of equipment cleanliness. GAP guidelines state that equipment that contacts produce should be visibly clean and free of dirt and debris (USFDA 1998). While sanitizers such as chlorine or quaternary ammonia have been used for years as part of the cleaning procedures in citrus packinghouses, there has until recently been little emphasis on the actual cleaning of the equipment prior to sanitizer application. Brushes used to clean and polish citrus fruit can become impacted with dirt and debris over time. In addition, heavy soil can build up on side rails and deliveries, particularly early in the process line where fruit has not been washed. As a result, cleaning products and methods traditionally used in the food processing industry are becoming more common to citrus packinghouses. For example, manually operated or automated systems are available to rinse, apply a commercial grade foaming equipment cleaner, rinse the cleaner, and apply a sanitizer. Computer based operating systems also provide the opportunity for automated documentation of the facility cleaning process. Development of a daily cleaning and sanitation procedure can help maintain the equipment in a visibly clean condition, and may provide additional sanitation benefits affecting both fresh fruit quality and safety.

In the packinghouse environment, there are many tools available to enhance food safety programs and record keeping requirements. Recycled wash water must be maintained properly to prevent it from becoming a source of potential microbial contamination (Bartz and Showalter 1981; Zhuang et al. 1995). Chlorine, supplied either as gas or as sodium or calcium hypochlorite is often used to prevent the buildup of quality and safety microorganisms of concern. There are many commercially available systems capable of balancing the oxidation-reduction potential (ORP) and the pH of the solution to maintain optimal levels of chlorine in its most active form. Accidental release of chlorine gas can occur if the pH of chlorine solutions drops too low. Automated ORP systems should have a warning mechanism that alerts packinghouse personnel if the pH drops below 6 or the chlorine level rises above maximum label rates. ORP systems can be equipped with data logging features that easily address documentation requirements for recycled water quality.

Antifungal compounds are often applied in the packinghouse to reduce spoilage associated with citrus pathogens (see Chapter 13). These materials may be applied in soaps, non-recovery sprays, dip or soak tanks, or as a component of a gloss coating. Fungicides applied in dip or soak tanks present multiple food safety challenges, as the concentration of pesticide and microbial load in the tank is more difficult to control than in a typical non-recovery application. For example, dip tanks utilizing imazalil, a systemic fungicide used to control *Penicillium* sp. on citrus, are typically heated once a day to a temperature sufficient to kill resistant mold spores and many types of bacteria. However, during the day, the solution is recycled and maintained at temperatures that are not lethal to most microorganisms. As fruit passes through the tank, it will often bring in some water on its surface and strip some of the fungicide out of the solution as it sits in the tank. This process will vary according to processing speed, fruit characteristics, dwell time and fungicide concentration. As a result, the fungicide concentration and the residue left on the fruit can fluctuate throughout the day. These systems require more frequent monitoring than non-recovery applications to ensure treatment solutions contain the proper concentration. Non-recovery applications are typically mixed daily or several times per week, and the concentration can be calculated based upon known volumes or mass of solution and pesticide additives. Written records should be maintained each time a new solution of fungicide is mixed. Non-recovery applications also have the potential to be calibrated to the specific volume of fruit to ensure residues are optimal for benefit without being excessive. This can be accomplished using relays or a programmable logic controller (PLC) controlled application unit that senses the amount of fruit entering the applicator and then adjusts its rate of application up or down to match the fruit volume. It is possible to obtain real time output of application rate or obtain daily use rates for pesticide application record keeping purposes. Flow control devices used to optimize application rates provide significant protection against over-application of pesticides and reduce the likelihood of over tolerance residues.

GAP programs for fresh produce are not developed for complete risk elimination. Even with the best available preventive measures, trace levels of contaminants found in the environment will still be unavoidably introduced to some fruit during production and handling operations. Though not a guarantee of absolute safety, the implementation of GAP programs provides increased assurance to consumers by preventing gross contamination of fruit during pre-harvest, harvest, and post-harvest operations.

Good Manufacturing Practices (GMP)

In the food industry, the current Good Manufacturing Practices (GMP, GMPs, or cGMP) are a set of general federal regulations that apply to all foods. However, the Code of Federal Regulations (CFR) Title 21, section 110.19 provides a specific exemption of GMP to establishments engaged solely in the harvesting, storage, or distribution of raw agricultural commodities which are ordinarily cleaned, prepared, treated, or otherwise processed before being marketed to the consuming public. Based on this exemption, citrus fruit production and packing operations are not governed by GMP in the United States. Thus, whether or not to implement a packinghouse GMP program is a matter of private business decision. On the other hand, GMP is mandatory in fresh-squeezed juice, fresh-cut fruit, and other processed food operations.

Compared to unsheltered groves, the environment of a citrus packinghouse or processing plant is much more controllable, and thus suitable for implementing a more aggressive sanitation plan to create and maintain hygienic conditions. In general, GMP for fruit packing or processing is set to cover all areas of food sanitation to include personnel, buildings and facilities, equipment and utensils, and production and process controls. A checklist for preventing direct or indirect in-house contamination may include the following areas: 1) pest control, 2) structure and layout, 3) maintenance, 4) cleaning and sanitizing, 5) personnel, 6) restrooms, 7) water and ice supply, 8) chemicals, 9) ventilation, 10) waste disposal (USDA 2002; Marriott 1994). Rodents, insects, or other animals are major sources for food contamination with bacteria, filth, and foreign materials; their presence in the facility should not be allowed. An improper layout of operations in a facility can increase the likelihood of contamination through excessive employee traffic, wind and dust drafts, inadequate water drainage or other means. Poorly designed and maintained external conditions can also increase the likelihood of indirect product contamination. Proper facility maintenance is needed to avoid deterioration of the building and equipment due to defects such as a leaky roof, cracking floor, frayed conveyor belts, or pitted product-contact surfaces. Such conditions may trap wastes and harbor bacteria. Direct or indirect food contact surfaces can transmit contaminants if not thoroughly cleaned and sanitized. Therefore, an effective sanitizing operation is needed, provided that the methods themselves used in the operation will not result in chemical contamination or product adulteration. In addition, good housekeeping of all areas (such as staff lounge, locker rooms, and restrooms) is vital to minimize indirect product contamination.

The best facility sanitation operation can be defeated if the facility personnel do not maintain a high degree of personal cleanliness and pay attention personal hygienic practices to avoid food contamination (USDA 2002). Ill employees who can transmit foodborne disease pathogens should not come in contact with food or equipment used in operation. Good hygienic practices are not to be fully expected without providing sufficient restroom facilities. The restrooms and hand washing stations must be kept clean and functional with abundant hygiene supplies. Water and ice are potential reservoirs and carriers of filth, chemicals, and bacteria if not reasonably protected. Sources of unsafe water supply may include the use of untested water, open vessels of water, cross-connection of plumbing, back-siphonage, or back flow from a contaminated source to the supply system (USDA 2002). Recycled water is often utilized in the post-harvest environment, and should be maintained in such a manner as to prevent washing or dipping treatments from becoming sources of potential contamination. Agricultural or plant chemicals such as cleaners, sanitizers, rodenticides, insecticides, and machine lubricants may pose a risk of contaminating product if not handled with care; they must be used following manufacturers' instruction, have proper labeling, and be stored in a restricted area. Condensation in a facility may carry contaminants to adulterate food products through dripping on exposed food, equipment, and packaging material; thus, proper ventilation is required to allow adequate air exchange and drying. Processing wastes are likely to decompose quickly and are an attractant to rodents, insects and other animals. Failure to dispose of these wastes in a timely manner may result in direct and indirect contamination.

In practice, the development of a specific GMP program relies heavily on documentation of operating procedures. The creation of written Sanitation Standard Operating Procedures (SSOPs) is the backbone of GMP. These procedures, when followed, should be designed to control risk factors that can affect product safety or wholesomeness. SSOPs are usually supplemented by additional documentation that is generated in the monitoring of the overall program. Routine check lists, product inspection reports, and operating logs are examples of some of the supplemental documents used to verify that SSOPs are being followed. Table 5.1 is an example of a packinghouse daily cleaning schedule and Table 5.2 is an example of SSOPs for sanitizing packinghouse brush bed.

Hazard Analysis and Critical Control Point (HACCP)

A Hazard Analysis and Critical Control Point (HACCP) program is complementary to an existing GMP program. The HACCP process was originally developed to prepare food with a high assurance of safety for use in the space program (Marriott 1994). HACCP programs use seven logical principles: 1) conduct a hazard analysis; 2) identify the critical control points (CCPs) in the process; 3) establish the critical limits; 4) establish monitoring procedures; 5) establish corrective actions; 6) establish verification procedures; and 7) establish documentation and recording-keeping procedures (Juice HACCP Alliance 2002). It begins with a hazard analysis that identifies any relevant food safety risk factors that could impact the product prior to reaching the consumer.

The preparation steps for a hazard analysis include assembling a HACCP team, describing and identifying the food and its intended use, and developing and verifying a process flow diagram. A written hazard analysis can then be executed by completing the following steps: 1) list all potential physical, chemical, and biological hazards; 2) assess the likelihood of occurrence and the severity of health consequences in the absence of control for each identified hazard; 3) identify measures to control hazard identified as reasonably likely to occur; 4) review the current process to determine weather modifications are needed; and 5) identify CCPs (USFDA 2003).

In practice the CCPs and critical limits are established after hazard analysis to control any significant hazards that are not sufficiently removed by the pre-existing GAP and GMP programs. CCP is a point, step, or process at which a control measure can be applied and at which control must be performed to reduce a specific hazard to an acceptable level (USFDA 2003). The pasteurization temperature used in juice processing is an example of a potential CCP common to the citrus industry. CCPs must be monitored to ensure that the process is functioning properly. Deviations from the HACCP plan and failure at a CCP need to be anticipated so that problem-solving alternatives are documented ahead of time. The corrective actions are predetermined, defined and documented prior to the occurrence of the problem. HACCP plans must be validated and verified to ensure that the program will actually meet the goal when implemented.

Disease outbreaks involving fresh fruit juice in the late 1990s, including unpasteurized orange juice, have raised regulatory concerns regarding the

TABLE 5.1. An Example of a Packinghouse Daily Cleaning Schedule and Record

Daily Sanitation Control Record		Date:		
Firm:	Mark S/U			
Address:				
Products being processed:	Pre-Op	4-hour	8-hour	Post-Op
Condition	Time:	Time:	Time:	Time:
1. Safety of water and ice:				
a. Water faucets and fixtures have anti-siphoning devices				
2. Condition and cleanliness of food contract surfaces, including utensils, gloves, and outer garments:				
a. Equipment and utensils are adequately cleaned				
b. Sanitation strength (ppm) is correct				
c. Food contact surfaces and utensils are clean and sanitized.				
d. Gloves/garments contacting food are clean and sanitary.				
3. Prevention of cross contamination:				
a. Employee practices do not result in food contamination (hand washing, personal belonging storage, no eating, drinking or smoking)				
b. Personnel/hand sanitzer strength is adequate (ppm)				
c. Facility grounds are in good condition				
d. Waste is removed from processing areas				
e. Floors have adequate drainage/no standing water				
f. Facility building in good repair				
g. Incoming and finished product stored separately				
h. No drip (water or other substance) over product or packaging materials				
i. Safety-type lighting in use				
j. Non-food contact surfaces clean				

TABLE 5.1. (Continued) An Example of a Packinghouse Daily Cleaning Schedule and Record

k. Packaging materials protected from contaminants				
l. Separate color-coded sanitation equipment used				
4. Hand washing and toilet facilities:				
a. Toilet facilities are clean, sanitary and in good repair				
b. Adequate hand washing and sanitizing supplies				
5. Adulteration:				
a. Food-grade chemicals identified and stored properly				
b. Food, food-packaging materials and food contact surfaces protected from adulteration				
c. Equipment in good repair				
6. Toxic compounds:				
a. Pesticides, cleaners, sanitizers and other hazardous compounds identified and stored properly				
b. Properly labeled containers and containment used				
7. Employee health:				
a. Employee health conditions are acceptable				
b. Employees have no infected lesions				
8. Pests:				
a. No pests visible in plant				
b. Pest control devices properly deployed				
Comments and Corrections:				
Report by:				
S = Satisfactory/U = Unsatisfactory				

Adapted from: Seafood HACCP Alliance Course (Seafood HACCP Alliance 2000).

microbial safety of fruit juice in general. In 2001, Food and Drug Administration (FDA) issued regulations requiring juice processors to adopt a HACCP program and meet a 5-log microbial reduction requirement in the juice (US-

TABLE 5.2. An Example of SSOP for Packinghouse Brush Bed

SOP	Daily cleaning
1	Manually remove all loose fruit and debris from the washer and discard them into proper trash containers
2	Rinse brushes and sponges with a high volume sprayer to help remove loose debris
3	Turn washer on and apply foam cleaner to fruit contract surfaces. Follow manufacturer instructions of cleaning products.
4	Rinse surfaces with clean water.
5	Turn on washer and rinse again with clean water.
6	Turn washer on and use a high volume sprayer to treat all surfaces with an approved contact fruit sanitizer, such as Quanternary Ammonium at 200 ppm. Wear rubber gloves and goggles when handling sanitizing materials. Read product labels and MSDS for specific safety procedures and protective gear.
7	Rinse with clean water

SOP	Annual cleaning
1	Clean or replace brushes and sponges
2	Clean or replace all wipers, squeegees, and flicker bars.

FDA 2001). Although a HACCP program is not required for producers of fresh citrus fruit, its principles in risk analysis and CCP have been considered for citrus post-harvest management for years (Beattie and Revelant 1992). Facing ever-tightening scrutiny from the FDA and consumers to improve food safety, many fresh-cut fruit operations have already adapted HACCP programs.

GMP and HACCP are programs used throughout the food processing industry to identify and mitigate food safety risks. Both GMP and HACCP plans are regulatory requirements in many segments of the United States food industry. Failure to comply with GMP or HACCP requirements results in the end product being defined as adulterated, and can be the cause of costly recalls or product destruction. This is a significant contrast to the GAP programs implemented in the produce industry. GAP carries no regulatory penalty, as it is merely guidance for the industry. Current GAP guidelines identify potential sources of food safety problems and provide significant freedom to the individual business in the manner in which they choose to address risk factors. Nevertheless, the terminal retail market has sought compliance from the citrus industry with current guidance documents. Consolidation of retail chain stores has significantly increased their influence in the produce industry, thus it is anticipated that food safety programs and documentation requirements will continue to evolve in the trade in the years ahead.

CURRENT PERSPECTIVES

The increased focus on food safety, liability, and risk management in the produce market has affected the way in which citrus packers conduct business. The evolution from farm-based packing operations to sophisticated food processing establishments is still in progress. While the momentum for this change is being driven from the retail market, potential regulatory action in the future could increase the pace of this process. Some of the changes underway in the industry are described in the following subsections.

Facilities

The types of facilities used to pack and supply fresh citrus to the world markets vary a great deal in terms of their technology and infrastructure. It is not uncommon for very successful operations to be conducted in facilities that are several decades old. In such cases, these facilities far predate the emergence of food safety concerns recently associated with fresh produce. Food safety concerns such as ease of cleaning, pest exclusion, and materials of construction were not recognized when older facilities were built. It is not uncommon to find open buildings, wood floors and equipment manufactured from non-stainless steel throughout the produce industry, including citrus. Such facilities present many challenges in addressing good agricultural practice concerns, and may require development of specific strategies to comply with GAP guidelines. For example, doors and windows may need to be installed to improve pest exclusion, and a pest control program and daily facility cleaning and sanitation procedures can further mitigate pest issues. Non-stainless steel equipment surfaces may need to be treated with chemical resistant coatings or replaced to improve their cleanability and reduce pitting and corrosion caused by the use of various sanitizers.

The facility alone does not guarantee food safety. Updated sanitary practices employed within the facility are as critical to the success or failure of the overall program. Perhaps the most significant impact that food safety has had on citrus packing facilities is that it is now considered a criterion for new equipment purchases or facility renovation, whereas this was typically not the case as recently as the mid 1990s.

Traceback

Citrus fruit is typically packed into cardboard cartons for shipment to distant markets, although reusable plastic crates are becoming more common in some markets. In many countries, the carton must contain written information that declares what type of protective coating and post-harvest fungicides have been applied to the fruit within. In addition, bar codes applied via ink or stickers to the outside of the carton may contain more detailed information, such as the date harvested, harvest site, packing date, etc. These bar codes represent the primary means of locating fruit in the distribution channel if there are quality or safety concerns.

Carton labeling is the primary means of notification for the distributor and retailer, but fruit is often removed from the carton for retail display.

As a result, the consumer may not have the opportunity to view the carton labeling information. The standardization of individual fruit labeling with coded stickers provides the opportunity to convey information to the retailer and consumer on a single fruit basis. In the future, it may be possible to use bar codes or similar technology to print labels at the packinghouse which will contain all relevant information to track the individual fruit back to the grove from which it was harvested.

Auditing

Retailers in many markets now require that written records be kept of the programs and monitoring practices dealing specifically with food safety risk factors. As a result, a number of private firms and some governmental agencies now provide auditing and information management services throughout the produce industry to deal specifically with emerging retail concerns with food safety risk management. The lack of a single authority capable of setting uniform standards to govern produce specific food safety issues has created significant logistical issues for producers. The different influences and points of emphasis in different geographical regions, coupled with the variance between different auditing firms, presents a significant challenge to produce companies seeking to market products in international trade.

Inspection and audit services required by various retail chains focus on the relevant issues highlighted in CODEX (2001), FDA GAP or similar guidelines. Typically, these audits assign a specific point value to individual items, and individual ratings are summed to determine an overall score. Labeling and segregated storage of pesticide chemicals, visible cleanliness of harvesting or packing equipment, and maintaining an active pest control program are just a few examples of the types of practices that may be evaluated during an audit. Some retailers now require a specific minimum score that must be obtained in the audit in order to qualify as a potential supplier. The retail chain may elect to conduct the audit through one of its agents, or require that the grower/packer contract with an approved auditor or auditing firm whose standards the retailer recognizes and accepts. Some private audit firms and the USDA provide results via an Internet web-site, and the data management aspect of food safety auditing has become an increasingly popular feature for retailers. Growers and packers should verify that these Internet based data management services are secure and tamper resistant, as sensitive information about their operations which will influence retail buying decisions is contained in these web-based programs.

Globally, there are fresh citrus producers who have implemented GMP or HACCP programs, although the specific requirements and focal points vary based upon the laws of the producing country. In some cases, HACCP programs have been broadened to include quality parameters as well as food safety. This can result in confusion for citrus import and export operations, as the standards and nomenclature vary across national boundaries. In addition to many private firms, universities and some large grower organizations have become active in providing information and training programs to facilitate the education of produce growers, packers and shippers. The overall trend is that third party audit programs are driving the industry toward the GMP model of documentation and monitoring.

REFERENCES

BEATTIE, B. and REVELANT, L. (Editors). 1992. Guide to Quality Management in the Citrus Industry. Australian Horticultural Corporation, Sydney, Australia.

BARTZ, J. A. and SHOWALTER, R. K. 1981. Infiltration of tomatoes by aqueous bacterial suspensions. Phytopathology 71, 515-518.

BEUCHAT, L. R. 1996. Pathogenic microorganisms associated with fresh produce. J. Food Prot. 59: 204-216.

BHAT, G. P. and SUROLIA, N. 2001. In vitro antimalarial activity of extracts of three plants used in the traditional medicine of India. Am J. Trop. Med. Hyg. 65, 304-8.

BOLLES, H. G., DIXON-WHITE, H. E., PETERSON, R. K., TOMERLIN, J. R., DAY, E. W., JR. and OLIVER, G. R. 1999. U.S. market basket study to determine residues of the insecticide chlorpyrifos. J. Agr. Food Chem. 47, 1817-1822.

BUCHANAN, R. L., EDELSON, S. G., MILLER, R. L. and SAPERS, G. M. 1999. Contamination of intact apples after immersion in an aqueous environment containing *Escherichia coli* O157:H7. J. Food Prot. 62, 444-450.

CHUN, D. and McDONALD, R. E. 1987. Seasonal trends in the population dynamics of fungi, yeasts, and bacteria on fruit surface of grapefruit in Florida. Proc. Fla. State. Hort. Soc. 100: 23-25.

CODEX ALIMENTARIUS. 2001. Proposed draft code of hygienic practice for the primary production, harvesting, and packing of fresh fruits and vegetables. http://www.fao.org.

DABBAH, R., EDAARDS, V. M. and MOATS, W. A. 1970. Antimicrobial action of some citrus fruit oils on selected food-borne bacteria. Appl. Microbiol. 19, 27-31.

D'AQUINO, M. and TEVES, S. A. 1994. Lemon juice as a natural biocide for disinfecting drinking water. Bull Pan. Am. Health Organ. 28, 324-330.

de CASTILLO, M. C., DE ALLORI, C. G., DE GUTIERREZ, R. C., DE SAAB, O. A., DE FERNANDEZ, N. P, DE RUIZ, C. S., HOLGADO, A. P. and DE NADER, O. M. 2000. Bactericidal activity of lemon juice and lemon derivatives against *Vibrio cholerae*. Biol. Pharm Pull. 23, 1235-1238.

EUROPEAN COMMISSION. 2002. Risk profile on the microbiological contamination of fruits and vegetables eaten raw. http://europa.eu.int.

HANKIN, L. and PYLYPIW, H. M., Jr. 1991. Pesticides in orange juice sold in Connecticut. J. Food Prot. 54, 310-311.

JOINT INSTITUTE OF FOOD SAFETY AND APPLIED NUTRITION (JIFSAN). 2002. Improving the safety and quality of fresh fruit and vegetables: a training manual for trainers. University of Maryland. http://www.jifsan.umd.edu.

JUICE HACCP ALLIANCE. 2002. Juice HACCP Training Curriculum. National Center for Food Safety and Technology, Chicago, IL.

KELSEY, F. 1997. High pressure washer. University of Florida. Packinghouse Newsletter, W. F. Wardowski (Editor). 180, 2-3. http://www.postharvest.ifas.ufl.edu.

KILCHER, L. 2001. Organic agriculture in Cuba: the revolution goes green. J. Agri. Tropics Subtropics 102:185-189.

KIMBALL, D. A. 1999. Citrus Processing: A Complete Guide, 2nd Edition. AspenGaithersburg, MD.

LIANG, Z., MITTAL, G. S. and GRIFFITHS, M. W. 2002. Inactivation of *Salmonella Typhimurium* in orange juice containing antimicrobial agents by pulsed electric field. J. Food Prot 65, 1081-1087.

LINTON, M., McCLEMENTS, J. M. J. and PATTERSON, M. F. 1999. Inactivation of *Escherichia coli* O157:H7 in orange juice using a combination of high pressure and mild heat. J. Food Prot. 62, 277-279.

MARRIOTT, N. G. 1994. Principles of Food Sanitation. 3rd Edition. Chapman & Hall, Inc., New York, NY.

MEAD, P. S., SLUTSKER, L., DIETZ, V., McCAIG, L. F., BRESEE, J. S., SHAPIRO, C., GRIFFIN, P. M. and TAUXE, R. V. 2001. Food-related illness and death in the United States, Emerging Infectious Diseases 7, 516-521.

MURDOCK, D. I. and BROKAW, C. H. 1957. Some specific sources of contamination in processing frozen concentrated orange juice- 1. handling and preparing fruit for extraction. Proc. Fla. State. Hort. Soc. 70, 231-237.

MURDOCK, D. I., FOLINAZZO, J. F. and BROKAW, C. H. 1953. Some observations of gum-forming organisms found on fruit surfaces. Proc. Fla. State. Hort. Soc. 66, 278-281.

NOTERMANS, S., IN'T VELD, P., WIJTZES, T. and MEAD, G. C. 1993. A user's guide to microbial challenge testing for ensuring the safety and stability of food products. Food Microbiol. 10, 145-167.

NATIONAL ADVISORY COMMITTEE ON MICROBIOLOGICAL CRITERIA FOR FOODS (NACMCF). 1999. Microbiological safety evaluations and recommendations on fresh produce. Food Control. 10, 117-143.

PAO, S. and BROWN, G. E. 1998. Reduction of microorganisms on citrus fruit surfaces during packinghouse processing. J. Food Prot. 61, 903-906.

PAO, S., BROWN, G. E. and SCHNEIDER, K. R. 1998. Challenge studies with selected pathogenic bacteria on freshly peeled Hamlin orange. J. Food Sci. 58, 359-362.

PAO, S. and DAVIS, C. L. 1999. Enhancing microbiological safety of fresh orange juice by fruit immersion in hot water and chemical sanitizers. J. Food Prot. 62, 756-760.

PAO, S. and DAVIS, C. L. 2001A. Transfer of natural and artificially inoculated microorganisms from orange fruit to fresh juice during extraction. Food Sci. Tech. (lwt). 34, 113-117.

PAO, S. and DAVIS, C. L. 2001B. Comparing attachment, heat tolerance and alkali resistance of pathogenic and non-pathogenic bacterial cultures on orange surfaces. J. Rapid Meth. Automation Microbiol. 9, 271-278.

PAO, S., DAVIS, C. L., FRIEDRICH, L. M. and M. E. PARISH, M. E. 2002. Utilization of fluorogenic assay for rapid detection of *Escherichia coli* in acidic fruit juice. J. Food Prot. 65, 1943-1948.

PAO, S., DAVIS, C. L. and KELSEY, D. F. 2000. Efficacy of alkaline washing for the decontamination of orange fruit surfaces inoculated with *Escherichia coli*. J. Food Prot. 63: 961-964.

PAO, S., DAVIS, C. L. and PARISH, M. E. 2001. Microscopic observation and processing validation of fruit sanitizing treatments for the enhanced microbiological safety of fresh orange juice. J. Food Prot. 64, 310-314.

PAO, S., DAVIS, C. L., KELSEY, D. F. and PETRACEK, P. D. 1999. Sanitizing effect of fruit waxes at high pH and temperature on orange surfaces inoculated with *Escherichia coli*. J. Food Sci. 64, 359-362.

PAO, S. and PETRACEK, P. D. 1997. Shelf-life extension of peeled oranges by citric acid treatment. Food Microbiol. 14, 485-491.

PARISH, M. E. 1997. Public health and nonpasteurized fruit juices. Crit. Rev. Microbiol. 23, 109-119.

PARISH, M. E. 1998A. Coliforms, *Escherichia coli* and *Salmonella* serovars associated with a citrus-processing facility implicated in a salmonellosis outbreak. J. Food Prot. 61, 280-284.

PARISH, M. E. 1998B. High pressure inactivation of Saccharomyces cerevisiae, endogenous microflora and pectinmethylesterase in orange juice. J. Food Safety 18, 57-65.

PETRACEK, P. D., KELSEY, D. F. and DAVIS, C. 1998. Response of citrus fruit to high pressure washing. J. Amer. Soc. Hort. Sci. 123, 661-667.

RANGARAJAN, A., BIHN, E. A., GRAVANI, R. B., SCOOTT, D.L. and PRITTS, M. P. 2001. Food safety begins on the farm, a grower's guide. Cornell Good Agricultural Practices Program. http//www.gaps.cornell.edu.

RITENOUR, M. A., SANCHEZ, T. N., and KELSEY, D. F. 2000. Quaternary ammonia injury on grapefruit peel. University of Florida. Packinghouse Newsletter. M. A. Ritenour (Editor). 192, 1-4. http://www.postharvest.ifas.ufl.edu.

RITENOUR, M. A., SANCHEZ, T. N., and KELSEY, D. F. 2001. Update on grapefruit quaternary ammonia injury. University of Florida. Packinghouse Newsletter, M. A. Ritenour (Editor). 193:3-4. http://www.postharvest.ifas.ufl.edu.

SEAFOOD HACCP ALLIANCE. 2000. Sanitation control procedures for processing fish and fishery products: Example SSOP plan and sanitation control records. Seafood HACCP Alliance Course. http://seafood.ucdavis.edu.

SEEMAN, B. K., SUMNER, S. S., MARINI, R. and KNIEL, K. E. 2002. Internalization of *Escherichia coli* in apples under natural conditions. Dairy Food Environ. Sanit. 22, 667-673.

SHOMER, R., COGAN, U. and MANHEIM, C. H. 1994. Thermal death parameters of orange juice and effect of minimal heat treatment and carbon dioxide on shelf-life. J. Food Process. Preserv. 18, 305-315.

SOFFER, R. and MANHEIM, C. H. 1996. Effect of minimal heat treatment and carbon dioxide on shelf-life of grapefruit juice. Fruit Process. 96, 99-101.

TAKAHASHI, Y., OHTA, H., YONEI, H. and IFUKU, Y. 1993. Microbicidal effect of hydrostatic pressure on satsuma mandarin juice. Int. J. Food Sci. Technol. 28, 95-102.

U.S. DEPARTMENT OF AGRICULTURE (USDA). 1998, 1999, 2000. Pesticide Data Program Annual Summary. http//www.ams.usda.gov/pdp.

U.S. DEPARTMENT OF AGRICULTURE (USDA). 2002. Qualified through verification (QTV) program for the fresh-cut produce industry. File Code 151-B-4. http://www.ams.usda.gov/fv/qtv.htm.

U.S. FOOD AND DRUG ADMINISTRATION (USFDA). 1998. Guidance for industry: guide to minimize microbial food safety hazards for fresh fruits and vegetables. http://www.fda.gov.

U.S. FOOD AND DRUG ADMINISTRATION (USFDA). 2001. Hazard analysis and critical control point (HACCP); procedures for the safe and sanitary processing and importing of juice; final rule. Fed. Regist. 66, 6138-6200.

U.S. FOOD AND DRUG ADMINISTRATION (USFDA). 2003. Guidance for industry: juice HACCP small entity compliance guide. http://www.fda.gov.

VARGAS, I., SANZ, I., MOYA, P., and PRIMA-YUFERA, E. 1999. Antimicrobial and antioxidant compounds in the nonvolatile fraction of expressed orange essential oil. J. Food Prot. 62, 929-932.

WEI, C. I., BALABAN, M. O., FERNANDO, S. Y. and PEPLOW, A. J. 1991. Bacteria effect of high pressure CO_2 treatment on foods spiked with *Listeria* or *Salmonella*. J. Food Prot. 54, 189-193.

WEI, C. I., HUANG, T. S., KIM, J. M., LIN, W. F., TAMPLIN, M. L. and BARTZ, J. A. 1995. Growth and survival of *Salmonella Montevideo* on tomatoes and disinfection with chlorinated water. J. Food Prot. 58, 829-836.

WEIER, T. E., STOCKING, C. R. and BARHOUR, M. G. 1974. Fruit, seed, and seedling. *In* Botany, and Introduction to Plant Biology, 5th ed. John Wiley & Sons, New York.

ZHUANG, R. Y., BEUCHAT, L. R. and ANGULO, F. J. 1995. Fate of *Salmoella Montevideo* on and in raw tomatoes as affected by temperature and treatment with chlorine. Appl. and Environ. Microbiol. 61, 2127-2131.

6

Part 1

Production Trends Around the World

Argentina

Roberto Varela

Citrus fruit was introduced in Argentina in the 17th century. The citrus industry became important at the beginning of 20th century due to the contribution of pioneers in the field who set an example of courage and work. The domestic market was developed and organized between 1940 and 1950. At the beginning of the 1970s, Argentina began to send fresh citrus fruit overseas. During this period the citrus industry concentrated mainly on fresh fruit even though then was also a considerable increase in citrus processing.

Production Areas

Citrus producing areas of Argentina (Fig. 6.1) are located in two main regions: the Northwest (NOA) made up of Tucuman, Salta, Jujuy, and the Northeast (NEA) constituted by Buenos Aires, Entre Rios, Corrientes, and Misiones. The NOA region has a defined summer rainfall season compared to the NEA where rains are evenly distributed throughout the year. The climate makes big differences that are reflected in different sanitary problems and distinctive fruit type production in each region. A non-citrus area separates the two regions which are approximately 600 km away from each other.

Tucumán, Salta and Jujuy are the most important citrus producing provinces in the NOA region. Lemons are produced in Tucumán, while late oranges and grapefruit are cultivated in Salta and Jujuy.

The NEA region produces mainly oranges (Valencias and navels) and tangerines (Ellendale, Satsuma, Clementina and Nova) with a low percentage of lemons and grapefruit. Main plantings are located in Corrientes and

129

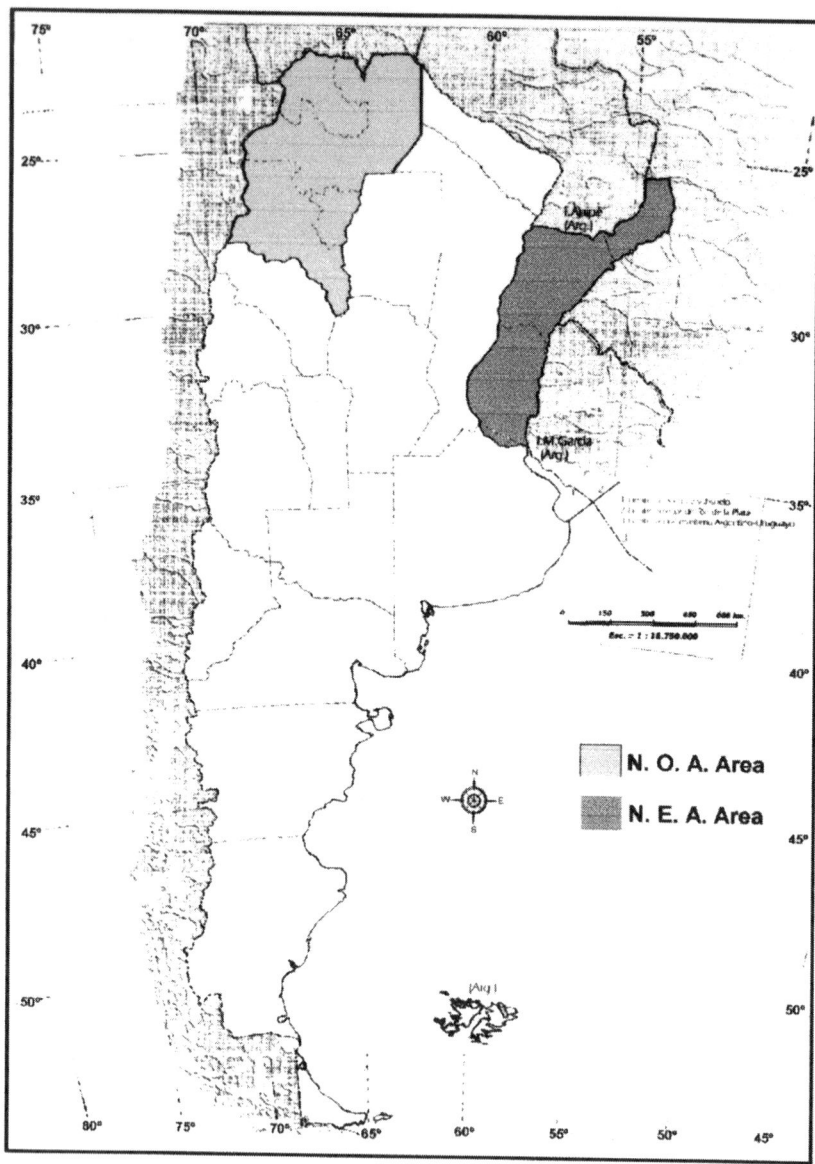

Fig. 6.1. Citrus producing areas in Argentina.

Entre Ríos provinces followed by Misiones and Buenos Aires. Two new small areas are developing; one is in Formosa province (NEA), with grapefruit and the other is in Catamarca province (NOA) with oranges and mandarins.

Citrus Varieties and Rootstocks

Argentina has PROCITRUS, a nationwide citrus budwood program, which will enhance the uniformity and high quality of propagation material reaching the nursery industry. The objective of the program is to obtain, maintain and distribute disease-free horticultural superior plant material (scion varieties and rootstocks) for the production of commercial citrus nursery trees nationwide. Plant material is free of tristeza, psorosis, exocortis, cachexia, canker and variegated clorosis (CVC).

Control of citrus nurseries are carried out by law since 1998 using a certification system implemented by the Secretaria de Agricultura, Ganadería, Pesca y Alimentación (SAGPyA). A new Citrus Nurserymen Association for the NEA region was established in 2000.

This program is responsible for the replacement of old varieties for new types demanded by overseas markets will determine the evolution of the citrus industry in Argentina. In the future this increase in plant density will be definitely more important than acreage increase.

The primary varieties grown include:

- Oranges: Valencia, Valencia Seedless, Salustiana, Newhall, Navelina, Lane late, Frost Navel, Delta and Midknight

- Mandarins: Satsuma, Nova, Clementina, Ellendale, Murcott, Fortune.

- Lemons: Eureka, Frost Lisbon, Limoneira 8-A, Génova Nucelar, Santa Teresa, and Tahiti Lime

- Grapefruit: Foster, Foster seedless, Hennninger's Ruby, Star Ruby, Mutation La Toma, Rio Red, and Marsh Seedless.

Budded citrus trees on sweet orange (*Citrus sinensis* Osbeck) were planted at the beginning of the 19th century in Argentina. Soon after many trees died due to the fungus disease, *Phytophthora*. Sour orange (*C.aurantium* L.) became the second rootstock used but after the discovery of tristeza it is only used as rootstock for lemons.

Main commercial rootstocks are *Poncirus trifoliata* (L.) Raf. (Concordia, Rubidoux and Flying Dragon), Cleopatra mandarin (*C. reshni* Hort. Ex Tanaka), Troyer and Carrizo citranges [*C.sinensis* (L.) Osb. × *P. trifoliata* (L.) Raf.], Swingle citrumelo [*C. paradisi* Macf. × *P. trifoliata* (L.) Osb.], sour orange (*C.aurantium* L.), Rangpur lime (*C. limonia* Obsbeck), Rough lemon (*C. jambhiri* Lush.) and Volkamer lemon (*C. volkameriana* Pasq.)

Trifoliate orange is predominantly used in the NEA region where oranges and tangerines are mainly produced for the fresh market. During the last decade, Flying Dragon began to be used commercially as a semi-dwarfing rootstock for Lisboa lemons in Tucuman. Cleopatra mandarin and Rangpur lime are the secondly most used rootstocks in Argentina. Cleopatra is a good rootstock for the NOA region whereas Rangpur is used in both regions. Rough lemon is mainly used as rootstock for navels and lemons in areas where freeze hazard is low. Troyer and Carrizo citranges are used in low percentage for oranges and tangerines while Swingle citrumelo is used only for grapefruit.

Trials established in both regions are testing new rootstocks developed by the Citrus Breeding Program of the Obispo Colombres Experimental Station in Tucuman. Premium fruit production (top quality-best production) will give Argentinean citrus growers better competitiveness level at international markets.

Production and Destination

Argentina was the seventh world fresh citrus producer in the year 2001. It produced the 4.22% of citrus in the world and exported 5.38% of world trade citrus. Throughout the country the citrus industry has an important level of employment and quantity of facilities such as: 5000 citrus growers, 400 packinghouses, 14 processing plants and around 100,000 workers.

The citrus plantation area (Table 6.1) for the same year is 156,230 ha in the country. Those plantings are separated in two big areas, 62,753 ha in the NOA and 93,477 ha in NEA. The area planted by variety is divided in 44,357 ha of lemon, 60,691 ha of oranges, 38,923 ha of mandarin and 12,259 ha of grapefruit.

The yearly citrus production increased from 1,690,000 to 2,808,310 tons per year, between 1989 and 2001. Lemons are largely responsible for the increase since other varieties like oranges and mandarins have remained stable. Grapefruit has decreased, following the world trend. Citrus utilization (Table 6.2) is approximately 44% domestic, 40% processing and 16% export.

Table 6.1. Total Argentina Area Planted in ha (2001)

Province	Orange	Mandarin	Grapefruit	Lemon	Totals
Buenos Aires	7,250	640	310	560	8,760
Catamarca	850	1,000	70	80	2,000
Entre Ríos	20,486	22,963	1,649	1,679	46,777
Corrientes	17,300	8,200	600	3,390	29,490
Misiones	2,800	3,200	450	2,000	8,450
Jujuy	4,260	1,550	820	1,798	8,428
Salta	4,545	770	7,860	1,850	15,025
Tucumán	3,200	600	500	33,000	37,300
Totals	60,691	38,923	12,259	44,357	156,230

Source: La Actividad Citricola Argentina 2002.

Table 6.2. Supply and Distribution of Argentina Citrus Fruit (2001)

Variety	Processing	Domestic Fresh	Export Fresh	Totals	Percent by Variety
	----------------- metric tons -----------------				
Lemon	859,531	95,630	237,792	1,192,953	47.15
Mandarin	45,909	334,982	36,279	417,170	16.49
Orange	143,040	515,964	100,463	759,467	30.02
Grapefruit	71,122	65,840	23,655	160,617	6.35
Totals	1,119,602	1,012,416	398,189	2,530,207	100.00
Percent by Distribution	44.25	40.01	15.74	100.00	

The domestic per capita consumption fell down from 43.98 kg per year in 1984 to 28.13 kg per year in 2001. This was due to the great development of new products that replaced citrus and other fruits from them historical uses, like dessert.

Argentine fresh citrus exports between 1990-2000 are seen in Figure 6.2. It shows that lemons exportation has grown more than 300%, grapefruit has fallen 70%, orange 58% and mandarin 20%. The decrease of oranges and mandarins are due to climatic conditions in the last two years. Grapefruit consumption in the world is decreasing and tending to red pulp varieties. Argentine is the largest lemon producer in the world and the number two exporter. Though lemon is not a table fruit, it has excellent added value by processing, the use is full with high added value of its by-products.

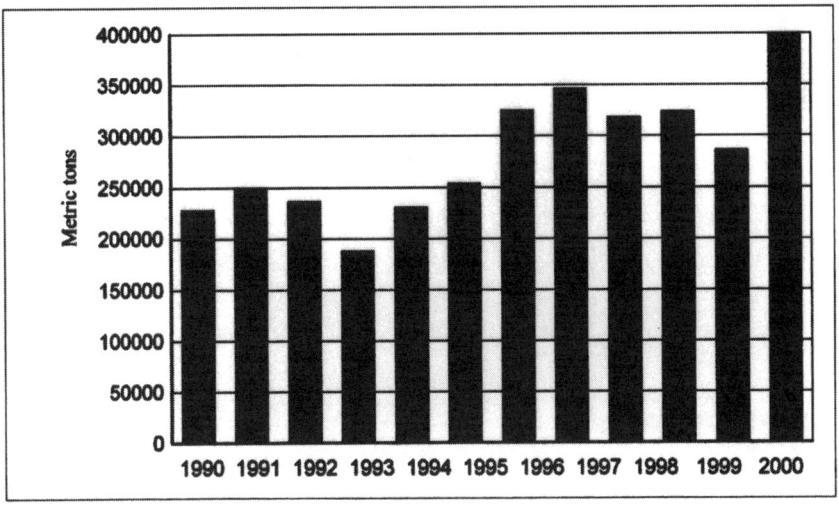

Fig. 6.2. Argentina fresh citrus exports (1990-2000). Source: INTA (1990-2000).

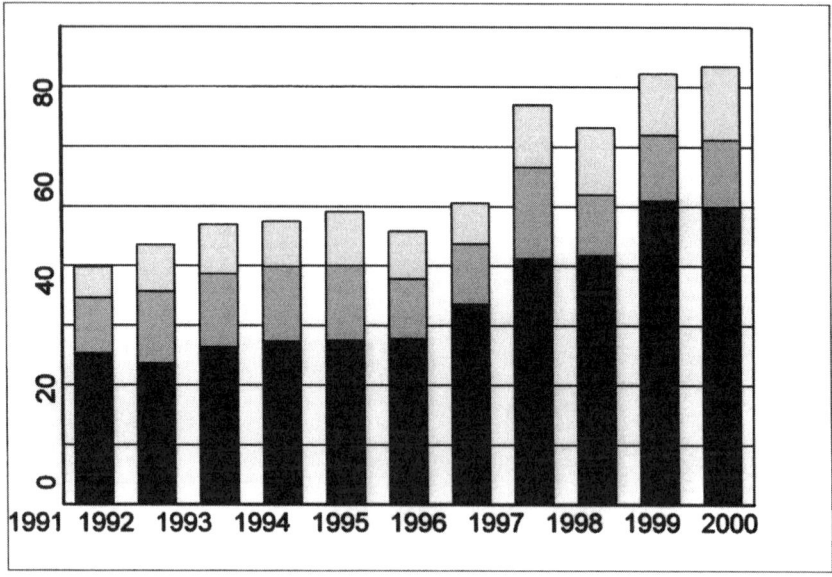

Fig. 6.3. Argentina production (metric tons × 10) of concentrated frozen citrus products (1991-2000).

Citrus Processing

Argentina became the fifth world citrus processing country with 1,119,602 tons of fresh citrus in 2001. Figure 6.3 illustrates the evolution of citrus processing. The products and by products for all citrus varieties in 2000 were 72,200 frozen concentrate juice, 4,130 tons essential oils, 770 tons of frozen pulp 43,000 tons of dehydrated peel. Lemon accounts for 71% of processing.

REFERENCES

ANDERSON, C. M. 1990. The Citrus Rootstock Situation in Argentina, pp. 23-28. *In* Annais. First Int. Seminar on Citrus Rootstocks. L. C. Donadio (Editor), 242 p. Bebedouro, S. Paulo, Brazil.

ANDERSON, C. M., COSTA, N. B., FABIANI, A. and PLATA, M. I. 1999. Procitrus: the Citrus Asociación Tucumana del Citrus. http//:www.atcitrus.com Budwood Improvement Program for Argentina. Proc. France. Federación Entrerriana del Citrus. VISCN, 149-153.

FOGUET, J. L., BLANCO, A., STEIN, B. and GONZALEZ, J. 1994. Resultados preliminares del Programa de Mejoramiento Genético de Portainjertos Cítricos. Rev. Ind. Y Agricola de Tucumán. Tucumán, Argentina. Tomo 71 (1-2), 41-47.

INFORMES CITRÍCOLAS 2001. Instituto Nacional de Tecnología Agropecuaria (INTA). Recopilado e impreso por FEDERCITRUS.

INSTITUTO NACIONAL DE ESTADÍSTICA Y CENSOS (INDEC). Dirección de Coordinación de Delegaciones. http//:www.indec.mecon.gov.ar

LA ACTIVIDAD CITRÍCOLA ARGENTINA. Reporte anual 2002. Federación Argentina del Citrus (FEDERCITRUS).

6
Part 2

Mexico

Thomas H. Spreen, Arturo Bocardo, and Ronald P. Muraro

INTRODUCTION

Mexico ranks as the third largest citrus producing country in the Western Hemisphere after Brazil and the United States. The industry in Mexico has a proud history dating back to the 17th century when the Spanish introduced citrus trees in northeast Mexico. Today, Mexico ranks as the largest producer of Persian limes, which are primarily produced for export to the United States and Europe. The Mexican market still prefers the Mexican or key lime, which is also widely cultivated. Mexico also has a large orange industry; nearly all orange production is consumed in the domestic market where it is purchased fresh and juiced at home.

An overview of the structure of the Mexican citrus industry is provided in this part. Among the factors that have influenced the evolution of this industry are the strong land tenure laws, the freezes of the 1980s, and the economic union with the United States and Canada through the North American Free Trade Agreement (NAFTA).

Production Zones for Citrus

Citrus is produced in many states in Mexico. The combination of cold and low rainfall makes citrus production marginal in north central Mexico. The largest producing state is Veracruz, which extends along Mexico's eastern coast. Other major producing states in eastern Mexico include San Luis Potosi, Tamaulipas, and Neuvo Leon. Commercial production can also be found in Tobasco, Campeche, and the Yucatan. A smaller, yet important production region for oranges can also be found along Mexico's western coast in Sonora and Sinaloa. In southwest Mexico, the states of Colima and Michoacan, Guerrero, and Oaxaca are the primary producers of Mexican limes that play an integral role in the diet of most Mexicans. Citrus production by state and variety is shown in Table 6.3. A map of Mexico is shown as Figure 6.4 and the main citrus producing states are highlighted.

Citrus Varieties Produced in Mexico

The citrus varieties produced in Mexico are, in order of importance, oranges, limes, grapefruit, and tangerines. In this section, oranges, limes, and grapefruit production and consumption are discussed in more detail. Tangerine production is quite small and nearly all tangerine production is consumed in the domestic market.

Fresh Oranges

With 30 percent of the country's total fruit acreage and the highest level of consumption, oranges are the most important citrus fruit produced in the country (Mondragon *et al.* 1998). In the 2000-01 season, orange production was 3.2 million MT (78 million boxes). This total production places Mexico

TABLE 6.3. Citrus Production in Mexico by State, 2001

State	Limes	Oranges and Grapefruit
	----------------- Thousand MT -----------------	
Baja California Sur	0.0	20.3
Campeche	13.1	54.8
Colima	502.1	6.1
Chiapas	3.0	21.6
Guerrero	58.6	0.0
Hidalgo	1.9	89.2
Jalisco	32.4	5.3
Michoacan de Campo	301.0	2.8
Nuevo Leon	0.0	343.2
Oaxaca	205.4	47.1
Puebla	31.6	200.2
Quintana Roo	0.0	20.8
San Luis Potosi	0.0	296.1
Sonora	0.0	177.4
Tabasco	87.0	166.2
Tamauilpas	0.0	379.7
Veracruz-Llave	276.6	1,95.0
Yucatan	34.1	187.5
Totals	1,546.7	4,003.4

Citrus in Mexico

Fig. 6.4. Citrus producing states in Mexico.

as the third largest orange producing country in the Western Hemisphere (after Brazil and the United States). Although oranges are produced throughout much of Mexico, the most important producing states are Veracruz, Nuevo Leon, Tamaulipas, San Luis Potosi and more recently Tabasco. Until 1982 Nuevo Leon was the leading producing state, but a series of freezes struck during the early 1980s and damaged most of the local area planted with oranges and resulted in higher domestic market prices. Veracruz became the largest orange-producing state in Mexico, with a planted area that represents nearly 45 percent of the country's total production area. This series of freezes also devastated Florida and increased the international price for fresh oranges. Such phenomenon spurred a major orange production expansion in the country that more than doubled the total land area planted to oranges during the 1980-1995 period. Today, the area planted to oranges in Mexico is estimated to be 808,000 acres (USDA/FAS 2003).

About 90 percent of the oranges cultivated in Mexico are late Valencia, and the rest is mainly early Valencia. These varieties are cultivated under tropical conditions and are not exported as fresh fruit to the United States, the closest open market for Mexico, because of quality constraints. Only the states located in western Mexico, i.e., Sonora and Sinaloa, have weather conditions that allow production of fruit that can be exported to the international fresh orange market. For instance, Sonora, a relatively young state in orange production and the leading exporting-state of fresh oranges into the United States, has a 6 percent of its total area planted with Navel oranges. This percentage is similar in places such as Montemorelos, Nuevo Leon and Cd. Victoria, Tamaulipas, but production in those locations is not stable as these states are subject to periodic freezes.

Another major problem that limits the exports of fresh Mexican oranges is the presence of the Mexican fruit fly. Except for Sonora and Sinaloa, the other producing states are not fruit fly-free zones. The Unites States requires that oranges produced in fly-infested regions be fumigated with methyl bromide. This treatment, however, seems to be unsuitable for the fresh market because it is expensive and tends to burn the external surface of the fruit. A significant effort is underway to establish more fruit fly-free zones in Mexico, but the characteristics of citrus production on these areas limits the effectiveness of this effort.

Most orange trees in Mexico are planted on sour orange rootstock (Citrus aurantium). These standard-size trees yield crops of excellent quality. Sour orange rootstock, however, is highly susceptible to the viral disease, tristeza, when used with any scion except lemon or lime. During the period of 1990/96, nurseries in Veracruz produced approximately 315,000 orange trees on Tristeza-resistant rootstocks. In 2000, the federal governmental agency in charge of the agricultural sector (SAGAR) published an emergency regulation to implement a National Emergency Mechanism to prevent the spread of and eradicate the brown citrus aphid and citrus tristeza virus in Mexico. Brown citrus aphid was first detected in the states of Yucatan and Quintana Roo, and tristeza has been detected in Baja California. As part of this regulation, citrus from these areas have to be washed and packaged in order for them to be transported into other states.

Production practices for oranges differs across the country. In Veracruz, for example, about 90 percent of the planted area is non-irrigated while in Nuevo Leon, which represents 8 percent of the total area planted in Mexico, about 85 percent irrigated (Mondragon et al. 1998). The cost of production also varies by state. In Veracruz, the average cost of production for a traditional grove with little cultivation is approximately US$200/acre, whereas the average for a more intensively managed grove is about US$450/acre (Mondragon et al. 1998). Fertilization and pest control accounts for most of the difference between these figures.

Countrywide orange yields average 105 boxes/acre. Orange yields differ widely depending on the production area. In Veracruz yields range from 100 to 200 boxes, and in Nuevo Leon yields range from 120 to 150 boxes/

acre. In San Luis Potosi yields range from 70 to 130 boxes/acre. Among the factors that explain this variance are weather, input levels, terrain and tree density. In Veracruz, for example, average tree density is 80 trees per acre, but new Valencia trees are planted at higher densities, ranging from 125 to 150 trees per acre.

Persian and Key Limes

The second most important citrus crop in Mexico is limes. Two varieties are produced and consumed in Mexico: the Mexican lime, also known as the key lime in the United States, and Persian limes, also called Tahiti lime in the United States (Roy *et al.* 1996). The most popular lime in Mexico is the Mexican lime, but as a result of increasing prices, consumption is shifting to Persian limes, which are generally larger and contain more juice than Mexican limes. Mexican limes have a longer shelf life, however, which is attractive in Mexico with its lack of refrigeration. Since lime production is highly sensitive to freezing weather, lime production in the United States is limited to extreme south Florida and parts of southern California. The devastating impact of Hurricane Andrew in 1992 (Attaway 1999) that struck the main lime producing area of Florida, Dade County, combined with the eradication efforts in Florida to control citrus canker, has placed Mexico as the dominant supplier of limes to the U.S. market, accounting for approximately 90 percent of total U.S. consumption. In addition, there has been an upward trend in lime consumption in the United States with per capita consumption tripling from .5 pounds in 1985 to 1.5 pounds in 2000 (USDA/ERS 2003). The other export markets for Mexico are France and Japan, but they are small relative to the U.S. market.

The total area planted for both Persian and Key limes is approximately 305,000 acres, representing 25 percent of the total area planted with citrus. Because of favorable international prices, this share has recently been changing. Some producers have been switching to Persian limes from oranges or grapefruit. Of this total area, 80 percent is planted with Key limes and 20 percent is planted with Persian limes. Production of Key limes is found mainly along the Pacific coast, in the states of Colima, Michoacan, Guerrero and Oaxaca, and Persian limes are grown in the states of Veracruz, San Luis Potosi, Tamaulipas, Hidalgo, and more recently Oaxaca and Tabasco. Veracruz is the largest Persian lime producer in Mexico, representing about 80 percent of total national production. The major producing states for Key limes are Colima and Michoacan.

Contrary to oranges, Persian lime groves in Veracruz are irrigated by micro-jet irrigation or other irrigation systems. Michoacan and Colima, have irrigation in most of the Key lime groves. This factor facilitates year round production, but represents a higher cost of production relative to the cost for orange production. The cost of production for Persian limes in Veracruz can be as high as US $400/acre whereas the cost of production for Key limes in Oaxaca, Colima and Michoacan can vary from US $300 to US $500 per acre. This is due to higher prices for imported inputs such as pesticides, fertilizers and other agrochemical products (Roy *et al.* 1996).

The predominant production system for Key limes is an intercropping system in Colima, which usually includes coconut palm trees planted in between Key lime trees. This cultural practice has a negative impact on yields per hectare, reducing yields generally up to 50 percent in comparison with conventional groves. Yields for Key lime range from 2.8 to 4.8 MT/acre while Persian limes yields range from 2 to 4.8 MT/acre.

Fresh Grapefruit

Grapefruit represents the second lowest portion of citrus production and consumption in Mexico, with tangerines being the lowest. With a total area of 24,438 acres, which is only 2 percent of the total citrus production area, grapefruit has not economically attractive to Mexican growers. There are two types of grapefruit planted in Mexico: the red table varieties produced in Michoacan, Tabasco, Nuevo Leon and Veracruz, and the white fleshed varieties produced in Tamaulipas and Veracruz. The red table variety is produced for export to the United States and Europe while the white fleshed variety is mainly produced for juice production or for peeled slices that are frozen and then exported. Veracruz is the major producer of grapefruit accounting for about 70 percent of national production, and also has the highest yield in the country with an average of 230 boxes/acre. The other grapefruit producing states average yields of 160 boxes/acre. The planted area in Veracruz and Nuevo Leon, two of the most important producing states, has not experienced significant change in recent years. Due to better weather conditions and lower cost of production, the state of Michoacan is becoming an important player in the national grapefruit industry.

Fresh Versus Processing Utilization

Most citrus growers in Mexico gear their production toward domestic fresh consumption. Utilization in the fresh domestic orange market usually ranges between 80 and 90 percent. A major difference between the Mexican market for oranges and its U.S. counterpart is that in Mexico, most oranges are sold in bulk and are home-squeezed to obtain orange juice. Consumption of processed orange juice or any other processed citrus juice in Mexico is negligible. Processors based their production on international markets, and processed utilization depends on international prices. Since the international price has been low in recent years, many processing plants in Mexico have stopped operating and only few remain in operation. The main product produced by processors is the frozen concentrate orange juice (FCOJ). Processing plants compete with the fresh domestic market for the supply of fruit. Since the fresh market represents a better price for producers, processing plants are supplied only after the fresh market is satisfied.

Land Tenure and Citrus

As a consequence of the revolution of 1917, Mexico enacted one of the strongest land reform laws found in Latin America. As a result, several large tracts of land in private ownership were appropriate by the state and divided among peasant farmers. These collections of small farmers are called *eijidos* and play a prominent role in citrus production in Mexico. In the more humid regions along the east coast of Mexico, a larger proportion of land is in the *eijido* system. Approximately 50 percent of the citrus trees found in Veracruz are in *eijidos* (Mondragon *et al.* 1998). A similar percentage is found in the state of San Luis Potosi.

The implications of the strength of the *eijido* system in citrus production Mexico is that citrus growers in Mexico are typically much smaller compared to their counterparts in other major citrus producing countries. Even though the land tenure system in Mexico was modified in 1992 as a result of the Reform of the Land Reform, citrus production remains highly fragmented, with limits on individual land ownership. Hence, Mexico citrus growers often lack technological know how and access to capital. As a consequence, fruit yields in Mexico are low compared to other major citrus producing countries and fruit quality is often below international market standards.

Another consequence of the fragmented ownership structure is that the marketing system for oranges in Mexico is primitive compared to other major citrus producing regions. Fruit brokers, called coyotes, dominate the first sale of oranges. These coyotes, in turn, sell fruit to other coyotes and wholesalers. Eventually, the allocation between fresh and processed utilization is established. It may be several days, however, before the fruit is ultimately presented for sale in the fresh market or sent to the processing plant. As a result, juice yields are often low and juice quality is adversely affected.

International Markets

Mexico has signed nine trade agreements with different countries all over the world. These trade agreements represents an opportunity for citrus production in Mexico, but they also entail a series of challenges for the citrus industry. Among the most important trade agreements signed are NAFTA, The European Union Trade Agreement (Garcia-Chavez *et al.* 2004) and more recently, the agreement with Israel that allows Mexico unlimited exports of fresh oranges and FCOJ. The resulting impact of these trade agreements is uncertain for the future of the Mexican citrus industry. Given that Mexico is afforded preferential access to the United States market under NAFTA, an extension of the North American free trade zone to the entire Western Hemisphere as proposed in the Free Trade of the Americas, would adversely affect its fledging processing industry. With its proximity to the United States, however, Mexico does possess major advantages in the export of fresh fruit and high transportation cost products such as not-from-concentrate citrus juices.

REFERENCES

ATTAWAY, J. A. 1999. Hurricanes and Florida Agriculture. Florida Science Source, Longboat Key, FL.

GARCIA-CHAVEZ, L. R., GREENE, G., SPREEN, T. H., SANO, D. and ANDREW, C. O. 2004. Transitions in the Mexican Sugar Industry: An Analysis of the Production and Marketing Systems. Florida Science Source, Longboat Key, FL.

INEGI (Instituto Nacional de Estadística, Geografia e Informatica). 2002. Anuario Estadistico Aguascalientes, Mexico.

MONDRAGON, J. P., SPREEN, T. H., ANDREW, C. O. and MURARO, R. P. 1998. Oranges in Eastern Mexico: An Economic Analysis of Production and Marketing Channels. Florida Science Source, Lake Alfred, FL.

ROY, M., ANDREW, C. O. and SPREEN, T. H. 1996. Persian Limes in North America: An Economic Analysis of Production and Marketing Channels. Florida Science Source, Lake Alfred, FL.

USDA/ERS (United States Department of Agriculture/Economics Research Service). 2003. Fruit and Tree Nuts, 2002 Annual Summary. Washington, DC.

USDA/FAS (United States Department of Agriculture/Foreign Agricultural Service). 2003. "Citrus Annual Report." Mexico City: U.S. Embassy, various issues.

Japan

Isao Iwagaki

Most citrus orchards in Japan are located not far from the coast in southwestern Japan, between north latitudes 30 and 35 degrees, on slopes of up to 300 m where cold air does not linger in winter and drainage is good during the humid season. Satsuma mandarins make up 65% of all Japanese citrus production followed by Iyokan, Natsudaidai, Hassaku, Ponkan, and various other old and new varieties. Ninety-five percent of Japanese citrus trees are grafted on trifoliate orange, the rest on Yuzu, Sunki, and other rootstocks. Shiikuwasha and Flying Dragon are rootstocks used experimentally. Independent citrus growers have farms or orchards of 1.0 to 3.0 ha and grow table fruit for the domestic market. Citrus production figures for 1999 and 2000 are given in Table 6.4, and the production areas are shown in Fig. 6.5.

Production Trends

In the latter half of the 1970s, Japan produced about 4 million tons of citrus; 3.5 million tons of Satsuma mandarin as well as 300 thousand tons of Natsudaidai and the other varieties. Since then, Satsuma and Natsudaidai production has steadily decreased. There were increases in the production of Iyokan, Hassaku, and navel oranges in the 1980s, but in the last 10 years the production of these fruits also has decreased. During the past 20 years, the Japanese position in the world production of citrus has dropped from one of the first three to last of the first ten countries.

Interestingly, the production of such other varieties as Ponkan, Tankan, Kiyomi, Shiranuhi, some acid citrus fruits, has increased yearly although the total quantity is not large (15% of national production) (Fig. 6.6).

TABLE 6.4. Citrus Production in Japan: Averages for 1999 and 2000

Common name	Scientific name	Production (1000 ton)	Major production areas (Prefecture)
Wase Satsuma	*C. unshiu* Marc. var Praecox Tanaka	705.3	Ehime, Wakayama, Kumamoto
Common Satsuma	*C. unshiu* Marc.	436.8	Ehime, Shizuoka, Wakayama
Iyokan (Miyauchi iyo)	*C. iyo* Hort. ex. Tanama	188.4	Ehime, Wakayama, Saga
Natsudaidai (Amanatsu)	*C. natsudaidai* Hayata	84.5	Kumamoto, Ehime, Kagoshima
Hassaku	*C. hassaku* Hort. ex. Tanaka	67.1	Wakayama, Hiroshima, Ehime
Navel orange	*C. sinensis* Osb.	19.1	Wakayama, Hiroshima, Shizuoka
Ponkan[a]	*C. reticulata* Blanco	37.9	Kagoshima, Ehime, Kumamoto
Shiranuhu[a]	Kiyomi × Ponkan	19.8	Kumamoto, Ehime, Hiroshima
Kiyomi[a]	Wase Satsuma × Trovita orange	16.8	Ehime, Wakayama, Kumamoto
Yuzu (acid fruit)[a]	*C. junos* Sieb. ex. Tanaka	16.9	Kochi, Tokushima, Ehime
Total		1592.6	

Source: Ministry of Agriculture, Forestry and Fisheries.
[a]Average for 1998 and 1999

Various explanations have been offered to account for the current state of Japanese citrus production and consumption trends. Sales of Satsuma mandarin and the other leading varieties have suffered a severe blow due to imports of citrus fruit. Japan imports about 500 thousand tons of oranges, lemons, and grapefruit every year, and there are no restrictions on citrus juice importation. Moreover, Japanese consumers no longer must depend on a limited number of commodities because dietary habits have become diversified. Citrus fruits now compete with citrus juices, other tree fruit, strawberries, melons, and snacks and cakes of various kinds, as well as soft drinks. Consumers are unwilling to purchase large packages of citrus fruit and dislike the labor of peeling and clearing away the peels and segment membranes. This is especially true of the younger generations.

VARIETIES AND CULTIVARS

Satsumas

Traditionally, Satsuma mandarin's many cultivars have been divided into two varieties; Wase Satsuma (matures October to November) and Common Satsuma (matures November to December). A new classification proposed

Fig. 6.5. Major citrus producing prefectures and big cities (●) in southwestern Japan.

for the convenience of growers giving the corresponding cultivars is shown in Table 6.5.

The growth of very early wase Satsuma trees is weak, but the use of a vigorous rootstock is not attractive because fruit with a low sugar content generally is the result. Aoshima, a late season Satsuma, is the leading cultivar in Shizuoka Prefecture. It produces high quality fruit (12-13 °Brix). Trees of Aoshima are vigorous and have a broader canopy than other Satsuma mandarin trees. The very dwarf rootstock Flying Dragon is being tested for Aoshima at some experiment stations and citrus areas.

Iyokan

Iyokan apparently is a tangor. Its fruit is medium-large (200-300 g), easily peeled, and very fragrant. Its segment membrane is not as thick as that of Natsudaidai or Hassaku. An early maturing mutant, Miyauchi Iyo, was found in 1952, and its planting increased rapidly from 1975 to 1985. The fruit has a thin rind, is seedless and the eating quality is much better than that of the common cultivar. Miyauchi Iyo is picked before January and stored until

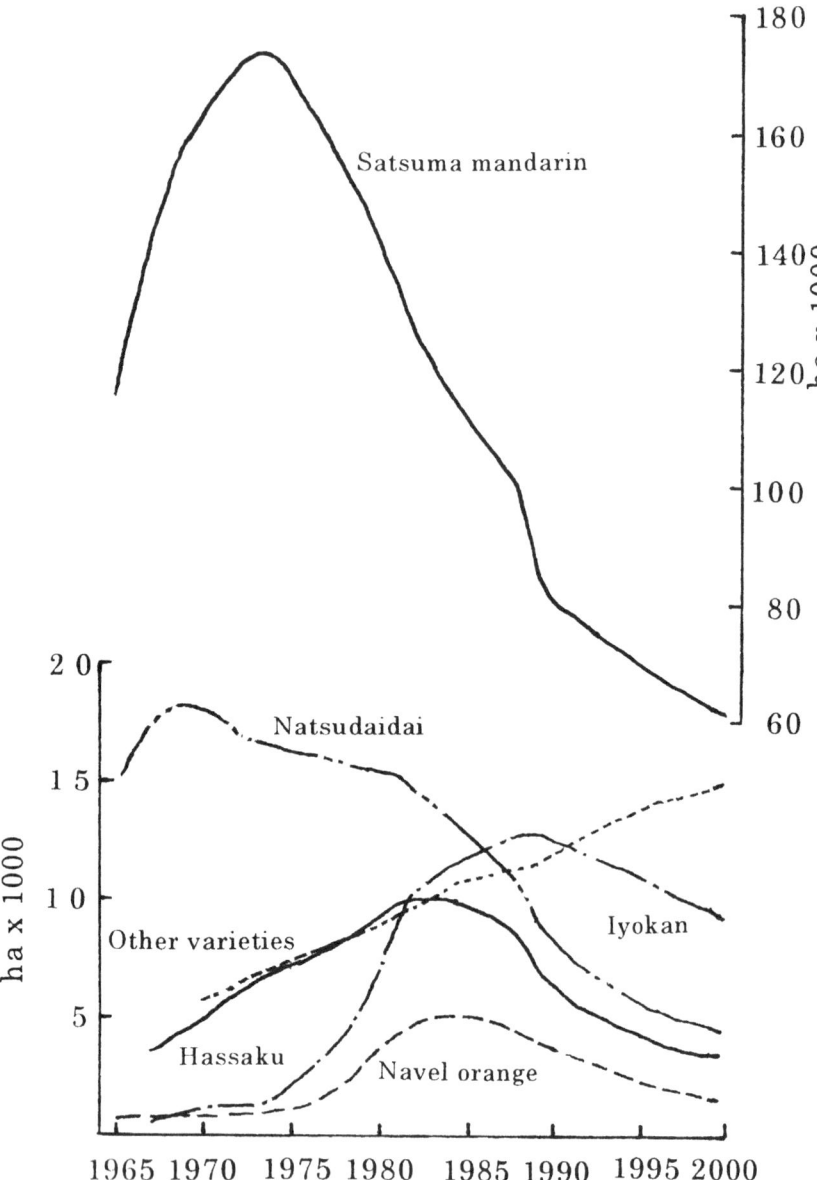

Fig. 6.6. Production area changes of citrus varieties in Japan (1965-2000).

shipment which takes place from December to April, the peak coming in February-March. One defect of this mutant is weak tree vigor. Shiikuwasha is used in Ehime Prefecture as a vigorous rootstock or root for inarching.

TABLE 6.5. Leading Satsuma Mandarin Cultivars and Hectares Farmed in 1999

Varieties	Cultivar classification in order of maturation	Cultivars: hectares
Wase Satsuma	Very early Wase Satsuma	Ueno: 2,678; Nichinan No. 1: 2,450, Miyamoto: 1,601, Iwasaki: 1,319
	Wase Satsuma	Miyagawa: 11,438, Okitsu: 8,043, Haraguchi: 1,027
Common	Mid season Satsuma	Nankan No. 20: 2,194, Mukaiyama: 1,342
Satsuma	Common Satsuma	Otsu No. 4: 2,452, Hayashi: 2,019, Owari: 1,971, Nankan No. 4: 1,783, Sugiyama: 1,734
	Late season Satsuma	Aoshima: 7,116

Source: Ministry of Agriculture, Forestry and Fisheries.

Natsudaidai

Natsudaidai seems to be a hybrid of pummelo and another citrus. Its fruit is large (400-500 g), has a thick rind, 20 to 30 seeds, and is very sour (contains 2-3% acid). An early maturing cultivar that has less than 2% acid was found as limb sport and named Kawano Natsudaidai in 1950. Generally, the less acidic type of Natsudaidai cultivars are termed Amanatsu (sweet Natsudaidai). Kawano Natsudaidai, Beni-Amanatsu (a reddish-rind mutant registered in 1975), and some new cultivars also have been designated Amanatsu. The Brix and acidity of Amanatsu reach 11% and 1.5% from March to April. People use knives to peel the fruit and eat the individual segments.

Hassaku

Hassaku seems to be of pummelo-mandarin parentage, with pummelo predominating. Its fruit is large (350-400 g), has 20 to 30 seeds, a thick rind, and a bitter taste like grapefruit. Unlike grapefruit, the fruit is not juicy, and the segment membrane is thick. Hassaku fruit drops readily at cold temperatures. An abscission layer appears to be easily formed in the fruit stem. The fruit therefore is harvested before the end of December and stored until shipment which takes place from January to May.

Kiyomi

Kiyomi originated from a Miyagawa wase (Satsuma mandarin) × Trovita orange cross made at the Fruit Tree Research Station Okitsu Branch and was registered in 1979. The fruit is oblate and medium large at about 200 g. The flesh is tender and juicy and has a rich orange color and orange-like aroma. The seed is mono embryonic although the fruit usually is seedless.

The Kiyomi tree has moderate vigor and grows upright when young. As it grows, it spreads due to the weight of the fruit, and its slender branches droop. Like Satsuma mandarin, Kiyomi is resistant to cold, as well as being resistant to scab and moderately resistant to canker. Kiyomi production has increased rapidly in the past 10 years from 6,892 tons in 1989 to 18,900 tons in 1999.

Shiranuhi

Shiranuhi (Dekopon) is second generation Kiyomi crossed with Ponkan. The fruit of Shiranuhi and Kiyomi mature in March. Although shape and size may vary, Shiranuhi generally is oval and weighs 250 to 300 g. It frequently has a large collar (Fig. 6.7). The rind is orange, rather rough, and easy to peel. The Shiranuhi fruit accumulates large amounts of soluble solids and has excellent flavor, but sometimes high acid is a problem. Its flesh is deep orange and tender, and the segment membrane is thin. The flower produces little pollen, and the fruit usually is seedless.

Because of lack of vigor, Shiranuhi trees sometimes do not grow well. Good soil conservation and thinning of young fruit therefore are very important practices. Shiranuhi trees often are grown in vinyl greenhouses. Production was 33 tons in 1990 and 21,274 tons in 1999. It outproduced Kiyomi in 1998.

GROWERS

Fruit growing in Japan is very labor intensive as shown in Table 6.6. The average owner-grower has about a 3 ha farm that includes a 1.5 ha Satsuma mandarin orchard. He produces 31.4 tons of Satsumas per hectare. Depending on conditions (e.g., location of the orchard, soil, climate, and skill of the grower) it is possible to produce 45 tons of Satsumas per hectare annually. Nationwide, per hectare Satsuma mandarin production based on total Japanese production divided by the total bearing area, averaged 23.9 ton/ha in 1989 and1990 and 21.9 ton/ha in 1999 and 2000.

There is no single explanation as to how individual growers with such a small establishment are able to support their families. They may produce vinyl house Satsumas or premium fruit, such as Shiranuhi, for sale in fancy fruit shops. Little outside labor is used, co-operators being family members or relatives. They may be part-time growers who receive money from other employment. Government support of agriculture also provides considerable financial help to individual owner-growers.

The biggest socioeconomic problem is the aging of Japanese agriculturists and lack of next generation successors. About 80% of the owner-growers are more than sixty years old. Younger agriculturists need to be educated as to the importance and attractiveness of fruit growing. Additionally, projects to reconstruct present hilly orchards into large flat ones that will cut down on labor and permit mechanized citriculture are being implemented (Fig. 6.8).

Fig. 6.7. Shiranuhi (Dekopon), A hybrid of Kiyomi and Ponkan with typical large collar.

TECHNIQUES FOR PRODUCING QUALITY FRUIT

Mulching

In summer, sugar begins to accumulate in the juice of the Satsuma mandarin fruit. The percentage of sucrose in the total sugar increases from September up to harvest. Citric acid, the main acid in the fruit, rapidly decreases after September.

Various techniques which subject roots to water stress during the period of active sugar accumulation are used to increase sugar distribution in the fruit. Of these, mulching is the most effective and practical. Drying the soil by covering it with impermeable vinyl or polyethylene film has been a common practice. New mulching materials, porous mulches, first were tested in mandarin orchards in 1989. Polyethylene nonwoven fabric with numerous micro holes, through which water vapor can pass but rainwater can not is one such mulch. After mulching, the soil dries out gradually. A white, polyethylene, nonwoven porous fabric, Tybec, has become increasingly popular over the past 10 years. Its use increases the Brix and improves the color of the rind. Solar radiation reflected off the surface of this white mulch reaches the inside of the tree canopy as diffused light.

There may be little air exchange in the soil if impermeable mulch is applied over a wide area. When porous mulch is used, there is no oxygen

TABLE 6.6. Working Hours of an Average Farm Household that Mainly Grows Satsuma Mandarin (1999)

Operation	Hours/hectare
Pruning and training	200.1
Weeding and cultivation	162.8
Young fruit thinning	365.3
Disease and pest control	187.2
Harvesting and processing	621.1
Other	287.9
Shipping labor	235.5
Total	2059.9

Source: Ministry of Agriculture, Forestry and Fisheries.

deficiency problem. In the event of sudden heavy rain, drainage must be provided for collected rain water. The timing of fertilizer applications is a considerable problem because of the long mulching period during the summer and autumn months. Prior mulching, fertilization, and the installation of an under mulch drip irrigation system are recommended. In 2001, in Ehime Prefecture about 10% of the Satsuma mandarin orchards used porous mulch.

Ethychlozate

Foliar applications of ethychlozate (ethyl 5-chloro-1H-3-indazolyl-acetate) are used to thin out young fruit, accelerate maturity, and prevent fruit from developing a puffy rind. This compound belongs to the plant growth regulator auxin group that includes naphthaleneacetic acid (NAA); the main fruit-thinning agent before the registration of ethychlozate. The main reason why ethychlozate causes fruit to drop is that the ethylene evolved in response to stimulation by the agent causes the development of an abscission layer. The compound ethephon, which causes the greatest ethylene evolution, has a very marked effect on fruit drop. NAA is second in ethylene production. Of these three chemicals, ethychlozate evolves the least amount of ethylene, but its effects last for a longer period (a week). These characteristics account for the mild effect of ethychlozate when used as a thinning agent.

Ethychlozate has been registered for various purposes, but mainly it is used to accelerate maturation. To do this, 67-100 ppm ethychlozate should be applied twice; the first application at 50-60 days, the second at 70-80 days after full bloom. Ethychlozate applications advance rind coloring by 5-10 days, and fruit with 0.5-1.0 higher Brix can be expected. This accelerator has negligible effects on the citric acid concentration.

Fig. 6.8. A steep, complicated hilly area leveled by mechanized means to develop a flat orchard of about 140 ha in Shimizu, Shizuoka prefecture. Tybec mulch is popular in this area.

Satsuma Mandarin in Vinyl Greenhouses

The culture of wase Satsuma in heated vinyl greenhouses started in 1970. The main objective of growing this variety in a vinyl greenhouse is to ensure market competitiveness by early shipping of a high quality product. Production of greenhouse Satsuma has increased over the years, the largest harvest being 70,800 tons in 1993. Since then production has decreased gradually to 62,300 tons in 2000 because the selling price is not as attractive as before.

Very early wase Satsumas and wase Satsumas are cultivated in vinyl greenhouses. Miyagawa, one of the most popular wase Satsuma cultivars, is a leader because of its high fruit quality and because, compared with other cultivars, growth is easily managed under vinyl greenhouse conditions.

Two main cultivation systems are used in growing Satsuma mandarin in vinyl greenhouses; early shipping and late shipping types. For early shipping, heating is started in early December, and the fruit is harvested before the end of July. Trees are pruned immediately after harvesting, and the summer-cycle shoots which sprout thereafter bear fruit during the next season. This also is called the early heating cultivation type or summer fruiting-shoot type. For the late shipping type, heating is begun in January, and the fruit harvested from August to early October. Pruning is done immediately before the vinyl covering is put up or heating begun. Spring-cycle vegetative shoots, which sprout after heating, bear fruit the next season. This also is called the standard heating cultivation type or spring fruiting-shoot type.

REFERENCES

IWAGAKI, I. 1991. The citrus industry in Japan. Chronica Hort. 31, 49-50.
IWAGAKI, I. 1997. Citrus production in Japan: New trends in technology. Food & Fertilizer Technology Center, Taipei, Ext. Bull. 440, 1-11.
MINISTRY OF AGRICULTURE, FORESTRY AND FISHERIES, 1998-2000 Annual Reports.
MUKAI, T. and KADOYA, K. 1994. Fruit trees: Citrus, pp. 14-22. *In* Horticulture in Japan. Asakura, Tokyo.

Israel

Ron Porat and Mena Davidson

HISTORICAL BACKGROUND

Cultivation of citrus fruits in Israel dates back to ancient times. Historical reports indicate the cultivation of ethrogs (*Citrus medica* Linn) for Jewish religious purposes as early as 136 B.C.E., lemons in the eleventh century C.E. and oranges in the fourteenth century. However, commercial production began in 1832, with exports at an annual rate of 500,000 boxes (40 kg each) and increased to 1.5 million boxes in 1913.

Since the late 1920s and following the establishment of the modern State of Israel in 1948, the citrus industry became one of the most important economical sectors, and fresh citrus fruits formed the new country's largest exporting products commodity. However, following the industrial development during the early 1980s the importance of the citrus industry in the Israeli economy has markedly declined. Nowadays, fresh citrus fruits form 20% of the total amount of agricultural exports from the State of Israel and provide 2% of its total income from exports.

GEOGRAPHICAL DISTRIBUTION

Israel is located on the east coast the Mediterranean Sea and has a subtropical climate, optimal for citrus growing. Traditionally, most of the citrus groves in Israel were planted in the warm and humid areas of the central coastal plain; for example, in the 1930s 85% of the citrus orchards in Israel were located in this region. However, because of the rapid urbanization and industrial development of the coastal area, many of the new plantations in the last 15 years were established in new regions of the country, especially in the dry and sandy southern areas and in the hot inland valleys (Fig. 6.9). In 2002, only 47% of the citrus-growing area remained near the coast, with 35% in the south and 15% in the inland valleys (Fig. 6.9). The massive transfer of citrus groves from the crowded central plain to the unsettled flat desert lands in the south allowed the planting of large groves, suitable for modern mechanization, and was therefore characterized by a major change from small groves belonging to private farmers, to large commercial groves owned by farming cooperatives. In fact, it appeared that the yield and quality of the fruit grown in the dry south region were just as good as those of the fruit grown in the humid coastal area, and the trees and fruit suffered much less from pathological diseases, such as *Alternaria citri*.

PRODUCTION TRENDS

Following the establishment of the State of Israel in 1948, a great boost was initiated in the development of the citrus industry, which brought a significant rise in the production rates, to 530,000 tons in 1960 and a peak of 1,700,000 tons in 1970 (Fig. 6.10). These high production rates continued till 1980, but then, for a variety of reasons, such as lower profits to the grower because of a lower value of European Currencies as compared with US$, expensive labor costs, rapid urbanization of the central coastal plan and the aging of the trees that were not replanted, all together brought to lower yield production and led to deterioration in quality and in fruit size. Therefore, citrus production rates in Israel gradually declined to 1,010,000 tons in 1990 (Fig. 6.10). During the last 10 years, other problems, such as shortage of irrigation water and the increased cost of labor, have led to a further reduction in citrus production, to only 703,000 tons in 2000 (Fig. 6.10).

Till the 1970s Shamouti oranges were by far the most common citrus cultivar grown in Israel, and accounted for about half of the total production. However, because of a gradual decrease in its yields and the development of new attractive citrus varieties, Shamouti became less profitable to the growers, and nowdays all orange varieties together (Shamouti, Navel, Valencia) form only 34% of the total citrus yield (Table 6.7). Other citrus cultivars, such as grapefruit, easy peelers, lemons and exotics provide 50, 13, 2 and 1%, respectively, of the total citrus output (Table 6.7). It should be noted that since the 1970s Israel has become an important producer of grapefruit for both the European and Far East markets. In the last few years, however, many of the new orchards have been planted with new easy-peeling varieties, especially Or and Mor, which are new locally bred products, therefore, a significant increase in the production of mandarins is expected to take place in the near future.

Region	Citrus area (% of total)
1. Coastal area	47
2. Northern coast	3
3. Inland valleys	15
4. South	35

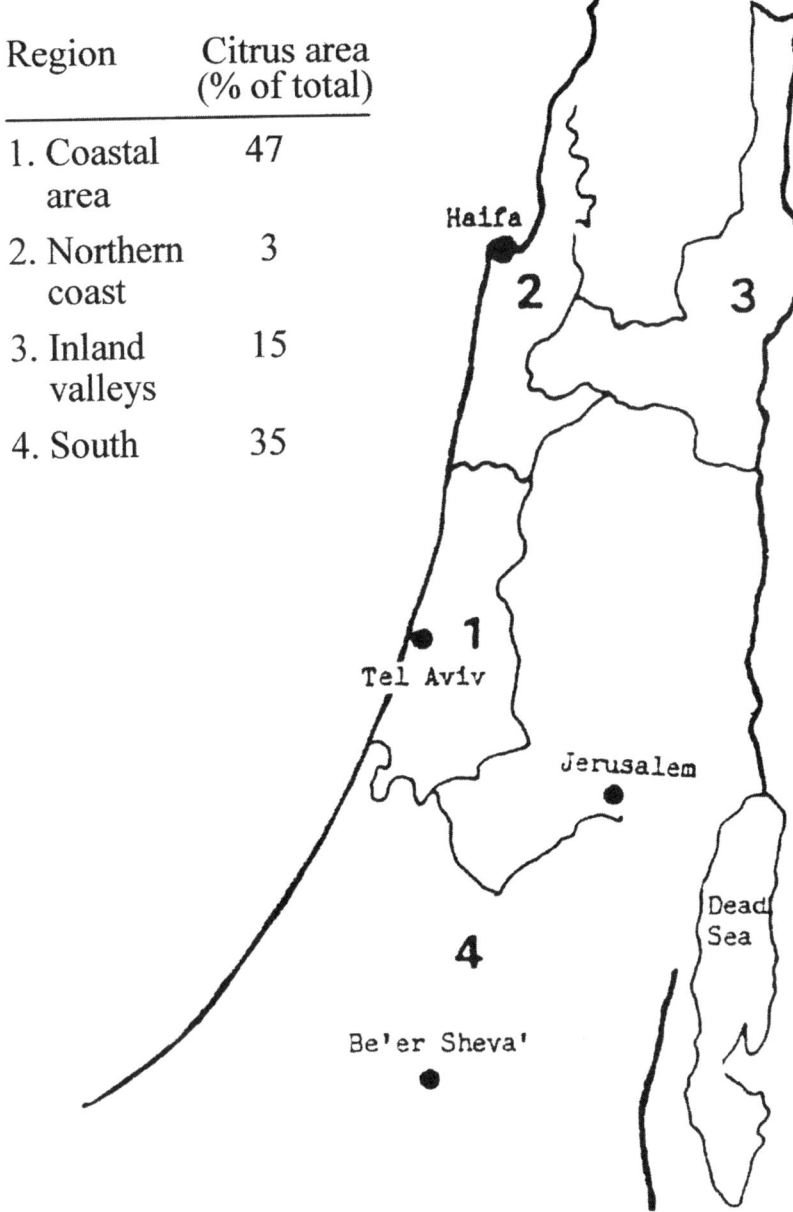

Fig. 6.9. Distribution of the citrus-growing areas in Israel in 2002.
Source: Israel Citrus Marketing Board.

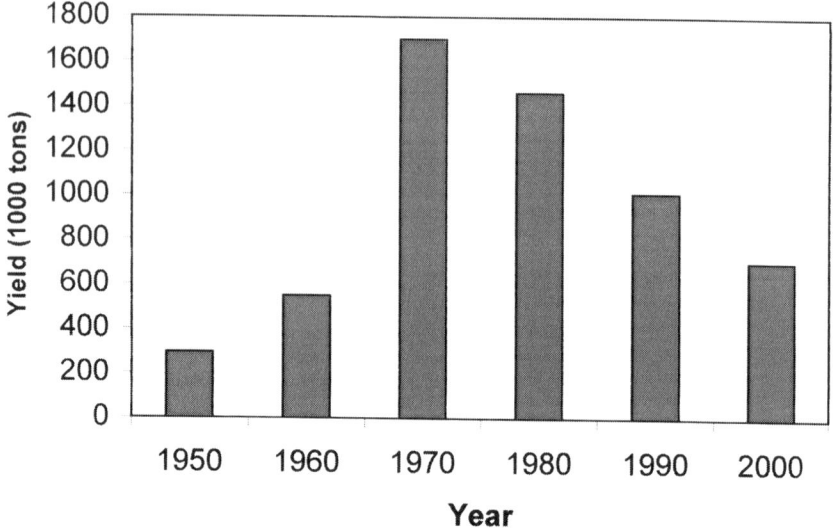

Fig. 6.10. Total production of citrus fruits in Israel during the years 1950 till 2000. *Source: Israel Citrus Marketing Board.*

The utilization of citrus crops in Israel is summarized in Table 6.7, and it can be seen that about one third of the production of oranges, grapefruit and mandarins is destined for export. Another third of the oranges and mandarins and two-thirds of the grapefruit are used for processing by local products companies, and the rest are sold for local fresh fruit consumption (Table 6.7).

EXPORT AND MARKETING

In general, the citrus industry in Israel is export oriented. For many years almost all of the exports were destined for Western Europe, especially to the UK, Scandinavia, Germany, France, and Benelux. For example, just 10 years ago, in 1992, 93% of all the citrus fruit exported from Israel was shipped to Western Europe. However, because of significant competition from other countries, such as Spain and Morocco, in the European market, many efforts have been made in recent years to direct the exports to other, new markets. Figure 6.11 shows the distribution of the exports of citrus fruit from Israel to various destinations around the world in 2001. It can be seen that most of the exports (74%) were still oriented towards Western Europe. However, other markets have also been developed, and 18% of the Israeli citrus crops, especially grapefruit and Oroblanco (Sweetie), are currently shipped to the Far East (Japan, Hong Kong, Singapore and Korea), another

TABLE 6.7. Utilization of the Major Citrus Crops in Israel during 2001

Type	Total yield (1,000 tons)	% of total production		
		Export	Processing	Local Market
Oranges	218	33	39	28
Grapefruit	316	30	64	6
Mandarins	81	37	32	31
Lemons	16	0	6	94
Exotics	8	62	0	38
Total	637	20	50	30

Source: Israel Citrus Marketing Board.

7% are shipped to Eastern Europe and 1% to America (Fig. 6.11). All of these fruit are marketed under the Jaffa brand that is known for its high quality perception and gives Israeli citrus premium.

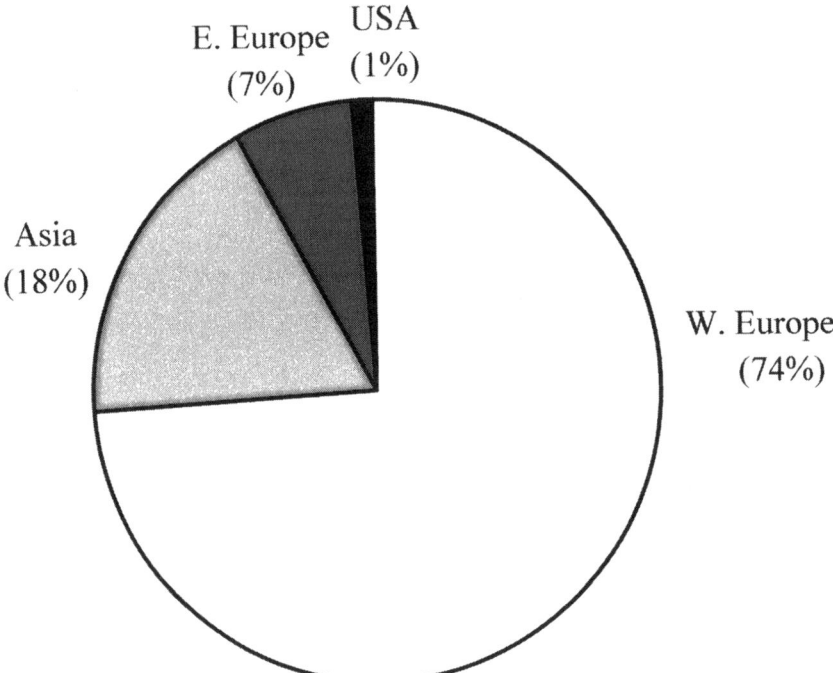

Fig. 6.11. Distribution of the exports of citrus fruit from Israel to various destinations around the world in 2001.
Source: Israel Citrus Marketing Board.

CURRENT STATUS AND FUTURE PERSPECTIVES

Currently, the citrus industry in Israel is undergoing some major changes and is facing some critical decisions. First; because of the rapid urbanization in the central coastal plain, many of the old citrus groves that were planted there have been displaced, and new plantations have been established in the periphery. This activity has enabled the choice of varieties to be changed and the production of new, attractive and promising easy-peeling varieties to be increased. Second, Israeli agriculture is now suffering from a severe shortage of irrigation water and, therefore, the entire citrus industry is now undergoing a massive transition towards irrigation with purified recycled water. Already about half of the citrus groves are irrigated with recycled water, and this trend will probably continue. Third; because of the current political crisis with the Palestinian Authority, the citrus industry in Israel is suffering from shortage of workers, which has led to a significant increase in labor costs. Hopefully, solution of this crisis in the near future will allow many Palestinian workers to come back and work in Israel.

In light of these adjustments, we consider that in the near future the citrus industry in Israel will stabilize itself at around 20,000 hectares with a predicted production rate of 800,000 tons per year. Of this amount, 300,000 tons will be destined for export, 300,000 tons will be processed and 200,000 tons will go to the local fresh fruit market. Overall, production will comprise more or less 30% oranges, 30% grapefruits, 30% mandarins and 10% lemons and exotic fruits.

REFERENCES

AARONSON, A. 1914. The world's production of citrus fruit (in Hebrew). Bull. Jewish Agr. Exp. Stn. 1.

CHORIN, Y. 1963. Citrus in Israel (in Hebrew). Sifriat Hassadeh Publishing House, Tel Aviv.

ISRAEL CITRUS MARKETING BOARD. Personal communication.

OPPENHEIMER, H. 1968. pp. 401-429. In Encyclopedia Hebraica (in Hebrew). The Encyclopedia Publishing Co., Ltd., Israel.

REGEV, H. and BUCH, E. 1970. The citrus groves in Israel, 1969 (in Hebrew). Spec. Ser. 316. Central Bureau of Statistice, Government of Israel.

6

Part 5

Southern Africa

Graham H. Barry and Etienne Rabe

INTRODUCTION

Southern Africa ranks only 13th in world citrus production, producing about 1.53 million tons of citrus (or 1.5% of world citrus production) in 2001. Yet, Southern Africa is the third largest exporter of fresh citrus in the world after Spain and the United States of America (FAO 2001). If total US export production is subdivided by state, then Southern Africa ranks second to Spain as an exporting region. Citrus production in Southern Africa has a strong fresh fruit export imperative; approximately 60% of the crop is exported, 30% processed and 10% consumed locally (CIAMD 2001). Income from exports exceeds 92% of total citrus income. The Southern African citrus-producing region (Fig. 6.12) comprises four countries, viz. South Africa (93% of total production in the region), Swaziland (5%), Zimbabwe (1%), and Moçambique (Mocambique) (<1%) (Barry 1996; CIAMD 2001). The citrus industry is the largest horticultural industry in South Africa in volume, and the second largest agricultural industry in value after the deciduous fruit industry. Over 20 million citrus trees or 58,000 hectares of citrus are currently planted in Southern Africa (Rabe 2001).

Due to a broad climatic range, from semi-tropical to Mediterranean, a diverse range of citrus cultivars are produced from late February/early March through late September/mid October. The Southern African citrus production region comprises six main producing regions, which are further sub-divided into 40 sub-regions.

Previously, citrus marketing in South Africa was under the auspices of a statutory marketing board that appointed the South African Co-operative

Fig. 6.12. Citrus production regions of Southern Africa (Barry 1996).

Citrus Exchange as the sole exporter in a single-channel, co-operative marketing system. The neighboring citrus-producing countries, Swaziland, Zimbabwe and Moçambique, voluntarily participated with the South African Co-operative Citrus Exchange. However, in 1998, the South African citrus industry was liberalized, allowing for the so-called de-regulation of the industry and the implementation of free-market principles, and the appointment of more than one export agent. By 2002, there were in excess of 100 registered citrus exporters in South Africa.

HISTORICAL PERSPECTIVE OF CITRUS PRODUCTION IN SOUTHERN AFRICA

The first citrus trees planted in South Africa were introduced to the Cape of Good Hope (present day Cape Town) from St. Helena Island in 1654 (Cartwright 1977), and were referred to as the St. Helena orange trees. On 25 July 1661, seven years later, the seedling orange and lemon trees produced their first fruit. The entry in the Journal of Jan van Riebeeck, the Commander of the Cape of Good Hope, reads:

This afternoon the Commander Riebeeck and his wife picked the first two lemons off a young tree growing in the Company's garden.

They were a fine yellow colour and of the large St. Helena type. It was one of the young trees which we had caused to be brought from the island some time ago and it is to be hoped that more trees will soon begin to bear.

Therefore, Commander van Riebeeck must be recognized as the founder of the South African citrus industry with 1,162 young orange, lemon and shaddock trees planted by 1661. South Africa's first citrus orchards were, therefore, planted more than 100 years before those in California where citrus fruit were first grown in San Diego in 1769 (Cartwright 1977). But California and Florida, serving a vast market in the northern states of the USA were soon to be nearly 100 years ahead of every country in the world where oranges were cultivated, even the fruit merchants of Europe, Portugal and Spain.

In South Africa the rise of the citrus industry was slow. It was almost 300 years before it was realized that it might be possible to ship oranges to cities 10,000 km away. Since the first orange trees were planted at the southernmost tip of Africa, the citrus industry has proliferated until today where there are 58,000 hectares planted, and the export of citrus has grown from 3,000 cases of oranges in 1907 to more than 58 million 15 kg-cartons of citrus in 2001, making South Africa and its neighboring territories the third largest exporter of citrus in the world.

The St. Helena orange trees were the ancestors of all the citrus trees that eventually spread through Southern Africa from the Cape to beyond the Limpopo River. There is no record of the importation of any other citrus seedlings or budwood from any source whatsoever until 1850 when Navel orange budwood was imported from Bahia, Brazil, and grafted by Mr. W. Tuck of Grahamstown (Cartwright 1977). In the early 20th century many new varieties were introduced from California, including Washington Navel and Valencia Late oranges.

In the early days of citrus marketing, virtually every citrus grower in South Africa had his own, registered, brand name for his fruit. These brands appeared on every box of fruit they sold. Some of the names were very well known on the London market. However, with the growth of the co-operative movement among the citrus growers and the rise of the Co-operative Citrus Exchange Company, it was eventually decided that all South African export fruit should be sold under one name only. The name chosen was "OUTSPAN", the brand name of Amanzi Estates. Mrs. Cecily Niven, daughter of Sir Percy Fitz-Patrick, and her husband Jack Niven, generously agreed to make the name available to the Exchange. Thereafter all other brand names fell into disuse until deregulation of the South African citrus industry in the late 1990s. Outspan is a word used in southern Africa at the time to describe a welcome halt in the course of a long wagon journey when the oxen had the yokes lifted from their necks and went off to the nearby water to drink. The verb means to unyoke, the noun a resting-place for travelers and draft animals (Cartwright 1977).

CURRENT PERSPECTIVE AND PRODUCTION TRENDS

Total citrus production decreased slightly from 700,000 tons in 1975 to 650,000 tons 10 years later. In the late 1980s production increased to between 800,000 and 850,000 tons, remaining at that level until 1994 when total production reached 930,000 tons, and exceeded 1 million tons in 1995. Since then production has continued to increase at more than 50,000 tons per annum, and production is expected to exceed 1.6 million tons by 2002 (Fig. 6.13) (CIAMD 2001; FAO 2001). Current production (2001) of 1.53 million tons was produced from about 35,000 hectares of mature bearing trees, giving an average yield in excess of 40 tons per hectare.

The trend of increased production over the past 25 years has been due to astonishingly rapid developments of new citrus orchards. The planting rate during the early 1980s was about 700,000 trees per annum. In the mid 1980s the planting rate increased to more than 1 million trees per annum

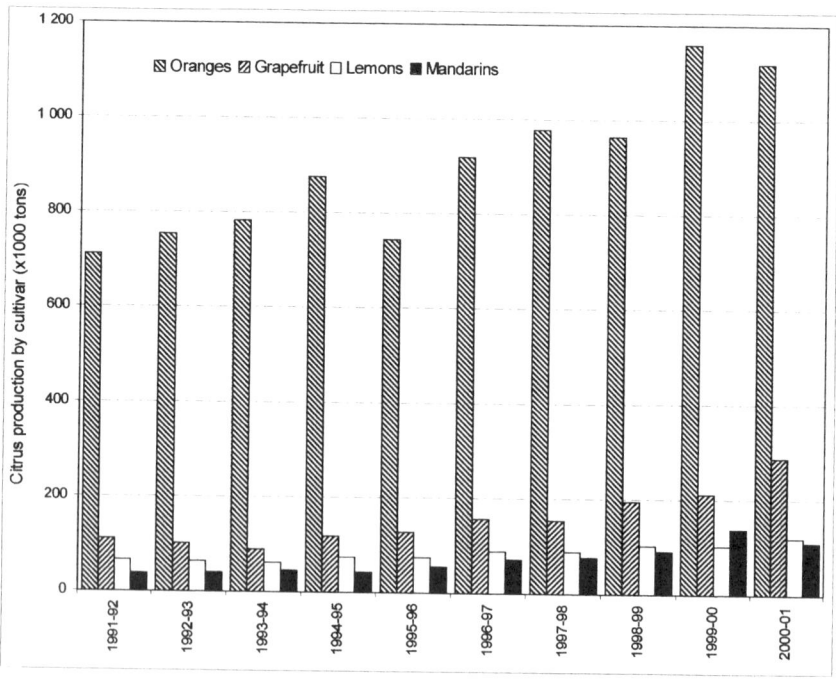

Fig. 6.13. Citrus production trends in Southern Africa by variety group over the past 14 years (CGA 2005; FAO 2005).

(≈2,600 hectares p.a.) (Barry *et al.* 1996). These planting trends can be explained by a severe drought followed by improved agricultural conditions; the devaluation of the local currency against that of South Africa's major trading partners, dramatically favoring export industries; the availability of virus-free, superior budlines from the Citrus Improvement Programme (CIP); and new, sought-after cultivars became available, e.g., Star Ruby grapefruit, Clementine mandarin, Delta Valencia and Midknight Valencia oranges. During the mid 1990s, the northern production region experienced a severe drought, old orchards were removed, and after the drought of the mid 1990s there was a tremendous planting boom; nearly 30 million buds were supplied to commercial citrus nurseries via the CIP from 1993 to 2001 (Du Toit 2002). This budwood supply translates into about 32,000 hectares planted or to be planted between 1994 and 2002 with peak plantings in 1998 (6,500 hectares), followed by a dramatic decline by 2001 (2,200 hectares) (Rabe 2001). During the past several years, Navel, Delta Valencia, Midknight Valencia, and Turkey Valencia oranges, Star Ruby grapefruit, Clementine mandarin, and lemons were the main cultivars planted.

CULTIVAR PORTFOLIO

The cultivar range in Southern Africa is composed of 70% sweet oranges (42% Valencia oranges, 26% Navel oranges and 2% midseason oranges), 16% grapefruit (7% white, 1% pink, 8% red), 7% mandarins (2% Satsuma mandarin, 4% Clementine mandarin, 1% others), and 7% lemons (almost exclusively Eureka lemon) (Barry *et al.* 1996; CIAMD 2001). The greatest growth in the 1990s was in Star Ruby grapefruit, Midknight Valencia and Delta Valencia oranges, and Satsuma and Clementine mandarins. In the late 1990s and early 2000s there was, in general, a planting slump mainly due to poor market performance, whereafter Turkey Valencia, Cara Cara Navel orange, and late-maturing mandarins were the main cultivars planted.

Numerous locally developed cultivars have attained commercial importance in Southern Africa. The development of these cultivars has been primarily through the discovery of chance mutations in orchards and as nucellar lines, rather than from an active breeding program.

The maturity periods of the various cultivars produced vary according to production region, but, in general, citrus is exported from Southern Africa from March through October (Fig. 6.14).

1. *Oranges.* Valencia oranges, including Delta Valencia and Midknight Valencia, and Navel oranges, primarily dominate the Southern African citrus industry. Navel orange production contributes 26% to the total citrus crop in Southern Africa. The commercial cultivars produced are Navelina, Palmer (a local nucellar Navel orange selection), Bahianinha, Washington, Robyn® (a local late-maturing selection), and Lane Late. Promising re-

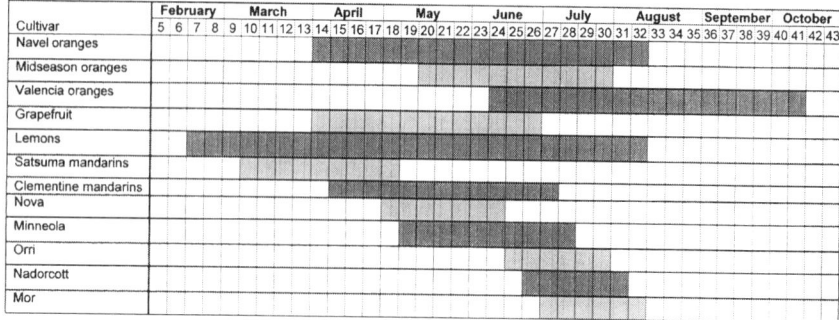

Fig. 6.14. Approximate maturity periods of citrus cultivars produced in Southern Africa.

cently developed local late-maturing selections include Royal Late Navel®, Cambria Navel® and Witkrans Navel®. There is also considerable grower interest in Cara Cara (red-fleshed) Navel and the late-maturing Australian selections, such as Autumn Gold®, Barnfield®, Summer Gold®, Powell® and Chislett®, amongst others.

Midseason oranges contribute approximately 2% to the total citrus crop. The main commercial cultivars are Tomango (>50% of midseason oranges), Clanor (≈30%) and Shamouti (≈10%). Tomango and Clanor are locally developed oranges. Semi-commercial cultivars produced are Seville, Moro, Tarocco and Salustiana oranges.

Valencia orange is the principle citrus cultivar group produced in Southern Africa, contributing 42% to the total citrus crop. Historically, seeded Valencia selections were primarily produced (52% of Valencia oranges), e.g. Valencia Late, Olinda, Du Roi, Amanzi and McClean (the latter two being local nucellar selections). However, the trend has shifted to two locally-selected seedless selections in the past 15 years, e.g. Delta (25% of Valencia oranges) and Midknight (<20% of Valencia oranges). More recently, the availability of new Plant Breeders' Rights (PBR) protected, locally developed, earlier-maturing selections, such as Turkey® and Bennie®, has maintained interest in planting Valencia oranges in the hot production regions of Southern Africa.

2. *Grapefruit and shaddocks (pummelos)*. Grapefruit contribute 16% to total citrus production. The commercial grapefruit cultivars are separated into three groups, viz. i) white-fleshed (46%): Marsh and Nartia, ii) pink-fleshed (5%): Redblush, and iii) red-fleshed (49%): Star Ruby. Semi-commercial cultivars include Ray Ruby and Henderson (pink), and Nelruby® and Rio Red (red). In recent years, market share has dramatically shifted from Marsh to Star Ruby; white-fleshed grapefruit had a stormy ride in the late 1990s and early 2000s, whereas pink-fleshed grapefruit have largely been replaced by the deeply pigmented cultivars, particularly Star Ruby. Star Ruby

grapefruit has been a success story in Southern Africa; the local nucellar selection was selected from seedlings derived from the Texas Star Ruby, and is superior to the original Star Ruby source. Excellent grower returns led to a planting boom in the late 1980s through mid 1990s. However, the current high production may pose marketing problems and reduced prices in the near future. Nartia is a locally developed selection of Marsh, favored for its apparent lower susceptibility to citrus tristeza virus. Nelruby® is a deeply pigmented cultivar, derived from nucellar Ray Ruby, and performs particularly well under hot, arid and calcareous conditions where Star Ruby is not well-adapted. Recently a naringin-free red cultivar was discovered and will be marketed as Flamingo™.

Production of shaddocks (pummelos) remains low; less than 1,000 tons are produced. The main cultivars produced are Pomelit®, a locally developed pink-fleshed cultivar of exceptional eating quality, and Java, with small-scale production of Oroblanco® and Melogold®, both California-bred cultivars.

3. *Lemons and limes.* Lemons contribute 7% to the total citrus crop. The predominant cultivar planted is Eureka, despite its limited rootstock options, and makes up >95% of total lemon production. Lisbon and Fino lemons have been planted to a lesser extent, especially in replant situations where a wider rootstock choice is possible with these cultivars, and, more recently, Limoneira 8A and Genoa lemons have been planted. In the late 1990s, the Agricultural Research Council-Institute for Tropical and Subtropical Crops' breeding program released a totally seedless lemon cultivar. Eureka Seedless™ lemon is expected to command a major marketing presence in the near future. Bearrs selection of Tahiti (Persian) lime is produced on a small scale under semi- to sub-tropical climatic conditions.

4. *Mandarins.* Satsuma mandarins contribute 2% to total citrus production. A local nucellar selection of Miho Wase is the main commercial cultivar, and Owari contributes a small amount to Satsuma mandarin production. Clementine mandarin contributes 4% to total citrus production. The main commercial cultivars are Nules, Oroval, SRA 63, SRA 92 and Marisol. Recently, Clemenpons®, an early-maturing Nules type, is being planted. Other mandarins contribute 1% to total citrus production. Minneola tangelo, Tambor (= Ortanique™), Thoro Temple, and Nova tangors fall into this group. More recently, later-maturing selections, such as Nadorcott® (= Afourer™) from Morocco, and Mor® and Orri® from Israel, are expected to play an important role in filling the late season market gap.

CITRUS PRODUCTION REGIONS

The Southern African citrus industry is characterized by sheer diversity, where geographical, topographical and resultant climatic diversities exist.

The citrus production regions of Southern Africa range from latitudes 17°S to 34°S (Fig. 6.14), and are closely linked to river valleys where suitable climatic, soil and water conditions occur for citrus production. Elevation has a large influence on the prevailing climatic conditions and hence cultivar choice in each region.

Examples of climatic diversity are the semi-tropical areas of the low-lying eastern seaboard (Zimbabwe, Moçambique, and Limpopo, Mpumalanga and Kwazulu-Natal provinces of South Africa), the higher lying subtropical areas (Nelspruit, Letaba, Zimbabwe middleveld), and the cool coastal areas of the Eastern and Western Cape.

The northern and eastern areas of Southern Africa are all summer rainfall areas, whereas the Western and Southern Cape enjoy a Mediterranean-type climate with winter rainfall. In the Eastern Cape a bimodal rainfall pattern exists with rains mostly occurring in spring and the fall.

A broad climatic range from semi-tropical to Mediterranean-type climates has numerous, distinct advantages resulting in a wide range of cultivars being successfully produced from late February/early March through to late September/mid October. Any natural and/or phytosanitary disaster can also not equally affect all regions, and the supply of fruit from Southern Africa as a whole is thus fairly stable from year to year. However, this diversity also has disadvantages in terms of variability in quality of the same cultivar produced in different areas, and peculiar problems associated with differing cultural practices and management philosophies. The distance from the ports also poses unique logistical problems that result in cost considerations.

Following initial work by Bozalek (1974), the boundaries of the established citrus production regions were defined, not according to specific topographical features such as elevation or climatic factors such as temperature, but rather loosely according to the performance of various cultivars in the areas concerned. The Southern African citrus producing region comprises six main climatic zones or production regions that are further subdivided into 40 sub-regions or commercial production regions.

The main citrus-producing regions are classified according to prevailing climatic differences and are loosely defined according to cultivar adaptation and the performance of the various cultivars in the areas concerned. For example, the hot regions are seen as good grapefruit and Valencia orange producing areas. Similarly, the cool and cold regions produce good quality Navel oranges and mandarins. The summer temperatures of the cool and cold regions can exceed that of the hot regions. The major difference between the regions, distinguishing it as predominantly suited to a specific cultivar, is the night temperatures. An area with relatively high winter and summer night temperature (hot, humid region) produces high quality, thin-rinded grapefruit with low naringin levels. Cool areas with lower summer night temperatures, but high day temperatures with long sunshine hours produce high quality Navel oranges with good sugar and acidity levels.

1. The *hot* production region is split into i) *hot, humid* (<300 meters elevation) and ii) *hot, dry* (300 to 600 meters elevation) regions, and is suitable for the production of high quality grapefruit and Valencia oranges, and to a lesser extent midseason oranges and certain mandarin types such as Minneola tangelo. A small amount of lemons, Tahiti limes and pummelos are also produced in this region. Approximately half of the total citrus crop is produced in the hot, humid and hot, dry production regions. Two-thirds of the Valencia oranges and virtually all the grapefruit are produced in the hot production areas. These areas are relatively low-lying and occur on the eastern seaboard of Southern Africa in southern Zimbabwe, southern Moçambique, and Limpopo, Mpumalanga and Kwazulu-Natal provinces of South Africa.

2. The *intermediate* production region is so-called because it falls between the hot, low-lying areas and cool, high-lying areas, i.e. between 600 and 900 meters elevation, and the consequent effect on temperature and, therefore, cultivar suitability. These areas form the higher-lying areas of Mpumalanga and Limpopo provinces. These areas are suitable for the production of Valencia and midseason oranges and lemons, and are marginally suitable for grapefruit (too cool) and Navel oranges (too warm).

3. The *cool, inland* production region is the high-lying (above 900 meters elevation) areas of North West and Kwazulu-Natal provinces, suitable for the production of Navel oranges and lemons, the warmer microclimates are suited to Valencia oranges, and to a lesser extent certain mandarins, such as Clementine, Nova and possibly Temple tangor.

4. The *cold* production region is composed of the semi-coastal areas situated in southern latitudes, between 32°30' and 34°30' S in the Eastern, Southern and Western Cape. High quality Navel oranges, Satsuma, Clementine and Nova mandarins, and lemons are produced in these areas, while the warmer microclimates in these areas are suitable for Valencia orange production.

5. The *semi-desert* region is relatively new in terms of citrus production and is characterized by extremes: hot summers and cold winters with the occurrence of frost due to advective conditions. In the cooler Vaalharts area, Navel and Valencia oranges are produced, whereas grapefruit and Valencia oranges are produced in the hotter lower Orange River area.

6. Due to *Zimbabwe's* more northerly latitude, ranging from 17°S to 22°S, higher elevations are required to produce similar conditions to those experienced further from the equator. Therefore, hot areas (lowveld) are at <900 meters elevation as opposed to 600 meters for South Africa, intermediate areas (middleveld) range from 900 to 1200 meters elevation, and cool areas (highveld) occur above 1200 m.

DESCRIPTION OF CITRUS PRODUCTION REGIONS BY GEOGRAPHIC AREA

1. *Limpopo Province.* Historically, the northern production region in South Africa supplied about 24% of total Southern African citrus exports. It is the largest production area in Southern Africa with about 14,000 hectares of citrus planted. This area is climatically diverse, comprising hot, dry and intermediate production regions. The largest sub-region within this area is the hot, dry Letsitele area where 33% of the export Valencia oranges are produced. Grapefruit are also produced in this sub-region.

2. *Central and Western Area (North West Province).* The Central and Western area is relatively small (3,000 hectares) with about 6% of the export crop being produced in this area. This area is higher lying than Limpopo Province and hence cooler. Navel and Valencia oranges and lemons are mostly produced.

3. *Mpumulanga Province.* Export production from the 10,000 hectares of citrus in Mpumalanga amounts to about 15% of total exports, with a large proportion of young trees. Nearly 80% of the grapefruit are produced in Mpumalanga and Swaziland areas. The area consists of two climatic zones, intermediate and hot, humid citrus production areas.

4. *Kwazulu-Natal Province.* Production from Kwazulu-Natal amounts to 5% from a relatively small area (3,000 hectares). Within the area, conditions vary from coastal sub-tropical to cool, riverine.

5. *Eastern Cape.* The Eastern Cape produces about 25% of Southern Africa's total citrus production from 14,000 hectares. The area is a cold production area (less than 2000 heat units; 13°C base temperature) producing excellent quality Navel oranges, lemons and mandarins. Midknight Valencia orange originates from this area. The main production areas are the Sundays River Valley (30 km from the coast), Gamtoos River Valley (60 km from the coast), and the East Cape Midlands (between 80 and 100 km from the coast).

6. *Western Cape.* The Western Cape production area has a Mediterranean-type climate typified by cool, wet winters and hot, dry summers. This region is traditionally a deciduous fruit and wine production area. Nevertheless, about 18% of the total citrus production of Southern Africa is derived from this area.

Citriculture dates back to the previous century in the Citrusdal area. It is currently the main citrus producing region of the Western Cape and is well-known for its Navel and Valencia oranges. The Paarl/Stellenbosch area initially concentrated on lemon production, but due to the need for the export-orientated deciduous fruit growers to diversify and an ideal climate, a mandarin industry developed during the early 1980s, especially Satsuma and Clementine mandarins. This subsequently spread north to Citrusdal and east to Swellendam, resulting in the Western Cape becoming the fastest growing citrus area in South Africa with 8,000 hectares planted.

7. *Swaziland:* Five percent of Southern Africa's exports are derived from Swaziland which has 2,000 hectares of citrus, half of which are less than six years old. The low-lying areas of Swaziland are hot, humid production areas, whereas the more mountainous, higher lying areas are classified as intermediate citrus production areas.

8. *Moçambique:* Moçambique produces less than 1% of the regions citrus exports and has less than 1,000 hectares under citrus. Most of the region comprises of tropical flood plain. Very little development is expected in Moçambique over the short term.

9. *Zimbabwe:* At present, Zimbabwe produces about 1% of the export crop from nearly 3,000 hectares. The area planted to citrus in Zimbabwe has increased four-fold in the past 10 years. Zimbabwe's climate is divided into four distinct seasons: i) a hot, dry season from September to November, ii) a hot, wet season from December to March, iii) a post-wet season during March/April with temperatures between 15°C and 20°C, iv) a cold, dry season from May to the end of August. During May/June minimum temperatures drop below 13°C and during July/August minimum temperatures range between 0 and 5°C.

MARKETS AND MARKETING

The strong fresh fruit export imperative of the Southern Africa citrus industry is the cornerstone of citrus production in the region. Net farm income from exports (approximately 60% of the total citrus crop is exported) exceeds 92% of total income of citrus producers (CIAMD 2001) as the domestic market is relatively small and cannot sustain high returns for large volumes of fruit.

Until the end of World War II, virtually all citrus exported from South Africa was marketed in the United Kingdom. By 1957, the export business had expanded to where South African citrus was sold in 48 countries (Cartwright 1977). Today, citrus produced in Southern Africa is sold in more than 60 countries. Whereas Europe has traditionally been the major export outlet (export destinations in 2001: 31% UK, 33% EU, 4% remainder of Europe), the Middle East (12%), Far East (10%) and Japan (6%) have become important markets. It is also anticipated that North American (4%; Canada and USA) will continue to grow as a market for Southern African citrus exports (CIAMD 2001). However, due to phytosanitary requirements, only specific magisterial districts in the Western Cape are currently permitted to export citrus to the USA.

Deregulation of the South African citrus industry in 1998, from a statutory single-channel co-operative marketing system to a voluntary multi-channel free-market marketing system, led to fragmentation and intra-industry competition and consequent downward spiraling of returns. By

2000, there were more 200 registered market agents in South Africa. Fortunately this number has now decreased to about 100, and the 10 largest exporters handle about 95% of the citrus exported. Since deregulation, returns to producers have plummeted and there is now a concerted effort by citrus producers and exporters to voluntarily group together to co-ordinate marketing issues. Collaboration among export agents for specific markets has begun establishing itself and is providing stability in the industry. In 2002, there were already changes from a fragmented and polarized industry to a market and customer focused citrus supply chain.

Future prospects for growth and development of the Southern Africa citrus industry are largely dependent on water availability and meeting market needs. The relatively low cost of production, climatic diversity, strong research and technical support base, ability to produce high-quality products, and magnitude of the Southern African citrus industry will ensure that the region remains a global player in the international citrus marketing environment.

CULTURAL PRACTICES

Citrus Improvement Programme and Nursery Practices

Most citrus nurseries in Southern Africa participate in the Citrus Improvement Programme (CIP). The CIP serves the citrus Industry via a centralized budwood supply farm (Citrus Foundation Block, CFB) near Uitenhage, close to Port Elizabeth. The CIP was developed in the late 1970s and early 1980s where the best producing trees (approximately 800 so-called Budwood Source Trees) of all cultivars were selected throughout South Africa. From these trees, budwood was supplied to nurseries for multiplication and propagation of trees. After a number of years of evaluation, three to five of the best producing trees were identified for each cultivar, budwood was taken from behind fruit, shoot-tip grafted for virus elimination, pre-immunized with a mild strain of citrus tristeza virus, and established at the CFB as budwood source trees. Currently the CFB supplies all certified propagation material to accredited citrus nurseries. A nuclear block of virus-free material of all cultivars is maintained at the Agricultural Research Council-Institute for Tropical and Subtropical Crops in Nelspruit.

Rootstocks

Until the late 1970s, the citrus industry used rough lemon as the principal rootstock. During the 1980s and more so in the 1990s, Troyer and Carrizo citranges, and Swingle citrumelo, gradually became the rootstocks of choice. This aspect is important for the future competitiveness of the Southern African citrus industry to produce fruit of high eating quality to compete with citrus production regions such as Argentina, Uruguay and Australia where trifoliate orange rootstock is preferentially used due to the cold tolerance it imparts on the scion.

Planting Time and Procedure

Since most nurseries are producing trees in containers, time of orchard establishment is not critical. However, in the colder, windy areas the preferred planting time is early spring (September/October). Nursery trees are commonly topped at 60 to 70 cm height to allow scaffold development to occur at a height of 40 to 60 cm. Recently, there is commercial interest in planting trellised, untopped trees for earlier production in slow-growing regions such as the Western Cape.

Spacing Trends

Citrus tended to be ranched in certain areas, especially the hot climatic regions. Due to increased establishment costs and the need for earlier economic break-even, and the need to have sunlight-, spray- and picker-friendly trees, there has been a move towards increasingly higher planting densities. Also, the new wave of technology development in tree size maintenance, particularly pruning, provide citrus producers with more confidence to plant at higher densities. In the hotter regions, where Valencia oranges and grapefruit are produced, spacings of 7×3 meters or 6×3 meters are commonly used, whereas in the cooler regions, where Navel oranges, and Clementine and Satsuma mandarins are produced, spacings as wide as 6×3 meters and as close as 4.5 or 5×2 meters are used.

Preplant Soil Preparation

The high potential soils of the northern areas with little or no need for pH correction is usually only ripped and land preparation costs are thus quite low. In the Western Cape region a lot of money is spent on proper ripping and ploughing. Soil pH correction and other ameliorants (phosphorus, sometimes micro-elements) are added in a double ploughing action. Expensive subsoil drainage systems are often required. In addition, in many cases ridging is considered to provide for added drainage or where the soil is high in clay content.

Windbreaks

Virtually all citrus orchards in Southern Africa have windbreaks. Many windbreak types have been tested or are commonly used. The most well-adapted windbreak tree throughout Southern Africa is beefwood or Casuarina (*Casuarina cunninghamiana* Miq.). *Pinus radiata* D. Don and silky oak (*Grevillea robusta* A. Cunn) are sometimes used. Deciduous type windbreaks are often used as secondary windbreaks in conjunction with beefwood in the Western Cape, e.g. Dutch alder (*Alnus cordata*) and Chinese poplar (*Populus simonii* [syn. *P. obtusa*]).

Row Orientation

Whereas it is not so critical to plant in north-south row directions in the northern regions (lower latitude, dry winters) it is still commonly done. In the more southern latitudes with the more extreme angle of the sun and where rain or dew can keep the tree wet for extended periods during harvest it is essential to plant in a north-south row direction.

Irrigation and Fertigation

Under-tree microsprinkler irrigation systems are most commonly used, while some orchards still use overhead sprinkler irrigation. More recently, however, drip irrigation systems have become increasingly common, with an increased use of drip fertigation where pH and electrical conductivity are controlled in a balanced nutrient solution is provided daily to restrict root system development in a bid to control tree phenology. To attain good eating quality, pre-harvest water stress (limited or deficit irrigation) is becoming an accepted practice, for example with Satsuma mandarin.

Fertilization

Fertilization of bearing trees is exclusively based on annual leaf analysis data from leaves from fruiting terminals and the previous history of the orchard with respect to yield, fruit size, quality and previous fertilization record. Phosphorus and potassium are applied as soil applications, whereas magnesium and the micro-elements (copper, boron, zinc, manganese and molybdenum) are applied as foliar applications, when required. Soil pH correction is achieved by the addition of calcitic or dolomitic lime, and water penetration or salinity problems are addressed by the application of gypsum.

Pruning

In some production regions there is a shift towards selective pruning by hand or with pneumatic pruning equipment. Most large orchards are, however, hedged and topped mechanically.

Insect Pests and Diseases

The hotter regions of Southern Africa are cursed by a spring and summer pest complex which can ruin an otherwise blemish-free crop in a relatively short time. The main problem is citrus thrips on young fruitlets necessitating the use of chemical control, thereby upsetting the natural enemy balance and causing repercussions of other pests, e.g. mites, later in the season. Organophosphate resistant red scale is a problem throughout. Mealybug poses particular problems, whereas fruit fly (Mediterranean and Natal) and false codling moth can be problematic in many regions in specific years. There is a concerted move towards IPM programs, introduction of predators and minimum chemical intervention. Soil-borne diseases are principally due to Phytophthora root rot and citrus nematode, and citrus black spot and Alternaria brown spot are the foliar diseases of commercial importance.

REFERENCES

BARRY, G. H. 1996. Citrus production areas of Southern Africa. Proc. Intl. Soc. Citriculture 1, 145-149.

BARRY, G. H., VELDMAN, F. J. and ALEXANDER C. J. 1996. The South African cultivar development programme and cultivar usage in Southern Africa. Proc. Intl. Soc. Citriculture 1, 156-158.

BOZALEK, S. J. 1974. Identification of citrus quality in production areas for the purpose of climatological analysis. Citrus & Subtrop. Fruit J. Aug., 13-17.

CARTWRIGHT, A. P. 1977. Outspan Golden Harvest: A history of the South African citrus industry. Purnell & Sons, Cape Town, South Africa.

CIAMD. 2001. Key citrus industry statistics 2001. Centre for International Agricultural Marketing and Development, Paarl, South Africa.

DU TOIT. 2002. Citrus Foundation Block statistics on budwood supply. Internal report, Capespan (Pty) Ltd., Uitenhage, South Africa.

FAO. 2001. Citrus fruit: fresh and processed. Annual statistics 2001. http://www.fao.org/ES/ESC/esce/escr/citrus/pdfs/bll2001.pdf

RABE, E. 2001. Southern Africa. Citrus 2001: A Florida perspective, an international outlook. Florida Grower. Mid-August, 35-37.

Australia

John Forsyth and Hugh Cope

INTRODUCTION

Citrus growing is a young but small, efficient and important Australian horticultural industry. Although only the fourth largest in the Southern Hemisphere (after Brazil, Argentina and South Africa) it is larger than Venezuela and Uruguay, producing 637,000 MT in 1998-1999 from 9.7 million trees (28,295 ha). However, it ranks only sixteenth in the world with 1% of total production. Over the last decade the Australian citrus industry has adjusted significantly in several ways, i.e., types and varieties planted, marketing and crop utilization, all aimed at the fresh fruit domestic or export markets and fresh (not from concentrate) orange juice (FAO 1999; Damiani 1999A).

Plantings remain generally concentrated in selected and more favorable areas of southeastern Australia (Fig. 6.15). However several new areas are now being planted especially where irrigation water is available together with suitable soils and climate, i.e., Emerald in Queensland and Bourke in NSW. Although overall production does not meet the current demand for processing oranges (mainly Valencia), a surplus of midseason navels, lemons, and grapefruit frequently occurs in local markets, resulting in poor demand and depressed prices. Exports of fresh fruit are increasing significantly from only 5%-10% in the 1980s to now averaging over 20% of annual production in the last five years.

Limited but increasing quantities of navels, lemons, grapefruit and mandarins are usually imported in the summer and autumn to supplement local supplies. Large quantities of frozen concentrated orange juice (mainly from Brazil and at wildly varying prices) continue to be imported annually to make up the shortfall in local supply.

Fig. 6.15. Citrus growing areas of Australia. In 1998-1999 the indicated southeastern region had 86% (including 17% non-bearing) of the plantings and 77% of the production.

Early History

Following seeds and trees arriving on the First Fleet to Sydney in 1788 from Rio de Janeiro and the Cape of Good Hope, citrus plantings gradually increased over the next hundred years, mainly in nearby coastal areas under natural rainfall. During the late 1800s, extensive new irrigated plantings were commenced along the inland Murray river by the Chaffey brothers with imported Washington navel and Valencia orange trees from California, establishing the Renmark and Mildura irrigation settlements. Similar, but later developments followed with irrigation from the Murrumbidgee river via a main canal at Yanco/Leeton and Griffith, when the first farms were allocated in 1912. These irrigated citrus areas continued to expand, aided by government soldier settlement programs and private schemes, after the World Wars and are now the important Riverland, Riverina and Sunraysia regions—see Fig. 6.15 (Bowman 1956).

Climate

Australia is basically a dry continent, but a range of climatic zones (tropical to arid) are now used for citrus growing. Coastal areas are generally mild to humid; although annual rainfall can exceed 1200 mm, supplementary irrigation is desirable for successful citriculture. The larger and now more important inland citrus areas are hotter and drier (650 mm of annual rainfall), making irrigation essential.

Problems of excessive wind, heat waves, drought, and frost periodically occur in most localities and can result in tree and crop damage or losses. Fruit maturity varies widely from early in the more northern Queensland and NSW coastal areas to much later in some southern colder inland areas. These wide climatic variations make it possible for some oranges, lemons, and grapefruit to be available for the fresh fruit market almost throughout the whole year.

A recent heat unit mapping project, together with further spatial analysis selection criteria for climate, topography, soil type, water availability and infrastructural requirements, has now identified new citrus growing locations that may be suitable for cool, warm or hot climate growing varieties which will further aid future planting decisions (Hutton 2001).

Soils and Topography

Coastal areas tend to be undulating, with citrus established only in selected localities where aspect, soil, drainage and water supply are suitable. Inland citrus areas are generally flatter on plains or low windblown ridges, usually adjacent to river systems. Irrigation is available by direct river pumping, bores or from government supply channel/pipe systems, as most horticultural properties are grouped together in scattered localities.

Recent Planting Trends

In the 1990s the Australian citrus industry was forced to make significant planting (and marketing) changes, due mainly to the decline in economic returns from growing Valencia oranges for processing and to the competition from Brazil. Some plantings were also replaced with the currently buoyant wine grapes. A large range of new (local or recently imported varieties and clones, i.e., early or summer navels and mandarins), together with increased fresh fruit export opportunities, greatly influenced the current planting trends.

The planting statistics for the main types grown in 1998-1999 are summarized in Table 6.8. Some trend highlights include the following, when compared with the 1988-1989 plantings:

- Total citrus plantings remain similar at 28,000 ha (after peaking in 1994 at 34,000 ha).

- For the areas surveyed (about 95% of plantings, excluding 'other NSW'—coastal declining 1,513 ha and Narromine stable 207 ha in 1993

TABLE 6.8. Australian Citrus Tree Plantings, 1998-1999. Number of Trees [× 10(3)]

Type	Bearing	Nonbearing and percentage		Total	Percentage of total trees
Oranges					
Navel winter[a]	1,578	374	(19%)	1,952	20
summer[b]	891	563	(39%)	1,454	15
(total navel)	1,952	910	(27%)	3,406	35
Valencia	3,849	188	(5%)	4,037	42
Other common	19	25	(20%)	44	—
Subtotal	6,337	1,150	(15%)	7,487	77
Mandarins[c]	885	803	(48%)	*1,688*	*17*
Lemons	209	83	(28%)	292	3
Limes	7	9	(56%)	16	—
Grapefruit	160	34	(18%)	194	2
Total	7,598	2,080	(18%)	9,678	
				(28,295 ha)	

[a]Winter navels are those varieties harvested from April to September i.e. Washington, Leng and Thomson.
[b]Summer navels are those 'new' varieties harvested from October to March ie Lane Late, Barnfield, Powell and Chislett.
[c]Mandarin summary plantings includes all types and hybrids i.e. common, satsuma, clementine tangor and tangelo.
Source: Damiani 1999A.

and the Northern Territory—slightly expanding from 50,000 trees in 1998 at Darwin and Katherine). Oranges now make up 77% of the plantings, mandarins 17%, lemons 3% and grapefruit 2%. (see Fig 6.16. for comparisons with 1988-1989).

- Total orange plantings declined 4% mainly Valencia (with a very low 5% now nonbearing due to removals and reworking trees); navel plantings increased from 29% to 35% mainly due to the new early and late maturing varieties becoming available and also increased export opportunities.

- Mandarins (especially in the early maturing Queensland growing regions) increased from 9% to 17%, with a high 48% nonbearing.

- Citrus plantings are now mainly concentrated in the following three inland regions of southeastern Australia (see Fig. 6.15 for locations) and they account for 86% of the total plantings:

Riverina 8,907 ha.—mainly Valencia and navel oranges; lesser grapefruit; lemons.

Riverland 8,429 ha.—Valencia and navel oranges; mandarins; lemons.

Sunraysia 7,067 ha.—Valencia and navel oranges; mandarins; grapefruit.

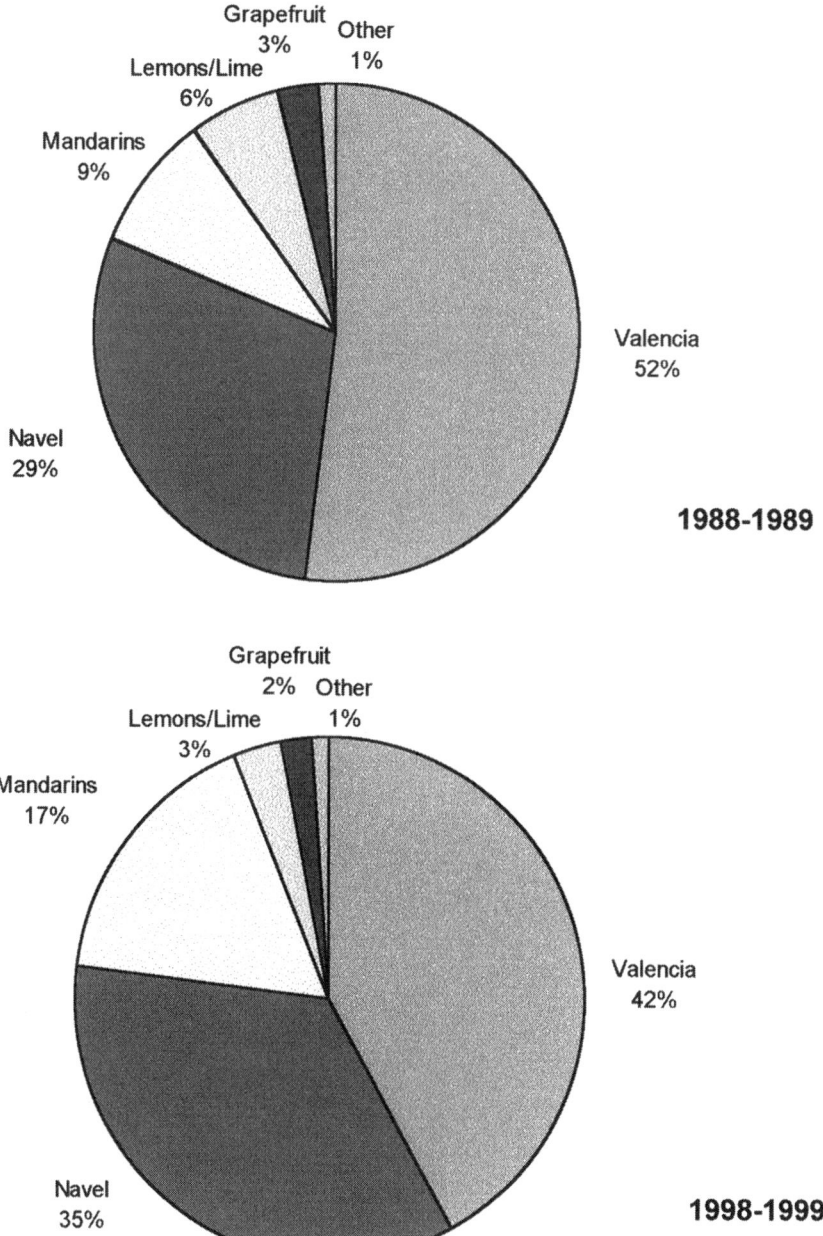

Fig. 6.16. Planting trends for the main citrus types grown in Australia1988-1989 compared with 1998-1999.

- Queensland (with early maturity) has 3,179 ha. planted, mainly to mandarins 80% (with a high 54% nonbearing) and lesser areas of navels and lemons.

- Minor plantings in Western Australia (712 ha.—100 growers) and the Northern Territory (30 growers) are mainly for local domestic markets together with some limited exports.

- Some other minor citrus types are also planted for local or niche markets and/or where micro climates are suitable, i.e., Seville oranges (marmalade); pummelo; Kaffir lime (fresh leaves); blood oranges; citrons and kumquats (ABARE 1994; Damiani 1999A).

Types and Varieties Grown. A large number of varieties are available, but only a small number have been historically grown commercially. Some are of older Australian origin like Imperial and Ellendale mandarins; Leng and Lane Late navels. However in the last 20 years many new varieties have become available from local discovery (especially navels) or have been imported. After a 20 year embargo, citrus budwood importations recommenced into Australia in 1986 with over 60 mainly public varieties imported to date. A few of the early importations are now being grown commercially, while others are still undergoing evaluation. The main types and varieties grown by 1998-1999 are shown in Table 6.9.

A large number of new and mainly late/summer navels have also been located since 1985. Many of these, i.e., Barnfield, Chislett and Powell are creating world wide interest. Some newer local mandarins, i.e., Taylor Lee, Mystique and Amigo with the older Yen Ben lemon are still under evaluation.

There are approximately 3,000 citrus growers in Australia. Of these 92% have less than 20 ha of citrus plantings. The largest number are located in the Riverland region with nearly 800 holdings but with 83% of 10 ha or less. Citrus plantings have been traditionally small and on typical family farms where several types are often grown and usually in conjunction with other horticultural crops, e.g., grapes, stone fruit and vegetables. Specialized large-scale citrus production has become more common, especially in new growing localities, i.e., Hillston, Bourke and Emerald or through property amalgamations and/or company ownership (Australian Citrus Growers).

Rootstock Trends. A limited number of rootstocks are available in Australia and depending on a number of factors (scion, virus disease tolerance and soil conditions like drainage, nematodes, salinity or pH), the following were the most popular in demand and supply trends for the 2000 seed season—Troyer (38% of the total), *P. trifoliata* (27%), Carrizo (9%), Swingle citrumelo (9%), rough lemon (6%), Benton citrange (5%) and Cleopatra mandarin (3%). There is interest in, but only limited supply to-date of two new Australian rootstocks for Eureka lemons—Cox mandarin and Fraser

TABLE 6.9. Main Citrus Types and Varieties Planted in Australia 1998-1999

Type	Standard variety	New variety (local/imported)	Under evaluation (imported)
Valencia	Late, Seedless		Delta, Midknight
Common	Hamlin, Joppa		Pera, Pineapple, Salustiana, Natal, Lima
Navel-winter	Washington, Leng, Thomson, Fisher	Navelina	Fukumoto, Cara Cara, Palmer, Newhall
-summer	Lane Late	Barnfield, Powell Chislett, Summer Gold Autumn Gold, Wilson, Rhode	Navelate
Mandarins	Imperial, Murcott Ellendale, Hickson, Minneola, Kara	Nules, Fremont Sunburst, Nova, Ortanique	Okitsu, Miho, Fortune, Fallglo, Daisy, Corsica 1&2, Afourer, Avana, Caffin
Lemons	Eureka, Lisbon, Meyer, Villa Franca	Fino, Verna	Limoneira 8a Lisbon, Allen Eureka
Limes	Tahitian, West Indian		
Grapefruit	Marsh,Thompson, Ruby	Oroblanco, Star Ruby	Rio Red, Henderson Flame, Ray

Source: Damiani 1999B, C, D; Sanderson 2001.

Seville hybrids. Source: Unpublished data from the two main seed suppliers—the Australian Citrus Propagation Association and the Queensland Citrus Improvement Society.

CULTURAL AND POST HARVEST PRACTICES

Australian citrus growers continue to adopt various new cultural, management and post harvest practices, to increase yields, improve fruit quality and market out-turns equal to world best practice and to ensure viable returns.

Bulk handling is used extensively throughout the industry both on and off the farm. Half-tonne bins are common (with the use of plastic bins increasing), and even larger capacity bins and road trailers are being used by many growers.

Because of the high cost of harvesting labor (A$45-A$50/MT), mobile power ladders for harvesting continue to be adopted widely (all values in this part are Australian dollars). Harvesting platforms or mechanical harvesting systems (butt and limb shaker or air) with associated fruit recovery and pickup equipment previously researched by Government Agencies, have not been developed further or accepted by growers.

Traditional square plantings of 188-260 trees/ha have now generally been replaced with double planting densities of 450 trees/ha. Excessive tree size in many older plantings grown on vigorous rootstocks (rough lemon and sweet orange) has been controlled by mechanical hedging and topping, to facilitate harvesting and other cultural practices. The newer double-planted trees are being lightly hedged on a regular early basis to provide hedge rows and to maintain cropping levels.

With the new emphasis on early and larger fruit sizes for increased fresh fruit production and marketing, some growers are commencing shaping trees by hand pruning and skirting younger trees—especially navels and mandarins at three-four years of age. Other cultural practices now being adopted more widely include crop regulation by chemical thinning, pruning and hand thinning of excessive fruitlets, to reduce alternate cropping and increase early fruit size, and the application of Giberallic acid (GA) to improve rind quality.

Extensive field research by the NSW Agriculture has shown that a mild bud-transmissible dwarfing factor, when innoculated into oranges growing on *P. trifoliata* or citrange rootstocks, offers potential to reduce normal tree size (25-50%) while maintaining tree health, earlier cropping and fruit quality. Although Graft Transmissible Dwarfing (GTD) was released to the industry in 1992, adoption has been slow and mainly on a regional trial basis by innovative growers. Densities of 1,000 trees/ha have been widely adopted with GTD size control, to achieve earlier production and more efficient use of resources, i.e., land and water.

Soil management varies with irrigation practice and locality, but regular cultivations are being replaced with a number of combined practices that usually involve a residual or knockdown herbicide (bromacil, diuron, krovar or glyphosate). Permanent blanket herbicide soil programs are common in the Riverina with furrow irrigation, while under-tree strip herbicides with inter-row sod or winter cover cropping or medic is practiced in most other areas. Some new plantings may also be on row mounds or raised beds with temporary narrow plastic row strips along the tree row.

The greatest recent changes continue in irrigation practices. Although furrow methods are still used extensively in some localities (Riverina), permanent overhead and portable systems are losing favor, particularly where water drainage, quality (salinity), supply, or cost problems exist. Limited interest was initially shown in trickle or drip irrigation, but now these and under-tree/low-level microjets systems or mini sprinklers are being installed extensively in new plantings or are replacing existing systems.

Normal ground applications or banding of single-strength (urea, nitram or superphosphate) artificial or mixed (NPK) fertilizers is still common practice. In some localities where organic farmyard manures are readily available, they are also applied to citrus plantings. Deficiencies of trace elements—particularly zinc, magnesium and manganese—are common and corrected by foliar sprays as required. Fertigation techniques are now normally coupled with new irrigation systems. Applications may also be required of lime, gypsum or dolomite, especially pre planting. Although a large number of citrus pests occur in Australia (scales, bugs, mites, aphids, thrips, weevils, beetles and caterpillars), only a small number may require special or regular control measures, depending on variety, market and growing locality. The pests most likely to require control include red scale (*Aonidiella aurantii*), Queensland fruit fly (*Bactrocera tryoni*), snow or white louse scale (*Unaspis citri*), citrus leaf miner (*Phyllocoptruta oleivora*), citrus rust mite (*Phyllocoptruta oleivora*), and black scale (*Saissetia oleae*).

Integrated Pest Management (IPM) has been widely researched and now broadly adopted in the Australian industry. For most common pests, IPM is a strategy which encourages the reduction of pesticide use by using a variety of controls in harmonious combination to contain or manage the pest below economic injury levels. It aims to maximize the use of biological (natural enemies—parasites, predators or pathogens) and cultural controls—to conserve natural enemies, good tree health, skirting etc. Selective, non-disruptive pesticides like petroleum spraying oil (PSO) are only applied when needed as determined by systematic monitoring of pests and their natural enemies. For example IPM control measures have been widely adopted for red scale, particularly in inland areas where parasitic wasps *Aphytis melinus*, and *A. lingnanensis* and the wasp *Comperiella bifasciata* have been released (Smith *et al.* 1997).

A similar low risk situation exists with citrus diseases, but the risk of damage to trees and fruit remains higher in a number of localities, especially coastal. Some common diseases that occur in Australia include root and collar rot (*Phytophthora citrophthora*), melanose (*Diaporthe citri*), septoria spot (*Septoria citri*); while black spot (*Guignardia citricarpa*) and citrus scab (*Sphaceloma fawcettii*) only occur in coastal areas. The cause of three citrus tree decline problems, 'blight', 'dieback' and 'sudden death' remain unsolved, and all can result in spasmodic tree losses or decline in bearing trees. The citrus nematode (*Tylenchulus semipenetrans*) can be a problem especially in replant sites.

A number of common virus diseases also occur e.g. tristeza - including the orange stem pitting strain (only in Queensland), exocortis, psorosis, tatter leaf and cachexia (xyloporosis). An important factor in keeping these virus diseases at their current low levels, was the commencement of the first budwood scheme in 1928, and the Australian Fruit Variety Foundation Repository of virus-indexed and horticulturally evaluated citrus source trees in 1977. The responsibility of producing true-to-type budwood of a known health status for commercial varieties to nurserymen and growers and maintaining the overall crop improvement program (importations, disease elimination and horticultural evaluation) is now with the Australian Citrus Propagation Association—trading as Auscitrus (Barkley 1998).

As previously mentioned, Emerald in Central Queensland is a new citrus area (Fig. 6.15), and although not endemic in Australia, citrus canker caused by the bacterium *Xanthomonas azonopodia* pv. citri was identified there in plantings within a 1,200 ha. property on July 6, 2004. As the industry had only recently developed a citrus biosecurity plan, the draft citrus canker plan was immediately put into action. A national approach and strategies to the outbreak, agreed to control and eradicate this new disease outbreak. Several previous incidents of the disease, most notable in the Northern Territory in 1912, 1991 and 1993 were all successfully eradicated by removing and destroying host plants in the wider vicinity of infected plants (Australian Citrus News 2005).

A Pest Quarantine Area (PQA) was immediately put into place and restricted the movement of all plants and plant material (including fruit). All trees were removed from this property (222,000 trees over 375 ha.) by the end of August. A second detection (October 2004) and more recently a third (May 2005) in adjoining properties, but all within the exiting PQA, will result in the removal of all commercial citrus (490,000 trees from seven properties) and with all residential trees together with any native citrus spp. trees within a 600 meter buffer zone.

On going surveys of all other commercial citrus growing areas, including the larger Central Burnett region of Queensland, has not detected any citrus canker. Normal interstate fruit trade (from outside the PQA), resumed from late July 2004, following national approval of market access protocols. Australia has been liaising with overseas trading partners to ensure continuity of fruit exports. All markets remain open, although some countries sought additional requirements for survey, treatment, inspections and certification to ensure them that all fruit is free of citrus canker. These details are correct as of August 1, 2005. Current information can be found on the Internet cites in Citrus Canker Outbreak in Australia (2004).

Hand spraying of agricultural chemicals was initially replaced by high-volume and pressure spraying units like the oscillating boom and some selected air-blast sprayers. Recent developments and research in spray application that will become more important in the future includes low-profile air-blasts (may be modified with an overhead hydraulic boom), air-blast with tower attachments, high-velocity with air-shear nozzles, rotary atomisers and multi-head type spray equipment (Smith *et al.* 1997).

Postharvest Handling and Treatment. The development of effective postharvest handling techniques has benefited the fresh fruit citrus industry. Packinghouses now carry out postharvest treatment procedures aimed at meeting higher standards of hygiene, quality control, improving packaging and reducing handling costs. Many also have Quality Assurance accreditation.

Only limited use is made of ethylene degreening, especially for early navels and mandarins, in some regions. Both the batch, or shot, and the now preferred trickle systems are used in specially constructed degreening rooms.

Fungicides are applied in a bulk dipping and/or packing line operation as soon as possible after harvest. The approved fungicides are not toxic to the fruit and include SOPP, carbendazim, thiabendazole, guazatine, imazalil EC and imazalil sulfate WSP). Waxing (sometimes with 2,4-D added) is routine practice throughout the industry. All products used are registered or approved by the national or state health departments. Cool storage is used by the industry when transport delays are likely to occur, for assembling large export consignments and when freshly delivered fruit cannot be packed immediately.

Some common postharvest diseases or disorder of navel oranges and mandarins grown in inland Australia include anthracnose, blue and green mold, septoria spot, sour rot, olleocellosis and chilling injury (Taverner 2001).

PRODUCTION

The production of citrus fruits in Australia has maintained a steady growth pattern since the 1970s, subject to variations brought about by seasonal factors and alternate cropping, up to a record total crop of 787,000 MT in 2000-2001, with 94% from the four main regions (see Table 6.10), valued at approximately A$400 million. This production was well above the 10 year average of 659,000 MT, while the prediction of 842,000 MT in 2009-2010 is an increase of 7% (ABARE 1996; Australian Citrus Growers).

Production trends for the main types now grown are as follows:

- Valencia oranges have basically peaked at 378,000 MT in 2000-2001 slightly above the 10 year average of 352,000 MT. The decline in plantings of Valencia oranges, with a now low 5% non bearing (see Table 6.8) is expected to result in reduced Valencia production levels in future seasons. This major adjustment is the result of over dependence on Valencia oranges for processing and widely fluctuating world prices of concentrate.

- Production of navel oranges during the last decade from 1990-1991, increased from 142,000 MT to 246,000 MT, an increase of 73%.

- A far greater increase in mandarins has also occurred from 41,000 MT to 116,000 MT (183%). Both navels and mandarins are predicted to increase further due to grower interest and relative high non-bearing plantings (27% and 48% respectively).

- Lemon production has remained static (34.000 MT to 33,000 MT), while grapefruit has declined overall (27,000 MT to 14,000 MT), reflecting the limited market growth for these two fruit types.

TABLE 6.10. Australian Citrus Production—1000 MT

Type	Production 2000-2001	Percentage	Predicted production[A] 2009-2010	Percentage
Navel	246	31	270	32
Valencia	378	48	349	41
Mandarins	116	15	168	20
Lemons/limes	33	4	39	5
Grapefruit	14	2	16	2
Total	787		842	

[a]Taking into account current tree numbers of non-bearing (Table 6.8); no further significant tree removals; average yields and favorable climatic conditions, the Australian total citrus production is predicted to increase a further 55,000 tonnes or 7%.
Source: Australian Citrus Growers 2001; Damiani 1999A.

MARKETING AND CROP UTILIZATION

The majority of the Australian production (80%) is consumed by the domestic fresh fruit and processing markets. Processing has traditionally been an important market for the industry especially with Valencia oranges. The percentage of the total Australian citrus crop delivered to processing factories increased from 23% in 1969-1970 to average about 60% in 1980s and mid 1990s. Over the same period fresh fruit exports increased from only 6% to a high 20% in 1999-2000.

In 1996-1997 to 1998-1999, 30% of the total orange crop was delivered to the domestic fresh fruit market, 49% went to processing and 21% were exported as fresh fruit. The comparable earlier percentages in 1989-1990 to 1991-1992 were 29%, 60% and 11% respectively (Damiani 2000).

Fresh fruit export had remained fairly constant at about 7% in the 1980s. The new focus by the industry on fresh fruit exports in the last decade, has achieved outstanding results. Exports have grown from almost 31,000 MT with a FOB value of A$22 million in 1988/89 to 180,000 MT (23% of production) with a FOB value of A$191 million in 2000/01. See Fig. 6.17 for some annual trends in fresh fruit exports. These exports makes citrus the largest fresh fruit exporter among the Australian horticultural industries (Australian Citrus Growers 2001).

Although Australia is only a small producer, opportunities exist to supply major northern hemisphere exports markets with out of season fresh fruit. The recent planting restructure has placed the industry in a better position to supply these niche counter season markets. However increased production in other southern hemisphere countries South Africa, Uruguay and Argentina will also increase competition in all markets.

Trends and marketing developments in the past export season included:

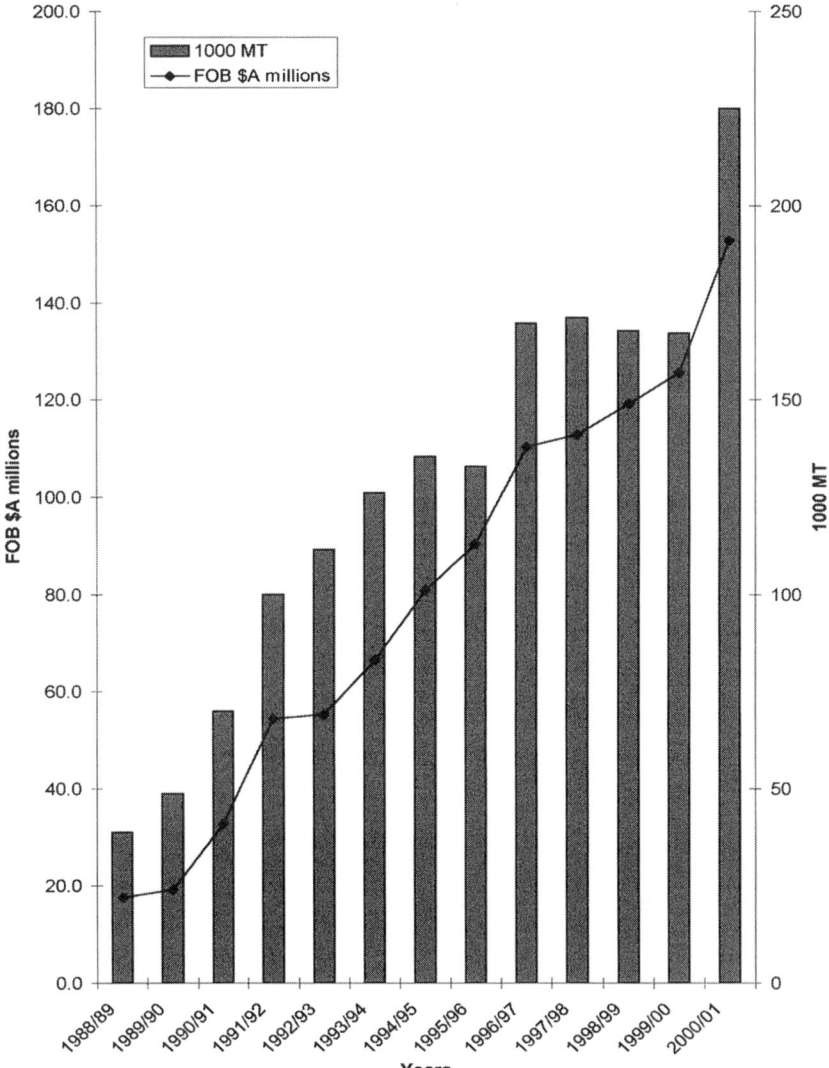

Fig. 6.17. Trends in volume and value of Australian fresh citrus exports.

- Of these exports 83% were oranges, (including currently 40% of total navel production) and 12% mandarins.

- Over 83% consigned to five major markets—the USA (22%), Hong Kong (20%), Malaysia (18%), Singapore (12%) and Japan (11%).

- The USA has developed into a major market in less than 10 years especially for navels—increasing from 5,228 MT in 1993-1994 to a record 26,406 MT in 1999-2000.

- Recent new opportunities in South Korea and Taiwan. The industry is investigating possibilities for exports to China, India, Pakistan and Bangladesh.

- Orderly marketing, promotions like 'Australia *fresh*', market access and quarantine issues being funded and developed.

- Recent industry fact finding report revealed new export opportunities and areas for future research and development. The project aimed to collate all existing information and produce a system that could be continually updated to identify market opportunities and assist growers and exporters in the long term planning of their business. A number of 'best prospects' were identified i.e. a supply window (currently) exist for Australian navels arriving in overseas markets in September/October; while a similar opportunity also exists for easy peelers in September and possibly August (Ferguson 2001).

The marketing of fresh citrus in Australia had previously been carried out in accordance with grade standards established by the state governments. The regulations covered quality, fruit size, maturity standards, and labelling of packages. In the mid 1990s these regulation were repealed, but the industry generally adopted many of the same standards on a voluntary basis.

Free trade between the states has placed some limitation on the ability of the industry to maintain the orderly marketing of citrus fruits on domestic markets, even where some quarantine restriction may be in force e.g. due to fruit fly free areas. Some citrus-producing regions and states have established citrus-marketing boards under state legislation to improve marketing—Riverina, Murray Valley (Sunraysia) and South Australia (Riverland), with influence over 77% of production.

TABLE 6.11. Distribution Trends of the Australian Valencia Crop

Market	Percentage of the total crop	
	1994-1995	1999-2000
Fresh exports	10	14
Fresh domestic	17	27
Juice fresh	41	53
Juice concentrate	33	6

Source: Damiani 2000.

These boards do not physically market the fruit but exercise some control of supply management factors, quality standards/maturity and coordination of exports, together with promotional activities in support of their marketing policy. The actual marketing of fruit is carried out by grower co-operatives, private packing companies, and individual growers in capital city wholesale or larger regional markets. Some direct selling to processors, supermarkets or larger retailers also takes place.

Exports are covered by regulations administered by the Commonwealth Department of Agriculture, Fisheries and Forestry, through Biosecurity Australian. The former Australian Horticultural Corporation—now Horticulture Australia Ltd. (HA), also plays a role in promotion, fact finding visits, together with powers to regulate horticultural exports through licensing both exporters and importers. The citrus industry uses these powers as an integral part of its market development strategies. Fresh citrus exports can be by grower co-operatives, private companies, and state or regional citrus boards. These organizations may unite and negotiate direct with buyers in overseas markets subject to any of the above HA requirements. For example the joint Riversun organization coordinates supply, shipping etc. for all exports to the USA from the three main producing regions to the one HA licensed importer. Similar import arrangements exist in Korea (three importers licensed), Thailand (14) and Taiwan (14) (Australian Citrus Growers 2001).

Current trends in packaging and marketing are aimed at reducing costs and improving the presentation and quality image of citrus fruit. Bulk bins are used in some areas for deliveries to retailers/supermarket chains with a view to reducing handling costs, and some experimentation has been carried out with returnable plastic crates. Net bags containing 3 kg of fruit have proved popular with consumers, and these packages account for a large part of the domestic market trade. Filling of the bags is normally carried out at the point of packing but can also be done at the market end of the operation. Work on vibration/volume filling packing and the use of plastic film wraps on individual fruits, particularly grapefruit has not been adopted except for volume filled smaller mandarins.

In particular for Valencia oranges, processing into juice has had become an important domestic outlet, i.e., for the five years to 1990-1995, 73% of production was processed. This increase has reflected the dramatic development of the overall citrus juice market. However within the processing market a new fresh (not from concentrate) orange juice market has also been developed (see Table 6.12 for the last five year trends) which now absorbs about 53% of Valencia production and was worth A$192 million in 2000-2001.

An interesting new development in processing has also been the growth in processed orange juice exports. They have grown from 9,628 KL in 1994-1995 to 16,420 KL 1999-2000. Major destinations are New Zealand, Japan and Hong Kong (Australian Citrus Growers 2001).

TABLE 6.12. Australian Imports of Orange Juice as Equivalent Fresh Fruit (MT)

Season	Imports (MT)
1994-1995	158,000
1995-1996	242,000
1996-1997	187,000
1997-1998	229,000
1998-1999	370,240
1999-2000	249,775

Source: Australian Bureau of Statistics 2001.

IMPORTS

In normal seasons the local production of all citrus in peak harvest and supply periods, exceeds the Australian market's demand, bearing in mind the industry's need for viable price maintenance. In the past, surplus fruit (small sized, blemished and packing over-runs) were offered to processors. Now an increased volume with a wider maturity period, is being produced for fresh fruit exports especially navels and mandarins. However, the total production of Valencia oranges is still not sufficient to provide for the total local juice market - although this is greatly influenced by prices offered by processors. This situation has existed since the early 1970s when the consumer demand for orange juice products started to increase dramatically.

The Australian juice market is in a unique situation. The trend for fresh (not from concentrate) orange juice has recently expanded and can only utilize local fruit (Table 6.12). However the current total annual demand for orange juice products is equivalent to over 600,000 MT of oranges. Domestic navel orange production provides about 55,000 MT of this total, and this juice is mainly used for blending and cordial production. Of the balance (in excess of 545,000 equivalent MT), Australian Valencia production, allowing for domestic and export fresh fruit market requirements, can supply only about 220,000 MT, thus leaving the equivalent 325,000 MT (six year average, Table 6.13) to be imported.

Before 1976, as the demand for imported orange juice concentrate increased, the domestic industry was placed under extreme economic pressure due to the disparity between Australian costs of production, under a high economic cost structure, and the price of orange juice concentrate manufactured in other countries (e.g., Brazil and Florida). From 1976 import tariff arrangements have been phased down by the Australian Government to the current minimum levels of protection against imports of orange juice concentrate.

With costs of production increasing and reduced tariff protection (now only 5% ad valorem), any major downward movement or wild fluctuations in the world price of orange juice concentrate places severe economic pres-

TABLE 6.13. Australian Imports of Fresh/Dried Citrus Fruits (MT)

Type	93/94	94/95	95/96	96/97	97/98	98/99	99/00
Oranges	6,689	7,315	10,267	12,682	12,683	6,250	14,300
Mandarins	432	1,560	781	1,028	978	484	676
Lemons/limes	1,347	1,610	1,870	1,653	3,005	2,056	1,663
Other	121	61	98	160	126	181	551
Total	9,396	11,343	14,093	16,271	17,644	9,684	17,983
Av. value/MT[a]	$999	$1,128	$1,151	$1,075	$1,234	$1,807	$1,334

[a]All values in Australian dollars.
Source: Australian Bureau of Statistics; Australian Citrus Growers 2001.

sure on the growing and processing sectors of the Australian industry and requires a reassessment of the current measures being provided to enhance the competitiveness of the industry. In recent years the Brazilian price of concentrate has resulted in grower returns falling to as low as A$A50 to A$100 per fresh fruit MT equivalent.

As a result in late 2001 following an industry request, the Federal Government announced a Productivity Commission inquiry into Australia's citrus growing and processing industries. The industry is currently experiencing a significant downturn through a combination of world factors including:

- Continued increased imports, particularly frozen orange concentrate.

- Historically low world orange concentrate prices, tends to set the domestic floor price across all markets.

- Continued high subsidies and tariffs in other citrus producing countries and markets (Davidson 2001).

Imports of fresh citrus fruits have also continued to increase during recent years. In 1999-2000 a record 17,983 MT were imported—mainly navel oranges from USA and Spain, lemons/limes from USA, Spain and New Zealand, but also smaller quantities of grapefruit and mandarins (See Table 6.13 for trends). These imports in the past were normally at the end of the Australian season. However with citrus now produced in a wider range of climatic region with earlier and later maturity, together with a far greater range of early and late varieties (especially navels and mandarins) the past seasonal shortfall in the local supply have been greatly reduced (Australian Citrus Growers 2001).

Increased imported fresh fruit competition can also be expected in the future from South Africa, Egypt, Florida, Japan, South Korea, Italy, Malaysia and New Caledonia (limes), subject to each negotiating import protocols, risk analysis and meeting quarantine requirements (Australian Citrus Growers 2001).

FUTURE OUTLOOK

Over the last decade the citrus industry has undergone many changes, especially in plantings and marketing. The future outlook for a more competitive and viable Australian industry will include:

- A favorable outcome from the Productivity Commission inquiry.

- The further reduced dependency on concentrate processing and the expansion of the fresh (not from concentrate) orange juice increasing local and export markets for processed juice.

- Identifying and meeting markets needs, especially for navels and mandarins of existing and new export markets and increasing these market outlets to represent over 30% of production.

- Meeting competition from an increased volume and range of fresh citrus imports.

- Additional planting of new varieties to further extend the availability of fruit for all markets—domestic, export and processing, especially in the very early and late maturity periods.

- The continued availability and price of irrigation water, together with electricity pumping costs.

- The ability of the industry to improve its overall efficiency by increasing high quality fruit yield and reducing costs of production, harvesting and marketing.

REFERENCES

AUSTRALIAN CITRUS GROWERS (ACG). Annual reports and statistical papers (Various issues).

AUSTRALIAN CITRUS GROWERS (ACG). 2001. Report to the Productivity Commission inquiry—Enhancing the performance of the citrus growing industry.

AUSTRALIAN CITRUS NEWS. 2005. Latest on citrus canker incursion. Aug./Sept. 81, 14.

AUSTRALIAN BUREAU OF STATISTICS. 2001. Fruit statistics Australia—Fruit growing industry and selected agricultural commodities Australia (Various issues).

ABARE. 1996. Australian Commodity Statistics 1994 and 1996 Fruits-Citrus.

BARKLEY, P. 1998. Citrus Diseases and Disorders. NSW Agriculture.

BOWMAN, F. T. 1956. Citrus-growing in Australia. Angus and Robertson, Sydney.

CITRUS CANKER OUTBREAK IN AUSTRALIA. 2004. Australian Government, Dept. Agr., Fisheries and Forestry: Dept. Primary Industries and Fisheries: and Australian Citrus Growers web sites.

DAMIANI, J. 1999A. 1998/99 Australian Citrus Planting Trends, Australian Citrus News July Vol. 75, 4-5.

DAMIANI, J. 1999B. Orange Planting Trends. Australian Citrus News August Vol. 75, 5.

DAMIANI, J. 1999C. Mandarins-Tangelo-'Easy-peels'. Australian Citrus News September Vol. 75, 11.

DAMIANI, J. 1999D. Lemons-Lime-Grapefruit. Australian Citrus News October Vol. 75, 2.

DAMIANI, J. 2000. The Australian Citrus Industry-Export for Profit. Australian Citrus News March Vol. 76, 3-4.

DAVIDSON, P. 2001. Agreement Reached on Productivity Inquiry & Short Term Assistance. Australian Citrus News July Vol. 77, pp. 1-3. And Industry inquiry begins. Australian Citrus News October Vol. 77, 1.

FAO. 1999. Citrus Fruit Fresh and Processed annual statistics.

FERGUSON, G. 2001. Developing a Citrus Export Market Intelligence System. Australian Citrus News July Vol. 77, 6.

HUTTON, R. 2001. Report on heat unit mapping project. Coastal Fruitgrowers' Newsletter No. 41 Spring, 3-4.

SMITH, D., BEATTIE, G. A. C. and BROADLEY, R. 1997. Citrus Pests and their natural enemies; integrated pest management in Australia. Department of Primary Industries, Queensland.

SANDERSON, G. 2001. Scion Evaluation report (3) in compile Proceedings, Citrus Breeding & Evaluation Workshop Dareton.

TAVERNER, P. 2001. A guide to the common postharvest diseases or disorder of navel oranges and mandarins grown in inland Australia. SARDI and HRDC Fact Sheet.

China

Xiuxin Deng

China is one of the most important native lands of citrus, and at present, several citrus species including Daoxian wild tangerine, and evergreen tri-foliate orange etc. are found in the wild state. The growing of citrus as an agricultural crop is recorded as far back in Chinese history as 2286 B.C. and the commercial industry has well developed in 10th century (Burke 1967). In 1178 A.D. of Song dynasty, Han described 27 citrus varieties commercially cultivated in Huangyan area of Zhejiang province in his book, Ju Lu (the monograph of citriculture), which maybe the first book of citrus in the world. Citrus production increased very slowly before 1980s, since the policy of emphasizing staple crops (Li 1996). This situation changed after 1983, since then, the production increased one fold about every 4 years, and reached to more than 10 million metric tons in 1999 (Table 6.14). Ms. Hu Zhaoling (1968) was the author of this section in the First Edition of this book, which was important to the current writing.

The important producing areas are situated in the provinces of Sichuan, Zhejiang, Hunan, Fujian, Guangxi, Hubei, Jiangxi, and Taiwan. Excluding Taiwan, the total citrus area was 1,282,800 ha and total production was 10,787,059 MT in 1999. The freeze at the end of 1999 killed many trees in the loose skin mandarin production area including Zhejiang and Hunan (Table 6.15). The production of 2000 and 2001 was less than that in 1999.

Most citrus are consumed as fresh fruits in the domestic market; about 300,000 MT of mandarin is used for processing of canned segments, about 50,000 MT for making orange juice.

In the recent years, a total of about 200,000 MT of citrus was exported mainly to the nearby countries and regions such as Philippines, Indonesia

TABLE 6.14. The Hectarage and Production of Citrus in China

Year	Hectares × 1000	Production 1000 MT	Year	Hectares × 1000	Production 1000 MT
1971		239	1986	672	2548
1972		308	1987	864	3224
1973		305	1988	955	2560
1974		337	1989	1026	4561
1975		336	1990	1061	4855
1976		281	1991	1123	6333
1977		398	1992	1087	5160
1978	178	383	1993	1126	6561
1979	215	555	1994	1142	6795
1980	260	770	1995	1214	8222
1981	274	798	1996	1280	8456
1982	324	939	1997	1350	10100
1983	353	1296	1998	1200	8590
1984	401	1499	1999	1283	10790
1985	507	1808	2000	12750	87830

Source: The Ministry of Agriculture of China (2001).

and Malaysia. Over 90% of the exported types were loose skin mandarin. In 2001, China exported about 170,000 MT of canned citrus segments to Japan and USA. At the same time, China imported about 70,000 MT fresh citrus fruit from USA, Australia, Israel and other countries. Orange juice consumption has been increasing. However, most of the juice was imported as concentrated orange juice from Brazil, USA and Israel.

PRODUCING REGIONS

Citrus-producing regions in China are located from 18 to 37 degrees north latitude; the annual mean air temperatures is 14.5°-27°C, the extreme minimum air temperatures is -9° to 0°C, and annual precipitation is generally above 1000 mm with most rainfall in spring and summer. The important citrus-producing region has been tentatively divided into one tropical and three subtropical districts based on climatic adaptability (Fig. 6.18). The most important are the subtropical districts and these are described more fully.

The northern subtropical producing district has an annual mean air temperature of 15°-17°C and annual rainfall of 750-1000 mm; the extreme minimum air temperature is commonly about -5°C. This district includes most citrus areas of Zhejiang, Jingsu, and Guizhou, and northern areas of Jiangxi and Hunan provinces. Satsuma mandarin is the main citrus crop in this district.

The middle subtropical producing district has an annual mean air temperature of 18°-22°C, and extreme minimum air temperature of 2°-3°C and annual rainfall above 1000 mm. This district comprises the Sichuan Basin;

TABLE 6.15. The Production Areas (excluding Taiwan) of Citrus in China

	1999		2000	
Provinces	Hectares	MT	Hectares	MT
Shanghai	4,500.00	133,860.00	4,800.00	101,765.00
Jiangsu	3,200.00	62,081.00	3,300.00	42,747.00
Zhejiang	132,900.00	2,120,078.00	125,230.00	971,896.00
Anhui	1,960.00	6,859.00	1,800.00	5,282.00
Fujian	148,600.00	1,589,142.00	137,900.00	1,206,027.00
Jiangxi	177,800.00	539,222.00	169,300.00	282,976.00
Henan	4,570.00	14,084.00	4,900.00	21,201.00
Hunan	245,800.00	1,496,568.00	247,900.00	1,259,254.00
Hubei	102,400.00	993,502.00	99,100.00	946,236.00
Guangdong	79,410.00	836,091.00	82,230.00	810,595.00
Guangxi	105,100.00	1,061,790.00	110,000.00	879,914.00
Chongqing	60,000.00	526,695.00	63,150.00	583,944.00
Sichuan	152,500.00	1,162,243.00	155,200.00	1,327,534.00
Guizhou	34,200.00	112,731.00	32,890.00	101,340.00
Yunan	17,600.00	89,435.00	19,500.00	91,640.00
Shanxi	11,030.00	29,588.00	12,050.00	35,155.00
Gansu	700.00	1,871.00	200.00	1,982.00
Hainan	600.00	11,219.00	2,230.00	13,741.00
Total	1,282,879.00	10,787,059.00	1,271,680.00	8,783,129.00

Source: The Ministry of Agriculture of China (2001).

the Gorge region of the Yangtze River; the southern part of the provinces of Zhejiang, Hunan, and Jiangxi; the western part of Hubei; and the middle part of the provinces of Fujian, Guangdong, and Guangxi. Sweet orange and mandarin including Ponkan and Satsuma mandarin are the main citrus types in this district, and pummelo is also produced.

The southern subtropical producing district has an annual mean air temperature of 22°-24°C and annual precipitation of 1200-2000 mm; snow and frost are rare. This district includes most of Taiwan province; the southern part of the provinces of Fujian, Guangdong, and Guangxi; Xishuangbanna region of Yunan province, and other areas. The main citrus types are Ponkan, Jiagan and sweet orange. Pummelo is also important.

CITRUS CULTIVARS

There are many varieties grown in China. In the past decade, varieties structure has changed, decreasing the proportion of mandarin and increasing that of sweet orange, especially navel orange (Zhang *et al.* 1992). For commercial cultivation, the varieties can be classified into three categories, i.e., for ornamental, for fresh fruit or processing and for medicine. For

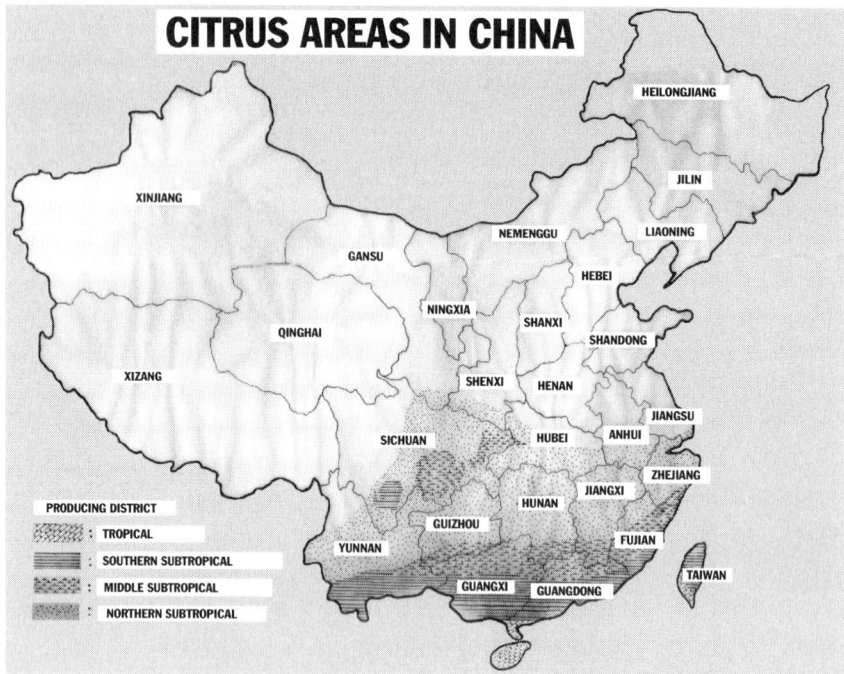

Fig. 6.18. Four citrus producing districts based on climatic adaptability are recognized in China.

ornamental, kumquat, nianju tangerine, and sometimes the citron are cultivated. Most of the mandarin and sweet orange are cultivated for fresh and processing. Trifoliate orange is grown in some area for making Chinese medicine. Based on the recent investigation, loose skin mandarin including tangerine, mandarin and tangor consists of about 60% of the total production, sweet orange 30%, pummelo 9.5% and rest for others.

Loose Skin Mandarins

Satsuma Mandarins lead in hectarage and yield in Chinese citriculture. Satsuma (*C. unshiu* Marc.) is mainly planted in the northern and middle subtropical citrus districts. During 1960-1990s, the hectarage of Satsuma increased more rapidly than that of other cultivars since the prolific performance and seedlessness and easy peeling trains. The main cultivars include Owari, Miyagawa wase, Okitsu wase and Guo qing No. 1 early Satsuma etc. In the past years, some of the Satsuma mandarin were in fact topworked with navel orange in the areas suitable for oranges.

Ponkan

Ponkan (*C. reticulata* Blanco) is also called Lugan in Fujian, and Baiju in Yunan. It is widely planted in Fujian, Taiwan, Guangdong, and Guangxi, and is also planted in some area in Zhejiang, Hunan and Hubei provinces.

Others

There are many kinds of loose skin mandarin types grown in China. Tankan (*C. tankan* Tan.) is commercially cultivated in the southern subtropical citrus district. Tankan is valued for is high productivity, late ripening (January-February harvest), and good performance in storage. However, its hectarage has been decreasing since the yellow shoots diseases and the lower net income compared to Lychee and longan in the southern subtropical area (Guangdong). Hongju (*C. tangerina* Hort. Ex. Tan.) is known for high yield and good outer-appearance and was important in Sichuan and Fujian provinces; its hectarage has decreased since 1990s. The small fruit mandarin, Nanfengmiju (*C. kinokoni* Hort. ex Tan.) is planted in Nanfeng county and nearby areas in Jiangxi province. Bendizao (*C. succosa* Hort. ex Tan.), a very flavorful tangerine is mainly grown in Taizhou of Zhejiang province.

Sweet Orange

Navel orange Sweet [*C. sinensis* (L.) Osb.] is second to mandarin in hectarage and yield in the Chinese citrus industry. Jincheng, Xuegan and navel orange account for more than 80% of the sweet orange production in this country. Navel orange is grown mainly in the three gorges areas, south part of Jiangxi, southern-west area of Hunan, Guilin area of Guanxi and some area in Sichuan; the cultivars include Newhall, Skagg's Bonanza and local strain Luo navel, Fengjie 72-1, etc. Jincheng is mainly planted in Chongqing and Xuegan in Fujian province. Summer orange Valencia occupies small hectarage in the Middle and upper reach of Yangtze river. However, recently Valencia's hectarage increased quickly in Chongqing. Other local varieties such as Dahong (deep red skin), Bingtang Cheng (acidless sweet orange) are planted in Hunan province. In 1980s, Hamlin was planted in south part of Hunan and other areas, but its hectarage is small.

Pummelo

Pummelo [*C. grandis* (L.) Osbeck] accounts for about 10% of the total production in China. The main varieties include Shatian, a very sweet cultivar mainly grown Guangxi, Jianghua county of Hunan and Meizhou of Guandong. Since 1990s, Guanxi pummelo, which is originated in Pinghe county of Fujian, was mainly grown in Fujian and some areas in Hunan and other provinces; this variety is selected from chance seedling in Pinghe county of Fujian, its flavor is rich with about 0.8% acid in the juice, prolific, seedless and juicy. Yuhuan pummelo, and Huyou, maybe the nature hybrids of orange with pummelo, are grown in Zhejiang province.

Kumquat

Kumquat is grown in China mainly for making preserved fruits and for ornamentals. The main cultivars include Luofu [*Fortunella margarita* (Lour.) Swingle], Luowen [*F. japonica* (Thumb.) Swingle], and Jindan (*F. crassifolia* Swingle). Jindan are consumed as fresh or preserved fruits and are used for ornamentals also. The main producing area of kumquat lies within Ningbo and Zhenhai counties of Zhejiang, Yunxiao county of Fujian, Suichuan county of Jiangxi, Liuyang and Lanshan counties of Hunan, and Rong-an and Yangshuo counties of Guangxi.

Citron

Citrus medica L. and fingered citron [*C. medica var. sarcodactylis* (Noot.) Swingle] are scattered in the middle and southern subtropical citrus districts, Jinhua of Zhejiang province is one of the main producing area for fingered citron. The citron is mainly used for medicinal and ornamental purposes.

Lemon

Lemon is not so commonly grown in China as the other types of citrus due to cold weather limitations. Eureka and Lisbon lemon [*C. limon* (L.) Burm.] are planted in Anyue of Sichuan and recently in Dehong district of Yunan.

ROOTSTOCKS

Trifoliate orange [*Poncirus trifoliate* (L.) Raf.] is an important rootstock in Chinese citriculture, and its fruit can be used as medicinal material. Trifoliate orange is planted mainly along the Yangtze River Valley as a fence plant. It is widely used as rootstock for nearly all the satsumas and kumquats in the various citrus areas, and also for other mandarins and sweet oranges in the middle and northern citrus-producing regions.

Suanju (*C. sunki* Hort. ex Tan.), Limeng (*C. limonia* Osbeck), Hongju (*C. tangerina* Hort. ex Tan.), and some other mandarins are used as rootstocks for sweet oranges and mandarins in the southern citrus-producing region, and in some cases Hongju, which is tolerant to citrus excortis viroid, is also used in the middle and upper reach of Yangtze River. Since the 1950s, Sanhuhongju (*C. erythrosa* Hort. ex Tan.) has been used as rootstock by certain orchards in Guangdong with good results. Goutoucheng (*C. aurantium* L.) is used as the main rootstock in the saline-alkali soil of the coastal region of Zhejiang.

PROPAGATION METHODS

Grafting is widely used in citrus propagation in China. Single-bud grafting in spring and single-bud side grafting and shield budding in autumn and spring are practiced. Many nurseries graft the bud at a height of 4-7 cm above the soil level, although higher position (15 cm above the soil) has been recommended by scientists and government since 1980s. After grafting a single shoot is encouraged, and cut back to a height of 40-50 cm. Three or four branches are usually kept. In general, two years are needed to produce nursery stock for planting. Most of the grafted trees are produced by the conventional method in the open field. Recently, sets of greenhouses were built by companies to produce grafted trees for new plantations. In south part of Jiangxi province, a simple and improved contain propagation method is widely used in the new plantation of navel orange. This method modified the classic method by growing the grafted trees from the open field in a plastic bag (with 15 kg of very fertile soil) in the spring, the bagged trees are planted to the new orchard after four months of intensive care. This modified method improves the growth of the young tree. Based on the observation, the tree can grow to 1.8 meter high for one year and flower after another year. This method is being gradually adopted in other locations.

ORCHARD PRACTICES

Chinese citrus orchards are established on hills, hilly land with a gentle slope, the alluvial soil along the rivers, and other flats including the flat land with high water tables where rice is usually planted.

The usual spacing of citrus orchards is 3.3 × 4 m (about 750 trees/ha), but a spacing of 4 × 5 m is also practices in some districts. During 1980-1990s, planned close planting (1200-1800 trees/ha) has been practiced in portions of some orchards for early production. Half of the trees will be removed when tree crowding occurs. In fact, many peasants would not like to cut the extra trees, which leads to the crowding of the orchard.

On the hills, terraces are usually prepared before citrus planting. Soil improvement procedures are carried out before and after planting where the orchard tilling depth is not deep enough for root development. In that case, one cubic meter (1 × 1 × 1 meter) planting hole or 1-m-wide and 1-m-deep planting ditch is prepared. In recent years, use of a 70-cm rather than 1-m-deep planting hole or ditch has been recommended in Jiangxi and in some other districts. The planting hole or ditch is usually filled with soil mixed with pig or cow dung, green manure, and weeds or compost. In some orchards, cake, bone meal, or calcium super-phosphate and lime are also mixed into the fill soil. After planting, a ditch about 40 cm deep is dug around the tree canopy each year, and organic fertilizers mixed with soil are used to fill up the ditch. In alluvial orchards, the depth of the planting hole or ditch is generally about 50 cm, and organic fertilizers are also used. In the flat land with high water tables, a mound is usually prepared for planting; after planting a ridge and ditch are prepared.

In addition to organic fertilizers, urea and ammonium sulfate are commonly used. In some orchards, especially flat orchards with high water tables, liquid fertilizers mixed with cake, pig dung, etc. are applied. Six to ten annual fertilizer applications in young groves and four to six in bearing orchards are recommended. In certain orchards urea spray for ex-root nutrition is practiced.

Flat orchards with a high water table are irrigated at intervals. The water usually stays in the ditch for a period of time to allow permeation through the ridge. In orchards on hilly land and those on other flat land, furrow irrigation is carried out in the dry season. In a limited number of orchards, sprinkling or drip irrigation is available.

In general, dead twigs are pruned off and the water sprouts are cut back every year. In some districts, the thinning and cut back of the bearing shoots are also practiced after harvesting. In orchards receiving good care, occasional summer sprouts and autumn shoots of young trees are pinched off when the shoots are about 1 cm in length, to induce uniform sprouting of summer shoot and autumn growth. All of the summer sprouts on trees at the initial bearing stage are pinched off to reduce fruit dropping and to induce a uniform autumn sprouting.

Recently, since the increased labor expense, simplified pruning is recommended to the farmers. This method consists of lower density of planting, and the open-center pruning. If the trees are crowding, one line of the trees will be removed; for a crowding tree, a branch in the center of the canopy is removed to let the sunlight enter into the trunk area. The simplified method saves a lot of labor. For the classic pruning, a skilled technician can prune just 8-10 trees a day, but for the simple method, 50 trees a day.

DISEASES, PESTS, AND COLD INJURY

Huanglongbing (citrus yellow shoot disease), which is prevalent in southern citrus-producing areas, is the most serious problem in the Chinese citrus industry. Citrus canker can be found in some area in Guangdong,

Guangxi, Fujian, south part of Zhejiang, Jiangxi and Hunan province. In these area, chemicals (copper mixture) are used 2-3 times a year provides good control. Citrus exocortis, Stem-pitting tristeza in some pummelo producing area, the tatter-leaf, scab, footrot, and anthracnose may cause damage in citrus areas. Red mite, rust mite, arrow headed scale, leaf miner are common pests in the orchard. Chinese citrus orchards are generally protected with insecticides and miticides applied 4 to 10 times per year. Periodic cold injury occurs in northern citrus-producing areas and causes serious damage there.

REFERENCES

BURKE, J. H. 1967. The commercial citrus regions of the world. *In* Citrus Industry, W. Reuther *et al.* (Editors). University of California, CA, USA. 1, 140-146.

LI, D. G. 1996. Citriculture. China Agr. Press, Beijing.

THE MINISTRY OF AGRICULTURE OF CHINA. 2001. Agriculture Statistical Data of China (2000), China Agr. Press, Beijing. 116-119.

ZHANG, W. W., DENG, X. X. and DENG, Z. A. 1992. Citrus germplasm preservation and varietal improvement works in China. Proc. VII Inter. Soc. Citriculture 1, 67-71.

ZHAOLING, H. 1968. China, pp. 199-204. *In* Fresh Citrus Fruits, W. Wardowski, S. Nagy and W. Grierson (Editors). Avi Publishing Co.

Uruguay

José Ortiz de Taranco

La Banda Oriental del Río Uruguay was the last American territory to be colonized by Spain. As a consequence of the Tratado de Tordesillas of 1494 it was the scene of serious border controversies between Spain and Portugal when the Colonia del Sacramento was founded by Portugal in 1680 in the eastern territory opposite Buenos Aires. The Colonia was strongly disputed by arms and diplomacy and it changed hands several times. Spain founded and fortified the port of Montevideo in 1724 to protect the territory of the Banda and the Río de la Plata from the Portuguese forages and the British pirates.

Before the settlement of the mentioned towns in its territory, the Banda Oriental was considered unproductive land because no gold or silver was found and the controversies about its limits were due to the geopolitics importance of the dominance of the northern coast of the Río de la Plata, entry to the heart of South America.

But since the beginning of the 17th century the famous Hernando Arias de Saavedra (Hernandarias) had introduced in the Banda Oriental the first heads of cattle during the period when the crowns of Spain and Portugal remained united under king Philip III. This introduction together with the one by the Jesuit missionaries from the Guaranitic Missions in Paraguay caused the expansion of the cattle that multiplied naturally, stimulated by the rich Uruguayan prairies criss-crossed by numerous rivers and streams. So in the 18th century the territory having a scarce population of nomad Indians became a "leather mine". The incipient industrial revolution of this century, that created a strong demand of leather for the manufacture of transmission belts for the new machines, found an inexhaustible supply in the Banda Oriental. Later on the economic importance of cattle raising greatly increased due to cured salted meat.

Consequently, the slow colonization of the land began and there followed the expansion and growth of fruit trees, mostly citrus, which has always taken place in the history of mankind.

There is no specific mention of the introduction of the first orange trees but there are references that the Presbyter Perez Castellanos grew some near Montevideo in mid 18th century. It is also known that the citrus came down by the Uruguay River to supply Buenos Aires from the Jesuitic Missions upstream. This is the reason why citrus expanded in the bank of the river during the 17th and 18th centuries particularly in the area of the present city of Salto. The two large citrus areas in Uruguay originated in this way. Citrus found an excellent environment for its expansion in these lands. The climatic conditions and the soil features make it possible to produce citrus of the best quality.

A favorable relation of acids and sugars is the result of mild winter frosts that give the fruit its excellent flavour and color, especially desirable for fresh fruit consumption. The yield per hectare obtained in this climate is lower than those of the tropical climates but the quality is superior in spite of the threat of the freezes.

When the República Oriental del Uruguay emancipated in 1830, the citrus culture continues to expand in the areas near the many towns and villages founded to colonize the country. Due to the fact that there were very few roads, the trade remained limited to the supply by small villages. Nevertheless, the supply to the city of Buenos Aires greatly increased by means of the waterway from the coastal region of the Uruguay River.

Citrus culture continued to grow in the 19th century due to the development of the railroad and the telegraph during the last quarter of the century. These means of communication, in a country with no mountains, allowed the slow economic integration of the entire territory. In the same way the enormous population growth that between 1850 and 1900 increased from 200,000 to 1,000,000 inhabitants as a result of immigration. The young nation that began to formulate laws and regulations not without internal conflicts that end in the first years of the 20th century.

Citriculture slowly gained the features of a commercial culture to supply the domestic demand as the population grew while at the same time the shipments to Buenos Aires continued to increase. In the twenties the government gave its support to production creating an experiment station and helping to eradicate plagues of locust that used to come in enormous flocks that darkened the sky from the Paraguayan Chaco.

So the cultivation of citrus strongly grew to such a point that already in the 1930s some pioneers, as Mr. Pedro B. Solari started to plan to export overseas. Two facts stopped the expansion of the Uruguayan citrus international markets. The first is the World War II that not only destroyed the potential consumer markets but also affected sea traffic. A German submarine torpedoed the ship that carried one of the experimental shipments by Mr. Solari and the small cargo was lost. On the other hand the national production until then was based on grafting on root stocks of bitter orange (*Citrus aurantium*) which was seriously affected by the citrus tristeza virus that attacked a great number of plants. The production improved when plants were slowly replaced by others grafted on trifoliate orange (*Poncirus trifoliata*), resistant to the disease.

The slow European recovery following the war, and also the slow recovery of Uruguayan citriculture was delayed until the 1960s. The start of the export trade of citrus later became important.

The serious freeze of 1967 again stopped the expansion until 1970. Since then the sustained growth of citrus and exports took place. This growth was guided by old pioneer families such as Solari, Caputto, Cerdeiras Alonso and Taranco (author's family). reinforced by the strong incidence of a large group of immigrants that came from Algeria, led by André Daricarrère. A little later Don Carlos Fraschini enthusiastically supported the development of citriculture.

The technical school created by the Israeli consultant Menashe Ben David, the advice of relevant professionals as Dr. Salibe from Brazil and the continuous study by Uruguayan producers and technicians made it possible for citriculture of the country to reach a high degree of specialization in a very short time. This positioned citrus in to be high quality, in spite of the relatively small volumes produced due to a small population of little more of 3 million inhabitants.

The production was oriented toward fresh fruit consumption due to the special features of climate and soil. Numerous packing plants with first generation equipment were installed beginning in 1980. Cold storage rooms, dock terminals on the Uruguay River and well-organized transportation rounded the needs of an industry in constant expansion. For more than thirty years the domestic market for fresh fruits was saturated so the expansion of the sector has aimed at the international market. The processing industry for juice and essential oils has developed to process fruit whose size and quality do not reach the necessary standards for fresh fruit export. In 2001 120,000 tons were marketed as fresh exports, 110,000 tons were processed and 113,000 tons were utilized in the fresh domestic market.

All this process of expansion has demanded the investment of huge capital. Similarly, the international trade of citrus handled by the supermarket chains, as well the sea transport, demand larger volumes and more uniform production, very far from the family production of 40 years ago. Trade is now conducted by great multinational firms that due to world globalisation take part in Uruguayan citriculture.

Fig. 6.19. North and south citrus producing areas in Uruguay.

The sector is of great economic importance, citrus being the second only to rice in agricultural export products from Uruguay. The great demand of labor needed in its culture and in packing plants as well as the different services demanded by the industry have a great social importance. The added value that through containers, packing materials, transport and services is incorporated to the agricultural products makes the activity an important part of the economy.

Nevertheless, the last decade has not been an easy one. The economic policy of the country, strongly influenced by the regional conditions of MERCUSUR (Mercado Común del Sur, the common market among Argentina, Brazil, Paraguay and Uruguay) has resulted in a gradual but constant

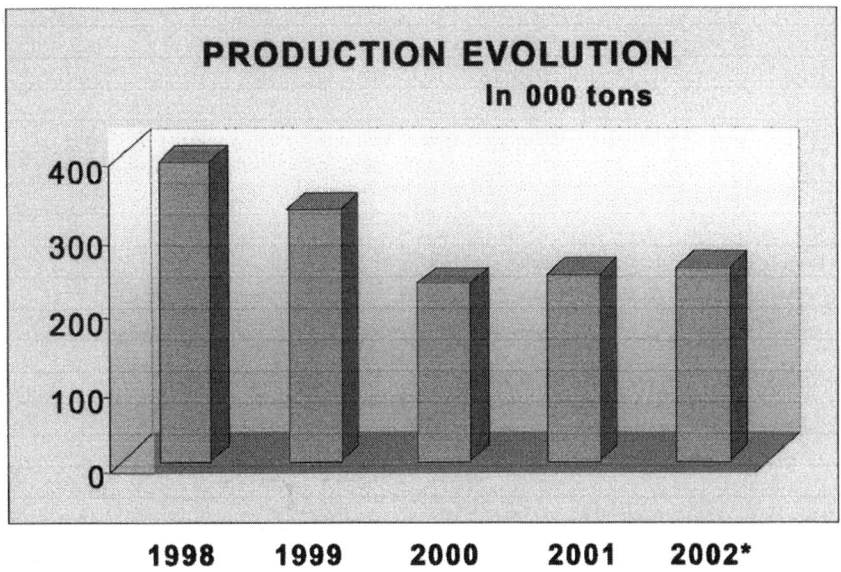

PRODUCTION EVOLUTION
In 000 tons

400

300

200

100

0

1998   1999   2000   2001   2002*

Fig. 6.20. Production of citrus in Uruguay.

process of the peso overvaluation. While domestic inflation was rising the devaluation of the Uruguayan peso against the dollar did not follow the same pattern, so a substantial increase of domestic costs in terms of foreign currency took place. The dollar appreciation against the European currency during the 1990s resulted in serious profit losses since Europe was the main market of Uruguayan citrus, and in turn it also paved the way for deep bank debt of the sector whose flexibility for negotiating was hindered by the naturally slow agricultural processes.

All the same, the sector is still moving forward and by being aware of the evolution of markets during the last ten years has replaced some varieties of citrus by ones in greater demand, such as mandarins that are easily peeled. It has also replaced some late varieties by some early ones, which are less, exposed to frosts and it has also developed some revolutionary technologies, such as utilizing temperature inversions for their control.

The economic crisis that has recently hit Uruguay as a result of the regional impact and which is being overcome by means of international help has resulted in a move towards a free-floating exchange ratio which will make our citrus more competitive. The appreciation of the Euro against the dollar will also be favorable to export.

The country also trusts that soon the long negotiations towards the opening of the North American market as well as the Chinese market will reach a successful agreement. Both will be of tremendous importance for

TABLE 6.16. Uruguay Citrus Production Volumes and Percentage for the Year 2001

Citrus type	Production metric tons	%
Lemons	46,447	14
Mandarins	97,000	28
Oranges	189,007	55
Grapefruit	10,063	3
Other	77	0
Total	342,594	100

the future expansion and success of our citriculture with a goal of being a supplier of counter-season fruit to the Northern Hemisphere.

A series of statistical data follows. This data was compiled by Ing. Marta Bentancour of the Comisión Nacional del Plan Citrícola that depends of the Ministerio de Ganadería, Agricultura y Pesca and where there are representatives of the active sectors of production. Our production area is now of 20,862 hectares with 6.36 million trees. The production exceeds 300,000 metric tons with 85% in the north and 15% in the south (Fig. 6.19). Total production has grown from 272 thousand tons in 1996 to 343 thousand tons in 2001. Climatic adverse conditions caused a significant reduction after 1998 season (Fig. 6.20). Over 15,000 people work in the sector, either stable or seasonal, which gives employment to 0.7 man per hectare.

Valencia and Navels account for 91% of oranges; Satsumas and Ellendales 51% of mandarins. New varieties, such as Clementines are growing in production during the last few years, due to market demand. Most Uruguayan lemons are a variety called Cuatro Estaciones and grapefruit represent only 3% of all citrus produced (Table 6.16).

Fresh fruit is exported primarily to Europe, and specially to the EU (Table 6.17), where a sanitary protocol audited by the EU has assured

TABLE 6.17. Fresh Citrus Exports in Metric Tons 1998 to 2001 to Major Destinations

Destination	1998	1999	2000	2001
Canada	4,195	2,395	1,735	1,667
Eastern Europe	17,825	20,228	18,603	15,279
Far East	1,735	3,176	1,229	1,650
Mercosur[a]	8,696	4,488	2,212	1,931
Arab Counties	2,146	877	136	512
Other Americas	199	212	45	596
Europe	95,640	88,838	51,301	75,873
Total	130,435	120,214	75,260	97,508

[a]Mercado Común del Sur, the common market among Argentina, Brasil, Paraguay and Uruguay.

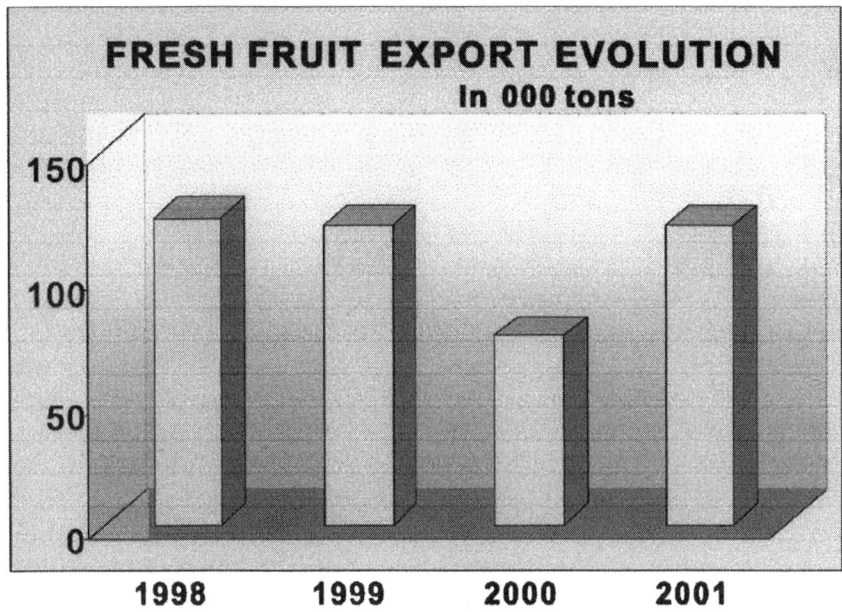

Fig. 6.21. Total citrus exports from Uruguay 1998 to 2001.

that important market through a very strict traceability program carried out
under the responsibility of the Uruguayan Official Authorities (Fig. 6.21).

REFERENCE

ORIZ DE TARANCO, J. 2001. Historia de la Citricultura del Uruguay. Tradinco, Montevideo.

6
Part 9

Spain

Salvador Zaragoza and Manuel Agustí

Citriculture plays an important role in the Spanish economy and is one of the first sources of income in the exports balance in Spain. Citrus culture generates jobs for many families because it involves the abundant use of hand labor. It provides year-round employment since many workers are retained for harvesting after field operations are completed. There are many ancillary enterprises: fertilizers, pesticides, machinery, packaging and others; which are dependent upon the citrus industry. On the other hand, many of the new plantings are made with a prior transformation of slightly producing drylands, which thanks to the irrigation set up and to the citriculture, provide an improvement in profitability.

History of Spanish Citriculture

The earliest references on the presence of citrus in the Spanish peninsula date to the seventh century and are attributed to Isidoro de Sevilla who mentioned the citron (*Citrus medica* L.) in his *Etymologies*. The sour orange (*C. aurantium* L.) was introduced much later, in the eleventh century, by the Arabs, and at the same time or afterwards the lemon (*C. limon* (L.) Burn. f.) and the *zamboa* or pummelo (*C. grandis* (L.) Osb.). The sweet orange (*C. sinensis* L.) probably arrived in Spain at the end of the 15th century or at the beginning of the 16th, through Italian and Portuguese sailors and the common or willow wild mandarin (*C. deliciosa* Ten.) was introduced in 1845 (Zaragoza 1993).

Until the end of the of the eighteenth century the evolution of the cultivation was slow, and were mainly used as ornamental plants, for medicinal purposes or in confectionery. The first large-scale plantings of orange trees

213

were established around 1830. In 1879 there were 8,362 ha under captivation, 80,000 ha in 1940, 200,000 in 1978 (Zaragoza 1993) and 300,000 at present.

Area Under Cultivation

Cultivation of citrus in Spain is carried out mainly along the Eastern coast (Levante) and Southern coast (Andalucía) in the river valleys, between 36° and 40.5° Hector N (Fig. 6.22). In other areas, with a few exceptions, the cultivation is restricted by the risk of freezes. The average annual rainfall is between 300 mm and 650 mm, (sometime more than 900 mm) and all the citrus area requires irrigation. In general, the soils are calcareous, low in organic matter and a pH between 7,5 and 8,5. The southwest of Spain is the exception with sandy and acids soils.

At present the area planted with citrus is about 300,000 ha. The hectarage is increasing since many years ago, and the last 10 years the mean of this increase is about 3,000 ha/year. The increase has been the result of the influence of trickle irrigation, that has favoured the use of land with climate and soil conditions suitable for citrus growing, and because of the difficul-

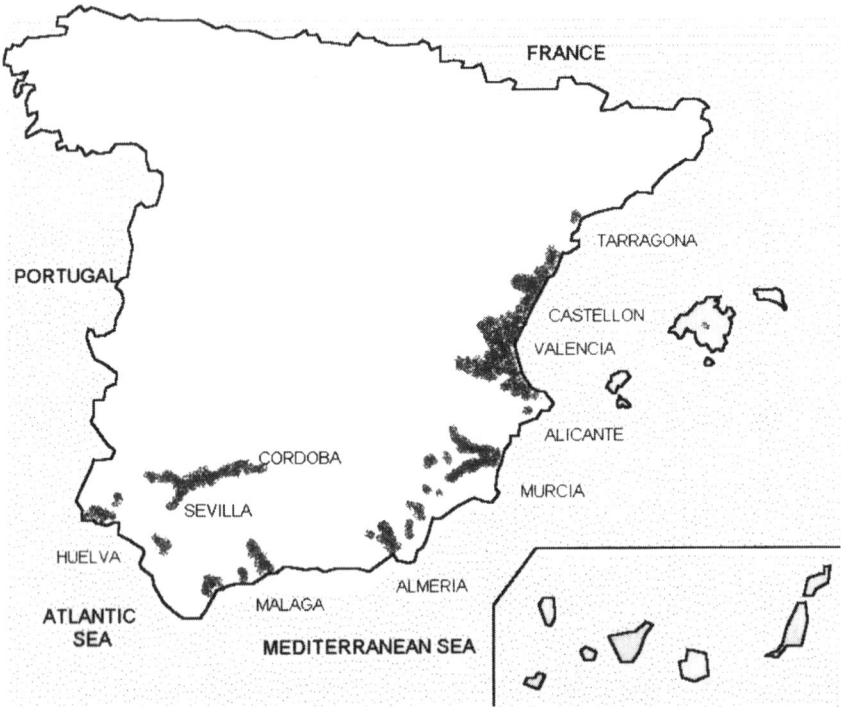

Fig. 6.22. Location of the major citrus growing areas in Spain.

ties to obtain good water sources suitable for conventional irrigation, or because of their orographic conditions, their transformation was a very expensive operation.

Most of the sweet oranges and mandarins are produced in the provinces of Valencia and Castellón, whereas lemon is basically cultivated in Murcia and Alicante. Sour orange is mainly produced in Sevilla. More than 80% of the area planted with citrus is concentrated in the eastern area.

Production and Varietal Distribution

Spain has traditionally cultivated many citrus varieties for fresh consumption, in order to meet the demands of the market throughout the year. The whole citrus production has increased near one million tons in the past 10 years (Table 6.18). In the season 2003-2004, the production reached more than 6 million tons from which the 51% are oranges, the 31% mandarins, the 17.5% lemons and the 0.5% others species. The average production, about 20 tons/ha, is low as a consequence of the new plantations and the constant replacement of plants for several reasons. The nurseries produce about 6 million plants annually for commercial orchards and gardening.

Orange varieties are mainly navel oranges, Navelina being the most important variety (1.2×10^6 tons/year), which represents near the 20% of total Spanish citrus production, followed by late navel oranges, Navelate and Lane late, Washington navel and others (400×10^3 tons). Valencia late sweet orange shows a slight increase during recent years (600×10^3 tons), whereas Salustiana remains stable (200×10^3 tons/year).

Spain produces nearly 1.2×10^6 tons a year of Clementine mandarin, mainly Clemenules (700×10^6 tons) and early maturing cultivars, such as Marisol, Oronules and Oroval (300×10^6 tons). Late maturing Clementine mandarins, mainly Hernandina, are produced in relative small quantities ($<100 \times 10^3$ tons/year). Hybrids and mandarin-like varieties are also produced (500×10^3 tons). Nova and Fortune mandarins the most important varieties; the latter is being reduced in production due to *Alternaria alternata* problems. Some quantities of Satsuma mandarin (250×10^3 tons) are also produced, mainly Owari and also Clausellina and Okitsu.

The most important variety of lemon grown in Spain is Fino (600×10^3 tons) followed by Verna (400×10^3 tons). The quantities are approximate and change slightly every season. Grapefruit and other *Citrus* species are produced in a very low quantities.

Although this is a varietal scheme that allows fruit marketing throughout the entire year, the seasonal distribution is markedly unbalanced and concentrated in November through January (Fig. 6.23). Because it saturates the market and, consequently, prices fall, research on obtaining early- and

TABLE 6.18. Production and Utilization of Citrus in Spain (tons × 10³)

	1993-94	1994-95	1995-96	1996-97	1997-98	1998-99	1999-00	2000-01	2001-02	2002-03
MANDARINS										
Production	1,626.4	1,749.3	1,683.9	1,507.1	2,099.0	1,749.2	2,042.3	1,819.0	1,778.1	2,010.0
Domestic	280.0	269.0	325.5	202.0	350.0	303.0	276.1	336.5	232.0	266.0
Processed	181.0	206.6	278.0	184.0	311.0	296.4	284.0	177.0	252.6	244.0
Wastes	50.2	78.0	46.8	13.4	114.6	47.6	165.6	162.4	108.5	130.2
Exports	1,115.2	1,195.7	1,033.6	1,107.7	1,323.4	1,102.2	1,316.6	1,143.1	1,185.0	1,369.8
ORANGES										
Production	2,674.0	2,759.2	2,512.0	2,281.8	2,786.0	2,623.7	2,811.4	2,708.8	2,923.7	2,935.0
Domestic	886.7	756.2	698.4	533.0	750.0	764.0	817.00	887.3	924.4	897.0
Processed	385.0	605.1	631.0	523.5	664.0	590.0	497.0	356.5	484.8	581.0
Wastes	127.0	97.7	58.9	29.5	90.7	55.4	67.4	278.5	65.7	48.1
Exports	1,275.3	1,300.2	1,124.1	1,195.8	1,281.3	1,214.3	1,430.0	1,186.5	1,448.8	1,408.9
LEMONS										
Production	662.0	622.08	499.3	665.8	968.2	860.1	745.8	845.9	1017.8	962.0
Domestic	128.4	115.8	74.8	60.0	110.0	105.0	125.0	130.0	140.0	140.0
Processed	105.0	160.0	96.0	187.0	272.0	268.4	141.0	168.6	218.0	187.0
Wastes	74.0	11.4	1.2	7.7	45.0	35.9	25.0	42.0	178.2	134.4
Exports	354.6	335.6	327.3	411.1	541.2	450.8	454.8	505.3	481.6	500.6
GRAPEFRUIT										
Production	31.5	36.4	29.0	20.1	32.1	27.7	31.9	27.0	31.0	37.0
Domestic	12.0	15.4	10.0	1.0	5.0	3.0	3.0	1.2	1.4	—
Processed	2.0	1.5	—	—	2.0	2.0	2.6	2.0	3.0	3.4
Wastes	0.5	0.5	1.1	0.5	1.0	0.7	1.0	—	—	—
Exports	17.0	19.0	17.9	17.6	24.1	22.0	25.3	23.8	26.6	33.6

Source CLAM (1995-2004)

TABLE 6.18. (Continued) Production and Utilization of Citrus in Spain (tons × 10³)

	Season									
	1993-94	1994-95	1995-96	1996-97	1997-98	1998-99	1999-00	2000-01	2001-02	2002-03
TOTAL										
Production	4,993.9	5,167.7	4,724.2	4,474.8	5,885.3	5,260.7	5,631.4	5,400.7	5,750.6	5,944.0
Domestic	1307.1	1,156.4	1,108.3	797.0	1,215.0	1,175.0	1,221.1	1,355.0	1,297.8	1,303.0
Processed	673.0	973.2	1,005.0	894.5	1,249.0	1,156.8	924.6	704.1	958.4	1,015.4
Wastes	251.7	187.6	108.0	51.1	251.3	139.6	259.0	482.9	352.4	312.7
Exports	2,762.1	2,850.5	2,502.9	2,732.2	3,170.0	2,789.3	3,226.7	2,858.7	3,142.0	3,312.9

Source CLAM (1995-2004)

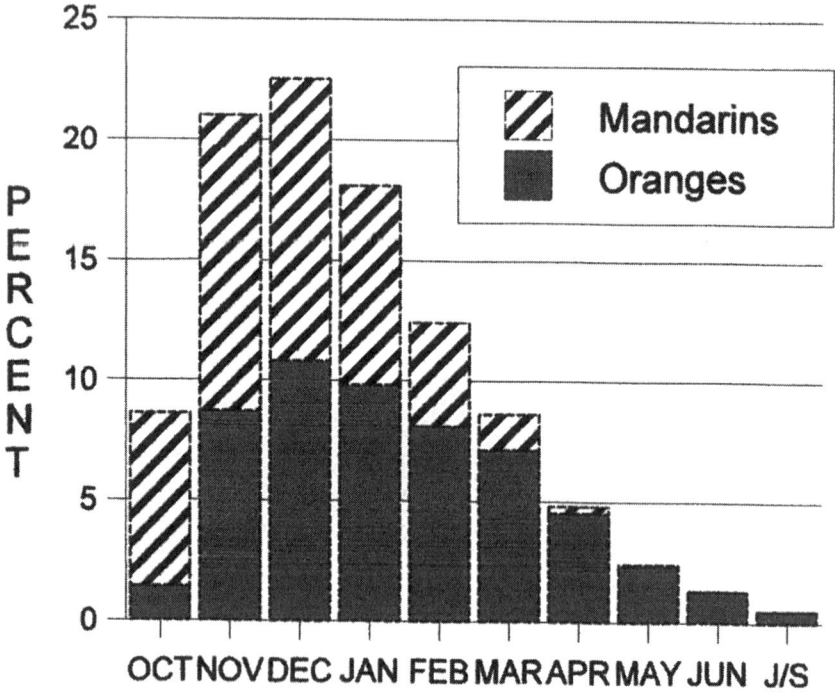

Fig. 6.23. Seasonal production of oranges and mandarins in Spain. Source MAPA.

late-maturing varieties and on the application of techniques capable of delaying harvest have been developed.

Destination of the Production

Most of the production (55%) is exported as fresh fruit, and only a small part (17%) is processed into jam, segments in syrup and juices of several types. Spain is the first exporter country of the world of fresh fruit, with more than 3.3 million ton in the 2002-03 season (Table 6.18). Half of the oranges (1.4×10^6 tons) and lemons (500×10^3 tons) production and more than 65% of mandarins production (1.2×10^6 tons) are exported. Navelina sweet orange, Clementine mandarins and Fino lemon the varieties exported in the greatest volume.

Germany (28%) and France (17%) are the main consumers of Spanish citrus fruits, followed by United Kingdom (11%), Holland (9%), Poland (8%) and Belgium and Italy (4% each). Other countries, such as USA, Canada, Czech Republic, Slovenia, Hungary, and others import around 80×10^3 tons a year. Domestic market consumes more than 650×10^3 tons (23% of total production).

Cultural Practices

One of the most relevant characteristics of Spanish citriculture is the extremely small orchards, specially in the Mediterranean coast where the average size of an orchard is about one hectare. Nevertheless, in Murcia and Andalucía orchards are frequently very large. Small or high tree densities which, in turn, makes it difficult for mechanization and significantly increases production costs. Average tree spacing ranges between 5-6 × 3-4 m, closer in mandarins and wider in lemons, 5.25 × 5.25 m being the most widely used.

Sour orange was the traditional rootstock in Spain. However, since 1972 rootstocks have been restricted to lemon, as a consequence of the spread of tristeza virus. At present there is still about 10% hectarage on sour orange. The new orchards of sweet oranges, mandarins and grapefruit are budded onto Carrizo citrange (*C. sinensis* (L.) Osb × *Poncirus trifoliata* (L.) Raf.) rootstock in higher proportion (75%), followed by Cleopatra mandarin (*C. reshni* Hort. *ex* Tan.) (8%) and Troyer citrange (4%). The alemov (*C. macrophylla* Wester), together with the *C. volkameriana* Ten. & Pasq. are the rootstocks most widely used for lemon. Sometimes the alemov is used in calcareous and saline soils with oranges or mandarins. There are other rootstocks, like Swingle citrumelo used in hard soils, but they are slightly expanded.

Topworking is a common practice and is performed by placing a varying number of patch buds on the suitable scaffold branches with the purpose that the foliage renewal occur as soon as possible. This operation entails a high amount of expense in adult trees, because this involves about two crops and around 4 years until the tree reaches its former size. During all the process of change, care must be taken with pruning, irrigation and fertilization, in order not to unbalance the plant. Special caution is required in order to use vegetative material free of diseases which can be transmitted by budding.

Pruning is a very expensive practice that is performed entirely by hand, with hatchet, handsaw and clippers. Young plants are shaped with 2-3 arms during the initial years. Marure mandarin trees are usually pruned once a year. Oranges, grapefruit and lemons, tend to be pruned annually, but because of high cost, are often pruned every two or three years. A man expends about 10-20 minutes in pruning an adult tree, plus a variable time to eliminate the cut wood, frequently burning it.

Fertilization is done either by conventional procedures or by fertigation, providing elements required according to studies made with Spanish soils and climatic conditions (Legaz and Primo-Millo 1988).

Nitrogen fertilization is done using ammonia sulphate ammonia nitrosulphate, ammonia nitrate or urea, at annual rates of 0.6-0.8 kg N per adult tree, with distribution two or three times a year depending on the soil's characteristics and type. Phosphorus and potassium fertilization is basically made in the spring, using calcium superphosphate and potassium phosphate at rates depending on their content in the soil; average annual maintenance rates range from 0.2 kg P_2O_5 and 0.3 kg K_2O per adult tree. Foliar applications are usually made in the spring and summer for correcting Mg, Zn and Mn deficiencies. The use of soluble or liquid fertilizers is increasing due to increasing trickle irrigation.

Spanish citriculture is absolutely depent on irrigation due to poor rainfall. Flood irrigation is still widespread, but trickle irrigation is markedly increasing recently. Amounts of water, irrigation dosage and the modules are variable, depending on the soil and the year, but general figures range 6000-7000 m^3 ha^{-1}. Trickle irrigation is used in about the 30% of the citrus hectarage and increases every year.

The structure of ownership, and narrow spacing make mechanization difficult. Soil is tilled several times a year, using small machinery or medium size tractors. Many orchards are treated with residual, contact, or translocation herbicides. The semi-non-tillage method is quite widespread, with plant cover in winter, and bare soil in summer.

The use of plant growth regulators (PGRs) contributes to improve production and fruit quality. PGRs increase fruit set of some Clementine varieties, such as Oronules, increase fruit size of some Clementine mandarins and hybrids, promote fruit coloring by using ethylene in degreening chambers, at a concentration of 2 to 5 mg l^{-1}; delay peel senescence of Clementine mandarin by applying gibberellic acid at a concentration of 5 to 10 mg l^{-1} before color break. PGRs and also control several physiological fruit disorders.

Harvesting cost is up to the trader who purchased the fruit. Harvesting is done by carefully cutting with special clippers. Growers can insure crops against freezing, hail, wind and flooding.

All aspects related to the Citrus Industry of Spain have been revised in depth by Agusti (2003).

Sanitation Conditions of Plantings

In general, pests are not serious problems. There are a wide variety of scales which are efficiently controlled with organo-phosphorate products. The most harmful is the California red scale (*Aonidiella aurantii* Maskell). Biological control with predators, *montrouzieri* Muls. and the vedalia (*Rodolia cardinalis* Muls.), is a common practice. The aphids *Toxoptera aurantii* B de F, *Aphis citricola* Van der Goot, *A. gossypii* Glover *and Myzus persicae* Sulzer and are controlled with contact or systemic aphicides. Fortunately *Toxoptera citricida* Kirkaldy does not exists in Spain.

The citrus red mite (*Panonychus citri* McGregor), is the most harmful mite. The Mediterranean fruit fly (*Ceratitis capitata* Wied.), is controlled with aerial sprays. The best time to begin the sprays is determined through flytraps with sex attractants. Wooly whitefly (*Aleurothrixus floccosus* Mask.) is efficiently controlled by its parasite *Cales noacki* How. The citrus leaf miner *(Phyllocnistis citrella* Stainton) is controlled by using abamectina and by its parasite *Citrostrichus phyllocnistoides.*

Insecticide spray liquid is applied with manual nozzles, through hoses, from movable mobile tanks with high pressure pumps. The use of integrated pest management (IPM) increases every year.

Nematodes are almost harmless in the Spanish citriculture.

The incidence of fungi damage, like of *Phytophthora* spp., in citrus cultivation is very limited. In some orchards with trees producing fruit close to the soil, this fungus potentially damages over mature fruit. Pathogenic bacteria have not been detected. Frequently many orchards are planted on ridges to better use the top soil and to avoid foot root problems.

Since 1982, the new plantings are being established with tristeza tolerant rootstocks and virus-free varieties recovered through the Citrus Variety Improvement Program of Spain (CVIPS) developed at the Instituto Valenciano de Investigaciones Agrarias (IVIA) (Navarro 1976).

Trends and Future of Spanish Citriculture

In Spain, citrus producing area increases 3,000 ha a year and Clementine production is increasing the most. This is especially remarkable in the southern regions where climate is warmer and the cost of land is cheaper than the Mediterranean coast. This trend of increasing producing area results in an average increase of production of 90,000-100,000 tons a year. In these new orchards mechanization and drip irrigation are common (Zaragoza 1993; Zaragoza and Hensz 1986).

The new plantings are being established with tristeza tolerant rootstocks and virus-free varieties. However, there are still old orchards affected by virus and fungi diseases that need to be renewed. This renewal program, based in the CVIPS, increases production and fruit quality. From time to time supply exceeds demand, particularly Clementine mandarin in November-January, and prices fall, sometimes dramatically, making it difficult to make a profit. Accordingly, new markets for fresh consumption, new and more efficient ways of commercialization, increased Clementine commercialization and/or new late Clementine-like varieties are needed.

For fresh consumption, fruit quality not only depends on the intrinsic fruit properties but on the mode of cultivation. Therefore, integrated and biological pest and disease management and alternative techniques to PGRs must be developed. Some PGRs and many pesticides are borne restrictions.

The small sizes of the orchards and the raising costs of production are the principal problems hindering mechanization of the Spanish citriculture. Finally, solutions against small holdings must be taken into account as soon as possible. Agricultural policy, financial aids and agronomical solutions are needed urgently.

REFERENCES

AGUSTÍ, M. 2003. Citricultura. Ed. Mundi Prensa, Madrid, Spain

CLAM. Les exportations d'agrumes du basin mediterranéen (Several years).

LEGAZ, F. and PRIMO-MILLO, E. 1988. Normas para la fertilización de los agrios. Generalitat Valenciana, Fullets Divulgació No. 5-88. Valencia.

MAPA. Ministerio de Agricultura, Pesca y Alimentación. Anuario de Estadística Agraria (Several years).

NAVARRO, L. 1976. The citrus variety improvement program in Spain. Proc. 7th Conf. Int. Organ. Citrus Virol., IOCV. Riverside, CA. pp. 198-203.

ZARAGOZA, S. 1993. Past and present situation of the Spanish citrus industry. Conselleria d'Agricultura I Pesca. Generalitat Valenciana.

ZARAGOZA, S. and HENSZ, R. A. 1986. Production Trends around the World. Spain. *In* Fresh Citrus Fruits, W. F. Wardowski, S. Nagy, and W. Grierson (Editors). AVI Pub. Co., Inc., Westport, CT.

7

Harvesting Techniques

Galen K. Brown

Fruit harvesting accounts for the largest part of the labor employed in the overall production of citrus. In most citrus-growing countries the seasonal supply and cost of labor for harvesting varies widely from year to year. By the mid-1990s in the United States, it was apparent that the majority of the seasonal laborers were migrant and undocumented, a situation that did not provide a foundation for future growth. In addition, the increasing adoption of free-trade agreements between countries had exposed the Florida citrus industry to international price competition that could only be met by cutting harvesting cost per unit by as much as 50%. These facts made it imperative to mechanize harvesting, and thereby greatly increase labor productivity (by more than 5 times) and reduce harvesting cost. In 1994 the Florida citrus industry decided to initiate a major harvesting research & development (R&D) program.

Mechanical harvesting of citrus fruit involves many horticultural, engineering, and economic factors that must be considered in a 'production system' approach in order to develop new efficient methods for harvesting. Careful examination of the various factors associated with picking citrus fruit reveals the complexity of the operation and the difficulties involved in converting from manual to mechanical harvesting. Many factors, such as fruit type, intended utilization, quality criteria, grove characteristics, need to maintain tree vigor and production, labor supply and cost, harvester capacity, required reduction in final product cost, all affect the basic approaches that can be considered as potentially successful mechanical harvesting methods. Florida groves were planted for hand harvesting and are quite variable. Many of the existing groves may have to be replanted to achieve the above cost and labor goals.

Despite the great amount of R&D work devoted to the mechanical harvesting of citrus during the past 40 years in the United States, all fresh-market citrus fruit and 97% of the processing fruit were still hand harvested during the 2003-2004 season. Recently, several mechanical harvesting systems have been developed for processed fruit, and commercial adoption and improvement of these systems is expected to continue. In this chapter, early R&D work on fresh market harvesting, and recent progress made on the mechanization of process harvesting are reviewed. Some of the systems developed for processed fruit may have application to fresh market fruit, if the need becomes acute. However, the fruit will need to be electronically inspected at high speed in the packinghouse for external and internal damage. Readers who are interested in the various harvesting attempts made prior to 1980 should refer to the earlier edition of this book and to O'Brien *et al.* 1983.

MANUAL PICKING

Picking is defined as the operation of separating the fruit from its supporting twig. Citrus fruit destined for processing is usually picked by grasping each fruit in the hand and giving it a jerk as it is twisted at an angle to the supporting twig (referred to as snapping). Fresh market fruit, however, is picked in many countries by clipping the supporting stem as close as possible to the calyx, which is attached to the peel, with a special clipper (Fig. 7.1). Clipping the fruit appears to be primarily a market requirement for some citrus fruit; except for loose skin mandarins there is no scientific evidence that correct hand snapping adversely affects the quality of the fruit (Hopkins and Loucks 1944). In a study that compared orange picking by snapping and clipping methods, no difference was observed between the two methods in incidence of rot during subsequent storage; however, labor productivity was 20% greater with the snapping method (Cohen *et al.* 1970).

The fruit-picking operation requires a series of activities including the movement of the hand to the fruit, detaching the fruit from the stem (Fig. 7.1), and the movement of the hand to the picking bag. The cycle is completed by emptying the bag into a suitable container located on the ground. Most fruit for fresh-market are now emptied into a plastic pallet bin, which helps minimize surface abrasion damage during transportation to a packinghouse. Fruit for processing are now emptied into a plastic conical tub, which is later emptied mechanically into a bulk truck. Each bin or tub typically holds 900 lb. (10 field boxes) of oranges, and are a standard measure of payment to the picker and measure of yield for the grove. Grove trucks haul the bins or bulk fruit to highway trucks outside of the grove.

On the average, in trees 15 to 25 feet tall about 40-50% of the fruit is picked while the worker is standing on the ground (Coppock and Jutras 1960; Schertz 1967). During the 1980 to 2000 time period, tree size was reduced through the planting of more compact trees and extensive use of mechanical topping and hedging. By 2004, typical mature tree height was 12 to 18 feet in Florida. The fruit above the picker's reach from the ground

Fig. 7.1. Hand picking citrus (top) using small clippers, snapping with wrist action (bottom).

still require the use of a ladder. The picker places the ladder against the tree, and with the picking bag supported from his shoulder, climbs the ladder to the top of the tree and begins to pick fruit from each side as he gradually descends to the ground (Fig. 7.2). This procedure is repeated with the picker moving around the tree until all the fruit has been picked. Today this usually requires from 6 to 12 ladder moves per tree, depending on the tree's size and shape.

The average labor productivity for process orange harvesting in Florida is about 900 lb./labor-hr. Pickers are 25% more productive during picking from the ground than during ladder picking (Schertz 1967). The lower productivity associated with ladder picking is attributed to the higher nonproductive time, and the slower and unsteady pace as a result of fatigue. Productivity is influenced by many variables, the major ones are tree height (Fig. 7.3; Fig 7.4) and fruit size (Coppock and Jutras 1960; Whitney *et al.* 1996). However, many other variables can influence labor productivity. The distribution of fruit over or within the tree and the radius of the tree's outer surface from the trunk (Brown *et al.* 1971) (Fig. 7.5) can have important influences. Terrain and weather conditions may also slow the worker, as does the handling of bins or tubs. The assessment of these variables is important, since in most cases pickers are paid on a piece-rate basis. Hence, a clear decision needs to be made as to the piece-rate pay that will apply to each grove situation.

Attempts were made to increase the labor productivity of manual harvesting by use of simple picking aids and improved picking methods. Since the number of fruits picked in one operational series has a direct bearing on the total time of the series, experiments were carried out with various intermediate containers attached to the picker which reduced the number of hand movements for transferring the fruit (Alper and Sarig, 1969). In addition, a device was developed to enlarge the holding capacity of the hand. Although both devices resulted in a 10% saving of time, they were clumsy to operate and disliked by pickers. Changes were also tried with the conventional citrus clipper, to make it possible to cut off the fruit and catch it with the same hand, but productivity did not increase.

Most citrus fruit is picked for the fresh market when the fruit are dry. Early in the morning the fruit are turgid, resulting in protrusion of oil cells, thus making the fruit subject to oleocellosis injury (Chapter 14).

POSITIONING MACHINES FOR HAND PICKING

Numerous studies have shown that the percentage of productive work time in a picking operation decreases with tree height (Fig. 7.4). This is caused by the additional time required to perform nonproductive work, such as positioning and climbing the ladder.

Fig. 7.2. Picking citrus fruit from a conventional ladder starting at top of tree.

Picker productivity, therefore, could be theoretically improved by using a mechanical device that would reduce or eliminate nonproductive operations and provide similar conditions when picking from heights as when on the ground. However, the motions involved in picking operations are quite complex, making it very difficult to design an efficient picker's aid. As a first step to circumvent these difficulties, studies were made to provide information on the fruit-bearing zone characteristics of citrus trees (Alper and Sarig 1969; Brown *et al.* 1971; Schertz and Brown 1965). In addition, analytical studies and experiments have established the proper relationships between the geometrical and structural configuration of fruit trees, fruit distribution, picking patterns, and picker's motion coordinates (Alper *et al.* 1976; Molitorisz and Perry 1966).

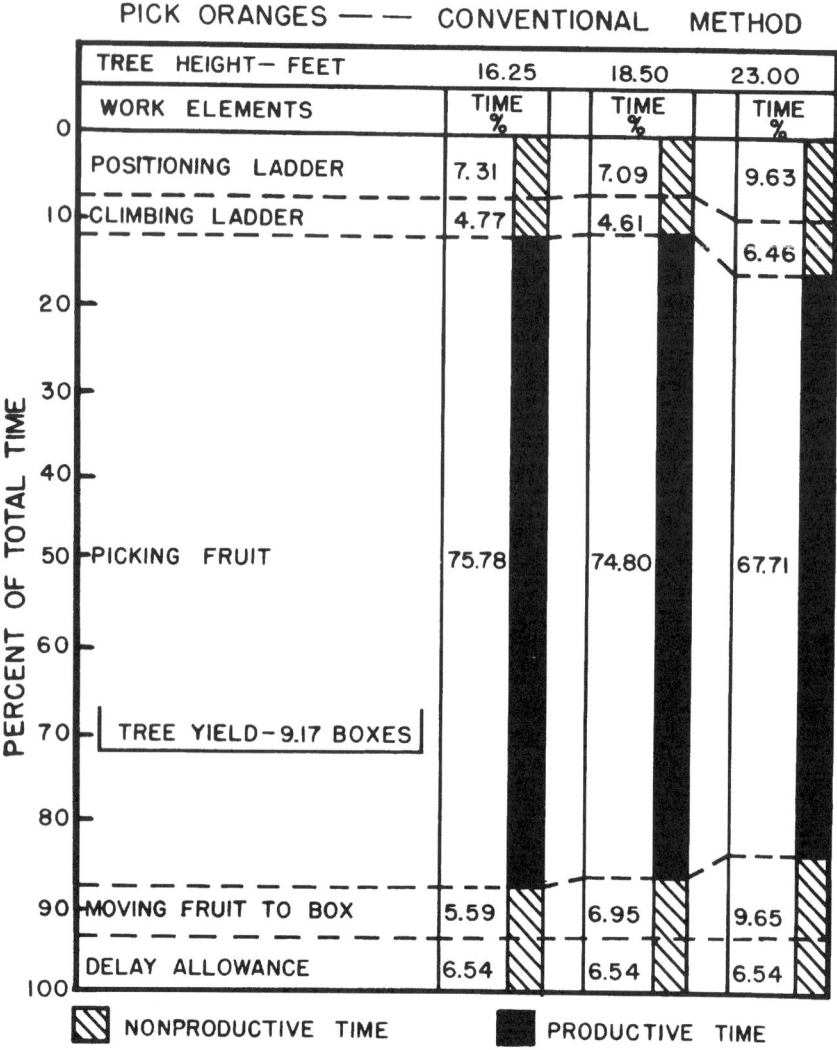

Fig. 7.3. Percentage of total picking time spent picking fruit from trees of different heights.

Many different models of mechanical positioners have been built in many places in the world in an attempt to quickly position the picker at the most favorable location and, hence, expedite fruit picking. The various machines can be divided into single- and multi-man positioning machines. From a kinematic viewpoint, however, they can be categorized into systems with two degrees or three degrees of freedom of motion. A ladder is also a

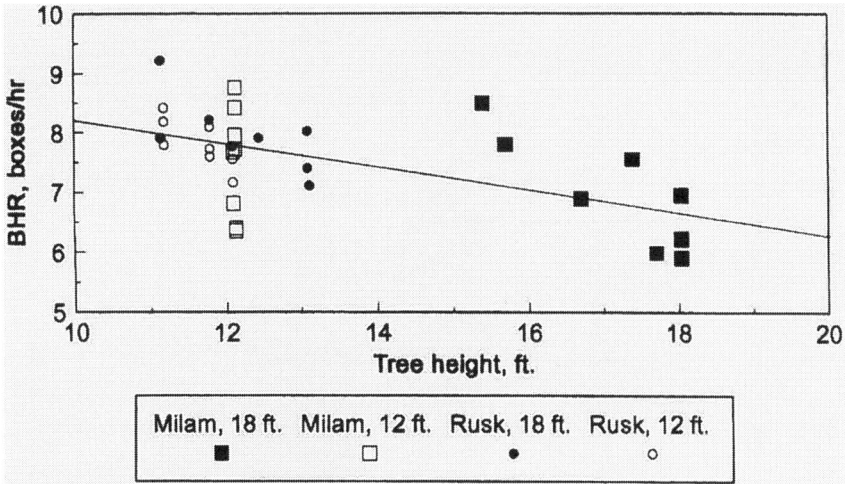

Fig. 7.4. Labor Prod vs Tree Height graph. Source: Whitney (1977).

picking aid that limits the freedom of motion to one degree (up and down, not considering the body motion). Examples of picking aids are shown in Figures 7.6 and 7.7.

In general, most single-man positioners have been designed with three degrees of freedom of motion, with the idea of eliminating all limitations on lateral movements, thus making it possible to minimize nonproductive time and pick in an uninterrupted process. However, if the tree coordinates do not conform to the machine motion coordinates (as is typical of most unshaped trees), the deficiency of such a mechanical positioning device becomes quite obvious, since a motion along any one coordinate results in a positive change relative to another coordinate. Many studies have shown that contrary to what was commonly believed, the "free choice" motion of a picker in control of a device resulted in 30% "nonproductive" motions performed by the picker during a picking cycle. This rather surprising result led to the idea that a programmed picking aid that limits freedom of motion might better minimize nonproductive time (Coppock and Jutras 1960; Molitorisz and Perry 1966). This "freedom-limited" machine should obviously be less complex and, hence, less expensive.

Results of time studies of the performance of various machines have indicated that the maximum productivity of pickers using a single-man positioning aid is twice that of pickers using ladders (Alper *et al.* 1967; Coppock and Jutras 1960; Perry 1965; Seamont 1969). However, with multi-man positioners and an increase in the number of pickers, labor productivity decreased. In the case of simpler devices—such as platforms—operated by a

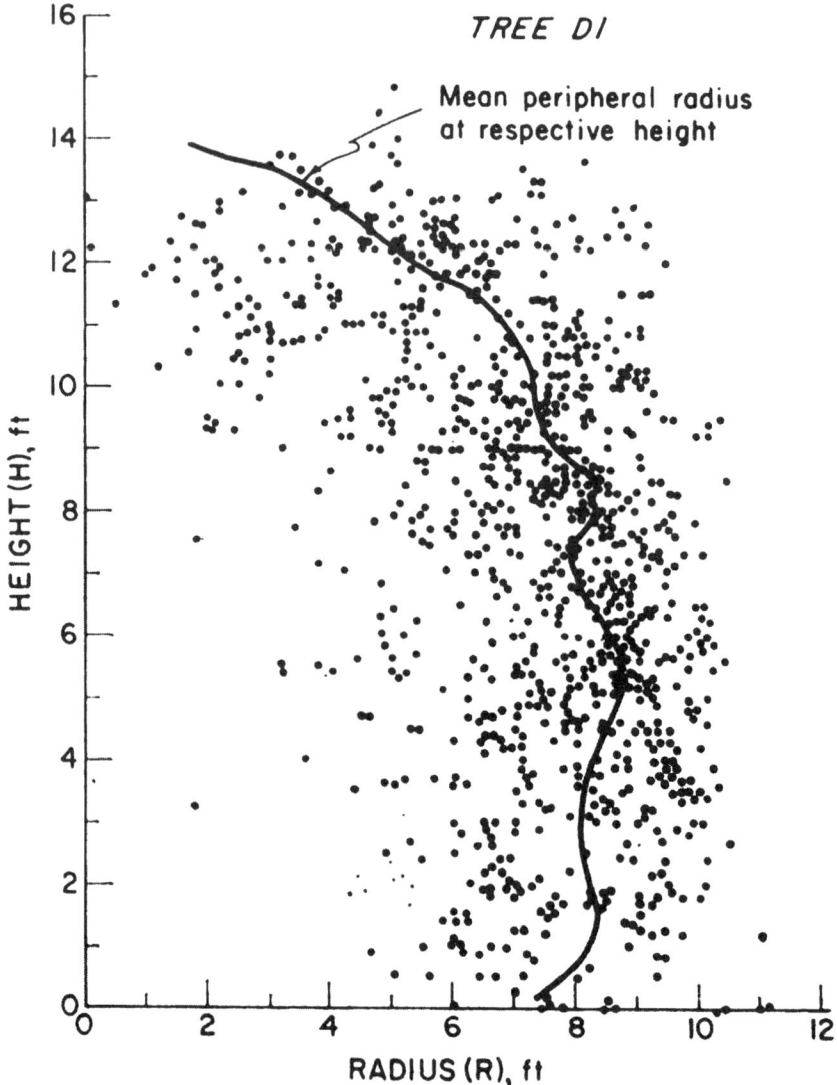

Fig. 7.5. Fruit location vs tree height and radius. Source: Brown *et al.* (1971).

large number of pickers, the output was the same or only slightly more than that of pickers using ladders (Berlage *et al.* 1972; Perkins *et al.* 1975). Nevertheless, even the increase in labor productivity made possible by the use of a single-man positioner, albeit not negligible, did not make the picking aid method economically competitive with standard methods. It was concluded

Fig. 7.6. Citrus Harvesting Systems single-man positioner.

that use of positioning machines for harvesting is not economically justified. The high cost of flexible aids was always the negative factor. Some success has been achieved by planting and maintaining high-density orchards (5 to 6 ft. wide trees) to match the dimensions of simpler and less costly multi-man positioners (Kollar and Brown 1996). It was also concluded that as long as picking is done manually, the potential for increasing productivity is limited to about a 25% gain at best. Therefore, the use of mechanical positioners as picking aids should be considered only as one tactic to tap an alternative labor supply until mechanical mass-removal or robotic multiple-removal systems can be successfully employed.

MECHANICAL HARVESTING METHODS

Mechanical harvesting is any method of removing fruit from the tree that does not require that a worker pick the fruit by hand. Most mechanized harvesting systems have been developed for fruit destined to be processed. For any mechanical harvesting system to be economical and practical, compared with skilled human fruit pickers, the fruit must be removed from the tree in multiples (successive areas of the tree) or in mass (entire tree at once). Machines for multiple fruit removal can be classified into those that physically contact the fruit and those that do not contact the fruit.

Fig. 7.7. Multi-picker platform for tree fruit harvesting. Source: O'Brien *et al.* (1983).

Direct Contact Machines

In direct contact machines, the detachment device makes physical contact with each fruit to cause detachment. Several detachment devices are arranged in multiples to detach several fruits at a time. Direct contact harvesters consist, in general, of two components: a picking head to detach the fruit, and a positioning mechanism to place the picking head over and around the tree. Several experimental picking heads were developed, pri-

Fig. 7.8. Pull-and-catch harvester.

marily in Florida and California; these partially duplicate the motions of a
picker's hand. See Sarig and Coppock (1986) for a description of devices
that were tried, but are not used today.

A unique direct-contact picking head was developed in California simu-
lating selective manual picking (Chen 1973). Each fruit was hooked by a
curved wire that protruded from the side of a tube which was inserted into
the fruiting canopy. Withdrawing the tube from the canopy caused a small
knife at the end of the wire to hook and cut the fruit stem. This was followed
by two other designs in Florida (Crunkelton 1991; Visser 1995) that used
rigid spring-action fingers along a tube to pull (snap) the fruit from the
stem. The Crunkelton design (Fig. 7.8) started extensive process harvesting
trials in Florida during the 2002-03 season, and might eventually help with
fresh-market harvesting. To fit the harvester, tree size can't exceed 16 ft. tall

and about 16 ft. wide. A mirror-image pair of harvesters is expected to average about 50-70 trees/hr (Brown 2002A, B).

The major drawback of all direct contact harvesting units is that their limited tree penetration can result in a low percentage of fruit removal. Reaching farther into the tree presents difficulties, especially in severely hedged groves where large limb stubs may be encountered. Another problem that hinders acceptable performance of some designs is the necessity of positioning the picking head around the tree canopy, which is time consuming and entails the use of expensive equipment. The general consensus is that the commercial potential of direct-contact harvesting units is limited, unless they can be successfully used in the selective harvesting of two-crop citrus (i.e., Valencia oranges harvested after the next season's crop blooms and sets) and the harvesting of fresh-market citrus.

Non-contact Machines

Shaking is a non-contact mass-removal approach to mechanical harvesting. Removal of fruit by shaking is a rather complex process. Fruit detachment is influenced on the one hand by characteristics of the tree (fruit weight, mechanical properties of tree branches, fruit detachment force, and natural frequencies of the fruiting limb and branches), and on the other hand by the dynamic characteristics of the specific oscillation imparted to the tree (e.g., frequency, amplitude, pattern, and duration of shake). Therefore, it is hard to predict the optimal shake for a specific fruit or cultivar; only actual trials to evaluate the various factors involved can ascertain the desired shaking conditions (Alper *et al.* 1976; Brown and Schertz 1966; Whitney 1999; Whitney *et al.* 2001).

Limb and Trunk Shakers. Fruit detachment may be achieved by applying an oscillating force to the trunk or scaffold limbs of a tree by a mechanical shaker and a clamp. Limb shakers (Fig. 7.9) with strokes of 6-8 in. and frequencies of 150-250 cpm can remove 80-90% of the crop with a field capacity of up to 25 trees/hr for early and midseason oranges (Brown and Schertz 1966; Whitney and Sumner 1977). However, the use of limb shakers has disappeared in all of the deciduous tree fruit and nut industries and is not a practical choice for today's commercial citrus harvesting.

Trunk shakers can remove fruit faster and more economically than limb shakers (Whitney 1999). Trunk shakers are adaptable to a wide variety of trees if the trunk has enough clear height to the first limbs, or the primary scaffold limbs can be clamped, and the low canopy foliage is skirted (cleared) to about 30 inches above the ground. Both mono-boom trunk shakers and trunk shake-and-catch harvest systems have been successfully designed for Florida citrus (Figs. 7.10 and 7.11). The major obstacle to wide adoption of trunk shakers is the fact that most Florida groves have short

Fig. 7.9. Limb shaker.

trunks, low skirts, and non-uniform spacing and alignment between trees. However, in 2001-02 harvesting, the mono-boom shakers averaged 134 trees/hr and the following hand clean-up crews averaged 19 field boxes per labor-hr (Fb/L-hr), and the trunk shake-and-catch systems averaged 125 trees/hr and 93 Fb/L-hr (Roka 2002).

Trunk shakers can't be used to the end of the Valencia harvest in Florida, because to remove a high percentage of the mature crop they also remove an excessive percentage of the following crop after it's diameter exceeds 0.75 in. (trunk shakers are not a selective method of harvest). Fruit abscission compounds are able to loosen the mature fruit, but not the developing fruit. This enables trunk shakers to be more selective (but not entirely) in Valencia harvest and to be used later into the Valencia season (See the following discussion on Fruit Abscission).

Foliage Shakers. These shakers, sometimes called canopy shakers, remove fruit by mechanically applying oscillating displacements to the outer canopy of the tree. The main advantage of the foliage shaker is that the stroke applied to remove the fruit can be controlled with greater precision than is possible when using a trunk shaker.

The shaking head of a foliage shaker consists of horizontal rows of flexible tines or rods, which are inserted into the fruiting canopy then oscillated to cause fruit detachment. The oscillations may be vertical, horizontal, or circular (Hedden and Coppock 1971; Whitney *et al.* 1973; Whitney 1999;

Fig. 7.10. Mono-boom trunk shaker.

Peterson 1998; Daniels 1999). This type of shaker lends itself to hedge-rowed trees that are 12-16 ft. tall and 12-16 ft. wide, so canopy penetration is nearly complete. The early shakers of this type were not able to deliver adequate stroke and quickly remove nearly all the fruit.

A stop-and-go area foliage shaker patented by Daniels (1999) was commercially used during the 2000 through 2002 harvest seasons to shake fruit to the ground. Cleanup crews picked up the fruit and gleaned the trees. However, the overall harvest operation did not decrease harvest cost, so it was rejected by growers. A somewhat faster foliage shaking and raking approach was patented by Hosking (2002) (Fig. 7.12), which is intended to use an integral simple fruit catching system under the tree. Development is continuing on the catching system. A circular tine-stroke of about 3-4 in., and frequency of about 200-250 cpm, are generally used. All fruit producing areas of the canopy must be penetrated by the shaker tines to achieve typical fruit removal of 75-85%. Gleaning is still required. This system can operate in taller, older, and irregular trees at 10-30 trees/hr where faster shake-and-catch systems can not operate.

Peterson (1998) developed a continuous-travel double spiked-drum canopy shaker for the Florida harvesting program. A horizontal tine-stroke of about 8 in., and frequency of 240-300 cpm, are generally used to get quick fruit removal. Down-the-row travel speeds of 66-176 ft./min. are reasonable. Tree spacings of 12-8 ft. in the row convert to harvest rates of 330-

Fig. 7.11. Trunk shake-and-catch system.

1320 trees/hr. Two manufacturers developed commercial single-drum shake-and-catch versions of this harvesting approach for the 2001-02 harvest season (Buist 2002; Stich 2001) (Figs. 7.13 and 7.14). A tractor-pulled continuous-travel canopy shaker is also offered (Fig. 7.15). In topped hedgerow groves that are well matched to the shaker, crop removal has averaged 90-95% (Roka 2002). In poorly matched groves (tree spacing of 15-20 ft. in the row and tops above 16 ft. fruit removal can fall to 60%. These foliage shakers are unsuitable for trees wider than 16 ft. or trees with fruit borne on inner limbs, since only the outer 5-6 ft. of canopy is shaken.

Air Shakers. Air shakers utilize pulsating air blasts (about 100 mph at 70 cpm) to detach the fruit from the twigs (Fig. 7.16). Air shakers do not attach to the trees and do not require topping and hedging, significant advantages over other shakers. Because no attachments are made, continuous, down-the-row operation is feasible, resulting in high harvester capacity. The main disadvantages of air shakers have been that power consumption is high, and high crop removal as well as harvester capacity are dependent on reducing the fruit detachment force by application of fruit abscission compounds to loosen the fruit.

Various configurations of air shakers have been designed and tested, achieving fruit-removal levels of 85-95% when the abscission compound causes good fruit loosening (Coppock and Donhaiser 1981; Whitney 1977; Whitney and Sumner 1977). However, without abscission compounds, fruit

Fig. 7.12. J H canopy shaker.

removal averaged only about 55%, which represents a significant reduction in harvesting effectiveness. Shake-and-catch air-shaker harvesting is impractical because the abscission compound causes about 50% of the fruit to drop before air harvesting begins, and the fruit is thrown, rather than dropped, by the action of the pulsating air.

Water Shakers. A water shaker generally uses the same principle to remove citrus as does an air shaker, except that water tends to remove the fruit by impinging on the fruit rather than by shaking the limbs (Whitney and Sumner 1977). However, availability of a high volume/min water source is a problem in most groves. Excess water and leaf shredding during harvest are also potential problems. A new 'Spray-Harvest' harvesting concept was proposed to the Florida Harvesting Program in September of 2001 (Adams 2001). This involves using compressed air to propel (by impulse) a wave of water droplets downward through the fruiting canopy, causing fruit detachment without shaking (Fig. 7.17). Fruit or leaf damage does not appear to result from this action. The inventor plans to continue developing and evaluating this unique harvesting approach.

Selective Harvesting. Most citrus varieties have only one crop on the tree at harvest time and, therefore, can be harvested in a once-over operation. Valencia orange trees, however, have both young fruit (which will develop into next year's crop) and mature fruit at harvest time. Hence, selective harvest-

Fig. 7.13. Korvan continuous canopy shake-and-catch system.

ing is required to maximize removal of mature fruit with minimum removal of young fruit, so as not to cause a reduction in the subsequent crop.

One approach is to stimulate the natural loosening process in mature fruit without affecting the young fruit, bloom, or leaves (Wilson *et al.* 1981). The use of abscission compounds to achieve this result has given predictable results, except at certain periods during the late Valencia harvest. Plant physiologists and biochemists are working to develop registerable inexpensive compounds that provide reliable results (Burns 2002). The recent work is focused on natural compounds.

The differentials in weight and detachment force young and mature fruit have been found to be useful for selective removal of mature fruit by different harvesting methods. Fruit removal by shake harvesting devices is influenced by fruit weight (*w, typically 0.35 to 0.45 lb. Avg.*) and detachment force (*F, typically 15 to 20 lb. Avg.*). Mature (large) fruit having a low detachment force are easier to shake off the tree than are young (small) fruit having a relatively high detachment force. Young fruit have a high F/w ratio, whereas mature fruit have a low F/w ratio and even lower after a fruit abscission compound is sprayed on the tree. The compound should not affect the F/w ratio of young fruit.

The F/w ratio of individual fruits on the same tree are different, and tend to be somewhat higher or lower at different locations in the tree. Trunk

Fig. 7.14. OXBO continuous-travel canopy shake-and-catch system).

shakers do not impart uniform vibration to every fruit on the tree, but they do provide better selectivity a few days after abscission compounds have been applied (Whitney *et al.* 2000). The canopy shakers appear to be more suitable for selective harvesting, because the vibration is more uniform on every fruit (Hedden and Coppock 1971; Peterson, 1998). Selectivity, with abscission, is improved with either shaker when the applied shake is less aggressive (lower frequency, shorter stroke, shorter shake period).

Mechanical designs such as the flexible-finger harvester (Chen 1973), or the rigid spring-action finger harvester (Crunkelton 1991), have shown promise of good selectivity due to fruit diameter differences between young and mature fruit, without the use of abscission compounds. Early experiments with these units also indicated they cause less damage to the fruit than do shake-and-catch methods of harvesting.

The need for selective harvesting exists also, to a much lesser extent, in grapefruit. Late in the harvesting season grapefruit trees have both mature fruit and the flowers of the next year's crop. Grapefruit trees, like orange trees, produce many times the number of flowers required for a normal crop. Only a small percentage of these flowers develop into mature fruit throughout the growing season. Adverse effects by shakers on subsequent yields have not been reported until the young fruit have grown larger than 0.5 in. diameter.

Fig. 7.15. OXBO tractor-pulled continuous-travel canopy shaker.

FRUIT COLLECTION METHODS

Various methods of fruit collection were developed to be compatible with fruit detachment methods. Basically, the detached fruit can either be simultaneously caught on catching surfaces or allowed to fall to the ground for later hand or mechanical pickup. Either method is suitable for fruit destined for processing. The pickup methods are generally more expensive than simultaneous catching, represent added risk that extreme weather can reduce fruit recovery or quality, and can result in the adherence of excessive amounts of wet soil that must be removed from the fruit at the receiving station of the processing plant.

Ground Pickup. The major advantage of the mechanical pickup method is its capacity to handle a large volume of fruit independently of any of the various fruit detachment systems. It is needed especially when abscission compounds are used to loosen the fruit for air harvesting, because a large pre-harvest fruit drop is needed prior to harvest to ensure that the fruit detachment force is very low (2-4 lb.). After the crop is on the ground,

Fig. 7.16. Continuous-travel air shaker.

hand workers can pick up 2-3 times more fruit/hr than when hand picking. Many hand pickers now hand-drop the crop to the ground, then pick it up. When machines are used for pickup the fruit must be accessible. This requires a reasonable amount of ground and skirt preparation. The ground should be smooth and free of holes or ruts (light disking will usually be adequate). The tree skirt must be clear for 24-30 in. above the ground to provide clearance for the machines. The individual fruits must be moved from the trunk line, or from under the tree canopy, to a windrow location for some pickup machines. Several methods of moving fruit into a windrow, that use tractor-mounted or self-propelled rakes, were developed in Florida (Churchill and Sumner 1977).

Two primary designs for windrow-style pickup machines were developed (Sumner and Churchill 1977) to work with the fruit rakes developed in the 1970s. These both use a rod-style chain belt (root crop vegetable belt) to pickup the fruit at ground level, discard soil and trash, and convey the fruit into the machine. One machine operates like a root crop harvester and digs a shallow layer of soil to lift the fruit. The other uses a flapper cylinder assembly mounted in front of and above the pickup chain to assist in loading fruit onto the chain at ground level. Gauge wheels mounted in front of either pickup head assembly follow the ground contour to control the elevation of the pickup chain. The fruit are discharged from the pickup chain to a series

Fig. 7.17. Continuous-travel spray harvester.

of conveyors and trash eliminators, pass by hand sorters who remove unwanted materials, and are finally dumped into a suitable container. Fruit
recovery obtained with these devices reached 98%, with a pickup rate of
about 1500 lb./min. during tests in the early 1980s. Neither of these systems
was adopted for commercial use, but they are now being re-evaluated.

Recently, two approaches for direct pickup, without the need to form a
windrow, have been designed. Both must move fruit from the trunk-line,
but then are able to pick up the fruit were they lay under the canopy or in
the drive row (Craven 2000; Stich 2001). Again, a smooth soil surface is desirable and some skirting is necessary. These machines should eventually be
more productive than the windrow-pickup systems, because they can re-
cover the crop in a single pass instead of two passes.

Catching Surfaces. The use of catching surfaces to collect fruit is usually
associated with shaking methods for fruit detachment. The simplest type of
catching surface consists of sheets laid on the ground beneath the tree being shaken. In a more advanced version, the sheets are connected to a
longitudinal towed conveyor. After fruit are shaken onto the sheets, the
sheets are mechanically rolled up and the fruit fall onto a conveyor, to be
discharged finally into a bulk container. The most common and widely used
catching surface is employed on mobile frames. These frames form inclined
surfaces beneath the tree, which direct the fruit to an appropriate handling

system. A trunk shaker is mounted on one of the frames. In its almost standard form, the system employs two self-propelled frames, one for each side of the row of trees (Fig. 7.18).

The design of all catching frames has to be compatible with a wide range of operating conditions, especially those associated with tree size and structure, and grove ground conditions. Trees with irregular short trunks and a low-hanging skirt foliage present major difficulties, which must be alleviated to ensure good performance (lb./hr, acres/season, and $/ton). Catching and conveying surfaces on the frames must be installed at a flatter angle than used for deciduous fruit crops (vase-shaped tall trunk trees), because existing citrus trees are not vase-shaped and have short trunks. Some of the fruit handling problems, encountered with standard shake-and-catch methods for fruit destined for processing, may be overcome with a "bulk cart". This cart is pulled behind the collector frame and can accumulate a grove-truck load of fruit (6,000 to 9,000 lb.), then periodically dump it to the highway truck within 1-2 min.

ECONOMIC CONSIDERATIONS

Over the past four decades significant efforts have been made to develop suitable mechanical harvesting methods for citrus. Research has been conducted on mechanical harvesting of both fresh and processed fruit, in various citrus-growing countries in the world. Until recently, however, no mechanical harvesting system has been acceptable to the Florida citrus industry. The major reasons for this were that the proposed systems were economically feasible only under a limited range of grove conditions, the supply of relatively low-cost seasonal hand labor remained adequate, and the competitive position of the Florida citrus industry was considered to be good in both domestic and international markets. It is now apparent that no single mechanical system can achieve economic feasibility under all conditions. Several new systems have therefore been developed that can be feasible for large segments of the Florida citrus industry (Roka 2002). Also, the supply of low-cost seasonal labor is decreasing, and Florida is now the high-cost producer in free-trade markets. Adoption of these new mechanical harvesting systems has started, and is expected to increase over the next 5-10 years (Brown 2002A, B).

It is difficult to accurately assess the present cost/unit for mechanical harvesting, but harvesting contractors indicate the potential cost savings can range from 10-50% (depending on grove type, grove yield, harvester type and cost, annual hours of operation, etc.). Many factors are still unknown or hard to estimate. If the supply of labor for hand picking decreases and mechanical harvesters fill the vacuum, or the overall cost for hand picking becomes prohibitive, the industry will gain the experience and new

Fig. 7.18. Fruit catching frames.

knowledge that are needed to optimize the operation of mechanical harvesters in future groves that will enable minimum costs and maximum profit to be realized.

In addition to strictly economic considerations, other factors are of practical importance when the acceptability of mechanical harvesting is analyzed. The management of manual harvesting crews is becoming more and more difficult, and maintaining harvesting crews that will deliver predictable quantities of quality fruit is becoming harder with time. On the other hand, the use of mechanical harvesting methods will, undoubtedly, create new machinery management problems.

PRESENT ASSESSMENT AND FUTURE TRENDS

Processed Fruit. Many systems have already been developed, and the necessary theoretical information has been obtained. Remaining obstacles include: the two-crop harvesting problem (selectivity) for Valencia oranges and all grapefruit (which might be solved by fruit abscission compounds or by selective harvest methods); and the replacement of many old-style (hand-harvest) groves with new-style groves that are well matched to the most productive and lowest cost methods of mechanical harvesting (Brown 2002A).

Fig. 7.19. Pellenc robot harvester.

The mechanization of processed citrus harvesting is inevitable. Successful industry-wide adoption will require an interdisciplinary effort involving growers, production managers, harvesting contractors, engineers, plant scientists, processors, and bankers. The optimum mechanized approach for citrus will most likely involve dwarf or semi-dwarf trees, a new shape for the tree, different tree and row spacing, changes in cultural and other production practices, and adoption of new pre- and post-harvest practices and new processing techniques. It is anticipated that the problem of maximizing fruit detachment will eventually be aided through the use of fruit abscission compounds (Burns 2002; Whitney *et al.* 2000). It is conceivable that with the development of new spraying techniques, variation of doses, and screening of new materials, that nearly complete mechanical removal will be obtained for all processed citrus (Young *et al.* 1999).

Fresh Fruit. The major harvesting problem that would continue to be the focus of future research is the maintenance of adequate quality for fresh-market fruit. All materials, those presently known and those yet to be explored, would be incorporated in a complete system to minimize damaged fruit. Nevertheless, based on past studies, it is reasonable to assume that mechanical harvesting of citrus will always be associated with some degree of fruit damage. Therefore, efforts should also be directed at developing methods of automatic external and internal damage detection, followed by removal of damaged fruit and its channeling to the processing industry. In addition, work has already been initiated toward the possible utilization of sophisticated techniques for harvesting that employ image analyzers, other artificial intelligence techniques, and robotic manipulators for individual fruit removal (Fig. 7.19) (Coppock 1983; Covington 1983; Tutle 1985; Harrell 1987; Pellenc *et al.* 1990; Kedem and Rubenstein 1991; Wang and Hardy 1995; Burks 2002). These, if proven successful, will simulate hand picking to provide the ideal system for picking high-quality fruit.

REFERENCES

ADAMS, J. 2001. The WetAir Picload and Roadside Goat. Proposal to FDOC Citrus Harvesting Research Advisory Council. Sept. 6. Lord & Others, Bradenton, FL 34205.

ALPER, Y. and SARIG, Y. 1969. Citrus harvest mechanization in Israel. Proc. Int. Soc. Citriculture, Vol. 2, 623-638.

ALPER, Y., FOUX, A. and LINOR, J. 1976. Detachment analysis for oranges in shaker harvest. Trans. ASAE 19, 1029-1033.

ALPER, Y., SARIG, Y. and RAVID, N. 1967. Experiments for the destination of fruit-bearing zones in citrus trees. Prelim. Rept. 553. Nat. Inst. Agr., Rehovot, Israel (Hebrew).

BERLAGE, A. G., R. D. LANGMO and YOST, G. E. 1972. Limitations of single- and multi-man platform harvesting aids. Bull. 609, Oregon State University Agr. Expt. Sta., Corvallis, OR.

BROWN, G. K. 2002A. Citrus harvesting program update for the 2000-2002 seasons. FDOC, Lakeland, FL.

BROWN, G. K. 2002B. Mechanical harvesting systems for the Florida citrus juice industry. ASAE Paper No. 021108. ASAE, 2950 Niles Road, St. Joseph, MI 49085.

BROWN, G. K. and SCHERTZ, C. E. 1966. Evaluating shake harvesting of oranges for the fresh market. Trans. ASAE 10, 577-578, 580.

BROWN, G. K., SCHERTZ, C. E. and HUSZAR, C. K. 1971. Fruit-bearing characteristics of orange and grapefruit trees in California. ARS 42-181. U.S. Dept. Agr., Agr. Res. Serv., Washington, DC.

BUIST, K. 2002. The Korvan harvester brochure. Korvan Industries, Inc., 270 Birch Bay Lynden Road, Lynden, WA 98264.

BURKS, T. 2002. The automated fruit harvester program. Project proposal, University of Florida, Bio & Ag Eng. Dept., Gainesville. Funded by the Florida Citrus Commission, July.

BURNS, J. K. 2002. Using molecular biology tools to identify abscission materials for citrus. HortScience 37, 459-464.

CHEN, P. 1973. Selective harvesting of 'Valencia' oranges with a flexible hook device. Trans. ASAE 16, 645-648.

CHURCHILL, D. B. and SUMNER, H. R. 1977. A new system for raking and picking up oranges. Trans. ASAE 20(4), 617-620.

COHEN, G. E., WAKS, J., SARIG, Y. and NADLER, A. 1970. Picking 'Shamouti' oranges by hand pulling. Prelim. Rept. 677. Nat. Univ. Inst. Agr., Rehovot, Israel (Hebrew with English summary).

COPPOCK, G. E. 1983. Robotic principles in the selective harvest of Valencia oranges. Proc. Int. Conf. Robotics and Artificial Intelligent Machines for Agr., Am. Soc. Agr. Eng., Tampa, FL.

COPPOCK, G. E. and DONHAISER, J. R. 1981. Conical air shaker for removing citrus fruit. Trans. ASAE 24, 1456-1481.

COPPOCK, G. E. and JUTRAS, P. J. 1960. An investigation of the mobile picker's platform approach to partial mechanization of citrus fruit picking. Proc. Fla. State Hort. Soc. 73, 258-263.

COVINGTON, R. O. 1983. Robotic fruit picking machine proposed. The Citrus Ind. 12, 22-25.

CRAVEN, M. 2000. A direct fruit pickup system for processed citrus. Proposal to FDOC Citrus Harvesting Research Advisory Council. Sept. Stackhouse Bros. Harvesting, Hickman, CA 95323.

CRUNKELTON, W. 1991. Mechanical citrus and other fruit picker. U.S. Patent No. 5,161,358.

DANIELS, M. 1999. Fruit harvesting device. U.S. Patent No. 5,946,896.

HARRELL, R. C. 1987. Economic analysis of robot citrus harvesting in Florida. Trans. ASAE 30, 298-304.

HEDDEN, S. L. and COPPOCK, G. E. 1971. Comparative harvest trials of foliage and limb shakers in 'Valencia' oranges. Proc. Fla. State Hort. Soc. 84, 88-99.

HOPKINS, E. F. and LOUCKS, K. W. 1944. Pulling versus clipping of oranges in respect to loss from stem-end rot and blue mold. Proc. Fla. State Hort. Soc. 25, 80-86.

HOSKING, J. 2002. Tree fruit harvester. U.S. Patent No. 6,425,233.

KEDEM, D. and M. RUBENSTEIN. 1991. Fruit Picking Device. U.S. Patent No. 5,005,347.

KOLLAR, G. and BROWN, G. 1996. Quality protected and labour efficient harvest of several fruits. Proc. 60th Ann. Mtng. Fla. Academy of Sciences. March 29-30, Melbourne, FL.

MOLITORISZ, J. and PERRY, R. 1966. Citrus harvest mechanization. Calif. Agr. (March), 8,9.

O'BRIEN, M., CARGILL, B. and FRIDLEY, R. B. 1983. Harvesting & Handling Fruits and Nuts. AVI Publishing Co., Westport, CT.

PELLENC, R., MONTOYA, J. L., D'ESNON, A. G. and ROMBAUT, M. 1990. Automated machine for detection and grasping of objects. U.S. Patent No. 4,975,016.

PERKINS, R. M., MROZEK, R. F. and NASH, P. A. 1975. Analysis of man positioning equipment for California citrus harvesting. Trans. ASAE 18, 221-226, 230.

PERRY, R. L. 1965. Harvesting aids and the outlook for mechanical harvesting. Calif. Citrog. 51, 61-70.

PETERSON, D. L. 1998. Mechanical harvester for process oranges. Appl. Eng. in Agr. 14(5), 455-458.

ROKA, F. 2002. Evaluating performance of citrus mechanical harvesting systems, 2001/02 season. Ann. Rept. to Citrus Abscission Registration Committee, FDOC, Lakeland, FL.

SARIG, Y and COPPOCK, G. E. 1986. Harvesting techniques. In Fresh Citrus Fruits, W. F. Wardowski, S. Nagy, and W. Grierson (Editors). AVI Publishing Co., Westport, CT.

SCHERTZ, C. E. 1967. Human energy expenditure for picking oranges. J. Agr. Eng. Res. 12, 281-284.

SCHERTZ, C. E. and BROWN, G. K. 1965. Determination of fruit bearing zones in citrus. Paper 65-129. Amer. Soc. Agr. Eng., Blacksburg, VA.

SEAMONT, D. T. 1969. Consistency of picker picking rates in oranges as a factor in influencing performance on man-positioning devices. Trans. ASAE 14, 911-913.

STICH, G. 2001. The OXBO Harvester brochure. OXBO Int'l. Corp., 7275 Byron-Batavia Rd., Byron, NY 14422.

SUMNER, H. R. and CHURCHILL, D. B. 1977. Collecting and handling mechanically removed citrus fruit. Proc. Int. Soc. Citriculture, Vol. 2.

TUTLE, E. 1985. Robotic fruit harvester. U.S. Patent No. 4,532,757.

VISSER, T. 1995. Fruit picker. U.S. Patent No. 5,428,947.

WANG, X. and HARDY, T. 1995. Automated fruit picker. U.S. Patent No. 5,426,927.

WHITNEY, J. D. 1977. Design and performance of an air shaker for citrus fruit removal. Trans. ASAE 20, 52-56.

WHITNEY, J. D. 1999. Field test results with mechanical harvesting equipment in Florida oranges. Appl. Eng. in Agr. 15(3), 205-210.

WHITNEY, J. D. and SUMNER, H. R. 1977. Mechanical removal of fruit from citrus trees. Proc. Int. Soc Citriculture, Vol. 2.

WHITNEY, J. D., BENSALEM, E. and SALYANI, M. 2001. The effect of trunk shaker patterns on Florida orange removal. Appl. Eng. in Agr. 17(4), 461-464.

WHITNEY, J. D., HEDDEN, S. L. and SUMNER, H. B. 1973. Harvesting 'Valencia' oranges with a vertical foliage shaker. Proc. Fla. Hort. Soc. 86, 41-48.

WHITNEY, J. D., WHEATON, T. A., CASTLE, W. S. and TUCKER, D. P. H. 1996. Orange grove factors affect manual harvesting rates. Trans. ASAE 39(2), 399-405.

WHITNEY, J. D., HARTMOND, U., KENDER, W. J., BURNS, J. K. and SALYANI, M. 2000. Orange removal with trunk shakers and abscission chemicals. Appl. Eng. in Agr. 16(4), 367-371.

WILSON, W. C., COPPOCK, G. E. and ATTAWAY, J. A. 1981. Growth regulators facilitate harvesting of oranges. Proc. Int. Soc. Citriculture. Vol. 2.

YOUNG, M. KOO, SALYANI, M. and WHITNEY, J. D. 1999. Effects of abscission chemical spray deposition on mechanical harvest efficacy of 'Hamlin' orange. Proc. Fla. Hort. Soc. 112, 28-33.

Plate 1. Stem-end rot caused by *Lasiodiplodia theobromae.* Note the irregular margins of the lesion.

Plate 2. Stem-end rot caused by *Phomopsis citri.* Note the smooth margin of the lesion.

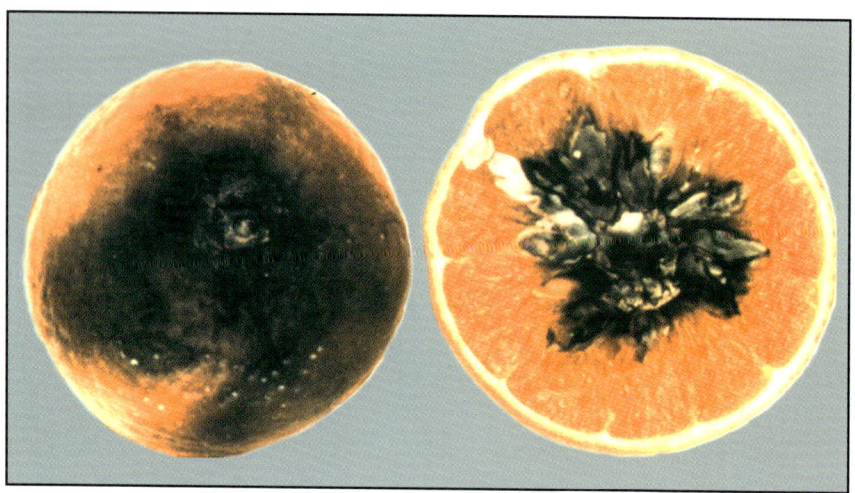

Plate 3. Black rot caused by *Alternaria citri*.

Plate 4. Anthracnose on Sunburst tangerine, caused by *Colletotrichum gleosporioides*.

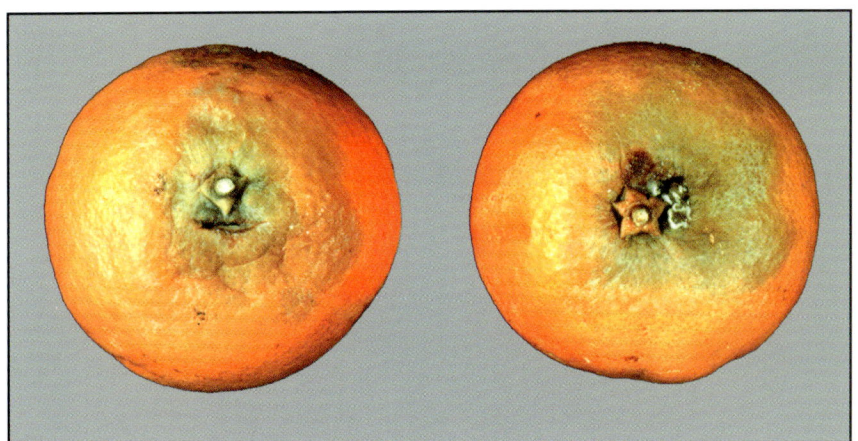

Plate 5. Brown rot caused by *Phytophthora* spp.

Plate 6. Green mold caused by *Penicillium digitatum.* Note the large white mycelia margin of the lesion.

Plate 7. Blue mold caused by *Penicillium italicum.* Note the narrow mycelial margin of the lesion.

Plate 8. Sour rot caused by *Geotrichum citri-aurantii.* Note the lack of discoloration in the very soft lesion, and lack of spores at this stage. Later, a spare white surface mycelium will develop with chains of hyaline arthrospores.

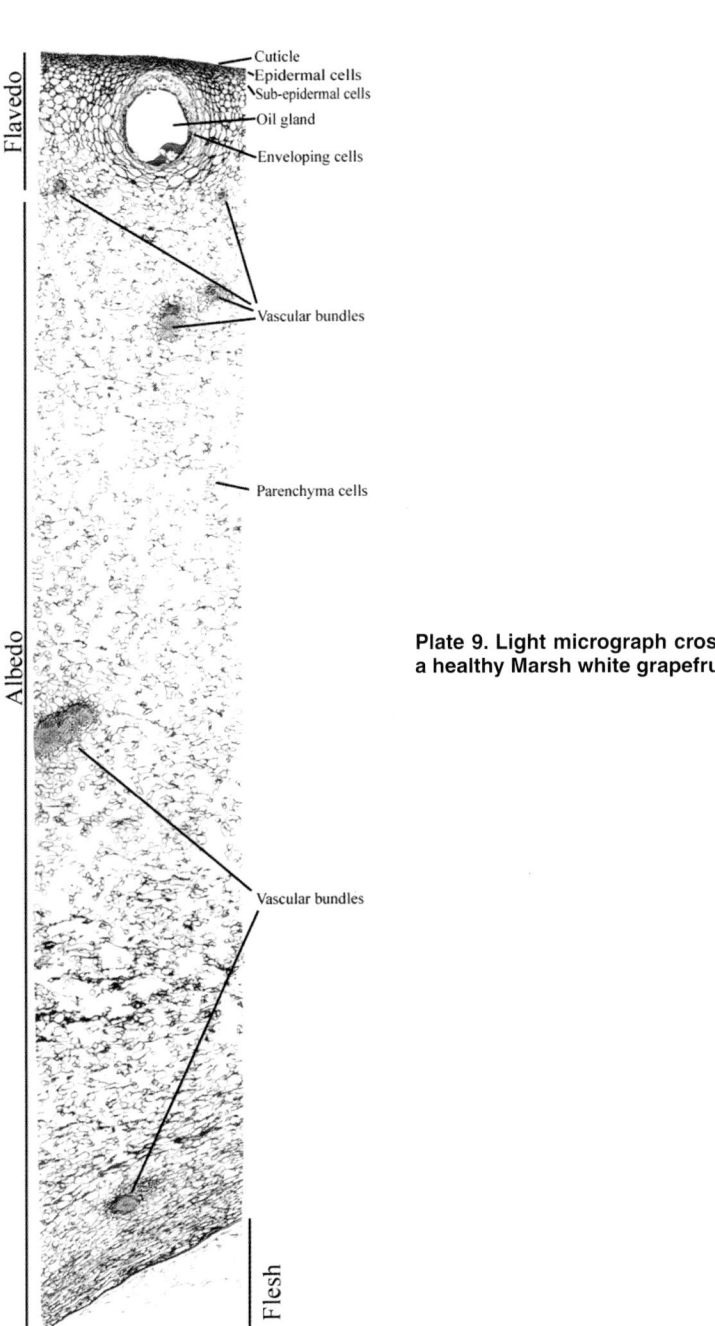

Flavedo

Cuticle
Epidermal cells
Sub-epidermal cells
Oil gland
Enveloping cells

Vascular bundles

Albedo

Parenchyma cells

Vascular bundles

Flesh

0.5 mm

Plate 9. Light micrograph cross-section of a healthy Marsh white grapefruit peel.

Plate 10. Spray damage (green spotting) of Marsh white grapefruit.

Plate 11. Wind scar damage of Marsh white grapefruit.

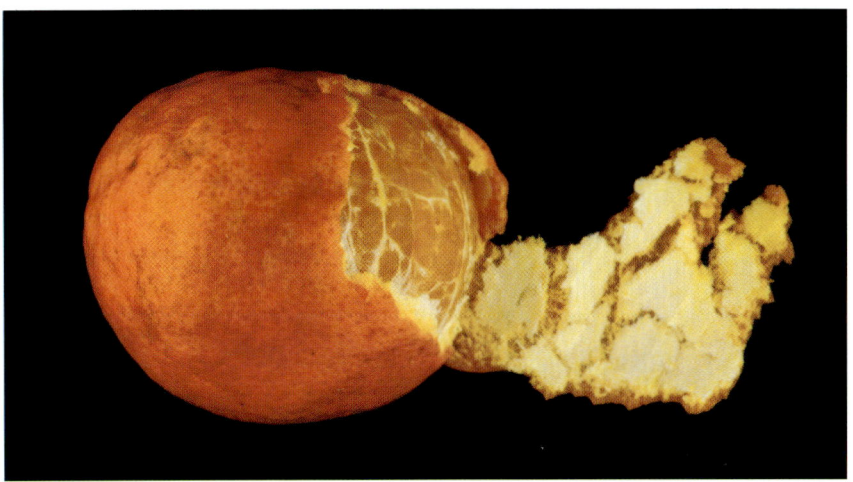

Plate 12. Creasing of Fallglo tangerine.

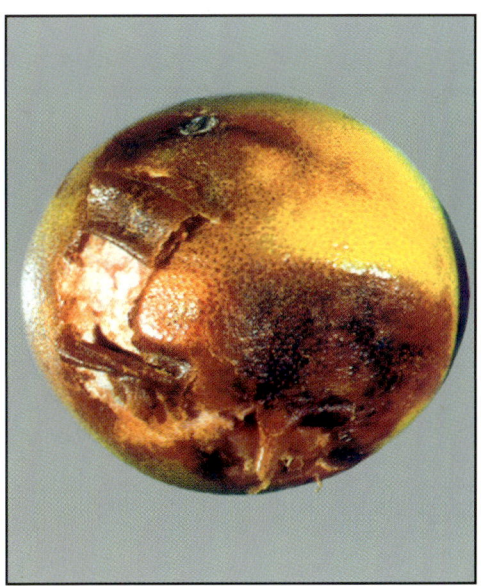

Plate 13. Sloughing of red grapefruit.

Plate 14. Blossom end clearing of red grapefruit (courtesy of J. Burns, Univ. Florida).

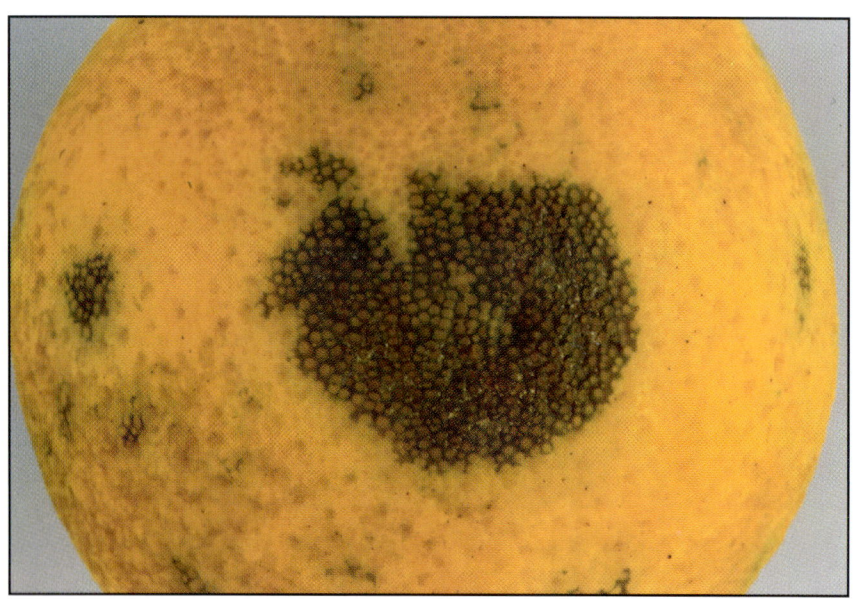

Plate 15. Oleocellosis of Hamlin orange.

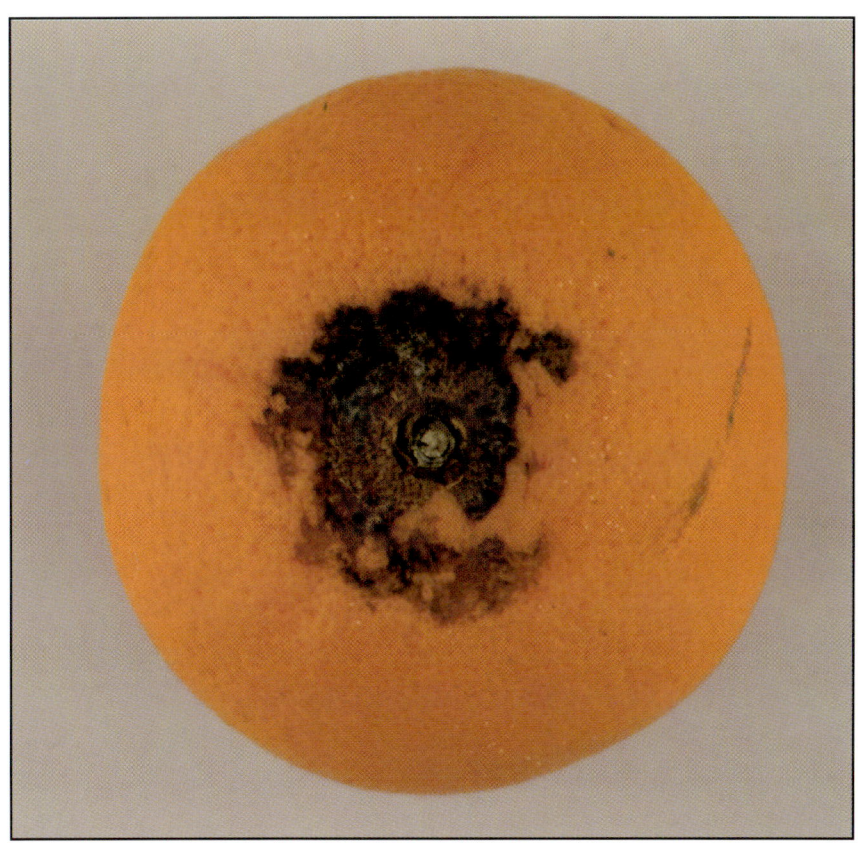

Plate 16. Aging of California Washington navel orange.

Plate 17. Stem end rind breakdown of Valencia orange.

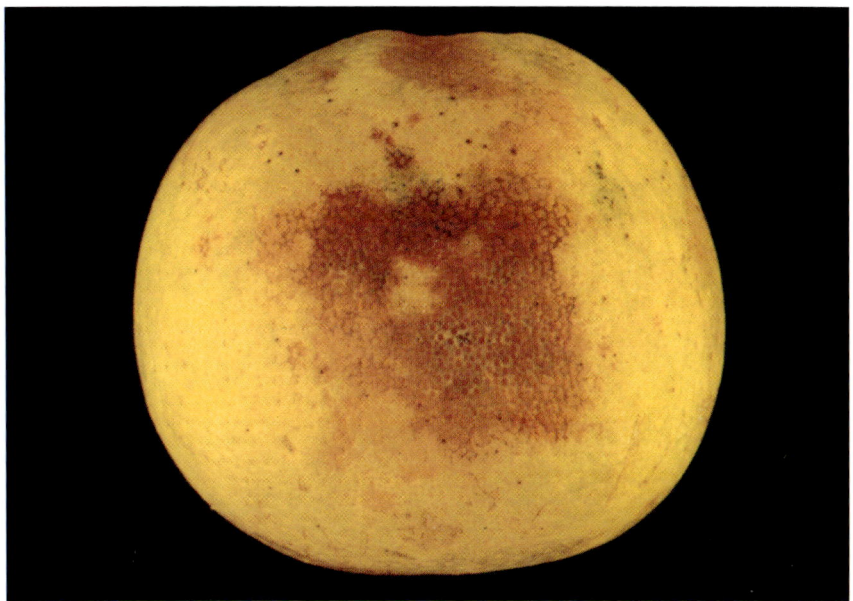

Plate 18. Chilling injury of Marsh white grapefruit.

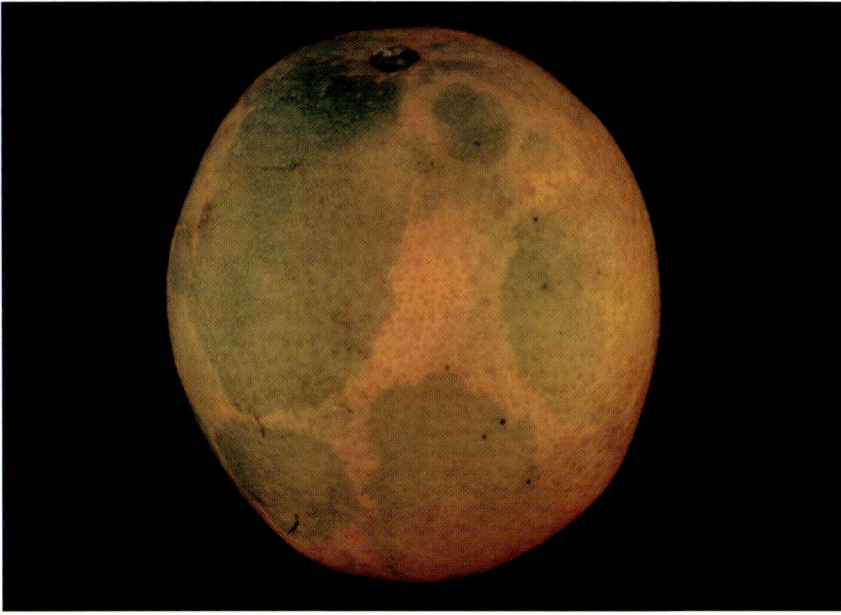

Plate 19. Drench damage (green ring) Marsh of white grapefruit.

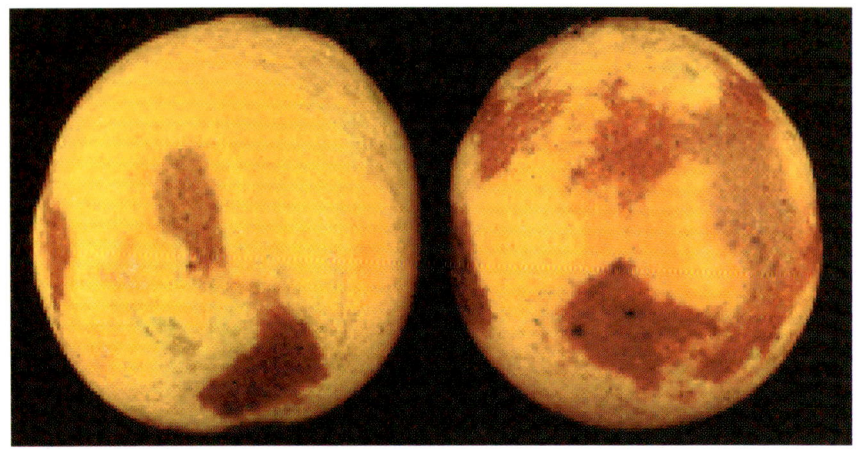

Plate 20. Ethylene damage of Ambersweet orange.

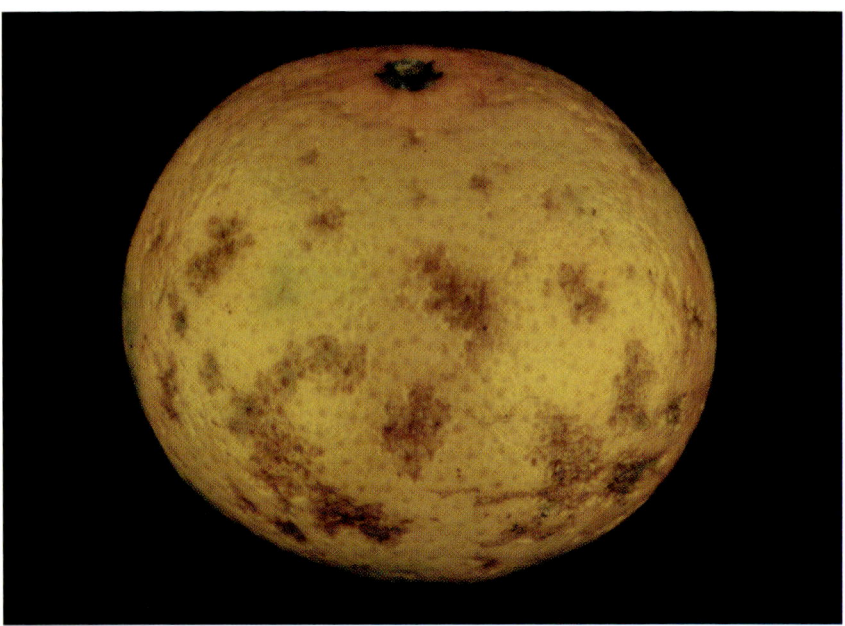

Plate 21. Postharvest pitting of Fallglo tangerine.

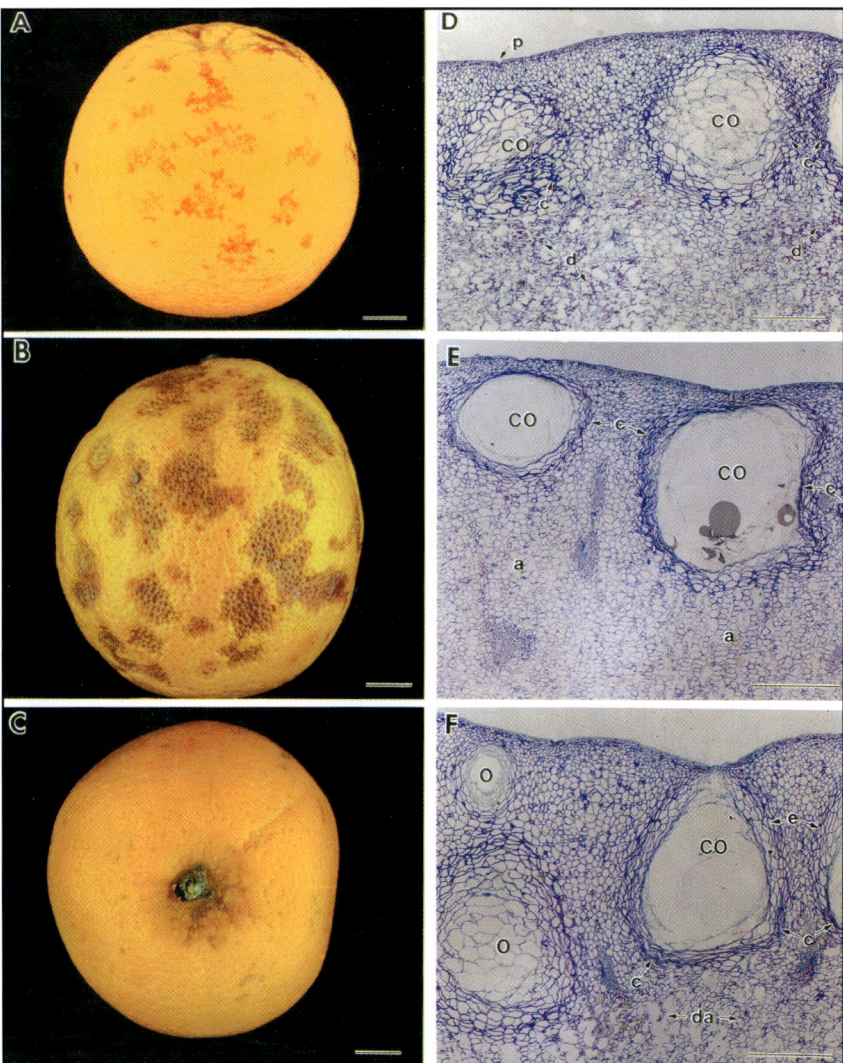

Plate 22. Postharvest pitting (early A, D and advanced B, E stages) and stem end rind breakdown (early stage C, F) of California Washington navel orange. Peel cross-section notation: O, healthy oil gland; CO, collapsed oil gland; e, healthy enveloping cells; c, collapsed enveloping cells; p, pit; a, healthy auxiliary cells; da, damaged auxiliary cells. Bars equal 1 cm for fruit, 0.5 mm for peel cross section.

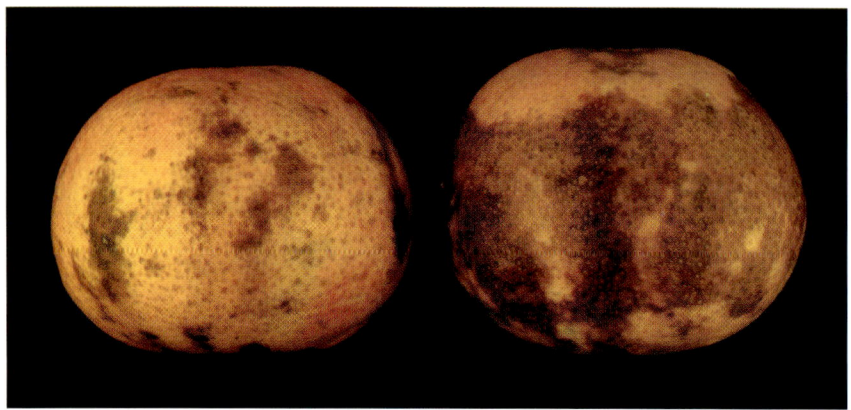

Plate 23. Zebra skin of Fallglo tangerine.

Plate 24. Color add test using plastic electrical tape to shield part of the fruit from the dye.

Plate 25. Mediterranean fruit fly.

Plate 26. Citrus canker on Valencia orange fruit and leaves.

8

Transportation to the Packinghouse

Mark. A. Ritenour, William Grierson, and Wilfred F. Wardowski

Transportation of fruit from the tree to the packinghouse is usually treated as a purely mechanical-economic operation. On this basis, several very detailed reports are available, e.g., Bowman *et al.* (1971), Phillips and Grierson (1960), and Sherkin (1977). The most comprehensive report on the economics of the transportation of harvested citrus fruit is incorporated in a study by Stevenson and Kellogg, Ltd., Toronto, under contract with the Canadian International Development Agency (Reid 1976). The Canadian study was designed to aid developing countries (initially Cuba) that were beginning or expanding their citrus industries (Sherkin 1977).

The movement of fruit from tree to packinghouse may be minimal and involve pickers simply carrying fruit to the packing area in or near the field (Wardowski and Bonnell 1983), or distant, involving transport of harvested fruit 200 km (124 miles) or more from the field to the packinghouse. During the 1980-81 season, the estimated average cost of hauling (transporting) Florida citrus to fresh fruit packinghouses and to processing plants was 10.3, 12.6, 15.2, and 19.0% of the total picking and hauling costs for tangerines, tangelos, oranges, and grapefruit, respectively (Hooks 1983). These differences are largely attributable to differences in picking costs; the smaller and frailer the fruit (e.g., tangerines vs. grapefruit), the higher the cost of picking relative to the cost of transportation. Per unit transportation costs are not necessarily affected by the type of fruit. During the 2003-04 season, hauling charges 30 miles or less averaged $0.41 per box for all fresh citrus varieties (Muraro and Hebb 2004).

As demonstrated by the history of fresh fruit bulk handling in Florida (Phillips and Grierson 1957, 1960; Prosser *et al.* 1955), legal, psychological, and sociological factors may impede the adoption and successful functioning of a particular transportation system. Thus, economic and mechanical considerations are often not the only, or the major, constraints on tree-to-packinghouse transportation.

SOME PRINCIPLES

Before considering some of the many components and their combinations involved in tree-to-packinghouse transportation systems, it is well to consider some of the principles involved, many of which are commonly overlooked or misunderstood.

Containers

Picking and hauling of fruit almost invariably involves at least two types of containers: some form of picking bag, sack, pail, etc., and some larger container for transportation of picked fruit to the packinghouse.

Picking containers must be no larger than a picker can handle conveniently without tiring. Metal-framed canvas bags with two shoulder straps holding up to 20 kg can be handled by most pickers, regardless of their age or gender, and will cause minimal damage to the fruit. The 40-kg "jumbo" single-strap picking bag generally favored in Florida (Fig. 8.1) accounts for much unnecessary damage to fruit, severely limits the availability of pickers, and cannot be recommended by the authors for citrus for the fresh fruit market. Both bags have a bottom-flap for easier and more gentile transfer of the fruit to a larger container.

Fig. 8.1. Picker with single strap picking bag.

Fruit is almost inevitably transferred to another larger container soon after it is picked. Transportation containers can be of three kinds: manually handled, mechanically handled, or integrated with the grove-to-packinghouse vehicle. Regardless of the type, citrus containers have to be more durable than apple or pear containers, which are used annually for one or two trips to the orchard and then hold fruit in storage for months. Citrus harvesting containers typically make approximately 50 round trips per year, although the number of trips varies considerably with the length of the harvesting season, which can be year-round for California packinghouses packing both Washington navel (early) and Valencia (late) oranges.

Manually handled containers, handled by laborers without mechanical assistance, should not hold over 20 kg of fruit. Larger field boxes are hard on the fruit and difficult for workers and severely limit the type of labor that can be employed. Even for reasonably able-bodied men, any manual container that cannot be lifted, loaded, and dumped with comparative ease will inevitably invite much rough handling, particularly as workers tire at the end of the working day.

Mechanically handled containers are usually large containers, called pallet boxes or bins, that incorporate a pallet base and hold so much fruit that they must be mechanically handled. In the field, they are often picked up from the bottom by some type of forklift equipment. When soil conditions preclude using forklift equipment in the grove, they have to be picked up by some cranelike device such as the Florida Lightning Loader, which requires special strengthening of the upper edge of the pallet box (Fig. 8.2). In all cases, the bottom (pallet base) must be absolutely rigid to avoid fruit damage. When degreening is involved (Chapter 10), pallet boxes must permit sufficient ventilation, as discussed later. Typical designs for pallet boxes are described by Wardowski and Grierson (2002). There are many other versions of mechanically handled containers other than pallet boxes. An early California version used large shallow containers holding about 7000 kg, each carried on a single-axle trailer with a mechanical tipping device to roll it off at the packinghouse (Greene and Cook 1959). A particularly successful version of such a container was once used in South Australia where the large container had swing-down legs and the highway truck drove out from under it at the packinghouse. As in most fresh market citrus-producing regions of the world, Australia now uses the pallet box system (Taverner 2002).

Vehicle-integral containers can be either prime movers (having their own engine) or trailers pulled behind a prime mover of some kind. In many circumstances, such containers are economically preferable, but many noneconomic factors relating to labor practices, local highway laws, special unloading arrangements, and degreening requirements may limit their use.

Fig. 8.2. Hydriodic pallet bin top lift loader transferring bins between semi flatbed and modified truck, known in Florida as a goat.

Sources of Fruit Damage Related to Transportation

Container Contact. Worldwide, attitudes toward fruit damage are conditioned by the far greater volume of research on noncitrus fruits for which a major hazard is fruit-on-fruit damage. This damage most typically results in bruising characterized by internal cell rupture and consequent detrimental metabolism of cell contents. Most bruising of such fruits occurs on impact, but depth in a pallet box can be a factor, largely as an interaction with time during storage (Mohsenin *et al.* 1962). Such fruit to fruit bruising generally does *not* occur in citrus fruits; the equivalent is oleocellosis (Chapter 14). Obviously, fruit to fruit damage can also occur from clipped fruit with sharp residual stems, which never should be allowed.

Most citrus fruit damage during tree-to-packinghouse transportation is caused by contact between the fruit and some other object, very commonly the surface of the container used for transportation. As the size of the container increases, the percentage of fruit in contact with the container decreases. Thus, all else being equal, the proportion of fruit damaged by the container decreases in going from field boxes to pallet boxes to bulk fruit vehicle, as was confirmed in a long series of studies in Florida (Prosser *et al.* 1955).

Fruit Depth. In a cooperative USDA and University of Florida study (Grierson 1970), Dancy tangerines (a very decay-susceptible variety) were handled from tree to packinghouse in old-fashioned field boxes, with a fruit depth of 30.5 cm, and in pallet boxes filled to depths of 33, 51, and 66 cm. Half the samples were degreened in the harvesting containers and half were not, and all were put through a simulated marketing test. There was no consistent correlation between decay losses and type of container, regardless of depth.

In another study in cooperation with Coca-Cola Foods Division (W. Grierson unpublished data), pallet boxes were filled with Dancy tangerines to depths of 30.5, 46, and 61 cm and trucked 120 km. All fruit were removed by hand and the bottom layers of fruit were carefully examined for fruit injuries and used for decay studies. No correlation was found between fruit damage or decay and the depth of fruit above the evaluated fruit. Such studies provide no support for the use of expensive shallow pallet boxes for transporting tangerines.

When damage occurs in the bottom of pallet boxes, it is almost invariably attributable to faulty pallet boxes or pickers having dropped the fruit roughly into the pallet box instead of lowering it in gently. Sharp edges, slivers, nail or bolt heads, etc., are obvious causes of fruit damage. A more serious, but harder to detect, pallet box failure is flexing of the bottom when the box is picked up or put down. Any flexing of the bottom causes distortion of the bottom layer of fruit with consequent injury. A surprising amount of injury is caused by overfilling of pallet boxes (Fig. 8.3). When other pallet boxes are stacked on overfilled ones, the runners of the box above can cause very serious damage, often in the form of distinct oleocellosis "belly bands" around the fruit.

Nonfruit Inclusions. Serious fruit injury, often erroneously blamed on pallet box handling, can occur due to inclusion of stems, twigs, or other trash among the fruit. Unfortunately, the development of pallet boxes and similar fruit-handling methods seems to have coincided with an apparently worldwide deterioration in picking standards. Certainly in Florida packinghouses, trash removal has become an essential part of fruit receiving. One pregrader in a Florida packinghouse claimed that she had pulled everything except tree roots from incoming fruit.

A more subtle form of damage during transportation to the packinghouse is found in sandy districts when sand is allowed to get among the fruit, usually from the pallet box above. Such sand not only can cause disfiguring injuries but also can carry soilborne decay organisms such as sour rot (see Chapter 13). In districts with sandy soil, lower pallets should be left open, i.e., with no stringers (boards) below the runners. In addition, care should be taken when placing pallets in the field that dirt is not

Fig. 8.3. Crushed oranges from overfilled lower pallet bin by placement of upper bin.

kicked up into the bottom of the pallet boxes. Some packinghouses pressure wash pallet boxes after each use to remove any sand picked up from the field (Fig. 8.4).

Rough Roads. Careless driving can cause serious fruit damage. Although driving habits should be controllable, the quality of road surfaces often is not. Wherever possible, grade dirt roads to remove potholes, bumps, and ruts. Reroute trucks to avoid roads in poor condition. In various studies with deciduous fruits in pallet boxes, it has been found that a high proportion of the fruit damage associated with rough road conditions is due to the top layers of fruit bouncing around. Bumps in the road and vibration often cause the most injury to product placed directly above the trailer axles. Such damage can be expected with very turgid citrus fruits. Florida lemons, which mature during the rainy season, are commonly so turgid that it has become accepted practice to leave harvested lemons in pallet boxes overnight to allow turgor pressure to decline before highway transport. Utilization of more expensive air ride suspension systems can greatly reduce injury due to bumps or vibrations during transport compared to steel spring suspension systems. Reducing air pressure can also reduce transportation damage.

Degreening

Degreening is thoroughly discussed in Chapter 10. It is technically possible to degreen fruit held in bulk-handling vehicles. One Florida

Fig. 8.4. Pressure washing pallet bin for sanitation and to remove refuse.

cooperative successfully degreened fruit in bulk semitrailers modified as though for fruit fly fumigation (Grierson and Hayward 1959). Economically, however, there is no justification for tying up expensive road vehicles during degreening except in unusual or emergency circumstances.

Sanitation

With the spread of various citrus diseases worldwide, issues of field and packinghouse sanitation have become very important. Good equipment and personnel cleaning and sanitation procedures can limit the spread of economically important weeds, insects, fungi, and bacteria into and throughout an area. In California, sanitation practices are being implemented to limit the spread of the glassy-winged sharpshooter that is an effective vector for Pierce's Disease and other strains of *Xylella* (Citrus Research Board 2001). In Florida, to aid in the eradication of citrus canker (*Xanthomonas axonopodis* pv. citri), strict sanitation procedures for equipment and personnel are now required (Fig. 8.4). Many of the compounds (e.g. quaternary ammonia) used for sanitizing equipment are not registered for direct contact with fresh produce and my cause fruit injury

(Ritenour *et al.* 2000). Thus, field and packinghouse decontamination operators must be diligent to insure that fruit not be sprayed with unlabeled sanitizers. Some sanitizers must be rinsed off equipment and pallet boxes before the surface contacts fresh fruit.

The increased use of plastic pallet boxes in the past 10 years is partly due to their ease of cleaning compared to wood pallet boxes. Plastic pallet boxes are also lighter, cause less fruit abrasion, have lower maintenance costs, and do not absorb moisture from the fruit during storage. However, they are more expensive than wooden bins. Furthermore, plastic pallet boxes made of high density polyethylene (HDPE) were reportedly weakened by some compounds (e.g., certain surfactants in drench solutions and quaternary ammonia), but the surfactants were replaced with ones that do not effect the plastic and newer polypropylene pallet boxes are much more resistant to these compounds.

Increased attention to documenting sanitation and food safety related practices will also increase the need to include identifying information on every truck delivering fruit to the packinghouse and likely every pallet of fruit on the truck. Mechanisms where packed fruit at destination markets can be quickly traced back to the packinghouse, field block, production records, and even harvester are increasingly becoming a part of a company's food safety program. Use of computers, GPS (global positioning systems), and GIS (geographic information systems) are making such data collection easier, more automated and are an integral part of the increased use of precision agriculture.

Management Considerations

No one system of tree-to-packinghouse transportation will ever be the best for all circumstances. How economical any given system will be in any particular circumstance will depend on various management considerations that are often overlooked.

Labor. Since World War II there has been a worldwide fascination with labor-saving equipment, whether or not appropriate methods are available. Many such false starts have been due to regarding modernization as merely replacing people with machines, instead of regarding machines as something to multiply the productivity of workers who can then be drawn from a far wider pool of available labor. Replacing a crew of workers who handle field boxes manually by a truck-mounted pallet box hoist means entrusting an expensive piece of machinery to a single worker who becomes so productive that a better wage can be paid to obtain someone skilled and reliable, and who can be hired regardless of gender or physical strength.

Highway Laws. Local and state highway laws can completely preclude certain transportation methods that are perfectly legal elsewhere. Regulations may even vary for different roads within a given district. One Florida packer had to abandon use of expensive grove-to-packinghouse equipment because it could not meet the minimum speed limit of 64 kph where it had to travel on a federally regulated interstate highway. Complete knowledge of such local laws should be a prerequisite for a manager choosing any transportation system that uses public highways.

Tree-to-Roadside Distance. An important consideration in selecting crew size and tree-to-roadside hauling equipment is the tree-to-roadside distance. With too few pickers per hauling unit, expensive equipment is underutilized. With too many pickers, the fruit cannot be moved to the roadside fast enough and highway equipment is underutilized. In solving this equation, the average tree-to-roadside distance is critical. An example of this relationship is given by Grierson *et al.* (1962). They found that a large tractor carrying four pallet boxes on front and rear forks could service 18 pickers when the average tree-to-roadside distance was 76 m but could only service 10 pickers when the average distance extended to 760 m. An unexpected finding in a similar study with a truck-mounted hydraulic hoist was that the driver tended to pace the pickers rather than *vice versa*. The faster the driver took away full pallet boxes, the faster the pickers tended to pick. This made it profitable to pay the driver a small bonus based on the volume of fruit handled.

Roadside-to-Packinghouse Distance. The type of highway hauling equipment selected is limited by the roadside-to-packinghouse distance. For example, a straddle truck (or straddle trailer) is much more expensive than a flatbed truck or trailer; however, its loading and unloading time is minimal and no labor is involved in these operations. Thus a straddle truck spends most of the working day on the road, not parked to load or unload, but it must make many trips per day to pay for its extra initial cost. As hauling distance increases, the number of these quick turnarounds decreases; at some point a straddle truck ceases to have any economic advantage over a flatbed truck. On the other hand, as roadside-to-packinghouse distance decreases there comes a point at which whatever vehicle brings the fruit to the roadside might just as well take it on into the packinghouse. Obviously, packinghouses drawing their fruit from both near and distant sources may need to combine two or more systems to achieve optimum efficiency.

Pooling of fruit from various sources permits many economies, particularly when harvesting systems have to be coordinated with degreening systems for much of the season. The California lemon industry, faced with presorting incoming fruit into four or five color categories followed by long curing periods, long ago instituted sampling systems (Thym and Smith 1948). This made it possible to pay according to fruit quality while still benefitting from the many efficiencies involved in pooling crops. However, it is often necessary to keep various sources of fruit separate such as to satisfy

TABLE 8.1. Equipment and Activities Associated with Some Grove-to-Packinghouse Citrus Transportation Systems

Activity	Bulk system	Pallet box and forklift system	Pallet box and hydraulic hoist system	Straddle trailer system	Container train system	Hillside monorail or cable system
A. Gather full field containers (or contents) and move to roadside.	A small single-axle grove truck with hydraulic device dumps contents of field containers into large cagelike container.	One man driving a farm tractor with single or double forks picks up full pallet boxes and takes them to roadside.	One man drives a small single-axle grove truck with hydraulic lifting device to place full pallet boxes onto truck.	A grove fork gathers several containers at a time, and accurately positions them on empty timber bed (bolster).	Tractor driver connects to full wheeled container and tows to roadside orienting container pointing toward facility.	Pickers position full bags, pails, etc., on cable system that moves fruit to road on steep hillsides.
B. Transfer to long-distance vehicle and transport to facility.	Fruit dumped into bulk highway trailer using a scissorlike mechanism on grove truck. Full highway trailer delivered to facility.	The tractor driver drives directly to a highway vehicle and positions boxes.	Grove truck load transferred to highway vehicle using hydraulic lifting device. A second man drives the full highway vehicle to facility.	A highway tractor pulling a straddle trailer backs over bolster. Trailer hydraulic lifts and transports at high speed to facility.	There is no transfer to long-distance vehicle. Tractor driver connects ten wheeled containers to each other and tows them to facility.	Workers transfer fruit to vehicles for transportation to packinghouse.
C. Unload cargo and reload any empty containers. Vehicle returns to grove.	Trailer backed down a ramp, tailgate opened, and fruit rolls onto a takeaway conveyor belt.	Common industrial fork-truck used to unload fulls and load empties back onto highway vehicle which returns to grove.	Common industrial fork-truck used to unload fulls and load empties back onto highway vehicle which returns to grove.	Boxes lowered onto bolster. Trailer backed over bed with empty boxes. Boxes are lifted and transported to grove.	Fork-truck lifts 1-ton pallet off wheeled bed and replaces with empty box. Tractor tows empties back to grove.	Containers are unloaded by hand or with lift trucks.
D. Unload empties and place in grove.	Bulk bins never leave the grove and are repositioned for harvesting.	Tractor driver unloads highway vehicle and distributes empty pallet boxes throughout grove for harvesters.	Lifting device on grove truck used to unload empty pallet boxes from highway vehicle and distribute for harvesting.	Empties are lowered onto empty bolster. Grove fork driver then distributes empties throughout grove for harvesting.	Tractor driver distributes empty wheeled containers by detaching them as he drives through the grove.	Empty picking containers are returned by cable system up mountainside.

Source: Adapted from Sherkin (1977).

fruit fly protocol requirements or to implement trace back procedures as part of a food safety program. Although fruit-sampling systems are universal in Florida canneries, most efforts to introduce them to fresh fruit packinghouses have failed.

MAJOR TRANSPORTATION SYSTEMS

The efficient transportation of fruit requires an integrated system from harvesting through receiving facilities. Each system component is linked to preceding and following components and must be coordinated with complex harvesting, transportation, and fruit processing schedules. Bowman *et al.* (1971) and Sherkin (1977) have described various fruit transportation systems in Florida, California, and Israel. The activities involved in some of the more common grove-to-packinghouse transportation systems are described by Sherkin (1977), and discussed below.

Bulk System

In Florida, all cannery fruit is hauled to processing plants in bulk trucks. At one time, a very successful modification of this system was used for fresh fruit by a few packinghouses. The development of this very economical system and the reasons for its current disuse in Florida are described in the final section of this chapter since much of this research may prove useful elsewhere.

Pallet Box and Forklift System

Perhaps the most common system in use today involves pallet boxes handled in groves by some form of hydraulic forklift equipment. For long distances from the tree to the roadside, an intermediate vehicle may be loaded by a forklift at the picking area and unloaded at the roadside by another forklift. Pallet boxes are loaded onto flatbed semitrailers for the highway haul to the packinghouse. This is a versatile system, but can be limited by soil type (too sandy, too muddy, or too easily compacted) and by tree spacing (maneuvering forklifts can be difficult in closely grown groves and can cause unacceptable tree damage). Forklift trucks unload full pallet boxes at the packinghouse and reload empty pallet boxes (Fig. 8.5).

Pallet Box and Hydraulic Hoist System

Forklifts mounted on very large farm tractors were used with only limited success in Florida (Grierson *et al.* 1962). On any but the most level groves, Florida's light sand soils make use of forklifts difficult or impossible.

Fig. 8.5. Industrial forklifts are often used to handle full and empty pallet bins.

They were rapidly replaced by a versatile hydraulic hoist (Lightning Loader), usually mounted on a stripped-down 1.22-m wide truck (goat) (Fig. 8.2). A typical goat will pick up eight or ten full pallet boxes, carry them to the roadside and transfer them to a waiting semitrailer. Handling at the packinghouse is identical to the pallet box and forklift system described in the previous section.

Other Systems

Most commercial fresh citrus production regions of the world have now adopted some form of the above pallet box and forklift or hydraulic hoist system. Below are some systems that have been previously used in different parts of the world but are currently much less common.

Straddle Trailer System

In California the grove forklift and straddle system was once common for handling fresh citrus fruit. Two, three, or four full containers were moved to the side of the grove by a grove forklift truck. The containers were precisely placed on a timber frame bed (bolster), which usually held 32 pallet boxes stacked four high, but could hold as few as four pallet boxes.

A highway straddle trailer backed over the full bolster and picked up the full pallet boxes. The load was delivered at highway speeds to the packinghouse where the load of full pallet boxes was placed on a bolster in the packinghouse yard and a load of empties picked up; then the straddle returned to the grove with a turnaround time seldom exceeding 10 min. Smaller loads could be pulled at slower speeds with a farm tractor.

Container Train System

The container train system was once used for fresh citrus fruit in Israel, South Africa, and elsewhere. The container was mounted on a two-wheel frame as a trailer and held about 1 MT, equal to about two or three pallet boxes. The full containers were pulled by a tractor to the roadside where ten were connected in a line pointing towards the packinghouse, and then pulled to the packinghouse by the tractor.

The full containers were lifted off the trailers and empty containers were positioned back on the wheeled frame. The empty ten-unit container train was towed back to the grove for the harvesters.

Hillside Monorail or Cable System

The Japanese developed and continue to use monorail and cable systems to move citrus fruit down steep terraced mountain slopes. These same systems are also used to move equipment and materials up for production practices. In 1977, 63% of the Japanese citrus orchards were planted on slopes of 15 degrees or more (Yamada *et al.* 1982). The monorail system has numerous variations including human and Gasoline power. In one study, a gasoline-powered system was more efficient than hand carrying for distances greater than 16 m, and was generally twice as efficient as hand carrying (Yamada *et al.* 1982).

FLORIDA BULK-HANDLING EXPERIENCE

A review of nearly 30 years of research and commercial experience in bulk handling of fresh citrus in Florida illustrates many of the principles and pitfalls involved in transporting fruit from grove to packinghouse. Bulk handling means doing away with containers altogether and conveying the fruit from tree to packinghouse in bulk trucks or trailers. Since this would be far less costly than using the manually handled field boxes then in use, a University of Florida-USDA project on fresh fruit bulk handling was set up at the Citrus Experiment Station, Lake Alfred, in 1948. Initially, only two real problems were foreseen: finding some way to degreen fruit in bulk, and avoiding any increase in fruit damage.

Stationary bins were developed in each of which approximately 6000 kg of fruit was degreened on baffles of cider press cloth, chosen because it was soft, porous, strong, and approved for food contact use. A system was set up at Chase & Co., Windermere. in which pairs of pickers filled two-wheeled carts holding approximately 800 kg each. Farm tractors pulled trains of carts from the groves onto an inclined ramp at the packinghouse where they were discharged from the side without uncoupling from the tractor. A vertical elevator delivered the fruit to rows of cloth-baffle bulk degreening bins, which performed well (Prosser *et al.* 1955). The system was efficient and economical and resulted in less fruit damage than with the traditional manually handled field box system used at the time. However, virtually no other packinghouse in Florida could adopt the system because none other had its packinghouse in the midst of surrounding groves and Florida highway laws prohibited pulling more than one trailer behind a prime mover. Because nearly all Florida packinghouses had to transport their incoming fruit over public highways, various methods of hauling bulk loads of fresh fruit were attempted Some of this early work is reported in Prosser *et al.* 1955.

An outstanding success was the system devised for Haines City Citrus Growers Association (C.G.A.). Two critical items were designed and built in this very large cooperative's own workshops. The first was a truck-mounted vertical loader. The second was a semitrailer body that hauled a tractor and about 10 two-wheeled carts to the citrus groves. Pairs of pickers filled the carts, which were pulled individually and discharged from the rear into the loader. Specially modified semi trailers discharged loads of about 17,000 kg from the side onto a belt at the packinghouse where the fruit went into very large (ca. 8000-9000 kg) cloth baffle bins. Initially, some fruit damage was detected by stain tests (Roistacher *et al.* 1956) and by an increased decay in holding tests. The origin of this was located only when a colorimetric paper was devised that reacted differentially to peel oil and to juice from damaged fruit (Grierson 1958). The damage that had been occurring in loads traveling on rough roads was due to uneven loading. Damage occurred in loads ridged down the center, but not in flat loads no more than 1.22 m deep. Such loading was obtained by simple modification of a standard loading chute (Bowman *et al.* 1971). This limited loads to about 410 kg (10 boxes) per 30.5 cm of truck body, about 75% of a normal loading for the cannery. At this point, the packinghouse had a very successful and economical system (Phillips and Grierson 1957).

However, the cart-vertical loader-semitrailer system was not readily adaptable to very short hauls, mixed plantings, or small growers. Haines City C.G.A.'s solution to this was a bulk grove truck that held approximately 3700 kg of oranges and officially was called the Chapman Automatic Loader after its inventor, Cecil Chapman (Phillips and Grierson 1960; Tidbury 1958). It was commonly called the Sputnik because it was invented in 1957, the year the first Russian Sputnik satellite was launched, and it operates in groves near the packinghouse like a satellite. This ingenious vehicle had a system of padded baffles throughout the truck body to minimize fruit damage and was filled by a hydraulically operated hopper at the rear. Six pickers pooled their earnings and emptied their picking bags into the hopper operated by the vehicle driver. When two Sputniks worked with one crew of six pickers, sustained picking rates 40% above the expected norm were regularly recorded.

When the whole system was running smoothly, the return on investment in setting up the system was calculated at 33% per year. Essentially, the system depended on crew discipline. Pickers had to be willing to pool their earnings. In addition, no trash could get into the bulk loads, where it could do great damage. The vertical loader had to be moved with each cartload in order to lay in the required flat, even loads. With each passing year, the quality of the workers degenerated until enforcement of these simple precepts became increasingly difficult. After about 20 years of operation the great bulk bin degreening system was termite riddled and had to be torn down and replaced. By then, the very successful continuously operating pallet box degreening rooms had been developed (Grierson and Wardowski 1973; see Chapter 10), and the full bulk-handling system, with its increasingly difficult labor management problems, was abandoned for pallet boxes handled by Lightning Loader hoists in the grove and by lift trucks at the packinghouse.

REFERENCES

BOWMAN, E. K., SPURLOCK, A. H., HEDDEN, S. and GRIERSON, W. 1971. Modernizing handling systems for Florida citrus from picking to packing line. USDA Marketing Res. Rept. 914.

CITRUS RESEARCH BOARD. 2001. California Citrus Industry Guide: Glassy-winged Sharpshooter and related bacterial diseases. Citrus Research Board. 18 p. www.citrusresearch.com (or http://citrusent.uckac.edu/GWSSmanual2.pdf)

GREENE, P. H. and COOK, P. H. 1959. Bulk handling, production service, grower operations. Calif. Citrogr. 44 (5), 147, 163.

GRIERSON, W. 1958. Indicator papers for detecting damage to citrus fruit. University of Florida Agr. Exp. Stn. Circ. S-J02.

GRIERSON, W., COWART, F. M., CHEN, S. C. T., SPURLOCK, A. H. and GRIZZELL, W. G. 1962. Handling Florida oranges in pallet boxes. USDA Marketing Res. Rept. 529.

GRIERSON, W. 1970. Managing tangerines for larger returns. Citrus Ind. 51 (6), 5, 7, 9, 11-12.

GRIERSON, W. and HAYWARD, F. W. 1959. Fumigation of Florida citrus fruit with ethylene dibromide. Proc. Am. Soc. Hort. Sci. 73, 267-277.

GRIERSON, W. and WARDOWSKI, W. F. 1973. Development of mechanization programs for harvesting and handling citrus fruits, pp. 633-649. Proc. Int. Soc. Citriculture, Vol. 3.

HOOKS, R. C. 1983. Estimated cost of picking and hauling fresh Florida citrus, 1980-81 season. University of Florida Econ. Inf. Rept. 188.

MOHSENIN, N., GOEHLICH, H. and TUKEY, L. D. 1962. Mechanical behavior of apple fruits as related to bruising. Proc. Am. Soc. Hort. Sci. 81, 67-77.

MURARO, R. P. and John W.H. 2004. Budgeting costs and returns for Indian River citrus production. UF/IFAS Extension, http://EDIS.ifas.ulf.edu/FE527.

PHILLIPS, R. V. and GRIERSON, W. 1957. Cost advantages of bulk handling citrus through the packinghouse. Proc. Fla. State Hort. Soc. 70, 171-177.

PHILLIPS, R. V. and GRIERSON, W. 1960. Cost advantages of bulk handling: II. The Chapman automatic loader. Proc. Fla. State Hort. Soc. 73, 231-235.

PROSSER, D. S., JR., GRIERSON, W. F., THOR, E., NEWHALL, W. F. and SAMUELS, J. K. 1955. Bulk handling of fresh citrus fruit. University of Florida Bull. 564.

REID, J. N. A. 1976. Personal communication. Toronto, Canada.

RITENOUR, M, NG-SANCHEZ, T. and KELSEY, D.F. 2000. Quaternary Ammonia Injury on Grapefruit Peel. Packinghouse Newsletter 192, 1-4.

ROISTACHER, C. N., KLOTZ, L. J. and EAKS, I. I. 1956. A color indicator for detecting surface injuries to fruit. Calif. Citrogr. 41 (6), 239-242.

SHERKIN, R. 1977. An evaluation of alternative harvested fruit transportation systems, pp. 277-283. Proc. Int. Soc. Citriculture, Vol. 1.

TAVERNER, P. 2002. Personal communication. Adelaide SA, Australia.

THYM, A. M. and SMITH, R. J. 1948. Mechanized sampling. Calif. Agr. 2 (10), 8, 14.

TIDBURY, G. E. (958. Bulk harvesting of orchard fruit. Commonwealth Agr. Bureau (England) Digest No. 1.

WARDOWSKI, W. F. and BONNELL, J. M. 1983. Observations on citrus in China. Proc. Fla. State Hort. Soc. 96, 361-366.

WARDOWSKI, W. F. and GRIERSON, W. 2002. Pallet boxes for Florida citrus. Fla. Agr. Ext. Circ. 443.

YAMADA, Y., SHICHIJO, T. and KAZUYOSHI, H. 1982. Saving the labor of fruit-picking and carriage at slope orchard of satsuma mandarin. Bull. Fruit Research Stn., Ser. B. (Okitsu) 9, 1-22 (Japanese with English summary).

9

Coordination of Fresh Fruit and Processing Outlets

William Grierson and Wilfred F. Wardowski

It is normal for a citrus crop to be grown either for the fresh fruit market or for processing; the latter typically involves a minimal pesticide spray program and some form of bulk harvesting and hauling. However, though a crop intended for the cannery is unlikely to be used for the fresh fruit market, the reverse is a common occurrence. For most fresh fruit markets some blemished fruit has to be graded out, and this often goes to the cannery; occasionally an entire crop initially intended for the fresh fruit market may be sent to the processor. Thus neither the economics nor the physical handling of fresh and cannery crops can be considered entirely separately, and how well use of these two outlets is coordinated can determine the profitability of a given crop. Oranges suitable for frozen orange concentrate can usually be switched from fresh fruit to processing with little financial loss. However, alternative disposition of grapefruit, tangerines, tangelos, and lemons can involve far more difficult financial decisions.

ECONOMIC CONSIDERATIONS

Pest-Infested Crops

Occasionally some insect or disease can become thoroughly entrenched early in the season before the grower is aware of it. In a humid climate such as Florida's, the fungus *Diaporthe citri* (Faw.) Wolf can infest wind scars on newly formed fruit during a rainy postbloom to cause the disfiguring disease melanose. A tangerine crop with an early heavy infestation of chaff scale *(Parlatoria pergandii* Comst.) can look perfect unless closely examined under a hand lens; but after color change it would be so disfigured by persistent green spots as to be unmarketable under almost any fresh fruit grades, even when such grades and standards are set to accommodate local priorities (Grierson and Ting 1978; see also Chapter 2).

As Albrigo (1978) has pointed out, such pest infestations can be detected early in the growing season if the developing crop is checked often and closely enough. Although the particular criteria of fresh fruit grade standards differ locally, the basic principle for deciding whether to save a fresh fruit crop or convert it to processing use is the same. If the crop will not return a reasonable profit on the fresh fruit market, calculate whether it is better to retrieve what is possible via the processing outlet. If so, then early in the season any fresh fruit sprays that are no longer justified should be stopped and the crop sent to the cannery when it is at maximum cannery value (in Florida, usually determined by pounds solids per acre) by the least expensive harvesting route.

A particular problem arises when a crop is to be harvested from an area infected with an insect or disease that is currently subject to a legal eradication campaign. This occurs in many citrus districts when an infestation by a fruit fly, such as the Mediterranean fruit fly, *Ceratitis capitata* (Wied.), complicates harvesting and transportation. In such cases, free movement of fruit is typically confined to within the infected area unless fumigated. Obviously, all fruit for shipment from the infested area has to be fumigated, though not necessarily for cannery fruit when the processing can be done within the quarantine area. When the processing plant is outside the quarantined area, cannery crops and packinghouse eliminations for processing have to be fumigated before leaving the quarantined area.

Pests for which there is no eradication treatment, such as citrus canker, *Xanthomonas* spp., can be ruinously expensive. At the time of first writing this chapter, a canker eradication program in Florida involved total destruction, not only of infected trees and fruit, but also of adjacent trees. Following the spread of canker by a series of hurricanes, the eradication program was abandoned early in 2006. Chapter 17 includes a thorough discussion of this and other regulatory issues, and provides internet addresses for up-to-date information.

Crops Damaged by Climatic Hazards

Pests can usually be controlled, but the weather can not. Moreover, post-1973 increases in fuel costs have made frost protection by grove or orchard heating too expensive except for exceptionally valuable citrus cultivars. There are severe economic limitations on what degree of freeze damage allows for economic separation of damaged from undamaged fruit. Sometimes it is not economically possible to try to separate No. 1 grade fruit from a frost-injured crop. Then the first option is to seek a lower grade fresh fruit outlet. Failing that, frost-injured crops should go directly to the cannery by the cheapest possible route, which is not via the packinghouse (see also Chapter 11).

Frost is, by far, the most dramatic, climatic hazard and one for which the effects are most easily documented (Attaway 1997). Other climatic hazards include extreme drought, with consequent loss of size and turgor, and excessive bloom set resulting in an excess of very small fruit that are expensive to pick and essentially worthless on the fresh fruit market. In all such cases, any hope of profit is diminished by delaying the decision as to whether to send the crop to the packinghouse or to the cannery.

Packout and Profitability

The obvious, unfortunately, constantly needs to be restated. A packinghouse exists only to pack fruit and its profitability therefore depends both on the number of units (usually cartons) packed per day and the percentage of packable fruit handled. Each blemished fruit removed by graders not only costs some considerable amount to handle from the tree to the grading table to the cannery, but it also displaces a packable fruit that could have contributed to the profits of the packinghouse.

Grierson (1957), in an economic study of Florida fresh fruit (oranges, grapefruit, and tangerines), considered all costs from growing to sale F.O.B. packinghouse and produced graphs, tables, and formulas illustrating (1) the effect of packout on final overall profit or loss; (2) typical packouts from a representative cooperative growers association; and (3) when it would have been more profitable to send the whole crop to the cannery rather than running it through the packinghouse. This study was later updated for tangerines only (Grierson *et al.* 1960; Grierson 1970). Other such studies reported on grade-lowering factors depressing packouts in a representative group of packinghouses (Grierson 1958) and throughout the whole season in a single large cooperative packinghouse (Grierson and Oberbacher 1959). In this latter study, fruit graded out for excessive green color cost an average of 7.2¢ per box (40 kg) delivered in to the packinghouse, even though normal degreening practices were followed. Individual packinghouses were observed to pack as little as 12% of a crop of particularly blemished grapefruit and up to virtually 100% of a bright, clean crop of tangerines. Then, as now, there was little effort to calculate the packout below which it would have been cheaper to send a given crop directly to the cannery rather than trying to pack it, even though a formula for doing so has long been available (Table 9.1).

A packinghouse, like any other business, must do more than break even. It must make a profit and the extent of that profit varies directly with packout; the magnitude of the relationship between profit and packout increases sharply with increasing differential between fresh and cannery prices. That this obvious relationship is very commonly ignored is attributable to (1) lack of coordination between managers responsible for growing and packing; (2) emphasis on reducing costs of the individual operations (e.g., growing, harvesting, packing, and processing) rather than concentrat-

TABLE 9.1. Packout to Break Even

$$X = 100 \times \frac{G + H + Q + T - E}{F + Q + T - (E + P)}$$

where

X = packout to break even
G = per box[a] cost of growing
H = per box cost of picking and hauling
P = per box cost of packing two 4/5-bu containers
Q = per box cost of running eliminations through packinghouse
T = per box cost of delivering eliminations to cannery
E = per box price received for eliminations
F = FOB price fresh fruit (per 1 3/5 bu)

Example based on costs and prices for tangerines in 1969-1970.

$$X = 100 \times \frac{1.40 + 1.33 + 0.45 + 0.07 - 1.00}{7.50 + 0.45 + 0.07 - (1.00 + 2.17)}$$

Packout to break even is 46%.

[a]The Florida box is legally defined as 90 lb (40.9 kg) oranges, 85 lb (38.6 kg) grapefruit and 95 lb (43.1 kg) tangerines.
Source: Grierson (1970).

ing on maximizing overall net returns; and (3) archaic accounting systems, usually originally set up when packinghouses packed blemished fruit as No. 2 or No. 3 grades and the cannery outlet was negligible (Grierson 2002). A particularly striking example was encountered in the Grierson (1970) study in which a cooperative was returning $0.93 per box (about 43 kg fruit) to its growers for tangerine eliminations (packinghouse discards for juice). Their statements read simply as follows:

Price at cannery	$1.00 per box
Haul to cannery	- 0.07 per box
Return to grower	$0.93 per box

This perpetuated the illusion that growers were making money on their blemished tangerine eliminations and that the cooperative cannery had a very cheap source of fruit. A more detailed accounting revealed the following:

Cost of growing	$1.40 per box
Cost of harvesting and hauling to packinghouse	1.33 per box
Cost of handling through the packinghouse	0.45 per box
Cost of hauling to the cannery	0.07 per box
Total costs	- 3.25
Price at cannery	+ 1.00
Net loss	- $2.25

Moreover, applying $3.18 of the actual $3.25 total cost for eliminations against the in-grade packed fruit resulted in apparent returns so low from in-grade fruit as to give very little incentive to the growers to invest sufficient money to improve cultural practices enough to raise the proportion of packable fruit.

This situation is particularly obscured when crops are sold by growers to independent packers. This 1970 study therefore included calculations as to what an independent packer could afford to pay for crops of tangerines according to the proportion of packable fruit, assuming a modest 10¢ per box profit (Fig. 9.1). At 1970 costs and prices, such an independent buyer-

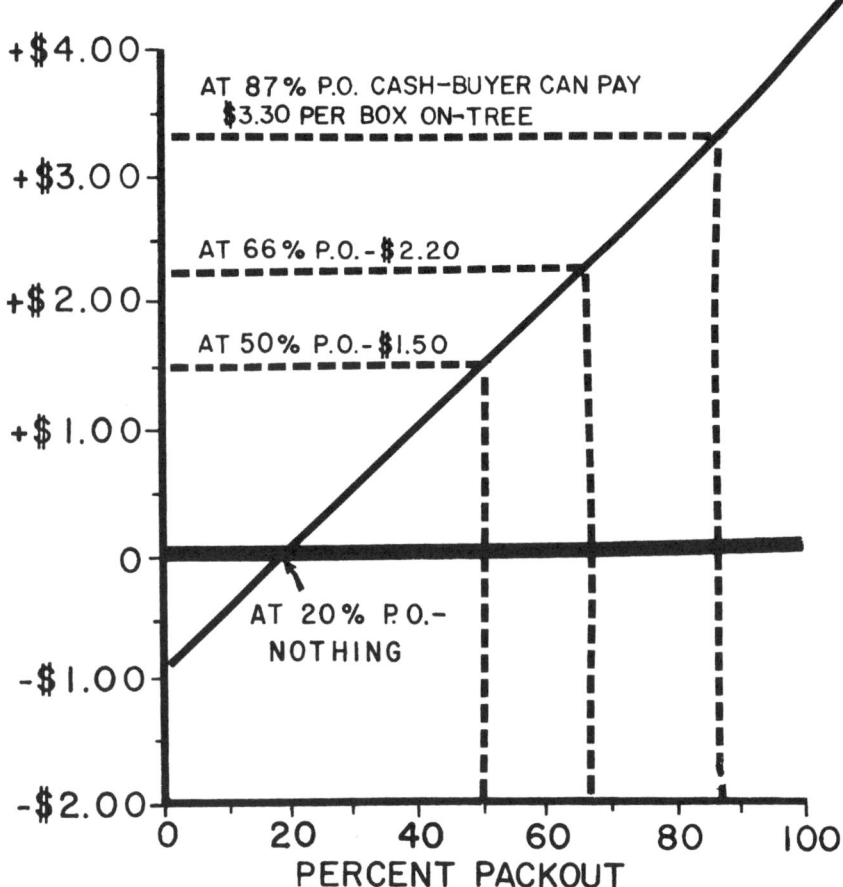

Fig. 9.1. On-tree price for tangerines that would yield a 10¢ per box profit for packer at different packouts (P.O.), based on average costs and prices for 1969-1970. *From Grierson (1970).*

packer could not afford to pack a crop packing out only 20% even if he paid nothing for it. He would lose money even if he sent it direct to the cannery. (That season, pick and haul costs averaged $1.33 and cannery prices for tangerines averaged $1.00).

Price/Packout Relationship

Because fresh fruit prices often vary widely from year to year, there is an understandable tendency to cut costs when low prices are anticipated. This fails to recognize that an increased packout is necessary to break even as fruit prices decline. Table 9.2 is taken from Grierson (1957); the dollar values are long out of date and seedy grapefruit are no longer being shipped, but the principles still stand. In the 1955-1956 season, grapefruit prices, at $2.05 per packed box, were very low. The following season the price averaged $2.71, 32% higher. At the $2.05 price, a 52% packout was necessary to break even; when the average price was $2.71, the break-even point was reached at 25% packout. Raising packout from 60% to 70% would have increased profits by 123% in the low-price year, but by only 28% in the following season when prices were higher. In the low-price season of 1955-1956, abandoning a fresh fruit spray program and sending the entire crop to the cannery would have resulted in a loss, even if growing costs had been halved (data not shown in Table 9.2).

Decay: Fresh vs. Processing Losses

Occasionally, a crop may be determined to have a very high decay potential. Typical examples include a crop found to be infested with brown rot

TABLE 9.2. Returns from Seedy Grapefruit as Related to Prices and Packout, 1955-1956 and 1956-1957 per Box Shipped to Fresh Fruit Market

	1955-1956		1956-1957	
	F.O.B.	Eliminations[a]	F.O.B.	Eliminations[a]
Average price for season[b]	$2.05	$0.48	$2.71	$0.65
Estimated costs	1.53	1.04	1.53	1.04
Profit or loss	+0.52	-0.56	+1.18	-0.39
Packout to break-even	52%		25%	
Profit per box at 60% packout	8.8¢		55.2¢	
Profit per box at 70% packout	19.6¢		70.9¢	
Increase in profit due to	10.8¢ per box		15.7¢ per box	
10% higher packout	(123% increase)		(28% increase)	

[a]Price for eliminations taken as average season price for seedy grapefruit for juice less 2¢.
[b]Average prices for season (both F.O.B. and cannery) supplied by Florida Citrus Mutual.
Source: Grierson (1957).

(Phytophthora citrophthora (Sm. and Sm.) Leonian or *P. parasitica* Dastur) for which there are no effective postharvest fungicides; an early grapefruit crop already developing diplodia stem-end rot *(Diplodia natalensis* Pole-Evans) after ethylene degreening; lemons seriously infested with fungicide-resistant *Penicillium* molds during postharvest curing; or any crop known to have suffered unusual damage due to particularly careless harvesting. In such crops, an unacceptable amount of fruit is likely to be lost during marketing, and very serious consideration should be given to taking a lower price at the cannery rather than selling as fresh fruit, particularly on distant markets.

Fruit graded out as decayed on arrival at the cannery represent only the economic loss of the cannery delivered in price (i.e., the cost of growing plus harvesting and hauling and the canner's mark-up). However, decayed fresh fruit in the market represent a very serious economic loss. By the time they show up on a distant market, their loss represents not only the original cost of the fruit at the packinghouse, but also the cost of handling through the packinghouse, plus the cost of the container, plus the cost of transportation to the market, plus wholesale and retail marketing costs. Additionally, the economic loss due to damage to the shipper's reputation is intangible but real. Moreover, in these days of energy conservation, the losses in wasted energy inputs are a serious consideration.

HARVESTING

Since harvesting is discussed in Chapter 7, only those aspects pertaining to fresh fruit and cannery coordination are considered here.

Fresh Fruit Market Only

Harvesting crews should never be switched back and forth between fresh fruit and cannery harvesting, as happens constantly when citrus organizations are involved in both fresh fruit and cannery operations. Pickers who have been employed to harvest for the cannery soon lose any respect at all for the living fruit that they so casually abuse. It is difficult enough to maintain good practices and discipline among purely fresh fruit crews without exposing them to cannery harvesting methods. Most particularly, cannery crews are accustomed to deliberately drop fruit to the ground, whereas fruit for the packinghouse should never touch the ground.

Fresh Fruit Market and/or Cannery

As mentioned above, citrus crops are usually grown and harvested specifically for either packinghouse or cannery. Of those going to the packinghouse, fruit too blemished for the fresh fruit market are usually graded out and sent to the cannery. The reverse is never (as far as these authors know) done, although this could be very profitable in districts producing large volumes of oranges for juice. When a crop destined for the cannery includes a high proportion of bright fruit that would fetch a premium on the fresh fruit market, there is no way of skimming it out as the fruit enters the cannery. Grierson and Wardowski (1977) have proposed a highly mechanized system whereby this could be done at minimal cost. Available equipment and expertise can obviously be put together into several different versions of a basically efficient layout. As has been pointed out by Grierson and Atkins (1968) every component necessary for such an integrated cannery plus fresh fruit operation is already in use somewhere within the United States and elsewhere.

Any such system would, however, be dependent on avoiding unnecessary harvesting damage. With reasonable crew discipline and modified equipment, fresh fruit have been successfully handled as bulk loads with no more damage than in field boxes (Bowman *et al.* 1971; Phillips and Grierson 1957). Transportation to the processing plant should be with minimum delay, because oranges by being left out in the sun and wind can suffer more harm than by being handled several times (McCornack and Grierson 1965).

Mechanical Harvesting

Grierson (1968) and Rackham and Grierson (1971) reported reasonable success in simulated fresh fruit marketing of mechanically harvested Valencia (late) oranges and seedy grapefruit, particularly when the fruit was protected with a preharvest benomyl (Benlate) spray for postharvest decay control. Damage to early and midseason oranges and to seedless grapefruit was considerably higher and it is not economically practical to invest in expensive mechanical harvesting systems for use only on specific varieties. A later report (Grierson and Wilson 1983) concludes that large-scale mechanical harvesting of processing fruit, but not of citrus fruit for the fresh fruit market, was then possible.

PACKINGHOUSE HANDLING

It has been traditional for grading to be almost the last operation in a fresh fruit house. By the time fruit reaches the graders, it has usually received treatments such as degreening, washing, color-add, fungicide applications, and waxing. Like so many firmly entrenched customs, this practice arose as a result of historical conditions that no longer generally prevail. When several grades of fresh fruit were being packed simultaneously, it was logical to carry out all treatments to the fruit prior to the grader, who consigned fruit to various market grades. In districts such as

Florida, where cannery fruit predominates, it has become normal to pack only one grade. Fruit that does not make this grade is consigned to the cannery. In such a situation, it becomes logical to remove cannery fruit from the line as soon as possible. The advantages are fourfold: (1) fruit eliminated at the beginning of the line can be replaced by increasing the dump rate proportionately (see Chapter 12); (2) expensive fresh fruit treatments (see Chapter 15) are not wasted on cannery fruit; (3) packinghouse overhead costs are reduced in proportion to the increased number of boxes packed; and (4) cannery fruit does not acquire residues of fungicides, waxes, color-add solvents, etc., that may carry through in certain products (Grierson and Wardowski 1977). Such residues can present legal problems, as well as an unnecessary economic burden.

CONCLUSION

The ultimate logical goal of citrus growing and marketing, as of all agricultural endeavors, should be to maximize the net return per hectare, to the general benefit of all concerned. Sometimes this is lost sight of when growing, harvesting, packing and processing are separate businesses under different ownership or different managers under common ownership. Increasingly, however, huge companies or cooperatives control every stage from budding nursery trees to selling fresh fruit and a wide range of citrus products. Whatever the case, there should be a more intimate coordination between growing, harvesting, packing and processing in order to maximize net returns per hectare. Unfortunately, citrus accounting methods seldom, if ever, encourage such maximizing of financial returns (Grierson 2002).

REFERENCES

ALBRIGO, L. G. 1978. Occurrence and identification of preharvest fruit blemishes in Florida citrus groves. Proc. Fla. State Hort. Soc. 91, 78-81.

ATTAWAY, J. A. 1997. A history of Florida citrus freezes. Florida Science Source, Longboat Key, FL.

BOWMAN, E. K., SPURLOCK, A. H., REDDEN, S. and GRIERSON, W. 1971. Modernizing handling systems for Florida citrus fruit from picking to packingline. USDA Marketing Res. Rept. 914.

GRIERSON, W. 1957. The effect of pack-out on grower profits. Proc. Fla. State Hort. Soc. 70, 21-27.

GRIERSON, W. 1958. Causes of low pack-outs in Florida packinghouses. Proc. Fla. State Hort. Soc. 71, 166-170.

GRIERSON, W. 1968. Effect of mechanical harvesting on suitability of oranges and grapefruit for packinghouse and cannery use. Proc. Fla. State Hort. Soc. 81, 53-61.

GRIERSON, W. 1970. Managing tangerines for larger returns. Citrus Ind. 51 (6), 5, 7, 9, 11-12.

GRIERSON, W. 2002. Attention fresh fruit production managers. Citrus Ind. 83 (2), 20-21.

GRIERSON, W. and ATKINS, C. D. 1968. Improving packinghouse and processing plant technology and efficiency. Proc. Inst. Food Agr. Sci. Citrus Conf., University of Florida, May

14-15. Reprinted: Fresh fruit plants face adjustment. Citrus World 5 (2), 7, 14, 18; 5 (3) 12-13, 19.

GRIERSON, W. and OBERBACHER, M. F. 1959. Pack-out as affecting profits of citrus packinghouses with particular reference to fruit color. Proc. Fla. State Hort. Soc. 72 254-258.

GRIERSON, W., OBERBACHER, M. F. and THOMPSON, W. L. 1960. Fruit color, grove practices and fresh-fruit pack-out with particular reference to tangerines. Proc. Fla. State Hort. Soc. 73, 97-100.

GRIERSON, W. and TING, S. V. 1978. Quality control of fruit and products: Quality standards for citrus fruits, juices and beverages, pp. 21-27. Proc. Int. Soc. Citriculture.

GRIERSON, W. and WARDOWSKI, W. F. 1977. Citrus packinghouse procedures relating to citrus processing, pp. 128-140. In Citrus Science and Technology, Volume 2. S. Nagy, P. E. Shaw and M. K. Veldhuis (Editors). AVI Publishing Co., Westport, CT.

GRIERSON, W. and WILSON, W. C. 1983. Mechanical harvesting and citrus quality: Cannery vs. fresh fruit crops. HortScience 18 (4), 40709.

McCORNACK A. A. and GRIERSON, W. 1965. Practical measures for control of stem-end rind breakdown of oranges. Fla. Agr. Exp. Stn. Circ. 286.

PHILLIPS, R. V. and GRIERSON, W. 1957. Cost advantages of bulk handling citrus through the packinghouse. Proc. Fla. State Hort. Soc. 70, 171-177.

RACKHAM, R. L. and GRIERSON, W. 1971. Effect of mechanical harvesting on quality of Florida citrus fruit for the fresh fruit market. HortScience 6 (2), 163-165.

10

Degreening

Wilfred F. Wardowski, William M. Miller, and William Grierson

As discussed in Chapters 1 and 2, the external color of citrus fruits often relates more to climatic conditions than to internal maturity. Many cultivars mature internally while their peel color is still green and unacceptable to the consumer, who usually associates green with immaturity.

A hundred or more years ago, it was common practice to deliberately wilt the peels of citrus fruits (a process known by such terms as: "curing," "quailing," or "sweating") to supposedly make them tougher and less liable to handling damage (Hume 1926). When kerosene (paraffin) stoves were used in this process, it was frequently noted that the green color tended to disappear. Sievers and True (1912) showed that some combustion product from kerosene stoves was responsible for this color change, and Denny (1923, 1924A, B) identified this product as ethylene. As ethylene became increasingly available from the petrochemical industry, it gradually replaced the combustion products from kerosene as a means to degreen citrus fruits. In some districts where industrial ethylene was not readily available, acetylene (evolved by dropping calcium carbide into water) was occasionally used. This practice is, however, dangerous because explosive concentrations are commonly encountered.

Today the physiological effects of ethylene and its role in degreening are well understood. Current research and commercial practice are concentrated on finding the conditions of temperature, humidity, air circulation, and ventilation at which ethylene is most efficacious, and on finding the most efficient and economical methods of providing such conditions.

THE DEGREENING ATMOSPHERE

Ethylene

Chemical and Physical Properties. Ethylene, $CH_2 = CH_2$, the simplest of all unsaturated hydrocarbons, is a gas at temperatures above -103.9°C. It is explosive at concentrations between 3 and 34%. This need never be a hazard in a packinghouse since efficient degreening concentrations range between 0.0001 and 0.1% (1 to 1000 $\mu l/l$; 1 to 1000 ppm).

Physiological Effects. Ethylene is a natural growth regulator (hormone) produced by many plant tissues and most fruits, either as a response to stress or as an integral part of the maturation of climacteric type fruits causing the "climacteric rise" in respiration in some fruits, but not in citrus (see Fig 1.6). Under the conditions of mild stress provided by cold (below 12.5°C) nights, citrus fruits evolve enough endogenous ethylene to degreen naturally. Postharvest degreening seeks to produce this effect with use of exogenous ethylene.

The most obvious effects of ethylene in degreening are changes in the plastid pigments of the flavedo, primarily the destruction of chlorophyll (Goldschmidt 1974) but also the development of characteristic yellow and orange carotenoids (Eilati *et al.* 1969; Stewart and Wheaton 1972; Abeles 1973). The optimum conditions for these two effects can differ. Ethylene-induced color changes are physiologically harmless and commercially beneficial. However, ethylene also promotes senescence (physiological aging) and so should be used with extreme discretion.

The most readily determined indicator of hastened senescence is a stimulation of respiration. For example, a 400% increase in the respiration rate of Valencia oranges subjected to 50 ppm ethylene for 24 hours was reported by Vines *et al.* (1965). Other workers have reported stimulation of respiration by ethylene in Washington navel oranges (Biale 1960; Aharoni 1968) and in lemons (Denny 1924B). When low dosages of ethylene are used, this stimulation disappears on removal of the fruit from the ethylene atmosphere, but the effect may persist if unnecessarily high levels are used (Cohen 1978A). Stimulated respiration is commonly an indication of other biochemical changes such as an increase in maturity index (or ratio, see Chapter 2) and in pectinesterase activity, which has been reported for many Spanish cultivars (Carreres *et al.* 1971) and for Navelina oranges and satsuma mandarins (Caro *et al.* 1971). Zamorani *et al.* (1973) observed an increase in juice content and decreases in weight, size, and acid in degreened Primofiori lemons; the extent of such changes was inversely related to the stage of maturity at which the lemons were picked. They considered that the effects of ethylene resembled those in slow curing of lemons in cool storage without ethylene (see Chapter 20). Ethylene has been reported to cause a 16- to 19-fold increase in evolution of volatiles from green lemons, ten times its effect on yellow lemons. More than 20 volatiles were involved, most particularly D-limonene, a-terpinene, terpindene, and geranial (Norman and Craft 1968). Although the physiological significance of this evolution is unknown, it affords another example of the manifold effects of this potent growth regulator.

Pathological Effects. Anything, such as ethylene, that hastens senescence inevitably increases susceptibility to decay. Other, more specific, effects of ethylene on decay relate to the pathogens endemic in the growing district and the particular cultivar involved.

Ethylene has to be used with particular care in areas (e.g., Florida) in which diplodia stem-end rot (*Diplodia natalensis* Pole-Evans) is endemic. The waterborne spores infect the developing fruit soon after petal fall. A fungal mycelium develops under the button (calyx) but will seldom penetrate the fruit unless the membrane below the abscission zone is in some way impaired. Ethylene causes such impairment and thus stimulates diplodia stem-end rot (Winston and Tilden 1935; Loucks and Hopkins 1946; Smoot *et al.* 1971). This stimulation is proportional to the concentration of ethylene and the duration of exposure (Grierson and Newhall 1955, 1960; Cohen 1979). Ethylene stimulates enzymatic activity in the abscission zone (Riov 1975; Rogers and Hurley 1971; Pollard and Biggs 1970) and any considerable exposure causes the buttons to fall off. In any event, the fungus has probably already penetrated the fruit. Phomopsis stem-end rot caused by *Phomopsis citri* Faw., is also stimulated by ethylene (Loucks and Hopkins 1946). However, this effect poses less danger than in the case of diplodia stem-end rot if only because *Phomopsis* is seldom prevalent until late in the season when little, if any, degreening is customary. The term "stem-end rot" is also used for a decay due to infection of dead or dying tissue in the button by *Alternaria citri* Ellis and Pierce. However, this slow-growing fungus is more of a hazard in long-term storage than in degreening despite any ethylene damage to the buttons.

Degreening induction of anthracnose decay (*Colletotrichum gloeosporioides* Penz.) involves a cultivar-specific and complex relationship. Ethylene both stimulates germination of the fungus and induces resistance on the part of the fruit. Which effect predominates depends upon the carotenoid pigments of the peel. Robinson tangerines mature enough that degreening reveals a deep orange color are resistant to anthracnose when degreened with up to 10 ppm ethylene, but not when degreened with 100 ppm (Brown and Barmore 1976, 1977).

Concentration and Duration. For any particular crop and circumstance, ethylene exhibits a very sharp threshold concentration. Levels above this threshold do not hasten degreening or improve post degreening color, but may cause serious losses from decay even when stem-end rots are not a major hazard (Table 10.1). Such threshold concentrations are usually not more than 5 ppm and seldom exceed 10 ppm; sometimes concentrations as low as 0.1 ppm give optimum stimulation of carotenoid pigment development (Stewart and Wheaton 1972). In a district in Spain where use of ethylene at 200 ppm or more was commonplace, M. Jimenez (personal communication) demonstrated excellent degreening with 0.5 ppm ethylene. Many commercial operators use too much ethylene, but greater numbers of packers around the world are using lower amounts.

Other conditions being constant, the time necessary for adequate degreening is principally dependent on initial fruit color which, in turn, is controlled

TABLE 10.1. Effect of Ethylene Concentration in Commercial Degreening Rooms on Mold Rot Incidence in Degreened Shamouti Oranges

			Mold incidence (%)	
Packinghouse	Ethylene (ppm)	CO_2 (%)	2 weeks	4 weeks
A	12.6	0.21	1	5
	14.3	0.15		
	13.4			
B	18.2	0.34	1	7
	25.2	0.35		
	22.0			
C	29.7	0.19	2	11
	21.7	0.29		
	27.7			
D	27.0	0.75	3	17
	39.6	0.92		
	42.8	0.96		
	33.1			
E	44.0	0.57	9	22
	26.0	0.34		
	65.0			

Source; Cohen (1979).

by fruit maturity and grove conditions, especially night temperatures. A crop from which a first picking takes several days to degreen will need steadily less degreening as the season advances. However, when a crop regreens in the spring, it is virtually impossible to degreen. Why this is so is not well known, but the higher chlorophyll b content may be a reason (Jahn and Young 1976).

Varietal Differences. Citrus fruits include many cultivars (varieties; representing several species and interspecific hybrids. Thus it is not surprising that there should be some differences among them in response to ethylene, but such differences are surprisingly minor. Typical studies report threshold concentrations as follows: for Marsh grapefruit, Robinson tangerine, and Bearss lemon approximately 5 ppm, the optimum being somewhat lower for Robinson and higher for Bearss (Jahn et al. 1973); for Shamouti and Washington navel oranges 5 to 10 ppm (Cohen 1978A; Cohen and Shuali 1976A); and for Michal Clementines and Eureka and Villafranca lemons between 3 and 5 ppm (Cohen and Shuali 1976B; Cohen et al. 1974).

Grierson and Newhall (1960) observed that when fruit were removed from the degreening room while still greenish, color change continued uninterrupted for 24 hours or more in Valencia oranges and Duncan grapefruit but ceased within 2 hours in Hamlin oranges. Jahn et al. (1969) later reported observing this same post ethylene effect.

Temperature

Degreening practices involve such a blend of local custom, mythology, and scientific data that it is difficult to lay down exact criteria. Each growing district must determine its own optimum degreening temperature, considering such variables as rapidity of chlorophyll degradation, desirable carotenoid buildup, and acceleration of decay and senescence consequent to degreening.

In California (where diplodia stem-end rot is not a hazard) it is customary to degreen at 24°C; temperatures as low as 18°C are sometimes used (Rose et al. 1951) and can achieve a very significant development of orange (carotenoid) pigmentation, particularly if degreening is prolonged for 7 or 8 days. In Israel, degreening is commonly done at 23 deg-25°C.

Eilati (1970) reported that throughout the first hours of degreening, the yellowness of the fruits was caused by the destruction of the chlorophyll and the carotenoids already present; after that stage, carotenoid pigments began to accumulate to produce the orange color. It seems that high temperatures (up to 30°C) accelerate chlorophyll destruction but at the same time impair carotenoid synthesis during the treatment (Eilati 1970; Stewart and Wheaton 1972; Jahn et al. 1973).

Shamouti oranges with an initial dark green color became yellow after 24 hours at 25°C and after 48 hours at 20°C. The difference in color due to the lower temperature persisted after degreening (Cohen 1978B). Degreening of Washington navel oranges at 25°C resulted in better color than degreening at 15°C (Aharoni and Lattar 1963); on the other hand, 35°C adversely affected color development. When Shamouti oranges were degreened at 35°C, fruits with an initial dark green color became a pale yellow after 60 hours; however, at 25°C a yellowish orange color developed. Color continued to develop after degreening only in fruits degreened at 25°C, whereas those degreened at 35°C remained pale yellow (Cohen 1979).

Jahn et al. (1973) found that loss of chlorophyll was faster at 30° than at 21°C, but 1 day after the beginning of treatment the fruit color was almost the same at both temperatures. It seems that the effect of temperature is different on fruit at different stages of maturity. Light green fruit degreened at 25°C became yellow only. However, in fruit initially greenish yellow, close to the color break, degreening at 35°C slowed down the rate of color development and the fruit achieved the typical yellow-orange color (Cohen 1978B).

Degreening is slowed down, above or below the optimum temperature. This optimum varies with the cultivar, citrus-growing area, stage of maturity, and other factors. For Florida oranges, the optimum temperature for chlorophyll degradation is sharply defined at 29°C (Grierson and Newhall 1953B, 1960). For Florida grapefruit, the optimum is less sharply defined, but the decrease in degreening rate at temperatures much greater or less than 29°C can be greater in grapefruit than in oranges. Because diplodia stem-end rot is a serious hazard in Florida, minimizing degreening time is critical and, therefore, 29°C is universally used in Florida. Unfortunately, virtually no buildup of carotenoid occurs at this temperature (Stewart and Wheaton 1972). This is why color-adding (Chapter 15) is resorted to in growing areas such as Florida, Brazil, Mexico, and Queensland where Diplodia is endemic.

Humidity

Physical and Physiological Effects. The most obvious result of degreening at too low a humidity is an undesirable softening of the fruit; not only are flaccid fruit unattractive, but they are also very subject to deformation after packing. When degreening humidity is less than optimum, fruit size can also diminish, even without obvious softening, resulting in significantly decreased packout (Deason and Grierson 1972). Differences in humidity during degreening also have less apparent but more complex physiological effects on plant respiration, enzymatic reactions, and physiological diseases (Grierson and Wardowski 1978). Differences in relative humidity (RH) between 70 and 90% do not affect color change (Cohen 1978B), but when humidity is low enough to result in severe wilting, color change can be greatly retarded (Hall et al. 1969).

Any existing peel injuries (oleocellosis, sand scratches, etc.) are sharply accentuated by degreening at too low a humidity. When oranges are susceptible to stem-end rind breakdown (Chapter 14), any drying between picking and waxing can cause development of this serious blemish (McCornack and Grierson 1965). For example, fruits degreened at 74% RH had three times as much rind breakdown as fruits degreened at 94% RH (Hopkins and McCornack 1958, 1960). High RH has been reported to enhance the healing of minor wounds in damaged peel after harvest, thus reducing mold development caused by *Penicillium digitatum* (Ismail and Brown 1975, 1979).

Blemishes occurring during, or exacerbated by, degreening are commonly referred to by dealers as "gas burn" on the erroneous presumption that they are caused by ethylene per se, rather than by low-humidity conditions. One very serious peel injury of Temples (a reputed tangor) was shown (under the unsophisticated conditions of 50 years ago) to be proportional to both concentration of ethylene and duration of exposure (Grierson and Newhall 1953A). It was later found that this ugly blemish was completely suppressed by degreening with minimal ethylene at a relative humidity of about 95%.

Control of Humidity. There are many advantages to degreening at as high a humidity as possible, without wetting the fruit. About 95% RH is desirable, but this cannot be achieved with manual controls. With the advent of very large pallet box degreening rooms, the use of automated controls for both temperature and humidity has become mandatory. In California, some packinghouses achieve cooling and very high humidities by circulating air through a cascade of temperature-controlled water over webs of nylon threads. The Florida system is cheaper and has proved very satisfactory. In this, a lithium chloride sensor (humistat) is located in the return side of the air stream, i.e., where the air is returning to the fan. It is important that the humistat be in the return air and the thermostat in the delivery air. The most commonly used humistat can be set for 94-95% RH. When the humidity falls below this level, the humistat activates humidifiers. Very effective humidifiers have pneumatic-hydraulic nozzles in which compressed air breaks up the water droplets into a fine mist (Raynor and Wardowski 1979). It is necessary to have about one horsepower (0.746 kW) of compressor capacity per nozzle.

Air Circulation

Adequate air circulation in degreening rooms is needed: (1) to equalize conditions of temperature, humidity, ethylene concentration, and possibly oxygen, throughout the entire air mass within the degreening room, (2) to deliver this correctly conditioned air to the surface of each and every fruit in the room, and (3) to remove unwanted products, largely CO_2 and possibly organic volatiles emanating from the fruit. These objectives are not accomplished by merely blowing air around the room, particularly when the fruit is being degreened in large pallet boxes (sometimes called bulk bins). Moreover, misuse of fan capacity can be very wasteful of costly energy.

The most effective air circulation is best achieved by arranging that the fruit to be degreened is located between areas of comparatively high and low pressures, respectively. The air will then move through (rather than around) the mass of fruit and economical fans rated against a minimum of head pressure (typically 2.54 cm water pressure) can be used effectively. Blowing air at the fruit is most inefficient, regardless of fan capacity.

Ventilation and Atmospheric Composition

It is certain that degreening rooms do not function satisfactorily without ventilation, which can be either intermittent or continuous. The latter is usually preferable because the fruit is constantly maintained at or near optimum humidity. Just why ventilation is so important is unclear. The usual explanation is that ventilation keeps the concentration of CO_2 (production of which by the fruit is stimulated by ethylene) sufficiently low to avoid counteracting the effect of ethylene (Burg and Burg 1967). However, the reported threshold values for CO_2 that impede degreening vary considerably from various growing areas and with various types of citrus. Grierson and Newhall (1960) found that degreening was inhibited by 1% CO_2 in a Florida packinghouse with massive bulk degreening bins (not pallet boxes) holding about 10,000 kg of oranges or grapefruit each. However, in controlled laboratory experiments Cohen (1973) found no inhibition of degreening of Shamouti oranges by 2.5% CO_2, nor of lemons by 5% CO_2, providing oxygen levels were normal. Others have reported that degreening of Shamouti oranges is markedly inhibited by 5% CO_2, an effect that is dependent on the relative concentrations of CO_2 and ethylene (Apelbaum et al. 1976; Young et al. 1962).

The effect of various oxygen levels on degreening is more of academic than practical interest since it is most unlikely that O_2 levels will vary enough in a well-run degreening room to affect degreening. Degreening of Shamouti (Cohen 1973), Hamlin, and Washington navel (Jahn et al. 1969) oranges with ethylene was not accelerated by a high level of oxygen (50%), nor did a low level (10-15%) inhibit peel color development. However, there was a slight inhibition of color development below 10% O_2. With several Spanish citrus fruit varieties, better fruit color developed and maturity was accelerated more when fruits were degreened in an atmosphere with 50% O_2 (and no ethylene) than in an atmosphere including 0.2% ethylene (Cessari and Paltrenieri 1967; Raciti and Martino 1966; Caro et al. 1971). The fruit color was better at 50% O_2 than at 80%. Under all these conditions, the CO_2 concentration in the atmosphere was normal. However, elevated O_2 levels (i.e., over 21%) are difficult and costly to achieve.

Florida recommendations for a ventilation rate of about one air change per hour (Wardowski 1996) are sometimes considered excessive and likely to cause undesirable lowering of humidity (Cohen 1977), especially since laboratory studies have found no differences in degreening with ventilation rates of 0.25 to 4.0 air changes per hour (Cohen 1973). This one air change per hour recommendation (which is often exceeded with impunity) is purely empirical, and it should be emphasized that its obvious success is related to the use of automated humidity control systems and the specific degreening room designs described later in this chapter.

A technique to measure fresh air exchange rates was developed (Miller 1989) for commercial degreening rooms. Rates from 0.6 to 16.5 air exchanges per hour were measured. The rooms with excessive air exchange were retrofitted to reduce air loss and reduce costs of heating and ethylene. Another benefit was better humidity control and faster degreening.

Monitoring and Control of Degreening Room Conditions

Temperature measurement and control has been achieved for many years in degreening rooms. Computer assisted monitoring and control in Florida citrus degreening was developed in recent years (Miller et al. 1997; Miller et al. 2000). Variables measured included fan operation, temperature, relative humidity, ethylene concentration and flow, and carbon dioxide levels. Ethylene at the desired low levels of 0 to 10 ppm is the most difficult variable to measure.

PRIOR FACTORS AFFECTING DEGREENING

Fruit Maturity, Tree Vigor, and Climatic Effects

Sometimes it is necessary to state the obvious. Grossly immature fruit are dark green and either fail to respond to degreening or respond to ethylene so slowly that the resultant fruit are not only immature and poor tasting, but also poorly colored, excessively prone to decay, and often disfigured by peel blemishes. Such problems are only encountered by ill-advised growers and packers who seek to "beat the market" in areas where severe standards for internal quality are not enforced. Degreening should only be attempted with fully mature, but aesthetically unacceptable, citrus fruits. When a citrus tree is in a state of vigorous growth flush, this vegetative condition extends to the fruit peel, which is thus very high in chlorophyll and low in carotenoids, and consequently hard to degreen. As the weather cools, particularly the night temperatures, the fruit become easier to degreen, eventually breaking color on the tree. Stearns (1942) and Stearns and Young (1942) noted that in Florida the effect of temperature on color break was sharply defined for oranges following the first 5 consecutive nights below 12.8°C, but was far less sharply defined for grapefruit. This observation has been clearly confirmed by 30 years of general observation at the Lake Alfred Citrus Research and Education Center.

Eilati (1970) reported that Israeli citrus began to show color break when average weekly minimum temperatures declined to 13°C, accompanied by a soil temperature of 16°C at a depth of 40 cm. Additionally, in cold, rainy winters a higher concentration of carotenoid pigments accumulated in the peel than in warm, dry winters. Young and Erickson (1961) found that when day and night temperatures were both independently controlled, the best-colored Valencia oranges were produced with 20°C day and 7°C night air temperatures and 12°C soil temperatures. Both controlled experiments and field observations indicate that low (7°-13°C) night air temperatures (sometimes unobtainable in subtropical climates) are critical in initiating natural color break.

Cultural Practices

Grierson and Newhall (1960) reviewed the effects of cultural practices on subsequent degreening. With a few later additions, only their review needs to be summarized here.

Rootstocks. Rootstocks, such as rough lemon (*C. jambiri* Lush.), that tend to produce particularly vigorous trees also tend to produce fruit that breaks color somewhat later than fruit from trees on less vigorous rootstocks, such as sour orange (*C. aurantium* L.) and Carrizo citrange. Bitters (1961) commented on an apparent interaction between rootstocks and climate in this regard. However, this is a difficult matter to determine precisely. Since rootstocks are selected primarily for adaptability to soil type and for disease resistance, it is hard to gather reliable data on comparable fruit from various rootstocks grown in suitably diverse climates.

Spray Programs. Spraying can have a sharp effect on degreening because summer oil insecticide sprays tend to lower soluble solids and delay color break in comparison with organophosphate sprays. This effect has been considerably reduced in the last 40 years by the use of more highly refined spray oils. Therefore some of the older reports indicating drastic differences between degreening of fruit receiving oil vs. phosphatic sprays (Grierson *et al.* 1960) must be reevaluated in the light of this later development.

No effect on fruit color was noted from organophosphate, fungicide, and nutritional sprays in extensive studies at the Citrus Research and Education Center, Lake Alfred, Florida. Gibberellin sprays are sometimes used to delay color break of grapefruit or to prolong the harvesting season of navel oranges or grapefruit (Chapter 4). This powerful growth regulator has profound effects on retention of chlorophyll (Lewis *et al.* 1964) and delayed development of peel carotenoids (Lewis and Coggins 1964).

Fertilizer Programs. The effect of fertilization on fruit color and color break has also been studied at the Lake Alfred Citrus Research and Education Center. No consistent effects have been noted except with nitrogen. However the delay in color break associated with nitrogen fertilization is an obvious corollary of prolonged growth flush due to excessive or late-applied treatments.

Cumulative Effects. Although the cumulative effect of these various climatic and cultural influences on fruit color are almost impossible to assess statistically, they are nevertheless real. In a study (Grierson and Oberbacher 1959) of blemishes lowering packout conducted throughout a whole season in a large Florida packinghouse, persistent green color caused a loss of over 7 cents per box (40.8 kg); in some seasons, 7 cents could mean the difference between profit and loss.

Packinghouse Treatments

With the exception of color sorting prior to degreening (which is not in general use), postharvest treatments either impede degreening or exert no consistent influence on degreening.

Bin Drenching. Drenching with benzimidazole or imazalil fungicides (Chapter 13) to reduce decay has little effect on degreening unless 2,4-D is included. Although 2,4-D definitely slows degreening, some delay is often tolerated when degreening fruits such as Arizona lemons or Israeli Shamouti oranges for which the market judges viability of the fruit on greenness of the buttons (Fig. 10.1).

Washing. The effect of washing prior to degreening varies considerably. Although Smoot *et al.* (1971) found that washing produced little, if any effect on degreening, Grierson and Newhall (1956A) reported that in 39 out of 44 individual experiments with two cultivars each of oranges and grapefruit, washing increased degreening time by an average of 26.7%. Such differences may relate to cultivar; they certainly relate to the initial color of the fruit. Degreening of very dark green fruit is clearly affected by washing, whereas this effect may be trivial or nonexistent once natural color break has started.

A special case is the washing of Robinson tangerines prior to degreening which reduces anthracnose decay due to mechanical removal of Colletotrichum appressoria from the surface of the fruit (Brown 1975A,B).

Waxing. Even though this treatment has long been known to drastically impede degreening (Grierson and Newhall 1960), there are still occasional attempts to degreen waxed fruit that have been graded out as being too green. This inhibition of degreening occurs with both natural waxes, such as carnauba, and synthetic resins, such as polyethylene (Aharoni *et al.* 1973).

Color Sorting. The sorting of fruit into color groups prior to degreening is very advantageous since each color group can be degreened only for the minimum time necessary to achieve satisfactory color. In an early study using hand sorting of Dancy tangerines (Grierson and Newhall 1956B), not only was subsequent decay very considerably reduced, but twice as much fruit could be degreened in the same facility due to the exclusion of well-colored fruit and the short time taken to degreen those lots that were already breaking color. Now that efficient automated color-sorting equipment is available (Gaffney and Jahn 1967; Jahn *et al.* 1967; Johnson 1981; Miller and Drouillard 1999), color sorting prior to degreening is commercially feasible to increase the capacity of existing degreening facilities and reduce subsequent decay.

DEGREENING ROOM DESIGNS

Traditional

As long as degreening was done in manually handled boxes (typically of 20- to 40-kg net capacity) and rooms were small (seldom holding more than 1000 such boxes), degreening room design was often inefficient, but seldom critically so. A usual pattern was to have some kind of central "stack"

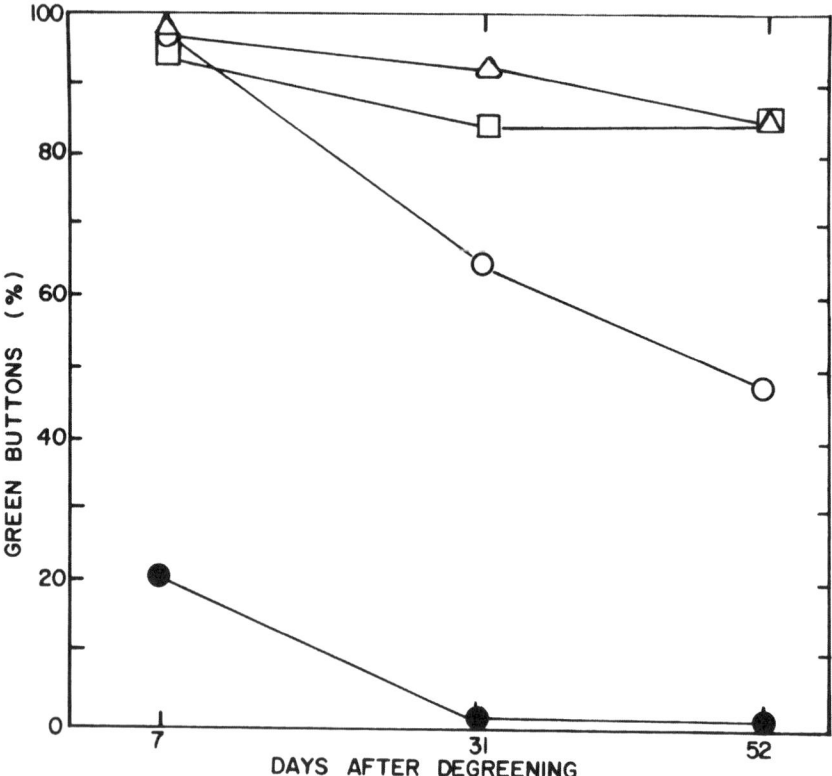

Fig. 10.1. Effect of prior treatments to Shamouti oranges on the percentage of green buttons (calyces) persisting after degreening, ○—○ = nondegreened control, no pretreatment; ●—● = TBZ only; △—△ = 3,4-D amine + TBZ; – = 2,4-D isopropyl ester + TBZ. *From Cohen (1977).*

equipped with a radiator and an upward-blowing fan. A particularly efficient type drew air from below a slatted wooden floor and discharged it above the fruit, thus creating a pressure differential between the vacuum area below the floor and the plenum area above the fruit. Grierson and Newhall (1960) have described the traditional designs. With the advent of large, hydraulically handled boxes holding 300-400 kg or more of fruit, such rooms proved slow, inefficient, and unsuited to lift truck handling.

Pallet Box (Bulk Bin) Degreening Rooms

Large pallet boxes handled by lift trucks clearly require very much larger degreening rooms, with quite different air distribution systems than do smaller manually handled boxes.

Ceiling Jet System. In California, a popular system of fast precooling rooms has been commonly adapted for degreening. In this system, a high air pressure (about 7.6 cm water pressure) is developed in a plenum above a false ceiling, which is pierced by conical delivery jets directed toward the floor. The stacks of pallet boxes are spaced about 23 cm apart in each direction, the delivery jets being located above the intersections of these spaces. This is an efficient precooling system (Mitchell *et al.* 1972), but when used for degreening it has several disadvantages. The fans responsible for maintaining the necessary air pressure in the plenum are more costly than low-pressure fans with a similar air volume per minute rated capacity; moreover, such fans take more energy to run than low-pressure fans. More energy also is used to drive warmed air to floor level (against convection) than when such a design is used for precooling in which convection supplements fan-derived air movement. Up to 20% of floor space is unoccupied due to the necessary spaces between the stacks of pallet boxes. Finally, lift truck handling is slow, as each stack of pallet boxes has to be exactly positioned on the marked floor area below the appropriate four ceiling jets.

Low-Pressure, Horizontal Airflow System. A system developed in Florida uses much less energy and less expensive fans, makes greater use of floor space, and facilitates rapid lift truck handling. In this system a false ceiling is also used, as a duct to deliver conditioned air (adjusted for temperature, humidity, ethylene content, and adequate ventilation) from one end of the room to the other. Thus fans rated against no more than 2.5 cm water pressure can maintain enough pressure differential across the mass of fruit to ensure a uniform air movement from one end of the room to the other. The pallet boxes are stacked tightly within the rows, which are separated by only 5 cm, indicated by yellow lines of "traffic paint" on the floor to guide the drivers. This system works best with pallet boxes having ventilated bottoms, nonventilated sides, and solid runners (stringers) oriented parallel to the direction of airflow (Wardowski and Grierson 2002). Most of the air then moves unimpeded through the channels provided by the closely abutted pallets, creating venturi action inducing a strong vertical movement, measured at as high as 15 m/min, through the fruit.

The first few such rooms delivered air to the front of the room and had short curtains above the fruit to prevent the air short circuiting, over the load. The time necessary for cool fruit to come into temperature equilibrium is, in part, a function of the length of the rows (Deason and Grierson 1971). Some of these rooms run well with rows as long as 15 pallet boxes (18 m) but obviously, when fruit comes in from the field cold, the longer the rows, the longer will be the initial temperature stabilization period. A considerable improvement was to deliver the conditioned air to wall ducts at the back of the room (Fig. 10.2D). Each wall duct supplies air to a single row of pallet boxes. An unexpected advantage turned out to be that such rooms

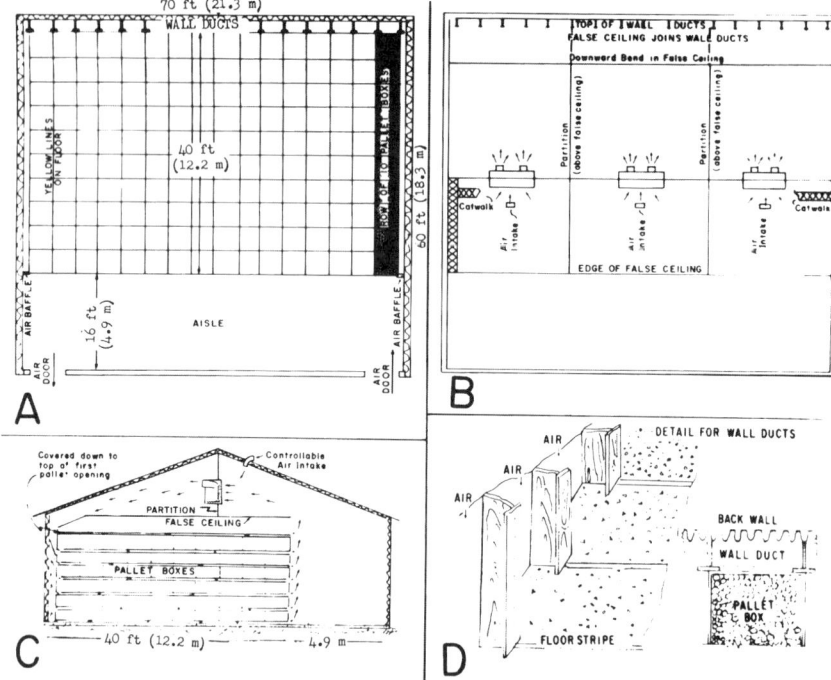

Fig. 10.2. Large pallet box degreening room for continuous operation. A-Plan view of degreening area showing wall ducts at rear of the room and location of the rows of pallet boxes (one row in place). B-Plan view of area over the false ceiling. Note the partitions separating the fan units and dividing return from delivery air. C-Longisection showing air circulation system. The 4.9-m aisle permits rapid lift truck maneuvering. D-Detail of wall ducts. These are made of heavy timber and also serve as safety stops for the lift trucks. When lighter material is used, they are attached to heavy metal "lift truck stops" embedded deep below the floor. A concrete curb would impede air flow under the bottom pallets and must not be used.
From Grierson (1972); Grierson and Wardowski (1973).

could be run for surprising periods with the door open (or a front curtain-wall raised) since any ambient air so introduced would be drawn into the return air stream and modified to degreening conditions before it is circulated through the fruit. A variation of this concept of low-pressure, horizontal airflow has been developed in Cuba (Torres and Pividal 1981).

Batch vs. Continuous Degreening Rooms

As long as degreening was done in small, manually operated rooms, the inefficiency of using a batch operation (individual degreening rooms) to supply a continuous operation (the packing line) was not readily apparent.

But as degreening rooms grew larger (500 pallet boxes, 200 MT net capacity, is not unusual in Florida and Texas) serious inefficiencies became apparent. Such rooms take so long to load and unload that they might be actually degreening for as little as 50% of the time, particularly as such large masses of fruit are necessarily slow to come to temperature. Moreover, during loading and unloading the fruit are being held under undesirably low humidity conditions. Also, energy demands are excessive because large amounts of fruit have to be warmed at the same time.

The next development was obvious as soon as it became apparent that wall duct rooms function regardless of the degree of loading of the room. A single row in an otherwise empty room degreens well, since the air from its wall duct cannot short circuit around it. This next advance was to have a single room that runs continually, like a cold room. Such a design for a 960-pallet box room is shown in Fig. 10.2. Note that the degreening area is a single large space into which fruit is placed as it arrives from the field and removed as it is degreened. The area overhead is partitioned so as to distribute the air from the three fan units to their appropriate wall ducts. When the full capacity is not needed, one-third or two-thirds of the room can be utilized despite the lack of any partitioning of the actual degreening area. These continuous degreening rooms are being constructed with 50% of the radiator capacity that used to be considered necessary.

It is critical that the thermostat be on the air delivery side of the fan(s) and the humistat in the return air stream, although the humidifier itself is in the delivery air, usually immediately in front of the fan. Once these two automatic controls are correctly set and ethylene flow and ventilation manually adjusted, such rooms run with little, if any, adjustment as long as degreening continues to be necessary.

This design shown in Fig. 10.2 is as efficient for refrigeration as for degreening, and some rooms have been constructed for use as degreening rooms at the beginning of the season and cold storage rooms when the degreening period is over. However, if later adaptation to refrigeration is contemplated, the necessary vapor barriers should be installed at the time that the room is built.

INTERMITTENT DEGREENING

When small degreening rooms were usual and batch degreening was the rule, most degreening was intermittent since it was customary to open the rooms for complete ventilation at least once a day. Continuous ventilation, though sometimes recommended (Grierson and Newhall 1960), did not become common until development of the large pallet box degreening rooms described in the previous section. Interest in intermittent degreening methods has, however, persisted for special uses.

The Japanese Experience

Although the total volume of citrus produced in Japan is very large (Chapter 6, Part 3), this production comes mostly from small family plantings, usually on precipitous hillsides. Moreover, degreening is only needed in the early autumn and then only in southwestern Japan. Thus pallet box handling and very large degreening rooms are clearly not suitable. Instead, a quite different degreening system has been developed (Kitagawa *et al.* 1971A,B; Kitagawa and Tarutani 1973; Kitagawa 1973).

In this method, fruit to be degreened (usually satsumas) are stacked as a rectangular block on a sheet of 0.2-mm polyvinyl chloride (PVC) surrounded by a wooden trough. A second sheet of PVC film is placed over the stack of fruit. The seal between the underlying and covering sheets of PVC film is made by filling the peripheral wooden trough with water. The underlying film and surrounding trough can be replaced with a nonporous floor and sand bags (Fig. 10.3). Ethylene (from cans holding 4.2 liters compressed to 600 ml or from "ethylene sieves," i.e., ethylene-absorbed molecular sieves that easily exchange C_2H_4 with moisture) is added to give approximately 1000 ppm C_2H_4. Typically, two such cans or 200 of the ethylene sieves are used for 120 20-kg boxes holding 2.4 MT of fruit. The seal is left intact for approximately 15 hours during which there is no apparent disappearance of chlorophyll. Laboratory tests indicate that ethylene rapidly equalizes between the external and internal atmospheres of the fruit, and during this period CO_2 may rise to 10-12% and O_2 fall to as low as 6.5-10%.

After about 15 hours, the covering film is removed. Degreening then starts and will typically be completed in 3 days at ambient temperatures but without appreciable buildup of carotenoid pigments. When the chlorophyll does not disappear completely after a single treatment, retreatment is effective.

An obvious question is whether the success of this distinctive degreening method is peculiar to satsumas. Kitagawa *et al.* (1978) found that satsuma (*C. unshiu* Marc.), three *C. sinensis* Osbeck cultivars (navel, Trovita and Valencia), two distinctively Japanese fruits, [Hassaku (*C. hassaku* Hort. ex Tan.) and Natsudaidai (*C. natsudaidai* Hay)] and Eureka lemon (*C. limon* Burm. f.) all could be degreened on a laboratory scale by this method. It worked most efficiently for satsuma and least efficiently for Valencia orange. The differences in effectiveness were not due simply to species (navel oranges degreened nearly as well as satsumas) but were most closely correlated with resistance to diffusion of ethylene out of the fruit after the seal was broken; the more rapidly ethylene diffused out of the fruit, the less efficient the degreening.

As discussed already, stimulation of diplodia stem-end rot is related to both the concentration of ethylene used and to duration of exposure. The Japanese method (which might well be useful for small packers anywhere)

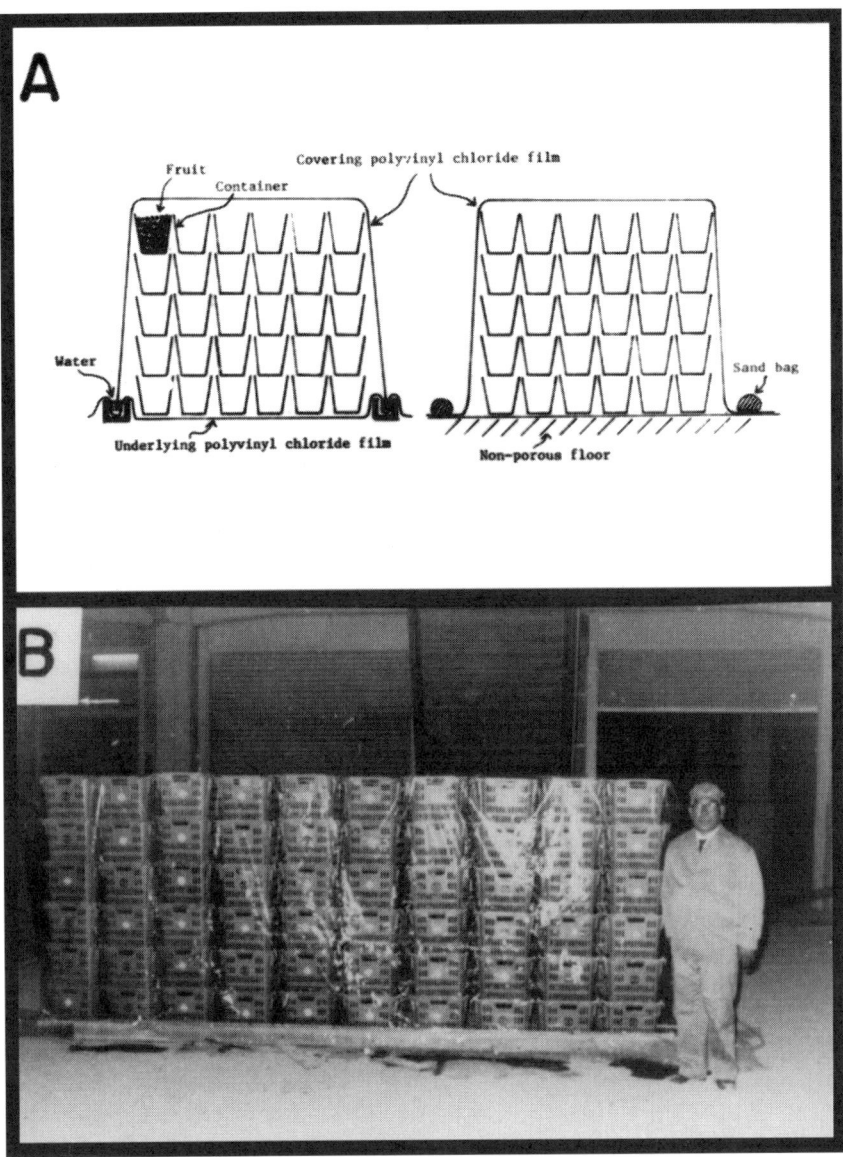

Fig. 10.3. Japanese sealed ethylene treatment. A-Cross-sectional view of sealing with two sheets of film and water (left), and one sheet of film and sand bags (right). B-9.6 MT of satsuma mandarins, (480 20-kg containers) undergoing sealed ethylene treatment for, 15 hours after which the overlying film will be removed.
From Kitagawa (1973).

involves use of a very high concentration of ethylene, but for an unusually short period. We know of no investigations into the use of this method in a growing area (such as Florida or Brazil) where endemic *Diplodia natalensis* is a major hazard.

The Israeli Experience

Comprehensive study of the degreening of Israeli citrus fruit, especially the role of ventilation and air composition in the degreening rooms, led to a modification of the commercial continuous ethylene flow method. The new intermittent method provides good degreening efficiency, results in better fruit quality, and requires less ethylene gas and energy needed to heat the rooms. This "intermittent" method was based on the following principles: (1) The degreening process and color change in fruit induced by ethylene continues virtually uninterrupted for at least 12-24 hours after the cessation of the gas treatment, following the removal of the fruit from the degreening rooms (Jahn *et al.* 1969; Grierson and Newhall 1960 N. B. As noted above, this does not apply). (2) The coloring of harvested fruit is controlled by hormones, and ethylene induces a biosynthetic process, the continuing effect of which is not related to the presence of ethylene (Eilati 1970). The Israeli approach combines reduced ventilation with intermittent degreening.

A ventilation rate of 0.25 to 0.50 air changes per hour produces an ethylene concentration optimal for degreening and maintains temperature and humidity conditions. This ventilation rate is lower than that used with the continuous flow method, thus, reducing the amount of energy required for heating (Cohen 1977, 1979).

In the Israeli system, fruit are exposed intermittently to ethylene and heating. An ethylene flow of 5-10 µg/ml and heating to 25°C are supplied to the degreening rooms for 12 hours a day, followed by a 12-hour interruption. These cycles are repeated throughout the degreening period, for longer periods early in the season and for shorter periods later in the season. During the intermissions, the ethylene concentration drops to 0-1 µg/ml and the temperature drops by only 1 deg-2°C. Throughout the degreening treatment, a continuous low ventilation rate of 0.25 to 0.5 air changes per hour (corresponding to about 0.5-1% fresh air per minute) and high humidity are provided. Under these conditions the atmospheric CO_2 buildup is between 0.06 and 0.19%; in identical degreening rooms using the continuous ethylene flow method CO_2 reaches 0.06 to 0.49% and higher. The period of time needed for degreening is the same with both methods (Cohen 1977, 1979). In the intermittent degreening method, fruit are exposed to ethylene gas for only half the time needed for the degreening process, and undesirable increases in ethylene concentration and temperature, which sometimes occur with the continuous degreening method, do not occur. This results in favorable conditions for the fruit, such as a decrease in respiration, weight loss, blemishes, and rot development. Color improvement in fruit degreened by the intermittent method is similar to that in fruit degreened by the continuous degreening method.

REFERENCES

ABELES, F. B. 1973. Ethylene in Plant Biology Academic Press. New York.

AHARONI, Y. 1968. Respiration of oranges and grapefruit harvested at different stages of development. Plant Physiol. 43, 99-102.

AHARONI, Y. and LATTAR, F. S. 1963. The effect of ethylene on the development of Navel orange peel color. Prelim. Rept. 426. Nat. Univ. Inst. Agr., Rehovot (Hebrew with English summary).

AHARONI, Y., LATTAR, F. S. and ANGEL, S. 1973. Peel color of oranges treated with ethylene before vs after waxing HortScience 8, 58.

APELBAUM, A., GOLDSCHMIDT, E. E. and BEN-YEHOSHUA, S. 1976. Involvement of endogenous ethylene in the induction of color change in Shamouti oranges. Plant Physiol. 57, 836-838.

BIALE, J. B. 1960. The postharvest biochemistry of tropical and subtropical fruits. Adv. Food Res. 10, 293-354.

BITTERS, W. P. 1961. Physical characteristics and chemical composition as affected by scions and rootstocks. *In* The Orange, Its Biochemistry and Physiology, W. B. Sinclair (Editor). University of California Press, Berkeley.

BROWN, G. E. 1975A. Factors affecting postharvest development of *Colletotrichum gloeosporioides* in citrus fruit. Phytopathology 65, 404-409.

BROWN, G. E. 1975B. Anthracnose, a serious decay of degreened Robinson tangerines. Proc. Fla. State Hort. Soc. 88, 308-311.

BROWN, G. E. and BARMORE, C. R. 1976. The effect of ethylene, fruit color, and fungicides on susceptibility of Robinson tangerines to anthracnose. Proc. Fla. State Hort. Soc. 89, 198-200.

BROWN, G. E. and BARMORE, C. R. 1977. The effect of ethylene on susceptibility of Robinson tangerines to anthracnose. Phytopathology 67, 120-123.

BURG, S. P. and BURG, E. A. 1967. Molecular requirements for the biological activity of ethylene Plant Physiol. 24, 144-152.

CARO, J., MUNOZ-DELGADO, L. and MUNOZ-DELGADO, J. A. 1971. Acceleration of degreening maturation in Navelina oranges and satsuma mandarins, pp. 121-128. *In* Proc. Congress Int. Froid, III (Spanish).

CARRERES, R., ALBERT, A. and REIG, A. 1971. The influence of refrigeration on the commercialization of citrus fruits. 129-136. In Proc. Int. Cong. Refrig. Vol 3.

CESSARI, A. and PALTRENIERI, G. 1967. Degreening of Washington navel oranges and Femminello citrons by means of oxygen and ethylene mixtures. Comptes Rend. XII Congress Int. Froid, III, 404-413.

COHEN, E. 1973. Effect of oxygen, carbon dioxide, ethylene and volatile compounds in the atmosphere on citrus degreening. Proc. Int. Soc. Citriculture 3, 297-301.

COHEN, E. 1977. Some physiological aspects of citrus degreening. Proc. Int. Soc. Citriculture 1, 215-219.

COHEN, E. 1978A. Ethylene concentration and the duration of the degreening process in Shamouti orange fruits. J. Hort. Sci. 53, 133-142.

COHEN, E. 1978B. The effect of temperature and relative humidity during degreening on the colouring of Shamouti orange fruit. J. Hort. Sci. 53, 143-146.

COHEN, E. 1979. The degreening of citrus fruit in Israel. Spec. Publ. 128. Agr. Res. Org., Bet Dagan (Hebrew, with English summary).

COHEN, E. and SHUALI, M. 1976A. Degreening of Washington (navel) oranges at different concentrations of ethylene, temperature and relative humidity. Alon HaNotea 31, 43-53. (Hebrew).

COHEN, E. and SHUALI, M. 1976B. Degreening of Michal clementines and the effect of different temperatures during the export on its quality. Alon HaNotea 31, 137-141 (Hebrew).

COHEN, E., SCHIFFMANN-NADEL, M. and UZIEL, M. 1974. Comparison between different varieties of lemon fruit after harvest. Alon HaNotea 8, 657-660 (Hebrew).

DEASON, D. L. and GRIERSON, W. 1971. Heating of citrus fruits during degreening and associated temperature gradients within the typical horizontal air flow degreening room. Proc. Fla. State Hort. Soc. 84, 259-264.

DEASON, D. L. and GRIERSON, W. 1972. Degreening at very high humidities: Humifresh-Filacell system vs. a pneumatic water spray system. Proc. Fla. State Hort. Soc. 85, 258-262.

DENNY, F. E. 1923. Method of coloring citrus fruits. U.S. Pat. 1,475,938.

DENNY, F. E. 1924A. Hastening the coloration of lemons. J. Agr. Res. 27, 757-769.

DENNY, F. E. 1924B. Effect of ethylene upon the respiration of lemons. Bot. Gaz. 77, 322-329.

EILATI, S. 1970. The changes in color of the ripening orange fruits as affected by endogenous and exogenous factors. Ph.D. Thesis. The Hebrew University of Jerusalem, Israel (Hebrew, with English summary).

EILATI, S., GOLDSCHMIDT, E. E. and MONSELISE, S. P. 1969. Hormonal control of colour changes in orange peel. Experientia 25, 209-210.

GAFFNEY, J. J. and JAHN, O. L. 1967. Photoelectric color sorting of early season Florida oranges before degreening. Proc. Fla. State Hort. Soc. 80, 296-301.

GOLDSCHMIDT, E. E. 1974. Hormonal and molecular regulations of the chloroplast senescence in citrus peel. In Plant Growth Substances. Hirokowa Press, Tokyo.

GRIERSON, W. and NEWHALL, W. F. 1953A. Should gassing of Temples be banned? Citrus Mag. 16 (2), 30-31,35. October.

GRIERSON, W. and NEWHALL, W. F. 1953B. Degreening conditions for Florida citrus. Proc. Fla. State Hort. Soc. 66, 42-46.

GRIERSON, W. and NEWHALL, W. F. 1955. Tolerance to ethylene of various types of citrus fruits. Proc. Am. Soc. Hort. Sci. 65, 224-250.

GRIERSON, W. and NEWHALL, W. F. 1956A. Degreening of citrus fruits. 185-188. In Annu. Rept. Fla. Agr. Exp. Stn. University of Florida, Gainesville.

GRIERSON, W. and NEWHALL, W. F. 1956B. Reducing losses in ethylene degreening of tangerines. Proc. Am. Soc. Hort. Sci. 67, 236-243.

GRIERSON, W. and NEWHALL, W. F. 1960. Degreening of Florida citrus fruits. Fla. Agr. Exp. Stn. Bull. 620.

GRIERSON, W. and OBERBACHER, M. F. 1959. Pack-out as affecting profits of citrus packing- houses with particular reference to fruit color. Proc. Fla. State Hort. Soc. 72, 248-254.

GRIERSON, W. and WARDOWSKI, W. F. 1973. Development of mechanization programs for harvesting and handling citrus fruits. Proc. Int. Soc. Citriculture 3, 633-649.

GRIERSON, W. and WARDOWSKI, W. F. 1978. Relative humidity as affecting the postharvest life of fruits and vegetables. HortScience 13 (5), 570-574.

GRIERSON, W., OBERBACHER, M. F. and THOMPSON, W. L. 1960. Fruit color, grove practices and fresh fruit pack-out with particular reference to tangerines. Proc. Fla. State Hort. Soc. 73, 97-100.

HALL, E. G., LEGGO, D. and SEBERRY, J. A. 1969. Ethylene degreening of citrus fruits. N.S.W. Dept. Agr. Div. Hort. Bull. H193.

HOPKINS, E. F. and McCORNACK, A. A. 1958. Prevention of rind breakdown in oranges. Citrus Mag. 21 (3), 18-23, 25.

HOPKINS, E. F. and McCORNACK, A. A. 1960. Effect of delayed handling and other factors on rind breakdown and decay in oranges. Proc. Fla. State Hort. Soc. 73. 263-269.

HUME, H. H. 1926. The Cultivation of Citrus Fruits. Macmillan Press, New York.

ISMAIL, M. A and BROWN, G. E. 1975. Phenolic content during healing of Valencia orange peel under high humidity. J. Am. Soc. Hort. Sci. 60, 248-251.

ISMAIL, M. A. and BROWN, G. E. 1979. Postharvest wound healing in citrus fruit: Induction of phenylalanine ammonia-lyase in injured Valencia orange flavedo. J. Am. Soc. Hort. Sci. 104, 126-129.

JAHN, O. L. and YOUNG, R. 1976. Changes in chlorophyll a, b, and the a/b ratio during color development in citrus fruit. J. Am. Soc. Hort. Sci. 101, 416-418.

JAHN O. L., YOST, G. E. and SOULE, J. 1967. Degreening response of color sorted Florida oranges. USDA, Agr. Res. Serv. Rept. 51-54.

JAHN, O. L., CHACE, W. G., JR. and CUBBEDGE, R. H. 1969. Degreening of citrus fruits in response to varying levels of oxygen and ethylene. Proc. Am. Soc. Hort. Sci. 94, 123-125.

JAHN, O. L., CHACE, W. G., JR. and CUBBEDGE, R. H. 1973. Degreening response of 'Hamlin' oranges in relation to temperature, ethylene concentration, and fruit maturity. J. Am. Soc. Hort. Sci. 98, 177-181.

JOHNSON, M. 1981. Electronic sorting/automated packaging for fresh citrus fruit. 826. Proc. Int. Soc. Citriculture 2, 826.

KITAGAWA, H. 1973. Coloring of satsuma mandarin (*Citrus unshiu* Marc.) with ethylene. Japan. Agr. Res. Quart. 7 (1), 43-46.

KITAGAWA, H. and TARUTANI, T. 1973. Studies on the coloring of satsuma mandarin: III. The relation of fruit condition and coloring by the treatment of sealing with ethylene for 15 hours. J. Japan. Soc. Hort. Sci. 42, 65-69 (Japanese with English summary).

KITAGAWA, H., ADACHI, S. and TARUTANI, T. 1971A. Studies on the coloring of satsuma mandarin: I. The relation of a method of ethylene treatment and degreening. J. Japan. Soc. Hort. Sci. 40, 190-194 (Japanese with English summary).

KITAGAWA, H., ADACHI, S. and TARUTANI, T. 1971B. Studies on the coloring of satsuma mandarin: II. Practical convenient method of coloring or degreening with ethylene using a plastic film. J. Japan. Soc. Hort. Sci. 40, 195-199 (Japanese with English summary).

KITAGAWA, H., KAWADA, K. and TARUTANI, T. 1978. Effectiveness of ethylene degreening of certain citrus cultivars. J. Am. Soc. Hort. Sci. 103, 113-115.

LEWIS, L. N. and COGGINS, C. W. 1964. The inhibition of carotenoid accumulation in navel oranges by gibberellin A_3 as measured by thin layer chromatography. Plant Cell Physiol. 5, 457-463.

LEWIS, L. N., COGGINS, C. W. and GARBER, M. J. 1964. Chlorophyll concentration in the navel orange rind as related to potassium gibberelate, light intensity and time. Proc. Am. Soc. Hort. Sci. 84, 127-186.

LOUCKS, K. W. and HOPKINS, E. F. 1946. A study of the occurrence of Phomopsis and Diplodia rots in Florida oranges under various conditions and treatments. Phytopathology 36, 750-757.

McCORNACK, A. A. and GRIERSON, W. 1965. Practical measures for control of stem end breakdown of oranges. Fla. Agr. Ext. Circ. 286.

MILLER, W. M. 1989. Measuring air exchange rates for citrus degreening rooms. Proc. Fla. State Hort. Soc. 102, 185-187.

MILLER, W. M. and DROUILLARD, G. P. 1999. Engineering Economic Analysis for Automatic Grading of Florida Citrus. Proc. Fla. State Hort. Soc. 112, 156-159.

MILLER, W. M., ISMAIL, M. A. and BUSLIG, B. S. 1997. Computer assisted monitoring and control in Florida citrus degreening. Proc. Fla. State Hort. Soc. 110, 201-204.

MILLER, W. M., ISMAIL, M. A., NELSON, B. and RICHARD, R. 2000. Review of sensor technologies for real time process control of ethylene in citrus degreening. Paper 006106, Milwaukee, WI, Am. Soc. Agr. Eng.

MILLER, W. M., NELSON, B., RICHARD, R. and ISMAIL, M. A. 2000. Ethylene measurement and control in Florida citrus degreening. *In* Integrated View of Fruit & Vegetable Quality, W. J. Florkowski, S. E. Prussia and R. L. Shewfelt (Editors). Technomic Publishing Co., Lancaster, PA.

MITCHELL, F. G., GUILLOU, R. and PARSONS, R. A. 1972. Commercial cooling of fruits and vegetables. University of California, Agr. Manual 43.

NORMAN, S. and CRAFT, C. C. 1968. Effect of ethylene on production of volatiles by lemons. HortScience 3, 66-67.

POLLARD, J. E. and BIGGS, R. H. 1970. Role of cellulase in abscission of citrus fruits. J. Am. Soc. Hort. Sci. 95, 667-673.

RACITI, G. and MARTINO, E. D. I. 1966. Degreening of several varieties of citron by ethylene and oxygen. Bull. Int. Inst. Ref. Commissions 4,5–Bologne, 257-262.

RAYNOR, A. and WARDOWSKI, W. F. 1979. Cold water mist humidification of citrus during degreening. Proc. Fla. State Hort. Soc. 92, 189-193.

RIOV, J. 1975. Polygalacturonase activity in citrus fruit. J. Food Sci. 40, 201-202.

ROGERS, B. J. and HURLEY, C. 1971. Ethylene and the appearance of albedo macerating factor in citrus. J. Am. Soc. Hort. Sci. 96, 811-813.

ROSE, O. H., COOK, H. T. and REDIT, W. H. 1951. Harvesting, handling and transportation of citrus fruits. USDA Bibliogr. Bull. 13.

SIEVERS, A. F. and TRUE, R. H. 1912. A preliminary study of the forced curing of lemons as practiced in California. Bull. 232. USDA Bureau Plant Industries.

SMOOT, J. J., MELVIN, C. F. and JAHN, O. L. 1971. Decay of degreened oranges and tangerines as affected by time of washing and fungicide application. Plant Dis. Rep. 55, 149-152.

STEARNS, C. R., JR. 1942. Color break studies, pp. 156-157. *In* Annu. Rept. Fla. Agr. Exp. Stn.

STEARNS, C.R., JR. and YOUNG, G. T. 1942. The relation of climatic conditions to color development in citrus fruit. Proc. Fla. State Hort. Soc. 55, 59-61.

STEWART, I. and WHEATON, T. A. 1972. Carotenoids in citrus, their accumulation induced by ethylene. J. Agr. Food Chem. 20, 448-449.

TORRES, M. A. and PIVIDAL, F. 1981. Degreening and color problems of Cuban Valencia oranges. Proc. Int. Soc. Citriculture 2, 761-764.

VINES, H. M., EDWARDS, G. J. and GRIERSON, W. 1965. Citrus fruit respiration. Proc. Fla. State Hort. Soc. 78, 198-102.

WARDOWSKI, W. F. 1996. Recommendations for degreening Florida fresh citrus fruits. Fla. Agr. Ext. Circ. 1170.

WARDOWSKI, W. F. and GRIERSON, W. 2002. Pallet boxes for Florida citrus. Fla. Agr. Ext. Circ. 443.

WINSTON, J. R. and TILDEN, R. W. 1935. Coloring or degreening of mature citrus with ethylene. U.S.D.A., unnumbered (mimeo.).

YOUNG, B. and ERICKSON, L. C. 1961. Influence of temperature on the color change in Valencia oranges. Proc. Am. Soc. Hort. Sci. 78, 197-200.

YOUNG, R. E., ROMANI, R. J. and BIALE, J. B. 1962. Carbon dioxide effect on fruit respiration. II. Response of avocado, bananas and lemons. Plant Physiol. 37, 416-422.

ZAMORANI, A., RUSSO, C. and MONACO, M. 1973. Effect of degreening on physical characteristics and juice composition of Feminello lemons. Proc. Int. Soc. Citriculture 3, 303-307.

11

Separation and Grading of Freeze-Damaged Fruit

William M. Miller, W. F. Wardowski, and William Grierson

Freeze damage in citrus fruits is normally widely scattered and the degree of damage varies greatly, not only among groves but within individual groves. Without the ability to separate damaged fruit, large amounts of sound oranges cannot go to the fresh fruit market because they include enough freeze-damaged fruit to prevent them passing any standard grades. Separating out this freeze-damaged fruit enables the grower to send his crop to the most profitable market, and enables the packinghouse operator to keep his packinghouse running. Methods of upgrading lightly to moderately damaged crops, to the point where they meet U.S. standards for fresh fruit shipments, are discussed in this chapter. It is helpful to understand how fruit freezes and the principles of specific gravity separation.

Citrus fruit that hangs on the tree after a freeze will be wholesome, although not necessarily packable. Specific gravity determinations can be used to estimate the cannery value of nonpackable crops (Stout 1964; Ting and Blair 1965). Any fruit that falls should NOT be picked up. A practical way to prevent pickers from picking up such drops is to disk or chop the grove immediately before picking.

HOW FRUIT FREEZES

Freeze injury of oranges tends to follow a definite pattern determined by the type of freeze. Most damage comes from radiation of the heat in the grove to a clear cloudless sky. When this is interrupted by the presence of the fruit, the bottom of the fruit tends to absorb heat radiated to it from the ground below. The top of the fruit radiates its heat to the sky above. It is this effect, rather than the slight difference in sugar content between the stem and stylar ends (Hass and Klotz 1935) that determines the basic freeze pattern. When a "wind freeze" condition prevails, the side of the fruit exposed to the wind tends to freeze first; and very sharp differences in amount of damage may prevail between the fruit on the windward and leeward sides of the tree.

The symptoms of freeze injury are principally due to membrane damage. This applies to both the tough carpellary membranes around the individual segments, to the very frail vesicular membranes of the juice sacs, and of the individual cells within the juice sacs. Initially, frozen areas within the fruit tend to be wet and mushy with the normal radial arrangement of the segment membranes distorted by the action of the formation of ice crystals. At this stage, frozen fruit cannot be mechanically separated from sound fruit. The injured portions dry out within 4-5 weeks, depending on the weather and state of maturity of the crop. A completely frozen fruit never shrivels because there is no membrane to be pulled inwards. The water diffuses to the outside leaving hollow dried up areas within apparently sound fruit (Fig. 11.1). Severely frozen fruit will usually drop, as much due to damage to the stem as to the fruit. Fruit lightly frozen while still immature will tend to remain on the tree, and the undamaged segments will often expand into the hollow areas where tissue was frozen.

A secondary symptom of freeze injury is the presence of white crystals of hesperidin between the carpellary membranes. Hesperidin is one of the normal components of orange juice, and its crystallization does not affect the wholesomeness of the fruit. Although relied upon in California (Bartholomew *et al.* 1950; Bennett and Albach 1981; Thomas *et al.* 1919) as an indication of severity of freeze damage, little correlation has been found in Florida between the presence of hesperidin crystals and the damage to be expected in a given crop (Grierson and Hayward 1959).

U.S. GRADES FOR FREEZE DAMAGE

One of the most restrictive citrus freeze-damage grade standards in the world is the U.S. grade for Florida oranges which is determined by the total volume of desiccated or mushy tissue, providing the fruit otherwise qualifies for the appropriate grade (Anon. 1967). This disorganized tissue is usually at the stem end; but when damage extends down the side of the fruit, it is assessed in terms of the volume of damaged tissue equivalent to slices across the stem end (Fig. 11.2).

U.S. No. 1 grade for Florida oranges allows no damage more than the volume of a 0.64-cm (¼-in.) slice off the flesh of the stem end. U.S. No. 2 grade allows damage not exceeding the volume of a 1.27-cm (11.0 ½-in.) cut off the flesh of the stem end. There is wide variation among types of citrus and varieties for the response to separation for freeze damage. Wardowski and Grierson (1972) discuss variation among Florida varieties and when separation is economically advantageous.

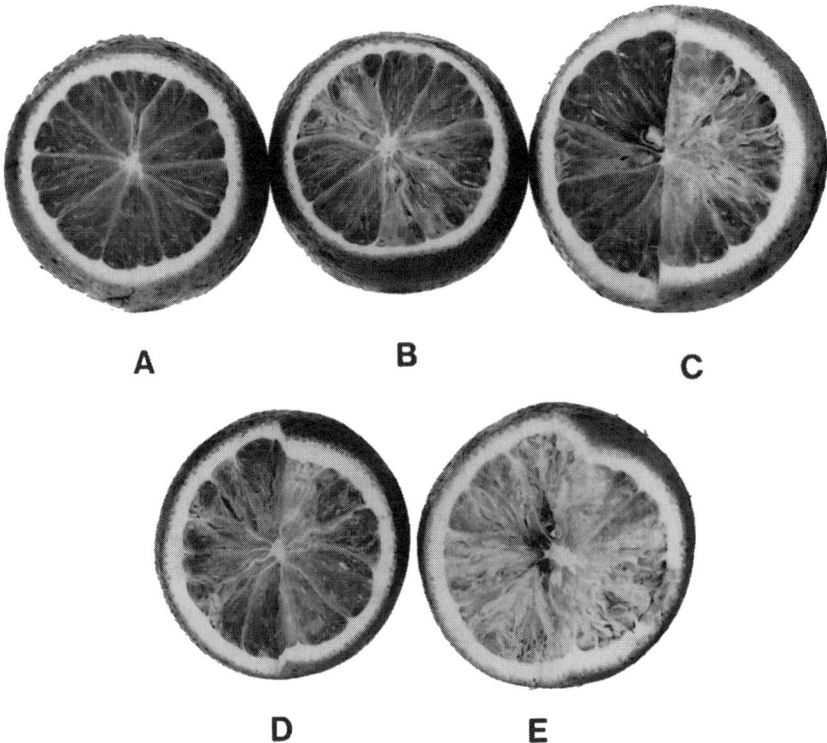

Fig. 11.1. Examples of freeze damage to citrus fruits. A. Shows only a trace of injury in one segment at the top of the orange after making a 0.64 cm (1/4 inch) cut. Adjacent segments have expanded to close up open space caused by injury. B. Shows dryness in several segments on the 0.64 cut. Another 0.64 cm cut would be necessary to determine grade for fresh fruit marketing purposes. C. Shows results of two 0.64 cm cuts and depicts damage that is scoreable against U.S. No. 1 grade but not against U.S. No. 2 grade. D. Shows the results of two cuts where injury is scoreable against No. 2 grade. E. Shows almost complete dryness in the fruit.
Courtesy Dr. G. F. Westbrook, Florida Dept Agr. and Consumer Services.

PRINCIPLES OF SPECIFIC GRAVITY SEPARATION

Specific gravity of injured fruit tends to decrease in the weeks following a freeze because of fruit dehydration. After a month or more, the specific gravity of damaged oranges is lowered enough to afford a means of separating sound from frozen fruit. This separation cannot be exact as long as the group of oranges to be separated includes those of varying size, shape, peel thickness, peel texture, and degree of hollow center. However, once desiccation is reasonably advanced, the more seriously damaged fruit can usually be separated on the basis of specific gravity.

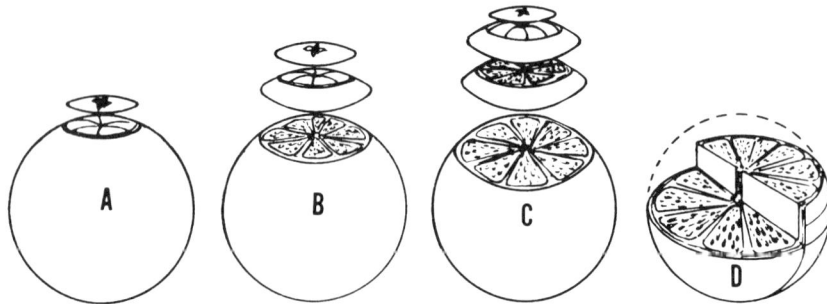

Fig. 11.2. To evaluate freeze damage in oranges, first cut a thin slice off the stem end to expose the flesh (A). Then remove a 0.64 cm (1/4 inch) slide and examine the orange (B). If damage does not extend below this 0.64 cm slice, the fruit automatically grades No. 1 as far as internal quality is concerned. If some damage is noted, make another 0.64 cm cut © and depending on the extent of damage noted, the fruit is graded No.1 or No. 2. Additional cuts may be made as needed to determine the full extent of damage-down to the middle of the orange (D) and, in some cases, even lower. Inspectors must balance the area of damage with its depth. A 10% tolerance is allowed on fruit graded for the fresh market. Oranges for concentrate must be "wholesome." *From Annon (1963).*

EMULSION SEPARATORS

The simplest type of specific gravity separator involves use of a fluid (commonly an emulsion of purified mineral spirits in water) whose specific gravity is frequently adjusted to be more than that of the damaged fruit, but less than that of the undamaged fruit. This will normally lie in a range between 0.90 and 0.95. Emulsion separators are virtually nonexistent today. More information can be found in Wardowski and Grierson 1972, and Wardowski *et al.* 1986.

Water Separators

Older types of specific gravity separators use water and rely not only upon differences in specific gravity, but also in buoyancy (Perry and Perkins 1968). These two properties are closely related, but the buoyancy of a submerged body is related not only to specific gravity but to its coefficient of friction as it moves through the water. Water separators are mostly superseded by electronic separators. More information can be found in Grierson and Hayward 1959, Wardowski and Grierson 1972, and Wardowski *et al.* 1986.

SETTING UP AN EFFICIENT SEPARATION SYSTEM

Any system in which the separator is installed in the direct line of fruit flow from dumping to packing is automatically inefficient. Not only is the flow of fruit to the house cut down drastically below normal economic levels, but the volume of fruit reaching the packers fluctuates with the degree of damage in each successive crop, making it extremely difficult to employ labor efficiently or to fill orders effectively. This flow is further cut down when the separators have to handle unpackable sizes, off-bloom, misshapen fruit, etc., that will then be graded out instead of being packed.

Ideally, the separator system should be able to run quite independently of the rest of the packinghouse, perhaps with an alternative route direct to the packing line (Fig. 11.3). In that way, a small crew can work long hours separating damaged crops and accumulating separated fruit which, when packed, will ensure a high rate of packout and efficient use of labor and machinery.

Electronic separators installed in the packing line can be operated through the night with a small crew, to supply fruit to a full day crew as needed.

Trash Elimination, Presizing, and Pregrading

It is extremely important to have efficient trash elimination, presizing, and pregrading. Every effort should be made to eliminate all obviously unpackable fruit prior to the separators. Where a separate line is set up, it is wise to include such measures as a sloping belt trash eliminator, chutes of spaced rod, and other measures to supplement the normal length of roller conveyor used for trash elimination. Accumulation of leaves, twigs, etc., can gravely impair efficiency of any separator.

Sampling and Control Station

For efficient separation, samples must be taken simultaneously from the eliminations and from the fruit going to the packinghouse. It must be possible to grade fruit quickly and make immediate adjustment on the machine. A recheck should be made as soon as the machine has settled down to the new adjustment (Fig. 11.4). Note in Fig. 11.4 that the operator can take fruit alternately from lines "A" (packinghouse) and "B" (eliminations), accumulating them on the cutting board. The operator's hands will be wet and messy nearly all the time. Therefore, provision must be made for him to keep records with wet hands. This is simply done by the use of "caps" cut off the fruit prior to the grade cut, as a tally. As each fruit is graded, the operator places the "cap" in the tally tray with the knife tip. When the grading is completed, the two samples can be counted, and the results recorded. This is important. A continuous, accurate record greatly helps efficiency of separation.

Separator Adjustment

If sampling indicates a need to adjust the machine, it should be done immediately and to a known degree. A remote control within reach of the operator can be used to move the adjustment vane of water separators with the adjustment numbered so the settings can be recorded. Direct communication with the control room for electronic separators is essential. The

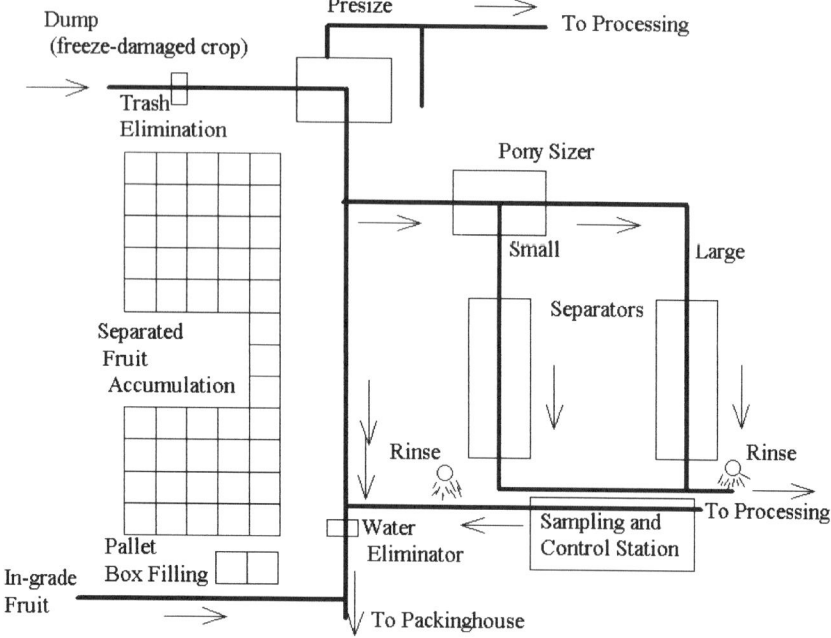

Fig. 11.3. An efficient layout for frozen fruit separation. Note these important features: (1) Trash is removed immediately. (2) Sound crops can be run directly into the packinghouse. (3) Severely damaged crops can be separated and sound fruit accumulated without running the rest of the house. (4) One crop can be separated while accumulated fruit from a previous separation is being packed. (5) Larger and smaller sized are segregated for more efficient separation except for electronic sizers which size each fruit. (6) Cannery and packinghouse lines can be sampled simultaneously for each machine and adjustments made form a single control station.
From Wardowski and Grierson (1972).

operator very soon gets to know the best setting for a given degree of damage and how much of a correction to make.

INTERNAL ELECTRONIC DETECTION METHODS

Considerable research has been done, initially in California (Johnson 1970), on detecting freeze damage to citrus fruits by means of X-rays or other electronic methods. Commercial installations were made in lemon and orange packinghouses. The grading equipment checked for internal drying resulting from freezing, granulation, crushing, or diseases. This method of separation provided a degree of accuracy unobtainable with emulsion and water separators. The variables of size, peel thickness, peel texture, and hollow centers can be minimized. There are no known current citrus applications of this technique.

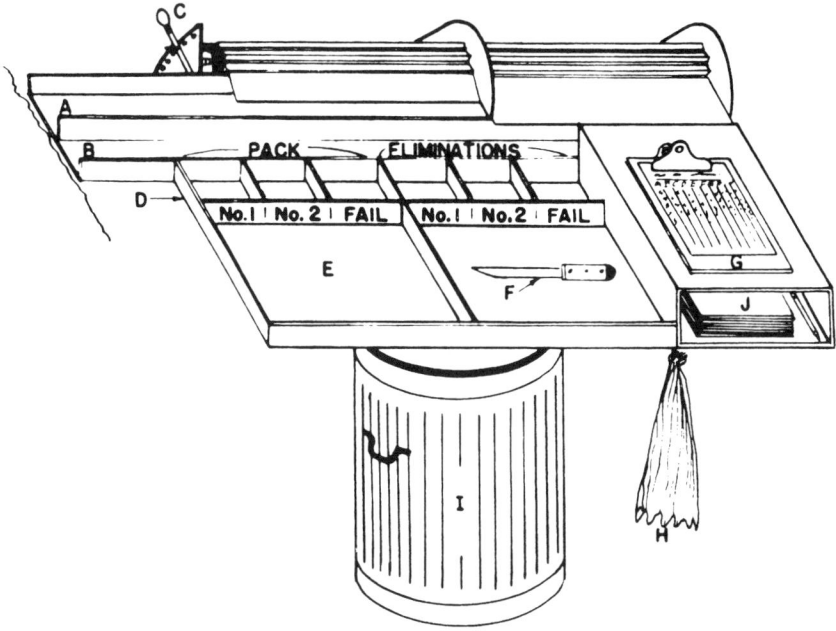

Fig. 11.4. Sampling and regulating station for freeze-damaged fruit separation. A. Packinghouse line. B. Eliminations. C. Remote control on selector vane and numbered settings, or direct communication line to the electronic sizer control room. D. Trays for tops of fruit kept as a tally. E. Cutting board for fruit from packinghouse line. F. Cutting board for fruit from elimination line and sharp knife. G. Clipboard with record sheets. H. Towel for operator to wipe hands before recording data. I. Garbage can (or cull chute for cut fruit. J. Shelf for supplies (record sheets, pencils, hone for knife, etc.). *From Wardowski and Grierson (1972).*

WEIGHT AND VOLUME ELECTRONIC DETECTION

Another electronic detection technique has been applied commercially. Electronic sensors can very accurately measure both dimensions and weight of individual fruit. If these measurements can be achieved accurately on a very uniform crop (peel thickness, hollow centers, etc.), it is possible to separate freeze-damaged citrus fruit without directly sensing internal desiccation or submerging the fruit.

Automatic evaluation of density is accomplished by analyzing real-time measurements of a fruit's mass and volume. Fruit must be singulated onto a roller or cup conveying system. It is critical that the fruit do not touch, as either the mass reading or image analysis for volume or both may be corrupted. Current automatic grading units function at rates of 8 to 10 objects per second per lane with 70 to 90% fill capacity. These same speeds are feasible for density sorting. The most critical measurement is the volume which is extrapolated from a two dimensional planar image on current camera systems implemented for automated fruit grading. Given that a fruit is an ideal sphere, required mass accuracy of ±3.2 g and dimensional accuracy of ±0.024 cm diameter are needed for a 1% rms error (Miller *et al.* 1988). Fruit may be assumed to be either oblate (typical grapefruit shape), prolate (typical lemon shape) or truncated sphere to increase the accuracy of the volume measurement.

Packers can further enhance breakpoints by combining size and density information. In general, larger fruit will have a lower density, so acceptable setpoints may be, for instance, 0.8 g/cm^3 on large fruit but 0.85 on fruit of a smaller size. Adjustments on the density thresholds as related to freeze damage are still required from crop to crop. However, it is easy to collect data on individual fruit or small lots and ascertain the average density levels for fruit varying from no freeze damage to severe internal desiccation.

In most packinghouses, this density sorting has been implemented as part of the final sizing. However, with the utilization of automatic sorting, the operation could be coupled with automatic pregrade sorting, thereby increasing the throughput of marketable fruit through the packingline.

REFERENCES

ANON. 1963. Fla. Citrus Mutual Triangle 12 (9).

ANON. 1967. United States standards for Florida oranges and tangelos. Fed. Regist. 32, 13492.

BARTHOLOMEW, E. T., SINCLAIR, W. B. and HORSPOOL, R. P. 1950. Freeze injury and subsequent seasonal changes in 'Valencia' oranges and grapefruit. Calif. Agr. Exp. Stn. Bull. 719.

BENNETT, R. D. and ALBACH, R. F. 1981. The nature of freeze-induced white spots on orange segment walls. J. Agr. Food Chem. 29, 511-514.

GRIERSON, W. and HAYWARD, F. W. 1959. Evaluation of mechanical separators for cold-damaged oranges. Proc. Am. Soc. Hort. Sci. 73, 278-288.

HAAS, A. R. C. and KLOTZ, L. J. 1935. Physiological gradients in citrus fruits. Hilgardia 9 (3), 181-127.

JOHNSON, M. 1970. A system for the seventies. Citrograph 55 (4), 129-130.

MILLER, W. M., PELEG, K. and BRIGGS, P. 1988. Automated density separation for freeze-damaged citrus. Appl. Eng. Agr. 4 (4), 344-348.

PERRY, R. L. and PERKINS, R. M. 1968. Separators for frost damaged oranges. Calif. Citrogr. 53 (8), 304.

STOUT, R. G. 1964. Specific gravity as a means of estimating juice yields of freeze damaged 'Valencia' oranges. Fla. Agr. Exp. Stn. Circ. S-150.

THOMAS, E. E., YOUNG, H. D. and SMITH, C. O. 1919. A study of the effects of freezes on citrus in California: II. Changes that take place in frozen oranges and lemons. Calif. Agr. Exp. Stn. Bull. 304.

TING, S. V. and BLAIR, J. G. 1965. The relation of specific gravity of whole fruit to the internal quality of oranges. Proc. Fla. State Hort. Soc. 78, 251-260.

WARDOWSKI, W. F. and GRIERSON, W. 1972. Separation and grading of freeze damaged citrus fruits. Fla. Agr. Exp. Stn. Circ. 372.

WARDOWSKI, W. F., NAGY, S., and GRIERSON, W. (Editors). 1986. Fresh Citrus Fruits. Van Nostrand Reinhold, New York.

12

Packingline Machinery

William M. Miller, W. F. Wardowski, and William Grierson

Extensive literature is available on individual packinghouse processes, such as degreening and fungicide applications, but minimal information has been compiled on individual components of the citrus packinghouse line and even less on assembling them into an efficient system.

Every packinghouse owner and every equipment supplier has their own ideas of what a packinghouse system should accomplish. However, there are basic principles that apply to virtually any citrus packinghouse line, regardless of the particular layout. Errors in proper choice and matching of packingline components are extraordinarily costly in money, labor inefficiency, reduced capacity, increased fruit losses and decay claims. Moreover, many design errors occur repeatedly and can be avoided if the principles herein are considered before equipment installation or packinghouse remodeling.

PRINCIPLES

Width of Equipment

Whatever the function of the individual component, a packingline is basically so much area for fruit conveyance. The amount of conveyor area needed can be calculated. Within reason, the wider and shorter the line, the less the initial cost for the following reasons:

A. As packingline length is much greater than the width, the building size is governed by the packingline length while width makes very little difference to the building area.

B. There is more initial cost in the sides of the line (framing, bearings, chains, drives, etc.) than in the span.

C. Electrical and plumbing costs relate more closely to the length than to the width of the line.

Capacity of the line depends on the width of conveying surface multiplied by its linear speed of forward travel. The wider a line, the slower the linear speed required for a given capacity. If the linear speed is high due to the initial design, extra capacity can only be obtained by running the line faster or the fruit deeper, adding potential damage from more abusive handling, or else by building an additional line. If the speed is low due to an initial design of wide equipment, capacity can be increased by merely speeding up operations where fruit treatment time is not a factor. When fruit treatment time is critical, the line can be redesigned with extra application equipment added at minimal cost. Plan for increased capacity and *start with the widest available equipment* and design for maximum capacity, not average capacity.

Sequence of Equipment and Processes

The conventional order of fruit treatments along the packingline goes back to the days when fresh fruit was paramount, several grades were packed, processed fruit was a small consideration, and residues of pesticides, etc., were usually not considered. Today, it is common to pack just one grade, though provision for an occasional second or fancy grade may be an advantage. Large amounts of fruit, >50% in the case of export grapefruit, may be graded out and sent to the processor where unnecessary chemical residues and fruit labels are to be avoided.

With these considerations in mind, it is apparent that every fruit not destined to be shipped as fresh fruit should be removed as soon as possible (Fig. 12.1). Immediately after dumping and trash elimination, over- and undersizes can be removed mechanically with a pre-sizer. Removal of fruit with exterior blemishes is often not possible until after washing, but provision should be made prior to the washer for removing all rotten or split fruit before they contaminate the rest of the fruit handling equipment. Washing should be followed by a water eliminator to remove excess water and grading should follow immediately. There is no reason to put fungicides, waxes, labels, and possibly color-add, on fruit that are eliminated for the processing plant. Additional costs are incurred by the packinghouse and excessive fungicide residues may result at the processing plant (Grierson and Wardowski 1973).

Grading immediately after the washer considerably reduces the amount of machinery necessary between the washer and the final sizer. Size and horsepower requirements of the remainder of the line can be decreased proportionately to the amount of fruit removed by grading. Alternatively, if the width of the line is not reduced, more packable fruit can be handled on it. In either case, machinery cost per box is decreased by grading immediately after washing.

The order in which the other operations are done depends, in part, on the types of fungicide and wax being applied. When SOPP (sodium ortho-phenylphenate) is used (Wardowski and Brown 1993), it may be combined with the wash soap, but any excess must be rinsed off to avoid fruit peel injury. Other

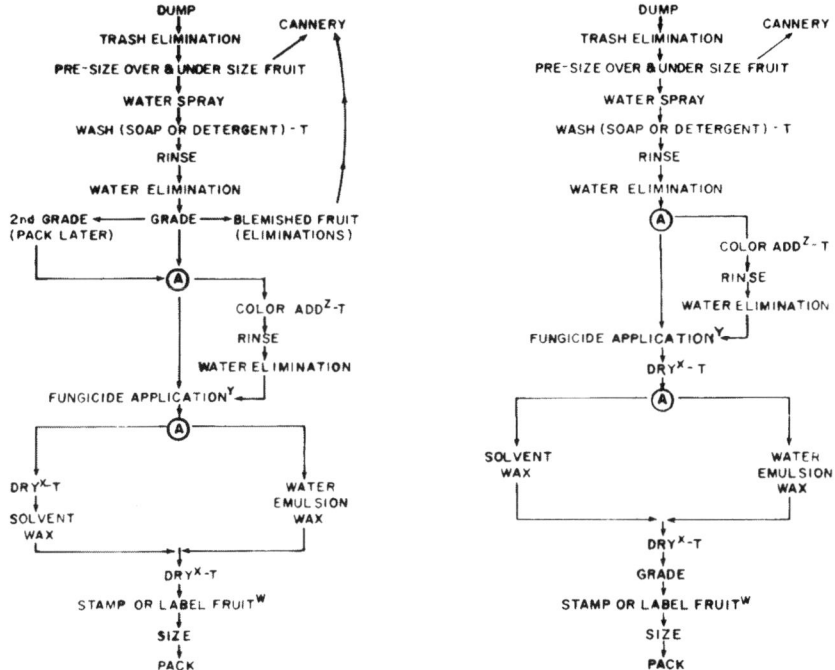

Fig. 12.1. Logical order for a packingline when only one grade is packed most of the time. Degreening and frozen fruit separation are not included here, being covered in separate chapters. T denotes time-dependent operation.

fungicides have to be applied to clean fruit and allowed to dry. The color-add process is best accomplished prior to fungicide applications, except for SOPP at the washer, as other fungicides are removed in the color-add emulsion.

Packing a Second Grade

Where a second grade is of minor importance, it is not logical to have a complete line of sizing and packing equipment for the second grade fruit. The fluctuation in volume between first and second grades precludes optimal use of equipment and labor. Instead, the second grade should be accumulated in pallet boxes (Fig. 12.2) and run on the same equipment after the No. 1 grade fruit is packed. With correctly sized equipment, this will not mean working a longer day.

Inventory-to-Inventory Packing

A logical approach for ultimate mechanization of packing and palletizing is to use an inventory-to-inventory system accumulating an inventory of

Fig. 12.2. Deceleration pallet box filler for citrus in Florida. Counter-weighted devices begin low in the pallet box and are gradually raised manually as the box fills. There are two pallet box fillers per fruit size to allow ample time to removed a full box and replace it with an empty box without interrupting the fruit flow.

sized, prepared fruit from which packing equipment draws one size at a time, and accumulating an inventory of packed, refrigerated fruit. Such broad considerations for a packinghouse layout are not considered in this chapter. Such a design change also involves changes in fruit harvesting schedules, inclusion of refrigeration, and other matters not discussed here. It should be noted, however, that an inventory-to-inventory system that packs one size at a time can utilize a standard single channel palletizer. Conventional packinghouses handling several sizes simultaneously can only use a mechanical palletizer by first investing in an extremely expensive accumulation system. Robotic palletizers may provide a versatile, less expensive palletizing system without a separate accumulation system.

THE BASIC PACKINGHOUSE LINE

Fig. 12.1 shows various packinghouse operations in logical order for a packinghouse in which only one grade is packed most of the time, or in which a second grade is a small proportion of the fruit packed regularly. Operations are indicated as being either time dependent or independent. That is, operations such as dumping, trash elimination, and pre-sizing do not involve retaining the fruit for a given length of time. Time dependent processes, on the other hand, take a certain length of time which must be taken into consideration in calculations to determine the necessary area of conveying surface, e.g., fruit drying.

Dumping

Dry dumping is highly recommended. If the machinery is well designed with unrestricted fruit flow, the fruit will suffer no appreciable damage. Dumping into water inevitably subjects fruit to fungal inoculum, some of which may be resistant to fungicides. Rotation and indexing of the bin to fixed positions during dumping assists in creating a uniform flow of fruit. Overhead canvas or belting can reduce the fruit's velocity, minimizing the chance for damage. Fruit-to-fruit contact is preferred over fruit-to-metal. The dumping sequence and fruit flow control are critical for uniform throughput and an efficient operation. De-stacking and stacking mechanisms are included in many dump systems. The arrangement should be arranged to facilitate forklift traffic. Bin cleaning and washing also may be included in this dumping process.

Trash Elimination

Few packinghouses have adequate provision for coping with the trash commonly included in deliveries of fruit from hand picking. Spaced metal rods parallel to the fruit flow are commonplace. A sloping belt trash eliminator (Grierson 1971) will remove most loose trash and deliver it to a conveyor or container. A vacuum brusher (Grierson 1971) can be used to remove loose sand, which is otherwise extremely injurious to the packingline equipment and fruit. Roller conveyors should always be self-cleaning, i.e., with angled supports that wipe the whole length of each roller with openings to shed trash (Fig. 12.3). Several pre-graders with clippers may be required to remove any adhering stems, and provision needs to be made for removing any grove debris plus rots and splits. Rots should be minimal if the grove has been chopped or disked immediately prior to picking.

Wetting

The fruit needs to be wet before it reaches the washer brushes. Dip or soak tanks are not recommended for the same reasons mentioned above for water dumps. After removal of rots and splits, a chlorinated water spray over rollers

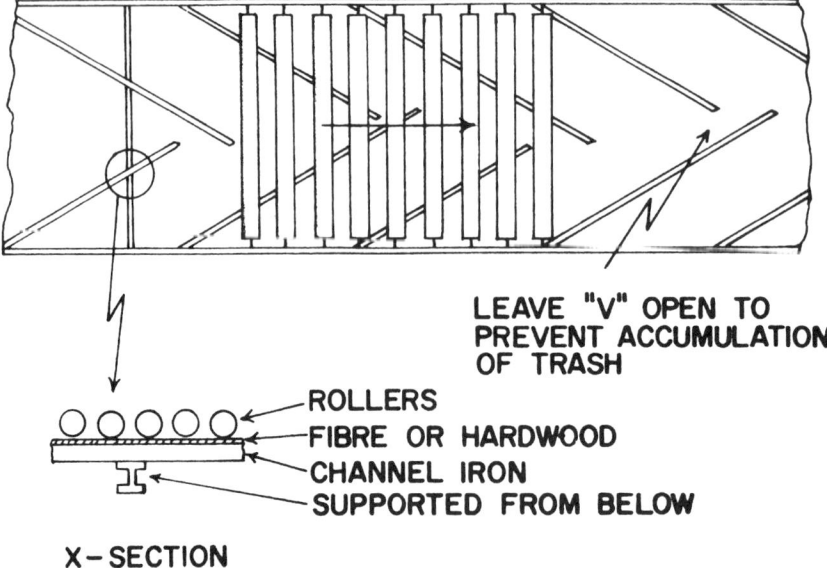

**LEAVE "V" OPEN TO
PREVENT ACCUMULATION
OF TRASH**

ROLLERS
FIBRE OR HARDWOOD
CHANNEL IRON
SUPPORTED FROM BELOW

X – SECTION

Fig. 12.3. Angled supports under roller conveyors. Spacing is such that every roller is supported by at least two supports at all times, wear is thus distributed evenly over the whole length of each roller, and the rollers are partially self-cleaning.

is satisfactory at 75 to 100 ppm free chlorine for pathogen lethality (Ritenour 2001). In handling fruit from canker quarantine areas in Florida, fruit treatment with SOPP or sodium hypochlorite is required (FDACS 2000).

Washing

Many packinghouses have increased packingline throughput without a proportional increase in either the length or width of their washer brush bed. In some cases, this change has led to ineffective cleaning of the fruit. Work in Australia (Jarrett and Tugwell 1975) has indicated a minimal 30-sec time interval for proper cleaning. In all cases, the washing time should remain above 20 sec. Such time requirements have been established for fruit in a single layer with all fruit in contact with the brushes. The relationship between packingline capacity and length of the brush bed for a 30-sec wash time is shown in Fig. 12.4. Problems such as sooty mold and sooty blotch may necessitate even longer cleaning times. Curves were generated for grapefruit and oranges assuming a 75% full brush bed. For conservative design, the curve for a 1.22 m wide unit would be used for 1.32 m wide washers commonly encountered. This slight overdesign incorporates a safety margin for peak fruit throughput conditions.

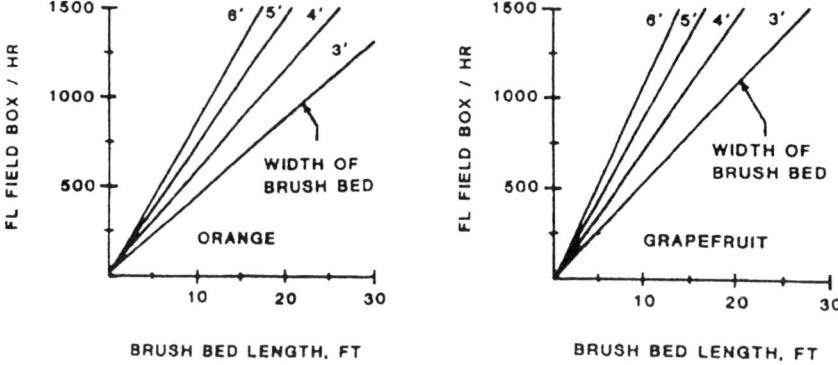

Fig. 12.4. Brush bed capacities for oranges and grapefruit (30 sec wash time).

Use of transverse rotating brushes is virtually universal, as is some form of controlled foam or drip application of soap. The applicator should be located immediately above the space between the first and second brushes, not immediately over a brush, because each row of fruit pauses between the brushes. Tumbler (wavy-pattern) or spiral wound brush designs are effective when fruit volume is not excessive. Also, more rigid brush fibers result in more effective cleaning but they may cause damage to sensitive-skinned fruit. Pre-wetting of the fruit is advisable. For all washers, a wipe-out, either manual or motor-driven, should be incorporated to remove fruit before abrasive damage occurs. As excessive brush speeds can also cause damage to the fruit, a 2 Hz maximum rotational speed is suggested. A roller-spreader conveyor prior to the washer is essential to provide uniform fruit delivery across the width of the brush bed. Having separate drives set at different rotational speeds for alternate brushes facilitates the brushing action. The bed should be laterally level so fruit do not migrate to one side. If new brushes are installed, a mid-season change is suggested when the fruit's peel is more mature and resistant to abrasive damage.

A study of washer efficiency in some Florida concentrate plants (Rejimbal and Bigler 1972) revealed two other very pertinent factors that are assumed to be similar for fresh fruit packinghouses. First, the postwash rinse was of critical importance. A 132 cm wide washer with ten spray nozzles each of 0.00013 m³/s was considered necessary for adequate cleaning. Second, washing efficiency was not affected by the amount of soil on the fruit.

For fruit to receive equal scrubbing action, a rotary washer has been proposed (Wardowski 1997). The washer has a solid bed of brushes around a central fruit delivery area with fruit discharge through a gated discharge at the outside perimeter.

To clean fruit more effectively, high-pressure washers (HPW) have been developed (Tate and Mullinaux 1999). Positive displacement pumps are used to generate system pressures from 690 to 5900 kPa. High flow rates of 0.003 m^3/sec to 0.032 m^3/sec necessitate water recycling. Petracek et al. (1998) found that HPW does not disrupt the peel integrity of sound fruit. However, rotted or physically damaged fruit rupture during washing due to the lack of peel integrity, the force of high pressure water, and the tearing action of the brushes. Secondly, HPW strips away many of the epicuticular wax platelets, but apparently does not abrade the peel surface. Thirdly, HPW stimulated an apparent ethylene wound response when fruit were washed under higher pressures and prolonged periods.

Rinsing

Thorough rinsing with potable water is required after fruit washing and is best accomplished over the last of the washer brushes or over a roller conveyor. Each fruit should pass under at least two nozzles.

Water Elimination

With increased fuel costs, it is far more economical to remove excess water mechanically rather than by heat and air movement. The common form of water eliminator consists of sponge rubber rollers (usually made up of sections of foam rubber or foam plastic known as "donuts"). The effectiveness of these foam rollers depends on the water being "wrung out" by spring-loaded wringer rolls underneath the rollers. For more efficient and economic operation, the wringer rolls are themselves wiped dry by neoprene blades held rigid between metal straps (Fig. 12.5). A less complicated, but efficient, water eliminator can be made from soft plastic brushes. Metal "flick bars" are placed underneath to barely touch the rotating bristles, throwing off much of the water (Fig. 12.5). Another possible technique eliminates water through the aerodynamic force of a high pressure blower (Miller 1986). Spaced rubber rollers have been implemented to provide increased open area, approximately six times over solid rollers, for air movement through fruit on a roller bed. As a general rule, it is less expensive to remove water mechanically than by the use of heated air.

Grading

The usual situation is that blemished fruit are removed and "in-grade" fruit are left on the line. It is normal to manually grade on a simple roller conveyor, although various improved grading stations have been configured (Bowman et al. 1975; Hunter et al. 1958; Malcolm and DeGarmo 1953).

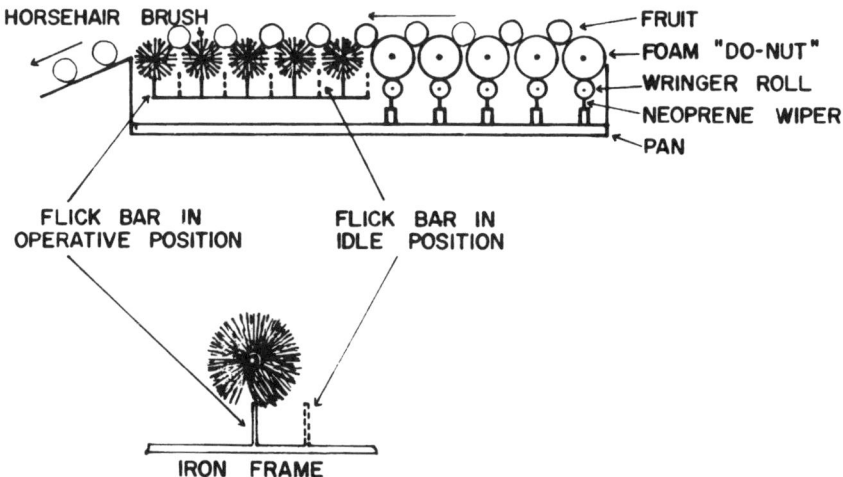

Fig. 12.5. Combined water-eliminator and fungicide-wax applicator. Top. Major components of the unit: sponge rubber rolls with wringer rolls wiped by neoprene wipers
constitute the water-eliminator section; horsehair brushes with flick bars follow as a
brushbed for application of water-emulsion wax or fungicide. Note that flick bars are
moved manually and are only in contact position when rinsing the brushes and never
when starting the motor. Bottom. Flick bar detail.

The common arrangement is for culls (unwholesome fruit) and eliminations (processing fruit) to be graded into chutes beside the grader, with a
second grade going to a conveyor down the center of the grade table. Points
to observe in designing and operating a grade table are as follows:

A. Good lighting is essential. An extensive study of lighting for apple
graders (Heft and Wiant 1962) resulted in a recommendation for 1900 lux
at the fruit surface using high output, cool white fluorescent lamps. This
should be very suitable for citrus grading. Minimizing glare and providing
a better contrast can be accomplished through gray PVC (polyvinyl chloride) rollers as opposed to the conventional white PVC.

B. A minimum of lifting should be required. Cull elimination chutes
are normally at the same height as the edge of the grade table. When a center belt is used, a lift of no more than 5 cm should be necessary to cross the
separator between the rollers and the center belt. It is most undesirable to
position one or more belts above the grading surface. The graders may be
required to remove an orange every 2 sec to a belt above the grading surface, equating to over 2700 kg lifted by each grader in the course of a
working day. If grapefruit were run all day, lifting more than 9000 kg (over
8 U.S. tons) in the course of an 8-hour day may result.

C. The number of grade positions is determined by the number of individual fruit per unit of time (Table 12.1), which also determines the

number of decisions to be made and consequent actions. For a 200 box per hour capacity, the inspection rate would vary from 16,000 fruit per hour for grapefruit to 47,000 for tangerines. Presuming a 60% packout with the 200 box per hour rate, approximately 6,400 grapefruit, 13,760 oranges or 18,800 tangerines would need to be physically removed. Ideally, the number of graders should vary with the type of fruit. However, the usual tendency in a packinghouse running the three types of fruit is to set the number of graders for oranges, which then means that tangerines are under-graded and grapefruit are over-graded.

D. There is a tendency for graders to reject a given number of fruit per unit of time, regardless of the fruit quality. Either rate of fruit flow or number of graders should be varied according to the proportion of fruit to be graded out.

E. With high packout fruit, a limitation is how many fruit the graders can observe per unit of time. With low packout crops, the limitation is the number of fruit the graders can inspect and discard per unit of time. A study in apple packinghouses showed that with good fruit and well designed grade tables, each worker could cope with over 7,000 fruit per hour. With poorly designed grade tables and low packout fruit, this value could drop to little more than 2,000 (Hunter *et al.* 1958). In most citrus packinghouses, each grader inspects more fruit per hour than in a typical apple packinghouse, so obviously they should be given as much consideration through proper design as possible.

F. An inexperienced grader should not check the grading of an experienced grader. When there is much difference in experience or skill, graders working on the same stream of fruit should be positioned with the least experienced upstream and the most experienced downstream. It is common, but highly inefficient, for 7 or 8 graders to observe the same stream of fruit. Fruit flow should be broken into several groups with no more than 3 or 4 graders per stream of fruit (Fig. 12.6). Not only is less fruit being re-inspected, but each time the stream of fruit is divided, the rate of forward travel can be reduced. For example, with four short grading lines instead of two long ones, the fruit passes before the workers at half the linear speed.

G. A very reasonable provision is to enclose the grading table area in an air-conditioned space to provide better conditions for grading. However, with the eliminations (off grade fruit) being tossed onto metal chutes, noise in such an enclosed area can be excessive. This is distracting for the graders and can reach illegal limits under OSHA regulations (OSHA 1974). A very simple and effective approach to reduce noise is to pad the undersides of the chutes with foam rubber. So used, foam rubber never wears out and the sound deadening results are just as effective as putting the foam rubber on the surface of the metal contacted by the fruit.

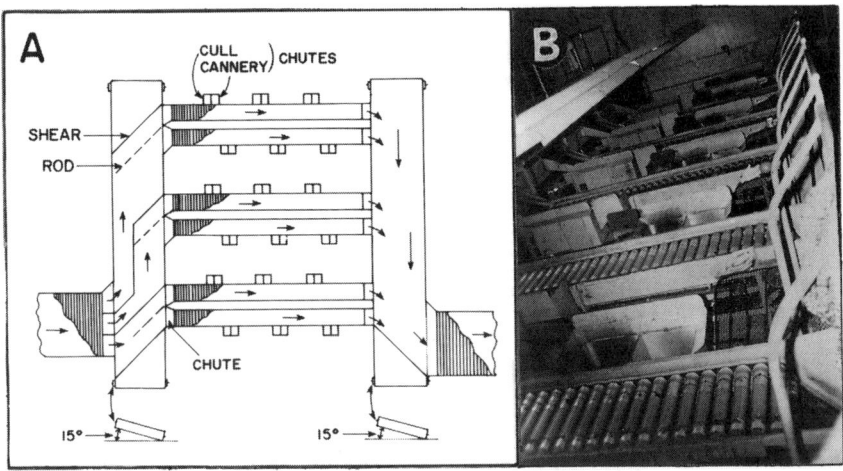

Fig. 12.6. Multiple grade tables. A. By contrast with a single long grading table, the stream of fruit divides into three standard width graders, speed of forward travel is slowed to one-third and each fruit is examined by one-third as many graders. B. Installed in a Florida citrus packinghouse.

H. A sharp limitation on the efficiency of the customary roller grading table is that rate of forward travel and speed of rotation of the fruit cannot be varied independently. This problem has been solved with various types of "reverse-roll" grade tables developed for the apple industry (Hunter *et al.* 1958) and are now commonly used for citrus. When properly used, they definitely increase the capacity of the workers as well as improving the grade. They must, however, be adjusted for the type and volume of fruit being run.

I. Automatic grading is now feasible for extensive pre-grading of citrus and a substantial number of packers have implemented this technology. The equipment should be sized for the maximum number of fruit handled. Since each fruit takes up one pocket, the number of lanes and the linear speed become the key design specifications. Also, illumination configurations are critical (Affeldt and Heck 1994). As with fruit washers, a roller-spreader to even the incoming fruit flow is essential. A section to allow two fruit in a pocket to be brushed off is needed especially in handling mandarin varieties and small oranges. Typically these units are based on a peak throughput such as 10 fruit per sec. However, a fill rate of 80% would be normal and should be taken into account in capacity determinations. A well-trained operator is critical for automatic grading implementation. The control room should be located so an operator can view both the incoming fruit and the exiting product streams. A maintenance schedule for cleaning camera lens, checking for broken conveyor parts, etc. should be established.

Automatic grading can be of great benefit when packout levels are low and the packingline throughput is constrained by the grading task. Weight and volume measurements can be incorporated to calculate fruit density. This criterion is important for separating fruit having natural internal drying or freeze-damage. It has been suggested that the best prospects for economic use of automatic grading equipment in Florida (Gaffney 1973; Miller and Drouillard 1998) might well be in a highly mechanized, combined fresh fruit and cannery operation (Grierson and Wardowski 1977).

Color-Adding

Color-adding (Chapter 17) is an optional treatment since it is only used on oranges, Temples, and tangelos—only on crops which do not have a distinctive varietal color due to climatic conditions (Long 1964). A logical arrangement is to have the color-add tank as a by-pass to the main line. The color-add tank is always a wide piece of equipment in which fruit are several layers deep and therefore advance very slowly. When fruit is not being color-added, it moves forward very quickly on a belt, and it is logical to have the belt in a straight line with no diversions, reducing fruit damage.

Color-adding is a time-dependent operation. For a given color-add emulsion, the intensity of color and the amount of residue is determined by the temperature of the emulsion and the fruit exposure time. Maximum conditions for both temperature and time are set in Florida (Florida Department of Citrus 1975).

The color-add process should be followed by a thorough rinse. Apart from the problem of excess color "bleeding" through the wax, there is a legal necessity for a good rinse as the Food and Drug Administration (FDA) maximum residue is 2 parts per million (ppm) of Citrus Red No. 2. Such rinsing is best done over washer-brushes or moving rollers rather than on a mesh belt or a slat conveyor on which the fruit does not rotate.

Waxing

As water waxes are predominantly used for citrus (Chapter 15), the water eliminator can be combined with a bed of horsehair brushes to also serve as a fungicide applicator (Fig. 12.5). For solvent wax application, water elimination was the first step in achieving the complete dryness necessary prior to solvent wax application. The more water removed by mechanical means at the water eliminator, the less that has to be removed with more expensive hot air drying.

Water wax applications, now used exclusively in Florida, consist of a water emulsion that is applied as a dip, foam, drip, or spray (Hall 1981) with drip or spray application more commonplace. Shellac, polyethylene and carnauba waxes are utilized. Either drip, spray, or spinner applications are utilized, the emulsion typically being applied over a bed of slowly rotating (not over 1.8 Hz) brushes. For this application, either horsehair or 50% horsehair/50% poly is superior to poly bristle, as the horsehair texture tends to hold the emulsion and wipe wax on the fruit rather than throwing it off by centrifugal force. The application of the emulsion can be by a bank of fixed or spinning nozzles, drippers, or a traveling nozzle system. In the spinning nozzle system, centrifugal force disperses the wax into a fine fog of emulsion. It is preferable to have two small nozzles on a traveling system rather than one large one so some wax coverage remains if one nozzle is blocked. Also, more uniform coverage results with multiple nozzles. Some waxing units have a flowrate controller which can be set for various types of citrus as the fruit surface area per box decreases with larger sized fruit. Another innovation incorporates finger sensors with switch closures mounted above a conveyor leading to the waxer. The fruit flow is monitored by this device regulating a pump or valve to provide proportional wax flow.

A convenient system for cleaning out wax applicator lines is to have a hot water or steam line connected to the emulsion delivery line with shut-off valves so that the emulsion can be shut off and the lines purged. Special precautions must be taken when packing for an export market with different regulations on waxes and/or fungicides from those of the domestic market (Carman and Lichty 1986). A brushbed used for application of wax, fungicide, or both, can contaminate fruit being run over it long after the changeover has been made. Efficient cleaning of the brushbed can be obtained by the use of flick bars under the brushes (Fig. 12.5). These bars are on a sliding rack under the horsehair brushes of the applicator. Except when rinsing, they are in an inoperative position with the flick bars between the brushes.

To clean a brushbed or change wax formulations:

1. Rinse out the wax lines and nozzles thoroughly. There is no point in cleaning the brushbed and then flushing out the nozzles onto the brushes.

2. Move the flick bar to its noncontact position and start the brushes.

3. Engage the flick bars so each will contact its corresponding brush.

4. Hose down for at least a minute with the flick bars in place and the brushes revolving.

5. After rinsing, leave flick bars in place for 20 sec or more to remove excess water which would dilute the wax.

6. Reposition flick bars into the noncontact position.

Fungicide Application

It should be noted that fungicides applied on the packingline fall into two classes, depending on whether they are used on unwashed or washed fruit. Sodium o-phenylphenate, as prepared for use on fruit, is an excellent detergent which penetrates into minor wounds on the surface of the fruit. It is usually applied at the washer followed by a water rinse. Other fungicides are best applied (usually over a brushbed) after pre-grading and before drying. Some fungicides may be incorporated in fruit waxes, however, the efficacy may decrease (Brown 1980, Chapter 13). It is important that fungicide application equipment be regularly checked and well maintained to assure the best possible decay control. More detailed fungicide application information has been compiled by Wardowski and Brown (1993).

Drying

The surface moisture drying rate of fresh citrus is influenced by three factors: surface area, humidity ratio difference, and mass transfer coefficient of water into the airstream. Surface area is determined by fruit variety and packingline capacity. Humidity ratio differences are determined from psychrometric conditions of the heated air and surface water temperature, which will approach the wet-bulb temperature of the dryer air as evaporation occurs. After evaporation, peel temperatures will approach the heated air dry-bulb temperature. The mass transfer coefficient is affected by the air velocity and geometric considerations such as fruit sphericity, layers of fruit, and type of conveyor, slat or roller (Miller 1981). Maintaining a full conveyor is essential to eliminate airflow by-passing the fruit.

The dryer moisture load varies with type of fruit. Tangerines with concave ends and a high fruit surface area per box have the greatest unit moisture load. With 0.9 g water per fruit and 300 tangerines per Florida field box, evaporation load is 270 g water per Florida field box. In contrast, grapefruit at 1.8 g per fruit and 90 fruit per field box has a calculated load of 162 g per Florida field box.

In water wax applications, other chemicals are vaporized which have latent heats of vaporization different than that of water. Furthermore, water may be chemically bound or may require additional drying to overcome tackiness of the wax. Dryers, after wax treatments, should always be in two sections, a short initial section and a longer final section. This design largely confines excess wax accumulation on the equipment to the first short section. Waxed fruit should not roll continuously while drying. This is usually achieved by using either a slat conveyor or dead rollers which are only supported by the pin chain at the sides so that they do not turn. Contact points between multilayered fruit are difficult to dry, and the fruit requires periodic rotation to expose contact areas as they progress through the dryer. The combination of hot air and brushing ("polisher-dryers") can be a source of damage to tender fruit and is strongly discouraged. Care should be exercised in fruit handling so that there is no contact between fruit and heated metal surfaces.

Some general procedures that are followed in Florida packinghouses include the following: minimum drying time of 2.5 minutes and a maximum air temperature of 60 deg-C. In cases where modular fan-heater units are utilized, the first dryer section can be set at higher temperatures since the constant evaporation rate retards excessive temperature increase of the fruit (Miller 1981). The temperature of the hot air that can be used without damaging fruit depends on several factors. The first of these is obviously the frailty of the fruit. Tender specialty fruit, such as degreened Robinson tangerines, should be heated as little as possible and never brushed. In contrast, mid-season grapefruit seldom suffer damage during drying.

Air recycling is an important energy conservation feature in dryer design. In most cases, heated air is not saturated with water vapor after passing over the fruit. The air can be further utilized in a multipass dryer, in an air-to-air heat exchanger, or by proportionally mixing with ambient air for recycling. The latter is the most straightforward and requires the least capital investment. A major advantage in a heat exchanger is that only sensible heat is transferred to the inlet air stream and latent heat, associated with moisture, is exhausted. Such exhaust air should be expelled to reduce humidity buildup in the packinghouse. This arrangement has the added advantages of reducing heat and humidity for the benefit of nearby workers. Insulation of the dryers also will save energy and reduce noise levels.

The optimum proportion of recycled air is governed by reduced energy losses through recycling and a reduction in drying potential as dryer air becomes more saturated. The driving force (humidity ratio difference) can be established for the heated air by knowing two of the following properties: dry-bulb temperature, wet-bulb temperature, dew point, or relative humidity.

Infrared drying may have significant potential for initial drying but is energy intensive also. The entire fruit surface must be exposed to the infrared radiation for complete drying. Hence, natural rotation of fruit on rollers and multilayering of fruit make entire drying from an infrared source difficult. However, partial initial drying by infrared has been used on citrus and other crops.

Sizing

Most citrus packinghouses worldwide now have optical sizing units using either line or area scan cameras. Capacity of these units should be based on a maximum unit count for a crop of high packout. These units size fruit in cups or between rollers providing finer resolution and less abrasive injury to fruit than mechanical sizers. Operators are able to easily adjust the size categories to maximize the output of desired sizes and to switch between types of fruit such as grapefruit and oranges. Fruit count to an individual drop can be controlled for loose-fill carton filling. Also, electronic weight sizing has been implemented and can be used to control packed carton weight. With a combination of these features, removal of naturally internally dried and freeze-damaged fruit with lower density is possible (Miller *et al.* 1988; Wardowski and Grierson 1972).

For a belt-and-roll sizer, efficiency depends on the relationship between the fruit contact speeds of the belt and roller. For example, on widely used Florida belt and roll sizers, the belts move at 1.1 m/s and the 7.6 cm diameter rollers turn at 1.7 Hz, giving a roller surface speed of 0.4 m/s. This ratio of 2.8:1 must be maintained to size the many types and shapes of citrus fruit likely to be sized in one day.

Fruit Labeling

Stamping of fresh produce has been supplanted by adhesive labels. The major impetus for this change has been the Universal Product Code (UPC) label requirements imposed by large grocery chains. Detailed information is available on the coding designations (Produce Electronic Identification Board 1995) for citrus and other fresh produce items.

The labeling is now done after sizing as the price look up (PLU) codes are specific to small and large produce items of the same variety. Direct interfacing with electro-optical sizers has been employed but multiple banks of stamping heads are required for each label designation. If brand identifying labels are placed on the fruit, 3 banks of labeling heads would be required. With mechanical sizing, fruit is conveyed to a roller grommet section with labeling units overhead to facilitate the label application. Bar code systems may someday replace the current UPC identification.

Fruit Packing

Details of fruit packing methods are not dealt with here. However, in any new equipment being set up, provision should be made for ultimate mechanization; the trend is sharply away from individual place packing to mechanized packing with an operator running one or several machines. Automated place packing is common for California citrus (Johnson 1981). Such systems should always allow for maximum flow to every machine, which is not possible when packing machines are merely substituted for people in a traditional packinghouse layout (Grierson and Wardowski 1973).

One common practice which damages citrus fruit is overfilling cartons. When cartons are filled higher than the carton top, the fruit rather than the carton bears the weight of the stacked cartons. Loose-fill packing requires a larger carton than place packing. Operations using such mechanical volume-fill systems may fill cartons upside down. Then when opened from the top, the "pack" looks surprisingly uniform. Although citrus fruit are approximately spherical when packed, they occasionally arrive in the markets severely flattened due to overfilling. It is better to have cartons appear less than full than to have them contain damaged or highly deformed fruit. Volume filling can be done on a fruit count or weight basis. This method takes advantage of mechanization, but makes for a less tailored appearing pack. The ultimate consumers rarely, if ever, see cartons of citrus fruit as they are opened, so the advantages of place packing are only useful to impress people in the wholesale markets and the back rooms of grocery stores. Volume or weight filling, common in bagging operations, may increase for carton operations as the cost and availability of packing labor become more prohibitive.

Major buyers commonly request bags filled by weight (e.g., 5 lb, 8 lb, etc.). Because federal regulations require that every bag must be at or over the declared weight, this means "giving away" a certain amount of fruit. This loss increases with fruit size. One small orange added to a slightly underweight bag is not big loss. One large grapefruit needed for the same purpose can mean a loss of 10 or 15% of the fruit in that bag.

Palletizing

Cartons of packed fruit are palletized by stacking on wooden pallets, or on fiberboard slip sheets. The pallet can then be moved by lift trucks. Typically, the least reliable labor in a citrus packinghouse is the set-off crew who stack fruit cartons on pallets. The work is quite arduous and monotonous.

Mechanical palletizers are commonly used by most large citrus packinghouses. They are expensive and require even more expensive accumulation systems to group and align enough cartons of one variety, grade, size and type of package (e.g., bagged vs. loose) to load a pallet. Mechanical palletizers eliminate a set-off work force but require several other employees with specific training, namely the palletizer operator(s) and people to direct cartons to the proper lanes in the accumulation system. Some form of simple robot may accomplish the palletizing task in the future. Such robots would not require precision accuracy and should compete economically with mechanical palletizer accumulation systems. Standardization in package size is beneficial for palletization but a diverse range of carton types has evolved in recent years.

MINIMIZING FRUIT DAMAGE ON THE PACKINGHOUSE LINE

Damage to fruit on the packinghouse line can take several forms. One of these is inoculation with decay organisms. This is very common when water dumps or soak tanks are used, even when a fungicide is put into the water. This is because there are several decay organisms, such as anthracnose (*Colletotrichum*), sour rot (*Geotrichum*), and various resistant strains of mold (*Penicillium*) which are not controlled by approved fungicides. A particularly subtle type of damage occurs due to excessive polishing. Fruit that has been through a hot polisher-dryer may appear beautiful when packed, but the peel can become crisp and brown a few days later. Therefore, polisher-dryers are not recommended. The third, and probably most common, type of damage is mechanical injury such as cuts and abrasions. Citrus fruits are comparatively resistant to bruising, but are very susceptible to decay after being scratched or scraped enough to cause small, often invisible, breaks in the peel.

Mechanical damage to fruit most commonly occurs at the transfer point between pieces of equipment or at corners. The most common locations for damage are discussed below. Studies have been undertaken to quantify impact damage with Instrumented Sphere technology (Miller and Wagner 1991). Impact damage is more prevalent at transfer drops, mechanical sizers and pallet bin dumpers.

Brushing

Abrasive damage occurs to fruit due to excessive brush speeds and excessive brushing time, especially with washer brushes having very stiff bristles. Although a stiff bristle may be needed for thorough cleaning, the brushing time nor the rotational speed should not be extended. To control brushing time, a continuous wipeout or one activated by interruption in fruit flow should be installed. Brushing time can be significantly altered by dump rate, pre-sizing and pre-grading in some cases. Since these factors vary, some wipeout mechanism is critical to prohibit excessive brushing action. Another helpful practice is to condition new brushes at the beginning of the season when the fruit peel is tender, and especially when sensitive fruit such as tangerines are packed. A plywood sheet lightly touching wet rotating brushes for 1 to 2 hours is effective to condition new brushes. Also, the installation of new brushes may be delayed until a midseason break when the fruit peel is more mature and less susceptible to injury.

Damage from brushes can be minimized by pre-wetting the fruit so that dry fruit is never on dry brushes. With this in mind, it is not advisable to use polisher dryers (soft brushes in heated dryers). Brush rotational speeds over 2 Hz for washers and 1.8 Hz for fungicide and wax applicators should be reviewed carefully for benefit vs. damage to the fruit peel. Fruit with brush damage (tiny scratches in the cuticle and possibly the outer layer of cells) is more subject to damage from contact with caustic chemicals or excess heat and will dehydrate during marketing. Fruit with visual damage from brushes will normally show an injury several hours or days after the damage occurs and thus after it is on its way to market.

Dumping

Today most dumping is from pallet boxes that empty approximately 400 kg of oranges at once. Cushioning material and overhead deceleration curtains can reduce the high impact levels of the first fruit discharged. It is imperative that this large mass of fruit be leveled out as rapidly as possible, both to avoid squeezing and scraping of the fruit and to make it possible to remove trash. In-line dumpers have been introduced that discharge fruit after 150 deg bin rotation. Some form of anti-surge device after dumping, such as 2 belt sections running at different speeds, is recommended.

Deliveries from Roller and Slat Conveyors

All deliveries from roller conveyors should be equipped with ejector slats on the drive shafts (Fig. 12.7). The deliveries from slat conveyors should be equipped with spinner rolls (Fig. 12.8). Chutes (transfer plates) from roller and slat conveyors should be aligned as an extension of a radius from the head shaft (Figs. 12.7 and 12.8). The slight drop from the roller to the chute will not damage the fruit, but a chute with too little slope on which flat or irregularly shaped fruit will not advance and can be very damaging. A minimum angle of 20 deg is suggested but the coefficient of friction is dependent upon the material selected (Miller 1988) and may call for a somewhat steeper angle.

Points of Impact

One common point of impact is when fruit drop onto a belt. Drops of several inches can be allowed onto a belt if it is not supported underneath at the point of impact (Figs. 12.7 and 12.9). Where the belt is carried on rollers, the rollers are removed at the point of impact; where the belt is carried on a pan, the pan should be cut away under the impact area. Rollers rather than pans for supporting the belts are always recommended, as dragging the belts over a metal pan can increase the horsepower requirements by as much as 30%.

Another point of impact is where fruit is delivered at right angles onto a belt, as from a dumper. A second point of impact is the side of the machinery. Most forms of padding wear away rapidly or build up with wax which catches debris and becomes abrasive. A very satisfactory bumper can be fabricated from plastic hose attached with Tee-bolts such as are used for attaching slats in a slat conveyor (Fig. 12.9). The bumper hose should be continued along the conveyor until the point at which the fruit is no longer rolling. The bumper can then be discontinued, and the fruit will continue on the belt without scraping against the sides, materially reducing the wear and tear on both the fruit and the equipment.

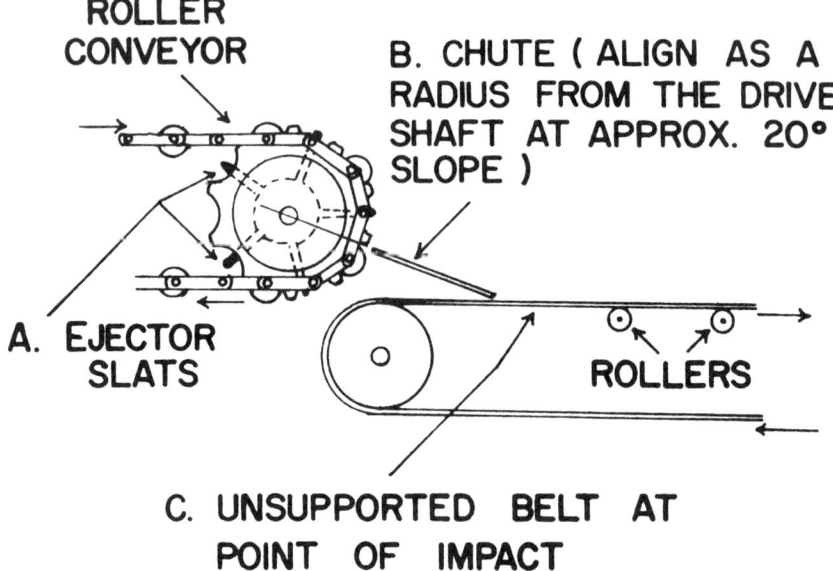

ROLLER
CONVEYOR

B. CHUTE (ALIGN AS A
RADIUS FROM THE DRIVE
SHAFT AT APPROX. 20°
SLOPE)

A. EJECTOR
SLATS

ROLLERS

C. UNSUPPORTED BELT AT
POINT OF IMPACT

Fig. 12.7. Delivery from roller conveyor to a belt. A. Ejector slats. B. Chute aligned as a radius of the head shaft. C. Delivery onto unsupported belt, where one roller having been removed.

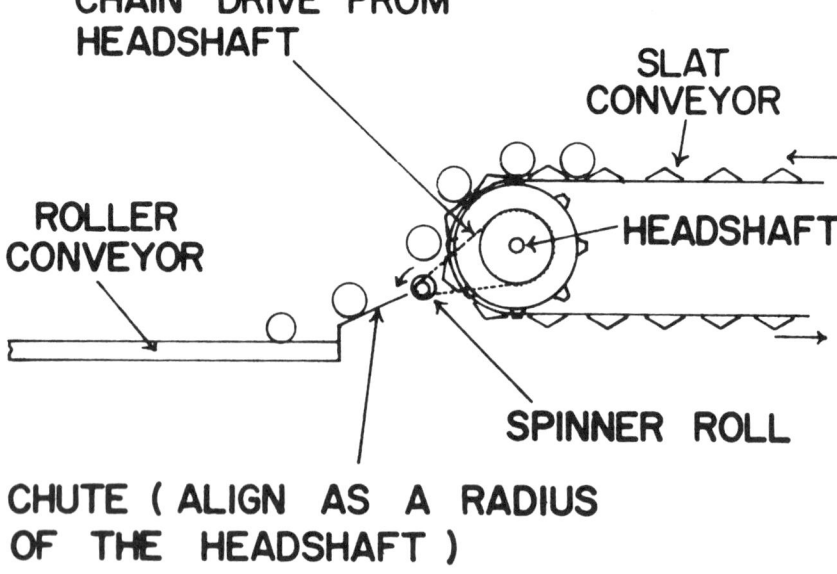

CHAIN DRIVE FROM
HEADSHAFT

SLAT
CONVEYOR

ROLLER
CONVEYOR

HEADSHAFT

SPINNER ROLL

CHUTE (ALIGN AS A RADIUS
OF THE HEADSHAFT)

Fig. 12.8. Spinner roll on a slat conveyor delivery.

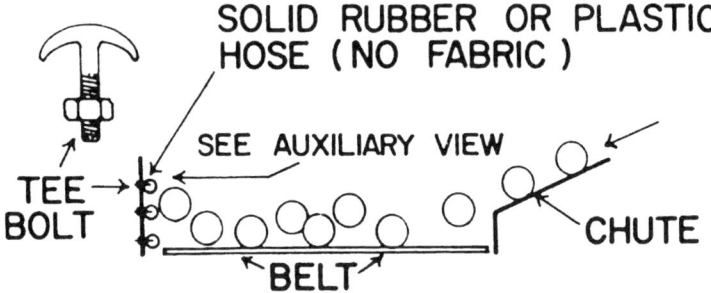

SOLID RUBBER OR PLASTIC
HOSE (NO FABRIC)

SEE AUXILIARY VIEW

TEE
BOLT

CHUTE

BELT

TEE-BOLTS INSERTED THROUGH SLITS IN HOSE NO
MORE THAN 15 cm ON CENTER WITH STAGGERED
PLACEMENT

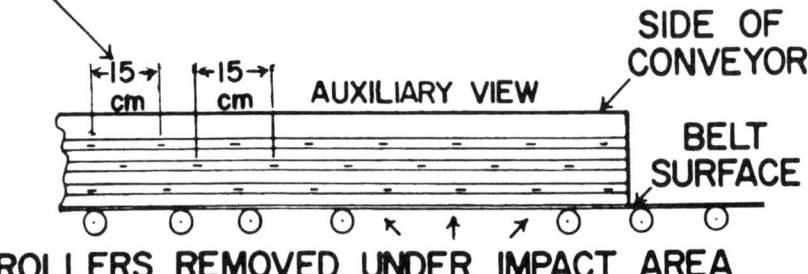

SIDE OF
CONVEYOR

15
cm
15
cm
AUXILIARY VIEW

BELT
SURFACE

ROLLERS REMOVED UNDER IMPACT AREA

Fig. 12.9. Solid rubber or plastic hose (no incorporated fabric) used as a bumper opposite a right-angle delivery.

Turns

More damage is done to fruit at turns of various kinds than anywhere else in a normal packinghouse. Most turns are at right angles and many involve delivery from one type of conveyor onto another. In general, over-the-end delivery from one conveyor to the other (Fig. 12.10) is preferable to the use of a shear (Fig. 12.11). When two belts intercept at right angles, the belt pulling the fruit out of the corner should be on the top (Fig. 12.12).

Where the fruit is to turn at right angles, a shear is most commonly used. Most fruit damage occurs at such turns, largely due to the common error of not cutting back the inside corner of the turn, thereby restricting the fruit flow and forcing it against what is usually a sharp edge at the inside corner (Fig. 12.11). It is preferable to keep the angle of a shear no more than 30 deg. However, there are many cases where this is not possible, particularly when shearing from a narrow belt onto a wider conveyor (Fig. 12.13). In such cases, rods should be used parallel to the shear and riding on the

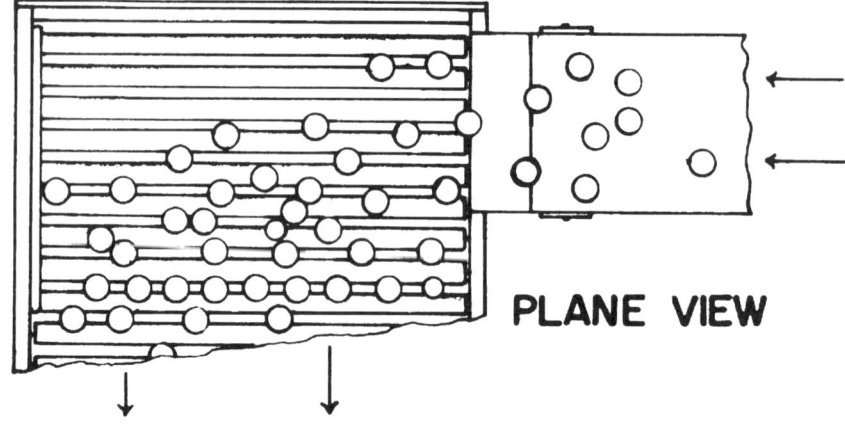

PLANE VIEW

X- SECTION

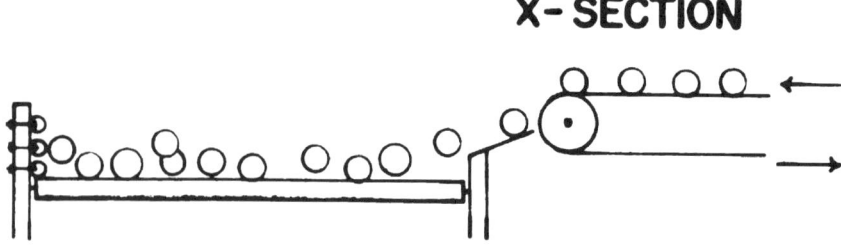

Fig. 12.10. Over-the-end delivery for a right-angle turn onto a belt, roller conveyor, or slat conveyor. This method is preferable to the use of a shear. Triangular delivery chute is necessary when delivering onto a slat conveyor but not essential for either a belt or roller conveyor.

delivery belt. In most instances, an 0.6 cm steel rod is adequate. Where several successive rods are used, they should increase in diameter. When fruit rapidly changes directions, as in bypass belts into and out of a color-add tank, the fruit flow can be aided, and damage minimized by sloping belts 5 deg in the direction of fruit exit.

The surface material of the shear contacting the fruit should be smooth and resist fruit wax accumulation. Metal shears should not be painted, and wooden shears are best covered with laminated plastic. At the beginning of the fruit line, where there may be twigs and leaves in the fruit stream, shears should be made self-cleaning by cutting out the downstream corner so twigs caught under the shear will be released (Fig. 12.14).

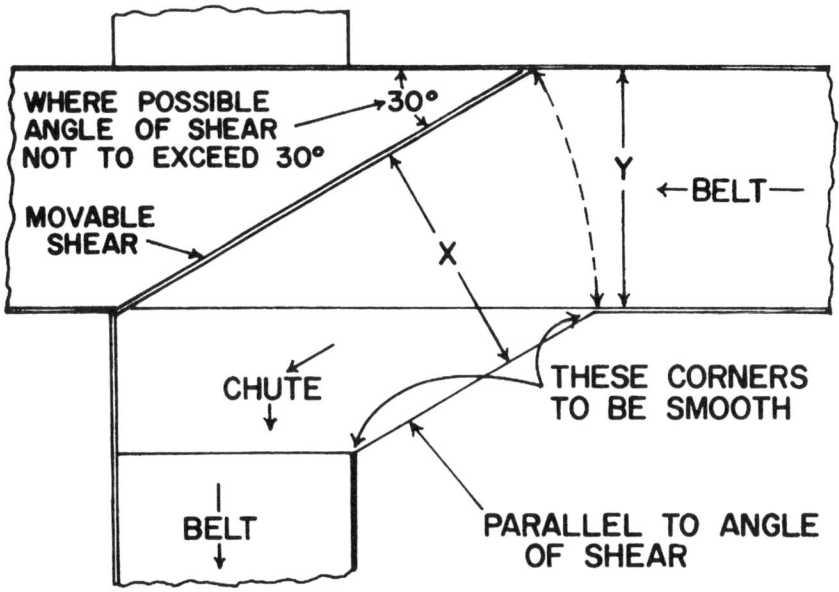

DISTANCE "X" TO BE NEVER LESS
THAN DISTANCE "Y"

Fig. 12.11. Cutting back the inside corner of a sheared turn thereby avoiding harmful constriction of the stream of fruit. A shear angle of 30 deg is optimum, but 40 deg can be used. A supporting plate that prevents the belt from sagging under the shear helps to minimize the change of fruit injury.

CALCULATING PACKINGLINE CAPACITY

The capacity of a given item of equipment or the size of equipment necessary to handle a given volume of fruit can be calculated. For this, it is necessary to know certain characteristics of both the fruit (Table 12.1) and of the equipment (Table 12.2). Note that all conveyor capacities in Table 12.2 are based on 100% utilization. Here 100% utilization is considered as the case where fruit is a single layer deep and at full capacity (i.e., no empty area). When these conditions do not exist, an efficiency factor should be incorporated into the capacity equations. In most instances, the actual utilization will be somewhat less than 100%, but will vary according to the machine and the matching of capacities for various machines. Maximum usage may be associated with either low or high packouts. For example, number of graders and belts for rejects should be based on low packout numbers. Packing stations and capacity of the fruit sizer should be based on anticipated high packout levels.

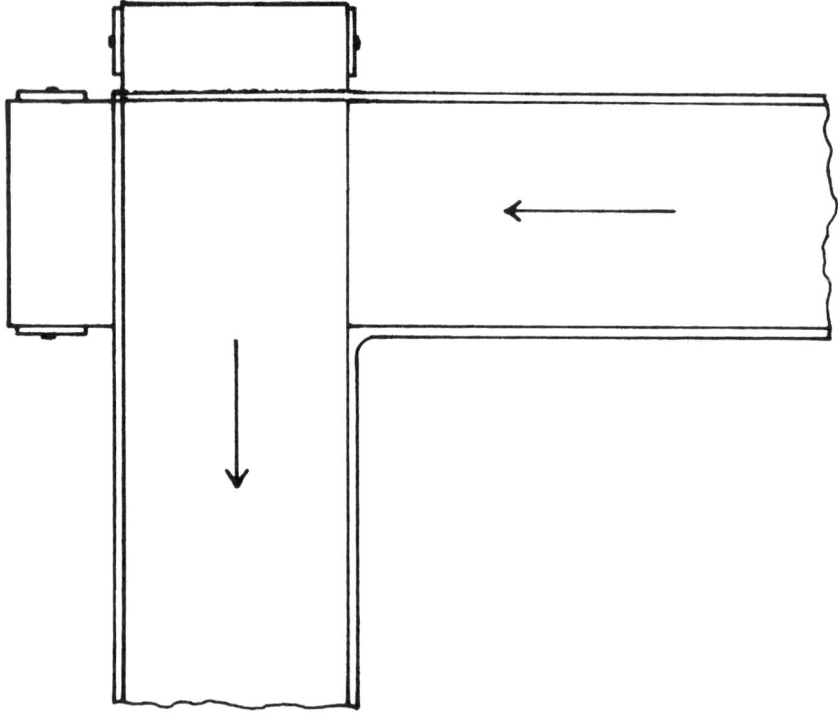

Fig. 12.12. When conveying fruit on two belts at the same elevation, the second (pull out) belt should be on top. Over-the-end delivery (Fig. 12.10) is preferred.

Fruit Characteristics

The capacity of a packinghouse line is governed by certain characteristics of the fruit, particularly fruit size, although weight and shape can also be limiting factors in certain circumstances. On belts, capacity is determined by the speed of the belt (Table 12.2) and by the area occupied by a box or other unit of fruit (Table 12.1). On slat and roller conveyors, capacity is determined by the number of linear feet when that same unit of fruit is lined up in a row. This ranges from 2.2 m for 10 kg of grapefruit to about 3.9 m for 10 kg of tangerines. Because of these factors, a belt that can carry 10 kg of grapefruit at a given speed can carry only 9.0 kg of oranges and less than 7.0 kg of tangerines. A slat or roller conveyor that can carry 10 kg of grapefruit can carry only 6.8 kg of oranges or 5.6 kg of tangerines.

It is in manual grading that the size of fruit becomes most critical. Not only is the fruit normally lined up in rows on rollers, which limits the capacity of a conveyor, but, more critically, each grader can make only a limited

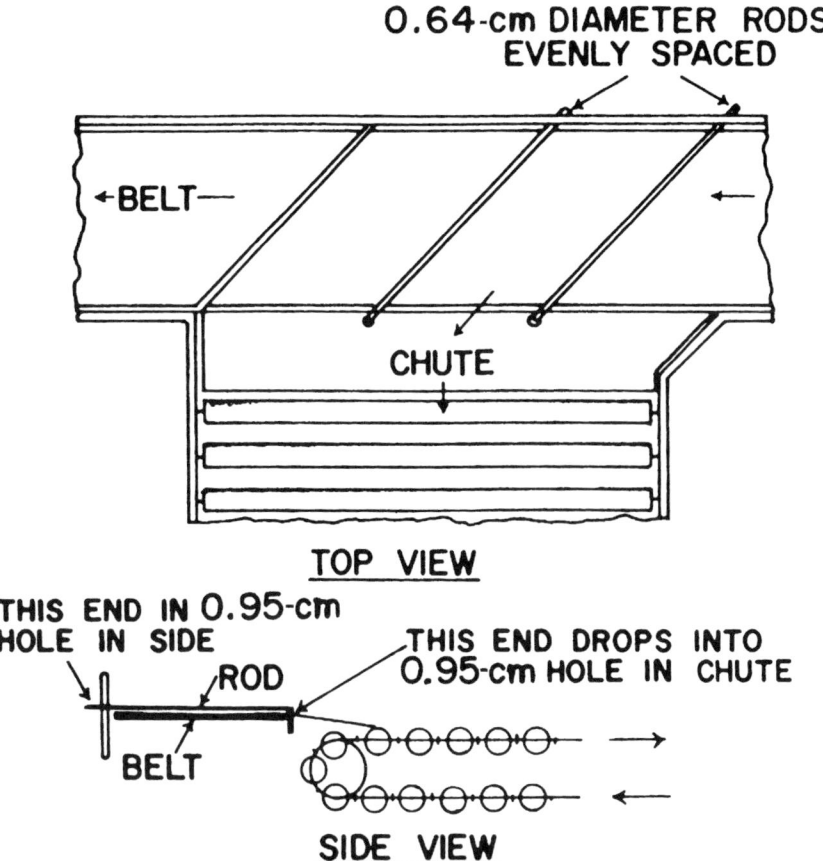

0.64-cm DIAMETER RODS EVENLY SPACED

←BELT—

CHUTE

TOP VIEW

THIS END IN 0.95-cm
HOLE IN SIDE

ROD

THIS END DROPS INTO
0.95-cm HOLE IN CHUTE

BELT

SIDE VIEW

Fig. 12.13. Use of diversion rods with a fixed shear. The rods are NOT fixed in place. They are inserted through holes in the chute and the side of the conveyor and ride on the surface of the belt.

number of decisions and motions per minute. There is also a human element, as has been noted previously, in that graders tend to throw out a given number of fruit per minute regardless of the condition of the fruit. Automatic grading is constrained by the number of fruit per unit time and proper distribution across grading lanes.

Equipment should never run at excessive speeds that cause damage to fruit through the packingline. However, lines are often operated above design capacity. In such situations the point at which damage first occurs when the line is speeded up or overcrowded becomes the limiting factor. This factor is compounded when handling varieties susceptible to mechanical injury such as tangerines or lemons which require greater conveying sur-

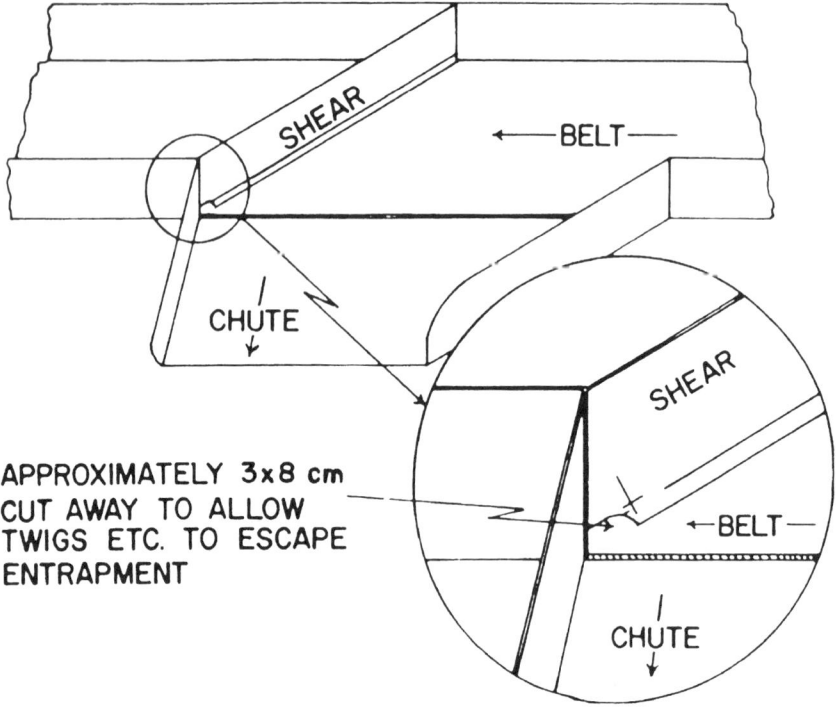

APPROXIMATELY 3x8 cm
CUT AWAY TO ALLOW
TWIGS ETC. TO ESCAPE
ENTRAPMENT

Fig. 12.14. Self-cleaning shear.

face area per box (Table 12.1). Electric, hydraulic or mechanical variable speed drives are available to change the linear speed of conveyors or the rotation speed of rollers or brushes.

Equipment Characteristics

Packinghouse machinery in the United States, and to a certain extent internationally, has standardized certain components. Such standardization is most helpful in equipment maintenance and in calculating equipment capacities. The amount of fruit per row will vary with the fruit characteristics and the width of the line, but once known, volume or weight of fruit per row or revolution of the machine can be computed.

Equipment characteristics of the machinery components most commonly used in Florida citrus packinghouses are compiled in Table 12.3. Deviation from such standard specifications, particularly in width of conveyor, can be expected to entail extra costs.

TABLE 12.1. Physical Characteristics of Citrus Fruit Relevant to Conveyor Design

Symbol[a]	Abbreviation	Characteristic	Grapefruit	Oranges	Tangerines
	lb/box	Pounds per Florida field box[b,c]	85[c]	90[c]	95[c]
	no./box	Average number of fruit per box	80	172	235
	U.S. Measures				
	in.	Average fruit diameter	4.1	3.0	2.8
a	ft²/box	Area (ft²) per field box[d]	7.9	9.1	11.3
	boxes/ft²	Field boxes per ft²	.126	.109	.088
	lb/ft²	Pounds (lb) per ft²	10.7	9.8	8.4
	no./ft²	Average number of fruit per ft²	10.1	18.7	20.7
1	ft/box	Linear feet per field box	27.3	43.0	54.8
	lb/ft	Pounds (lb) per linear foot	3.1	2.1	1.7
	Metric Measures				
	cm	Average fruit diameter	10.4	7.6	7.1
A	m²/10 kg	Area (m²) per 10 kilograms of fruit	.19	.21	.24
	kg/m²	Kilograms per m² of fruit	52.1	47.7	40.9
	no./m²	Average number of fruit per m²	108.7	201.2	222.7
L	m/10 kg	Linear meters per 10 kilograms of fruit	2.2	3.2	3.9
	kg/m	Kilograms per linear meter of fruit	4.6	3.1	2.6

[a]See Table 12.2.
[b]Florida field box = 4,800 in³ (approx. 2.23 U.S. bushels[x]).
[c]Florida legal measure.
[d]Assume nested pattern.
Note: Area per box and linear feet per box have been determined from statewide statistical analysis. Such figures may vary from theoretical values when fruit are not spherical, e.g., oblate for grapefruit, elliptical for lemons, etc.

TABLE 12.2. Formulas Involved in Conveyor Capacity

Value needed	Belt conveyor	Slat or roller conveyor[a]
U.S. measures[a]		
Capacity of a given conveyor (boxes[b]/hr)	$c = \dfrac{w \times s \times 60}{a}$	$c = \dfrac{60 \times rpm \times n \times w}{\ell}$
Necessary linear speed (ft/min for a given capacity)	$s = \dfrac{c \times a}{w \times 60}$	$s = \dfrac{c \times \ell \times r \times 2 \times \pi}{w \times n \times 60}$
Necessary drive shaft rpm for a given linear speed (ft/min)	$rpm = \dfrac{s}{\pi \times d}$	$rpm = \dfrac{s}{2 \times \pi \times r}$
Necessary rpm for a given capacity (boxes/hr)	$rpm = \dfrac{c \times a}{w \times \pi \times d \times 60}$	$rpm = \dfrac{c \times \ell}{60 \times n \times w}$
Metric measures[c]		
Capacity of a given conveyor (tonnes/hr)	$C = \dfrac{W \times S \times 6}{10 \times A}$	$C = \dfrac{RPM \times N \times W \times 6}{L \times 10}$
Necessary linear speed (m/min) for a given capacity	$S = \dfrac{10 \times A \times C}{6 \times W}$	$S = \dfrac{C \times L \times R \times 20 \times \pi}{W \times N \times 6}$
Necessary drive shaft rpm for a given linear speed (m/min)	$RPM = \dfrac{S}{\pi \times D}$	$RPM = \dfrac{S}{2 \times \pi \times R}$
Necessary rpm for a given (tonnes/hr)	$RPM = \dfrac{A \times C \times 10}{6 \times W \times \pi \times D}$	$RPM = \dfrac{C \times L \times 10}{6 \times W \times N}$

[a]U.S. measures: c = capacity (boxes/hr); w = width of conveyor (ft); s = linear speed (ft/min); a = area (sq.ft.) of a box spread 1 fruit deep; d = diameter of drum (ft); rpm = revolutions/min; n = number of fruit rows/sprocket revolution; ℓ = length of 1 box as a single row of fruit (ft); r = pitch radius, ft; π = 3.1416.

[b]A Florida box = 90 lbs oranges, 85 lbs grapefruit, or 95 lbs tangerines.

[c]Metric measures: tonne = 1,000 kg = 2,205 lbs.; C = capacity (tonnes/hr); W = width of conveyor in meters (m); S = linear speed (m/min); A = area (m²) of 10 kilograms (kg) of fruit; RPM = revolutions per minute; N = number of fruit rows/sprochet revolutions; L = length of 10 kg fruit in a single row; R = pitch radius, m; D = diameter of drum (m); π = 3.1416.

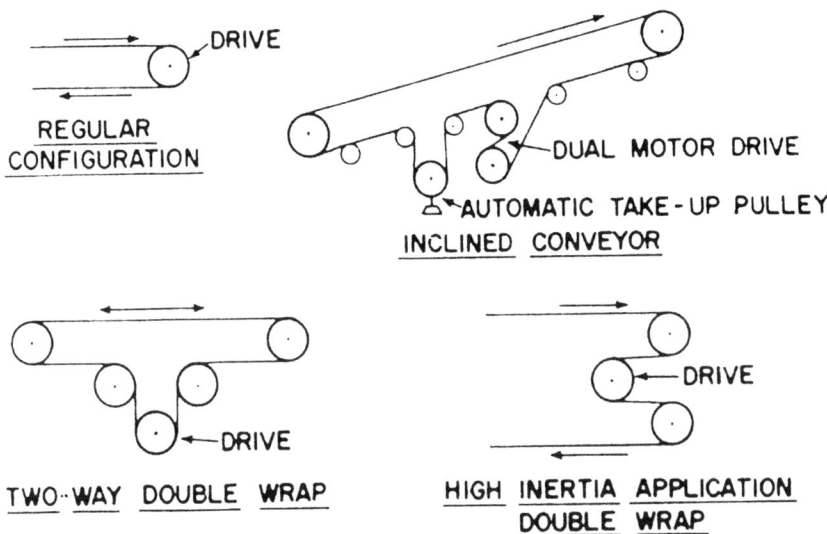

Fig. 12.15. Various belt drive configurations.

Standard Sizes and Components

Numerous sizes of belts, rollers, and slats are utilized throughout the citrus industry. Roller and slat conveyors are typically found in 15 cm width increments from 30 to 212 cm. Standard drum diameters for belt conveyors range from 15 to 45 cm. Normal belt widths are 35, 45 and 60 cm for small capacities with belts in 25 cm increments above 50 cm for larger fruit volumes. Typical belt drive configurations include single and multiple wraps (Fig. 12.15). Double-pitched roller chain is used for most roller and slat conveyor applications. Rollers are typically driven through D5 attachment pins. Chain size and number of sprocket teeth will depend upon design capacity of the system. With double pitch roller chain, sprockets with an odd number of teeth are preferred to reduce the wear factor by 0.5 as contact teeth alternate with each revolution. Sprockets for conveyor and elevator applications usually have the same diameter at both ends. Sprockets with more teeth will minimize wear and provide smoother operation. With this arrangement, only the carrying portion of the conveyor chain is under a high load. A list of typical components has been assembled in Table 12.3.

SAFETY CONSIDERATIONS

Safety is very important for the efficient operation of a packinghouse. Federal and state regulations frequently require certain safety precautions, such as guards on chains and bright paint, to highlight certain dangers. In

TABLE 12.3. U.S. Standard Equipment Dimensions

Belt Conveyors	Standard Sizes
Width (cm)	30.5, 35.6, 45.7, 61.0, 91.4, 121.9, 152.4
Drum diameter (cm)	15.2, 20.3, 25.4, 30.5, 35.6, 45.7
Roller and Slat Conveyors	
Width (cm)	30.5, 45.7, 61.0, 76.2, 91.4, 121.9, 152.4, 182.9, 213.4
Chain	RC2060 with D5 attachment (roller)
	RC2060 with A3 attachment (slat)
Rollers[a]	2 in. Aluminum tubing
	2 in. Sch. 40 steel pipe
	2 in Sch. 40 PVC pipe
Washers and Water Eliminators	
Brush length	(As required)
Brush diameter (cm)	15.2
Moisture eliminators (cm)	10.2 to 15.9 (various sizes)

[a]Pipe diameters are nominal. Sch. 40 2-inch-pipe is t.0 cm O.D.

the United States, the Occupational Safety and Health Administration regulates safety in the workplace. Insurance companies may require that safety be taught and practiced. Astute managers will encourage their employees to be safety conscious, keep their machinery and equipment in good repair and do everything possible to avoid accidents. An accident not only interrupts production, but also can be very expensive in terms of personal injury and workman's compensation settlements.

A safety checklist can be helpful to evaluate efforts to improve safety in the workplace. Such a list might include the following:

- Prepare a checklist of safety and ergonomic practices for your particular plant,

- Make sure that federal, state and local codes are followed,

- Assign one employee to be responsible for safety,

- Keep a record of accidents and work-related injuries,

- Inspect for tripping hazards,

- Properly mark areas of low overhead clearances and take precautionary measures,

- Inspect usefulness of guardrails and note absence of needed guardrails,

- Inspect for and eliminate sharp edges and burrs,

- Provide guards over all chains and rotating assemblies,

- Assure face and eye protection for bright flashes and sparks, e.g., welding equipment,

- Implement a safety awareness program and post hazard warnings where appropriate,

- Be sure that controls are readily accessible and that emergency "Stop" buttons are easily accessible, clearly marked and always painted red,

- Guard critical controls to prevent inadvertent operation,

- Train employees to respond to emergencies,

- Take precautions to avoid electric shocks,

- Provide lift trucks and other vehicles with governors or other speed controls. Where practical, mark "travel routes" for lift trucks with yellow highway paint,

- Reduce noise levels to meet standards and to prevent fatigue and interference with hearing,

- Provide adequate lighting, especially for critical locations such as grading,

- Protect workers from exposure to dryer heat, volatiles and chemical spills,

- Provide comfortable handles when lifting is required,

- Avoid unassisted lifting of heavy objects,

- Provide safe handling procedures for cleaners, fungicides and pesticides other potentially toxic substances,

- Design equipment to avoid fires and explosions,

- Pay close attention to all aspects of sanitation

- Continually train employees to work safely,

- Display prominently a notice board, "Days Since Accident Involving Time Off."

REFERENCES

AFFELDT, H. A., JR. and HECK, R. D. 1994. Illumination methods for automated produce inspection: design considerations. Appl. Eng. Agr. 10, 871-880.

BOWMAN, E. 1975. Efficiency in manually grading citrus fruit. Packinghouse Newsletter No. 73, University of Florida, AREC, Lake Alfred.

BROWN, G. E. 1980. Fruit handling and decay control techniques affecting quality, pp. 193-224. *In* Citrus Nutrition and Quality. ACS Symposium 143.

CARMAN, G. E. and LYCHTY, R. W. 1986. Pesticide Tolerances. *In* Fresh Citrus Fruits, W. F. Wardowski, S. Nagy, and W. Grierson (Editors). AVI Publishing Co., Inc., Westport, CT.

FDACS. Citrus packinghouses requirements for receiving fruit from citrus canker quarantine areas. Feb. 2000. http://doacs.state.fl.us/canker/packers.htm

FLORIDA DEPARTMENT OF CITRUS. 1975. Official rules affecting the Florida citrus industry, pursuant to chapter 601, Florida Statutes. Rule No. 20-32, Artificial coloring of fresh fruit.

GAFFNEY, J. J. 1973. Potentials for photoelectric grading equipment in the Florida citrus industry. Trans. 1973 Citrus Eng. Conf. XIX, Fla. Section, Amer. Soc. Mech. Engrs.

GRIERSON, W. 1971. Trash elimination. Packinghouse Newsletter No. 39. AREC-LA-71-41, University of Florida, Lake Alfred, FL.

GRIERSON, W. and WARDOWSKI, W. 1973. Development of mechanization programs for harvesting and packing citrus for the fresh fruit markets. Proc. Int. Soc. Citriculture (Spain) 111, 633-639.

GRIERSON, W. and WARDOWSKI, W. 1977. Packinghouse procedures relating to citrus processing, Chap. 2, pp. 128-140. *In* Citrus Processing, Science & Technology. Vol. 2. M. K. Veldhuis, S. Nagy, and P. E. Shaw (Editors). AVI Publishing Co., Inc., Westport, CT.

HALL, D. J. 1981. Innovation in citrus waxing. Proc. Fla. State Hort. Soc. 94, 258-263.

HEFT, M. E., JR. and WIANT, D. E. 1962. Lighting apple packing areas. Illuminating Engrs. 57 (6).

HUNTER, D. L., KAFER, F. and MEYER, C. H. 1958. Apple sorting: methods and equipment. Marketing Research Report No. 230. Agr. Marketing Service, Marketing Research Division, U.S. Dept. Agr.

JARRETT, L. D. and TUGWELL, B. L. 1975. Post-harvest handling of citrus fruit. Dept. of Agr. and Fisheries, South Australia, Sp. Bull. No. 11.75.

JOHNSON, M. 1981. Electronic sorting and automated packaging for fresh citrus fruit. Proc. Int. Soc. Citriculture 2, 826.

LONG, W. G. 1964. Better handling of Florida's fresh citrus fruit. Fla. Agr. Exp. Sta. Bull. 681.

MALCOLM, D. G. and DEGARMO, E. P. 1953. Visual inspection of products for surface characteristics in grading operations. Marketing Research Report No. 45, Production and Marketing Administration, U.S. Dept. Agr.

MILLER, W. M. 1981. Surface drying fresh citrus. University of Florida, Energy Information Fact Sheet EI-49.

MILLER, W. M. 1986. Mechanical dewatering techniques for fresh citrus. Energy Agr. 5, 225-238.

MILLER, W. M. 1988. Frictional properties in handling citrus. Proc. Fla. State Hort. Soc. 101, 182-184.

MILLER, W. M., PELEG, K. and BRIGGS, P. 1988. Automated density separation for freeze-damaged citrus. Appl. Eng. Agr. 4, 344-348.

MILLER, W. M. and WAGNER, C. J. 1991. Impact studies in Florida citrus packinghouses using an instrumented sphere. Proc. Fla. State Hort. Soc. 104, 125-127.

MILLER, W. M., WARDOWSKI, W. F. and GRIERSON, W. 2001. Packingline machinery for Florida citrus packinghouses. University of Florida, Coop. Ext. Serv. Bull. 239. http:// edis.ifas.ufl.edu/

OCCUPATIONAL SAFETY & HEALTH ADMIN. 1974. Occupational noise exposure. Federal Register 39 (125), 23596-23597.

PETRACEK, P. D., KELSEY, D. F. and DAVIS, C. 1998. Response of citrus fruit to high-pressure washing. J. Amer. Soc. Hort. Sci. 123 (4), 661-667.

PRODUCE ELECTRONIC IDENTIFICATION BOARD. 1995. To Coding Fresh Produce. Product Electronic Identification Board. 3rd Edition.

REJIMBAL, T. R., JR. and BIGLER, R. E. 1972. Cleaning efficiency of brush washers in citrus concentrate plants. Proc. Fla. State Hort. Soc. 85, 254-257.

TATE, D. A. and MULLINAUX, B. A. 1999. Method and apparatus for washing fruit. United States Patent Number 5,918,610. July 6, 1999.

WARDOWSKI, W. F. 1997. Packinghouse newsletter. Fla. Coop. Ext. Serv. No. 180.

WARDOWSKI, W. F. and BROWN, G. E. 1993. Postharvest decay control recommendations for Florida citrus fruit. Fla. Coop. Ext. Serv. Circ 359-A.

WARDOWSKI, W. F. and GRIERSON, W. 1972. Separation and grading of freeze damaged citrus fruits. Fla. Coop. Ext. Serv. Circ. 372.

13

The Biology and Control
of Postharvest Diseases

Joseph L. Smilanick, G. Eldon Brown, and Joseph W. Eckert

This chapter addresses the biology of pathogens that cause postharvest diseases of citrus fruit, with an emphasis on those typically encountered in the United States and the measures employed to manage them. Illustrations and descriptions of the symptoms and signs of citrus postharvest diseases exist in other publications (Amat 1988; Fawcett 1936; Klotz 1973; Smoot *et al.* 1971A; Snowdon 1990). Eckert and Eaks (1989) wrote a comprehensive review of the subject of citrus postharvest pathology and physiological disorders. Schirra (1999) assembled a collection of reviews on postharvest pathology and physiology of citrus fruit. Typical commercial postharvest practices employed to handle fresh citrus fruit have been described (Brown and Miller 1999; Kader and Arpaia 2002).

INTRODUCTION

Citrus fruits are produced mainly in subtropical areas, which may be up to several thousand miles from the major markets in temperate regions. Some may mature when consumer demand is weak or when markets are glutted, necessitating storage of the fruit until better marketing periods. Both circumstances may result in a lapse of one week to several months between the harvest and consumption of the fruit. It is under these circumstances that postharvest disease losses become significant. All of the important pathogens are fungi, which destroy a substantial portion of the fruit during this period and would cause unacceptable losses unless measures to control them are employed.

The actual loss of citrus fruits due to postharvest diseases is quite variable and depends upon the area of production, citrus variety, tree age and condition, weather conditions during the growing and harvest season, the extent of physical injury to the fruit during harvest and subsequent handling, the

339

effectiveness of fungicide treatments, and postharvest environment. In a summary of 12 years of inspections of commercial shipments of California and Florida citrus fruit in the New York produce market, penicillium decays, sour rot, and stem-end rot were present in 30, 9, and 5%, respectively, of the inspected shipments (Ceponis *et al.* 1986). In 2001, green mold had destroyed a total of 4.1% of the lemons among more than 6000 fruit examined in three inspections within a California lemon packinghouse (EcoScience Corp., personal communication). In a survey of eight lemon packinghouses, Coggins and coworkers (1992) reported sour rot was present among 2.3% of the fruit emerging from storage. In an earlier study, the total percentage of fruit lost to decay during both storage and subsequent marketing was about 8% in three California lemon packinghouses (Bancroft *et al.* 1984). The fruit examined were from commercial packinghouses that employed sanitation measures, fungicides, and temperature management regimes to minimize decay; losses among fruit handled without these measures can be much higher. For example, in Florida, among samples of several cultivars of untreated oranges, collected over a 5-year period, stem-end rot occurred in 13 to 42% of the fruit after storage at 21°C for three weeks (Table 13.1). Incidence among the early orange cultivars, Hamlin and navel, that were degreened with ethylene gas was particularly high; after storage for 3 weeks, 42 and 36% had stem-end rot, respectively (Table 13.1). In California in 2001, among five collections of untreated navel oranges from different groves, an average of 14% developed penicillium decay after they had been degreened with ethylene gas for several days at 20°C (Sunkist Growers, personal communication). Among smaller growers, especially organic growers and some of those in underdeveloped countries, where efficient transport, refrigeration, and chemical treatments are generally less available, losses are typically so high as to make sales to distant markets infeasible.

The relative importance of different postharvest diseases is influenced by the climate of the production area. Florida is a typical summer-rainfall production area, where stem end rot incidence is typically high. Fruit produced in areas characterized by low summer rainfall typically show a much lower incidence of decay after harvest. Penicillium diseases (green and blue molds) are responsible for major postharvest losses in citrus fruits shipped from California and other areas with a dry summer climate.

The percentage of fruit destroyed by postharvest diseases is only one measure of their economic impact. The unsightly appearance of rotten fruit within shipments, although the incidence may be comparatively low, repels wholesale buyers who may as a consequence abandon the affected producer and seek other sources. In addition to the losses of individual fruit, propagules produced from lesions on decaying fruit soil and contaminate the surrounding environment and adjacent fruit, initiating new cycles of decay and necessitating the cleaning and repackaging of the remaining healthy fruit. If the losses

TABLE 13.1. Decay of Freshly Harvested Florida Citrus Fruits Held at 21°C, 1971-1976, Orlando, Florida

Cultivar	Harvest season	No. of experiments	Percentage of fruit decayed[a]					
			After 2 weeks			After 3 weeks		
			S	P	M	S	P	M
Oranges								
Hamlin[b]	Oct.-Dec.	32	27	2	1	42	3	1
Hamlin	Dec.-Jan.	20	8	2	T	20	3	1
Navel[b]	Oct.-Dec.	14	13	1	1	36	2	1
Pineapple	Dec.-Feb.	14	16	4	T	31	6	1
Valencia	Feb.-May	17	6	2	1	13	2	1
Mandarins								
Dancy tangerine[b]	Nov.-Dec.	11	10	3	6	—	—	—
Dancy tangerine	Dec.	4	1	3	2	—	—	—
Temple[b]	Dec.	5	16	5	3	26	7	6
Temple	Jan.-Feb.	12	1	6	2	5	8	2
Robinson[b]	Sep.-Oct.	8	33	6	11	—	—	—
Robinson	Nov.	3	1	1	2	—	—	—
Grapefruit	Oct.-May	19	1	T	1	3	1	2

Source: Smoot (1977).
[a]S = stem-end rot; P = penicillium mold; M = miscellaneous decay; T = less then 0.5% incidence.
[b]Degreened with 5 ppm ethylene at 30°C and 90% relative humidity.

occur after shipment and far from the producer, the producer is usually billed for the added handling costs, which can exceed his returns. Expenses that begin at harvest typically surpass those to produce the fruit. For example, between 51 and 67% of the total cost of growing, harvesting, packing, marketing, and shipping California oranges and lemons occurred after the fruit were harvested (Eckert and Eaks 1989). Therefore, the loss of one fruit after harvest is more than twice as costly than the loss of one fruit before harvest.

DEVELOPMENT OF POSTHARVEST DISEASES

Certain postharvest diseases of citrus fruits are initiated by infection of the fruit during the growing season, whereas other diseases originate in injuries that are created during harvest and subsequent handling of the fruit.

Preharvest Fruit Infection

STEM-END ROTS. The stem-end rots of citrus fruit are diplodia stem-end rot, caused by *Lasiodiplodia theobromae* (*Botryosphaeria rhodina*) [(syn. *Diplodia natalensis* (*Physalospora rhodina*)], and phomopsis stem-end rot, caused by *Phomopsis citri* (*Diaporthe citri*). They are the principal postharvest diseases of citrus fruits produced in areas with a substantial rainfall during development of the immature fruit. These diseases are rare in production areas with a Mediterranean-type climate, characterized by peak rainfall during the winter and early spring, followed by a dry growing season. In summer-rainfall production areas such as the Gulf states of the United States, the West Indies, and southeastern Asia, spores of *L. theobromae* and *P. citri* are produced in pycnidia that develop on dead wood in the tree. The spores are splashed by rain onto developing fruits where they initiate an incipient infection in the button (calyx + disc) of the fruit (Brown and McCornack 1972). *L. theobromae* and *P. citri* do not aggressively attack the button during the period of fruit growth, but rather these fungi remain quiescent or develop saprophytically on necrotic tissue on the disc and the inner surface of the calyx. After harvest, the button undergoes senescence and begins to separate from the fruit. Fungi that had been quiescent in the button during the growing season resume active growth and enter the fruit proper through the abscission zone (Brown and Wilson 1968). The fungi then invade the central axis of the fruit and tissues of the peel, giving rise to a typical stem-end rot (Plates 1, 2).

Although *L. theobromae* and *P. citri* are present together in the calyx of the fruit at the time of harvest, the incidence of each disease is more or less seasonal. Diplodia stem-end rot (Plate 1) is most common early in the harvest season, whereas phomopsis stem-end rot (Plate 2) does not make its appearance until the late fall, winter, or spring months. Diplodia stem-end rot is prominent early in the harvest season because it develops faster than phomopsis stem-end at the higher ambient temperatures that prevail at that time of the year. Furthermore, the development of diplodia stem-end rot is enhanced by the ethylene degreening treatment used to remove green color from the peel of early-season fruit (Brooks 1944; McCornack 1972A, B; Porat *et al.* 1999). The recommended temperature for this operation is 28-29°C in Florida and 21-22°C in California, reflecting the physiological difference in fruit grown under different climatic conditions. Ethylene stimulates the growth of *L. theobromae* (Brown and Lee 1993), and increases polygalacturonase and cellulase activity in the fruit that hastens abscission of the stem-end button, a condition that increases stem end rot (Brown and Burns 1998). Ethylene treatment increases diplodia stem-end rot and decreases penicillium decay of early varieties (Tables 13.2 and 13.3). The elevated temperatures employed during degreening in Florida inhibit penicillium infection compared to the cooler temperatures used in California during degreening. As the harvest season progresses, however, the ambient temperatures decline and ethylene degreening is discontinued because the peel develops sufficient color naturally. The lower temperature and absence of ethylene are more favorable to the development of *P. citri*, so phomopsis

TABLE 13.2. Effect of Ethylene on Anthracnose, Stem-end Rot, and Green Mold of Citrus Fruits

Ethylene (µL/L air)	Percentage of infected fruit		
	Anthracnose[a]	Stem-end rot[b]	Green mold[b]
0	0	0	6
5	—	13	3
10	17	—	—
20	57	—	—
50	86	23	2

[a]From Brown and Barmore (1977). Robinson tangerines exposed to ethylene for 2 days and then stored for 1 week at 26°C and 100% relative humidity.
[b]From McCornack (1972B). Stem-end rot incited mostly by *Lasiodiplodia natalensis,* Valencia oranges exposed to ethylene for 2 days and then stored at 21°C for 4 weeks.

stem-end rot becomes the principal stem-end rot during this period (Smoot *et al.* 1971A).

Alternaria citri causes alternaria black rot and stem-end rot (Plate 3) that can be found most often in areas of low summer rainfall. The taxonomy of *Alternaria* pathogens on citrus is incompletely known (Peever *et al.* 2002; Simmons 1999), and it is likely *A. citri* will be renamed (Timmer *et al.* 2003). Other *Alternaria* spp., some identified as *A. citri,* cause brown spot, a preharvest disease found in Florida on mandarin oranges, but they differ from the postharvest isolates. Stem-end rot begins as the pathogen invades through the stem end of the fruit and grows into the peel and juice sacs in a manner similar to that observed with diplodia and phomopsis stem-end rots (Bartholomew 1926; Brown and McCornack 1972; Isshiki *et al.* 2003; Joly 1967; Schiffmann-Nadel *et al.* 1981). However, there are important differences in the etiology of these diseases that influence their occurrence in harvested fruit. Since infection by *A. citri* spores is not dependent upon rainfall during the growing season, this disease is an important postharvest problem of cit-

TABLE 13.3. Influence of Temperature and Relative Humidity (RH) on the Development of *Penicillium digitatum* in Oranges during Degreening and Subsequent Storage[a]

Degreening temperature (°C)	Percentage of infected fruit	
	55-75% RH	90-96% RH
27	71	89
30	93	63
33	97	21

[a]From Brown (1973). Fruit were degreened at each temperature and RH for 3 days, then the number of infected fruit recorded after 4 days additional storage at 20°C at 100% relative humidity.

rus fruits in all areas of production. *A. citri* grows saprophytically on dead plant materials in the citrus grove and the spores are transported by air currents, rather than by rain, to the flower or the developing fruit. The calyx cup is an effective receptacle for collecting airborne spores, which then become trapped under the sepals as the fruit enlarges. On navel oranges, *A. citri* may develop also as a saprophyte on the necrotic style of the flower and, thereby, gain entrance to the stylar end of the fruit. *Alternaria*, like the other stem-end pathogens, remains quiescent in the button and stylar end of the fruit until after harvest. Removal of the calyx at harvest by snap picking, which reduces diplodia stem-end rot, does not reduce alternaria incidence because it invades both the calyx and underlying tissue (Bartholomew 1926; Isshiki *et al.* 2003; Pelser 1977). The disease can be a serious market problem because, unlike the other stem-end rots, the fungus may grow abundantly in the central axis of the fruit without any external symptoms that would be obvious to the buyer. *Alternaria* is a less aggressive pathogen than either *L. theobromae* and *P. citri* and, therefore, causes a stem-end rot or stylar-end rot only in over-mature oranges or mandarins and on fruits that have been stored for long periods of time (Smoot *et al.* 1971A).

Alternaria black rot is a significant disease in California particularly among lemons, where stem-end infections develop, and occasionally among navel oranges, when cracks on the blossom end of mature fruit become infected. Diplodia and phomopsis stem-end rots are rare in California because of the scant precipitation during the growing season (Bartholomew 1926; Harvey 1946). Frost injury in the grove predisposes grapefruit to alternaria stem-end rot during storage (Schiffmann-Nadel *et al.* 1975B). The disease also is a major problem in the long-term storage (10 to 12 weeks) of Valencia oranges at 1°C in Florida because the low temperature and fungicide treatments suppress *L. theobromae* and *P. citri* to a much greater extent than alternaria black rot (Brown and McCornack 1972; Smoot 1969). Alternaria black rot may be accentuated by low-temperature storage of cultivars that are sensitive to chilling. Israeli workers reported that stem-end rots in grapefruit incited by *Alternaria*, *Phomopsis*, and *Fusarium* were more severe at 6° to 8°C than at 10° to 12°C (Schiffmann-Nadel 1969B; Schiffmann-Nadel *et al.* 1971). Greater growth of the pathogen at the higher temperature was a less important factor in disease development than the loss of host resistance (incipient chilling injury) at the lower temperature.

Anthracnose. Caused by *Colletotrichum gloeosporioides*, anthracnose (Plate 4) is a major decay of the Robinson cultivar of tangerine and certain other tangerine hybrids in Florida that are harvested early in the fall when long periods of ethylene degreening are required to give the fruit an attractive appearance (Smoot and Melvin 1967; Smoot 1977). In other citrus producing areas, anthracnose develops on rind injuries on mature fruit, irrespective of ethylene treatment (Timmer and Brown 2000). Anthracnose is a minor problem on oranges, grapefruit, and lemons, appearing only on fruits that have been harvested late in the season or cold-stored for long periods.

In summer-rainfall areas, spores of *C. gloeosporioides* are produced abundantly on dead plant parts and are dispersed by rain and wind to the developing fruits. The spores germinate on the fruit surface, giving rise to appressoria. As the season progresses and the fruit begin to mature, some of the appressoria germinate and send out infection hyphae that penetrate a short distance into the peel (Adam *et al.* 1949). However, most of the appressoria remain in an ungerminated state on the surface of the fruit (Brown 1975). Ethylene treatment causes a loss of chlorophyll and an increase in carotenoids in the fruit, and accelerates senescence of the peel, making it more susceptible to invasion by the infection hyphae of the pathogen (Brown 1975, 1977B, 1978; Brown and Barmore 1977; Table 13.2). Ethylene stimulates germination of conidia and the formation of appressoria, and can stimulate germination of appressoria, even in the absence of the fruit (Brown 1992). When the appressoria were removed from the surface of the green fruit before treatment with ethylene, the ethylene-treated fruit became orange and simultaneously developed resistance to invasion by *Colletotrichum* spores subsequently placed on the fruit surface. Brown (1978) has shown that penetration of an epidermal cell of an orange-colored fruit by an appressorial infection hypha caused the death of four layers of cells surrounding the infection hyphae. The necrotic cells formed a barrier to the hyphae, localizing the pathogen in the immediate area penetrated by the infection hyphae.

Brown Rot. Caused by several *Phytophthora* spp., brown rot (Plate 5) of citrus fruit usually develops from infections that take place in the grove prior to harvest. Motile spores of *Phytophthora* that develop on the surface of the moist soil or fallen infected fruit are splashed by rain onto fruit hanging on the lower skirt of the tree. Epidemics are associated with repeated rain events over a period of days, or wet foggy weather with temperatures from 18° to 25°C, although conducive temperatures for some Florida isolates were 23° to 30°C (Zitko *et al.* 1991). Most of the infected fruit develop on the tree within 1 m of the soil surface, although fruit higher in the tree may be infected as a result of wind-driven rains or in groves with a heavy cover crop (Fawcett 1936; Graham *et al.* 1998). The zoospores of *Phytophthora* may infect a fruit on its surface at any point; hence, this decay is not necessarily associated with the stem or stylar end of fruit. The susceptibility of the fruit increases with maturity, so the greatest incidence of infection occurs just before or during the harvest period.

Fruit infected with phytophthora brown rot have a characteristic pungent rancid odor, which immediately distinguishes this disease from fruit afflicted with the stem-end rots. The most serious aspect of phytophthora brown rot is that fruit infected before harvest may be inspected and graded before symptoms of the disease are visible. Infected fruit therefore become mixed with sound fruit in storage or in packages shipped to market (Klotz and DeWolfe 1961B). Tan spots become visible on the fruit after 3 days incubation at 25°C or after 10 days at 10°C. Under optimum conditions for decay development the entire fruit becomes tan to brown in about 7 days, but the hyphae of the fungus may not be visible on the surface of the fruit. A delicate white growth of mycelium does form on the surface of fruit stored under very high humidity conditions. Furthermore, the disease may spread from fruit to fruit under the normal conditions of lemon storage (Klotz and DeWolfe 1961B). Fruit infected with *Phytophthora* are readily colonized by the wound pathogens *Penicillium* and *Geotrichum*, which may transform the firm brown rot into a soft watery rot.

Many species of *Phytopthora* have been associated with brown rot, and although the symptoms caused by all are indistinguishable, their etiology varies (Graham *et al.* 1998). In California, *P. citrophthora* and *P. parasitica* probably account for 90% of the brown rot infections in California (Feld *et al.* 1979). In Florida, the restricted occurrence of severe brown rot on fruit was attributed to the limited distribution of *P. citrophthora* in these areas (Whiteside 1970). In both areas, *P. parasitica* is the major cause of phytophthora disease of the roots and trunks of the tree, but this species is less pathogenic to fruit than *P. citrophthora*. However, epidemics in 1994 to 1997 in Florida, which were associated with repeated rainfall events, were caused by *P. palmivora* and *P. nicotianae* (Graham *et al.* 1998). *P. nicotianae* was common in soil and confined to the lowest one meter of the canopy. In contrast, *P. palmivora* typically infected fruit above one meter in the canopy. It was found primarily found on fallen immature fruit and its populations in soil were smaller than those of *P. nicotianae*.

Postharvest Fruit Infection

Green (Plate 6) and blue mold (Plate 7), caused by *Penicillium digitatum* and *P. italicum*, respectively, and sour rot, caused by *Geotrichum candidum*, are usually initiated at wounds inflicted during harvesting and handling the fruit. These pathogens may invade fruit before harvest through injuries such as cracks or thorn wounds, or those made by insects such as fruit flies, fruit-piercing moths, and orange worms (Roth 1967; Huang 1990). Immature fruit that are inoculated long before harvest often drop from the trees, whereas inoculations made only 2 to 3 days before harvest often result in incipient infections that are not detectable at the time of harvest. These infections also are very difficult to eradicate by postharvest treatments.

Green and Blue Molds. Green mold, caused by *Penicillium digitatum*, is the most important postharvest decay of citrus fruits produced in areas with scant summer rainfall. Blue mold, caused by *Penicillium italicum*, is usually of lesser over-all importance, but may become the major problem under conditions that selectively suppress the development of green mold, such as storage below 10°C. Penicillium molds are important also in humid climates but tend to be overshadowed by the high incidence of diplodia and phomopsis stem-end rots in these areas (Table 13.1). A third pathogen, *Penicillium ulaiense,* causes whisker mold (Holmes *et al.* 1994). Although encountered frequently on fruit within packinghouses, its economic importance is very modest because whisker mold develops very slowly compared to green and blue molds and often occurs as a mixed infection within lesions caused by other pathogens.

Spores of *P. digitatum* and *P. italicum* that are formed on fruit rotting on the ground in the grove or in the packinghouse are transported by air currents to sound fruit. The spores do not germinate on the surface of fruit until the peel is injured; free water and nutrients are required for spore germination (Green 1932; Kavanagh and Wood 1971; Pelser and Eckert 1977). Spores situated in injuries that penetrate to the albedo layer of the peel usually bring about irreversible infection within 48 hr at 20° to 25°C (Smoot and Melvin 1961). Fruit held for 3 days after inoculation with spores of *P. digitatum* at room temperature will show areas around injuries on the rind that appear water-soaked, termed "blister rot" or "clear rot". The fungus invades most of the peel of the fruit in an additional 7 days and sporulates, resulting in the typical symptoms of green mold. The disease develops much more slowly below 10°C, and the rot usually does not develop beyond the blister stage if the fruit are stored at 1°C. An important problem associated with the occurrence of green and blue mold in loose-fill cartons or boxes is a condition termed soilage, caused by spores from a diseased fruit dispersing onto adjacent fruit in the same container. These spores may infect surface-contaminated fruit, but the immediate problem is the unacceptable appearance of soiled fruit. Green mold usually does not spread from fruit to fruit during storage, in contrast to blue mold. Fruit degreened with ethylene after harvest, particularly if degreened at 20°C and not protected by a prior fungicide application, typically have a high incidence green mold primarily because of this delay at temperatures conducive to decay development. Unlike stem-end rot, ethylene treatment alone has little direct impact on green mold incidence (Porat *et al.* 1999), although it has numerous physiological effects, such as a reduction in citral content in the peel of lemons (Ben-Yehoshua *et al.* 1995), increases in compounds associated with off-flavors with Shamouti oranges, such as acetaldehyde, ethanol, and ethyl acetate, and it markedly increased the susceptibility of the same fruit to chilling injury (Porat *et al.* 1999). Removal of ethylene from the storage atmosphere markedly reduced the incidence of decay among lemons (Wild *et al.* 1976) and penicillium decay of Valencia oranges (McGlasson and Eaks 1972), presumably because senescence of the fruit was delayed.

Blue mold is initiated in the same manner as green mold. Lesions of *P. italicum* grow more slowly than *P. digitatum,* but under cold conditions

(4°C), lesions caused by *P. italicum* were visible 16 days after the inoculation of Valencia oranges, while those of *P. digitatum* did not appear until 23 days had elapsed (Plaza *et al.* 2003A; Plaza *et al.* 2004). Therefore, blue mold is often more prevalent among fruit stored below 10°C, while green mold can overgrow blue mold in a mixed infection on fruit at warmer temperatures and is typically more common. Blue mold, in contrast to green mold, can spread by contact from fruit to fruit, resulting in pockets of decay involving several diseased fruit (Barmore and Brown 1982). Certain fungicide treatments such as borax and thiabendazole suppress the development of green mold more than blue mold and increase its prevalence (Gutter 1975).

Sour Rot. This disease (Plate 8) is second in importance only to penicillium decay as a wound-initiated disease of citrus fruits. The causal fungus, *Geotrichum candidum*, is widely distributed in citrus grove soils (Eckert 1959; Butler *et al.* 1965); therefore, fruit on the lower part of trees are most likely to be contaminated with this fungus. Virulent isolates are associated with citrus, while those from other sources are not virulent to citrus fruit (Butler *et al.* 1965; Hershenhorn *et al.* 1989), and some authors use *Geotrichum citri-aurantii* for those that attack citrus fruit rather than *G. candidum.* Brown (1979) observed that a larger amount of inoculum of *G. candidum* was associated with scarred fruit than with smooth fruit, reflecting the accumulation of soil particles on the former. *G. candidum* invades the peel of the fruit through injuries made by insects or by mechanical damage to the fruit during harvest (Roth 1967; Huang 1990). It does not readily infect through shallow injuries, especially on immature fruit. Postharvest gibberellic acid applications, that delay peel aging, reduce sour rot incidence (Coggins *et al.* 1992). Arthrospores of *G. candidum* will only germinate when water activity is high, unlike the more tolerant *P. digitatum* and *P. italicum* (Plaza *et al.* 2003A). Even with ripe fruit, the fungus may not develop an active decay lesion unless the peel has a relatively high water content and the inoculated fruit are held in a water-saturated atmosphere (Baudoin and Eckert 1982, 1985A, B), or if the fruit are submerged in water before inoculation (Cohen *et al.* 1991). Inoculation of fruit with a mixture of *G. candidum* and *P. digitatum* spores increases the development of sour rot (Morris 1982). Because of this synergy, treatments that control green mold can affect marked reductions in sour rot, even if the treatment has no activity alone on *G. candidum.*

The development of sour rot is limited not only by the resistance of immature fruit to infection, but also by the relatively high temperature required for optimum growth of *G. candidum.* Fruit temperatures lower than 10°C almost completely suppress the development of sour rot (Eckert and Eaks 1989; Plaza *et al.* 2004). Sour rot is a major disease problem on lemons that are stored at 15°C for several weeks or months before marketing, and on late-season oranges, grapefruit, or mandarin-type fruits that are not adequately refrigerated. Under these circumstances, this disease can cause heavy losses since the fungus grows at 15°C and elaborates pectolytic enzymes that completely macerate the fruit during the storage period. Portions of the diseased fruit drip on to underlying fruit or are dispersed by insects, resulting in rapid spread of the disease.

Two aspects of sour rot make it one of the most serious disease problems confronting the lemon industry of California. First, incipient infections created by contact with diseased fruit in storage are not visible to inspectors and infected fruit may enter into shipments destined for market. Secondly, sour rot is not efficiently controlled by any approved postharvest treatment (other than low temperature) and the fungus is resistant to the existing fungicides and those currently proposed for registration for the control of *P. digitatum* or *P. italicum.*

A wet soft decay of citrus fruit is associated with green and blue mold and sour rot. Dissolution of the rind and subsequent softening is due, in part, to the activity of pectolytic enzymes that degrade the middle lamella between the cells. *P. digitatum* produces an exopolygalacturonase that catalyzes the terminal hydrolysis of pectic acid, causing accumulation of free galacturonic acid (Barash and Angel 1970; Barmore and Brown 1979). Galacturonic acid together with the exopolygalacturonase of the pathogen and the pectin methylesterase of the host can cause maceration of the fruit peel. *P. italicum* and *G. candidum* produce endopolygalacturonases that cleave the _-1, 4-glycosidic bonds of pectic acid by random hydrolysis (Barash 1968; Barash and Eyal 1970; Barmore and Brown 1981; Hershenhorn *et al.* 1989). Galacturonic acid also accumulates during infection by these two pathogens. Polygalacturonases and galacturonic acid formed by their activity also are involved in the spread of decay from infected to healthy fruit in packed cartons. The acid and enzymes released during the decay process cause damage to the healthy peel, which allows the hyphae growing from the diseased fruit to penetrate the injured area of the adjacent healthy fruit (Barmore and Brown 1982). *L. theobromae*, a stem-end rot pathogen, also produces endopolygalacturonases in diseased oranges, but the enzyme activity is substantially less than in comparable tissue infected with *P. italicum* (Barmore *et al.* 1984).

CONTROL OF POSTHARVEST DISEASES

A consideration of the nature and development of postharvest diseases suggests several possible strategies that may reduce decay losses: (1) reduction of preharvest infection and contamination of fruit in the grove; (2) minimization of contamination of fruit in the packinghouse; (3) maintenance of fruit resistance to infection; and (4) application of suitable physical and chemical treatments to the harvested fruit to prevent development of the pathogens.

Sanitation

Pruning dead wood from citrus trees (Reichert and Hellinger 1932) and removing fallen fruit from the grove (Hough 1970) have been recommended as practices to reduce the amount of inoculum of *Lasiodiplodia* and *Penicillium* spp., respectively, available for contamination of citrus fruits before harvest. These practices have not been implemented on a broad scale, however, because the costs involved normally are not justified by the benefits realized. There may be situations, however, in which contamination from these sources is so great that such extraordinary measures would be appropriate.

Spraying the fruit in the grove with a fungicide to protect the button against the development of diplodia and phomopsis stem-end rots has also been considered, but thought not to be an efficient measure because spores of *L. theobromae* and *P. citri* are disseminated throughout the growing season and the button of the fruit is continuously susceptible to infection (Smoot and Melvin 1965B). However, several investigators have demonstrated that diplodia and phomopsis stem-end rots, as well as penicillium decay, can be controlled by a single spray of benomyl applied within 3 weeks of harvest (Brown 1974; Brown and McCornack 1969; Brown and Albrigo 1972). Benomyl, and more recently thiophanate methyl, have been applied experimentally before harvest in Florida and California to control stem-end rot and penicillium decay (Ritenour *et al.* 2004). This approach is valuable in situations where a postharvest treatment in a packinghouse is not done, such as before long periods of ethylene degreening or long transport of freshly harvested fruit in field bins. However, preharvest fungicide applications require much more material than do postharvest packingline applications and introduce the risk of the development fungicide resistant pathogen isolates in the groves.

Even after contamination of the fruit button by spores of *L. theobromae* and *P. citri*, the development of stem-end rot can be prevented by pulling the infested button from the fruit at harvest time rather than clipping the stem in the traditional manner of picking (Hopkins and Loucks 1944; Pelser 1977). Harvest by pulling the fruit (snap picking) is not recommended solely for the purpose of controlling stem-end rots, but may be an additional benefit of this more economical method of picking. Snap picking may increase penicillium decay, however, if the peel is torn when the button is pulled from the fruit, and it may increase alternaria black rot (Bartholomew 1926; Pelser 1977).

Brown rot, which is initiated by infection of mature fruit on the tree by zoospores of *Phytophthora* spp., is most effectively controlled by spraying the fruit on the skirt of the tree and the soil surface with a fixed copper fungicide or captan prior to the onset of the rainy season (Fawcett 1936; Klotz

1973; Pelser 1975; Schiffmann-Nadel 1969A). Incipient infections are difficult to eradicate by postharvest treatments. Control of the wound-invading pathogens *Penicillium* and *Geotrichum* spp. must also begin in the grove before harvest. Insects, such as fruit flies, fruit-sucking moths, and orange worms, that can inoculate fruit before harvest with *Penicillium* and *Geotrichum* must be controlled, since it is very difficult to prevent the development of decay from deep infected wounds by postharvest treatments (Hough 1970; Pelser 1975, 1977; Roth 1967).

Although little can be done to reduce the number of spores of *Penicillium* and *Geotrichum* spp. present in the grove during the growing season, picking boxes that are heavily contaminated with these fungi should be cleaned before subsequent use. Recycled lemon storage boxes are usually cleaned and disinfected before being refilled with a new lot of fruit. Lemon packinghouses in California have adopted stringent sanitation measures in order to discourage the selection of fungus strains that are resistant to fungicide treatments currently in use. Bins, packingline equipment, and the floors and walls of the packinghouse can be cleaned with steam or hot water, or sprayed with 30% isopropyl alcohol or 200 ppm or less of a quaternary ammonium sanitizer. These cannot contact the fruit directly, and if higher quaternary ammonia rates are used, treated surfaces must be rinsed with water (Anon. 2000). Dried residues of quaternary ammonia, but not chlorine, that contacted the peel of Marsh grapefruit caused injuries (Ritenour *et al.* 2003). After storage fruit are surface-sterilized with a solution of sodium hypochlorite or sodium *o*-phenylphenate before being admitted to the packing area. Sanitation is sometimes accomplished with aqueous solutions of other sanitizers, such as peroxyacetic acid, chlorine dioxide, or ozone. Packinghouse layouts are typically designed to minimize the exposure of fruit to airborne mold spores (Hall and Bice 1977; Bancroft *et al.* 1984). Residues of imazalil and thiabendazole reduce sporulation from blue and green mold lesions that develop from isolates of these pathogens sensitive to these fungicides, and this reduces the airborne inoculum produced inside storage rooms or packinghouses. Ozone gas at low concentrations (0.3 to 1 ppm) also reduces blue and green mold sporulation effectively when the gas is present, but it has little other effect on postharvest decay development on inoculated fruit (Harding 1968; Palou *et al.* 2001A). Sporulation was effectively controlled when ozone gas was applied to fruit in open storage boxes, returnable plastic containers, or field bins, but not to fiberboard boxes or plastic bags that impeded ozone penetration (Palou *et al.* 2001A; 2003). Ethylene removal can be also be accomplished by ozone, and minimizing ethylene by other means markedly reduced the incidence of decay among lemons (Wild *et al.* 1976) and penicillium and stem-end decay of Valencia oranges (McGlasson and Eaks 1972) during long storage.

Maintenance of Fruit Resistance to Infection

Wound Minimization and Healing. Mechanical injuries to the peel inflicted during harvesting and handling citrus fruit are the principal sites of infection by the wound-invading pathogens. While some mechanical injury is unavoidable during the harvest and processing of citrus fruit, the number and severity of these injuries is a consequence of the care exercised in these procedures. Powell (1908) found that, by training harvesters in California, the number of oranges with visible wounds could be reduced from 17% to less than 3%, with concomitant reductions in postharvest green and blue molds. In South Africa, Christ (1966) similarly observed that measures to reduce injuries dramatically reduced the incidence of green mold. Mechanical harvesting, by shaking the fruit from the tree, caused considerably more injury and decay than typically results from conventional harvesting by hand with a clipper (Rackham and Grierson 1971). Careful picking to minimize injuries is a time-honored recommendation, but the rising cost of labor, coupled with an indifference to careful picking, means that high levels of injury to the fruit will remain common.

Injuries likely to be infected by spores of *P. digitatum* or *P. italicum* are those two or more millimeters in depth into the peel or those that rupture oil glands (Bates 1933; Kavanagh and Wood 1971; Smoot and Melvin 1961). Inoculum of these fungi is typically ubiquitous in grove and packinghouse atmospheres and on fruit surfaces (Barkai-Golan 1966; Kelly and Austin 1985, Roth 1967). More superficial wounds may become resistant to infection through desiccation or by the formation of protective barriers that prevent the penetration by the germinating spores (Brown 1973). Oil glands of green lemons that resist infection contain high levels of the antifungal monoterpene aldehyde citral (Rodov *et al.* 1995B). Superficial injuries, involving the flavedo portion of the peel, possess the capacity to heal and may become resistant to infection by *Penicillium* and *Geotrichum* spp. Resistance of wounds deeper in the peel to infection is a consequence of defenses already present in the peel and those that occur after wounding and infection. The antifungal compound citral, a mixture of geraninal and neral, occurs in the peel of lemons and oranges. Citral, higher in concentration in fruit which resist infection such as immature lemons, persists longer after thermal curing, hot water treatment, or treatment with 2,4 dichlorophenoxyacetic acid or gibberellic acid, while ethylene accelerates citral decline (Ben Yehoshua *et al.* 1995). Exogenous applications of citral controlled green mold on inoculated lemons but visibly injured the flavedo (Ben-Yehoshua *et al.* 1992). After a wound is made, lignin-like materials accumulate in the flavedo tissue as resistance to infection develops (Brown *et al.* 1978). Chemical defenses also are induced, particularly if the wound is infected, which include the phytoalexins scoparone and scopolitin, and pathogenesis-related proteins, some of which include the antifungal enzymes chitinase, beta-1,3 endoglucanase, and phenylalanine ammonia lyase. In addition to infection by pathogens, chemical defenses are induced by biological control yeasts, hot water or air treatments, UV light, and compounds that induce defensive reactions in plants such as jasmonates and beta aminobutyric acid (Ben-Yehoshua *et al.* 1992; Ben-Yehoshua *et al.* 1995; Droby *et al.* 2002; Porat *et al.* 2002C). Wound healing is facilitated at warm temperatures, and has been used as a strategy to control green mold (Plaza *et al.* 2003B; Stange and Eckert 1994). In Florida, the usual degreening environment (29°C, 96% RH) reduces the incidence of green mold (Hopkins and Loucks 1948; Brown 1973; Table 13.3).

Calyx Vitality. The vitality of the tissues of the fruit calyx ("button") is a major impediment to the development of stem-end rots. Hence, chemical treatments and environmental conditions that delay the senescence of the button will also delay the onset of stem-end rots. A wax formulation containing 500 ppm 2,4-D (isopropyl ester) is applied to lemons to control alternaria stem-end rot during storage in California (Stewart *et al.* 1952) and to oranges and grapefruit in South Africa (Pelser 1975) and Israel (Schiffmann-Nadel *et al.* 1972) to control stem-end rots during long-distance shipment and prolonged storage of the fruit. Australian lemons treated with wax containing 500 ppm 2,4-D and 500 ppm gibberellin were stored in controlled atmospheres for 24 weeks without excessive decay (Wild *et al.* 1976).

Storage Temperature. Storage at low temperature and high humidity are beneficial to the maintenance of resistance to infection of both the peel and the button of the fruit, but the most obvious effect of low temperature is to retard the growth of pathogens in infected fruit. However, disease symptoms will appear a few days after the infected fruit are transferred to the ambient environment. Chemical fungicides can prevent or eradicate incipient infections and are usually regarded as supplementary measures to adequate environmental control. Low temperature maintains the quality of fresh fruit and retards the development and spread of infections that are not eradicated by the fungicide treatments.

Physiological Injury. Detrimental postharvest environments and poor handling practices can cause injuries exploited by wound-infecting pathogens. Controlled atmosphere injury, ice damage, water spot, oleocellosis, and stem-end rind breakdown are examples of physiological disorders that may be subsequently invaded by *Penicillium* spp. (Hatton and Cubbedge 1977; Hopkins and McCornack 1960; Smoot 1977; Schiffmann-Nadel *et al.* 1975B). Anthracnose, caused by *C. gloeosporioides*, typically appears only on fruit with other disorders such as sunburn, chemical injury, feeding injuries, or on fruit that are overripe or stored too long (Brown and Eckert 2000). Anthracnose of Robinson tangerines is instigated by subjecting green-colored fruit to ethylene during the degreening operation, a practice that stimulates germination of latent appressoria on the fruit surface. As the fruit develop more orange color, they become resistant to the disease. Some control of anthracnose has been achieved by preharvest sprays of ethephon, which releases ethylene and enhances the orange color and the resistance of the peel without triggering infection by the latent appressoria (Barmore and Brown 1978).

Common Postharvest Fruit Treatments

Among the postharvest treatments examined to control postharvest diseases are washing, thermal treatments, irradiation, biological control, and chemical fungicides. Chemical fungicides are the principal means employed in commercial fruit storage and shipment today. However, treatments that control fruit decay, yet leave no residue on the fruit, are preferable to many food regulation authorities and consumers. This line of reasoning has engendered a substantial amount of research on the use of other than conventional fungicides to control postharvest diseases.

Washing. The usual practice of washing citrus fruits, with a soap and sanitizer such as sodium ortho-phenylphenate (SOPP) or sodium hypochlorite (chlorine), after harvest is an effective method for removing or inactivating spores on the surface of the fruit. Chlorine is the sanitizer in most common use in high-pressure water washing devices because it is economical and can kill spores rapidly in water and on fruit. Brief immersion of lemons in 200 µg/ml free chlorine reduces populations of spores of *P. digitatum* and *G. citriaurantii* on the surface of the fruit by 99.9% (Smilanick *et al.* 2002). However, chlorine will not control decay from infections initiated by spores from inside wounds, even at very high rates. SOPP, more commonly used when washing is accomplished by brushing the fruit, will control infections from within wounds. Barkai-Golan (1966) reported that the peel was almost free from fungus spores (especially *Penicillium*) after the fruit were washed in a bath of SOPP, but the fruit were re-contaminated to their original level in the packinghouses by the time they were packed in shipping boxes. Florida investigators reported that washing citrus fruits with a non-fungicide cleaner before ethylene degreening reduced the population of pathogenic fungi on the fruit and decreased anthracnose and diplodia stem-end rot on several cultivars (Jahn *et al.* 1970; Brown 1975; Smoot and Melvin 1972; Smoot *et al.* 1971B). The washing treatment did not reduce the incidence of phomopsis stem-end rot, penicillium decay, or sour rot, however. High-pressure water washing, which effectively removes scale insects and soil, did not reduce the incidence of green mold or sour rot on lemons (Sorenson *et al.* 1999; Smilanick *et al.* 1999). Washing the fruit should always occur before fungicide applications, because washing can remove their residues and reduce their effectiveness (Cabras *et al.* 1999; Gutter 1969; Smilanick *et al.* 1999).

Immersion in Hot Water. This very old practice has increased in popularity in some packinghouses in California. This and other thermal treatments will be discussed at length later in this review. Several investigators (Fawcett 1936; Klotz and DeWolfe 1961A, B) have reported that incipient infections of *Phytophthora* in fruit incubated 30 hr at room temperature can be eradicated by immersing the fruit in 49°C water for 2-4 min. A milder heat treatment of 46°C gave similar results if the incubation period was shorter or the incubation temperature was suboptimal for the pathogen growth. The major problem with hot-water treatments is that turgid, freshly picked lemons develop oleocellosis (unsightly rind spots caused by the phytotoxicity of the released contents of ruptured oil glands to cells of the flavedo) if immersed immediately after harvest in hot water. Therefore, it is necessary to hold the fruit for 1 day in the packinghouse to allow them to lose some peel moisture before exposure to hot water. Gradual heating in hot water, over a period of 45 min to a core temperature of 45°C, was better tolerated by Valencia oranges than immersion in 53°C water for 12 min, although oil glands appeared collapsed after storage of the treated fruit (Williams *et al.* 1994). In practice, a 2-4 min hot-water treatment that heats the peel to a sufficient depth to reduce decay is likely to injure the surface cells (Klotz and DeWolfe 1961A; Palou *et al.* 2001B). Even if the hot water does not cause oleocellosis, it has been observed that hot water-treated lemons and oranges tend to develop secondary decays during storage (Harding and Savage 1964; Smoot and Melvin 1965A). Recently, very hot water applied briefly, for no longer than 30 seconds, in a low-pressure drench to fruit on rotating brushes has been employed. It accomplished moderately good control of green and blue molds at temperatures of 56°C and higher, and markedly reduced microbe populations on fruit surfaces (Porat *et al.* 2000A; Smilanick *et al.* 2003).

Application of Chemical Fungicides. Numerous fungicides have been evaluated for control of citrus fruit decay. The chemical properties of most citrus fungicides, influence of the mode of application on efficacy, methods of analysis, and the level of residues and their persistence in fruit have been discussed (Eckert 1967, 1977; Dezman *et al.* 1986; Papadopoulou-Mourkidou 1991). Fungicides can reduce decay losses by inhibiting the development of latent infections of the stem-end rot fungi, by inactivating spores in fresh wounds, by protecting the peel from infection at injuries that are inflicted after application of the fungicide, by inhibiting sporulation of *Penicillium* spp. on the surface of decaying fruit, and by inhibiting the contact spread of several diseases.

Postharvest fungicides have played an important role in developing distant markets for citrus fruits. The first compounds used—borax, sodium carbonate, sodium bicarbonate, and sodium *o*-phenylphenate—prevent infection of fresh injuries if fruit are treated within a day or two after harvest, depending upon the prevailing temperature. These compounds do not penetrate into the peel of the fruit to a significant extent; thus, the patho-gens must be inactivated before the hyphae grow beyond the wounded site. Fungicides developed over the past 30 years can penetrate a short distance into the peel and can prevent the development of stem-end rot by *L. theobro-mae* or *P. citri* in the fruit button and the sporulation of *Penicillium* spp. on the surface of the decaying fruits. The application of these fungicides to control the stem-end rots can be delayed for a few days after harvest if the fruit are not degreened with ethylene, which causes a rapid decline in the resistance of the button. To control green mold, most should be applied within 24 hours after infection, although this period can be longer if fruit temperatures are less than 15°C (Wild and Spohr 1989).

The general procedure involved in the sequence of fungicide treat-ments in California is shown in Fig. 13.1 and discussed in the rest of this section. The pattern is similar in Florida except that Florida lemons are stored more briefly, typically only 1-3 weeks, for color development. Discus-sion about the properties of these fungicides occurs later in this review.

Bin Drenching Treatments. Early-season oranges grapefruit, mandarins, Florida lemons and occasionally California lemons are degreened with eth-ylene gas to develop an acceptable orange or yellow color. This degreening treatment is known to increase penicillium decay in California and diplodia stem-end rot of early varieties in Florida (Brooks 1944; McCornack 1972).

Drenching oranges in field containers with a fungicide solution before degreening is an efficient means of disease control (Brown 1977A; Gutter 1977). Fruit in bins, often still loaded on field trucks, are transported through a tunnel and drenched (Fig. 13.2) with thiabendazole or imazalil before being placed in the degreening room (Eckert and Kolbezen 1964; Eckert *et al.* 1969A; Brown and Miller 1999). This procedure is highly effec-tive in reducing penicillium decay because it prevents infection of harvest-related injuries during the period that the fruit are held in the degreening room where the environment is optimum for fungus infection. An advan-tage the process offers is that the fruit are treated very soon after harvest; delays between harvest and treatment, particularly if they exceed 24 hours, reduce the effectiveness of decay control treatment (Fig. 13.3). Thiabenda-zole drench solutions are usually chlorinated to prevent the growth of nuisance microbes in the solution, and to prevent inoculation of the fruit by fungicide resistant *Penicillium* spp., *Geotrichum citri-aurantii*, or other pathogens that are not inhibited by the fungicides used in drenchers (Brown 1977A; Gutter 1977). Imazalil is not compatible with chlorine, so it is filtered or periodically heated for the same purpose. Some facilities in California add sodium bicarbonate to the drench solutions to provide some control of fungicide-resistant isolates. The bins should always be sanitized before reuse, particularly after degreening, because of the abundant con-tamination from decay that often occurs during this process.

Lemon and orange postharvest packinghouse operations

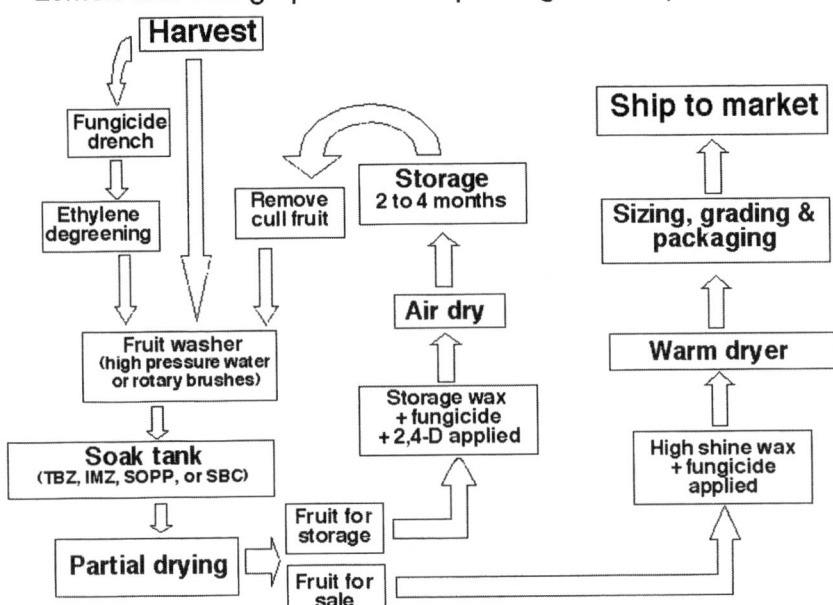

Fig. 13.1. Handling sequences for oranges and lemons within a packinghouse. The storage handling is typical only for lemons. TBZ, IMZ, SOPP, and SBC indicate thiabendazole, imazalil, sodium *ortho*-phenylphenol, and sodium bicarbonate, respectively.

Fungicides Applied in Cleaning Operations. After the degreening treatment, if scale insect removal or cleaning is needed, the fruit are washed under a high volume blast of water applied at a pressure of 100 to 200 pounds per square inch (700 to 1400 kPa). The water often contains 25 ppm chlorine, and in some facilities sodium bicarbonate is added at 1 to 3%. In some packinghouses, the fruit are washed by passage over rotating brushes where a soap is applied, which usually contains the fungicide sodium *o*-phenylphenol, followed by a spray of fresh water to rinse them. Sometimes the fungicide is formulated into a foam (Fig. 13.4). The purpose of these treatments is to remove soil, scale insects, and sooty molds, to remove or inhibit spores on surface of the fruit, and to inactivate spores in wounds.

In California for over 75 years, the standard method of cleaning oranges was to soak fruit for several minutes in a heated (43°C) solution of borax (sodium tetraborate decahydrate) or sodium carbonate within a day or two after harvest (Barger and Hawkins 1925; Eckert 1967). Soap or a detergent was usually added to the solution to clean the fruit at the same time. The borax treatment that was widely utilized in citrus packinghouses until recent times consisted of a solution of 4% borax and 2% boric acid at a temperature of

Fig 13.2. Commercial drenchers apply fungicides to fruit within field bins that pass through a drencher (top) or while the bins are loaded on trailers (bottom; courtesy C. Campos, FMC FoodTech, Riverside CA).

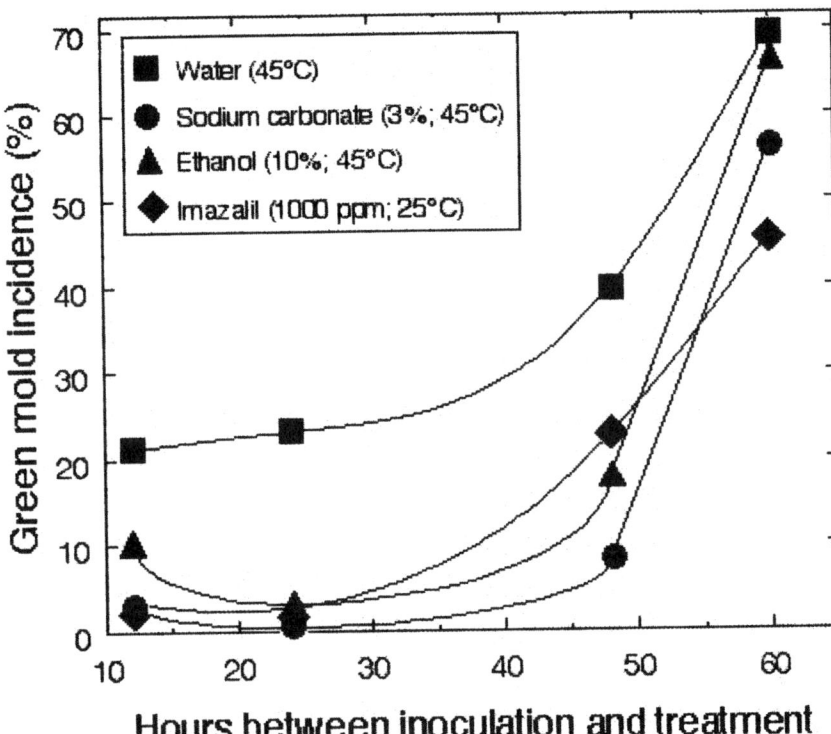

Hours between inoculation and treatment

Fig. 13.3. Influence of the interval between inoculation of lemons with *P. digitatum* and treatment by immersion in imazalil for 1 min or for 2.5 min in heated solutions of water, sodium carbonate, or ethanol. The temperature of the fruit during the interval period was 20°C. After treatment, the lemons were stored for 3 weeks at 10°C. *From Smilanick et al. 1995.*

43°C. The oranges are immersed in the solution for 2-4 min, then rinsed with a fresh water spray, and waxed. The water rinse reduces the effectiveness of the treatment but is required to remove borate residues from the surface of the fruit (Winston 1935). The application of a wax coating to prevent water loss is essential since the warm alkaline borax treatment removes a substantial portion of the natural wax from the fruit. The borax bath treatment remains only in occasional use in California, and has been abandoned elsewhere (Smoot 1977; Wardowski and Brown 1993; Pelser 1975, 1977). A practical problem with this treatment is that disposal of large volumes of rinse water containing high levels of boron must be accomplished. Beginning in the 1950s, borax was replaced to a large extent in both California and Florida by SOPP (sodium *o*-phenylphenol), which is somewhat more effective against both penicillium molds and stem-end rot fungi and constitutes a less serious water pollution problem than borax (Fig. 13.5).

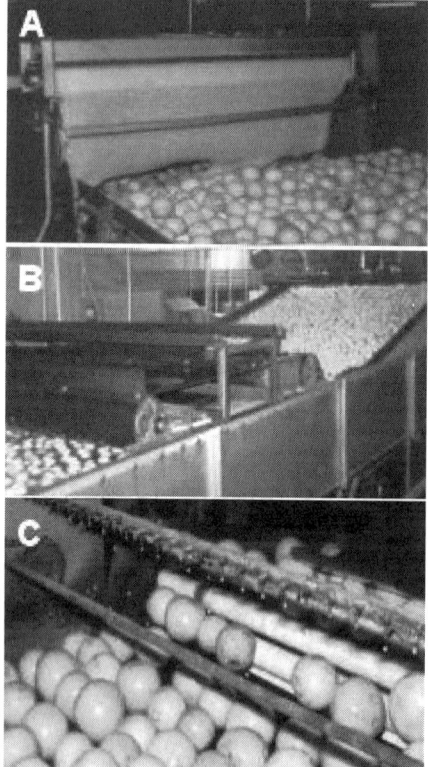

Fig. 13.4. Treatment of oranges by passage through foam containing 2% sodium orthophenylphenate (SOPP) (A), of lemons by immersion in an aqueous solution heated to 40°C containing 500 µg/ml imazalil (B), and of oranges by passage through rotating brushes where thiabendazole is dripped onto them through small emitters (C).

Currently, use of borax-boric acid and SOPP in large tanks has been largely replaced in California by sodium carbonate or bicarbonate. SOPP applied by other methods remains popular. Immersion in sodium carbonate or bicarbonate is a very old practice that has again become popular because it is effective and inexpensive (Barger 1928; Smilanick *et al.* 1995; Smilanick *et al.* 1999). Fruit are immersed or drenched for 1-4 min in a solution of 3% sodium carbonate or sodium bicarbonate at ambient or elevated temperatures followed by a brief fresh water rinse. They can also be applied effectively through high-pressure washer nozzles (Sorenson *et al.* 1999). Low-volume spray applications over rotating brushes are avoided because calcium carbonate scale accumulates on the brushes and the efficacy of the carbonates when applied this way is poor compared to tank or drench applications. Good control of penicillium rots and fair control of sour rot is obtained with these treatments (Palou *et al.* 2001B; Smilanick *et al.* 1997A; Smilanick and Sorenson 2001). Their effectiveness is lower in mandarins than lemons or oranges, but in all cases is improved by prolonging the duration of the treatment or heating the solution (Palou *et al.* 2001B, 2002B; Smilanick *et al.*

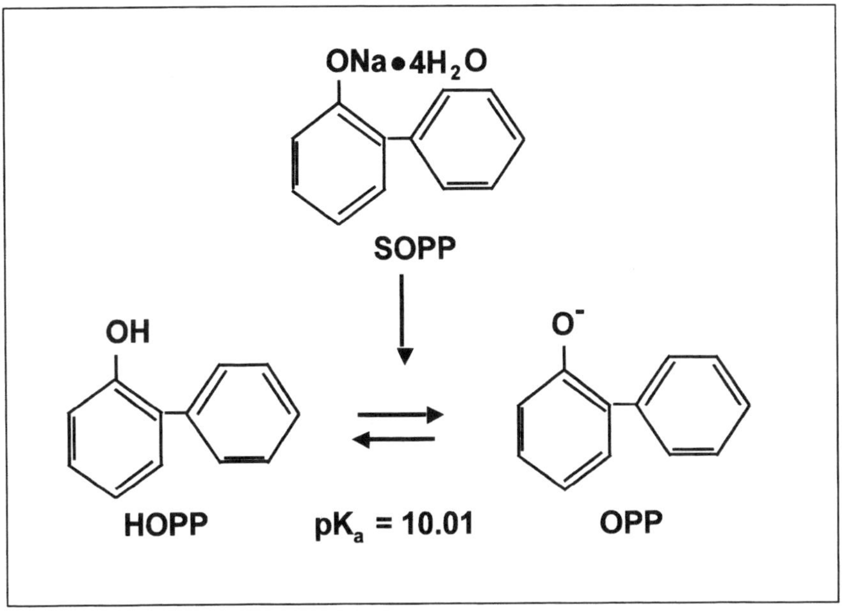

Fig. 13.5. Equilibrium between *ortho*-phenylphenate (OPP) and *ortho*-phenylphenol (HOPP) after dissolution of sodium *ortho*-phenylphenate tetrahydrate (SOPP) in water.

1997A). Liquid lime sulfur solution, which contains calcium polysulfide, is equal or superior in effectiveness when heated to the carbonates (Smilanick and Sorenson 2001) and has the advantage that used solutions can be disposed of in soil, where it is commonly used to adjust pH or improve water penetration. It was approved for postharvest use on citrus fruit in California and Arizona, but it has not become popular because of the objectionable sulfide odor it emits and its corrosiveness to some packinghouse equipment.

The use of heated solutions should be approached with caution. Harding and Savage (1964) observed that sodium carbonate treatment at 43°C predisposed mature lemons to decay without causing visible symptoms of heat injury. A one minute sodium carbonate treatment caused few or no visible rind injuries on five navel orange varieties when the solution was 44°C or 50°C, but many were injured at 56°C, and most all were harmed at 61°C (Smilanick et al. 1997A; Palou et al. 2001B). Good control of the penicillium decay does not require very high temperatures; most packinghouses do not heat the solutions above 41°C. The risk of fruit injury is higher with sodium carbonate than sodium bicarbonate, presumably because of the higher pH and sodium content of sodium carbonate (Larrigaudiere et al. 2002). A fresh aqueous solution containing 3% wt/vol sodium carbonate has a pH of about 11.5, while the pH of a 3% wt/vol sodium bicarbonate solution is about 8.3. The sodium content of sodium carbonate is 43.4%, while that of sodium bicarbonate is 27.4%. Spores survive long periods in these solutions, so chlorine is often added to sodium bicarbonate and maintained at a concentration of 200 µg/ml free chlorine. Chlorine slightly improves the effectiveness of the treatment (Smilanick *et al.* 1999) and rapidly kills spores of *P. digitatum* and *G. citri-aurantii* in the solution and on the surface of the fruit (Smilanick *et al.* 2002).

Similar to borax-boric acid treatments (Winston 1935), post-treatment rinsing also can reduce the effectiveness of carbonate treatments, but some rinsing is needed to eliminate weight and firmness losses that can result if the salts are left on the fruit during storage (Larrigaudiere *et al.* 2002; Smilanick *et al.* 1999). High-pressure water washing or other very rigorous fruit washing after treatment can greatly reduce the effectiveness of the treatment and should be avoided (Larrigaudiere *et al.* 2002; Smilanick *et al.* 1999). The mechanism of control of fungal growth by bicarbonate or carbonate treatment is unclear. It appears to be due in part to the presence of an alkaline residue in wounds that inhibits the development of penicillium spores at these sites (Marloth 1931; Green 1932), although equimolar solutions of the same pH prepared from sodium carbonate or bicarbonate salts are more effective than those prepared from potassium or ammonium salts, which suggests other factors may be important (Smilanick *et al.* 1999).

Fungicides Applied as Non-recovered Sprays, Tanks, and in Wax Formulations. Often, solutions are sprayed over fruit on rotating brushes and are not recovered and used again. Following tank or pressure washing citrus fruit, it is a standard practice to apply a second fungicide in foam (SOPP), in a water or wax solution dripped or sprayed over rotating brushes, or by immersion of the fruit in a tank of a fungicide (Fig. 13.4). A second application of a wax containing a fungicide is sometimes applied after aqueous spray or tank fungicide applications in order to deposit a uniform residue of the fungicide within the wax to control sporulation (Brown and Dezman 1990; Smilanick *et al.* 1997B). The most common compounds for such treatments are thiabendazole and imazalil.

COMMON FUNGICIDES

The most common compounds used for the fungicide treatments discussed in the previous section are examined in more detail in this section.

ortho-Phenylphenol

ortho-Phenylphenol has been used for forty years to control postharvest diseases of citrus fruits. Currently, only the sodium salt of *ortho*-phenylphenol (SOPP) is in use in the United States. The first product used was a tetrahydrate sodium salt with the trade name Dowicide A, and concentrations were reported as percent Dowicide A or percent Dowicide by commercial users. When calculated as the anhydrous salt, 2% (w/v) sodium *ortho*-phenylphenate tetrahydrate contains 1.45% anhydrous sodium *ortho*-phenylphenate, and failure to express the SOPP concentration without this distinction has caused much confusion in the literature. Sodium ortho-phenylphenate tetrahydrate is very soluble in water and hydrolyzes extensively in aqueous solutions; a 0.5% (w/v) solution of SOPP is approximately pH 11.2 and a 2.0% solution is pH 11.5. The concentrations of undissociated *ortho*-phenylphenol and of the *ortho*-phenylphenate anion are dependent on the concentration of SOPP and the pH.

ortho-Phenylphenol is a broad-spectrum biocide in comparison to most other organic fungicides used for control of postharvest diseases (Fig. 13.5). The undissociated phenol is lethal to microorganisms and is injurious to citrus fruits at concentrations of 200-400 mg/liter, depending upon the temperature of the solution and the period of contact. The dissociated form (ortho-phenylphenate ion) is not phytotoxic, and a solution of SOPP, containing excess alkali to suppress hydrolysis of the salt, is safe for treatment of harvested citrus fruits (Long and Roberts 1958; Eckert *et al.* 1969B). The intact waxy surface of citrus appears to be relatively impermeable to the ortho-phenylphenate anion as indicated by low residue levels in fruit treated at pH 11.8 (Fig. 13.6). However, the *ortho*-phenylphenate anion diffuses selectively into wounds where the surface of the fruit is ruptured and is soon hydrolyzed to *ortho*-phenylphenol in the presence of fruit acids and metabolic carbon dioxide. Rinsing the treated fruit with water removes most of the sodium ortho-phenylphenate residue from the surface of the fruit, but a substantial amount remains associated with wounds and prevents the development of pathogens at these sites (Eckert *et al.* 1969B). Residues are stable within rind tissues, except those within oil glands, which decline substantially during storage (Johnson *et al.* 2001). The concentration of *ortho*-phenylphenol is regulated by the solution pH and determines the phytotoxicity of the SOPP solution, as well as the residue level in treated citrus fruits (Hayward and Grierson 1960; Fig. 13.6). Fruit injury increases with solution temperature and contact time. In commercial packinghouses, episodes of fruit damage usually can be traced to a drop in pH of the SOPP solution caused by accidental dilution with tap water or the accumulation in the bath of acidic materials such as fruit debris, soil, and CO_2.

The benefits of SOPP when properly applied are twofold: (1) spores of fungi and bacteria on the surface of the fruit or in the cleaning solution are inactivated and (2) a residue of *ortho*-phenylphenol is deposited in wounds and prevents infection at these sites during storage or marketing. The solution recommended for soaking or flooding oranges in Florida contains 2% sodium *ortho*-phenylphenate tetrahydrate, 1% hexamine, and 0.2% sodium hydroxide

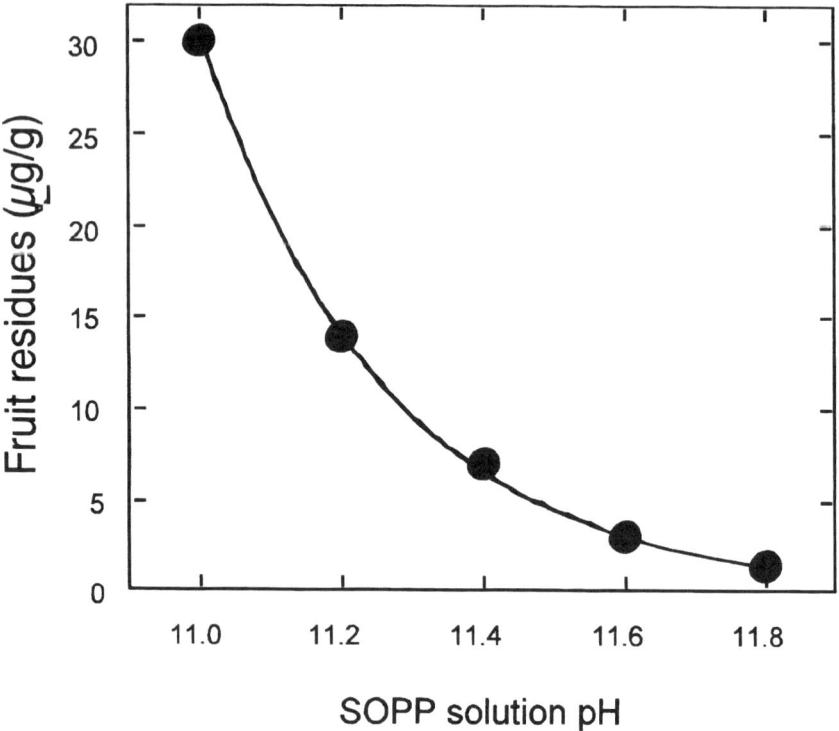

SOPP solution pH

Fig. 13.6. Influence of sodium ortho-phenyl phenol solution pH on residues of ortho-phenylphenol (SOPP) in oranges.
From Hayward and Grierson 1960.

(Wardowski and Brown 1993). The pH must be maintained in the range 11.5-12, and the solution is not heated. Hexamine precipitates free *ortho*-phenylphenol as the slightly soluble hexamine phenate (3:1) complex before the concentration of undissociated phenol reaches the threshold for phytotoxicity; hexamine also exerts a buffering effect upon the solution at about pH 11.8 (Hopkins and Loucks 1950; Long and Roberts 1958; Wardowski and Brown 1993). In addition, the hexamine *ortho*-phenylphenol precipitate reduces the concentration of *ortho*-phenylphenol in solution, thereby preventing excessively high residues, which are inevitable in fruit treated with solutions of SOPP without hexamine at pH values below 11.5. In other citrus-producing areas the bath for the treatment of oranges usually contains 0.5% SOPP at pH 11.5-12, and is heated to 32 to 38°C (Eckert 1977; Gutter 1977). Hexamine is not included in this formulation, but the pH is carefully maintained in the desired range. In the bath treatment, the fruit are submerged for 2-4 min in the SOPP solution, brushed, and finally rinsed with water sprays.

Foam application (Fig. 13.4) is sometimes used for treating citrus fruit with SOPP (Smoot 1977; Wardowski and Brown 1993). A solution containing 2% SOPP, 0.1% sodium dodecylbenzenesulfonate, and 0.2% sodium carbonate is agitated into a foam that drops as a curtain over fruit moving beneath it on a horizontal conveyor. The foam-covered fruit are brushed for about 15 sec before being rinsed in a spray of water. The foam treatment controls decay much less effectively than the bath treatment (Smilanick and Sorenson 2001), but has the advantage that pH control is facilitated because the foam is not recycled (Harding and Savage 1965). The foam treatment is less effective than the bath treatment, probably because the residues of SOPP are considerably lower on fruit treated with SOPP foam than on fruit submerged in a solution of SOPP (Rajzman and Apfelbaum 1968). The principle utility of this treatment is to minimize inoculum on fruit cleaning brushes.

Benzimidazole Fungicides

Four benzimidazole fungicides used on citrus fruit include carbendazim, thiabendazole, benomyl, and thiophanate methyl, however, only thiabendazole is now in common postharvest use (Fig. 13.7). All are systemic and share the common mode of action; they bind to tubulin and inhibit microtubule assembly within fungal cells (Davidse 1986). Benomyl and thiophante methyl slowly hydrolyze to carbendazim after application, which is also a potent fungicide (White *et al.* 1973). Treatment with these fungicides markedly reduces penicillium decay as well as diplodia and phomopsis stem-end rots (Brown *et al.* 1967; Crivelli 1966; Eckert *et al.* 1969A; Eckert and Kolbezen 1971; Gutter 1977; Pelser 1973; Wild *et al.* 1975). They do not, however, control sour rot, alternaria rot, or brown rot on citrus fruits and have little or no activity against these pathogens in vitro (Brown and McCornack 1972; López-García *et al.* 2003; McCornack 1974; Pelser 1973; Smoot 1977). Benomyl, and presumably thiabendazole, appears to penetrate to a limited extent into the superficial tissues of the fruit peel where it inhibits the development of latent infections of *Diplodia* and *Phomopsis* (Brown 1977A). Residues of benomyl, and presumably thiabendazole, on the fruit confer resistance to infection by *Penicillium* for several weeks after treatment (Brown and Albrigo 1972; McCornack 1974) and inhibit the growth of *Penicillium* on the surface of the treated fruit (Eckert and Kolbezen 1977; Eckert *et al.* 1979). Typically, benzimidazoles are applied after harvest to control postharvest decay, but if applied in groves before harvest they provide good protection of the fruit from postharvest decay (Kuramoto 1976; Ritenour *et al.* 2004).

Immersing fruit in an aqueous suspension of thiabendazole provides the most effective control of decay, but other application methods are common. Although thiabendazole is typically used at 500 µg/ml or higher in

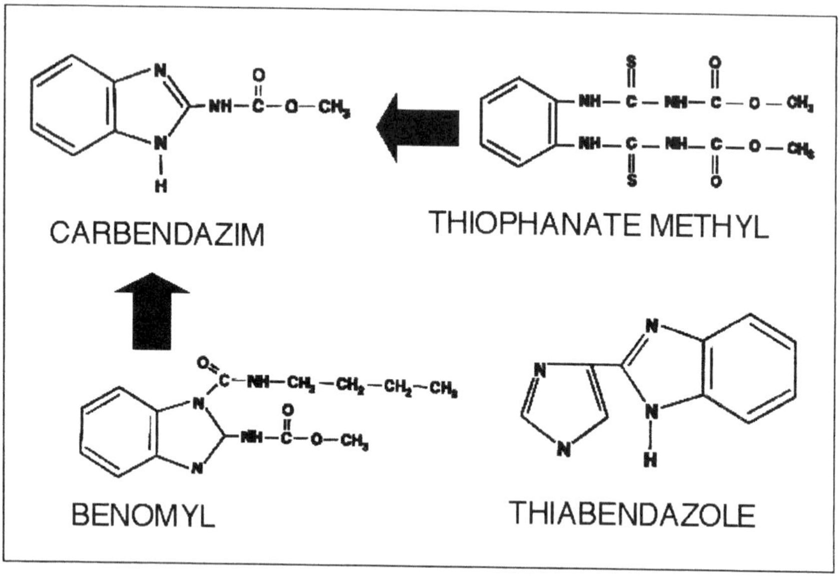

CARBENDAZIM

THIOPHANATE METHYL

BENOMYL

THIABENDAZOLE

Fig. 13.7. Benzimidazole fungicides used on citrus fruit. Benomyl and thiophanate methyl hydrolyze after application to carbendazim. Only thiabendazole is currently used after harvest on citrus fruit in the United States.

most applications, the solubility in water of the pure compound is only 25 µg/ml at 23°C. In many applications, a suspension of finely-divided thiabendazole particles is what is actually applied, while in other formulations thiabendazole is used with surfactants to improve its solubility (Eckert and Eaks 1989). As a consequence of its poor solubility, thiabendazole suspensions require constant agitation when used in tanks or recirculating systems, and residues of the thiabendazole are very easily removed by rinsing, washing, or waxing fruit after treatment (Norman *et al.* 1972; Cabras *et al.* 1999). Currently, thiabendazole is applied as a nonrecoverable spray in water dripped or sprayed over rotating brushes, by passing fruit through a high-volume, recirculating drench or tank containing aqueous thiabendazole suspensions, or a wax formulation containing thiabendazole is sprayed on to fruit on rotating brushes (Brown and Miller 1999; Eckert and Kolbezen 1971; McCornack 1974; Smoot and Melvin 1974; Wardowski *et al.* 1974). The most effective application methods are those that thoroughly wet the fruit with the fungicides and efficiently infiltrate wound infection sites, such as when fruit are drenched or immersed in tanks. Brown and Craig (1989) reported drenching oranges was more effective than non-recovery sprays over rotating brushes, although residues in the fruit were similar, and that aerosols failed to control green mold completely and only partially controlled stem end rot by *Lasiodiplodia theobromae*. Heating aqueous thiabendazole from 25°C to 52°C increased its effectiveness such that the concentration in which fruit were treated was decreased from 1500 to 200 µg/ml with no loss in effectiveness for the control of green mold (Schirra and Mulas 1995A). They reported water alone at 52°C provided substantial control of decay. When thiabendazole is applied in heated aqueous solutions, residues are higher and proportional to the concentration in the solution, while the length of time the fruit are in the solution has little impact on residues (Cabras *et al.* 1999). Increasing the pH of the solution increases thiabendazole residues; residues in oranges increased from about 0.5 to 1.2 ppm when the pH of the solution increased from 8.0 to 10 (Wardowski *et al.* 1974).

Fruit waxes influence thiabendazole efficacy. Suspensions of thiabendazole in water alone affect superior control of penicillium decay than those in wax emulsions (Pelser 1973; Gutter 1975; Gutter *et al.* 1974). For example, a reduction in green mold on lemons by about 50% was accomplished by a brief dip in only 10 µg/ml of thiabendazole in water, while in an emulsion finishing wax, 200 µg/ml thiabendazole was needed to obtain an equivalent level of control (Smilanick, unpublished). Similarly, for the control of stem-end rots, benzimidazole fungicides (benomyl, thiabendazole, and carbendazim) were more effective in water than in wax formulations (Brown 1984; Smoot and Melvin 1974; Pelser 1973). The practical consequence of this fact is to apply thiabendazole before waxing the fruit.

Presumably, some waxes dry and immobilize thiabendazole before it can move into inoculated wounds or under the button of the fruit where the stem-end pathogens reside in a quiescent state. Brown (1984) reported *P. digitatum* infections were controlled by benzimidazole fungicides in water or wax when the inoculated puncture wound was 1.0 mm in diameter. However, the wax formulation was less effective than the water formulation when the puncture wound was reduced to 0.3 mm in diameter, apparently reflecting a poorer penetration of the injury site by the fruit wax formulation. Application of a suspension of 4-6 g/liter thiabendazole in a water-wax formulation to citrus fruits results in a surface deposit of the fungicide, which inhibits sporulation of *Penicillium* on decaying fruit (Eckert *et al.* 1969A; Eckert and Kolbezen 1971; Gutter *et al.* 1974; Gutter 1977). *P. italicum* is usually more tolerant than *P. digitatum* to the benzimidazole fungicides; therefore, blue mold is the more prevalent decay on oranges treated with low concentrations of these compounds (Gutter 1975) and on lemons in storage rooms where benzimidazole-treated fruit are being recycled all season.

Aside from its antifungal action, thiabendazole reduces chilling injury in grapefruit and oranges stored at temperatures that normally cause cold-induced pitting of the fruit (Kokkalos 1974; Schiffmann-Nadel *et al.* 1975A; Wardowski *et al.* 1975; Schirra and Mulas 1995A).

Imazalil

Imazalil (Fig. 13.8) can be used interchangeably with thiabendazole and SOPP for control of several postharvest diseases, but the relative effectiveness of these fungicides varies with the fungal pathogen involved. Imazalil controls *P. digitatum* and *P. italicum* well on citrus fruits, including isolates of

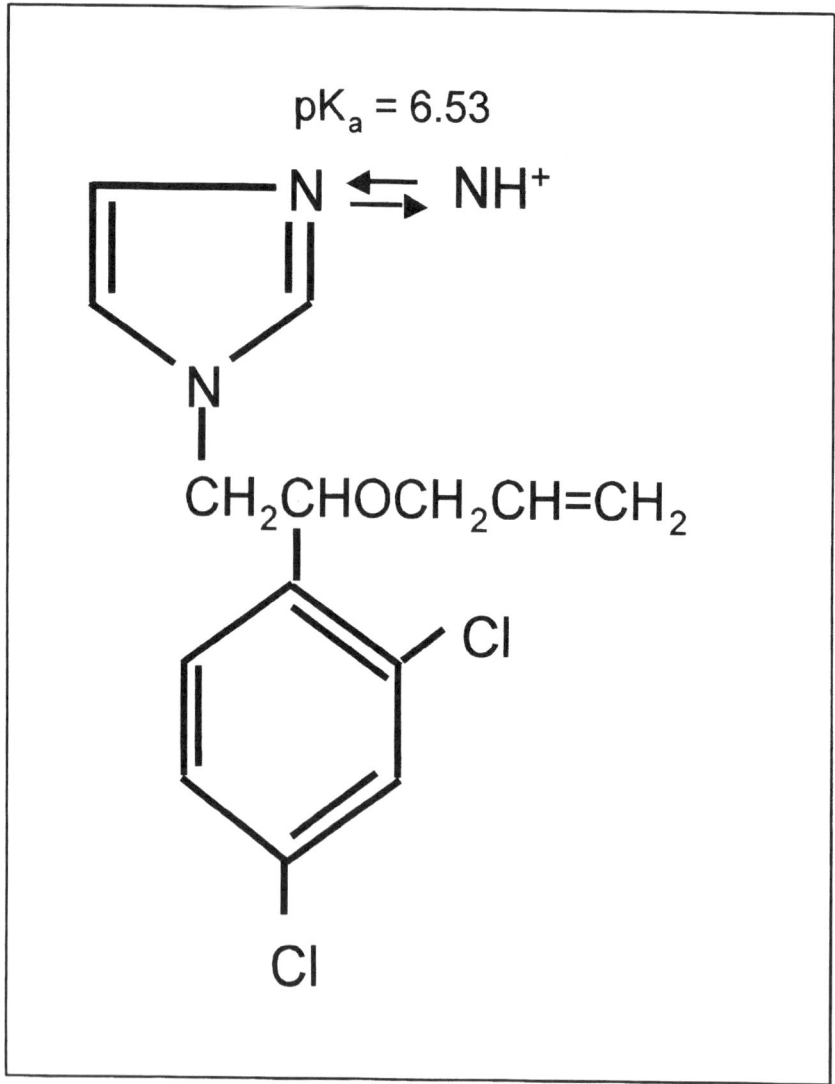

Fig. 13.8. Structure of imazalil.

these pathogens that are resistant to thiabendazole and SOPP (Gutter *et al.* 1981; Kaplan and Davé 1979; Laville 1973; Laville *et al.* 1977; McCornack *et al.* 1977; Pelser 1977). Imazalil applied in water controls penicillium decay by curative, protective, and antisporulant effects that at least equal, and perhaps are slightly superior to, those associated with benomyl or thiabendazole (Laville 1973; Laville *et al.* 1977; Eckert *et al.* 1981; Pelser and la Grange 1981). Imazalil is effective against penicillium decay when applied in water (500-1000 mg/liter active) as a dip, drench, or spray (Laville *et al.* 1977; Kaplan and Davé 1979; Tuset *et al.* 1981; McCornack *et al.* 1977; Gutter *et al.* 1981). Both the fungicidal activity and proportion of dissociated imazalil, which is the neutral and more lipophilic form of the molecule, increase as the pH increases (Holmes and Eckert 1999). The pKa of imazalil is 6.53, and it was about tenfold more toxic to *P. italicum* at pH 7 than pH 5.2 (Siegal *et al.* 1977). Imazalil effectiveness improves substantially when it was combined with sodium bicarbonate (Smilanick, unpublished) or when it was followed by sodium carbonate treatment (Smilanick *et al.* 1999), presumably because the high pH of these solutions increased imazalil activity.

The mode of application greatly influences imazalil residues and efficacy. Sprays are more effective when applied over brushes (Kaplan and Davé 1979) and imazalil residues are significantly higher when fruit are dipped in imazalil compared to those treated with a nonrecovery spray over brushes saturated with the fungicide (Brown and Dezman 1990). The effectiveness of imazalil in controlling penicillium decay and stem end rot caused by *Lasiodiplodia theobromae* is reduced in water waxes so that the concentration must be increased to 2-3 g/liter for activity equivalent to 1 g/liter in water (Pelser and la Grange 1981; Brown *et al.* 1983; Brown and Miller 1999). Brown (1984) reported that the poor eradicant action against *P. digitatum* provided by imazalil in a water-wax formulation was related to the reduced movement of the fungicide in the wax film and limited penetration into the fruit peel compared to the behavior of imazalil applied in water. The performance of imazalil in high solids finishing waxes can be inconsistent and very poor (Eckert *et al.* 1994; Kaplan and Davé 1979; Smilanick *et al.* 1997B). Imazalil moves into the rind of the fruit during treatment and most is absorbed by the epicuticular wax and cuticle during application and absorption continues while they are wet (Brown and Dezman 1990). They reported after 30-45 min, some of the fungicide had penetrated deeper than 1 mm into the rind of oranges, although about 40% of the applied imazalil remained on the surface after the fruit dried. Imazalil residues in fruit resist removal by washing and decline very slowly during storage (Cabras *et al.* 1999; Schirra *et al.* 1997). Cabras and coworkers (1999) reported 83% of the imazalil residue on oranges was present after 9 weeks of storage at 17°C, and only that portion of the imazalil on the fruit surface degraded during storage.

Imazalil is most effective when fruit are immersed in heated, aqueous solutions, and the improvement in efficacy is obtained without necessarily
increasing fungicide residues (Fig. 13.9; Schirra and Mulas 1995B; Schirra
et al. 1996; Smilanick *et al.* 1997B). Schirra and coworkers (1996) reported
that complete control of green mold on lemons with a 3 minute dip treatment with aqueous imazalil required 1500 µg-ml[-1] at 20°C, with residues of
5.05 µg-g[-1], while at 50°C, only 250 µg-ml[-1] was needed, with residues of 1.47
µg-g[-1]. At 50°C, a little as 50 µg-ml[-1] imazalil reduced green mold more than
95% (Schirra *et al.* 1997). Similarly, in California (Smilanick *et al.* 1997B),
control of green mold was better when lemons were immersed for 15 or 30
sec in 500 µg-ml[-1] aqueous imazalil at 37.8°C, compared to 4200 µg-ml[-1]
imazalil in a solvent wax sprayed on fruit at ambient temperatures. Residues
of about 3.5 µg-g[-1] imazalil deposited by the application of imazalil in wax
reduced the incidence of green mold on lemons from 94.4% among untreated controls to 15.1%, whereas an equal residue deposited by the
heated aqueous imazalil treatment reduced green mold incidence to 1.3%.

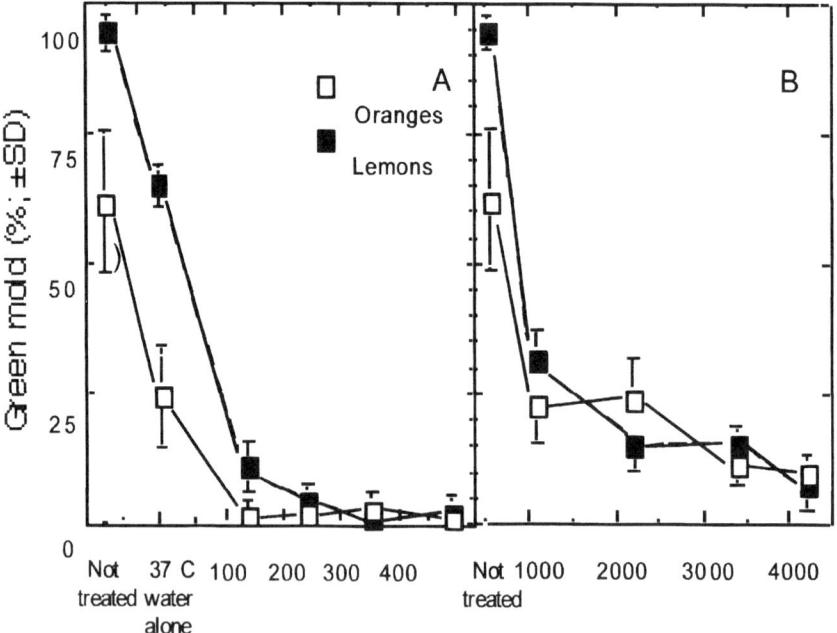

Fig. 13.9. Influence of imazalil concentration (µg-ml[-1]) and method of application on the
incidence of postharvest green mold of oranges and lemons. The fruit were (A) immersed for 15 sec in imazalil in water at 37°C or the fruit were (B) sprayed with imazalil
in wax over brushes at 23°C. All fruit were inoculated 24 h before treatment with spores
of *Penicillium digitatum.*
From Smilanick et al. 1997B.

Results with oranges were similar. Imazalil residues rise with increased imazalil concentration, temperature, and duration of treatment (Cabras *et al.* 1999; Smilanick *et al.* 1997B); residues in lemons and oranges increased 1.5 to 2-fold when the concentration or immersion period was doubled, or if the solution temperature increased 5 or 6°C. Other benefits of the use of heated, aqueous imazalil are an improvement in the resistance of fruit to chilling injury (McDonald *et al.* 1991; Schirra *et al.* 1995), which is mostly a consequence of the hot water treatment and not the fungicide (Rodov *et al.* 1995A), and a reduction in the amount of material needed and discharged to the environment as wastewater (Schirra *et al.* 1997). Negative aspects of the use of heated imazalil include an increased risk of injury compared to water alone, particularly at 50°C (Schirra and Mulas 1995A; Schirra *et al.* 1996), the cost to acquire a dip tank and the energy to operate it, and contamination of the imazalil tank by nuisance microbes or imazalil-resistant isolates of *Penicillium* spp., necessitating the use of periodic heating or filtration of the solution to remove this contamination.

The effectiveness of imazalil against other citrus pathogens is limited. Smoot and Hale (1977) reported that grapefruit sprayed with 1 g/liter imazalil in water had significantly less phomopsis stem-end rot after shipment to Japan; thiabendazole (1200 mg/liter) was more effective, however. Burger and Davis (1982) treated grapefruit with 600 mg/liter imazalil in water by dipping before storage. The imazalil treatment provided control of phomopsis stem-end rot equal to that with benomyl treatment (600 mg/liter). Brown (1981) reported that a water spray of imazalil (1000 mg/liter) significantly reduced phomopsis stem-end rot on artificially inoculated fruit, but benomyl gave more consistent results and was superior to imazalil if the spray treatments were applied 50 hours after inoculation of the fruit. Brown (1981) concluded from eight tests with degreened oranges naturally inoculated with *Diplodia* (*L. theobromae*) that benomyl gave more consistent control of the disease, although the superiority of the benomyl treatment was statistically significant in only one test. Similar results have been obtained in South African tests (Pelser and la Grange 1981). McCornack *et al.* (1977) observed that imazalil was equivalent to thiabendazole and benomyl in reducing stem-end rot of oranges naturally inoculated with *L. theobromae* and *P. citri.* Brown (1984) found that the effectiveness of imazalil against diplodia stem-end rot was greatly diminished by degreening oranges for 48-72 hours before treatment and applying imazalil in a water-wax formulation. These factors probably account for part of the reported variability in the performance of imazalil. Most investigators have reported that imazalil is not effective against sour rot (McCornack *et al.* 1977; Kaplan and Davé 1979; Eckert *et al.* 1981; Brown 1979; Smoot and Hale 1977; Schachnai and Barash 1982). Reports on the effectiveness of imazalil against alternaria rot are conflicting (Brown 1981; Tuset *et al.* 1981; Schiffmann-Nadel *et al.* 1981; Pelser

1977; Smoot and Hale 1977). The inhibitory activity of imazalil against *Alternaria* sp. and *Geotrichum* sp. in vitro is poor (López-García *et al.* 2003).

Sorbic Acid

Sorbic acid (CH_3-CH=CH-CH=CH-COOH), or its sodium or potassium salts, is a widely used preservative found naturally in some berries (Sofos 1988). It has been applied to citrus fruits in commercial packinghouses to control decay, although its use is not common. Among more than twenty organic acids and salts tested, potassium sorbate and sodium benzoate were the most effective for the control of green mold on oranges and lemons (Palou *et al.* 2002C). They were about equal in activity to each other and to sodium carbonate. Only sorbic acid has regulatory approval for postharvest use on citrus. Smoot and McCornack (1978) applied potassium sorbate (2%) in a non-recoverable water spray to seven cultivars of mandarins, oranges, and late-season grapefruits. Control of phomopsis stem-end rot and penicillium mold by potassium sorbate was at least equal to that provided by sodium *ortho*-phenylphenol. The sorbate treatment was generally less effective than thiabendazole and benomyl against penicillium strains that were sensitive to the benzimidazole fungicides. Gutter (1981) reported treatment of fruit with potassium sorbate alone did not substantially reduce green mold in inoculated fruit, but only delayed the onset of decay by one or two weeks. Palou *et al.* (2002C) similarly observed potassium sorbate effectiveness declined when post-treatment storage times were prolonged. Immersion of fruit in heated solutions of sorbic acid or potassium sorbate are the most effective methods of application (Kitagawa and Kawada 1984; Wild 1987). When applied to lemons by immersing the fruit in 50°C solution for 2 min in an aqueous 2% sorbic acid solution, control of sour rot as effective or better than sodium *ortho*-phenylphenol similarly applied (Kitagawa and Kawada 1984). Control of green mold by immersion 0.2 M solution of potassium sorbate at pH 7.9 heated to 40.6°C was superior on lemons than on oranges, probably due to rind pH differences (Palou *et al.* 2002C).

Sorbic acid treatment has been employed to manage fungicide-resistant strains of *P. digitatum*. Nelson *et al.* (1981) investigated the effect of adding 2% potassium sorbate to a water-base wax containing thiabendazole (3 g/liter) or benomyl (1 g/liter). They reported that the addition of potassium sorbate resulted in a significant reduction in penicillium decay in commercial shipments of lemons and grapefruit from packinghouses that were contaminated with benzimidazole-resistant spores. However, Wild (1987) reported the interaction of the combination was solely additive and no particular synergy was present to affect control of thiabendazole-resistant isolates.

Other Fungicides

Guazatine is a broad-spectrum water-soluble fungicide that can eradicate incipient infections of penicillium molds and sour rot (Fig. 13.10). Treatment of citrus within 1 day after inoculation (ambient temperature ca. 22°C and a guazatine concentration of 250-1000 µg-ml⁻¹) eradicated incipient infections of green and blue mold, including isolates that were resistant to fungicides now in practical use (Brown 1983; Hartill *et al.* 1977; Eckert *et al.* 1981; Tugwell *et al.* 1981; Kuramoto and Yamada 1976). Residues of the fungicide on treated fruit did not protect against subsequent infection at new inoculation sites nor did high treatment levels (2000 µg-ml⁻¹) inhibit sporulation of *Penicillium* on diseased fruits (Brown 1983; Gutter *et al.* 1981; Eckert *et al.* 1981; Tugwell *et al.* 1981; Hartill *et al.* 1983).

Guazatine was the first fungicide recognized to have strong activity against incipient infections of sour rot. Several investigators have demonstrated that guazatine (250-1000 µg-ml⁻¹) applied at room temperature within 24 hours after inoculation provides excellent control of sour rot (Pelser and la Grange 1981; Schachnai and Barash 1982; Eckert *et al.* 1981; Kuramoto and Yamada 1976; Brown 1979; Rippon and Morris 1981; Tugwell *et al.* 1981). Unfortunately, strains of *P. italicum* that are resistant to guazatine were isolated (Hartill *et al.* 1983; Wild 1983).

Guazatine does not appear to be effective against diseases caused by *Alternaria, Phomopsis,* or *Colletotrichum* on mandarins (Kuramoto and Yamada

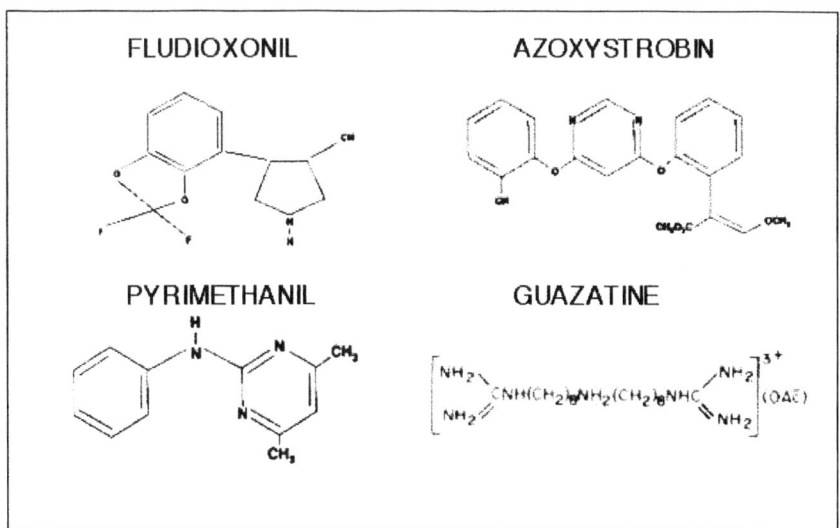

Fig. 13.10. Structures of several experimental fungicides evaluated for postharvest use on citrus fruit.

1976), but showed significant activity against diplodia stem-end rot when applied to oranges as a drench before degreening (Brown 1983). Benomyl (600 μg-ml⁻¹) was much more effective against diplodia stem-end rot than guazatine (1000 μg-ml⁻¹) when both treatments were applied as a nonrecoverable spray after degreening. Guazatine has been used commercially on citrus fruits for many years and residue tolerances have been established in many countries, but not the United States, where it can neither be used nor can fruit treated with it be imported.

Several promising new postharvest fungicides were identified recently and actions to obtain their regulatory approval are in progress. Many modern fungicides, including these promoted for citrus postharvest use, are classified as "reduced-risk" by the U.S. Environmental Protection Agency, which means their environmental and dietary hazards are perceived to be very low and this facilitates their regulatory approval (Adaskaveg *et al.* 2002). In addition to domestic regulatory approval, another significant regulatory issue is their approval by countries that import citrus fruit from the United States, because a substantial portion of the crop is exported. They include: 1) pyrimethanil, an anilino-pyrimidine; 2) fludioxonil, a phenylpyrrole; and 3) azoxystrobin, a strobilurin (Fig. 13.10). The mode of action of these compounds differs both from each other and imazalil, thiabendazole, and sodium orthophenyl phenate. Their efficacy does not exceed the current fungicides and their value is primarily in the management of *P. digitatum* isolates resistant to the existing fungicides. Brief immersion in a combination of fludioxonil and azoxystrobin controlled green mold on Valenica oranges as well as imazalil, but they were inferior to it when used alone (Cochran *et al.* 2003). None control sour rot.

Thermal Treatments

Heat treatments employed to control postharvest decay include hot water treatments, from 15 seconds to five minutes in duration, and thermal curing or conditioning treatments, where the fruit are subjected to elevated temperatures for up to several days. Both approaches inhibit growth of the pathogen, while wound healing proceeds in the fruit. The influence of postharvest thermal treatments on the interactions of pathogens with citrus fruit and other hosts has been reviewed (Schirra *et al.* 2000).

Hot Water Treatment. Particularly for producers of fruit where fungicide treatments must be avoided, hot water treatment may be of interest. In most work hot water treatments of one to five minutes were evaluated, while recently, very brief treatments (less than 30 seconds) have received considerable attention. Hot water treatment is most feasible and effective for the control brown rot, caused by *Phytopthora* spp. (Klotz and Dewolfe 1961A; Schiffmann-Nadel and Cohen 1966), moderately effective for control of green and blue molds (Porat *et al.* 2000A; Palou *et al.* 2001B; Smilanick *et al.* 2003), and not effective for sour rot (Smilanick *et al.* 2003) or *Diplodia* stem end rot (Brown and Baraka 1996). It was more effective on lemons and oranges than mandarin oranges (Palou *et al.* 2002B).

The risk of hot water injury to the fruit has been the primary barrier to the commercial implementation of this treatment and this issue deserves special attention and evaluation by those who want to employ this process. Many workers immersed citrus fruit in water at high temperatures, typically 50°C for up to three minutes, without injury to the fruit in extensively repeated trials (Houck 1967; Rodov *et al.* 1995A, Shirra *et al.* 2004). Even a brief water drench at temperatures as high as 63°C over rotating brushes treatments was tolerated by many varieties without injury (Porat *et al.* 2000A; Smilanick *et al.* 2003). However, Palou *et al.* (2001B) reported that although effective control of green mold was obtained with water treatments of oranges of one to several minutes duration at 50 to 55°C, this effectiveness was associated with rind injuries. Citrus fruit can vary widely in their tolerance to heat, even within the same variety. To control green mold, Houck (1977) recommended 5 to 10 min immersion of lemons in water at 51.7°C or 1 min at 54.4°C. This treatment was just tolerated by yellow, winter-harvested lemons, the most sensitive fruit he tested, and was readily tolerated by green, summer-harvested lemons, which were very resistant to heat injury and could tolerate much higher temperatures. Fawcett (1936) reported the tolerance of citrus fruit to hot water improved substantially if a period of 2 or 3 days elapsed between harvest and treatment, and he recommended this be done routinely. Porat and coworkers (2000A) evaluated a short hot water brushing treatment where citrus fruit were treated for seconds. A brief (20 sec) high volume, low pressure, hot water drench was applied over rotating brushes to Eureka lemons and Valencia oranges. Green mold incidence was reduced by 45 to 55% on Minneola tangerines, Shamouti oranges, and Star Ruby red grapefruit by a 20 sec treatment of 56°C water without injury to the fruit. Using similar treatments, Smilanick and coworkers (2003) reported green mold incidence was reduced from 97.9 and 98.0% on untreated lemons and oranges, respectively, to 14.5 and 9.4% by 30 sec treatment with 63°C water. The fruit were not injured by these treatments. Sour rot was not reduced by this treatment.

The mode of action of hot water has been studied. Sub-lethal hot water treatments at 50 to 53°C that did not kill *P. digitatum* spores caused a delay in germination and in the subsequent growth and sporulation of the pathogen (Schirra *et al.* 2000). These treatments increased resistance to infection and induced ß1-3 glucanases and chitinases in grapefruit (Pavoncello *et al.* 2001; Porat *et al.* 2000B). Nafussi and coworkers (2001) reported treatment of lemons for 2 min with water at 52 to 53°C caused a transient inhibition in the growth of *P. digitatum* for 24 to 48 hours, during which lignin production, scoparone, and scoletin accumulated in inoculated wounds and infections were delayed or stopped.

Hot water treatment can have other benefits, primarily increases in chilling tolerance and fruit surface sanitation. The resistance of Star Ruby grapefruit to chilling injury was greatly enhanced (Porat *et al.* 2000B). Natural rind surface microbe populations, most of which are not decay pathogens but can be of concern for produce sanitation or juice preparation purposes, are greatly reduced by hot water treatment (Pao and Davis 1999; Porat *et al.* 2000A; Smilanick *et al.* 2003). Commercial use of hot water alone is rare in the United States, but the technique is commonly used with dilute fungicide solutions or carbonate salts at lower temperatures. In addition to the risk of fruit injury, energy costs to heat water can also be a significant barrier to the implementation of hot water treatments.

Curing. Holding harvested fruit for one half to several days under humid conditions at 30°C or higher is termed a long-term curing treatment (Schirra *et al.* 2000). These temperatures delay or inhibit *P. digitatum* growth, reduce infections among fruit inoculated before treatment (Brown 1973; Fawcett and Barger 1927; Stange and Eckert 1994), accelerate acquisition of resistance to infection within wounds (Brown and Barmore 1983), and improve retention of the preformed antifungal compound citral (Ben-Yehoshua *et al.* 1995). Thermal death points for cultures of *P. digitatum*, *P. italicum*, and *Phytopthora infestans* are about 33°C. Other pathogens can tolerate this temperature and diseases they cause can be exacerbated with curing regimes that control penicillium decay, such as *G. citri-aurantii*, cultures of which become non-viable at 39°C and above, and *A. citri* and *L. theobromae*, both of which become non-viable at 42°C and above (Ben Yeoshua and Eckert 1989). Thermal inhibition alone does not predict curing efficacy, however, because blue mold (Plaza *et al.* 2003B) is not controlled by regimes that control green mold and these pathogens have similar thermal tolerances. Curing is rarely deliberately done commercially, although some control of green mold occurs as a consequence of ethylene degreening at 30°C, a common practice in Florida. Curing to reduce decay within individually shrink-wrapped citrus fruit has been well demonstrated (Ben-Yehoshua and Eckert 1989; Shirra *et al.* 2000). Reluctance to employ curing commercially exists because of concerns about accelerated weight loss during the curing period and the paucity of information about its impact on fruit quality.

Another class of thermal treatments have been developed to reduce chilling injury. These enable the use of lower storage temperatures that can delay senescence and in some cases decay of the fruit, because the growth of many pathogens is slowed or stopped and because lesions caused by chilling injury are eliminated, which can be sites of infection. Temperature conditioning employs a single postharvest pre-storage treatment before cold storage. For example, Hatton and Cubbedge (1983) kept grapefruit for 7 days at 16°C before the fruit were moved to long-term storage at 1°C and developed significantly less chilling injury than fruit stored constantly at 1°C, although the incidence of green mold and phomopsis stem-end rot was not reduced by this treatment. Intermittent warming employs repeated periods of warming the fruit during cold storage to reduce chilling injury so the fruit can be stored at lower temperatures (Davis and Hofmann 1973; Porat *et al.* 2003; Schirra and Cohen 1999).

Variable temperature regimes are rarely employed in the United States because of concerns about dehydration of the fruit during treatment (Plaza *et al.* 2003B), exacerbation of physiological disorders, such as rind break-down (Eckert and Eaks, 1989), or concerns about impacts on fruit flavor (Schirra *et al.* 2000). Schirra *et al.* (2004) described quality changes caused by two days treatment at 37°C of four blood orange varieties. Compared to constant 1°C storage, the warm treatment reduced subsequent chilling injuries that developed at 1°C, increased internal ethanol content three-fold or more, markedly increased maturity indices, significantly reduced titratable acidity, and greatly reduced the organoleptic quality. Exhaustive evaluation of this kind applied to more common citrus varieties is needed before thermal regimes can be employed.

Biological Control

The postharvest application of antagonistic microbes to citrus fruit to control postharvest decay was first investigated by de Matos (1983), who showed a *Rhototorula* sp., identified among many microbes isolated from lemon surfaces, and *Trichoderma viride* could significantly reduce green mold when co-inoculated with *P. digitatum*. Soon after this, Singh and Deverall (1984) reported dipping citrus fruit in whole *Bacillus subtilis* cultures or cell-free filtrates controlled *A. citri*, *G. candidum*, and *P. digitatum*. Since that time, a large volume of work in this area was published, and many other antagonists were identified and characterized, and several commercial products released for use on citrus and other fruit (El-Ghaouth *et al.* 2002; Janisiewicz and Korsten 2002). All aggressively colonize wounds on the fruit. Approved products cannot grow at human body temperature, to minimize risks that they could colonize humans, and themselves are not pathogens of other plants or animals (Janisiewicz and Korsten 2002; Smilanick *et al.* 1996). The first products, introduced in 1995, were Aspire, containing *Candida oleophila*, and various formulations of Bio-Save, containing *Pseudomonas syringae* pv. *syringae*. Recently, excellent control of green mold and good control of sour rot by another biological control approach, termed "bio-fumigation", which consisted of emanations from grain colonized by the filamentous fungus *Muscador albus* from open cups placed within boxes of lemons (Mercier and Smilanick 2003). The major antifungal volatiles produced by this fungus were 2-methyl-1-butanol, phenethyl alcohol, and isobutryic acid, although the mode of action is incompletely known (Mercier and Jiménez 2004).

Commercial use of postharvest biological control products for citrus has been modest, primarily because of issues about efficacy and secondarily because they do not control sporulation like some fungicides. Brown and Chambers (1996) reported significant control of green mold was obtained with these products, but the level of control and its consistency was usually less compared to thiabendazole or imazalil, and that diplodia and phomopsis stem-end rots were not controlled. Brown and coworkers (2000) reported that major factors influencing efficacy of *C. oleophila* was how quickly and thoroughly it colonized rind injuries. Colonization of puncture-related injuries that either encompassed only oil glands or individually ruptured glands occurred within 1 to 2 days at 21°C. Ruptured oil glands were colonized more effectively if treated 7 hr after injury rather than immediately. Peel oil was toxic to cells of *C. oleophila* but not to spores of *P. digitatum*. Colonization of larger puncture injuries by *C. oleophila* was comparable after 2 days at 21 and 30°C, but no colonization occurred at 13°C. *C. oleophila* colonized punctures more uniformly than individually damaged oil glands, and provided more effective control of green mold originating at punctures than at oil gland injuries. Droby *et al.* (2002) showed *C. oleophila* colonization induced pathogen resistance in grapefruit which was associated with elevated chitinase, endoglucanase, and phenylalanine ammonia lyase activities, phytoalexin accumulation, and they observed inhibited growth of *P. digitatum* germlings inside colonized wounds.

Commercial acceptance of biological control products will require reliable and high levels of efficacy. Particularly important is an improvement in eradication of infections 24 hr old at the time of treatment, because biological control treatments generally fail to control these (Brown and Baraka 1996; Smilanick and Denis-Arrue 1992; Smilanick 1994), while most fungicides do (Gutter 1969; Wild and Spohr 1989). Approaches to improve the efficacy of biological control agents that have been demonstrated or suggested include their use before or after thermal curing (Brown *et al.* 2000; Plaza *et al.* 2004) or hot water treatment (Brown and Baraka 1996; Obagwu and Korsten 2003), the addition of low rates of fungicides (Droby *et al.* 1993), their use with antifungal or substances such as 2-deoxy-D-glucose (El-Ghaouth *et al.* 2001) or sodium carbonate or bicarbonate (Teixidó *et al.* 2001; Obagwu and Korsten 2003), or with elicitors of natural defense processes such as chitosan (Fajardo *et al.* 1998) glycolchitosan (El-Ghaouth *et al.* 2000), or calcium chloride (Chalutz *et al.* 1992). Application of the antagonists to citrus groves before harvest of the fruit also significantly reduced postharvest decay (Huang *et al.* 1993).

Controlled Atmosphere Storage

Controlled or modified atmosphere storage was reported to cause modest reductions in the occurrence of postharvest diseases among stored citrus fruit in some studies, probably by changes in the physiology of the fruit, such as delayed senescence, decreases in chilling injuries, retention of rind and internal quality, or reduced ethylene generation, rather than inhibition of the pathogens by the atmospheres (Grierson and Ben-Yeoshua 1986; Singh and Singh 1996; Smoot 1969). The usefulness of controlled atmospheres for decay control of citrus fruit is limited by the off-flavors and rind injuries that develop at oxygen levels low enough, or carbon dioxide levels high enough, to inhibit these pathogens (Hatton and Cubbedge 1977; Houck and Snider 1969). Hatton and Cubbedge (1977), in a review of controlled atmosphere storage of citrus fruit, stated that it has been found to be generally of little or no advantage for extending the storage life of citrus fruits. They state that increased, rather than reduced, decay was mentioned in some studies as a limiting factor in the use of controlled atmospheres. Increased decay was a consequence of infections that occurred within rind injuries associated with the controlled atmospheres; if these injuries were not present, decay incidence was not affected.

Summary

The applications and major limitations of the fungicides and other measures currently employed to control decay of citrus fruits during storage and marketing are summarized in Table 13.4. Currently, the major limitations of these treatments are fungicide-resistant *Penicillium* isolates (discussed later in this chapter), poor control of sour rot and alternaria rot, and regulatory restrictions on acceptance of residues of certain compounds in some citrus-importing countries. Approaches that control fruit decay, yet leave no objectionable residue on the fruit, are preferable to many food regulation authorities and marketers. This line of reasoning has engendered a substantial amount of research on the use of other than conventional fungicides to control postharvest diseases and these efforts will continue.

FUNGICIDE-RESISTANT PATHOGENS

The intensive and continuous use of sodium *ortho*-phenylphenol, thiabendazole, and imazalil has resulted in a serious problem of fungicide-resistant strains of *P. digitatum* and *P. italicum* (Bus *et al.* 1991; Bus 1992; Eckert 1982; Eckert and Wild 1983; Holmes and Eckert 1999; Houck 1977). Treatment of fruit with one fungicide before storage usually results in the buildup of resistant isolates in the pathogen population, so that a structur-

TABLE 13.4. Effectiveness of Common Approved Treatments Against Postharvest Diseases of Citrus Fruits

| | Preharvest infection | | | Wound pathogens | | | |
| | Stem-end rots | | *Phytophthora* brown rot | *Penicillium* spp. | | *Geotrichum* sour rot | Comment |
Treatment	*Lasiodiplodia*	*Alternaria*		Infection	Sporulation		
Hypochlorite	–	–	–	–	–	–	—
Hot water	–	–	+	±	–	±	a
Na$_2$CO$_3$/NaHCO$_3$	–	–	±	±	–	±	b
ortho-Phenylphenol	–	–	–	±	–	±	b,c
Sorbic acid	±	–	–	±	–	–	b
Thiabendazole	+	–	–	+	+	–	c
Imazalil	±	±	–	±	+	–	c
Biological control	–	–	–	–	–	±	d
2,4-D	±	+	–	–	–	–	e
Gibberellic acid	?	–	–	–	–	±	e

The indicators +, ±, and – indicate control is excellent, good, or none, respectively.

a. Water temperature typically above 50°C, determined by length of contact and application method.

b. These are most effective as tank or drench treatments heated to 40°C or more, risk of phytotoxicity present, a brief water rinse after treatment is common.

c. Resistant *Penicillium* isolates common within some packinghouses.

d. Refers to *Pseudomonas syringae* pv. *syringae* strain ESC-10 (Bio-Save). Limited eradicant action, must be applied within hours of infection for best results. Sour rot efficacy data from Smilanick, unpublished.

e. These growth regulators are not fungicidal, they delay senescence and prolong natural resistance of the fruit to infection.

ally related fungicide (cross resistant) cannot be used effectively on the same lot of fruit after storage, although currently all of the fungicides now in use are not structurally related to each other. The problem of fungicide-resistant strains of *P. digitatum* and *P. italicum* is of worldwide importance (Fig. 13.11) but can be managed if the situation is recognized early and dealt with intelligently.

The handling sequence for oranges (Fig. 13.1) suggests how fungicide-resistant strains of *Penicillium* spp. are selected and proliferate. Early-season oranges may be drenched with a solution of thiabendazole or imazalil and then placed in an ethylene degreening room at 20°C. The fungicide deposited on the fruit suppresses the sensitive strains, which are dominant in the field population of *Penicillium* spp., thereby permitting fungicide-resistant strains to colonize the fruit and sporulate after several days, in the absence of competition with sensitive strains. When the fruit are subsequently

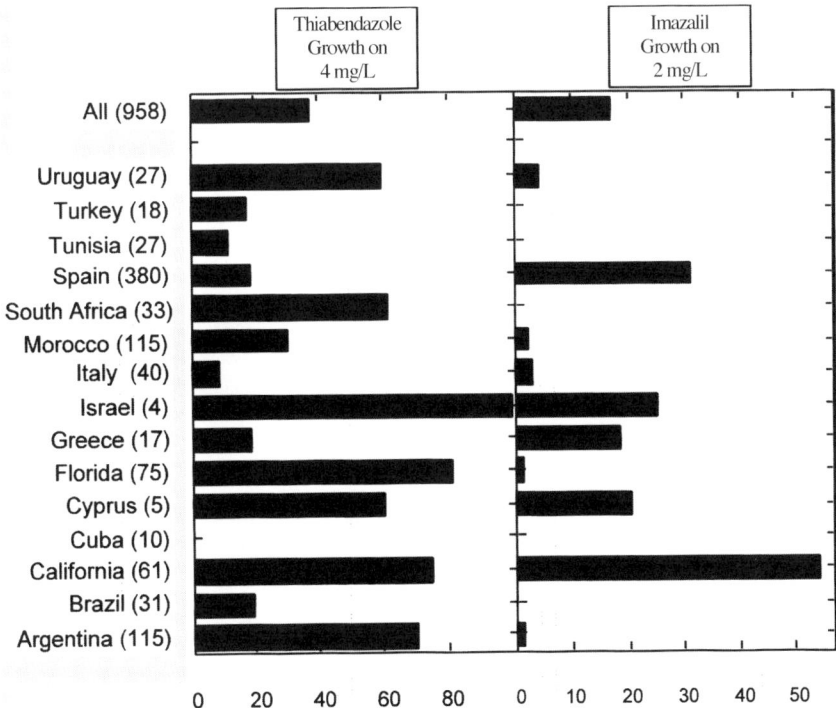

Figure 13.11. Frequency of isolates of *P. digitatum* from diverse geographic origins from decayed citrus fruit capable of growth on media amended with thiabendazole at 4 mg/L or imazalil at 0.2 mg/L. Numbers in parenthesis are the number of isolates evaluated. Most sensitive isolates cannot grow on media with concentrations of either fungicide above about 0.05 mg/L.
From Bus et al. 1991.

dumped from the field bins, spores of the resistant strains become airborne and can infect newly harvested fruit as they, in turn, are placed in the de-greening room. After degreening, the fruit—now contaminated with fungicide-resistant spores—receive a second treatment with the same fungicide in the wax formulation before shipment to market. Inevitably, the first fungicide treatment selects for resistant strains during the degreening period; therefore, the second treatment applied on the pack line fails to control fruit decay during marketing.

In California, lemons are commonly washed in a bath of sodium carbonate or bicarbonate or SOPP, coated with a wax formulation containing 2,4-D and thiabendazole, or imazalil, and then stored at 15°C for several months (Fig. 13.1). Resistant strains that are selected during the storage period contaminate sound fruit when the boxes are dumped after storage, leading to the failure of the second treatment of these same fungicides applied in the wax formulation before packing. The contamination of lemons entering storage with fungicide-resistant spores that have been selected by fungicide residues on the preceding fruit lot during storage is another situation that may create a difficult resistance problem.

Fungicide-resistant strains also frequently develop when lemons or oranges are packed, but are not shipped because of a weak market demand. These fruit remain in cold storage for several weeks before they are returned to the packinghouse for removal of decayed fruit from the cartons prior to shipment. Fungicide-resistant *Penicillium* spp., selected during storage by the fungicide deposits on the fruit, contaminate all fruit passing through the packinghouse, resulting in a great reduction in effectiveness of the final fungicide treatments.

The management of fungicide-resistance problems is currently an area of active research. The layout and management of most packinghouses is sufficiently unique that procedures to reduce development of resistant strains must be customized to specific circumstances. Two approaches dominate in the development of an overall strategy: (1) sanitation measures and antisporulant treatments to suppress the spore population to a very low level and (2) fungicide regimens that do not encourage the proliferation of fungicide-resistant strains in the spore population.

An effective sanitation program will reduce the level of resistant spores in a packinghouse and is critical to manage fungicide resistance problems. A program should include the following: (1) isolate affected lots and eliminate decayed fruit so as to minimize contamination of the packinghouse atmosphere with spores. The design of the packinghouse physically isolate and separate of "dirty" operations, such as repacking cartons or bin and box dumping, from "clean" operations, such sorting and packing equipment or storage rooms; (2) disinfect spore-contaminated fruit by spraying, pressure washing, or immersing them in a hypochlorite solution before they are conveyed into the packinghouse and disinfest the fruit-handling equipment and premises with an appropriate biocide; (3) if fruit are passed through tanks or re-circulating drenches containing fungicides, the solutions should contain hypochlorite or be periodically sanitized by heat or filtration to prevent an accumulation of fungicide resistant spores; (4) if possible, treat fruit before storage with an effective antisporulant fungicide such as imazalil. Antisporulant action has also been obtained by the use of ozone in the air of storage rooms, provided the fruit are in open bins or boxes with large vents so the gas can penetrate to the fruit (Harding 1968; Palou *et al.* 2002A; Palou *et al.* 2003). A study of the benefits of a sanitation program in three commercial lemon packinghouses in central California demonstrated that a reduction in spore inoculum reduced fruit decay due to thiabendazole-resistant *Penicillium* strains and improved the profitability of these operations (Bancroft *et al.* 1984).

Application of several fungicides in an appropriate sequence can prevent or at least delay the buildup of fungicide-resistant strains of *Penicillium* (Wild 1980; Eckert 1982; Eckert and Wild 1983). This strategy is especially valuable in situations where fruit are treated with fungicides both before and after storage or a holding period (e.g., degreening, lemon storage). The fungicides applied before storage are chosen on the basis that they will not encourage the proliferation during storage of *Penicillium* strains that are resistant to the fungicides applied after storage. The latter treatments are critical, since they must protect the fruit from decay during shipment and marketing. For example, lemons can be treated with sodium carbonate, potassium sorbate, borax, and/or imazalil *before* storage and with SOPP and/or thiabendazole *after* storage. The prestorage treatments in this case would not select for biotypes of *Penicillium* that are resistant to SOPP or thiabendazole. The success of this strategy depends upon an efficient sanitation program because the buildup of a large population of fungicide-resistant strains in the packinghouse could jeopardize the poststorage fungicide treatments.

The strategy employed is also influenced by which pencillium disease is most troublesome. The incidence of thiabendazole and imazalil resistance among *P. digitatum* isolates is common, while only thiabendazole resistance is common among *P. italicum* isolates and imazalil resistance is rare (Bus *et al.* 1991; Holmes and Eckert 1999), so imazalil presumably can be effective in managing thiabendazole resistant isolates of this pathogen. Another important aspect of resistance management is the fitness of resistant isolates. Isolates of *P. digitatum* resistant to benzimidazoles (Eckert and Wild 1983) or imazalil (Holmes and Eckert 1999) are less fit than sensitive isolates; the proportion of resistant spores declines rapidly after several cycles of co-inoculation with sensitive spores on fruit. Presumably, if the use of these products is stopped, they could be re-introduced later and their effectiveness would be to some extent restored.

REFERENCES

ADAM, D. B., McNEIL, J., HANSON-MERZ, B. M., McCARTHY, D. F. and STOKES, J. 1949. The estimation of latent infection in oranges. Aust. J. Sci. Res., Set. B: 2, 1-18.

ADASKAVEG, J. E., FORSTER, H., and SOMMER, N. F. 2002. Principles of postharvest pathology and management of decays of edible horticultural crops, pp. 163-195. *In* Postharvest Technology of Horticultural Crops. Pub. 3311, University of California Agr. and Natural Resources, Oakland, CA.

AMAT, S. R. 1988. Defectos y alteraciones de los frutos citricos en su comercializacion. Second ed., Lit Nicolau, Almassora, Spain.

ANON. 2000. Code of federal regulations, protection of the environment. Title 21, part 178.1010. Office of the Federal Register, National Archives and Records Administration, Washington, D.C.

BANCROFT, M. N., GARDNER, P. D., ECKERT, J. W. and BARITELLE, J. L. 1984. Comparison of decay control strategies in California lemon packinghouses. Plant Dis. 68, 24-28.

BARASH, I. 1968. Liberation of polygalacturonase during spore germination by *Geotrichum candidum*. Phytopathology 58, 1364-1371.

BARASH, I. and ANGEL, E. 1970. Isolation and properties of an exopolygalacturonase produced by *Penicillium digitatum* during infection of lemon fruits. Isr. J. Bot. 19, 599-608.

BARASH, I. and EYAL, Z. 1970. Properties of a polygalacturonase produced by *Geotrichum candidum*. Phytopathology 60, 27-30.

BARGER, W. R. 1928. Sodium bicarbonate as citrus fruit disinfectant. Calif. Citrograph 13, 164, 172-174.

BARGER, W. R. and HAWKINS, L. A. 1925. Borax as a disinfectant for citrus fruit. J. Agr. Res. 30, 189-192.

BARKAI-GOLAN, R. 1966. Reinfestation of citrus fruits by pathogenic fungi in the packing house. Isr. J. Agr. Res. 16, 133-138.

BARMORE, C. R. and BROWN, G. E. 1978. Preharvest ethephon application reduces anthracnose on Robinson tangerine. Plant Dis. Rep. 62, 541-544.

BARMORE, C. R. and BROWN, G. E. 1979. Role of pectolytic enzymes and galacturonic acid in citrus fruit decay caused by *Penicillium digitatum*. Phytopathology 69, 675-678.

BARMORE, C. R. and BROWN, G. E. 1981. Polygalacturonase from citrus fruit infected with *Penicillium italicum*. Phytopathology 71, 328-331.

BARMORE, C. R. and BROWN, G. E. 1982. Spread of *Penicillium digitatum* and *Penicillium italicum* during contact between citrus fruits. Phytopathology 72, 116-120.

BARMORE, C. R., SNOWDEN, S. E. and BROWN, G. E. 1984. Endopolygalacturonase from valencia oranges infected with *Diplodia natalensis*. Phytopathology 75, 735-737.

BARTHOLOMEW, E. T. 1926. Alternaria rot of lemons. Calif. Agr. Exp. Stn. Bull. 408.

BATES, G. R. 1933. Oil glands of citrus fruits as an avenue of infection. Nature 132, 751-752.

BAUDOIN, A. B. A. M. and ECKERT, J. W. 1982. Factors influencing the susceptibility of lemons to infection by *Geotrichum candidum*. Phytopathology 72, 1592-1597.

BAUDOIN, A. B. A. M. and ECKERT, J. W. 1985A. Development of resistance against *Geotrichum candidum* in lemon peel injuries. Phytopathology 74, 174-179.

BAUDOIN, A. B. A. M. and ECKERT, J. W. 1985B. Influence of preformed characteristics of lemon peel on susceptibility to *Geotrichum candidum*. Physiol. Plant. Pathol. 26, 15 1-163.

BEN-YEHOSHUA, S., and ECKERT, J. W. 1989. Studies of curing, water-saturated atmosphere and individual seal-packaging in reducing decay and extending life of harvested fruits. Final report for Binational Agr. Res. and Development Fund Project I-749-84, Beltsville, MD.

BEN-YEHOSHUA, S., RODOV, V., KIM, J. J., and CARMELI, S. 1992. Preformed and induced antifungal materials of citrus fruit in relation to the enhancement of decay resistance by heat and ultraviolet treatments. J. Agr. Food Chem. 40, 1217-1221.

BEN-YEHOSHUA, S., RODOV, V. FANG, D. Q., and KIM, J. J. 1995. Preformed antifungal compounds of citrus fruit: Effect of postharvest treatments with heat and growth regulators. J. Agr. Food Chem. 43, 1062-1066.

BERAHA, L., RAMSEY, G. B., SMITH, M. A. and WRIGHT, W. R. 1959. Factors influencing the use of gamma radiation to control decay of lemons and oranges. Phytopathology 49, 91-96.

BROOKS, C. 1944. Stem-end rot of oranges and factors affecting its control. J. Agr. Res. 68, 363-381.

BROWN, G. E. 1973. Development of green mold in degreened oranges. Phytopathology 63, 1104-1107.

BROWN, G. E. 1974. Postharvest citrus decay as affected by Benlate applications in the grove. Proc. Fla. State Hort. Soc. 87, 237-240.

BROWN, G. E. 1975. Factors affecting postharvest development of *Colletotrichum gloeosporioides* in citrus fruits. Phytopathology 65, 404-409.

BROWN, G. E. 1977A. Application of benzimidazole fungicides for citrus decay control. Proc. Int. Soc. Citriculture 1, 272-277.

BROWN, G. E. 1977B. Ultrastructure of penetration of ethylene degreened Robinson tangerines by *Colletotrichum gloeosporioides*. Phytopathology 67, 315-320.

BROWN, G. E. 1978. Hypersensitive response of orange-colored Robinson tangerines to *Colletotrichum gloeosporioides* after ethylene treatment. Phytopathology 68, 700-706.

BROWN, G. E. 1979. Biology and control of *Geotrichum candidum*, the cause of citrus sour rot. Proc. Fla. State Hort. Soc. 92, 186-189.

BROWN, G. E. 1981. Investigations with experimental citrus postharvest fungicides in Florida. Proc. Int. Soc. Citriculture 2, 815-818.

BROWN, G. E. 1983. Control of Florida citrus decays with guazatine. Proc. Fla. State Hort. Soc. 96, 335-337.

BROWN, G. E. 1984. Efficacy of citrus postharvest fungicides applied in water or resin solution water wax. Plant Dis. 68, 415-418.

BROWN, G. E. 1992. Factors affecting the occurrence of anthracnose on Florida citrus fruit. Proc. Int. Soc. Citriculture 3, 1044-1048.

BROWN, G. E. and ALBRIGO, L. G. 1972. Grove application of benomyl and its persistence in orange fruit. Phytopathology 62, 1434-1438.

BROWN, G. E. and BARAKA, M. A. 1996. Effect of washing sequence and heated solutions to degreened Hamlin oranges on *Diplodia* stem-end rot, fruit colour and phytotoxicity. Proc. Int. Soc. Citriculture 2, 1164-1170.

BROWN, G. E. and BARMORE, C. R. 1977. The effect of ethylene on susceptibility of Robinson tangerines to anthracnose. Phytopathology 67, 120-123.

BROWN, G. E. and BARMORE, C. R. 1983. Resistance of healed citrus exocarp to penetration by *Penicillium digitatum*. Phytopathology 73, 691-694.

BROWN, G. E. and BURNS, J. K. 1998. Enhanced activity of abscission enzymes predisposes oranges to invasion by *Diplodia natalensis* during ethylene degreening. Postharvest Biol. Tech. 14, 217-227.

BROWN, G. E. and CHAMBERS, M. 1996. Evaluation of biological products for the control of postharvest diseases of Florida citrus. Proc. Fla. State Hort. Soc. 109, 278-282.

BROWN, G. E. and CRAIG, J. O. 1989. Effectiveness of aerosol fungicide applications in the degreening room for the control of citrus fruit decay. Proc. Fla. State Hort. Soc. 102, 181-185.

BROWN, G. E., DAVIS, C. and CHAMBERS, M. 2000. Control of citrus green mold with Aspire is impacted by the type of injury. Postharvest Biol. Tech. 18, 57-65.

BROWN, G. E., and DEZMAN, D. J. 1990. Uptake of imazalil by citrus fruit after postharvest application and the effect of residue distribution on sporulation of *Penicillium digitatum*. Plant Dis. 74, 927-930.

BROWN, G. E., and ECKERT, J. W. 2000. Anthracnose, pp. 37-38. *In* Compendium of citrus diseases, Second Edition. L. W. Timmer, S. M. Garnsey, and J. H. Grahm (Editors). APS Press, St. Paul, MN.

BROWN, G. E., ISMAIL, M. A. and BARMORE, C. R. 1978. Lignification of injuries to citrus fruit and susceptibility to green mold. Proc. Fla. State Hort. Soc. 91, 124-126.

BROWN, G. E. and LEE, H. S. 1993. Interactions of ethylene with citrus stem-end rot caused by *Diplodia natalensis*. Phytopathology 83, 909-912.

BROWN, G. E. and McCORNACK, A. A. 1969. Benlate, an experimental preharvest fungicide for control of postharvest citrus fruit decay. Proc. Fla State Hort. Soc. 82, 39-43.

BROWN, G. E. and McCORNACK, A. A. 1972. Decay caused by *Alternaria citri* in Florida citrus fruit. Plant Dis. Rep. 56, 909-912.

BROWN, G. E., McCORNACK, A. A. and SMOOT, J. J. 1967. Thiabendazole as a postharvest fungicide for Florida citrus fruit. Plant Dis. Rep. 51, 95-98.

BROWN, G. E. and MILLER, W. R. 1999. Maintaining fruit health after harvest. *In* Citrus Health Management, L. W. Timmer and L. W. Duncan (Editors). APS Press, St. Paul, MN.

BROWN, G. E., NAGY, S. and MARAULJA, M. 1983. Residues from postharvest nonrecovery spray applications of imazalil to oranges and effects on green mold caused by *Penicillium digitatum*. Plant Dis. 67, 954-957.

BROWN, G. E. and WILSON, W. C. 1968. Mode of entry of *Diplodia natalensis* and *Phomopsis citri* into Florida oranges. Phytopathology 58, 736-739.

BURGER, D. W. and DAVIS, R. M. 1982. New fungicides for the postharvest control of stem-end rot in Texas grapefruit. HortScience 17, 976-977.

BUS, V. G. 1992. ED$_{50}$ levels of *Penicillium digitatum* and *P. italicum* with reduced sensitivity to thiabendazole, benomyl and imazalil. Postharvest Biol. Tech. 1, 305-315.

BUS, V. G., BONGERS, A. J. and RISSE, L. A. 1991. Occurrence of *Penicillium digitatum* and *P. italicum* resistant to benomyl, thiabendazole, and imazalil on citrus fruit from different geographic origins. Plant Dis. 75, 1098-1100.

BUTLER, E. E., WEBSTER, R. K. and ECKERT, J. W. 1965. Taxonomy, pathogenicity, and physiological properties of the fungus causing sour rot of citrus. Phytopathology 55, 1262-1268.

CABRAS, P., SCHIRRA, M., PIRISI, F. M., GARAU, V. L. and ANGIONI, A. 1999. Factors affecting imazalil and thiabendazole uptake and persistence in citrus fruits following dip treatments. J. Agr. Food Chem. 47, 3352-3354.

CEPONIS, M. J., CAPPELLINI, R. A. and LIGHTNER, G. W. 1986. Disorders in citrus shipments to the New York market, 1972-1984. Plant Dis. 70, 1162-1165.

CHALUTZ, E., DROBY, L., COHEN, B., WEISS, B., DAUS, A., WILSON, C. and WISNIEWSKI, M. 1992. Calcium-enhanced biocontrol activity of two yeasts antagonists of citrus postharvest diseases. Proc. Int. Soc. Citriculture 3, 1066-1069.

CHRIST, R. A. 1966. The effect of handling on citrus wastage. S. Afr. Citrus J. 387, 7-14

COCHRAN, A., TALLY, A., and TEDFORD, E. 2003. Evaluation of tank mixtures of fludioxonil and azoxystrobin for postharvest disease control on citrus. Phytopathology 93, S17.

COGGINS, C. W., ANTHONY, M. F. and FRITTS, R. 1992. Postharvest use of gibb on lemons. Calif. Citrograph 78, 11-14.

COHEN, E., COGGINS, C. W. and ECKERT, J. W. 1991. Predisposition of citrus fruits to sour rot when submerged in water. Plant Dis. 75, 166-168.

CRIVELLI, G. 1966. Ricerche sulla utilizzazione e commercializzazione degli agrumi. Nota V: Prove sul potere fungistatico del 2-(4'tiazolil) benzimidazolo sui Penicilli delle arance. Freddo 20, 25-29.

DAVIDSE, L. C. 1986. Benzimidazole fungicides: Mechanism of action and biological impact. Ann. Rev. Phytopathol. 24, 43-65.

DAVIS, P. L. and HOFMANN, R. C. 1973. Reduction of chilling injury of citrus fruits in cold storage by intermittent warming. J. Food Sci. 3, 871-873.

De MATOS, A. P. 1983. Chemical and microbiological factors influencing the infection of lemons by *Geotrichum candidum* and *Penicillium digitatum*. Ph.D. dissertation, University of California, Riverside.

DEZMAN, D. J., NAGY, S. and BROWN, G. E. 1986. Postharvest fungal decay control chemicals: treatments and residues in citrus fruits. Residue Rev. 97, 37-92

DROBY, S., HOFSTEIN, I. R., WILSON, C. L., WISNIEWSKI, M., FRIDLENDER, B., COHEN, L., WEISS, B., DAUS, A., TIMAR, D. and CHALUTZ, E. 1993. Pilot testing of *Pichia guilliermondii*: a biocontrol agent of postharvest diseases of citrus fruit. Biol. Control 3, 47-52

DROBY, S., VINOKUR, V., WEISS, B., COHEN, L., DAUS, A., GOLDSCHMIDT and PORAT, R. 2002. Induction of resistance to *Penicillium digitatum* in grapefruit by the yeast biocontrol agent *Candida oleophila*. Phytopathology 92, 393-399.

ECKERT, J. W. 1959. Lemon sour rot. Calif. Citrograph 45, 30-31, 35, 36.

ECKERT, J. W. 1967. Application and use of postharvest fungicides. *In* Fungicides, Vol. 1. D. C. Torgeson (Editor). Academic Press, New York, NY.

ECKERT, J. W. 1977. Control of postharvest diseases. *In* Antifungal Compounds, Vol. 1. M. R. Siegel and H. D. Sisler (Editors). Marcel Dekker Inc., New York, NY.

ECKERT, J. W. 1982. Case study 5: Penicillium decay of citrus fruits. *In* Fungicide Resistance in Crop Protection, J. Dekker and S. G. Georgopoulos (Editors). PUDOC, Wageningen, Netherlands.

ECKERT, J. W., BRETSCHNEIDER, B. F. and RATNAYAKE, M. 1981. Investigations on new postharvest fungicides for citrus fruits in California. Proc. Int. Soc. Citriculture 2, 804-810.

ECKERT, J. W. and BROWN, G. E. 1986. Postharvest citrus diseases and their control. *In* Fresh Citrus Fruits, W. F. Wardowski, S. Nagy, and W. Grierson (Editors). Van Nostrand Reinhold Co., New York, NY.

ECKERT, J. W. and EAKS, I. L. 1989. Postharvest disorders and diseases of citrus fruits. *In* The Citrus Industry, Vol. 5. W. Reuther, E. C. Calavan, and G. E. Carman (Editors). University of California Press, Berkeley.

ECKERT, J. W. and KOLBEZEN, M. J. 1964. 2-Aminobutane salts for control of postharvest decay of citrus, apple, pear, peach, and banana fruits. Phytopathology 54, 978-986.

ECKERT, J. W. and KOLBEZEN, M. J. 1971. Chemical treatments for the control of postharvest diseases of citrus fruits. 683-693. *In* Proc. 6th British Insecticide and Fungicide Conf., Vol. 3.

ECKERT, J. W. and KOLBEZEN, M. J. 1977. Influence of formulation and application method on the effectiveness of benzimidazole fungicides for controlling postharvest diseases of citrus fruits. Neth. J. Plant Path. 83 (Suppl. 1), 343-352.

ECKERT, J. W. KOLBEZEN, M. J. and KRAGHT, A. J. 1969A. Applications of 2-aminobutane and thiabendazole for the control of penicillium decay of citrus fruits. Proc. Int. Soc. Citriculture 3, 1301-1308.

ECKERT, J. W. KOLBEZEN, M. J. and KRAMER, B. A. 1969B. Accumulation of o-phenylphenol by citrus fruit and pathogenic fungi in relation to decay control and residues. Proc. Int. Soc. Citriculture 2, 1097-1103.

ECKERT, J. W., KOLBEZEN. M. J., RAHM, M. L. and ECKARD, K. J. 1979. Influence of benomyl and methyl 2-benzimidazolecarbaiiiate on the development of *Penicillium digitatum* in the pericarp of orange fruit. Phytopathology 69, 934-939.

ECKERT, J. W., SIEVERT, J. R. and RATNAYAKE, M. 1994. Reduction of imazalil effectiveness against citrus green mold in California packinghouses by resistant biotypes of *Penicillium digitatum*. Plant Dis. 78, 971-974.

ECKERT, J. W. and WILD, B. L. 1983. Problems of fungicide resistance in penicillium rot of citrus fruits, pp. 525-556. *In* Pest Resistance to Pesticides, C. P. Georghiou and T. Saito (Editors). Plenum Press, New York, NY.

EL-GHAOUTH, A., SMILANICK, J. L., BROWN, G. E., IPPOLITO, A., WISNIEWSKI, M. and WILSON, C. L. 2000. Application of *Candida saitoana* and glycolchitosan for the control of postharvest diseases of apple and citrus fruit under semi-commercial conditions. Plant Dis. 84, 243-248.

EL-GHAOUTH, A., SMILANICK, J. L., BROWN, G. E., IPPOLITO, A. and WILSON, C. L. 2001. Control of apple and citrus fruits in semi-commercial tests with *Candida saitoana* and 2-deoxy-D-glucose. Biol. Control 20, 96-101.

EL-GHAOUTH, A., WILSON, C., WISNIEWSKI, M., DROBY, S., SMILANICK, J. L. and KUR-STEN, L. 2002. Biological control of citrus postharvest diseases, pp. 289-312. *In* Biological Control of Crop Diseases, S. S. Gnanamanickam (Editor). Marcel Dekker, Inc., New York, NY.

FAJARDO, J. E. MCCOLLUM, T. G., MCDONALD, R. E. and MAYER, R. T. 1998. Differential induction of proteins in orange flavedo by biologically based elicitors and challenged by *Penicillium digitatum* Sacc. Biol. Control 13, 143-151.

FAWCETT, H. S. 1936. Citrus Diseases and Their Control. 2nd ed. McGraw-Hill, New York, NY.

FAWCETT, H. S. and BARGER, W. R. 1927. Relationship of temperature to growth of *Penicillium italicum* and *P. digitatum* and to citrus fruit decay produced by these fungi. J. Agr. Res. 35, 925-931.

FELD, S. J., MENGE, J. A. and PEHRSON, J. E. 1979. Brown rot of citrus: a review of the disease. Citrograph 65, 101-106.

GRAHAM, J. H., TIMMER, L. W., DROUILLARD, D. L. and PEEVER, T. L. 1998. Characterization of *Phytophthora* spp. causing outbreaks of citrus brown rot in Florida. Phytopathology 88, 724-729

GREEN, F. M. 1932. The infection of oranges by Penicillium. J. Pomol. Hort. Sci. 10, 184-215.

GRIERSON, W. and BEN-YEOHOSHUA, S. 1986. Storage of citrus fruits. *In* Fresh Citrus Fruits, W. F. Wardowski, S. Nagy, and W. Grierson (Editors). Van Nostrand Reinhold Company, New York, NY.

GUTTER, Y. 1969. Effectiveness of preinoculation and postinoculation treatments with sodium ortho-phenylphenate, thiabendazole, and benomyl for green mold control in artificially inoculated Eureka lemons. Plant Dis. Rep. 53, 479-482.

GUTTER, Y. 1975. Interrelationships of *Penicillium digitatum* and *P. italicum* in thiabendazole treated oranges. Phytopathology 65, 498-499.

GUTTER, Y. 1977. Problems of decay in marketing citrus fruits: Strategy and solutions around the world: Israel. Proc. Int. Soc. Citriculture 1, 242-244.

GUTTER, Y. 1981. Investigations on new postharvest fungicides: Israel. Proc. Int. Soc. Citriculture 2, 810-811.

GUTTER, Y., YANKO, U., DAVIDSON, M. and RAHAT, M. 1974. Relationship between mode of application of thiabendazole and its effectiveness for control of green mold and inhibiting fungus sporulation on oranges. Phytopathology 64, 1477-1478.

GUTTER, Y., SCHACHNAI, A., SCHIFFMANN-NADEL, M. and DINOOR, A. 1981. Chemical control in citrus of green and blue molds resistant to benzimidazoles. Phytopath. Zeit. 102, 127-138.

HALL, D. J. and BICE, J. R. 1977. Packinghouse strategies for the control of fungicide-resistant molds. Proc. Fla. State Hort. Soc. 90, 138-141.

HARDING, P. R., JR. 1968. Effect of ozone on Penicillium mold decay and sporulation. Plant Dis. Rep. 52, 245-247.

HARDING, P. R., JR. 1976. R23979, a new imidazole derivative effective against postharvest decay of citrus by molds resistant to thiabendazole, benomyl. and 2-aminobutane. Plant Dis. Rep. 60, 643-646.

HARDING, P. R., JR. and SAVAGE, D. C. 1964. Investigation of possible correlation of hot-water washing with excessive storage decay in coastal California lemon packinghouses. Plant Dis. Rep. 48, 808-810.

HARDING, P. R., JR. and SAVAGE, D. C. 1965. Use of foam washers for treating poststorage lemons with sodium orthophenylphenate. Plant Dis. Rep. 49, 332-334.

HARTILL, W. F. T., CANTER-VISSCHER, T. W. and SUTTON, P. G. 1977. An alternative fungicide to benomyl for the control of green mould in citrus. N.Z. J. Exp. Agr. 5, 291-292.

HARTILL, W. F. T., TOMPKINS, G. R. and KLEINSMAN, P. J. 1983. Development in New Zealand of resistance to dicarboximide fungicides in *Botrytis cinerea*, to acylalinines in *Phytophthora infestans* and to guazatine in *Penicillium italicum*. N. Z. J. Agr. Res. 26, 261-269.

HARVEY, E. M. 1946. Changes in lemons during storage as affected by air circulation and ventilation. USDA Tech. Bull. 908.

HATTON, T. T. and CUBBEDGE, R. H. 1977. Status of controlled atmosphere storage research of citrus fruits, pp. 250-259. Proc. Second National Controlled Atmosphere Research Conference, D. H. Dewey (Editor). Michigan State University.

HATTON, T. T. and CUBBEDGE, R. H. 1983. Preferred temperature for prestorage conditioning of 'Marsh' grapefruit to prevent chilling injury at low temperature. HortScience 18, 721-722.

HAYWARD, F. W. and GRIERSON. W. 1960. Effects of treatment conditions on o-phenylphenol residues in oranges. J. Agr. Food Chem. 8, 308-310.

HERSHENHORN, J., BEHR, L., BARASH, I. and ARSEE, T. 1989. Mode of sour rot formation as inferred from comparative studies with virulent and avirulent strains of *Geotrichum candidum*. J. Phytopathology 126, 257-271.

HOLMES, G. J. and ECKERT, J. W. 1999. Sensitivity of *Penicillium digitatum* and *P. italicum* to postharvest citrus fungicides in California. Phytopathology 89, 716-721.

HOLMES, G. J., ECKERT, J. W. and PITT, J. I. 1994. Revised description of *Penicillium ulaiense* and its role as a pathogen of citrus fruits. Phytopathology 84, 719-727.

HOPKINS, E. F. and LOUCKS, K. W. 1944. Pulling versus clipping of oranges in respect of loss from stem-end rot and blue mold. Proc. Fla. State Hort. Soc. 57, 80-86.

HOPKINS, E. F. and LOUCKS, K. W. 1948. A curing procedure for the reduction of mold decay in citrus fruits. Fla. Agr. Exp. Sta. Bull. 450.

HOPKINS, E. F. and LOUCKS, K. W. 1950. Prevention of the phytotoxic action of sodium o-phenylphenate on citrus fruits by hexamine. Science 12, 720-721.

HOPKINS, E. F. and McCORNACK, A. A. 1960. Effect of delayed handling and other factors on rind breakdown and decay in oranges. Proc. Fla. State Hort. Soc. 73, 263-269.

HOUCK, L. G. 1967. Hot water treatments for control of *Penicillium digitatum* green mold of Eureka lemons. Phytopathology 57, 99.

HOUCK, L. G. 1977. Problems of resistance to citrus fungicides. Proc. Int. Soc. Citriculture 1, 263-269.

HOUCK, L. G. and SNIDER, J. W. 1969. Limitations of modified atmospheres for decay control of citrus fruits. Phytopathology 59, 1031-1032.

HOUGH, A. 1970. Control of green mould by orchard sanitation. S. African Citrus J. 442, 11, 13, 15.

HUANG, J. 1990. A study on the original inoculum of citrus sour rot (*Geotrichum candidum*). Proc. Intl. Soc. Citriculture 4, 620-623.

HUANG, Y., DEVERALL, B. J., MORRIS, S. C. and WILD, B. L. 1993. Biocontrol of postharvest orange diseases by a strain of *Pseudomonas cepacia* under semi-commercial conditions. Postharvest Biol. Tech. 3, 293-304.

ISSHIKI, A., OHTANI, K., KYO, M., YAMAMOTO, H. and AKIMITSU, K. 2003. Green fluorescent detection of fungal colonization and endopolygalaturonase gene expression in the interaction of *Alternaria citri* with citrus. Phytopathology 93, 768-773.

JAHN, O. L. CUBBEDGE, R. H. and SMOOT, J. J. 1970. Effects of washing sequence on the degreening response and decay of some citrus fruits. Proc. Fla. State Hort. Sci. 83, 217-221.

JANISIEWICZ, W. J. and KORSTEN, L. 2002. Biological control of postharvest diseases of fruits. Ann. Rev. Phytopathol. 40, 411-441.

JOHNSON, G. D., HARSY, S. G., GERONIMO, J. G. and WISE, J. M. 2001. Orthophenylphenol and phenylhydroquinone residues in citrus fruit and processed citrus products after postharvest fungicidal treatments with sodium orthophenylphenate in California and Florida. J. Agr. Food Chem. 49, 2497-2502.

JOLY, P. 1967. The black decays of citrus fruits caused by Alternaria. Fruits 22, 89-95.

KADER, A. A. and ARPAIA, M. L. 2002. Postharvest handling systems: subtropical fruits, pp. 375-383. In Postharvest Technology of Horticultural Crops. Pub. 3311, University of California Agr. and Natural Resources, Oakland.

KAPLAN, H. J. and DAVE, B. A. 1979. The current status of imazalil: a postharvest fungicide for citrus. Proc. Fla. State Hort. Soc. 92, 37-43.

KAVANAGH, J. A. and WOOD, R. K. S. 1971. Green mould of oranges caused by *Penicillium digitatum* Sacc.—effect of additives on spore germination and infection. Ann. Appl. Biol. 67, 35-44.

KELLY, J. L. and AUSTIN, L. A. 1985. A quantitiative detection method for *Penicillium digitatum* and *P. italicum* in citrus packinghouses. Proc. Fla. State Hort. Soc. 98, 211-213.

KITAGAWA, H. and KAWADA, K. 1984. Effect of sorbic acid and potassium sorbate on the control of sour rot of citrus fruits. Proc. Fla. State Hort. Soc. 97, 133-135.

KLOTZ, L. J. 1973. Color Handbook of Citrus Diseases. 4th ed. University of California Press, Berkeley.

KLOTZ, L. J. and DEWOLFE, T. A. 1961A. Limitations of the hot water immersion treatment for the control of phytophthora brown rot of lemons. Plant Dis. Rep. 45, 264-267.

KLOTZ, L. J. and DEWOLFE, T. A. 1961B. Brown rot contact infection of citrus fruits prior to hot water treatment. Plant Dis. Rep. 45, 268-271.

KOKKALOS, T. L. 1974. Thiabendazole reduces chilling injury (pitting) of Cyprus-grown grapefruit. HortScience 9, 456-457.

KURAMOTO, T. 1976. Resistance to benomyl and thiophanate-methyl in strains of *Pencillium digitatum* and *P. italicum* in Japan. Plant Dis. Rep. 60, 168-172.

KURAMOTO, T. and YAMADA, S. 1976. DF-125, a new experimental fungicide for control of satsuma mandarin postharvest decays. Plant Dis. Rep. 60, 809-812.

LARRIGAUDIERE, C., PONS, J., TORRES, R. and USALL, J. 2002. Storage performance of clementines treated with hot water, sodium carbonate, and sodium bicarbonate dips. J. Hort. Sci. Biotech. 77, 314-319.

LAVILLE, E. 1973. Studies on the activities of R23979 and its salts on the penicillium decays (*P. digitatum and P. italicum*) of oranges. Fruits 28, 545-547.

LAVILLE, E. Y., HARDING, P. R., DAGAN, Y., RAHAT, M., KRAGHT, A. J. and RIPPON, L. E. 1977. Studies on imazalil as potential treatment for control of citrus fruit decay. Proc. Int. Soc. Citriculture 1, 269-273.

LONG, J. K. and ROBERTS, E. A. 1958. The phytotoxic and fungicidal effects of sodium o-phenylphenate in controlling green mould wastage in oranges. Aust. J. Agr. Res. 9, 609-628.

LÓPEZ-GARCÍA, B., VEYRAT, A., PÉREZ-PAYÁ, E., GONZÁLEZ-CANDELAS, L. and MARCOS, J. F. 2003. Comparison of the activity of antoifungal hexapeptides and the fungicides thiabendazole and imazalil against postharvest fungal pathogens. Int. J. Food Microbiol. 89, 163-170.

MARLOTH, R. 1931. The influence of hydrogen-ion concentration and of sodium bicarbonate and related substances on *Penicillium italicum* and *P. digitatum*. Phytopathology 21, 169-198.

McCORNACK, A. A. 1972A. Factors affecting decay and peel injury in temples. Proc. Fla. State Hort. Sci. 85, 232-235.

McCORNACK, A. A. 1972B. Effect of ethylene degreening on decay of Florida citrus fruit. Proc. Fla. State Hort. Soc. 84, 270-272.

McCORNACK, A. A. 1974. Control of citrus fruit decay with postharvest application of Benlate. Proc. Fla. State Hort. Soc. 87, 230-233.

McCORNACK, A. A., BROWN, G. E. and SMOOT, J. J. 1977. R23979, an experimental postharvest citrus fungicide with activity against benzimidazole-resistant Penicilliums. Plant Dis. Rep. 61, 788-791.

McCORNACK, A. A., WARDOWSKI, W. F. and BROWN, G. E. 1979. Postharvest decay control recommendations for Florida citrus fruit. University of Florida Agr. Ext. Circ. 359-A.

McGLASSON, W. B. and EAKS, I. L. 1972. A role for ethylene in the development of wastage and off-flavors in stored Valenica oranges. HortScience 71, 80-81.

MERCIER, J. and JIMÉNEZ, J. I. 2004. Control of fungal decay of apples and peaches by the biofumigant fungus Muscador albus. Postharvest Biol. Tech. 31, 1-8.

MERCIER, J. and SMILANICK, J. L. 2003. Control of green mold and sour rot of lemons and gray mold rot of grapes by biofumigation with Muscado albus. Phytopathology 93, S61.

MORRIS, S. C. 1982. Synergism of Geotrichum candidum and Penicillium digitatum in infected citrus fruit. Phytopathology 72, 1336-1339.

NAFUSSI, B., BEN-YEHOSHUA, S., RODOV, V., PERETZ, J., OZER, B. K. and D'HALLEWIN, G. 2001. Mode of action of hot-water dip in reducing decay of lemon fruit. J. Agr. Food Chem. 49, 107-113.

NELSON, P. M., WHEELER, R. W. and McDONALD, P. D. 1981. Potassium sorbate in combination with benzimidazoles reduces resistant penicillium decay in citrus. Proc. Int. Soc. Citriculture 1, 820-823.

NORMAN, S. M., FOUSE, D. C. and CRAFT, C. C. 1972. Thiabendazole residues on and in citrus. J. Agr. Food Chem. 20, 1227-1230.

OBAGWU, J. and KORSTEN, L. 2003. Integrated control of citrus green and blue molds using Bacillus subtilis in combination with sodium bicarbonate or hot water. Postharvest Biol. Tech. 28, 187-194.

PALOU, L., SMILANICK, J. L., CRISOSTO, C. H. and MANSOUR, M. 2001A. Effect of gaseous ozone on the development of green and blue molds on cold stored citrus fruit. Plant Dis. 85, 632-638.

PALOU, L., SMILANICK, J. L., USALL, J. and VINAS, I. 2001B. Control of postharvest blue and green molds of oranges by hot water, sodium carbonate, and sodium bicarbonate. Plant Dis. 85, 371-376.

PALOU, L., SMILANICK, J. L., MANSOUR, M., CRISOSTO, C. H. and CLARK, T. J. 2002A. Evaluation of ozone gas penetration through citrus commercial packages and control of green and blue mold sporulation during cold storage. Central Valley Postharvest Newsletter 11, 8-11.

PALOU, L., USALL, J., MUÑOZ, J. A., SMILANICK, J. L. and M.-J. VIÑAS, I. 2002B. Hot water, sodium carbonate, and sodium bicarbonate for the control of postharvest green and blue molds of clementine mandarins. Postharvest Biol. Tech. 24, 93-96.

PALOU, L., USALL, J., SMILANICK, J. L., AGUILAR and M.-J. VIÑAS, I. 2002C. Evaluation of food additives and low-toxicity compounds as alternative chemicals for the control of Penicillium digitatum and Penicillium italicum on citrus fruit. Pest Manag. Sci. 58, 459-466.

PALOU, L., SMILANICK, J. L., CRISOSTO, C. H., MANSOUR, M. and PLAZA, P. 2003. Ozone gas penetration and control of the sporulation of Penicillium digitatum and Penicillium italicum within commercial packages of oranges during cold storage. Crop Prot. 22, 1131-1134.

PAO, S. and DAVIS, C. L. 1999. Enhancing microbiological safety of fresh orange juice by fruit immersion in hot water and chemical sanitizers. J. Food Protect. 62, 756-760.

PAPADOPOULOU-MOURKIDOU, E. 1991. Postharvest-applied agrochemicals and their residues in fresh fruits and vegetables. J. Assoc. Off. Anal. Chem. 74, 745-765.

PAVONCELLO, D., LURIE, S., DROBY, S. and PORAT, R. 2001. A hot water treatment induces resistance to Penicillium digitatum and promotes the accumulation of heat shock and pathogenesis-related proteins in grapefruit flavedo. Physiologia Plantarum 111, 17-22.

PEEVER, T. L., IBANEZ, A., AKIMITSU, K. and TIMMER, L. W. 2002. Worldwide phylogeography of the citrus brown spot pathogen, *Alternaria alternata*. Phytopathology 92, 794-802.

PELSER. P. DuT. 1973. Influence of application method on the efficacy of benomyl and thiabendazole in controlling post-harvest rots of citrus fruit. Citrus Subtrop. Fruit J. 474, 12, 13, 16.

PELSER, P. DuT. 1975. Recommendations for the control of post-harvest decay of citrus fruits. South African Co-op. Citrus Exchange, Pretoria.

PELSER, P. DuT. 1977. Development of alternaria and diplodia rots in stored grapefruit and lemons as influenced by snap picking. Citrus Subtrop. Fruit J. 519, 5, 7, 9.

PELSER, P. DuT. and ECKERT, J. W. 1977. Postharvest handling of South African citrus fruit. Proc. Int. Soc. Citriculture 1, 244-249.

PELSER, P. DuT. and LA GRANGE, J. M. 1981, Latest developments in the control of postharvest decay of citrus fruits in South Africa. Proc. Int. Soc. Citriculture 2, 812-814.

PLAZA, P., USALL, J., SMILANICK, J. L., LAMARCA, N. and VIÑAS, I. 2004. Combining *Pantoea agglomerans* (CPA-2) and curing treatments to control established infections of *Penicillium digitatum* on lemons. J. Food Prot. 67, 781-786

PLAZA, P., USALL, J., TEIXIDO, N. and VIÑAS, I. 2003A. Effect of water activity and temperature on germination and growth of *Penicillium digitatum*, *P. italicum* and *Geotrichum candidum*. J. Appl. Microbiol. 94, 549-554.

PLAZA, P., USALL, J., TEIXIDO, N. and VIÑAS, I. 2004. Effect of water activity and temperature on competing abilities of common postharvest citrus fungi. Int. J. Food Microbiol. 90, 75-82.

PLAZA, P., USALL, J., TORRES, R., LAMARCA, N., ASENSIO, A. and VIÑAS, I. 2003B. Control of green and blue mould by curing on oranges during ambient and cold storage. Postharvest Biol. Tech. 28, 195-198.

PORAT, R., DAUS, A., WEISS, B., COHEN, L., FALLIK, E. and DROBY, S. 2000A. Reduction of postharvest decay in organic citrus fruit by a short hot water brushing treatment. Postharvest Biol. Tech. 18, 151-157.

PORAT, R., PAVONCELLO, D., PERETZ, J., WEISS, B., DAUS, A., COHEN, L., BEN-YEHOSHUA, S., FALLIK, E., DROBY, S. and LURIE, S. 2000B. Induction of resistance to *Penicillium digitatum* and chilling injury in 'Star Ruby' grapefruit by a short hot-water rinse and brushing treatment. J. Hort. Sci. Bio. Tech. 75, 428-432.

PORAT, R., McCOLLUM, T. G., VINOKUR, V. and DROBY, S. 2002C. Effects of various elicitors on the transcription of a ß-1,3-endoglucanase gene in citrus fruit. J. Phytopathology 150, 70-75.

PORAT, R., WEISS, B., COHEN, L., DAUS, A., and COHEN, E. 2003. Effects of intermittent warming and temperature conditioning on the postharvest quality of oroblanco citrus fruit following long-term cold storage. HortTechnology 13,70-74.

PORAT, R., WEISS, B., COHEN, L., DAUS, A., GOREN, R. and DROBY, S. 1999. Effects of ethylene and 1-methylcyclopropene on the postharvest qualities of 'Shamouti' oranges. Postharvest Biol. Tech. 15, 155-163.

POWELL, G. H. 1908. The decay of oranges while in transit from California. USDA Bull. 123, Bureau of Plant Industry.

RACKHAM, R. L. and GRIERSON, W. 1971. Effect of mechanical harvesting on keeping quality of Florida citrus fruit for the fresh fruit market. HortScience 6, 163-165.

RAJZMAN, A. and APFELBAUM, A. 1968. Survey of o-phenylphenol residues found in marketable citrus fruit. J. Sci. Food Agr. 19, 740-744.

REICHERT, I. and HELLINGER, E. 1932. Further experiments on the control of diplodia stem-end rot of citrus by pruning and spraying. Hadar 5, 142-143.

RIPPON, L. E. and MORRIS, S. C. 1981. Guazatine control of sour rot in lemons, oranges and tangors under various storage conditions. Sci. Hort. 14, 245-251.

RITENOUR, M., NG-SANCHEZ, T. and KELSEY, D. F. 2003. Peel injury on 'Marsh' grapefruit from quaternary ammonia. HortTechnology 13, 656-660.

RITENOUR, M., PELOSI, R. R., BURTON, M. S., STOVER, E. W., DOU, H. and McCOLLUM, T. G. 2004. Assessing the efficacy of postharvest fungicide applications to control postharvest diseases of Florida citrus. HortTechnology 14, 58-62.

RODOV, V., BEN-YEHOSHUA, S., ALBAGLI, R. and FANG, D. Q. 1995A. Reducing chilling injury and decay of stored citrus fruit by hot water dips. Postharvest Biol. Tech. 5, 119-127.

RODOV, V., BEN-YEHOSHUA, S., FANG, D. Q., KIM, J. J. and ASKENAZI, R. 1995B. Preformed antifungal compounds of lemon fruit. citral and its relation to disease resistance. J. Agr. Food Chem. 43, 1057-1061.

ROTH, G. 1967. Citrus fruit decay in South Africa caused by *Penicillium digitatum* Sacc. Phytopath. Zeit. 58, 383-396.

SCHACHNAI, A. and BARASH, L. 1982. Evaluation of the fungicides CGA64251, guazatine, sodium o-phenylphenate, and imazalil for control of sour rot on lemon fruits. Plant Dis. 66, 733-735.

SCHIFFMANN-NADEL, M. 1969A. Research on phytophthora diseases of citrus fruit in Israel. Proc. Int. Soc. Citriculture 3, 1201-1205.

SCHIFFMANN-NADEL, M. 1969B. Stem-end rot diseases in refrigerated and non-refrigerated storage of citrus fruit. Proc. Int. Soc. Citriculture 3, 1295-1299.

SCHIFFMANN-NADEL, M. and COHEN, E. 1966. Influence of grove temperatures on the effectiveness of heat treatment of *Phytophthora*-infected citrus fruit. Plant Dis. Rptr. 50:867-868.

SCHIFFMANN-NADEL, M., LATTAR, F. S. and WAKS, J. 1971. The response of grapefruit to different storage temperatures. J. Am. Soc. Hort. Sci. 96, 87-90.

SCHIFFMANN-NADEL, M., LATTAR, F. S. and WAKS. J. 1972. The effect of 2,4-D applied in waxes on the preservation of 'Marsh Seedless' grapefruit and 'Valencia' orange during prolonged storage. HortScience 7, 120-121.

SCHIFFMANN-NADEL, M., CHALUTZ, E., WAKS. J. and DAGAN, M. 1975A. Reduction of chilling injury in grapefruit by thiabendazole and benomyl during long-term storage. J. Am. Soc. Hort. Sci. 100, 274-272.

SCHIFFMANN-NADEL, M., WAKS. J. and CHALUTZ, E. 1975B. Frost injury predisposes grapefruit to storage rots. Phytopathology 65, 630.

SCHIFFMANN-NADEL, M., WAKS, J., GUTTER, Y. and CHALUTZ. E. 1981. Alternaria rot of citrus fruit. Proc. Int. Soc. Citriculture 2, 791-793.

SCHIRRA, M. 1999. Advances in postharvest disease and disorder control of citrus fruit. Research Signpost, Trivandrum, India.

SCHIRRA, M., CABRAS, P., ANGIONI, A. and MELIS, M. 1996. Residue level of imazalil fungicide in lemons following prestorage dip treatment at 20 and 50°C. J. Agr. Food Chem. 44, 2865-2869.

SCHIRRA, M., CABRAS, P., ANGIONI, A., D'HALLEWIN, G., RUGGIU, R. and MINELLI, E. V. 1997. Effect of heated solutions on decay control and residues of imazalil in lemons. J. Agr. Food Chem. 45, 4127-4130.

SCHIRRA, M. and COHEN, E. 1999. Long-term storage of 'Olinda' oranges under chilling and intermittent warming temperatures. Postharvest Biol. Tech. 16, 63-69.

SCHIRRA, M., D'HALLEWIN, G., BEN-YEHOSHUA, S. and FALLIK, E. 2000. Host pathogen interactions modulated by heat treatment. Postharvest Biol. Tech. 21:71-85.

SCHIRRA, M. and MULAS, M. 1995A. Improving storability of 'Tarocco' oranges by postharvest hot-dip fungicide treatments. Postharvest Biol. Tech. 6, 129-138.

SCHIRRA, M. and MULAS, M. 1995B. Influence of postharvest hot-water dip and imazalil-fungicide treatments on cold-stored 'Di Massa' lemons. Adv. Hort. Sci. 9, 43-46.

SCHIRRA, M., MULAS, M. and BAGHINO, L. 1995. Influence of postharvest hot-dip treatments on Redblush grapefruit quality during long-term storage. Sci. Tech. Inter. 1, 35-40.

SCHIRRA, M., MULAS, M., FADDA, A. and CAULI, E. 2004. Cold quarantine responses of blood oranges to postharvest hot water and hot air treatments. Postharvest Biol. Tech. 31,191-200.

SIEGAL, M. R., KERKENAAR, A. and KAARS SIJPESTEIJN, A. 1977. Antifungal activity of the systemic fungicide imazalil. Neth. J. Pl. Pathol. 83 (Supplement 1), 121-133.

SIMMONS, E. G. 1999. *Alternaria* themes and variations. Classification of citrus pathogens. Mycotaxon 48, 263-323.

SINGH, V. and DEVERALL, B. J. 1984. *Bacillus subtilis* as a control agent against fungal pathogens of citrus fruit. Trans. Br. Mycol. Soc. 83, 487-490.

SINGH, A. and SINGH, R. 1996. Quality of kinnow mandarins as affected by modified atmosphere storage. J. Food Sci. Tech. 33, 483-487.

SMILANICK, J. L. 1994. Strategies for the isolation and testing of postharvest biological control agents, pp. 25-41. *In* Biological Control of Postharvest Diseases—Theory and practice, C. L. Wilson and M. E. Wisniewski (Editors). CRC Press, Boca Raton, FL.

SMILANICK, J. L. and DENIS-ARRUE, R. 1992. Control of green mold of lemons with *Pseudomonas* species. Plant Dis. 76, 481-485.

SMILANICK, J. L., MARGOSAN, D. A. and HENSON, D. J. 1995. Evaluation of heated solutions of sulfur dioxide, ethanol, and hydrogen peroxide to control postharvest green mold of lemons. Plant Dis. 79, 742-747.

SMILANICK, J. L., GOUIN-BEHE, T., MARGOSAN, D. A. and BULL, C. T. 1996. Virulence on citrus of *Pseudomonas syringae* strains that control postharvest green mold of fruit. Plant Dis. 80, 1123-1128.

SMILANICK, J. L., MACKEY, B. E., REESE, R., USALL, J. and MARGOSAN, D. A. 1997A. Influence of concentration of soda ash temperature, and immersion period in the control of postharvest green mold of oranges. Plant Dis. 81, 379-382.

SMILANICK, J. L., MICHAEL, I. F., MANSOUR, M. F., MACKEY, B. E., MARGOSAN, D. A., FLORES, D. and WEIST, C. F. 1997B. Improved control of green mold of citrus with imazalil in warm water compared to its use in wax. Plant Dis. 81, 1299-1304.

SMILANICK, J. L., MARGOSAN, D. A., MLIKOTA, F., USALL, J. and MICHAEL, I. F. 1999. Control of citrus green mold by carbonate and bicarbonate salts and the influence of commercial postharvest practices on their efficacy. Plant Dis. 83, 139-145.

SMILANICK, J. L. and SORENSON, D. 2001. Control of postharvest decay of citrus fruit with calcium polysulfide. Postharvest Bio. Tech. 21, 157-168.

SMILANICK, J. L., AIYABEI, J., MLIKOTA GABLER, M., DOCTOR, J. and SORENSON, D. 2002. Quantification of the toxicity of aqueous chlorine to spores of *Penicillium digitatum* and *Geotrichum citri-aurantii*. Plant Dis. 86, 509-514.

SMILANICK, J. L., SORENSON, D., MANSOUR, M., AIEYABEI, J. and PLAZA, P. 2003. Impact of a brief postharvest hot water drench treatment on decay, fruit appearance, and microbe populations of California lemons and oranges. HortTechnology 13, 333-338.

SMOOT, J. J. 1969. Decay of Florida citrus fruits stored in controlled atmospheres and in air. Proc. Int. Soc. Citriculture 3, 1285-1289.

SMOOT, J. J. 1977. Factors affecting market diseases of Florida citrus fruits. Proc. Int. Soc. Citriculture 1, 250-254.

SMOOT, J. J. and HALE, P. W. 1977. Evaluation of decay control treatments and shipping containers for export of grapefruit to Japan. Proc. Fla. State Hort. Soc. 90, 152-154.

SMOOT, J. J. and McCORNACK, A. A. 1978. The use of potassium sorbate for citrus decay control. Proc. Fla. State Hort. Soc. 91, 119-122.

SMOOT, J. J. and MELVIN, C. F. 1961. Effect of injury and fruit maturity on susceptibility of Florida citrus fruit to green mold. Proc. Fla. State Hort. Soc. 74, 285-287.

SMOOT, J. J. and MELVIN, C. F. 1965A. Reduction of citrus decay by hot-water treatment. Plant Dis. Rep. 49, 463-467.

SMOOT, J. J. and MELVIN, C. F. 1965B. Grove inoculation studies with stem-end rot fungi. Phytopathology 55, 1077.

SMOOT, J. J. and MELVIN, C. F. 1967. Postharvest decay of speciality hybrid citrus fruits in relation to degreening time. Proc. Fla. State Hort. Soc. 80, 246-250.

SMOOT, J. J. and MELVIN, C. F. 1972. Decay of degreened citrus fruit as affected by time of washing and TBZ application. Proc. Fla. State Hort. Soc. 85, 235-238.

SMOOT, J. J. and MELVIN, C. F. 1974. Decay control of oranges with benomyl by three methods of postharvest application. Proc. Fla. State Hort. Soc. 87, 234-236.

SMOOT, J. J., HOUCK, L. G. and JOHNSON, H. B. 1971A. Market Diseases of Citrus and Other Subtropical Fruits. USDA Agr. Handbook 398.

SMOOT, J. J., MELVIN, C. F. and JAHN, O. L. 1971B. Decay of degreened oranges and tangerines as affected by time of washing and fungicide application. Plant Dis. Rep. 55, 149-152.

SNOWDON, A. L. 1990. A Color Atlas of Post-harvest Diseases and Disorders of Fruits and Vegetables. Volume 1: General introduction and fruits. CRC Press, Boca Raton, FL.

SOFOS, J. N. 1988. Sorbate Food Preservatives. CRC Press, Inc., Boca Raton, FL.

SOMMER. N. F., MAXIE, E. C., FORTLAGE, R. J. and ECKERT, J. W. 1964. Sensitivity of citrus fruit decay fungi to gamma irradiation. Radiat. Bot. 4, 317-322.

SORENSON, D., SMILANICK, J. L. and MARGOSAN, D. A. 1999. Postharvest high pressure washing of citrus fruit with sodium bicarbonate to control green mold. Phytopathology 89, S74.

STANGE, R. R., JR. and ECKERT, J. W. 1994. Influence of postharvest handling and surfactants on control of green mold of lemons by curing. Phytopathology 84, 612-616.

STEWART, W. S., PALMER, J. E. and HIELD, H. Z. 1952. Packing-house experiments on the use of 2,4-dichlorophenoxyacetic acid and 2,4,5-trichlorophenoxyacetic acid to increase storage life of lemons. Proc. Am. Soc. Hort. Sci. 59, 327-334.

TEIXIDÓ, N., USALL, J., PALOU, L., ASENSIO, A., NUNES, C. and VINAS, I. 2001. Improving control of green and blue molds of oranges by combining *Pantoea agglomerans* (CPA-2) and sodium bicarbonate. Eur. J. Plant Path. 107, 685-694.

TIMMER, L. W. and BROWN, G. E. 2000. Biology and control of anthracnose diseases of citrus. *In* Colletotrichum. Host Specificity, Pathology, and Host-pathogen Interaction, D. Prusky, S. Freeman, and M. B. Dickman (Editors). APS Press, St. Paul, MN.

TIMMER, L. W., GARNSEY, S. M., and BROADBENT, P. 2003. Diseases of citrus. *In* Diseases of Tropical Fruit Crops, R. C. Ploetz (Editor). CABI Publishing, Cambridge, MA.

TUGWELL, B. L., GILLESPIE, K. and GLENN, T. 1981. Guazatine for postharvest mold control of citrus fruits. Proc. Int. Soc. Citriculture 2, 818-820.

TUSET, J. J., PIQUER, J., GARCIA, J., MARTINEZ, J. M. and ROCA, M. 1981. Activity of imidazole fungicides to control postharvest citrus decay. Proc. Int. Soc. Citriculture 2, 784-787.

WARDOWSKI, W. F., ALBRIGO, L. G., GRIERSON, W., BARMORE, C. R. and WHEATON, T. A. 1975. Chilling injury and decay of grapefruit as affected by thiabendazole, benomyl, and CO_2. HortScience 10, 381-383.

WARDOWSKI, W. F. and BROWN, G. E. 1993. Postharvest decay control recommendations for Florida citrus fruit. Fla. Coop. Ext. Service Circular 359-A.

WARDOWSKI, W. F., HAYWARD, F. W. and DENNIS, J. D. 1974. A flood-recovery TBZ fungicide treatment system for citrus fruits. Proc. Fla. State Hort. Soc. 87, 241-243.

WHITE, E. R., BOSE, E. A., OGAWA, J. M., MANJI, B. T. and KILGORE, W. W. 1973. Thermal and base-catalyzed hydrolysis products of the systemic fungicide, benomyl. J. Agr. Food Chem. 21, 616-618.

WHITESIDE. J. O. 1970. Factors contributing to the restricted occurrence of citrus brown rot in Florida. Plant Dis. Rep. 54, 608-612.

WILD, B. L. 1980. Resistance of citrus green mold *Penicillium digitatum* Sacc. to benzimidazole fungicides. Ph.D. Dissertation. University of California, Riverside.

WILD, B. L. 1983. Double resistance by citrus green mold *Penicillium digitatum* to the fungicides guazatine and benomyl. Ann. Appl. Biol. 103, 237-241.

WILD, B. L. 1987. Fungicidal activity of potassium sorbate against *Penicillium digitatum* as affected by thiabendazole and dip temperature. Sci. Hort. 32, 41-47.

WILD, B. L., McGLASSON, W. B. and LEE, T. H. 1976. Effect of reduced ethylene levels in storage atmospheres on lemon keeping quality. HortScience 11, 114-115.

WILD, B. L., RIPPON, L. E. and SEBERRY, J. A. 1975. Comparison of thiabendazole and benomyl as post-harvest fungicides for wastage control in long-term lemon storage. Aust. J. Exp. Agr. Animal Husb. 15, 108-111.

WILD, B. L. and SPOHR, L. J. 1989. Influence of fruit temperature and application time on the effectiveness of fungicides in controlling citrus green mold, *Penicillium digitatum*. Austral. J. Exp. Agr. 29, 139-142

WILLIAMS, M. H., BROWN, M. A., VESK, M. and BRADY, C. 1994. Effect of postharvest heat treatments on fruit quality, surface structure, and fungal disease in Valencia oranges. Austral. J. Exp. Agr. 34, 1183-1190.

WINSTON, J. R. 1935. Reducing decay in citrus fruits with borax. USDA Tech. Bull. 488.

ZITKO, S. E., TIMMER, L. W. and SANDLER, H. A. 1991. Isolation of *Phytophthora palmivora* pathogenic to citrus in Florida. Plant Dis. 75, 532-535.

14

Physiological Peel Disorders

Peter D. Petracek, D. Frank Kelsey, and William Grierson

INTRODUCTION

Physiological peel disorders reduce the shelf life and degrade the appearance of fresh citrus fruit. Most disorders do not affect the quality of the edible portion of the fruit. However, cosmetic damage often reduces fresh fruit marketability and consequently motivates researchers to determine the cause of peel disorders and develop preventative strategies to reduce their severity. While the incidence of most disorders is typically low, even under conditions conducive to triggering the problem, economic losses can be substantial due to market pressure to produce defect and blemish free fruit.

In several ways, physiological peel disorders are characteristically elusive. First, disorders appear and disappear unpredictably. Many disorders result from periodic failure of the peel and unmanaged stress, and consequently are sporadic and fitful. Recreating the conditions that likely stimulate the disorder is often unsuccessful and thus attempts to study the disorder are often unproductive (Eckert and Eaks 1989). Second, disorder symptomology and etiology are not necessarily unique or constant. A single disorder may have multiple symptoms while multiple disorders may have similar symptoms. Similarly, stress factors (e.g., nutritional imbalances, overmaturation, rough handling during harvest and packing, chemical and fruit coating treatments, high or low humidity at harvest, and high or low temperature at harvest, during handling or storage) do not necessarily stimulate a single disorder. Grierson (1981) proposed etiological classification of defects, but this system has not been adopted because of the complex interactions involved in the culture, maturation, harvesting, and marketing of citrus fruits and the cumulative impact of these practices on expression of disorders. Third, disorder terminology is not systematic or consistent among researchers. Terms such as pitting, peel collapse, and staining are at once both descriptive and vague.

Unlike a disease, which can be positively identified by isolating the causal pathogenic organisms, there are typically no single factors that critically define a disorder. Since much of disorder diagnosis relies on visual inspection and knowledge of previous handling, the process of disorder diagnosis is an art form as much as a science. The potential to misdiagnose and mistreat a problem is consequently great. The recent definition of postharvest pitting provides an example. When fruit with postharvest pitting were observed in March 1994, several experienced researchers agreed that the collapsed peel was due to chilling injury. When the packinghouse manager who provided the damaged grapefruit insisted that the fruit had never been exposed to cold storage, we set out to prove him wrong. In fact, we could reproduce the characteristic collapse of oil glands only when coated fruit were stored at non-chilling temperature (Petracek et al. 1995). Thus, "chilling injury" was actually "non-chilling injury."

Many diagnostic books, booklets, pamphlets, and articles have been published to provide keys for defining, identifying, and diagnosing citrus peel disorders including Amat 1988; Brown 1998; Browning et al. 1995; Eckert and Eaks 1989; Fawcett and Lee 1926; Klotz and Fawcett 1941; Knorr, 1973; Petracek et al. 1997A; Smoot et al. 1971; Sunkist 1974; and Whiteside et al. 1988. One key to classifying and understanding disorders is through the anatomy. The general anatomy of the peel (Schneider 1968) and oil gland development (Turner et al. 1998) have been previously described. The citrus peel consists of flavedo (outer most part of the peel), which is comprised primarily of cuticle, epidermal cells, sub-epidermal (hypodermal) cells, and oil glands, and albedo (internal spongy white part of the peel), which is comprised primarily of parenchyma cells interspersed with vascular bundles (Plate 9). Most disorders begin in the flavedo (e.g., chilling injury, postharvest pitting, oleocellosis, zebra-skin), but some target the albedo (e.g., creasing). Previous publications on the anatomy of disorders include chilling injury of white grapefruit (Petracek and Davis 2000; Platt-Aloia and Thomson 1976), oleocellosis (Shomer and Erner 1989), a preharvest pitting of Fortune mandarin (Vercher et al. 1994), postharvest pitting of white grapefruit (Petracek and Davis 2000), and physical preharvest damage of white grapefruit (Petracek and Davis 2000).

In this review, physiological peel disorders are defined as any non-pest induced malady. They include man-made artifacts such as harvesting procedures and chemical application and cover storage and transit conditions after harvest. Distinguishing between man-made artifacts and purely physiological disorders is quite difficult because different causes can produce identical results. Categorization of disorders by cause assumes the knowledge of the chronology and cause of the disorder. Classification also implicitly suggests that the cause occurs during a defined period of time. However, predisposition of fruit to a disorder may occur months prior to the appearance of the symptoms. For example, oleocellosis is commonly considered to be caused by physical mishandling of the fruit. Nevertheless, preharvest blemishes due to extruded peel oil can be caused by certain extreme, preharvest weather conditions (Fucik 1972; Klotz et al. 1968). Agusti (1999) provides an excellent review on the effects of preharvest factors (e.g., nutritional, environmental, and cultural) on postharvest fruit quality.

This review considers physiological blemishes of citrus fruits regardless of whether they are caused by weather, nutrition, handling, or postharvest conditions. The disorders listed below were selected because they are apparently defined as distinct disorders and are currently or have been relatively common in incidence. Disorders that are likely manifestations of other disorders (e.g., Noxan or Nuxan's blemish of Shamouti orange may be rumple of lemon and brown stem may be stem end rind breakdown or aging) are not listed. Unusual disorders such as blue albedo may be important, but are considered too rare to include. Disorders are listed according to when they predominantly are discernible.

PEEL DISORDERS

I. Preharvest Related Disorders

Nutritional Disorders and Spray Damage

Boron Deficiency. The symptoms of boron deficiency are raised bumps on the surface of the fruit which, when cut open, reveal gummy pockets in the albedo (Bryan 1950; Browning et al. 1995). Diagnosis is complicated because these symptoms are identical with those produced by arsenic toxicity when arsenate sprays, used to lower fruit acidity of grapefruit (Knapp et al.1984), have been used in excess.

Exanthema, Ammoniation, Copper Deficiency. Now that citrus tree nutrition is better understood, ugly skin blemishes in the form of black or brown raised lesions are seldom seen. The cause is copper deficiency, but the term "ammoniation" arose because the condition was most commonly seen when nitrogen was used in apparent excess on copper-deficient soils (Browning et al. 1995; Smoot et al. 1971).

Pineapple Pitting. Pineapple pitting is characterized by the collapse of small areas of the shoulder and cheek of the Pineapple orange peel. Pitted areas may coalesce and darken with time (Browning et al. 1995; Smoot et al. 1971). Although the disorder appears in other orange cultivars, Pineapple oranges are especially susceptible. The disorder is discernible at picking, but tends to develop sharply after harvest, particularly if the fruit are held at low humidity. To a marked extent, the tendency for pineapple pitting increases with cropload. Pineapple pitting is classified as nutritional disorder because incidence increases when potassium levels in adjacent leaves decreases (Grierson 1965). However, the relationship between nutritional program and the disorder incidence is not clear. Translocation of nutrients within the tree, particularly under the stress of abnormally heavy crops, may be involved. **Spray Damage (Plate 10).** Foliar application of pesticides may cause a phytotoxic response if applied incorrectly. Phytotoxicity due to spray damage may be due to incompatible tank mix chemical combinations, incorrect application rates or timings, or the incorporation of phytotoxic active ingredients or adjuvants (Albrigo and Grosser 1996). Spray damage is often characterized by streaks of damaged or non-degreened cells running longitudinally down the fruit surface, or by rings at fruit to fruit or leaf to fruit contact points.

Weather Related Disorders

Endoxerosis, Internal Decline, Wither Tip. Endoxerosis of lemons develops only on the tree. Internal tissues within the stylar end collapse, discolor, and may disappear leaving cavities. Endoxerosis is difficult to detect by external appearances. Affected fruit are particularly susceptible to alternaria decay. This problem is most common in arid growing areas and in lemons from trees subjected to water stress (Klotz 1978; Smoot *et al.* 1971).

Freeze Injury. The peel of citrus fruits is very much less vulnerable to freezing injury than are the internal membranes and juice vesicles. Externally uninjured fruit can contain large areas of completely desiccated tissue, typically at the stem (proximal) end of the fruit (Chapter 11). As with most other blemishes, how much freeze damage is permitted varies with local regulations (Grierson and Ting 1978). Internal freeze damage may grow progressively worse after initial grading, a serious matter if fruit are to be many weeks in transit to export markets (Hatton *et al.* 1977; Kitagawa and Kawada 1979).

Peel-pitting of Fortune Mandarin. Fortune mandarin peel-pitting is characterized by an undulated peel surface and damaged epidermal and sub-epidermal cells (Vercher *et al.* 1994). Cold temperature and low humidity weather stimulate peel-pitting (Vercher *et al.* 1994; Agusti *et al.* 1997). Both anatomy and etiology suggest that peel-pitting of Fortune mandarin is chilling injury that develops on the tree. Peel-pitting may be reduced by preharvest GA3, calcium nitrate (Zaragoza *et al.* 1996), or pinolene (Agusti *et al.* 1997) applications and postharvest ethylene (Lafuente *et al.* 2004) treatment.

Sunburn. While still attached to the tree, citrus fruits are surprisingly resistant to insolation injury. A temperature of 44.4°C with a relative humidity of 20% has been recorded as necessary to cause sunburn injury to Valencia (Ketchie and Ballard 1968). An interesting exception to this usual resistance to insolation injury occurs with the Honey tangerine, a natural citrus hybrid of increasing importance in Florida and, to a lesser degree, elsewhere. This cultivar is anomalous in having unusually stiff, rigid petioles, which tend to make the fruit grow "blossom end up," making it peculiarly susceptible to sunburn (Smoot *et al.* 1971). Such injury results in a flat side to the fruit, hard in texture and usually yellow when the rest of the fruit surface is still green. Once picked, citrus cultivars are subject to sunburn injury, which can occur in a very few hours between picking and delivery to the packinghouse. Sunburn typically causes flat, pale, leathery areas on the exposed side of the fruit.

Water Spot. Water-soaked areas of the peel in which epidermal cells have been ruptured by endosmosis can occur on various citrus varieties, but is most typically a problem of navel oranges grown under usually low humidity conditions that are then subjected to an anomalous cool, wet period (Scott and Baker 1947; Klotz 1975; Riehl and Carman 1953; Smoot et at. 1971). The problem relates to the basic characteristic of citrus fruit continuing cell division in the peel during fruit enlargement. Anything that delays maturity of such proliferating epidermal cells, most particularly oil sprays (Simanton and Trammel 1966), can accentuate the problem.

Wind Scar Damage (Plate 11). Small (<1 cm in diameter) citrus fruits are so susceptible to abrasion injury that just rubbing against a leaf can cause lesions that expand to large silvery or tan blemishes as the fruit enlarges (Dodson 1966; Elmer *et al.* 1973; Freeman 1976; Smoot *et al.* 1971). Wind scar is a particular problem in areas in which very high winds coincide with the immediate postbloom period. Wind scar is sometimes confused with the corky or silvery spots that occur due to epidermal ruptures in periods of rapid fruit enlargement (Tal and Monselise 1965; Turrell *et al.* 1964A) and can be controlled with growth regulators (Goren *et al.* 1976).

Maturity Related Disorders

Creasing (Plate 12). Creasing is characterized by grooves or furrows which are irregularly distributed on the surface of the fruit indicating underlying areas in which the albedo is discontinuous or completely absent (Browning *et al.* 1995; Smoot *et al.* 1971). Creasing occurs on oranges and mandarins of various types, usually when the fruit is very mature. It is a serious condition on thin-skinned fruit and may cause them to split open under pressure in packing or transit (Gilfillan and Stevenson 1977). This has traditionally been regarded as a preharvest condition that did not progress after harvest. Thus, it is of particular interest to note a report that severe creasing developed in Robinson tangerine after harvest (Nagy *et al.* 1982).

The exact cause of creasing is unknown. GA3 sprays can reduce creasing (Bar-Akiva 1975; Bower 2000; Gilfillan *et al.* 1974; Monselise *et al.* 1976) thus indicating that creasing may be largely a maturation related disorder. Other factors such as rootstock, water relations, and nutrition (Treeby *et al.* 2000) may play a role. Potassium nutrition in particular appears to be an important factor. The results of various studies on the relationship between nutritional programs and the incidence of creasing vary widely, and various other factors most likely interact with potassium nutrition (Bar-Akiva 1975; Embleton *et al.* 1971; Grierson 1965; Jones *et al.* 1967; Reese and Koo 1974, 1975). Early season foliar applications of calcium reduced Australian navel orange creasing 29% (Treeby *et al.* 2000). More recently, Storey and Treeby (1994) suggested that differential growth or water stress may stimulate creasing.

Puffiness. Puffiness is the separation of the peel from the pulp. It is rare in oranges, but occurs frequently in the various mandarin-type varieties. Puffiness usually occurs on the tree, making the fruit at first difficult, then impossible to handle (Clark and Stearns 1941), but it can also develop in storage (Smoot *et al.* 1971). Advancing maturity, vigor of the tree, and weather (particularly irregular water supply) are involved (Grossenbacher 1941; Kuraoka 1962). The most detailed research on puffiness has been conducted in Japan because mandarin varieties (*Citrus unshiu* Marc.) are so important there, and because much of the crop is stored. Japanese research shows that puffiness has a dual origin: shrinking, often to near disappearance, of the albedo from undetermined causes and swelling of the flavedo from external moisture (Kuraoka 1962). Preharvest GA3 sprays have provided significant reduction in puffiness, but at the expense of poorer fruit color (Kuraoka *et al.* 1977). Puffiness of tangerines (Kuraoka *et al.* 1977; Smoot *et al.* 1971) can develop after harvest as well as before.

Rind Staining of Navel Oranges. This disorder occurs when the peel is so physiologically overmature that the epidermal wax has softened and handling causes reddish-brown blemishes (Eaks 1964). Susceptibility is greater for some rootstocks (Rubidoux sour and rough lemon, in particular) and for trees receiving high nitrogen fertilization (Eaks 1969). In California, rind staining is routinely prevented by the use of GA3 sprays to delay peel senescence (Coggins and Eaks 1967).

Rumple of Lemons. This disorder superficially resembles creasing of oranges, but its etiology and development are quite different, the epidermal furrows being due to necrosis of the albedo beneath them (Knorr and Koo 1969). In advanced cases, the necrotic tissues blacken and coalesce. Rumple is strongly maturity related, appearing at the end of the season and usually on lemons that have colored on the tree. It can progress in storage and develop de novo up to 3 weeks after harvest, but only to a minor degree (Oberbacher and Knorr 1965). Rumple has been reported from Florida and various Mediterranean areas such as Sicily, Cyprus and Turkey.

Sloughing (Plate 13). Sloughing is a dramatic peel injury of red grapefruit in which the peel develops large, moist, chocolate-brown areas that slough off under slight finger pressure. Sloughing develops several days after shipment and only occurs with very early pickings (Grierson and Newhall 1958; Grierson and Patrick 1956; Browning *et al.* 1995). In the 1950s, sloughing caused some severe losses for Florida growers and shippers of red-fleshed grapefruit.

In response, maturity standards were raised enough to delay the first harvest of the season by about 10 days. Sloughing has rarely been seen since then.

II. Harvest Related Disorders

Blossom-End Clearing of Grapefruit (Plate 14). Blossom-End Clearing (BEC) of grapefruit is also called stylar-end clearing, waterlog, and wet bottom. Mature, heavy, thin-skinned, seedless grapefruit are very vulnerable to this form of handling injury, which is usually caused by dropping. About 24 hr after dropping such grapefruit, a translucent area several centimeters in diameter may appear at the stylar end due to rupture of the cells of both the albedo and of the adjacent juice vesicles (McCornack 1966). Such injured fruit soon decay. BEC susceptibility increases with temperature (Echeverria and Burns 1994) and decreases with fruit size (Echeverria *et al.* 1998).

Oleocellosis (Plate 15). Oleocellosis is also known as oil spotting, oleo, bruising, green spot, and, erroneously, "gas burn." Citrus fruits carry the means of their own destruction in the oil cells (glands) of the flavedo, the oils being toxic to the surrounding epidermal cells. Rupture of oil cells inevitably results in necrosis of the adjacent epidermis causing an initial grade-lowering blemish and ultimately an open invasion site for fungal pathogens. Almost all oleocellosis results from human activities, especially during harvest (Eaks 1969; Nel *et al.* 1974; Smoot *et al.* 1971; Wardowski *et al.* 1976), although the resultant lesions may not darken enough to be clearly visible until much later. However, in rare cases, oleocellosis can be induced by weather; this occurs when turgid fruit on water-satiated trees are subjected to sudden cold. Shrinking of the peel against the turgid flesh can cause extrusion of peel oil causing discrete spots (Turrell *et al.* 1964B), large "scalded" areas (Fucik 1972), or concentric rings of small lesions (concentric ring stipple) when drops of dew distribute the peel oil (Klotz *et al.* 1968).

Monetary losses from oleocellosis are increasing world wide as care in picking declines. All types of citrus are susceptible to oleocellosis, but limes, lemons, and navel oranges are so susceptible that when moisture supplies are ample, early morning picking can be inadvisable or impossible (Eaks 1969; Grierson *et al.* 1971; McCornack 1970; Pantastico *et al.* 1966; Wardowski *et al.* 1976). For such tender fruits, the use of a pressure tester to determine when turgidity is decreased enough to permit picking is advisable (Cahoon *et al.* 1963; Oberbacher 1965; Wardowski *et al.* 1976). Colorimetric papers can be used to detect where in the harvesting or packing operation oleocellosis is occurring (Grierson 1958). Very little oleocellosis originates on well-designed packinghouse machinery (Miller *et al.* 2001).

Red Colored Lesions. Superficial wounds, no deeper than the flavedo, often develop a reddish color in the lesion and surrounding peel. This has been attributed to a reaction by peel tissue denoting resistance to infection by Penicillium digitatum (Kavanagh and Wood 1967). However, involvement of Penicillium is not necessary and under conditions of a well run Florida degreening room (29°C and 90 + % RH), true wound healing can occur involving development of lignin and colored polyphenolic compounds (Ismail and Brown 1979).

Stylar-End Breakdown of Limes. Stylar-end breakdown (SEB), a disorder similar to BEC, first appears as a water-soaked, tan-colored area typically near the nipple at the stylar end of seedless limes (i.e., Persian or Tahiti). The lesion spreads rapidly over the surface of the fruit and is commonly followed by Penicillium mold, to which a healthy lime is virtually immune. The cause of SEB is unknown, but the explanation is simple. When a juice vesicle in a mature, turgid lime is broken, the contents are toxic to the adjacent cells, as are the contents of these cells to those adjacent to them, and so the lesions spread (Davenport and Campbell 1977; Grierson *et al.* 1971; Pantastico *et al.* 1966). Usually SEB is initiated by rough handling, but intense field heat can initiate vesicle rupture, and thus may explain why SEB occurs occasionally on the tree (Davenport and Campbell 1977).

III. Postharvest Related Disorders

Aging (Plate 16) and Stem-End Rind Breakdown (Plate 17). As already noted, classifying the various causes of physiological disorders is not easy. Stem-end rind breakdown (SERB) illustrates this well. It is initiated by an ill-defined imbalance in nutrition involving nitrogen and potassium (Chapman 1958, 1965), but its development as an economic concern depends on handling procedures between picking and packing, although the resulting ugly lesions do not usually develop until after shipment (McCornack and Grierson 1965).

SERB involves collapse and subsequent darkening of the epidermal tissues around the stem end of oranges, particularly on the smaller sizes (and occasionally other types of citrus). The most distinctive feature is a narrow (2 to 5 mm) ring of undamaged tissue immediately around the calyx, this limited area having no stomata and an unusually thick layer of cuticular wax (Albrigo 1972). Oranges with SERB meet with considerable buyer resistance at both wholesale and retail levels because they appear to be old and are unattractive. Further financial losses are caused by the greatly increased amount of decay in oranges that have developed SERB. Aging of oranges and grapefruit (Smoot *et al.* 1971), which can occur after long-term storage, is almost indistinguishable from SERB, except that the characteristic narrow ring of healthy cells does not tend to persist around the calyx.

The development of SERB by susceptible crops can be prevented or greatly diminished by never letting the fruit dry out in the period between picking and waxing. Susceptible crops should be transported to the packinghouse as soon as possible after picking and held under humid (>90%

RH) conditions until washing and waxing (McCornack and Grierson 1965). Excessive brushing should be avoided and detergents used in the washing process should be thoroughly rinsed from the fruit surface to prevent desiccation during subsequent transport and storage.

Chilling Injury (Plate 18). Chilling injury (CI) is a common disorder characterized by the collapse of discrete areas of the peel that form sunken lesions which tend to coalesce. CI is induced by low temperature (below 10°C) storage of citrus fruit and symptom development is exacerbated by transfer to room temperature. CI is particularly common on grapefruit (Pantastico *et al.* 1968; Smoot *et al.* 1971) and limes (Pantastico *et al.* 1968). The demarcation between lesion and healthy epidermal tissue is very sharp. The reason for the patchy development of CI in citrus is not understood. When CI of banana, avocado, limes, and grapefruit was studied using 10-mm disks of peel tissue in tissue culture, the banana and avocado disks behaved uniformly, but CI developed randomly on the lime and grapefruit disks, indicating that this localized chilling resistance persisted even after transfer to tissue culture (Vakis *et al.* 1971). Purvis and Yelenosky (1993) found that CI could develop on grapefruit of potted trees.

The interaction between harvest date and response to storage temperature is striking. As early as 1936, it was reported that grapefruit harvested very early (November 6) were immune to CI while those harvested in mid-December began to show susceptibility. Late-harvested fruit (beginning by early April) were severely affected by CI at 0°C. In contrast, similar lots of fruit held at 5.5°C were susceptible at the beginning and end of the season, but resistant in midseason (Harvey and Rygg 1936). This latter result parallels later findings in Florida for storage at 4.5°C (Grierson 1974; Grierson and Hatton 1977). Grapefruit stored at 10°C are extremely susceptible to CI early in the season, resistant by midseason, and show little evidence of late-season susceptibility (Chace *et al.* 1966).

At very low temperatures, a general, superficial scalding may occur instead of pitting. It is typically reddish or tan-colored and can occur on most susceptible types of citrus fruits. Browning of the albedo and of the carpellary membranes is reported to be peculiar to lemons (Smoot *et al.* 1971). In grapefruit and tangelos, the oil glands may darken (Smoot *et al.* 1971). Watery breakdown can occur in various types of citrus held at too low, but not freezing temperatures. The general appearance is as though the fruit had been hard frozen, then thawed (Smoot *et al.* 1971). The various manifestations of CI may be associated with a particular range of storage temperature.

Postharvest temperature regimes have be used to mitigate CI effects. Intermittent warming throughout the storage period (Davis and Hoffman 1973; Hawkins 1921), stepwise lowering of temperature (Hatton and Cubbedge 1980; Pantastico *et al.* 1968), and prestorage heat treatments (Klein and Lurie 1992; McDonald *et al.* 1993; Wild and Hood 1989) can mitigate CI. Delayed storage (Hawkins 1921) can reduce CI. CI in the form of storage pitting is reduced or its incidence delayed by holding at very high humidity (Pantastico *et al.* 1968).

Storage atmosphere, postharvest chemical treatments, and coatings can affect CI incidence. Very high initial concentrations of CO_2 can mitigate CI, particularly of grapefruit (Brooks *et al.* 1936; Hatton *et al.* 1975; Vakis *et al.* 1970; Wardowski *et al.* 1973). However, the effect is not always consistent (Hatton *et al.* 1975; Wardowski *et al.* 1975). Low levels of CO_2 generated within semipermeable film packages have sometimes given good control of CI (Wardowski *et al.* 1973), but this effect was completely absent for late grapefruit picked after the trees had again bloomed (Wardowski *et al.* 1975). Yuen *et al.* (1995) found that pre-storage treatment of a number of varieties with low levels of ethylene (≤ 10 ppm) stimulated CI. In contrast, Lafuente *et al.* (2004) found that ethylene (2 ppm) treatment of Fortune mandarin during storage reduced peel pitting. Methyl jasmonate (Meir *et al.* 1996) and squalene (Nordby and McDonald 1990) treatments have shown some degree of protection from CI. CI is reduced by fungicides such as thiabendazole (Kokkalos 1974; McDonald *et al.* 1991; Schiffmann-Nadel *et al.* 1972; Schirra *et al.* 1995; Wardowski *et al.* 1975; Wild and Hood 1989) and imazalil (McDonald *et al.* 1991; Schirra *et al.* 1995) potentially through inhibition of cytochrome P450 oxidase. Despite these numerous confirmations, however, CI inhibition by fungicides is not consistent (Brown *et al.* 1998). Also, diphenyl (a vapor-phase fungicide) considerably increased susceptibility to CI (McCornack 1976). The response of Florida-grown waxed grapefruit and limes has been exactly opposite: waxing mitigated CI of grapefruit (Davis and Harding 1960; Grierson 1971; Pantastico *et al.* 1968) and exacerbated CI of limes (Grierson 1971; Hatton and Reeder 1967; Pantastico *et al.* 1968). Even more curiously, CI of California grown limes was less on waxed limes (Eaks and Masias 1965). The mechanisms by which these chemicals and coatings affect CI are not understood.

The interaction among climatic factors, tree condition, PGRs, and susceptibility to CI was investigated further. Midwinter in Florida is typically a drought period, so finding a strong positive correlation between resistance to CI and deviation of winter temperature above the norm indicated a possible benefit from preharvest stress (Kawada *et al.* 1978). Reduction of CI by delayed storage (Grierson 1974; Kawada 1980) was interpreted as an indication that subjecting grapefruit to water stress either pre- or postharvest reduced susceptibility to CI. Thus, it is not surprising that resistance to CI was found to be correlated with peaks in abscisic acid (ABA), the typical PGR of stress resistance (Kawada 1980).

Observations from other studies have not been integrated into any overall hypothesis on CI. Hypobaric pressure storage gives almost complete control of CI of limes and grapefruit (Pantastico *et al.* 1968). There is a differential response to respiratory inhibitors by chilling-sensitive and chilling-resistant flavedo tissue (Purvis 1980). The midwinter resistant period coincides with peaks in reducing sugars (Purvis *et al.* 1979) and proline (Purvis 1981) in grapefruit peel.

Storage pitting of lemons, commonly known as peteca, is similar to CI in etiology and symptomology. Peteca is stimulated by wax application and brush damage and reduced by ethylene degreening and storage before waxing (Wild 1991). Although peteca is a postharvest disorder, Klotz (1978) reported that it sometimes develops preharvest.

Drench Phytotoxicity (Plate 19). Recycled postharvest fungicide drenches require constant monitoring and changing of solution. However, long term, unmonitored reuse of drench solution can lead to chemical accumulation including salts, preharvest agrichemicals washed from the fruit, and even motor oil from the truck. If the drench solution is phytotoxic, the citrus peel may be damaged. Touching points between two fruit are particularly susceptible to damage since these points hold water longer and thus chemical against the peel for a longer duration. The result is characteristic off-colored circles and annuluses where the chemical was held. The most common disorder attributed to recycled fungicide drenching occurs on early season grapefruit and Fallglo tangerine in Florida, and has been termed as the "green ring" disorder due to characteristic green circles at fruit contact points in the bin that are evident after degreening (Ritenour and Dou 2000). These green rings may become necrotic during subsequent handling and storage.

Ethylene Damage (Plate 20). Degreening with excess rates of ethylene by itself may stimulate peel degradation. Ethylene damage or "gas burn" has become less common due to improved control of ethylene levels and temperatures during degreening. To reduce the risk of ethylene damage on ethylene sensitive varieties such as Fallglo tangerine, some citrus handlers allow their fruit to "degas" after degreening and prior to waxing to avoid trapping ethylene in the fruit. However, ethylene diffuses quickly out of fruit (Petracek 1994) and the time between degreening and the waxer is probably sufficient for degassing of most fruit. For sensitive varieties such as Fallglo, a short duration (6-12 hours) exposure to ethylene to initiate degreening followed by storage under high relative humidity with no exogenous ethylene has resulted in market acceptable color development with lower incidence of peel disorders. Reducing ethylene exposure can have the additional benefit of reducing the incidence of stem end rot and anthracnose decay.

The effects of ethylene on peel degradation are not understood. Ethylene stimulates phenylalanine ammonia lyase (Lafuente *et al.* 2001; Lafuente *et al.* 2004) which may in turn stimulate a phytotoxic response as has been implicated in ethylene induced russet spotting in lettuce (Hyodo *et al.* 1978).

Postharvest Pitting (Plate 21). Postharvest pitting (PP) is a physiological citrus peel disorder characterized by clusters of collapsed oil glands scattered over the fruit surface (Plate 21; Plate 22A, B). A characteristic anatomical symptom of PP is the collapse of the cells enveloping the oil glands (Plate 21D, E; Petracek and Davis 2000). PP was initially misidentified as CI because the peel collapsed during postharvest storage. However, early studies quickly showed that PP developed during postharvest storage at non-chilling temperatures (Petracek *et al.* 1995). Wax application exacerbates PP possibly through hypoxic respiration (Petracek *et al.* 1998A). PP has been studied in Temple (Petracek *et al.* 1997B) and navel orange (Alferez and Zacarias 2001) and has been observed in other citrus crops including red grapefruit, Hamlin and Valencia orange, and Sunburst tangerines (unpublished). Fallglo tangerines are particularly susceptible to PP (Petracek *et al.* 1998B).

PP incidence is increased by low humidity handling after harvest (Alferez and Zacarias 2001) and decreased by early season GA3 applications (unpublished). Profiles of peel oil volatiles are different among pitted and non-pitted fruit and vary between Fallglo and white grapefruit (Dou 2003). Foliar application of GA3 reduces PP of Fallglo during initial storage, but its effects decrease as time in postharvest storage increases (Ritenour and Stover 1999). In practice, PP can be greatly reduced by using more gas-permeable coatings and aggressive low temperature storage (Petracek *et al.* 1999).

California navel oranges provide a good example of the difficulty encountered in clearly defining a physiological disorder. Navel orange rind breakdown (NORB) is a commonly used term to describe physiological peel disorders occurring on navels after harvest in California. The term may be more of a "catch all" for navel peel disorders, rather than a specific disorder with distinct, discernible causes. In white grapefruit and Fallglo, etiology and symptomology of PP are typically distinct from other disorders. Similar to white grapefruit and Fallglo, PP of California navels initially appears as the collapse of clusters of oil glands scattered over the surface of the fruit (Plate 22A, B) with the primary damage occurring in the cells enveloping oil glands (Plate 22D, E). Also similar to white grapefruit and Fallglo, California navel PP is stimulated by high temperature storage of coated fruit (Table 14.1). However, in several of our studies on California navels, we observed a disorder with SERB-like collapse of cells in the ring around the stem scar (Table 14.1; Plate 22 C). Similar to PP, these SERB-like symptoms increased with storage temperature (Table 14.1). Unlike PP, the SERB-like symptoms were reduced by application of carnauba or shellac based coatings (Table 14.1). We attempted to distinguish fruit that visually appeared to have either PP or SERB by differences in anatomy or internal gas profile. California navels that developed either PP or SERB were both anatomically characterized by oil gland damage and did not have apparent

Table 14.1. Effects of storage temperature and coating formulation on peel disorders, and internal gas level California navel orange.[a]

Storage tempera- ture (°C)	Coating applied	Peel disorder (% incidence)		Internal gas level (%)			
		Postharvest pitting	SERB	O_2	CO_2	Ethanol	Acetaldehyde
21	No coating	0.0	16.8	17.7	1.9	0.06	0.009
21	Carnauba	23.4	7.9	12.8	5.2	0.46	0.018
21	Shellac	26.3	8.5	7.3	6.3	0.98	0.042
13	No coating	2.8	11.6	18.1	1.8	0.04	0.007
13	Carnauba	20.7	1.9	16.9	2.8	0.06	0.007
13	Shellac	16.4	2.8	9.3	5.2	0.18	0.008
4	No coating	0.9	0.9	18.1	1.8	0.02	0.000
4	Carnauba	0.0	5.9	15.5	2.9	0.02	0.005
4	Shellac	5.1	5.1	18.3	1.2	0.11	0.014
Storage temperature[b]		***	*	***	***	***	***
Coating[b]		***	n.s.	***	***	***	***
Storage temperature × Coating[b]		***	n.s.	n.s.	n.s.	**	*

[a]Fruits were harvested 5 May 1997, coated and placed in storage 8 May 1997. Pitting and SERB incidence (n = 3 cartons of 36 fruit) and internal ethanol and acetaldehyde (n = 10 fruit) were determined 14 d after coating application. Internal O_2 and CO_2 (n = 10 fruit) were determined 19 d after coating application. Mean internal gas levels and mass loss for 10 fruit per treatment.

[b]Level of significance for main treatment and treatment interaction: *, **, or *** for $P \leq$ 0.05, 0.01, or 0.001.

distinguishing anatomical traits (PP, Plate 22D, E; SERB, Plate 22F). In general, fruit with PP had somewhat higher ethanol levels regardless of storage at 21 or 13°C, but the distinction from SERB was not consistent (Fig. 14.1). PP and SERB in California navels may be related by physiology or only symptomology.

Rindstaining of Navelina Oranges. Rindstaining of Navelina oranges is considered to be both a preharvest and postharvest disorder that is characterized by the collapse and drying of the flavedo and eventually by the darkening of the affected area over time (Sala *et al.* 1992; Lafuente and Sala 2002). Navelina rindstaining is suppressed by low temperature storage (2°C), and is stimulated by increasing humidity during high temperature (22°C) storage (Lafuente and Sala 2002). Navelina harvested during or after dry weather are more susceptible (Lafuente and Sala 2002). Rindstaining occurs in non-waxed fruit (Sala *et al.* 1992). Although water loss may be an important trigger, Sala *et al.* (1992) found no relationship between total epicuticular wax content and susceptibility. Reduction in incidence due to high humidity degreening was attributed to ethylene rather than high humidity (Lafuente and Sala 2002).

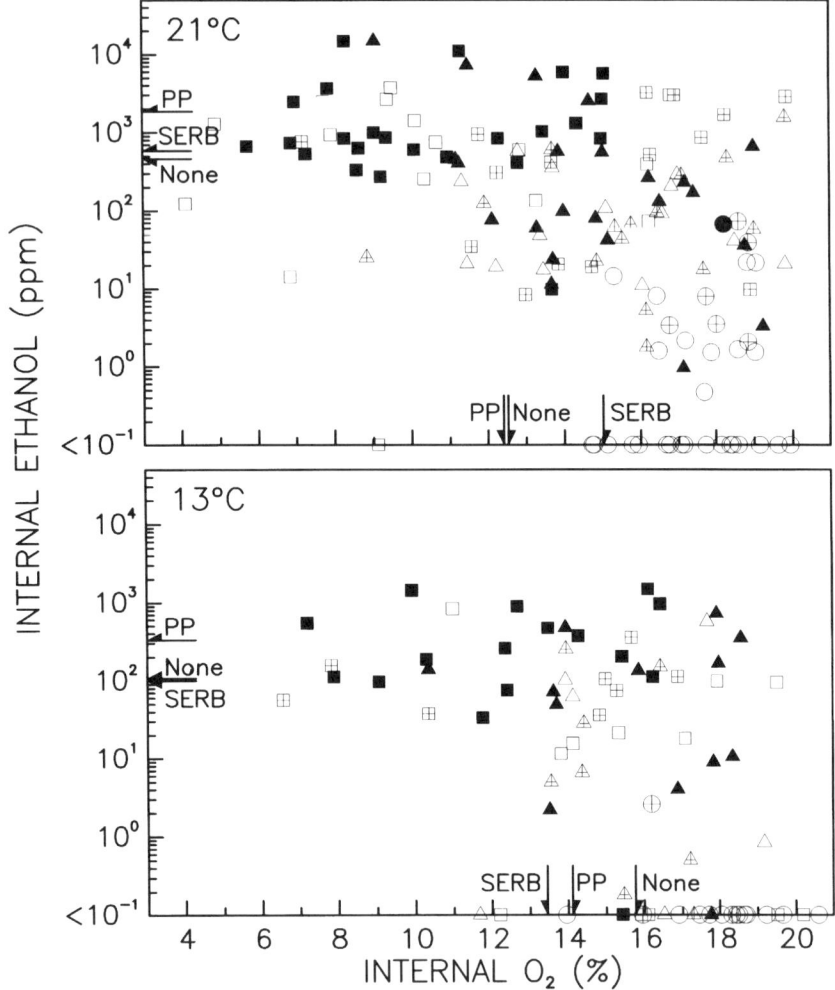

Fig. 14.1. The influence of storage temperature and coating application on internal O$_2$ and ethanol levels and the development of postharvest pitting and stem end rind breakdown of navel oranges. Internal gas levels of fruit with clearly defined peel disorders (postharvest pitting, PP, solid symbol; stem end rind breakdown, SERB, crossed symbol; no disorder, None, open symbol) were determined 21 days after coating application (shellac-based coating, square; carnauba-based coating, triangle; no coating, circle). Arrows represent average internal O$_2$ and ethanol levels of coated fruit only.

Navelina rindstaining is apparently distinct from other disorders. Rind-staining of Navelina is different from 1. rindstaining of navel oranges, which is stimulated by peel over maturation, 2. CI, which is stimulated by low temperature storage, or 3. PP, which is stimulated by postharvest coatings. Still, the similarities among Navelina rindstaining and other disorders suggests potential physiological connections.

Sanitizer Phytotoxicity. Sanitizers which are used in canker quarantine protocols or in packinghouses to control disease organisms can cause significant peel damage if they come in contact with fruit. Accumulation of residual materials such as quaternary ammonia on plastic bins may injure fruit when rehydrated (Ritenour *et al.* 2003). Early morning dew or postharvest drenching could trigger the rehydration phenomenon under field conditions.

Zebra Skin (Plate 22). In contrast to water spot of navel oranges, zebra skin of tangerines is caused not by water on the surface of the fruit, but by a sudden excess of soil water taken up by tangerine trees that had been in a state of moderate to severe drought stress (Grierson and Brown 1966; Grierson and Koo 1958; Grierson *et al.* 1965). In such circumstances, albedo and flavedo cells may rupture. When this happens, the fruit tends to decay and soon fall. If not ruptured, such suddenly distended cells will lose their dangerously high turgor pressure if fruit are not picked for 5-7 days after the rain or irrigation that caused the problem. However, if affected fruit are harvested during this period, normal handling in harvesting containers and on packingline machinery will rupture the distended epidermal cells causing a blackening of the peel over the individual fruit segments; hence, the term "zebra skin." This condition is exacerbated by ethylene degreening (Grierson and Newhall 1956) and by brushing (Grierson *et al.* 1965). When tangerines have a wide range of color (as when picking from multiple blooms early in the season), the combination of ethylene degreening and brushing exacerbates zebra skin more severely in fruit picked full green or full orange than in fruit just breaking color (Grierson and Newhall 1956).

DEFINING AND STUDYING CITRUS DISORDERS

Correct diagnosis is the foundation on which physiological disorder research is built. There is a tendency to quickly diagnose a problem. For example, random pocking is often attributed to sand damage, various forms of collapsed or damaged peel after harvest is called oleocellosis, brown or soft tissue near the stem end is called stem end rind breakdown, and peel damage that occurs during postharvest storage is called either chilling injury or, more recently, postharvest pitting. The following approach is useful in elucidating underlying causes of peel disorders and is more productive in problem solving than typical postmortem guessing based solely on visual observations.

1. Document symptomology: When observing a disorder for the first time it is important to have detailed notes on visible appearance, a record of the symptoms with photographs, and a catalog of both notes and pictures in a database. Similar symptoms will likely

appear over time. Citrus handlers have an adage: We saw it last year, we see it now, and we will see next year. Thus, even though citrus disorders are elusive, they may also be redundant and return annually.

2. Establish etiology: One key is to gather information on production and handling procedures quickly after the disorder appears. Frequently, there is a lack of reliable detailed information and an assertion that everything was done correctly or the same as in previous seasons. Obtaining a true chronology requires persistence and luck. Time lapse videos of fruit during postharvest storage can also provide an accurate visual chronology of events as the disorder progresses (Petracek *et al.* 1998B).

3. Recreate the causal conditions: This is the most difficult part as Eckert and Eaks (1989) noted on the elusive nature of citrus disorders. Citrus is unique in that a single crop may be harvested over a period of several months. The physiology of the fruit and its environment change significantly over this period, which no doubt contributes to the elusiveness of disorder research. In essence, susceptibility changes, handling may not be exactly repeated, and the re-generation of the problem may not readily occur. Nonetheless, the re-creation of the disorder is necessary to determine which factors control the disorder and to eventually establish a biochemical understanding of the process.

4. Identify critical defining factors: Histology, although time consuming, is still one of the best ways to define a disorder. Many disorders have characteristic patterns of degradation. In general, chilling targets epidermal cells, oleocellosis targets sub-epidermal cells, postharvest pitting targets enveloping cells of the oil gland, and creasing targets the parenchyma cells of the albedo. In contrast, physical damage is characterized by non-targeted damage and secondary pathogens in the flavedo. In addition to anatomical definition, biochemical molecular or genetic stress markers may ultimately be identified as the processes of physiological peel disorder development becomes understood.

POTENTIAL AREAS OF FUTURE RESEARCH

There are a number of opportunities in citrus disorder research. Cultivar, environmental conditions, and cultural practices can significantly impact the incidence and severity of disorders. In approaching research of this type, first identify methods to study the nature of susceptibility. This may lead to developing citrus fruit that can be stored longer and under a greater number of conditions. Second, determine the earliest events of the disorder. This may result in finding the key to the processes that control how stress triggers a disorder and how disorders can be controlled. Third, find markers that define and distinguish disorders including chemical or genetic indicators, and anatomical signs. The primary challenge is to develop methods that unambiguously define apparently similar physiological peel disorders.

REFERENCES

AGUSTI, M. 1999. Preharvest factors affecting postharvest quality of citrus fruit, pp. 1-34. *In* Advances in Postharvest Diseases and Disorders Control of Citrus Fruit, M. Schirra (Editor).

AGUSTI, M., ALMELA, V., ZARAGOZA, S., GAZZOLA, R. and PRIMO-MILLO, E. 1997. Alleviation of peel-pitting of 'Fortune' mandarin by the polyterpene pinolene. J. Hort. Sci. 653-658.

ALBRIGO, L. G. 1972. Ultrastructure of cuticular surfaces and stomata of developing leaves and fruit of the 'Valencia' orange. J. Am. Hort. Sci. 97, 761-765.

ALBRIGO, L. G. and GROSSER, J. W. 1996. Methods for evaluation of spray chemical phytotoxicity to citrus. Proc. Fla. State Hort. Soc. 109, 52-57.

ALFEREZ, F. and ZACARIAS, L. 2001. Postharvest pitting in navel oranges at non-chilling temperature: influence of relative humidity. Acta Hort. 553, 307-308.

AMAT, S. R. 1988. Defectos y Alteraciones de los Frutos Citricos en su Comercializacion. Lit. Nicolau, Almassora, Spain 153.

BAR-AKIVA, A. 1975. Effect of foliar application of nutrients on creasing of 'Valencia' oranges. HortScience 10, 69-70.

BOWER, J. P. 2000. Prediction and physiology of creasing. Proc. Intl. Soc. Citriculture IX Congr. 1089.

BROOKS, C. BRATLEY, C. O. and McCOLLOCH, L. P. 1936. Transit and storage diseases of fruits and vegetables as affected by initial carbon dioxide treatments. USDA Tech. Bull. 519.

BROWN, G. E. 1998. Identification of diseases, peel injuries and blemishes of Florida fresh citrus fruit, Florida Department of Citrus, Lakeland.

BROWN, G. E., PETRACEK, P. D., CHAMBERS, M., DOU, H. and PAO, S. 1998. Attempts to extend the market availability of 'Marsh' grapefruit with storage at 2-3C. Proc. Fla. State Hort. Soc. 111, 268-273.

BROWNING, W. H., McGOVERN, R. J., JACKSON, L. K., CALVERT, D. V. and WARDOWSKI, W. F. 1995. Florida Citrus Diagnostic Guide. Florida Science Source, Longboat Key FL.

BRYAN, O. C. 1950. Malnutrition symptoms of citrus with practical methods of treatment. Fla. State Dept. Agr. Bull. 93.

CAHOON, G. A., GROVER, B. L. and EAKS, I. L. 1963. Cause and control of oleocellosis on lemons. Proc. Am. Soc. Hort. Sci. 84, 188-198.

CHACE, W. G., JR., HARDING, P. L., SMOOT, J. J. and CUBBEDGE, R. H. 1966. Factors affecting the quality of grapefruit exported from Florida. USDA Marketing Res. Rept. 739.

CHAPMAN, H. D. 1958. The citrus industry of South Africa. Calif. Citrograph 43, 179-181.

CLARK, C. K. and STEARNS, C. R., JR. 1941. Puffy tangerines in the packinghouse process. Proc. Fla. State Hort. Soc. 54, 45-52.

COGGINS, C. W. and EAKS, I. L. 1967. Gibberellin research on navel oranges. Calif. Citrograph 52, 457, 486, 489-490.

DAVENPORT, T. L. and CAMPBELL, C. W. 1977. Stylar-end breakdown in 'Tahiti' lime: Aggravating effects of field heat and fruit maturity. J. Am. Soc. Hort. Sci. 102, 484-486.

DAVIS, P. L. and HARDING, P. L. 1960. The reduction of rind breakdown of 'Marsh' grapefruit by polyethylene emulsion treatments. Proc. Am. Soc. Hort. Sci. 75, 271-274.

DAVIS, P. L. and HOFFMAN, R. C. 1973. Reduction of chilling injury of citrus fruits in cold storage by intermittent warming. J. Food Sci. 38, 871-873.

DODSON, P. G. C. 1966. Damage to citrus fruit by wind. S. African Citrus J. 393, 4-5, 7, 11.

DOU, H. 2003. Volatile differences of pitted and non-pitted 'Fallglo' tangerine and white 'Marsh' grapefruit. HortScience 38, 1408-1409.

EAKS, I. L. 1964. The effect of harvesting and packing house procedures on rind staining of central California 'Washington' navel oranges. Proc. Am. Soc. Hort. Sci. 85, 245-256.

EAKS, I. L. 1969. Rind disorders of oranges and lemons in California. Proc. Int. Soc. Citriculture 3, 1343-1354.

EAKS, I. L. and MASIAS, E. 1965. Chemical and physiological changes in lime fruits during and after storage. J. Food Sci. 30, 509-515.

ECHEVERRIA, E. and BURNS, J. 1994. Handling and storage conditions that affect blossom end clearing development in grapefruit. Proc. Fla. State Hort. Soc. 107, 243-245.

ECHEVERRIA, E., BURNS, J. and MILLER, W. 1998. Progress on blossom end clearing in grapefruit. Proc. Fla. State Hort. Soc. 111, 255-257.

ECKERT, J. W. and EAKS, I. L. 1989. Postharvest disorders and diseases of citrus fruits. The Citrus Industry 5, 179-260.

ELMER, H. S., BRAWNER, 0. L. and EWART, W. H. 1973. Scarring and silvering on Central Valley navels. Calif. Citrograph 58, 335-338.

EMBLETON, T. W., JONES, W. W., LABANAUSKAS, C. K. and PLATT, R. G. 1971. Leaf analysis and phosphorus fertilization of oranges. Calif. Citrograph 56, 101, 114.

FAWCETT, H. S. and LEE, H. A. 1926. Citrus Diseases and Their Control. Agr. Bot. Sci., C.V. Pipe, McGraw and Hill Co., NY.

FREEMAN, B. 1976. Artificial windbreaks and the reduction of windscar of citrus. Proc. Fla. State Hort. Soc. 89, 52-54.

FUCIK, J. E. 1972. A physiological rind disorder on 'Valencia' oranges. Proc. Rio Grande Valley Hort. Soc. 26, 13-18.

GILFILLAN, I. M., and STEVENSON, J. A. 1977. Effect of creasing severity on splitting and decay of export oranges. Citrus Subtrop. Fruit J. 518, 5-7.

GILFILLAN, I. M. STEVENSON, J. A. and KOEKEMOER, W. 1974. Gibberellic acid reduces creasing in late season navels. Citrus Subtrop. Fruit J. 482, 4-5.

GOREN, R., MONSELISE, S. P. and BEN MOSHE, A. 1976. Control of corky (silvery) spots of grapefruit by growth regulators. HortScience 11, 421-422.

GRIERSON, W. 1958. Indicator papers for detecting damage to citrus fruit. Fla. Agr. Exp. Stn. Circ. S-102.

GRIERSON, W. 1965. Factors affecting postharvest market quality of citrus fruits. Proc. Trop. Reg., Am. Soc. Hort. Sci. 9, 65-84.

GRIERSON, W. 1971. Chilling injury in tropical and subtropical fruits: IV. The role of packaging and waxing in minimizing chilling injury of grapefruit. Proc. Trop. Reg., Am. Soc. Hort. Sci. 15, 76-88.

GRIERSON, W. 1974. Chilling injury in tropical and subtropical fruit: V. Effect of harvest date, degreening and peel color on chilling injury of grapefruit. Proc. Trop. Reg., Am. Soc. Hort. Sci. 18, 66-73.

GRIERSON, W. 1981. Physiological disorders of Citrus fruits. Proc. Int. Soc. Citriculture 2, 764-767.

GRIERSON, W. and BROWN, G. E. 1966. "Zebra-skin" of tangerines as related to pre- and post-harvest handling. Citrus Ind. 47, 8-10.

GRIERSON, W. and HATTON, T. T. 1977. Factors involved in storage of citrus fruits: A new evaluation. Proc. Int. Soc. Citriculture 1, 227-231.

GRIERSON, W. and KOO, R. C. J. 1958. Peel injury of tangerines as influenced by water relations in the grove and subsequent handling practices. Citrus Mag. 21, 110.

GRIERSON, W. and NEWHALL, W. F. 1956. Reducing losses in ethylene degreening of tangerines. Proc. Am. Soc. Hort. Sci. 67, 236-243.

GRIERSON, W. and NEWHALL, W. F. 1958. Sloughing. *In* Florida Guide to Citrus Insects, Diseases and Nutritional Disorders in Color. R. M. Pratt (Editor). Fla. Agr. Exp. Stn.

GRIERSON, W. and PATRICK, R. 1956. The sloughing disease of grapefruit. Proc. Fla. State Hort. Soc. 69, 140-142.

GRIERSON, W. and TING, S. V. 1978. Quality control of fruit and products: Quality standards for citrus fruits, juices and beverages. Proc. Int. Soc. Citriculture, 21-27.

GRIERSON, W., McCORNACK, A. A. and HAYWARD, F. W. 1965. Tangerine handling. Fla. Agr. Ext. Serv. Circ. 285.

GRIERSON, W., WARDOWSKI, W. F. and EDWARDS, G. J. 1971. Postharvest rind disorders of 'Persian' limes. Proc. Fla. State Hort. Soc. 84, 294-298.

GROSSENBACHER, J. G. 1941. Loose skinned tangerines. Proc. Fla. State Hort. Soc. 54, 44.

HARVEY, E. M. and RYGG, G. L. 1936. Field storage studies on changes in the composition of the rind of the Marsh grapefruit in California. J. Agr. Res. 52, 747-787.

HATTON, T. T. and CUBBEDGE. R. H. 1980. Preconditioning Florida grapefruit to prevent or reduce chilling injury in low-temperature storage. HortScience 15, 432.

HATTON, T. T. and REEDER, W. F. 1967. Quality of 'Persian' limes after different packinghouse treatments and storage in various controlled atmospheres. Proc. Trop. Reg., Am. Soc. Hort. Sci. 11, 23-32.

HATTON, T. T., CUBBEDGE, R. H. and GRIERSON, W. 1975. Some effects of prestorage, Hort. Rev. 4, 247-271. carbon dioxide treatments and delayed storage 'Marsh' grapefruit. Proc. Fla. State Hort. Soc.

HATTON, T. T., SMOOT, I. J. and HALE, P. W. 1977. Internal freeze damage in Florida grapefruit held in Florida and similar fruit shipped and held in Japan during late spring. Proc. Fla. State Hort. Soc. 90, 154-156.

HAWKINS, L. A. 1921. A physiological study of grapefruit ripening and storage. Agr. Res. 22, 263-278.

HYODO, H., KURODA, H. and YANG, S. F. 1978. Induction of phenylalanine ammonia-lyase and increase in phenolics in lettuce leaves in relation to the development of russet spotting caused by ethylene. Plant Physiol. 62, 31-35.

ISMAIL, M. A. and BROWN, G. E. 1979. Postharvest wound healing in citrus fruit: Induction of phenylalanine ammonia-lyase in injured 'Valencia' orange flavedo. J. Am. Soc. Hort. Sci. 104, 126-129.

JONES, W. W., EMBLETON, T. W., GARBER, M. J. and CREE, C. B. 1967. Creasing of orange fruit. Hilgardia 38 (6). 231-244.

KAVANAGH, J. A. and WOOD, R. K. S. 1967. The role of wounds in the infection of oranges by *Penicillium digitatum* Sacc. Ann. Appl. Biol. 60, 375-383.

KAWADA, K. 1980. Some physiological and biochemical aspects of chilling injury of grapefruit (*Cirrus parudisi* Macf.) with emphasis on growth regulators. Ph.D. Thesis, University of Florida.

KAWADA, K., GRIERSON, W. and SOULE, J. 1978. Seasonal resistance to chilling injury of 'Marsh' grapefruit as related to winter field temperature. Proc. Fla. State Hort. Soc. 91, 128-130.

KETCHIE, D. O. and BALLARD, A. L. 1968. Environments which cause heat injury to 'Valencia' oranges. Proc. Am. Soc. Hort. Sci. 93, 166-172.

KITAGAWA, H. and KAWADA, K. 1979. Marketing of Florida grapefruit in Japan. Proc. Fla. State Hort. Soc. 92, 241-245.

KLEIN, J. D. and LURIE, S. 1992. Heat treatments for improved postharvest quality of horticultural crops. HortTechnology 2, 316-320.

KLOTZ, L. J. 1975. Water spot of navel oranges. Calif. Citrograph 60, 439-441.

KLOTZ, L. J. 1978. Fungal, bacterial and non-parasitic diseases and injuries originating in the seedbed, nursery and orchard. *In* Citrus Industry, Vol. IV. W. Reuther, E. C. Calavan, and G. E. Carman (Editors). University of California, Berkeley.

KLOTZ, L. J. and FAWCETT, H. S. 1941. Color Handbook of Citrus Diseases, University of California Press, Berkeley.

KLOTZ, L. J., DEWOLFE, T. A., TURRELL, F. M., PLAIT, R. G. and MILLER, M. P. 1968. Concentric ring stipple of grapefruit. Calif. Citrograph 53, 15&156.

KOKKALOS, T. I. 1974. Thiabendazole reduces chilling injury (pitting) of cyprus-grown grapefruit. HortScience 9, 456-457.

KNAPP, J. L., TUCKER, D. P. II. and FASULO, T. R. 1984. Florida citrus spray guide, 1984. Univ. of Fla. Ext. Circ. 393-J.

KNORR, L. C. and KOO, R. C. J. 1969. Rumple-a serious rind collapse of lemons in Florida and Mediterranean countries. Proc. Int. Soc. Citriculture 3, 1463-1472

KURAOKA, T. 1962. Histological studies on the fruit development of the satsuma orange with special reference to peel-puffing. Memoirs, Ehime Univ. (Sect. VI) 8, 106-154.

KURAOKA, T., IWASAKI, K. and ISHII, T. 1977. Effect of GA, on puffing and levels of GA-like substances and ABA in the peel of satsuma mandarin (*Citrus unshu* Marc.). J. Am. Soc. Hort. Sci. 102, 651454.

LAFUENTE, M. T. and SALA, J. M. 2002. Abscisic acid levels and the influence of ethylene, humidity and storage temperature on the incidence of postharvest rindstaining of 'Naveline' orange (*Citrus sinensis* L. Osbeck) fruit. Postharvest Biol. Technol. 25, 49-57.

LAFUENTE, M. T., SALA, J. M. and ZACARIAS, L. 2004. Active oxygen detoxifying enzymes and phenylalanine ammonia-lyase in the ethylene-induced chilling tolerance in citrus fruit. J. Agr. Food Chem. 52, 3606-3611.

LAFUENTE, M. T., ZACARIAS, L., MARTINEZ-TELLEZ, M. A., SANCHEZ-BALLESTA, M. T. and DUPILLE, E. 2001. Phenylalanine ammonia-lyase as related to ethylene in the development of chilling symptoms during cold storage of citrus fruits. J. Agr. Food Chem. 49, 6020-6025.

McCORNACK, A. A. 1966. Blossom-end clearing of grapefruit. Proc. Fla. State Hort. Sci. 79, 258-264.

McCORNACK, A. A. 1970. Peel injury of Florida navel oranges. Proc. Fla. State Hort. Soc. 83, 267-270.

McCORNACK, A. A. 1976. Chilling injury of 'Marsh' grapefruit as influenced by diphenyl pads. Proc. Fla. State Hort. Soc. 89, 200-202.

McCORNACK, A. A. and GRIERSON, W. 1965. Practical measures for control of stem-end rind breakdown of oranges. Fla. Agr. Ext. Circ. 286.

McDONALD, R. E., McCOLLUM, T. G. and NORDBY, H. E. 1993. Temperature conditioning and surface treatments of grapefruit affect expression of chilling injury and gas diffusion. J. Amer. Soc. Hort. Sci. 118, 490-496.

McDONALD, R. E., MILLER, W. R., McCOLLUM, T. G. and BROWN, G. E. 1991. Thiabendazole and imazalil applied at 53C reduce chilling injury and decay of grapefruit. HortScience 26, 397-399.

MEIR, S., PHILOSOPH-HADAS, S., LURIE, S., DROBY, S., AKERMAN, M., ZAUBERMAN, G., SHAPIRO, B., COHEN, E. and FUCHS, Y. 1996. Reduction of chilling injury in stored avocado, grapefruit, and bell pepper by methyl jasmonate. Can. J. Bot. 74, 870-874.

MILLER, W. M., WARDOWSKI, W. F. and GRIERSON, W. 2001. Packingline machinery for Florida citrus packinghouses. Univ. Fla. Coop Ext. Serv. Bull. 239. http://edit.ifas.ufl.edu/

MONSELISE, S. P., WEISER, M., SHAFIR, N., GOREN, R. and GOLDSCHMIDT, E. E. 1976. Creasing of orange peel: Physiology and control. J. Hort. Sci. 51, 341-351.

NAGY, S., WARDOWSKI, W. F. and ROUSEFF, R. L. 1982. Postharvest creasing of 'Robinson' tangerines. Proc. Fla. State Hort. Soc. 95, 237-239.

NEL, J. G., JACOBS, C. J. and SWARTS, D. H. 1974. Cold storage of citrus: Mechanical handling of fruit and its effect on rind disorders. 1964-1974. Dept. Agr. Tech. Serv. (South Africa), Agr. Res. 98, 98-99.

NORDBY, H. E. and McDONALD, R. E. 1990. Method for protecting citrus fruit from chilling injury and fruit protected thereby. U.S. Patent 4,921,715.

OBERBACHER. M. F. 1965. A method to predict the postharvest incidence of oleocellosis on lemons. Proc. Fla. State Hort. Soc. 78, 237-240.

OBERBACHER, M. F. and KNORR, L. C. 1965. Increase of rumple and decay in lemon fruits during storage. Proc. Am. Soc. Hort. Sci. 86, 260-266.

PANTASTICO, E. B., GRIERSON, W. and SOULE, J. 1966. Peel injury and rind color of 'Persian' limes as affected by harvesting and handling methods. Proc. Fla. State Hort. Sac. 79, 338-343.

PANTASTICO, E. B., SOULE, J. and GRIERSON, W. 1968. Chilling injury in tropical and subtropical fruits: 11. Limes and grapefruit. Trop. Reg., Am. Soc. Hort. Sci. 12, 171-183.

PETRACEK, P. D. 1994. Ethylene degassing of grapefruit. HortScience 29, 535.

PETRACEK, P. D. and DAVIS, C. 2000. Ultrastructure comparison of postharvest pitting, chilling injury, and preharvest physical damage of white grapefruit peel. Proc. Intl. Soc. Citricult. IX Congr. 1079-1083.

PETRACEK, P. D., DAVIS, C. and DOU, H. 1997A. Identification of postharvest pitting of citrus fruit (fold-out color brochure), Florida Department of Citrus, Lakeland, Fla.

PETRACEK, P. D., DOU, H. and MALIK, I. 1997B. A postharvest pitting of Temple oranges stimulated by high temperature storage and wax application. Proc. Fla. State Hort. Soc. 110, 211-214.

PETRACEK, P. D., DOU, H. and PAO, S. 1998A. The influence of applied waxes on postharvest physiological behaviour and pitting of grapefruit. Postharvest Biol. Technol. 14, 99-106.

PETRACEK, P. D., MONTALVO, L., DOU, H. and DAVIS, C. 1998B. Postharvest pitting of 'Fallglo' tangerine. J. Amer. Soc. Hort. Sci. 123, 130-135.

PETRACEK, P. D., HAGENMAIER, R. D. and DOU, H. 1999. Waxing effects on citrus fruit physiology, pp. 71-92. *In* Advances in Postharvest Diseases and Disorders Control of Citrus Fruit.

PETRACEK, P. D., WARDOWSKI, W. F. and BROWN, G. E. 1995. Pitting of grapefruit that resembles chilling injury. HortScience 30, 1422-1426.

PLATT-ALOIA, K. A. and THOMSON, W. W. 1976. An ultrastructural study of two forms of chilling-induced injury to the rind of grapefruit (*Citrus paradisi* Macfed). Cryobiology 13, 95-106.

PURVIS, A. C. 1980. Respiration of grapefruit and orange flavedo tissue in relation to chilling and non-chilling temperatures and respiratory inhibitors. Proc. Am. Soc. Hort. Sci. 105, 209-2 13.

PURVIS, A. C. 1981. Free proline in peel of grapefruit and resistance lo chilling injury in storage. HortScience 16, 160-161.

PURVIS, A. C. and YELENOSKY, G. 1993. Inducible chilling injury of grapefruit on trees. HortTechnology 3, 69-69.

PURVIS, A. C., KAWADA, K. and GRIERSON, W. 1979. Relationship between midseason resistance to chilling injury and reducing sugar level in grapefruit peel. HortScience 14.

REESE, R. L. and KOO, R. C. J. 1974. Responses of 'Hamlin', 'Pineapple', and 'Valencia' orange trees to nitrogen and potash applications. Proc. Fla. State Hort. Soc. 87, 1-5.

REESE, R. L. and KOO, R. C. J. 1975. Effects of N and K fertilization on internal and external fruit quality of three major Florida orange cultivars. J. Am. Soc. Hort. Sci. 100, 425- 428. 227-229.

RIEHL, L. A. and CARMAN, G. E. 1953. Water spot on navel oranges. Calif. Citrograph 7, 7-8.

RITENOUR, M.A. and DOU, H. 2000. Factors contributing to the "green ring" disorder of fresh market citrus. Proc. Fla. State Hort. Soc. 113:297-299.

RITENOUR, M. A. and STOVER, E. 1999. Effects of gibberellic acid on the harvest and storage quality of Florida citrus fruit. Proc. Fla. State Hort. Soc. 112, 122-125.

RITENOUR, M. A., NG-SANCHEZ, T. and KELSEY, D. F. 2003. Peel injury of 'Marsh' grapefruit from quaternary ammonia. HortTechnology 13, 656-660.

SALA, J. M., LAFUENTE, T. and CUNAT, P. 1992. Content and chemical composition of epicuticular wax of 'Navelina' oranges and 'Satsuma' mandarins as related to rindstaining of fruit. J. Sci. Food Agr. 59, 489-495.

SCHIFFMANN NADEL, M., CHALUTZ, E., WAKS, J. and LA'ITAR. F. S. 1972. Reduction of pitting in grapefruit by TBZ during long-term storage. HortScience 7, 394-395.

SCHIRRA, M., MULAS, M. and BAGHINO, L. 1995. Influence of postharvest hot-dip fungicide treatments on Redblush grapefruit quality during long-term storage. Food Sci. Technol. Int. 1, 35-40.

SCHNEIDER, H. 1968. The Anatomy of Citrus. The Citrus Industry, Volume II. 1-85. University of California, Berkeley.

SCOTT, F. M. and BAKER, K. C. 1947. Anatomy of 'Washington' navel orange rind in relation to water spot. Bot. Gaz. 108, 459-475.

SHOMER, I. and ERNER, Y. 1989. The nature of oleocellosis in citrus fruits. Bot. Gaz. 150, 281-288.

SIMANTON, W. A. and TRAMMEL, K. 1966. Recommended specifications for citrus spray oils in Florida. Proc. Fla. State Hort. Soc. 79, 2630.

SMOOT, J. J., HOUCK, L. G. and JOHNSON, H. B. 1971. Market diseases of citrus and other subtropical fruits. USDA Agr. Handbook 398.

STOREY, R. and TREEBY, M. T. 1994. The morphology of epicuticular wax and albedo cells of orange fruit in relation to albedo breakdown. J. Hort. Sci. 69, 329-339.

SUNKIST GROWERS, I. 1974. Citrus Defects Market Handbook, USA.

TAL, D. and MONSELISE, S. P. 1965. Corky (silvery) spots on the rind of citrus fruits. Isr. J. Agr. Res. 15, 73-81.

TREEBY, M. and STOREY, R. 1996. Albedo breakdown research. Austral. Citrus News 72, 7.

TURNER, G. W., BERRY, A. M. and GIFFORD, E. M. 1998. Schizogenous secretory cavities of Citrus limon (L.) Burm. F. and a reevaluation of the lysigenous gland concept. Inter. J. Plant Sci. 159, 75-88.

TURRELL, F. M., MONSELISE, S. P. and AUSTIN, S. W. 1964A. Effects of climatic district and of location in tree on tenderness and other physical characteristics of citrus fruits. Bot. Gaz. 125, 158-170.

TURRELL, F. M., ORLANDO, J. and AUSTIN, S. W. 1964B. Researchers forge a link between rind-oil spot and foggy weather. West. Fruit Grow. 18, 17-18.

VAKIS, N., GRIERSON, W. and SOULE, J. 1970. Chilling injury in tropical and subtropical fruits. 111. The role of C02 in suppressing chilling injury of grapefruit and avocados. Proc. Trop. Reg., Am. Soc. Hort. Sci. 14, 89-100.

VAKIS, N., GRIERSON, W., SOULE, J. and ALBRIGO, L. G. 1971. A tissue culture technique for studying chilling injury of tropical and subtropical fruits. HortScience 5, 472-473.

VERCHER, R., TADEO, F. R., ALMELA, V., ZARAGOZA, S., PRIMO-MILLO, E. and AGUSTI, M. 1994. Rind structure, epicuticular wax morphology and water permeability of 'Fortune' mandarin fruits affected by peel pitting. Ann. Bot. 74, 619-625.

WARDOWSKI, W. F., GRIERSON, W. and EDWARDS, G. J. 1973. Chilling injury of stored limes and grapefruit as affected by differentially permeable packaging films. HortScience 8, 173-175.

WARDOWSKI, W. F., ALBRIGO, L. G., GRIERSON, W., BARMORE, C. R. and WHEATON, T. A. 1975. Chilling injury and decay of grapefruit as affected by thiabendazole, benomyl and CO_2. HortScience 10, 381-383.

WARDOWSKI, W. F., McCORNACK, A. A. and GRIERSON, W. 1976. Oil spotting (oleocellosis) of citrus fruit. Fla. Coop. Ext. Serv. Circ. 410.

WHITESIDE, J. O., GARNSEY, S. M. and TIMMER, L. W. 1988. Compendium of Citrus Diseases, Amer. Phytopathol. Soc., St. Paul, MN.

WILD, B. L. 1991. Postharvest factors governing the development of peteca rind pitting on 'Meyer' lemons. HortScience 26, 287-289.

WILD, B. L. and HOOD, C. W. 1989. Hot dip treatments reduce chilling injury in long-term storage of 'Valencia' oranges. HortScience 24, 109-110.

YUEN, C. M. C., TRIDJAJA, N. O., WILLS, R. B. H. and WILD, B. L. 1995. Chilling injury development of 'Tahitian' lime, 'Emperor' mandarin, 'Marsh' grapefruit, and 'Valencia' orange. J. Sci. Food Agr. 67, 335-339.

ZARAGOZA, S., ALMELA, V., TADEO, F. R., PRIMO-MILLO, E. and AGUSTI, M. 1996. Effectiveness of calcium nitrate and GA3 on the control of peel-pitting of 'Fortune' mandarin. J. Hort. Sci. 71, 321-326.

15

Washing, Waxing and Color-adding

David J. Hall and David Sorenson

The typical purchaser of citrus fruits makes their decision based on the appearance of the fruit. Clean, well colored, glossy fruit free of blemishes, has a better chance of being selected. For this reason it is often said that the consumer "buys with their eyes" (Taverner 2001B). The manager of one of Florida's largest packinghouses, when asked about the importance of appearance in marketing, said "its not important at all, it's CRUCIAL" (Dunnahoe 2001). That this attitude is not new is illustrated by comments made in a patent filed in 1929. "This matter of shine or polish on fruit is of extreme importance from a marketing standpoint. Of two different lots of fruit of the same grade and quality, that lot which shows the better shine or polish will practically always bring a substantially higher price per box in the market" (Brogden and Trobridge 1933).

Upon arrival at the packinghouse citrus fruits are typically dirty and unattractive. During growth they have accumulated a layer of dust, dirt, mold, bacteria, spores, and preharvest spray. A fungicidal drench before degreening may also have contributed additional dirt to the surface of the fruit. In preparation for market this accumulation of soil, etc. must be removed. During washing the natural waxy coating of the fruit is removed to a great extent and, unless replaced, will lead to rapid dehydration. Therefore a coating is applied to prevent this. At one time the coatings used in commercial production consisted entirely of wax (beeswax, carnauba, paraffin, etc.). Therefore, these coatings are commonly referred to as waxes regardless of their makeup.

In a commercial packinghouse the processes of preparing the fruit for market by washing, color-adding (if used), and waxing are carried out consecutively. Since these processes all involve the use of liquids the entire line from the dump to the dryer is referred to as the "wet line".

DUMPING

The wet line begins with emptying the fruit from field containers onto the process line, this process is usually referred to as dumping and the equipment used as the dump. There are many variations on dumping but they all have the same aim, to provide a smooth flow of fruit with minimum surges. It is also desirable that dumping be accomplished with minimum injury to the fruit, (Miller *et al.* 2001; Chapter 12). Variable speed belts, bin dumps with hydraulically controlled lids, and dumping into water have all been used. Relatively new to Florida is the bin tipper. This inverts the bin onto an angled moving belt, which feeds the bin up to a place where the fruit falls onto the feed belt with the aid of a brush. This method has proven to be extremely gentle.

While dumping into water is very gentle and evens out surges, it is generally discouraged because of its potential for spreading postharvest diseases (Miller *et al.* 2001; Wagner and Sauls 2000; Anonymous 2001B). Some smaller packinghouses have successfully used water dumps by the use of a sanitizer in the dump water (Ritenour *et al.* 2001). At least one small packinghouse has used the chlorination of their dump tank water to meet the requirements of a citrus canker quarantine (Crawford 2001).

Grading to remove trash, rots, split fruit and obviously misshapen fruit immediately following the dump is suggested. A presizer to eliminate undersized fruit is also common. By eliminating fruit that will not be packed, there is a savings on equipment and process chemicals needed further down the line.

Many packers begin wetting the fruit soon after the dump with sprays over the process line. Plain water, cleaning compounds and or approved sanitizers (chlorine, ozone, chlorine dioxide, or sodium orthophenylphenate (SOPP)) may be used. In Florida, some packers were able to satisfy citrus canker quarantine (Crawford 2001) with a chlorinated spray over a long conveyor ahead of their washer.

WASHING

The washing process may be accomplished in a number of ways, and include both mechanical and chemical procedures. In any case they will always include a brushing stage. The washing process also often includes a fungicidal treatment. In Chapter 12 Fig. 12.1 illustrates the common sequences for packlines. Chapter 13, Fig. 13.1 illustrates the sequence that might be used for a storage line. The aim of this process is to prepare the fruit (usually lemons) for relatively long-term storage before preparing them for shipment. After storage the fruit would normally be run over a pack line as illustrated in Chapter 12. There is considerable flexibility in the design of these lines. The placement and number of grading stations may vary and some processes may be mandated by local regulations. An example of the later is the requirements of Citrus Canker regulations in Florida; wherein a treatment of either 200 ppm chlorine at pH 7 for 2 minutes or an SOPP treatment for 45 seconds must be used (Crawford 2001).

Another variation would be in the case of Florida packers who will process fruit into bins for storage until such time as they may wish to pack the fruit fresh or sell for use in freshly squeezed juice products. In such a case a hybrid shipping/storage wax might be used. At times this fruit will be packed for shipping without further processing beyond grading, sizing, and packing into bags or cartons.

Cleaning Products

There are a number of chemical products used to enhance cleaning. For the most part these are supplied as concentrated solutions of alkaline salts (silicates, carbonates, and/or phosphates) with one or more anionic detergents. Currently most commercial products are designed to have a pH between 10.5 and 12.0 when applied.

One method commonly used in California for preparing lemons for storage (storage line) is to pass the fruit through a heated tank (~105°F/ 41°C) containing sodium carbonate (soda ash) or sodium bicarbonate at about 3% concentration for 3-4 minutes. This solution, containing a soap or detergent is then flooded over the fruit as it is brushed for 15-30 seconds. The wash fluid is then recirculated back to the tank. For oranges and grapefruit, tanks containing 0.35 to 0.5% Dowicide A (SOPP Tetrahydrate) have been used on pack lines.

In another method the fruit is fed directly to a brusher where the cleaning solution is applied onto the entering fruit. The applicator may be a foam generator, a drip applicator or a spray. In any case the application is applied over the first two or three brushes and is not recirculated. Brushing continues for up to 60 seconds whereupon the fruit is rinsed.

When using cleaning compounds in a brush washer, the packer needs to give attention to the amount of product applied, too much can be worse than too little. While a lot of foam gives the appearance that something is happening, the fact is that foams are mostly air and reduce the amount cleaner contacting the surface of the fruit. Ideally a cleaning compound will be formulated to give enough foam to ensure adequate coverage and that the foam will almost completely die down before the rinse. Excessive foam, wastes chemical and in extreme cases will reduce the effectiveness of the brusher by coming between the fruit and the brushes.

Currently the only fungicide incorporated in formulated fruit cleaners in the United States is the sodium salt of o-phenylphenol (SOPP). The concentration used varies, as does the method of reporting the concentration. When first used in the United States, The only product available was the tetrahydrate form of the sodium salt and was sold as "Dowicide A". At that time concentrations were reported as percent Dowicide A or percent Dowicide, this method was used by commercial operators and could be called the commercial concentration. When calculated as the anhydrous salt, 2% SOPP tetrahydrate becomes 1.45% SOPP anhydrous. Much confusion exists in the literature when this distinction is not made.

One possible problem that needs attention is the potential build-up calcium deposits on washer brushes. Hard water may react with some of the components of the cleaning product and form hard nodules on the washer brush bristles. These can be injurious to the fruit. Many commercial formulations contain sequestering agents to combat this but these add to the cost of manufacture.

A special consideration in cleaning citrus is sooty mold. Sooty mold is a massive superficial fungal growth of *Capnodium, Cladosporium* or *Meliola* spp. which live on the honey dew produced by insects such as aphids and mealybugs. Black mats of interwoven fungal strands (hyphae) may cover large areas of the fruit, especially around the stem end. This dark fungal mat is very difficult to remove, especially from creases and irregularities in the peel (Browning *et al.* 1995; Snowden 1990; Gillespie 1986).

Specially formulated cleaners containing solvents that assist in loosening the mold have been used in California and Florida since the early to mid 1970s. Ideally these are applied 1-2 minutes before the brusher to allow time for the cleaner to penetrate the sooty mold. Packinghouses that use a drencher to apply fungicides before degreening have had success using these specially formulated cleaners in the drench. Where sooty mold is only an occasional problem, and scale insect removal is not a high priority these special cleaners can be very useful to the citrus packer. Where the expense of a pressure washer is justified, these special cleaners are not necessary.

Washers

The single largest advance in fresh fruit washing was the introduction of the transverse brush washer and waxer (Holzcker 1938). In these the length of the brush is oriented across the flow of fruit. Before the 1930s, packlines used brushes oriented in the direction of fruit travel. The fruit traveled down the valley formed by two brushes in parallel. As a fruit entered at one end it would push the others along. At that time the practical limit for brushes was 52 inches (1.3 M) and mechanical considerations made machines more than 5 brushes wide impractical.

Since 5 brushes give 4 channels for fruit, a process requiring 30 seconds of brushing would have a maximum theoretical capacity of about 1600 kg of oranges per hour (Miller *et al.* 2001). On the other hand a 5 brush transverse washer, since it uses the entire area of the brush bed, would have a capacity of about 4000 kg per hour. In addition machines could be much longer than 5 brushes with consequently greater capacity. Despite the superiority of the transverse brush washer/waxer Dr. Grierson (2002) reports that lateral brush machines were still in use when he began working in Florida in the early 1950s.

Today improved materials and construction techniques have made longer brushes possible. Washers as wide as 96 inches (2.4 M) have been built and some as wide as 84 inches (2.1 M) are in service in California at this writing. Two disadvantages of brushers this wide are that longer brushes can begin to warp under the weight of the fruit and unless extraordinary care is taken fruit migration can become extreme. In most cases it has proven more practical to use two narrower washers in parallel.

The earliest washer (and waxer) brushes were made by using a drilled wooden core with natural fiber material stapled into the holes. These early brushes had several problems. The first was that the fill material was subject to rapid wear and brushes needed regular replacement. Another was that when the brushes dried out between seasons, the wooden cores could split and the bristles could break off necessitating replacement. A third is that natural fibers tend to rot with subsequent loss.

Brush Selection and Speed

Modern washer (and waxer) brushes are constructed in two distinct manners, either the bristles (fill material) is clamped in a continuous metal channel that is then spirally wound around a central core (spiral brush), or tufts of the fill material are stapled in holes spaced around a central core (tufted brush). Modern tufted brushes use a polyethylene sleeve over a metal core, Stainless steel staples hold the tufts in place.

Spiral brushes are manufactured as either right or left handed, referring to the direction of the spiral wrap. Right and left handed brushes must be alternated in a washer. If not, the fruit will tend to crowd to one side of the washer as the brush will act as a screw pushing the fruit right or left. This effect will be cancelled by alternating these brushes.

Spiral brushes have both advantages and disadvantages. An advantage is that the back and forth push of the spirals will cause a slight wobble to the fruit as it progresses through the brusher. A disadvantage is that the small space between channels allows for a build up of dirt and decay organisms. Tufted brushes are neither right or left handed. They are also easier to clean and their construction resists the build up of dirt and decay organisms.

Regardless of brush constructions most brushes are trimmed so that the bristles are of an equal length giving a uniform diameter of between 4 ½ to 4 ¾ inches (11.4 to 12.1 cm). This is referred to as a straight trim. A variation is the tumbler trim where the brushes are trimmed so that the fruit encounters a series of peaks and valleys as it progresses through the washer. These prevent the fruit from turning on a single axis as it progresses through the washer and ensures that all surfaces of the fruit receive brushing.

Modern brushes are constructed using synthetic bristle materials such as polyethylene. There are two conflicting views regarding the best material for cleaning. Some advocate a stiff bristle based upon the idea that the tip of the bristle is doing most of the cleaning. A common bristle of this type has either an "X" shaped cross section or a cross section that is round to oval. Advocates of softer bristles recommend a triangular shaped cross section. The theory behind this idea is that the edges of the bristles clean by scraping the surface of the fruit, maintaining that in a rotary brush the triangular bristle wiggles as it drags across the fruit surface. All other things being equal, both types of bristle produce clean fruit and as long as the stiff bristles are not so stiff as to scratch the fruit surface, there is not normally any detectable difference in injury to the fruit.

It is commonly assumed that new brushes are more injurious than brushes that have had a little wear. This is born out in a very limited test conduct at the University of California in Riverside (Eaks). In order to minimize this, many packers will run several loads of cull fruit over new brushes. Others will lay a sheet of plywood on top of their brushes and let the machine run for an hour or so. Either process is called wearing in. This may not be necessary with modern soft bristled brushes.

A major consideration is brush speed. For California and Florida citrus varieties, speeds of in excess of 120 rpm are not usually recommended. Higher speeds have been used and recommended in the past but modern chemicals and brush materials have achieved good cleaning with reduced danger of fruit injury.

With increased pressure on production the temptation packers often speed up their processing line allowing shorter periods of time for each operation. A minimum of 30 seconds in the washer is recommended for good cleaning. The temptation is to speed up the brushes and/or use stiffer brushes. This is not good practice as it can cause damage to the fruit. Widening the washer and other equipment is a better solution to the needs of increased production. A small increase in width of a washer can add significant capacity (Wardowski 1982).

Rotary (Centrifugal) Washer

A recent innovation in washer design was introduced into Florida in the mid 1990's. The design embodies two disc shaped brushes, one above the other. The top disc remains stationary while the bottom disc rotates (Washnock and Thomas 1996.). Fruit is fed into the center of the top and proceeds through the machine by centrifugal force. The bottom brush rotates at 16 to 18 rpm and the direction of rotation is changed regularly (usually daily) to prevent permanent brush deflection. The first of these units was installed in Waverly Florida. It had an 8 foot diameter brush bed and replaced a 60 brush 48 inch wide brusher (Wardowski 1997).

Compared to the brusher it replaced, the Rotary Brusher had fewer bearings, 2 vs. 120, used less horsepower, 2 vs. 5. Also, since the fruit was brushed on all sides and does not rotate on an axis, the stem and blossom ends of the fruit received equal treatment with the sides. Another feature of the design allowed the fruit to be discharged in any direction relative to the direction of feed. The second unit in the same packinghouse was used to make a 90° turn in their mandarin line. In addition to this, because of the design, fruit migration as experienced in a transverse brush washer, is virtually nonexistent.

On the negative side the machine is not currently in production and only two examples are known to have been installed in a packinghouse currently closed to consolidation. Another drawback is that while it does an excellent job of cleaning round fruit, varieties that are slightly flattened or elongated are difficult to clean. (Mincey 2002)

Pressure Washing

A recent innovation, the pressure washer is usually installed in addition to the usual washing process (Tavener 2001A). A bank of nozzles delivers water at pressures of up to 580 pounds per square inch (psig). The usual range is 150 to 250 psig over about 12 brushes with a 15 to 35 second exposure to the spray. A typical system might consist of 6 to 12 banks of 15 to 20 nozzles each delivering 0.6 to 1.4 gallons (2.3 to 5.3 liters) per minute. The banks of nozzles would be mounted 5 inches (127 mm) apart so that the spray may be directed between the brush valleys. With 3 to 4 inches (75 to 100 mm) between nozzles, an installation on a 6 foot (2.8 meter) wide washer could have up to 288 nozzles and deliver about 1580 gallons (6000 liters) per hour. Even though these are maximum figures it is obvious that considerable volumes of water are involved.

One important factor in pressure washer design is the height of the nozzles above the fruit. Nozzles should be mounted as close to the fruit as practical, as the pressure impacting on the fruit drops dramatically with small increases in distance (Petracek *et al.* 1998). Adequate cleaning depends upon the impact on the surface of the fruit, therefore one nozzle mounted higher than another would require a higher pressure at the nozzle, for the same impact. Higher pressures require greater horsepower, which means greater initial and operational cost.

In practice units with as few as 5 banks of nozzles and using pressures as low as 150 psig have given adequate removal of scale when most of the scale is dead or parasitized (Walker *et al.* 1999). When there is a high percentage of live scale, higher pressures are needed (Walker *et al.* 1996).

There is considerable variation in the installation and operation of pressure washing systems, depending on the citrus varieties to be cleaned, the cleaning problems encountered and the practical aspects of installation. While 7 inches (17.8 cm) is typical, installations with anywhere from 6 to 10 inches (15.2 to 25.4 cm) above the brush bed have been encountered. Units using water at the rate of as much as 3000 gallons (11,356 liters) per hour are not unusual.

Because of the high volumes involved, it is necessary to recirculate the water. It is also necessary to chlorinate this water to prevent the accumulation and spread of decay organisms. Another important consideration is the build-up of dirt and debris in the recirculating water. Most systems use some sort of screening or filtering system to remove debris and by continuously replacing a portion the system volume. As a general guideline, replacing the volume at the rate used by a conventional rinse line has been adequate (Katz 1995).

This system has been quite efficient in removing both sooty mold and scale insects. Where removal of scale insects is not a consideration, lower pressures (100 psig) have been used with success for sooty mold removal (Cunningham 2002).

Some advantages of High-Pressure washers are that they can clean without the use of chemical cleaning compounds, which decreases disposal problems. On the other hand, experiments in Australia have demonstrated that incorporating various cleaning compounds in the pressure washing fluid gives improved removal of sooty mold at lower pressures (Cunningham 2002). While this increases disposal problems, the economy of lower horsepower requirements in both initial equipment and operating costs may be well worth considering.

In addition to sooty mold removal, pressure washers are also very efficient in the removal of scale insects (Honiball *et al.* 1979; Katz 1995; Walker *et al.* 1996; Walker *et al.* 1999; Taverner 2001A; Cunningham 2002). They are often able to clean fruit that would be otherwise nearly impossible to clean sufficiently for market demands.

Some drawbacks of the system are that the pumps needed are quite expensive and use considerable horsepower requiring as much as 400 hp to run higher pressure systems (Katz 1995). Other drawbacks are that the pressures used tend to cause excessive brush wear, there is the possibility of damage to some varieties of fruit (Petracek *et al.* 1998) and, when live scale insects are removed, they leave their mouthparts embedded in the peel.

Mouthparts left behind by live scale insects allow cellular exudate to leak to the surface of the fruit, which serves as a substrate for secondary mold growth (Giliomee and Swanepoel 1979). It has also been reported that when large amounts of scale are removed from the fruit, the exudate on the surface interferes with the waxing process to the point that a satisfactory appearance is not obtainable. Small amounts of scale (less than 5% coverage) are of little concern and several techniques for the prevention of secondary mold growth have been developed (Pelser 1993). Directing the spray into the valleys between brushes can minimize the brush wear problem. Some California packinghouses have solved this problem by alternating the brushes with brush sized PVC rolls, and directing the nozzles so that the majority of the spray force is directed to strike the fruit above the edge of the roll.

In using pressure washers, consideration also needs to be given to the effect of pressure washing on postharvest decay. In tests on fruit treated with carbonates (See Chapter 13), pressure washing before treatment improved decay control while pressure washing after treatment greatly reduced decay control (Smilanick *et al.* 1999). By using the carbonate treating solution as the pressure washing fluid, this loss of decay control is eliminated. Similar effects may be true with other treatments.

Hot Water Brushing

Hot water brushing is another innovation, which is not strictly a washing process, but is incorporated, in the wash line. See Chapter 13. Cleaned fruit is subjected to 125°-144°F (52°-62°C)water sprays for 15-20 seconds. This has resulted in lower decay rates especially with the penicillium molds (Fallik *et al.* 2001; Porat *et al.* 2000; Lanza *et al.* 2000). Tests in California have not demonstrated efficacy against sour rot (Smilanick 2002). One advantage of this system is that, if it immediately precedes the waxer, the surface of the fruit has been heated which greatly enhances water elimination and waxing (see waxing below).

WATER ELIMINATION (DEWATERING)

After the fruit is cleaned it is important that excess water be eliminated from the fruit surface to prevent dilution of process materials. In the case of some waxes, bar wax, solvent wax, etc. the fruit should be completely dry for good coverage and adhesion of the wax film. The water waxes do not require as thorough drying but any excess water will dilute the wax and increase the energy required for drying. Water elimination is accomplished in several ways, each with its advantages and disadvantages.

Brush Polishers. Originally common as a prelude to solvent waxing a brush polisher typically consisted of a section of transverse horsehair brushes rotating at 120 to 160 rpm. In the past speeds as high as 225 rpm have been used (Anonymous 1962). Often fans either heated or unheated would be mounted above the brush section to aid in drying. With the demise of solvent wax in the United States many packinghouses have retained these polishers as prelude to their water wax applicator. The advantage of the brush polisher is that it thoroughly dries the fruit as well as imparting a temporary shine prior to waxing. The polisher also warms the surface of the fruit, which improves the drying and subsequent shine of water wax.

The disadvantages of the polisher are high initial cost, high maintenance cost, and the friction that dries and warms the fruit causes some injury which has the potential of reducing shelf life. The brush polisher dryer is not recommended (Miller *et al.* 2001).

Foam Rolls. The most common method of water elimination in United States packinghouses is foam rolls. These rolls are typically made up of 1 to 2 inch thick donut-shaped (torus) disks of foam rubber packed on a metal core and arranged in the same manner as a transverse brush washer. These donuts are either made of latex foam or polyurethane foam. A typical installation will consist of foam rolls to about half the number of washer brushes. A "wringer roll" is necessary to squeeze excess water. For greater efficiency a wiper blade on the wringer roll will prevent water from being redeposited on the foam roll (Fig. 15.1, Fig. 12.5).

The disadvantage of foam rolls are their cost. Latex foam is expensive and often in short supply. Also a set of rolls usually will only last one season and if, once wet, they are allowed to dry out for an extended period, they begin to disintegrate rapidly. Also the wringer rolls require precise adjustment, too tight and they will tear the donuts, too loose and water elimination will be less than optimum. The wiper blades also need regular cleaning.

Polyurethane rolls avoid many of these problems, they are in good supply, are usually available at a lower initial cost, and can endure repeated wetting and drying. Unfortunately they are not as efficient in removing water as are latex rolls.

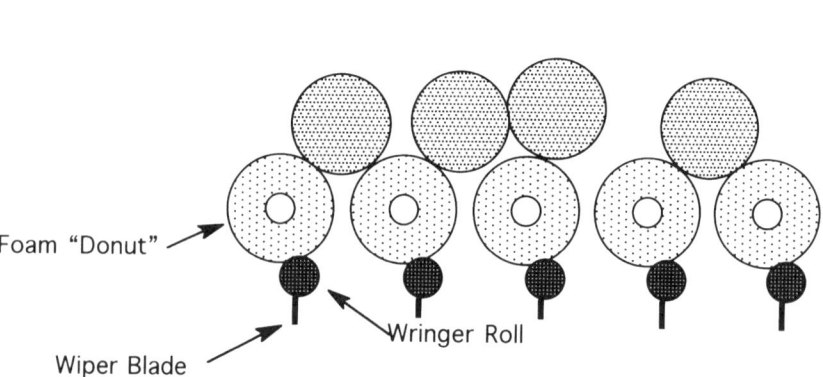

Fig. 15.1. Donut water eliminator with wringer rolls and wiper blade.

Brushes with Flicker Bars. Where water elimination is less critical regular brushes can be used to remove excess water. By mounting a bar of metal or other material below the brush where it contacts about ½ inch of the bristles as they rotate, excess water will be knocked off (Fig. 15.2, Fig. 12.5). The disadvantages of this system are that it is not a very efficient water removal system, and that the brushes tend to wear excessively.

Solid Rolls. Clean brass has the property of repelling water so that passing wet fruit over a section of brush size brass rolls was once a common method of dewatering. A rubber blade mounted against the underside of the roll, a few degrees past the center in the direction of rotation, would wipe excess water from the roll making these the most efficient of their time. Once a very common type of water eliminator, the brass roll eliminator is rarely seen in United States packinghouses today.

The brass roll eliminator had the disadvantage of being initially expensive and requiring regular maintenance. The wiper blades need regular cleaning as any hard material caught between blade and roll could cause damage to the soft brass. The same principle has been embodied in the use of smooth surfaced PVC rolls with wiper blades. Tests by the University of Florida has determined that these are the most efficient method of water removal, using less than 5% of the energy required for heated air (Miller 1986).

High Velocity Air (Air Knife). A wide, yet very narrow stream of air at high velocity will blow considerable water from the surface of wet fruit. This method of water elimination has been tried experimentally but as yet has not come into common commercial practice. The main drawback with this method is its expense. Considerable volumes of compressed air are required and compressors capable of producing large volumes of clean (oil free) air are expensive.

Rubber Disk. A relatively new method of removing excess water. These are constructed of a series of stiff rubber, or similar material, approximately

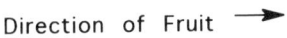
Direction of Fruit ➤

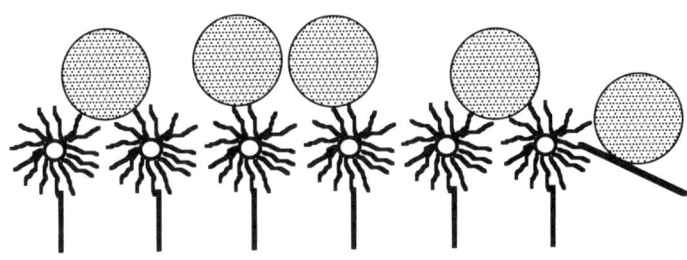

Fig 15.2. Brush water eliminator with flick bars.

⅜ inch thick, disks mounted on a core with spacers between the disks so that there is a gap between them. The gap spacing is usually 1-½ inches but other spacings are used, depending upon the variety processed. High velocity fans mounted above the water eliminator section blow down through the fruit, thus expediting water removal (Fig. 15.3).

LIGHT FRUIT SEPARATION

If the lot of fruit being processed is going to be subjected to a wet separation procedure to remove light fruit due to freezing or drying (Chapter 11), it will be diverted either before or after a water elimination step. If a water separator is used then the fruit will be diverted before the water elimination section and returned to the main line for water elimination. If a solvent emulsion based specific gravity separator is used the fruit will be diverted after water elimination to reduce the chance of changing the specific gravity of the fluid. In such a case a second water eliminator is necessary after the excess emulsion is rinsed off the fruit.

In modern packing houses separation of low specific gravity fruit can take place at the sizer. Modern machines have been developed that are able

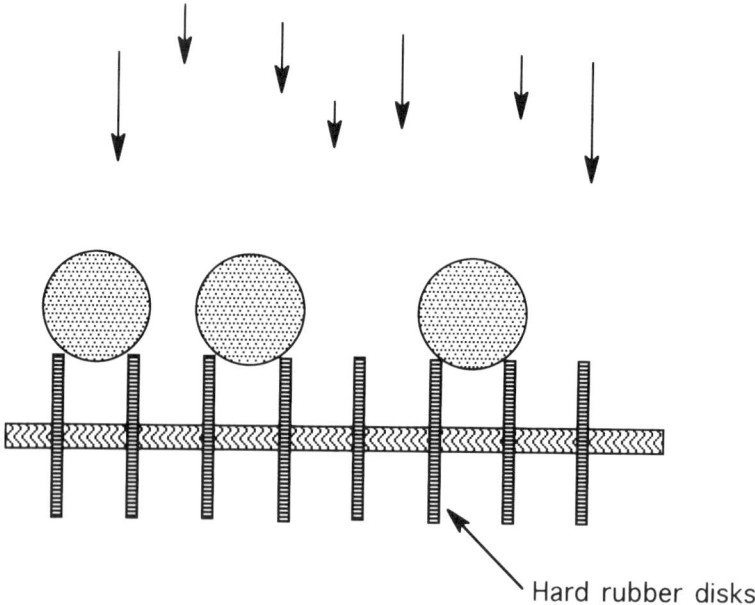

Air Flow from fans or blower

Hard rubber disks

Fig. 15.3. End view of a disk type water eliminator.

to measure both weight and volume accurately enough to equal and even exceed the wet methods used up to now (Chapter 12).

If the fruit is to be color-added, a water elimination section should follow the color-add rinse.

THE COLOR-ADD PROCESS

Probably the most abused product in fresh fruit processing in Florida is color-add. The basic process involves flooding a water solution containing an oil soluble dye at a controlled temperature and for a specified length of time. These products come in two forms, soap-based formulas and emulsified solvent based formulas. In either case the product dilutes to form a solution that weakly holds the dye until it contacts the fruit, the dye is then deposited onto the fruit and is strongly bound to the surface. When correctly applied the dye will not come off during subsequent processing.

The method of application, and equipment used have remained constant over the last half-century or more. Drawings illustrating application equipment in a United States Patent filed in 1947 (Gerwe and Fisk 1950) are essentially identical to equipment built in the last few years.

The typical color-add tank has a large reservoir of 500 to 1500 gallons over which a flat roll conveyor passes. Perforated flood pans above the conveyor allow the color solution to rain down upon fruit as it passes under. The dye solution is pumped from the reservoir to a distribution or weir box, which supplies the pans. Sufficient solution needs to be fed to the pans to allow a constant flooding of the fruit as it passes the entire length of the tank and to flood over the end of the pan section to quickly wet the incoming fruit with dye solution. Contrary to the practice with other conveyors in a packinghouse, the conveyor in a dye tank is designed to run with the fruit stacked in a triple layer during operation.

The solution is heated by circulation through a heat exchanger. This should be accomplished by a separate system with a thermostat controlled by measuring the temperature of the solution just below the applicator conveyor.

In Fig. 15.4 the fruit flow is from left to right while the solution is flooded over the fruit from overhead pans. The color-add solution is drawn from a reservoir through a heat exchanger to a tank at the top right of the machine (The Weir Box in the drawing). From there it flows along perforated pans where it drips onto the fruit below. Excess color-add drains back to the reservoir tank.

In the United States the color-add process is regulated by both state and Federal Laws. Under Federal Law the dye used must be certified by the United States Food and Drug Administration and only one dye, Citrus Red No. 2, is permitted (Anonymous 2001A).

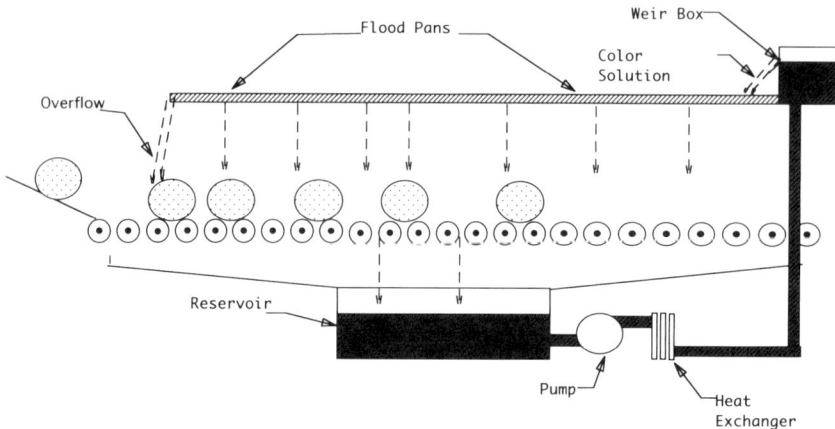

Fig. 15.4. Color-add flood recovery application tank.

Some United States states prohibit the use of color-add while others strictly regulate its use. Florida specifies the varieties that may be color-added, the time and temperature used in application as well as limiting the intensity of color that may be applied (Florida Dept. of Citrus 2002).

Soap Color

The soap-based formula, while usually cheaper by the gallon, is quite expensive to use and has a narrow range of intensity as far as added color is concerned. In addition the soap-based formulations are "tricky" to use and require much closer attention to the color-add operation than many packinghouses are willing to give.

A typical soap-color formulation is designed to be used at a dilution of 20 or 25:1. A major problem with soap color is that it is very sensitive to calcium and magnesium hardness in the make-up water. In addition to that, it is also very sensitive to acid conditions and works best at a pH between 9 and 11. Excessive hardness and/or acid can be often be recognized by the accumulation of a scummy build-up on the edges of the tank and the surface of the solution. Soap color formulations may not be mixed with solvent color formulations, without the danger precipitation of dye or soap. For these reasons the soap-based formulations have essentially disappeared from commercial use.

Solvent Based Products

The emulsified solvent type products are much simpler to use, and have the advantage to the packer that they may be used with much less attention.

While all formulations are based on emulsifiers and solvents, different manufacturers have varying emulsifier bases that significantly affect the performance of the product (Hall and Bowers 1989). One color-add product has a base dilution factor of 300:1. Another product on the market, using a different emulsifier system, has a base dilution factor of 200:1. Despite base dilution factors, many packers desire a very dark color on their fruit and often use the products at two to four times the recommended concentration.

The color-add process is extremely temperature sensitive. A drop of 2°F. will give a noticeable decrease of color intensity. In our experience this is generally true of all products available in Florida. The temperature indicators used in most dye tanks used in Florida are not sensitive enough to give an accurate indication of the true solution temperature. An additional problem is that the automatic temperature regulators used are not accurate enough to keep the temperature within 1 or 2 degrees of the desired temperature.

The interaction of time and temperature is illustrated in an unpublished laboratory demonstration conducted by D. Hall. In a series of trials, marked locations on several fruit were marked and the L*a*b values of each location were measured with a Minolta CR-200 Chromameter. The fruit were then treated with commercial dilutions of a standard, solvent based, color-add product for different times and temperatures. After treatment the L*a*b values were once again measured. The increase in the "a" value (red) was then calculated. For fruit treated for 4 minutes at 110°F, 115°F and 120°F the "a" value increased +12.8, +14.9 and +17.1 respectively. There were corresponding decreases in the "L" and "b" values. In another set of trials, comparing the effect of time at various temperatures, an increase of 90 seconds (from 2.5 to 4.0 minutes) at 110°F, 115°F and 120°F resulted in an additional increase in the "a" value of 1.1, 2.0, 5.2 respectively. From these results it is obvious that both time and temperature are important controlling factors in the final appearance of the fruit.

During use, the volatile solvents used in color-add formulations are driven off by elevated temperatures and solution agitation. In a well designed and maintained applicator, operated under optimum conditions as to time temperature, and process rate, this rate of solvent loss is proportional to dye use and is of no concern. When conditions are not at optimum, the use of an emulsifiable supplemental solvent, referred to as a booster or additive, is used to replace this loss.

During operation the pH of the tank will tend to drop due to the take up carbon dioxide from the air, and from the acid in broken or damaged fruit. The pH of soap based products must be maintained between 7 and 8 for optimum results, whereas pH is not as critical a factor with solvent based color-add. In a soap based product an acid pH will cause a soap scum to form and precipitate the dye, resulting in spotty or uneven color. Solvent based products will work over a wide range of pH, however, the best performance is seen when it is kept between 6 and 8. The preferred material for pH adjustment is trisodium phosphate (TSP). It is alkaline enough to require small quantities, is relatively safe to handle, and the phosphate adds a small measure of corrosion protection in steel tanks.

There are several potential problems associated with the color-add process. Most of these are caused by using too much dye. In order to get a color of greater intensity, rather than increasing the time or temperature of exposure, some operators increase the amount of dye concentrate used. Excessive dye can result in uneven coloring and spotting where the fruit contact each other during the process.

Another condition known as "ringing" occurs when the fruit turn freely on conveyor rolls in the tank and the dye concentration is too high. This appears as a dark band of color around the fruit. This condition also has occurred when excessive silicone anti-foam is used in the dye solution. The latter is usually caused when the circulating pump begins sucking air due to clogged screens or low solution levels. The first response to excessive foam is often to add more antifoam rather than address the basic problem. The manufacturers of color add solutions provide compatible antifoam products. Under normal operating conditions, no more than one addition at the recommended dose should be made during a normal day's operation.

The most common error made in the use of color-add is using too much dye concentrate. The manufacturers design the balance of dye, solvents, co-solvents and emulsifiers to give optimum performance at the recommended dilution. In their formulations they allow some leeway in their use, but there is a practical limit. As color-add concentrate is added to the solution, so to are all of the other ingredients. In such cases one can approach the point where the dye is more strongly held by the solution than the fruit surface. In such cases adding more dye results in weaker, irregular color.

The operator of a color-add system needs a simple method of evaluating the effect of the color-add application. If the fruit have been properly treated, it is often difficult to discern just how much dye has been added. A quick method of evaluating this is by wrapping a single band of plastic electrician's tape around the fruit, then running that fruit through the process. After removing the tape, one may compare the before and after effect quite clearly (Plate 24).

A simple method of determining the effect of changes in the dye solution may be accomplished by a procedure that can be performed in the packinghouse. In this procedure one takes a sample of the tank solution and measures out a volume, in milliliters, equivalent to a multiple of the volume of the tank in gallons. For example if the tank held 600 gallons of solution one would measure out 600, 1200, ml., etc. Then, after heating the solution to the operating temperature, one immerses fruit in the solution, preferably with a tape wrap as above, for the same time as the fruit are exposed in the tank. After evaluating the color, add buffer or booster and evaluate again. Using this method one ml. of booster or color concentrate, per 600 ml. solution would be the equivalent of adding one gallon to the tank. By the same token, one ml of a 120 gm per liter TSP solution would be equivalent to adding one pound of TSP per 600 gallons.

If it is necessary to determine the actual amount of dye on a fruit, the simplified method of chloroform extraction and colorimetric (490nm) determination (Ting 1955) for the old Citrus Red No. 32 has been found to work quite well for the current Citrus Red No. 2 (Hayward 1964).

WAXING

Before shipping or storage the natural wax coating removed during the washing process needs to be replaced. The packinghouse may use one or more of several products, depending upon the immediate and ultimate destination of the fruit. There are three basic types of waxes used on citrus, storage waxes, combination shipping and storage waxes, and shipping waxes.

Fruit destined for long term storage and then subsequent use either as fresh fruit or for fresh squeezed juice are usually coated with an easily removable storage wax. These waxes are usually emulsions of either the nonionic or anionic types and are composed of paraffin wax and or oil, natural waxes such as carnauba or synthetic waxes such as oxidized polyethylene. Their common features are that they have little noticeable shine, and that standard packinghouse washers easily remove them.

In the California lemon packing industry, the great majority of the crop is coated with a storage wax, then held until needed for the fresh market. This can amount to several months storage. When needed for shipment as fresh fruit, the lemons are washed to remove the storage wax, and then coated with a high shine shipping wax. At present high shine waxes of the shellac/resin type are favored in the markets.

WAXES

Coatings used for citrus are referred to as generically as waxes even if they contain no actual wax. The reason for this that the earliest waxes were simple compositions of paraffin wax alone or a combination of various other waxes such as beeswax, carnauba, spermaceti, etc. These were applied by pressing a block of wax against a brush, which then transferred the wax to the fruit. Subsequent brushes would spread and polish the wax coating.

Wax formulation and application is an art that involves balancing many factors. Among these are cost, shine, drying rate, fruit respiration, durability, and water resistance. Also the packer needs to consider application method, ease of equipment cleanup, and compatibility with other processes. Since the formulation must also be composed of materials that are compatible with applicable food laws, the list of materials available to the formulator is extremely limited (Hall 1981). There are no all-purpose waxes that satisfy all requirements equally well. Increasing shine and durability, usually means an increase in cost, lowering cost means losing or reducing some other desirable quality. Therefore, most formulators have several products available to meet specific requirements.

There are two main types of wax products available to the packer. Shipping waxes and storage waxes. Each is designed for specific purposes. A third type, the storage/shipping wax has been offered to the trade recently. These products generally have good fruit respiration qualities and durability. However, they are more expensive to use and are weaker in other factors such as shine.

The formulation type may also categorize waxes. Solvent waxes refer to those that are composed of resins dissolved in a petroleum distillate carrier. Water wax refers to those formulations that use water as their main component. These may be further categorized as emulsion or shellac/resin waxes. There are also solid or bar waxes. Of these types the water-based formulations currently dominate the industry.

Solvent Waxes

At one time the solvent waxes dominated citrus waxing. By the mid 1970's about 90% of Florida's citrus was shipped with solvent wax from the Food Machinery Company (FMC). In Florida, their brand "Flavorseal" was nearly synonymous with solvent wax (Hall 2003). In California and Arizona virtually all lemons and a significant portion of other citrus varieties were packed with solvent wax. There were however, two other major suppliers of solvent wax, the Brogdex Company and Pennwalt-Decco.

Since the mid 1980's, solvent wax has not been used in the United States and its use elsewhere in the world has not been reported. Three factors contributed to this; the high price of petroleum solvents, concerns over air pollution, and the inability to incorporate fungicides with the wax.

Users of this type of wax often mistakenly believed that they did not need a drier for their fruit, simple unheated fans above a long slatted or roller conveyor was all that was needed. While this was true, much energy was expended before waxing in order to have the fruit dry enough to receive the coating.

Bar Waxes

The solid or bar waxes are still used in a few very low volume operations. Simple and very inexpensive to use, they give very little shine and complete, uniform coverage is difficult to obtain. For smaller packers this type of wax is a practical alternative in that it does not require a complex application system, nor does it require a post-wax dryer. While still found at the occasional roadside fruit stand operation catering to local or tourist trade, no commercial citrus shippers in the United States use this type of wax today.

The future of this type of wax is uncertain. One factor that may result in greater use is the growing market for organically grown and packed produce. Formulations are possible that would meet the requirements of those organic programs that are similar to the United States National Organic Program (USDA 2002).

Water Waxes

As noted, there are three main categories of water waxes: storage, shipping or shine waxes and hybrid storage/shipping waxes.

Storage waxes are designed to act as anti-transpirants for citrus that is to be held in relatively long term storage. For lemons in California this may be as long as 150 days. Oranges and grapefruit are often held for up to 90 days in Florida, mainly for use in juice products marketed as fresh squeezed.

These waxes are generally emulsions, and are designed to be easily removed by washing when the fruit is removed from storage. Originally anionic emulsions of paraffin wax and or mineral oil were used. Their great drawback was that the emulsion was sensitive to water hardness and would tend to be unstable. This was a minor problem before the introduction of the fungicides thiabendazole and benomyl. When these fungicides were mixed into the storage wax, the unstable emulsion would tend to precipitate the fungicide resulting in uneven application.

In recent times nonionic emulsions based on oxidized polyethylene have become more common. These emulsions are very stable under all conditions normally encountered in a citrus packinghouse. In any case, the concentrated emulsion is diluted at the packinghouse for use based upon the anticipated term of storage. One of the great advantages of this type of wax is that no drying after application is required. The wax is not sticky and the moisture content of the coating soon reaches equilibrium with the storage room atmosphere.

The California lemon industry routinely treats lemons with these removable waxes for storage. Then, washes them off when the fruit is passed over a conventional packline for the application of a shine or shipping wax. In Arizona some packers use this type of wax as a fungicide carrier on fruit prior to degreening. A similar procedure is used on oranges in Spain (Dunnahoe 2001).

Hybrid storage/shipping waxes are viewed with mixed feelings by many packers. They are usually used when a packer is processing fruit where some of the lot will be shipped immediately as fresh, and the rest to be held for later determination whether it will be sold as fresh fruit or sent for juice processing. These waxes have been described as combining both the best and worst features of both types at the same time. Good formulations give good shrinkage control during storage but are much more expensive than conventional storage waxes. Their initial shine is not as good as dedicated shipping waxes, but it generally holds up well in storage. They are not easily removed so rewaxing the fruit with a fresh coat before latter shipping is not a good practice as too much wax on the fruit is detrimental.

Shipping waxes, also known as shine waxes, are designed to improve the appearance of the fruit while reducing weight loss during shipping and marketing. They may contain resinous materials such as shellac, natural and synthetic resins. There are no generally accepted terms for these waxes. Various suppliers refer these to as, shellac, resin or shellac/resin waxes. Some formulations may be based on an emulsion of oxidized polyethylene ("Poly" or polyethylene wax) or a natural wax such as carnauba. These formulations usually contain some shellac and or other resinous ingredients (Hall 1981).

These shipping waxes usually contain anywhere from 12 to 18% non-volatile components (solids). It is a mistake to compare waxes solely on the basis of solids content as different ingredients behave differently in any given formulation as to controlling weight loss and gas exchange.

A variation of this type of wax is a very high solids (20-30%) wax that has an extremely high viscosity. It is designed to be applied at a rate much lower than most, usually at a rate of about one gallon per 25,000 pounds of fruit (3000 Kg/L). This type of wax is best applied using air nozzles. These waxes give a very good initial shine but are very poor in controlling weight loss.

Since the fruit must continue to carry on respiration, it is important that the wax allow an adequate exchange of oxygen and carbon dioxide while reducing weight loss. The rate of weight loss and respiration are greatly dependent upon storage conditions; therefore, these become important factors in choosing a shipping wax.

The packer must consider his own market needs to choose a shipping wax. There is no single wax that satisfies every need. Table 15.1 gives the qualities to be expected from well formulated examples of each type of wax.

Since citrus is usually sold by weight, the control of weight loss or shrinkage between the shipper and the buyer is of great importance. However the packer cannot stop all weight loss without encountering the off flavor development related to poor gas exchange (Peeples *et al.* 1999). Rapid turnover and proper storage temperatures in the marketing channels can minimize some of this. Because of the concern over possible off flavor development, some advocate using a wax with less shine and better gas exchange. In the final analysis, the packer must select the coating that will provide the greatest returns.

While instruments for the measurement of gas exchange are available, they are generally impractical for routine quality control of wax applica-

TABLE 15.1. Characteristics of Wax Types

Wax type	Durability	Appearance-shine	Gas exchange	Weight loss reduction
Solvent wax	Fair	Very High	Poor[a]	Low[b]
Shellac/resin	Good	High	Moderate	High
Emulsion	Very good	Moderate	Good	Fair

[a]The poor gas exchange properties of solvent wax is minimized by the generally poor coverage in the applicator.

[b]The generally poor coverage with this type of wax contributes to greater weight loss. Hand dipped fruit are usually completely sealed and will go into anaerobic respiration.

tions. A simple quality control procedure is to measure the rate of weight loss of waxed fruit over a specific time period as compared to a standard. Methods used differ between workers. Absolute weigh loss, that is just the percentage of loss, is meaningless. A comparison with fruit of the same lot is necessary, as there are great differences due to variety and growing conditions. One method is to compare the rate of weigh loss with washed but not waxed fruit while another is to compare the rate of weight loss of washed and waxed fruit with unwashed fruit. In the former method, a ratio can be calculated to compare with an established standard. Those using the latter method usually seek to apply wax at a rate to achieve the same rate of weigh loss as the unwashed fruit. (Hall 1981)

Another common mistake in evaluating waxes is the arbitrary comparison of solids content. One might assume that an 18% solids wax is superior to a 16% solids wax. This may not be necessarily true. With waxing, the end result is the only important consideration. A high solids wax may be so because a large quantity of filler material has been added to boost solids, or to control viscosity, while a lower solids wax may be composed entirely of ingredients that increase the technical efficiency of the wax. The four cornerstones of wax selection are; efficiency in application (includes cost of product), appearance at the point of sale, shrinkage control, and lack of off flavor development.

Another consideration in comparing waxes is the difference between the wax coating applied in a commercial applicator and that applied by hand. An normal commercial wax/applicator combination will usually apply wax at the rate of one gallon per 5,000-10,000 pounds (600-1,200 Kg/L) of fruit while hand waxing is often at a rate of 1 gallon to 2,000-4000 pounds (240-480 Kg/L). To compensate for this many workers dilute the commercial wax before applying (Ben-Yehoshua 1967; Ben-Yehoshua et al. 1970; Hall 1981). Based upon comparative weight loss studies, it has been found that a dilution of 60-70 parts wax with water to make 100, closely approximates a commercial coating when used for hand waxing.

FUNGICIDES

One advantage with the water based waxes is the ability to incorporate many common fungicides into the wax, thus combining applications. When using fungicides such as imazalil or thiabendazole the recommendation is to use approximately double the rate in a separate water based system (Brown 1983). Since most water based applications apply at the rate of one gallon per 2,000 to 4,000 pounds of fruit per gallon (240-480 Kg/L) there is little difference in cost and a great savings in energy costs of extra drying.

DEFECTS

Whiting. Several conditions can result in the waxed citrus developing white areas, which the uninformed sometimes mistake for pesticide residues. These are variously called, blushing, rewetting, chalking, powdering, fracturing, shattering, dusting, etc. Often these terms are used interchangeably without regard to the cause. These conditions and their causes are:

Dusting, and Powdering. When high shine resin/shellac waxes are applied under conditions of relative humidity significantly lower than the wax was designed for, the wax particles will dry before laying down to make a smooth coating on the fruit. This irregular surface will easily fracture and cause a white power to form. This can be easily tested by lightly brushing two pieces of fruit against each other and noticing if a powder forms. If the powder will wipe off leaving a shiny surface, this condition is confirmed. Adjustment of the plasticizers in the wax formulation will usually eliminate this condition.

Fracturing and Shattering. This is characterized by flakes of wax separating from the surface of the fruit. In some cases it is similar to rewetting as described below. It is the result of a wax coating that is too brittle. This can be caused by formulations that have too little plasticizer additives, also to some extent by fruit that have not been thoroughly cleaned. The wax film does not flex and as the fruit shrinks, the film separates from the surface of the fruit then flakes off. Experienced formulators are aware of this problem. When it does occur, the most likely cause is poor cleaning.

Blushing, Rewetting, and Chalking. When refrigerated fruit are brought out to warmer conditions condensation will often form. When this condensate develops between the surface of the fruit and the wax film, it will lift the film away from the surface of the fruit causing a white appearance to develop. If the fruit is undisturbed until the condensate dries, the wax film will often lay down with no apparent effect. But, if the fruit is handled during this time, the film may be broken and trapped air will give it a white appearance in this area. One factor that greatly contributes to this condition is poor cleaning.

Applicators

Regardless of the formulation used, coverage, or uniform application, is a very important factor in waxing. A coating that is not uniform can affect the appearance and keeping qualities of the fruit. Fruit that have too little wax may be dull in appearance and shrink excessively. Fruit with too much wax may not dry properly, may develop off flavors, and may exhibit such effects as flaking or whiting.

The earliest applicators involved pressing a bar of wax against the underside of the first one or two applicator brushes, relying on transfer to carry wax to the fruit, many low volume packers still use this system. Other early methods involved passing the fruit through a curtain of foam (Cunning 1955), using overhead brush in a tray to flick the wax onto the fruit below (Kalmar 1974), and spraying a molten version of the bar wax onto the fruit (Burwick *et al.* 1944).

The recommended brush for wax application is contains a mixture horsehair and polyethylene bristles. The horsehair provides a wicking action to hold and spread the wax while the polyethylene bristles lend support to the brush and prevent the matting of the horsehair. The function of the brush is to spread the applied wax over the surface of the fruit. Typical brush beds consist of 8 to 12 brushes, the wax is delivered at the first 4 to 6 brushes and the remaining brushes assist in spreading the wax uniformly over the surface of the fruit. It is recommended that normally the brush speed not exceed 80 rpm. One caution regarding these brushes is that horsehair is soluble under alkaline conditions, therefore strong alkaline cleaners should not be used to clean the brushes. It is possible to dissolve the horsehair, leaving a normal looking brush that will lose its effectiveness and will waste wax. Regular inspection of the brushes should be carried out.

The applicators major function is to supply a controlled quantity of wax to the fruit for spreading by the brushes. The earliest applicators used fine nozzles of the type used in oil burners. These are available in several types but the most commonly used nozzles were rated to deliver from 1 to 5 gallons of hour at 80 to 100 psi. The hollow cone, 90° pattern is the most favored. Stainless steel construction is necessary for water waxes. Most applicators operate these nozzles at 25 to 50 psi. Lower pressures can result in dripping and a collapsed cone, while higher pressures can cause fogging and drifting.

The method of controlling wax delivery rates depends upon the system used. Those using spray (oil burner) nozzles control delivery by regulating the pressure to the nozzle, usually using a pump with a pressure regulator. Drip type, spinners, and air nozzles control delivery rates by means of an adjustable metering pump. These systems may be further modified by the use of various fruit flow sensors, to turn the delivery on or off, or the change the delivery rate.

The solvent wax applicator was a special case in that it did not use brushes but sprayed the wax onto the fruit as it passed under the nozzles on a live roll conveyor. Relatively even distribution of the wax was achieved by a controlled flow of large volumes of air (Kalmar 1942). Enough air was introduced by blowers to virtually eliminate the fire/explosion hazard that would normally be expected, by diluting the solvent fumes to a point below their lower flammable limit. This type of wax usually did not cover the fruit completely, thus minimizing the effects of too little gas exchange.

Several delivery methods have been used in an attempt to deliver a uniform coating to the fruit each has its advantages and disadvantages. Some of these are:

Foam. A beater or aerator is used to generate a foam curtain through which the wax passes (Cunning 1955). These are rare as they are messy and often tend to leave a foamy residue on the fruit which detracts from its appearance. Wax application rates were controlled by varying the depth of the liquid in the reservoir and the speed of the beater.

Traveling Nozzles. One or more spray nozzles reciprocate across the brush bed delivering a fine spray of wax. The nozzles commonly used are of the oil burner type described above. Their main disadvantage is that while the nozzle is delivering wax at one end of its path, none is being delivered at the other. This results in more wax at each side of the brush bed as compared to the middle. Since fruit often travel slower along the sides of a brush bed, as compared to the middle, a uniform coating is difficult to obtain. Some have minimized this by installing mechanical clean-outs to keep the fruit moving. Various systems involving multiple nozzles or application paths, overlapping banks of counter traveling nozzles, and high speed travel have been used (Straley 1959; Lewis 1984). Each has its advantages but they all have the common problem of mechanical complexity.

Fixed Nozzles. A bank of nozzles giving continuous coverage to the entire application area. Unless very small nozzles or some other method of controlling the amount of wax delivered, this system could result in over waxing. Two approaches have been used to overcome this drawback. The simplest is to use a drip type applicator with many small droplets being delivered over a wide area. The second involves using sensors to determine the rate of fruit flow which is fed to a computer that controls solenoids to start and stop the wax flow to individual nozzles (Creason *et al.* 1989).

Air Nozzles. A adaptation of the air driven spray nozzles used in paint application, these nozzles are fed by a low volume pump where a controlled stream of air dispersed the wax. These nozzles are usually part of a traveling nozzle system. Their main drawback is that a very delicate balance of air and wax flow must be maintained. Wax build-up at the nozzle orifice will upset this balance. Also if the air pressure is to high the wax can become atomized into the packinghouse atmosphere and will build up on the surfaces it contacts. If the wax particles are atomized too finely they will dry in the air and not coat the fruit. This type of applicator has proven to require a very high level of maintenance. While troublesome, these nozzles are capable of being an excellent delivery system, especially with high viscosity waxes.

Spinners. A relatively recent innovation has been the spinner applicator. These are sometimes called controlled droplet applicators or CDAs. A high speed motor drives a disc mounted above the waxer brushes onto which a low volume stream of wax is directed. As the disk spins it slings the wax out into a circular pattern above the brushes and onto the fruit. Application is controlled by varying the rate of wax delivery, and the speed of disk rotation. This type of applicator depends heavily on the waxer brushes to spread the wax uniformly. This type of applicator is gaining acceptance with many citrus packers when combined with a computer controlled application system.

Whichever application method is used, certain features will provide for the best coverage. The first is that the application area should be long enough so the fruit will receive full coverage. Four to 7 brushes are usually enough for most applicator types. The second is that there should be enough brushes following the applicator to ensure an even spreading of the wax film. A number of brushes equal to one and one half the number of applicator brushes is usual.

When fruit flow through the system is not uniform, a means of controlling the rate of wax delivery becomes important. Surges and gaps in the fruit flow can result in over-waxing some fruit and under-waxing others. While the waxer brushes do much to even this out, they cannot cope with the extremes that might be encountered. A simple flag operated switch has been used to stop the wax when the fruit flow is interrupted. More sophisticated systems have been developed that use various types of sensors to detect not only the presence of fruit, but by feeding the information to a microprocessor, to adjust the rate of wax delivery at the applicator. These systems can be quite expensive and their use cannot be justified on wax savings alone. However some users of these systems feel that the improved consistency of application is worth the extra cost.

DRYING

The final step in waxing is drying. Whatever method is used, it must accomplish the function of removing the solvent, usually water, used in the wax formulation. In designing the drying system the considerations of initial cost, operating cost, and desired speed. Among the things to consider are cost of utilities, local climatic conditions and the availability of skilled labor. More complex systems may require maintenance skills that are not readily available. The discussion herein principally applies to water based wax systems. Notable exceptions to this are the use of storage waxes, solid waxes, and solvent waxes. See the discussion of each of these under waxing.

Drying is generally done in tunnel type dryers. The important variables that require concern are time, dryness of fruit entering the waxer, and how much coating was applied to the fruit. Another variable is the type of coating used. In 1987 trials at the University of Florida indicated that a wax based on Polyethylene emulsion dried in less than half the time taken by a shellac based wax (Miller and Verba 1987).

In every case where water based formulations are used, air capable of carrying away the water needs to move across the surface of the fruit to be dried. Drier air, coupled with good movement across the fruit will rapidly accomplish this. The drying operation will need to remove approximately 0.2 grams of water from each fruit treated with a typical water wax. Additionally the fruit itself will contribute up to 1.8 grams per fruit to the dryer load (Miller 1981), depending upon the variety.

There are several approaches used in the industry. The simplest is a flat conveyor with fans blowing down on the fruit. Heating this air will reduce its relative humidity, thus increasing its capacity to carry away more water. Several approaches have been used to increase drying and efficiency of energy use, but all rely on air capable of taking up moisture moving across the surface of the fruit. Very low volume packing lines in a dry climate might just run the fruit onto a long conveyor and allow the fruit to air dry. One or two partial turns; ether by live rolls or a delivery onto a second conveyor will turn the fruit so that all sides will be dried more evenly.

In modern, high volume, packing operations drying requires a considerable expenditure of energy. In fact, drying often requires the largest expenditure of energy in packinghouse operations. Many methods have been tried to reduce this cost.

Some of these include:

❏ Enclosing the dryer bottom to contain the heated air. Each heated fan still draws outside air into the system

❏ A cascade system whereby air enters the dryer at the exit end and is the successively passed through heater/fans to exhaust at the entrance end.

❏ Recirculation of a portion of the dryer air through a system of ducts. Bringing in from 10 to 50% fresh air continuously (Lewis 1981; Rose 1982).

❏ Enclosing the entire drying operation inside an enclosed room to in order to recirculate wasted heat.

❏ A recently developed concept dryer that uses high pressure blower fans to move air through the fruit stack from above and below has been developed by Sunkist Growers in California (Mulligan and Orman 2000).

❑ Drying the air by moisture absorbers before heating it. This then requires some method of regeneration of the absorbent (Bowman and Miller 1982).

❑ Drying the air by refrigeration below the dew point then rewarming the air before applying to the fruit. This method has demonstrated a reduction in energy costs by as much as 50% as compared to conventional dryers (Owen-Turner 1988).

Due to the high cost of energy any procedure that will reduce this cost will benefit the profitability of the packer. Capturing the heat from cold storage refrigeration units and using it in the dryers is an option currently being explored. Using solar energy to supplement the some of the methods enumerated above is also an option to be considered in designing a pack line.

MARKING/LABELING

While not a part of the wet line, the final step before sizing and packing is the labeling of individual fruit. With the introduction of Universal Product Code (UPC) numbers, many packers are required by their customers to label the individual fruit. This is usually accomplished by applying a small self-adhesive label to the waxed fruit. One objection to most of these systems is that many labels do not remain on the fruit and come off onto subsequent equipment.

A new system in development uses a computer driven laser writer to burn the information directly into the skin of the fruit. The resulting scar shows as white against the background color of the commodity. While the contrast is quire striking with dark colored fruits and vegetables (red peppers, eggplant, etc.), it is nearly invisible on the lighter skinned varieties of citrus. This has been overcome by applying a contrasting dye immediately after the laser. This system was tried for a season (2003-04) in one Florida packinghouse, but did not gain ready market acceptance and has since been removed.

REFERENCES

ANONYMOUS. 1962. Washing, cleaning citrus fruit. Chapter 9 Section 1. Sunkist Field Manual. Sunkist Growers, Inc., Van Nuys, CA

ANONYMOUS. 2001A. Citrus red No. 2. 21 CFR 74.302. U.S. Gov. Printing Office.

ANONYMOUS. 2001B. Postharvest handling of citrus - Washing and Cleaning. South Australian Res. Dev. Inst. http://www.sardi.sa.gov.au/hort/cit_page/hand_was.htm.

BEN-YEHOSHUA, S. 1967. Some physiological effects of various skin coatings on orange fruit. Israel J. Agr. Res. 17(1), 17-27.

BEN-YEHOSHUA, S., GARBER, M. J. and HUSZAR, C. K. 1970. Use of a physiological parameter as means for operational control of orange skin-coating in packing plants. Trop. Agr. 42(2), 151-155.

448   David J. Hall and David Sorenson

BOWMAN, E. K. and MILLER, W. M. 1982. Economics of an adsorption-solar energy regeneration method for surface drying citrus fruit. Am. Soc. Agr. Eng. SER 82-003.

BROGDEN, E. M. and TROBRIDGE, M. L. 1933. Art of coating. U.S. Pat. 1,940,530. Filed June 5, 1929.

BROWN, G. E. 1983. Application of fungicides in water waxes. Packinghouse Newsletter No. 135. University of Florida, IFAS, Lake Alfred.

BROWNING, H. W., McGOVERN, R. J., JACKSON, L. K., CALVERT, D. V. and WARDOWSKI, W. F. 1995. Florida Citrus Diagnostic Guide. Florida Science Source, Lake Alfred, FL.

BURWICK, L., CHARLES, W. COTHRAN, D. and CUMMING, T. G. 1944. Preparation of fresh fruit for market. U. S. Patent 2,364,946.

CREASON, K. C., SALKA, J. A. and HOLLAND, R. R. 1989. Fruit waxing method. U.S. Pat. 4,842,880. Filed Jul. 21, 1988.

CUNNING, T. G. 1955. Method of Coating Fruits and Vegetables. U.S. Pat. 2,703,760. Filed Jan. 25, 1952.

CUNNINGHAM, N. 2002. Sooty Mould Cleaners and High Pressure Washing. Packer Newsletter. No 67. South Australian Res. Dev. Inst. Adelaide.

CRAWFORD, B. 2001. Citrus Canker Compliance Agreement, Packing House. Fla. Dept. Agr. Cons. Serv. Bob Crawford, Commissioner.

DUNNAHOE, F. 2001. Personal communication. Dundee, FL.

EAKS, I. L. Undated. Effect of brushes and brushing practices on rind injury to central California Navel oranges. Univ. Calif. Mimeo Report of Res. Proj. 1822. Riverside.

FLORIDA DEPARTMENT OF CITRUS. 2002. Official Rules Affecting the Florida Citrus Industry. State of Fla. Dept. of Citrus. Lakeland, FL.

FALLIK, E., TUVIA-ALAKAI, S., COPEL, A., WISEBLUM, A. and REGEV, R. 2001. A Short hot water rinse and brushes: a technology to reduce postharvest losses - 4 Years of research. Acta Hort. 553, 413-416.

GERWE, R. D. and FISK, J. M. 1950. Method of Coloring Citrus Fruit. US. Patent 2,507,438.

GILIOMEE, J. H. and SWANEPOEL, T. G. 1979. Fungal growth on citrus fruit as a result of mechanical red scale removal. Citrus Subtrop. Fruit J. 550, 5.

GILLESPIE, K. 1986. Sooty mould. Packingshed Newsletter. No. 26, Dept. Agr. Waikerie South Australia.

GRIERSON. W. 2002. Personal communication. Winter Haven, FL.

HALL, D. J. 1981. Innovations in citrus waxing—an overview. Proc. Fla. State Hort. Soc. 94, 258-263.

HALL, D. J. 2003. Twentieth century developments in handling Florida's fresh citrus fruit—an overview. Proc. Fla. State Hort. Soc. 116, 369-374.

HALL, D. J. and. BOWERS, M. D. 1989. Peel disorders of Florida citrus as related to growing area and color-add formulations. Proc. Fla. State Hort. Soc. 102, 243-246.

HAYWARD, F. W. 1964. Color-adding. In Better Handling of Florida's Fresh Citrus Fruit. Bul 681. Agr. Expt. Sta. University of Florida, Gainesville.

HOLZCKER, R. 1938. Apparatus for the skin treatment of citrus fruit. U.S. Patent 2,119,914. Filed Jan. 20, 1938.

HONIBALL, F., J. H GILIOMEE, J. H. and RANDALL, J. H. 1979. Mechanical control of red scale Aonidiella auranti (Mask.) of harvested oranges. Citrus Subtrop. Fruit J. 549, 17-18.

KALMAR, A. F. 1942. Apparatus for treating fruit. U.S. Patent 2,283,372.

KALMAR, A. F. 1974. Apparatus for coating fruit. U.S. Patent 3,818,859.

KATZ, M. 1995. High-Pressure Washing boosts packout. Citrograph 80(8), 3,6,7.O, G. R. 2000. Evaluation of hot water treatments to control postharvest green mold in organic lemon fruit. Proc. Int. Soc. Citriculture, IX Congr. 1167-1168.

LANZA, G., di MARTINO ALEPPO, E., STRANO, M. C. and REFORGIATO RECUPERO, G. 2000. Evaluation of hot water treatments to control postharvest green mold in organic lemon fruit. Proc. Int. Soc. Citricult. IX Congr. 1167-1168.

LEWIS, P. J. 1981. Drying apparatus for aqueous coated articles and method. U. S. Patent 4,291,472. Filed Sep. 8, 1978.

LEWIS, P. J. 1984. Apparatus and method for controlling the application of liquid substances to surfaces of fruit. U.S. Patent 4,477,483.

MINCEY, J. 2002. Personal communication. Fort Pierce, FL..

MILLER, W. M. 1981. Surface drying fresh citrus. Energy Info. Fact Sheet EI-49. Fla. Coop. Ext. Serv., University of Florida, Gainesville.

MILLER, W, M. 1986. Dryer fundamentals. Packinghouse Newsletter No. 144. University of Florida, Lake Alfred.

MILLER, W. M. and VERBA, W. L. 1987. Citrus wax drying evaluation via infrared thermometry. Proc. Fla. State Hort. Soc. 100, 32-34.

MILLER, W. M., WARDOWSKI, W. F. and GRIERSON, W. 2001. Packingline machinery for Florida citrus packinghouses. Fla. Coop. Ext. Serv. Bull. 239. April 2001. University of Florida, Lake Alfred.

MULLIGAN, D. J. and ORMAN, C. R. 2000. Drying apparatus for coated objects. U. S. Patent 6,023,852.

OWEN-TURNER, J. 1988. Cold air drying of wax on citrus fruit. Packingshed Newsletter. No. 33. Dept. Agr. Waikerie, South Australia.

PEEPLES, W. W., ALBRIGO, L. G., PAO, S. and PETRACEK, P. D. 1999. Effects of coatings on quality of Florida Valencia oranges stored for summer sale. Proc. Fla. State Hort. Soc. 112, 126-130.

PELSER, P. and DuT., P. 1993. Prevention of post-harvest *Cladosporium* sooty mould development on descaled fruit. Citrus J. 3(2), 23-25.

PETRACEK, P. D., KELSEY, D. F. and DAVIS, C. 1998. Response of citrus fruit to high-pressure washing. J. Amer. Hort. Soc. 123(4), 661-667.

PORAT, R., DAUS, A., WEISS, B., COHEN, L., FALLIK, E. and DROBY, S. 2000. Reduction of postharvest decay in organic citrus fruit by a short hot water brushing treatment. Posthavest Biol. Technol. 18(2), 151-157.

RITENOUR, M. A., SARGENT, S. A. and BRECHT, J. K. 2001. Sanitizers for citrus packinghouse recirculated water systems. http://postharvest.tfrec.wsu.edu/REP2001A.pdf.

ROSE, B. W. 1982 Fruit dryer. U.S. Patent 4,352,249.

SMILANICK, J. L. 2002. Personal communication. Santa Barbara, CA.

SMILANICK, J. L., MARGOSAN, D. A., MILKOTA, F. USALL, J. and MICHAEL, J. F. 1999. Control of citrus green mold by carbonate and bicarbonate and the influence of commercial postharvest practices on their efficacy. Plant Disease 83(2), 139-145.

SNOWDEN, A. L. 1990. A Color Atlas of Post-Harvest Diseases & Disorders of Fruits and Vegetables. Vol. 1. CRC Press, Inc. Boca Raton, FL..

STRALEY, J. B. 1959. Apparatus for spraying waxy substances onto fruit surfaces. U.S. Pat. 2,898,881. Filed Nov 30, 1955.

TAVERNER, P. 2001A. The changing role of high pressure washers. Citrus Packer Newsletter No 62. South Australian Res. and Develop. Inst., Adelaid.

TAVERNER, P. 2001B. The quest for the perfect shine. Packer Newsletter. No 66 page 1,2. South Australian Res. and Develop. Inst., Adelaid

TING, S. V. 1955. Determination of artificial coloring agents on oranges and in orange products. Proc. Fla. State Hort. Soc. 69, 157-160.

USDA. 2002. National Organic Program. U.S. Code of Federal Regulations Title 7 Part 205. U.S. Govt. Printing Office. Washington, DC.

WAGNER A. B. and SAULS, J. W. 2002. Packingline operations. Texas Agr. Ext. Serv. Texas A&M Univ. http://aggie-horticulture.tamu.edu/citrus/12292.htm.

WALKER, G. P., MORSE, J. G. and ARPAIA, M. 1996. Evaluation of a high-pressure washer for postharvest removal of California red scale (Homoptera: Diaspididae) from citrus fruit. J. Econ. Entomol. 89(1), 148-155.

WALKER, G. P., ZAREH, N. and ARPAIA, M. 1999. Effect of pressure and dwell time on efficiency of a high-pressure washer for postharvest removal of California red scale (Homoptera: Diaspididae) from citrus fruit. J. Econ. Entomol. 92(4), 906-914.

WARDOWSKI, W. F. 1982. Washer capacity. Packinghouse Newsletter No. 127. University of Florida, Lake Alfred.

WARDOWSKI, W. F. 1997. Rotary (round) washer. Packinghouse Newsletter No. 180. University of Florida, Lake Alfred.

WASHNOCK, J. T. and THOMAS, H. L. 1996. Centrifugal packingline machine. U.S. Patent 5,557,821. Filed Mar. 27, 1995.

16

Packaging and Unitization

Jean-Pierre Emond and Maria Cecília do Nascimento Nunes

The fresh citrus fruits market comprises an important part of the trade in fresh horticultural crops around the world (Hern 1986). Although a considerable part of the citrus production is intended for processing, the fresh consumption is very important. Therefore, along with a good temperature management the choice of a suitable package is crucial to maintaining the quality of fresh citrus fruits throughout the handling chain, i.e., from the grower to the consumer. Unlike other sorts of fruits as for example strawberries or raspberries, which have a relatively short shelf life and thus need to be consumed within a short period of time, citrus fruits may have a considerable long shelf life (from 2 weeks to 6 months depending on the type of citrus) if stored and packed under optimum conditions. Certain types of citrus fruits like for example grapefruit, lemon, lime, and certain orange cultivars, which have a long shelf life, are not always immediately put on the market. These types of citrus fruits are usually harvested, and stored at the packing facility or transported to the distribution centers where they are temporary stored until commercialization. Therefore, a package capable of maintaining a good quality during transport as well as during such waiting periods would be recommended. The package should be strong enough to allow stacking without collapse or cause pressure damage to the fruit from the weight of other containers eventually placed on top of it. Besides, it should provide some protection against excessive water loss from the fruit but at the same time allowing adequate O_2 and CO_2 exchanges and heat removal.

Currently, citrus fruits are commonly transported in cartons, standard boxes, half-boxes, wire-bound boxes, fruit crates made of corrugated fiberboard or wood, plastic container and sometimes in net bags depending upon the country of origin and target market.

COMMERCIAL CONTAINERS AND PACKAGING MATERIALS

North America

Ever since the early 1950s that the fiberboard or wire-bound boxes used to pack grapefruit, oranges or lemons, with capacities of 16 to 18 kg (35 to 40 lb) have replaced the previously used boxes of 59 to 49 L (1 3/5 or 1 2/5 bushel). The change from big to smaller containers resulted from the increased demand of wholesale and retail stores on easily handled containers (Ryall and Pentzer 1979). Today, oranges, grapefruit and tangerines are packed in two piece telescopic corrugated fiberboard crates and only very few producers still use wood wire-bound crates. Florida oranges are usually packed in standard pack sizes containing from 64 to 163 fruits per 4/5-bushel (29.8 lb/13.4 kg) container while in California each container holds from 24 to 270 oranges. In Texas and other States other than Florida, California and Arizona 7/10-bushel containers include 24, 32, 36, 40, 48, 56, 64, 72, 88, 113, or 138 oranges per container (USDA 2001). Oranges are also pre-packed in 4-4.5 kg or 5-3.6 kg (4-10 lb or 5-8 lb) plastic bags and shipped in 21.8 or 22.7 kg (48 or 50 lb) cartons.

Grapefruit are in general pre-packed in consumer pack units (6 count) 4 kg (8 lb) polyethylene bags (ventilated), or in consumer packs (10 count) 2 kg (5 lb) polyethylene bags, or shipped in 21.8 or 22.7 kg (48 or 50 lb) cartons. In Texas and other States other than Florida, California and Arizona 7/10-bushel containers include 18, 23, 27, 32, 36, 40, 48, or 56 grapefruit per container (USDA 2001).

For tangerines, three different package sizes are usually used for shipping: 18.1 or 19.5 kg (40 or 43 lb) 4/5-bushel crates, or 11.3 kg (25 lb) cartons mostly used by Arizona and California growers (Table 16.1). A standard pack of tangerines includes 100, 120, 150, 176, 210, 246 or 249 fruits per pack (USDA 1999).

Europe and Eastern Mediterranean

In a study conducted on the European preferences for packaging fresh fruits and vegetables, Risse *et al.* (1990) reported that demand of receivers and consumers depended not only upon supply or price but also, and most of all upon quality of the fruits and the packaging. European markets require metrically identified pallet dimensions and have established (Organization of Economic Cooperation and Development) two size basic units which are 120 × 100 cm and 120 × 80 cm. European receivers usually demand a full telescopic fiberboard box containing 12 to 17 kg per box for imported citrus fruits. Grapefruit and oranges are usually placed-packed by layers of 3 to 6 depending on their size, and the number of fruit per box indicates the size. In Europe, smaller grapefruit (size 40-64) are preferred to larger fruits (Risse *et al.* 1990).

TABLE 16.1. Common Shipping Containers used for Citrus Fruits in North America

Oranges	Grapefruit
50 lb. (22.7 kg) cartons, 5 10 lb. (4.5 kg) film bags	50 lb. (22.7 kg), 10 5lb (2.3 kg) film bags
48 lb. (21.8 kg) cartons, 6 8 lb. (3.6 kg) film bags	48 lb. (21.8 kg) 6 8 lb (3.6 kg) film bags
48 lb. (21.8 kg) 1 1/5 bushel crates (Israel)	40 lb. (18 kg) 4/5 bushel cartons/crates
43 lb. (19.5 kg) 4/5 bushel crates/cartons	40 lb. (18 kg) 7/10 bushel cartons (Texas)
40 lb. (18 kg) 7/10 bushel cartons (Texas)	34 lb. (15.4 kg) cartons (Arizona and California)
40 lb. (18 kg) cartons, 8 5 lb. (4.5 kg) film bags	20 lb. (9 kg) 7/20 bushel cartons
38 lb. (17 kg) cartons (Arizona and California)	17 lb. (7.7 kg) cartons (Arizona and California)
4 10 lb. (4.5 kg) bags	18 lb. (8.2 kg) bags
5 8 lb. (3.6 kg) bags	10 to 11 lb. (4.5 to 5 kg) cartons, single layer (Arizona and California)
	5 lb. (2.3 kg) bags
	8 5 lb. (2.3 kg) bags
	5 8 lb. (3.6 kg) bags (Texas)
	4 10 lb. (4.5 kg) bags (Texas)
Lemons	**Limes**
42 lb. (19 kg) 4/5 bushel cartons	40 lb. (18 kg) cartons (California and Mexico)
38 lb. (17 kg) cartons (Arizona and California)	38 lb. (17 kg) cartons, bruce box (Florida)
36 lb. (16.3 kg) cartons/crates (Chile and Spain)	10 lb. (4.5 kg) cartons, pony box
	2 lb. (1 kg) mesh bag
	True count box (Mexico)
Tangerines	**Mandarins**
43 lb. (19.5 kg) 4/5 bushel cartons/crates	43 lb. (19.5 kg) 4/5 bushel cartons/crates
40 lb. (18 kg) 2/5 and 4/5 bushel cartons	25 lb. (11.3 kg) cartons (Arizona and Florida)
25 lb. (11.3 kg) cartons (Arizona and California)	
Tangelos	
43 lb. (19.5 kg) 4/5 bushel cartons/crates	
40 lb. (18 kg) bags:5 8 lb. (3.6 kg) or 8 5 lb (2.3 kg)	
40 lb. (18 kg) cartons (Arizona, California	
40 lb. (18 kg) 2/5 and 4/5 bushel cartons	
30 lb. (13.6 kg) 1/2 bushel cartons	
25 lb. (11.3 kg) 1/2 bushel cartons	

Source: The Packer (2002).

According to the European Commission Regulation (2001) citrus are classified in three classes: Extra class, Class I and Class II, according to their quality. The size of the citrus is also a requirement as fruit below a certain size are excluded (Table 16.2). Citrus fruits size is determined by the maximum diameter of the equatorial section of the fruit and then packed by count (Table 16.3). For fruit arranged in regular layers, in packages or in unit consumer packages, the difference between the smallest and the largest fruit, within a single size, in the case of citrus fruit packed by count must not exceed the values shown in Table 16.4.

The packages and their contents should also be in agreement with regulated presentation and marking for uniformity, packaging, presentation, identification, nature of produce, origin of produce, commercial specifications, and official control mark Consequently, the contents of each package must be uniform and contain only citrus fruit of the same origin, variety or commercial type, quality and size, and appreciably of the same degree of ripeness. A package should be used in order to adequately protect the citrus fruits. The material used inside the package must be new, clean and able to avoid external or internal damage of the product. The use of materials, particularly paper or stamps of trademarks are allowed but have to be done with non-toxic ink or glue. If the fruit is wrapped, a thin, dry, new, and odorless paper should be used. Citrus fruits are usually arranged in regular layers in packages, loosely in packages or in bulk bins, or in individual packages for direct sale to the consumer of a weight less than 5 kg (11 lb) either made up by number of fruit, or made up by net weight of the package. According to Risse *et al.* (1990) packaging should be functional and attractive (multicolored shipping containers) and the trend should be for smaller units of a maximum of 10 to 12 kg per shipping container.

COMPATIBILITY EUROPE AND NORTH AMERICA

In a global market trend, many packaging associations have agreed to develop a common footprint standard. The purposes of such standard consist of reducing the number of sizes, optimizing pallet utilization as well as protecting citrus by improving stacking strength due to a more uniform pressure on

TABLE 16.2. Minimum Size for Citrus Fruits According to European Regulations

Citrus fruits	Minimum size
Lemons	45 mm
Mandarins	45 mm
Clementines	35 mm
Oranges	53 mm

Source: European Commission Regulation (2001).

TABLE 16.3. Uniformity for Packing Citrus Fruits According to European Regulations

	Size (mm)	Maximum difference between fruit in the same package (in mm)
Lemons	45-90	7
Mandarins	50 and above	9
	43-56	8
	35-48	7
Oranges	84-110	11
	70-92	9
	53-76	7

Source: European Commission Regulation (2001).

boxes. In a context of distribution to retail stores in a mixed load configuration, common footprint reduces time required for pallet build-up, increases pallet stability as well as decreasing significantly damages from odd shape boxes stacking. Common footprint can be found in corrugated, solid board and reusable plastic containers (Figures 16.1, 16.2, 16.3, 16.4, 16.5, 16.6).

The standard has a half and a full size common footprint container. Box height can vary depending of the requirements in terms of protection and counts. More than the footprint, each box must have an interlocking system compatible with half and full boxes.

For the full size configuration, the dimensions are 597 mm × 398 mm (23 1/4 in. × 15 11/16 in.) and for the half-size configuration, the dimensions are 398 mm × 298 mm (15 11/16 in. 11 11/16 in.).

UNITIZATION

When fiberboard boxes are loosely filled, they should be loaded lengthwise or crosswise on their bottoms. If they are hand stacked, they should be loaded in an airflow pattern. This type of pattern allows better cooling by the refrigeration system or by ventilation when the ambient temperature is close to the desired transit temperature.

TABLE 16.4. Approximate Size, Weight, and Number of Pieces of Fruits per Package (North America)

Trays	Size	Weight	Number of fruit
1	¼ bushel	10-15 lb (4.5-6.8 kg)	12-16 oranges; 8-12 grapefruit
2	½ bushel	20-25 lb (9-11.3 kg)	24-36 oranges; 16-24 grapefruit
3	¾ bushel	30-35 lb (13.5-15.8 kg)	36-48 oranges; 24-36 grapefruit
4	1 bushel	40-45 lb (18-20.3 kg)	48-64 oranges; 32-48 grapefruit

Source: USDA (1999, 2001).

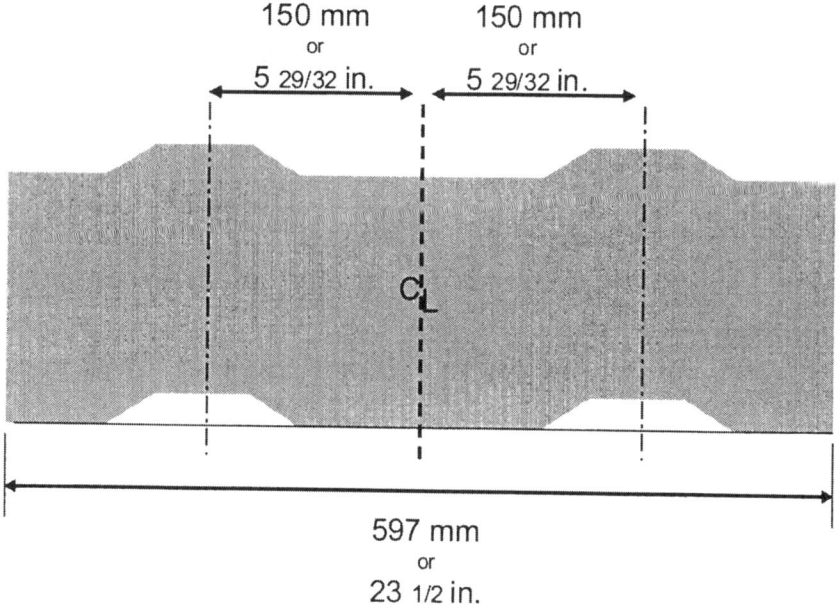

Fig. 16.1. Front view full size container.

In Florida, the boxes are usually unitized on slipsheets while in California they are unitized on pallets. The use of slipsheets requires specialized equipment for handling at shipping and receiving terminals, but studies conducted comparing costs of using slipsheets vs. wooden pallets showed cost advantages for the slipsheet system (Hearn 1986). The slipsheet measures 132.1 × 101.6 cm (includes a 10.2 cm clamp lip on 101.6 cm edge) with a 25.4 cm center die-cut hole. Slipsheets are usually constructed of double-wall, corrugated fiberboard with a board weight of at least 31.3/15/19 kg (113.4 kg Mullen test). Boxes are arranged on the slipsheet in a single-chimney interlocking-box stacking pattern (Fig. 16.7), nine boxes per layer, six or seven layers high. Boxes in lower layers are stacked in register, directly on the top of the other, and the pattern of boxes in the two upper layers of the stacks is reversed to provide stack stability.

Disposable wooden pallets measuring 106.7 × 88.9 cm are used, and the citrus boxes are stacked as shown in Figure 16.8; shipping containers are stacked seven per layer, seven layers high with tape, plastic strapping, or mesh netting around the horizontal perimeter for added stability (Hearn 1986).

As a continuation of the new trend of standardization, the new common standard footprint containers (described previously) allows a unique stacking pattern with five full size containers per layer. The last two layers are

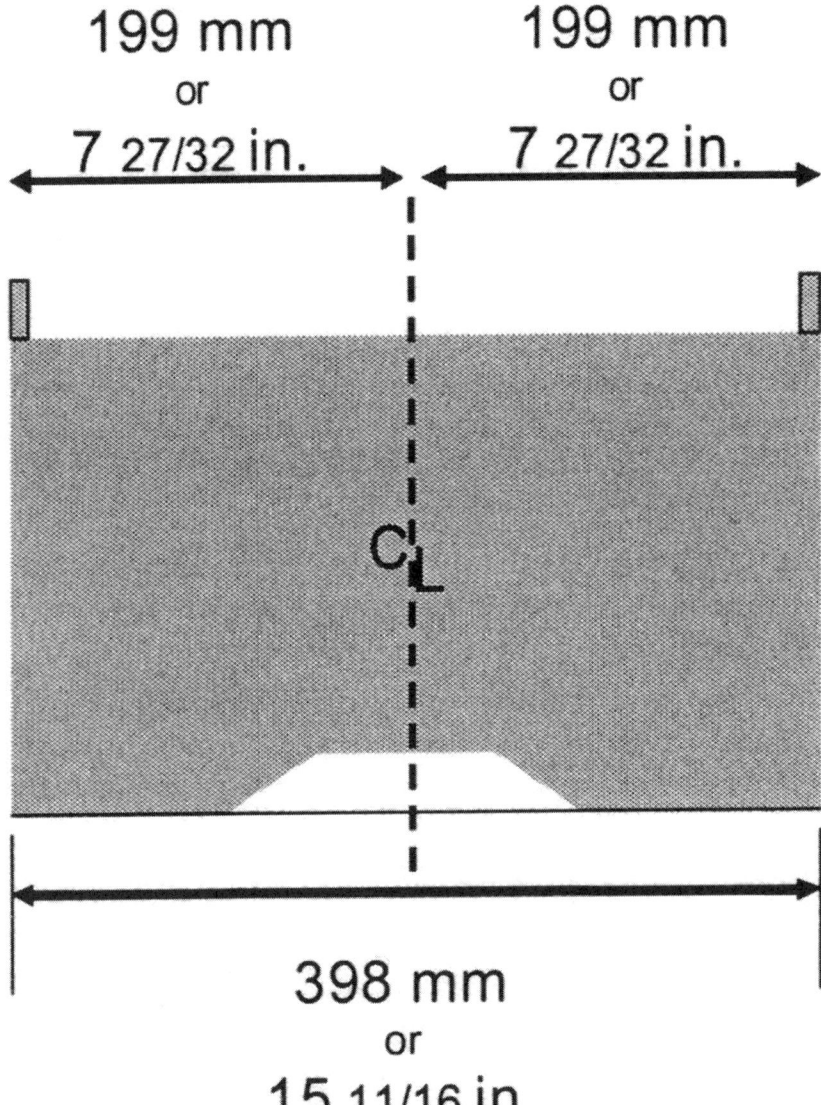

199 mm
or
7 27/32 in.

199 mm
or
7 27/32 in.

C L

398 mm
or
15 11/16 in.

Fig. 16.2. Side view full size container.

usually cross-stacked to lock the whole pallet for stability (Fig. 16.9). For mixed load pallet, half size containers can be stacked with full size containers as shown in Figure 16.10.

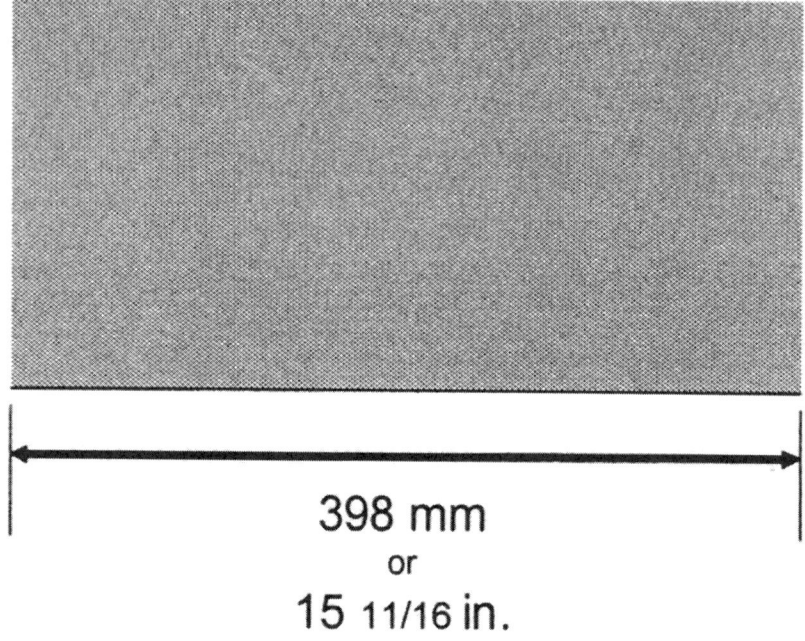

398 mm
or
15 11/16 **in.**

Fig. 16.3. Front view half size container.

CHOICE OF TYPE OF CONTAINER AND PACKAGING MATERIAL

Corrugated Container

Many types of corrugated container are used to ship citrus. Most of them are very suitable due to their smooth inside surface. However, unless they are wax treated, corrugated boxes are known to absorb water of about 10% to 15% of their weight. So citrus may lose water due to their interaction with the corrugated box.

It is important to remember that corrugated boxes can lose more than 50% of their strength if they are exposed to wet environment.

In order to not affect their strength, corrugated boxes are limited to about 5% opening. The location and the number of vents must take into account the air flow pattern during cooling but also the strength of the box. To improve cooling performance and distribution, some companies offer a honeycomb type system. The system using ventilation pads are excellent to achieve uniform cooling and good ventilation during shipping.

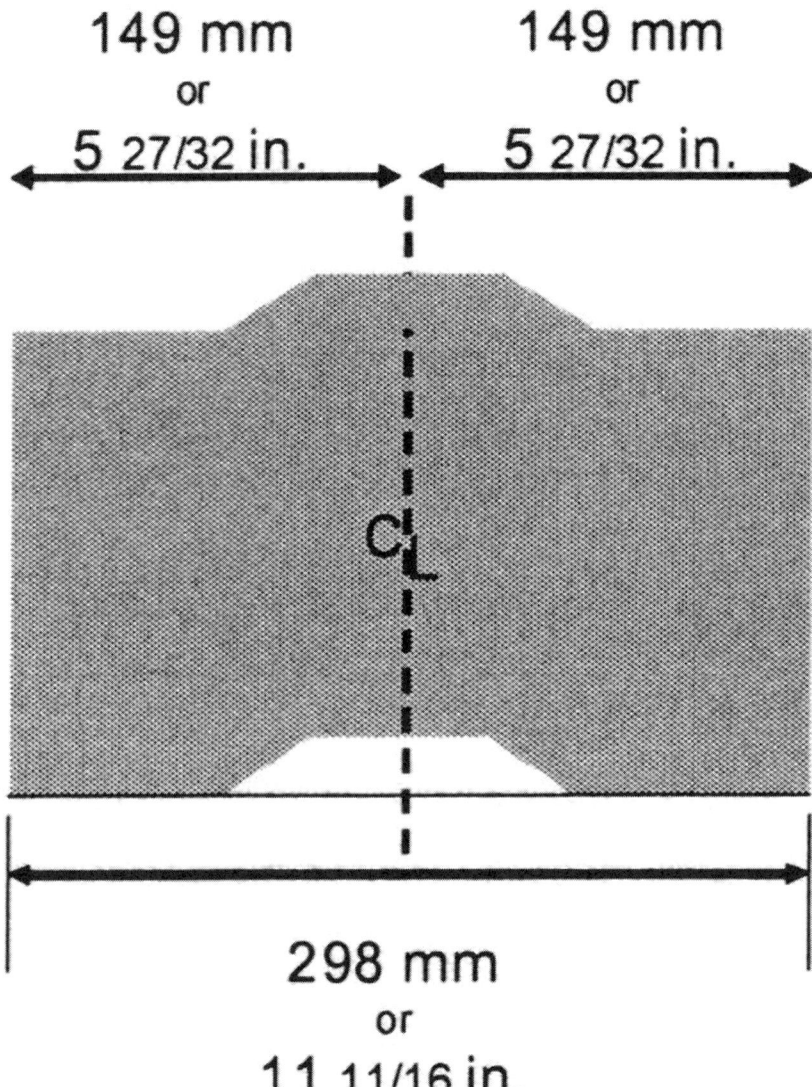

Fig. 16.4. Side view half size container.

Solidboard Container

Solidboard refers to laminated products made primarily from 100% recycled paperboard. Commonly used in Europe where wax-coated corru-

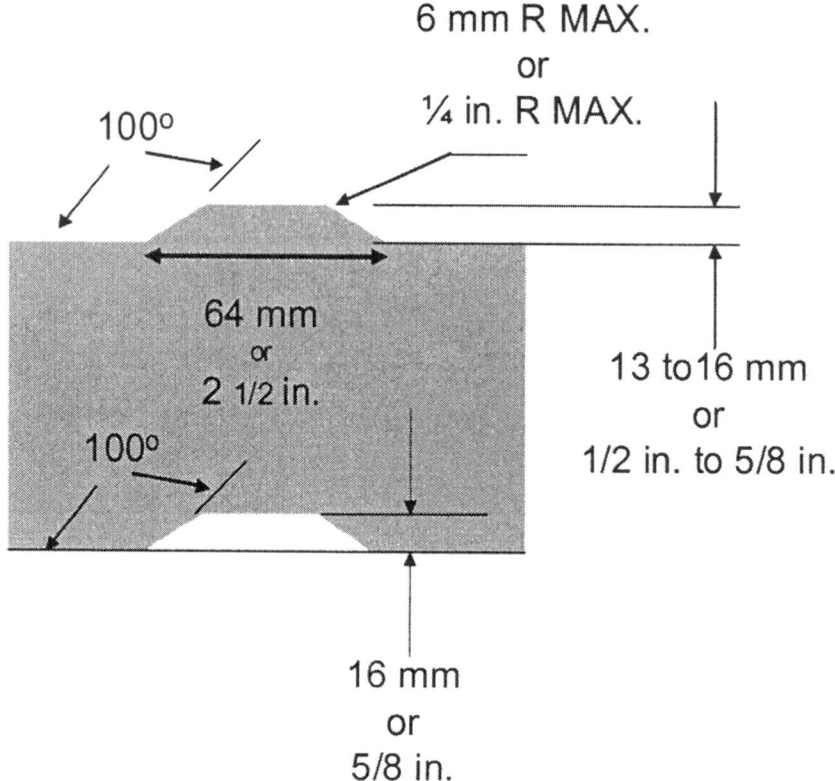

Fig. 16.5. Dimension requirements.

gated is prohibited due to its non-recyclability, the solidboard container is a good solution because of its strength, structural integrity even when wet.

Such containers take about 2% moisture compared to 15% for regular corrugated containers. Because solidboard containers do not take moisture, their strength during transportation is not reduced. An advantage of the solidboard container is its capabilities for high quality printing. Some examples of this new type of container are presented in Figures 16.11 and 16.12.

Reusable Plastic Container

As seen with many types of produce, reusable plastic containers are also used with citrus. The advantages are: smooth surface, strength, optimal ventilation and reusability. The disadvantage is mainly lost of water from citrus if exposed to a dry environment. Figure 16.13 presented a typical counter-ready reusable plastic container for citrus.

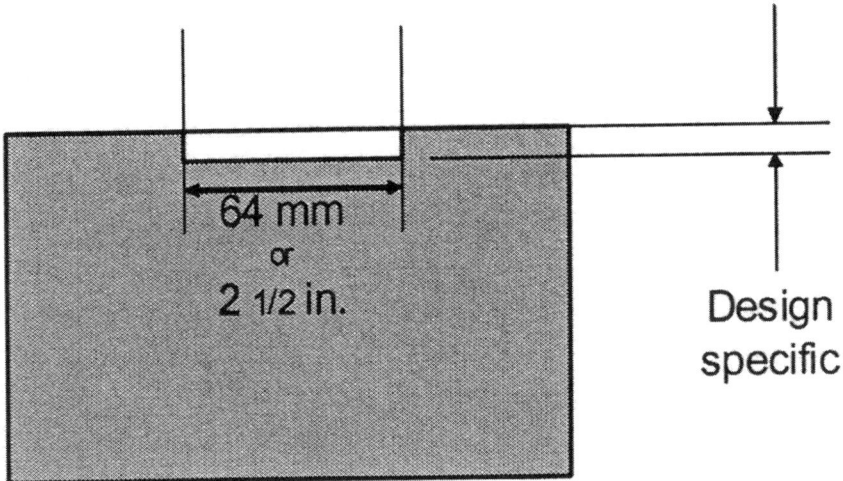

Fig. 16.6. Bottom dimension requirements.

Others

Within the common carton fiberboard boxes or plastic containers, several types of plastic materials have been used to keep citrus fruits either from being damaged or to protect against excessive loss of moisture from the fruit during shipping and storage. Loss of moisture during shipping or storage of citrus fruits is one of the major causes of loss of quality and salable weight (Albrigo *et al.* 1991; Cohen *et al.* 1990; Rodov *et al.* 2000; Ben-Yehoshua *et al.* 2001).

Packaging materials such as pads or liners, molded trays and cells, plastic film liners, plastic bags or individual seal packaging are used to protect the fruit, avoid excessive loss of moisture and thus offer a better quality product to the consumer. Besides, packaging citrus in bags or bag-masters at the packinghouse is not only a good way to avoid repacking of the fruits at the distribution center but also a good way to supply consumers with convenient single units (Albrigo *et al.* 1991). However, citrus bags are today sold by weight and not by count and loss of weight during shipping or storage may result in rejection of the loads due to under filling. Therefore, according to Albrigo *et al.* (1991) the bags need to be packed with extra weight to compensate fruit weight loss, which may eventually occur during shipping or storage. However, calculating how much extra fruit weight should be placed inside each bag is not always obvious and may vary from 0.5% to 5.8% depending on the cultivar, variation within cultivars, weather conditions and type of wax used. Albrigo *et al.* (1991) suggested that weight of fruit to be packed to compensate loss of fruit weight during shipping or stor-

Fig. 16.7. Shipping containers with single-chimney stacking pattern contains nine boxes per layers high on 132.1 × 101.6 cm slipsheet.

age may be calculated using the following formula: initial bagged fruit weight required = net weight delivered/(1-moisture loss %)^t, where t = time from packing to sale.

Packaging of citrus fruits with suitable plastic films rather than in carton boxes or plastic mesh bag may help not only to reduce loss of salable weight

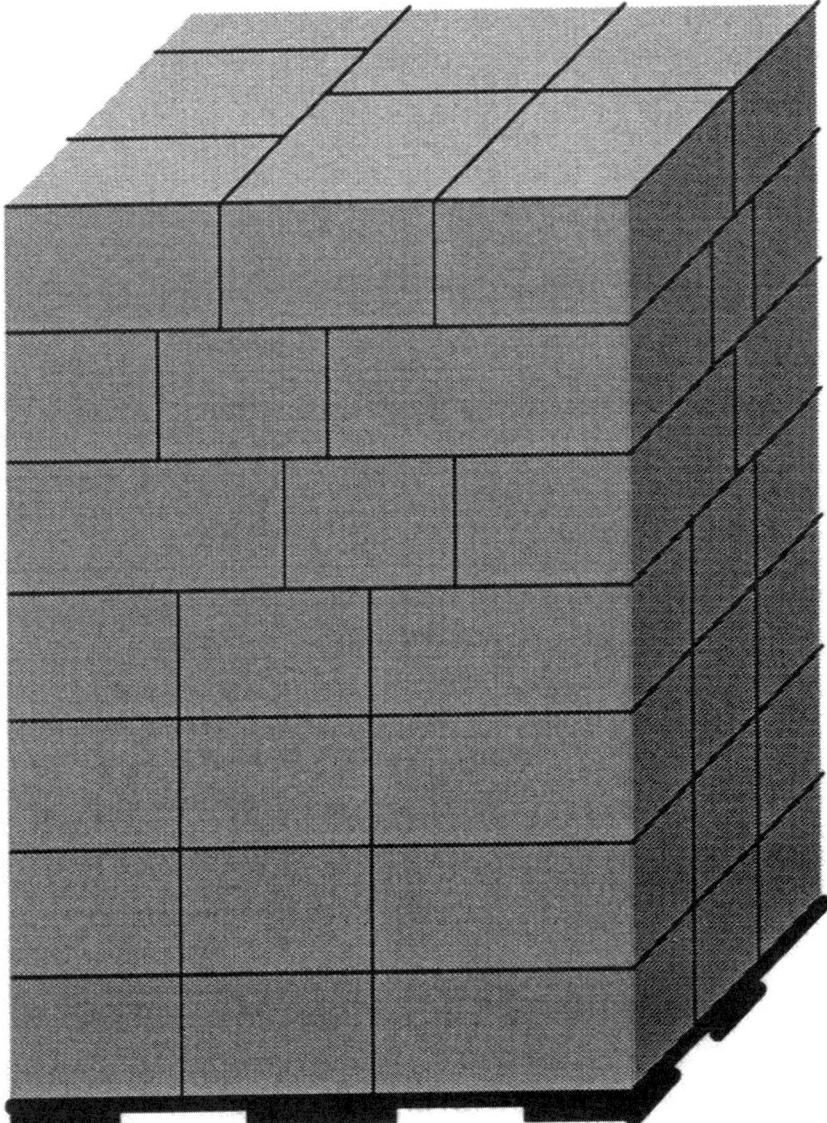

Fig. 16.8. Shipping container with tight stacking pattern contains seven boxes per layer, seven layers high, on 106.7 × 88.9 cm wooden pallet.

by controlling loss of moisture, but also to reduce certain serious physiological injuries. For example, in Israel the superficial flavedo necrosis in Shatoumi oranges (*C. sinensis*, Osbeck), locally known as noxan, is a serious

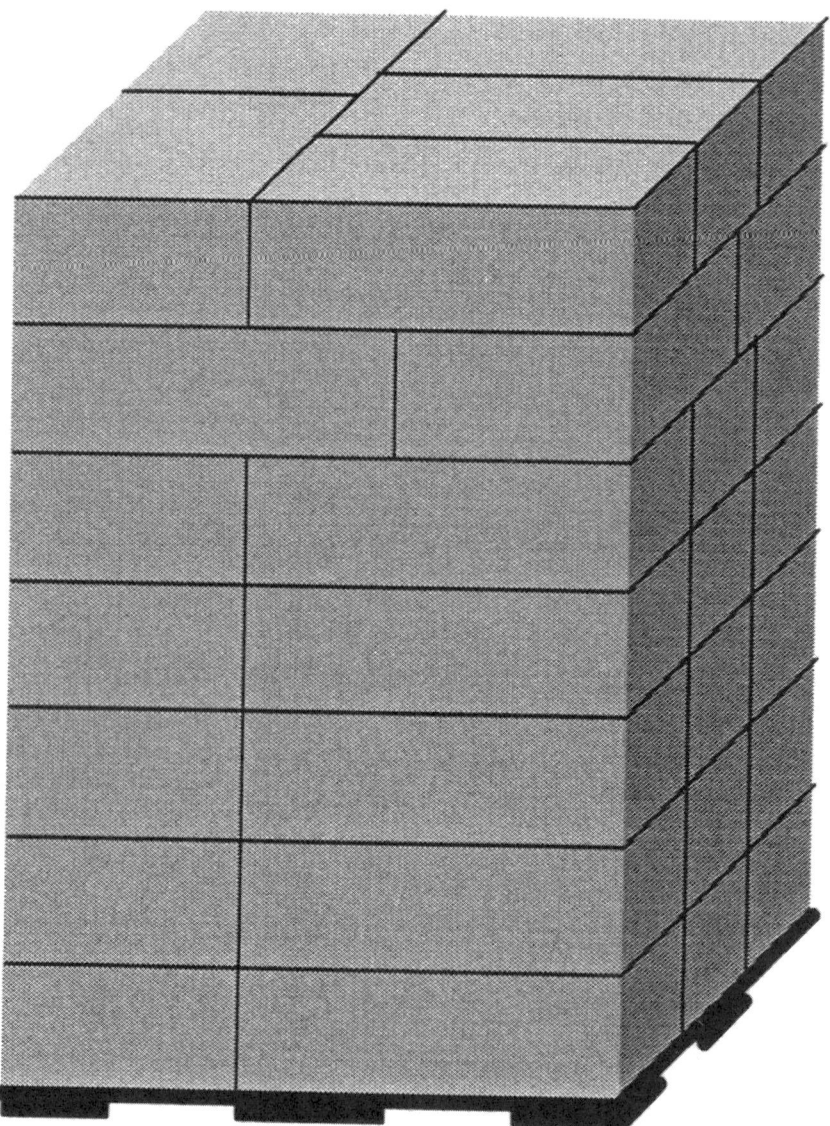

Fig. 16.9. Standard common footprint full size containers stacked five per layer with last two layers cross-stacked for locking the whole pallet.

physiological peel blemish that has been correlated with loss of moisture during storage (Ben-Yehoshua *et al.* 2001; Peretz *et al.* 2001). However, damage which develops after harvest of the fruits in the form of pits on the flavedo is impossible to be detected at the packinghouse, and may develop

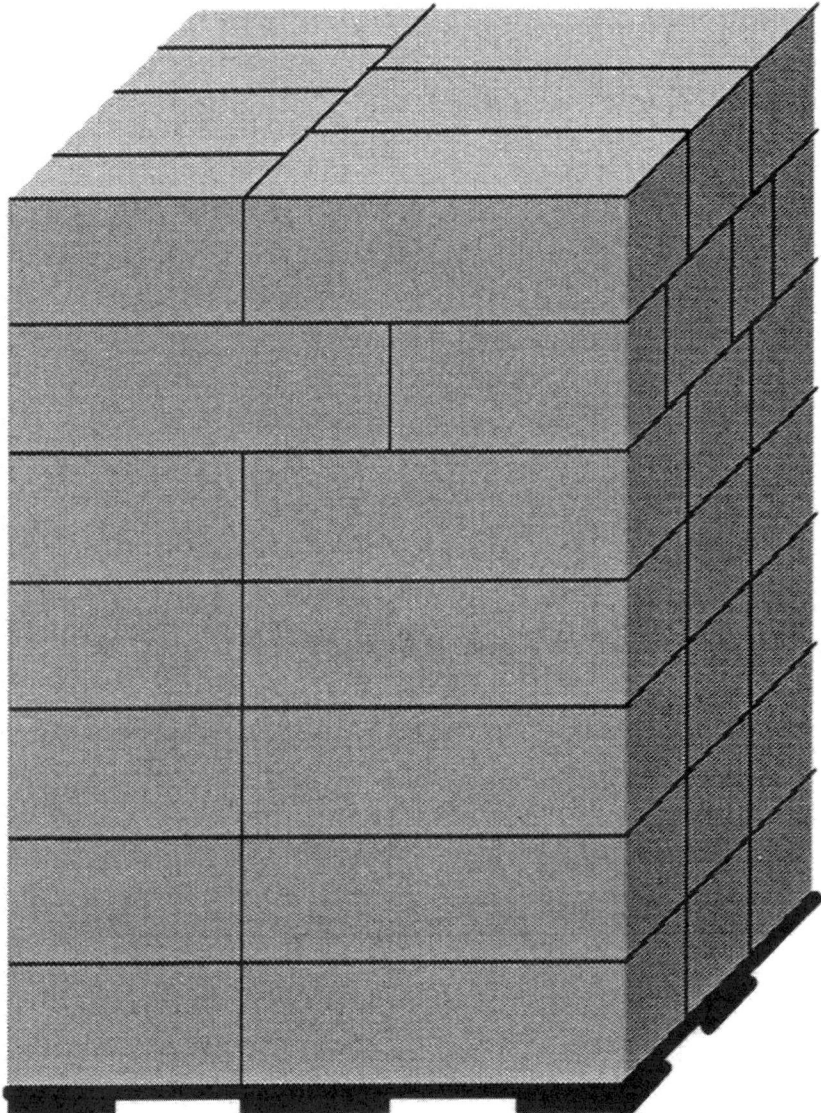

Fig. 16.10. Standard common footprint half and full size containers with last two layers cross-stacked for locking the whole pallet.

later obliging the exporters to repack the fruits and therefore, increasing their final cost. Recent studies demonstrated that this problem might be minimized by the use of adequate storage and transit temperatures combined with an adequate packaging (Ben-Yehoshua *et al.* 2001; Peretz *et al.*

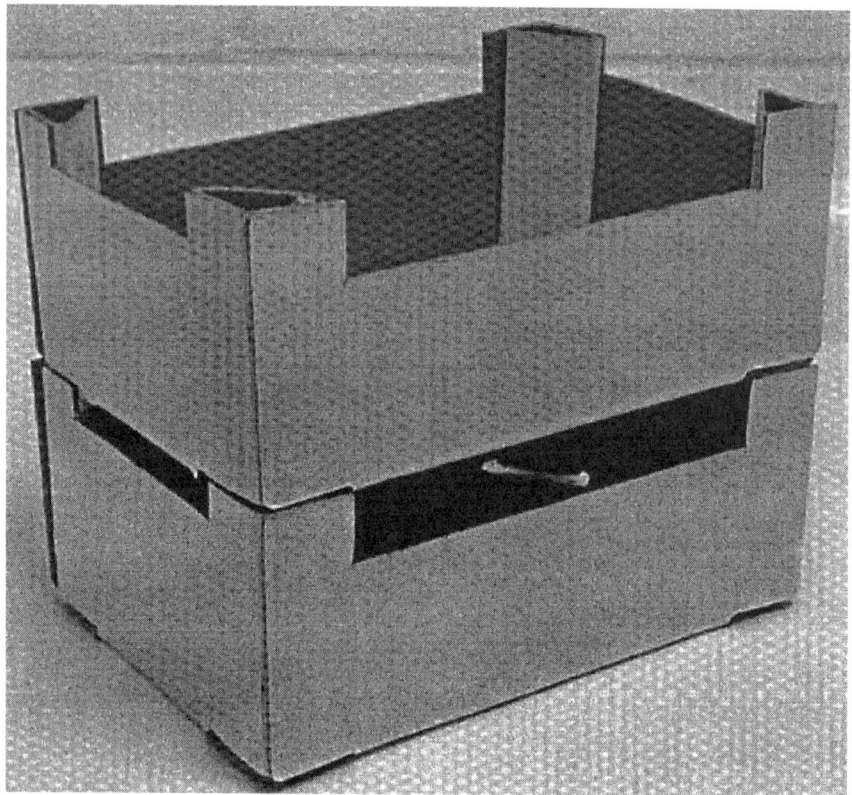

Fig. 16.11. Clementine boxes made with solidboard.

2001). The authors reported that the noxan incidence was much lower at 6°C than at 20°C and that because of the decrease in weight loss during storage. Furthermore, packaging of the fruits using either individual shrink seal packaging with high density polyethylene (HDPE), or packaging fruit in HDPE, or in low density polyethylene (LDPE) plastic bags or using LDPE, HDPE or LDPEH plastic liners reduced simultaneously noxan incidence and weight loss during storage compared to fruits stored in carton containers (Ben-Yehoshua *et al.* 2001).

In another study Cohen *et al.* (1990) reported that sealing individual green Eureka lemons in HDPE film reduces weight loss and preserves firmness of the fruits when compared to non-sealed fruits, which may loose approximately 10 times more weight during storage that sealed lemons. The same authors also reported that after 6 months the quality of seal-packed lemons was higher than that on non-sealed fruits. Likewise weight loss of Oroblanco grapefruit either individually sealed packed in a polyole-

Fig. 16.12. Tray pack boxes made with solidboard.

fin plastic film or packed in cartons with perforated polyethylene liners was significantly reduced when compared to weight loss of grapefruit packed in regular cartons (Rodov *et al.* 2000). Individually sealed grapefruit had the lowest weight loss and higher firmness and elasticity when compared to fruits in perforated polyethylene liners, but the later were more effective than water waxing for weight loss reduction (Rodov *et al.* 2000). The same authors reported that for Oroblanco grapefruit, individual seal packaging is the best way to control water loss during shipping and when not feasible plastic liners should be used rather then waxing, since they are more efficient at controlling loss of moisture from the fruit. In addition, the slight increase in CO_2 level in individually sealed fruits may contribute to delay senescence of the fruits and thus, prolong their shelf life. Also, seal packaging in HDPE plastic films may inhibit development of chilling injury symptoms in citrus fruits (Kale and Adsule 1995).

However, we should bear in mind that plastic film packaging may in some situations contribute to increase the condensation inside the package affecting not only the presentation of the product as well as increasing the risk of decay development. In addition, packing and transporting citrus fruit in plastic bags should always be avoided when fruit are not adequately precooled before being packed. When the warm fruit is packed in polyethylene plastic film bags and then placed inside carton boxes, it is very

Fig. 16.13. Counter-ready reusable plastic container for citrus.

difficult or almost impossible to bring down the fruit temperature to an optimal, during transit. Furthermore, when citrus fruits are packed in perforated polyethylene plastic liners a decay controlling treatment should be used to avoid development of decay (Rodov *et al.* 2000).

REFERENCES

ALBRIGO, L. G., BURNS, J. K. and HUNT, F. M. III. 1991. Weight loss considerations in preparing and marketing weight-fill bagged citrus. Proc. Fla. State Hort. Soc. 104, 74-77.

BEN-YEHOSHUA, S., PERTZ, J., MORAN, R., LAVIA, B. and KIM, J. J. 2001. Reducing the incidence of superficial flavedo necrosis (noxan) of 'Shamouti' oranges (*Citrus sinensis*, Osbeck). Postharv. Biol. Technol. 22, 19-27.

COHEN, E., LURIE, S., BEN-YEHOSHUA, S., SHALOM, Y. and ROSENBERGER, I. 1990. Prolonged storage of lemons using individual seal-packaging. J. Amer. Soc. Hort. Sci. 115, 251-255.

EUROPEAN COMMISSION REGULATION (EC). 2001. Laying down the marketing standard for citrus fruit. Official Journal of the European Communities No. L 244 of 14.9.2001.

HEARN, C. J. 1986. Production trends around the world. *In* Fresh Citrus Fruits, Wilfred F. Wardowski, Steven Nagy and William Grierson (Editors). AVI Book, New York.

KALE, P. N. and ADSULE, P. G. 1995. Citrus. *In* Handbook of Fruit Science and Technology; Production, Composition, Storage and Processing, D. K. Salunkhe and S. S. Kadam (Editors). Marcel Dekker, Inc., New York, NY.

PERETZ, J., MORAN, R., LAVIE, B. and BEN YEHOSHUA, S. 2001. Postharvest treatments of high relative humidity (RH) and low temperatures reduced the incidence of superficial flavedo necrosis (noxan) of 'Shamouti' oranges (*C. sinensis*, Osbeck). Acta Hort. 553, 301-302.

RISSE, L. A., BONGERS, A. J. and BUS, V. G. 1990. European references for packaging of selected fresh produce. Proc. Fla. State Hort. Soc. 103, 230-232.

RODOV, V., AGAR, T., PERETZ, J., NAFUSSI, B., KIM, J. J. and BEN-YEHOSHUA, S. 2000. Effect of combined application of heat treatments and plastic packaging on keeping quality of 'Oroblanco' fruit (*Citrus grandis* L. × *C. paradisi* Macf.). Posthav. Biol. Technol. 20, 287-294.

RYALL, A. L. and PENTZER, W. T. 1974. Handling, Transportation and Storage of Fruits and Vegetables. Vol. 2. Fruits. AVI Publishing Company, Inc., Westport, CT.

THE PACKER. 2002. Availability and Merchandising Guide. Published by The Packer, Lincolnshire, IL, USA.

USDA. 1999. United States Standards for Grades of Tangerines. USDA, Agric. Mktg. Serv., Washington, DC.

USDA. 2001. United States Standards for Grades of Oranges and Grapefruit (Texas and States Other Than Florida). Rules and Regulations. Federal Register Vol. 66, Number 185, 48785-48789. http://www.ceris.purdue.edu/fedweb/0109/24/0000.html

17

Plant Pest Regulations

Timothy S. Schubert, Xiaoan Sun,
Gary Steck and Susan E. Halbert

INTRODUCTION

Plant pests occur to some degree whenever and wherever plants are grown, and citrus is certainly no exception. Some of these pests (using the term in the broad sense of the Federal Plant Pest Act of 1957 to include insects, mites, mollusks, nematodes, pathogens, invasive and parasitic plants, etc.) are serious impediments to citrus production and have limited geographical ranges for one reason or another. These two facts—the negative impact of these pests on citrus growth and production and their limited geographical range—are the principle reasons for regulatory plant protection in the citrus industry and in agriculture and ecosystem protection generally. This chapter focuses upon governmental plant pest regulations and procedures that affect the movement of fresh citrus produce in domestic and world trade because the fruit may harbor and further distribute threatening exotic pests. In general, the more a plant commodity circulates in international commerce, the greater the risks of spreading exotic pests. Regulatory plant protection mitigates those risks.

The three main modes of pest distribution amenable to regulatory plant protection are trade, tourism, and scientific endeavors aimed at crop improvement (McGregor 1978). Experience in recent times suggests that in addition to the tourism element, actual immigration and relocation of residents should be added to that list. Simply stated, regulatory agencies design regulations to limit the unnecessary distribution of plant pests with the commodity or propagation material. Regulatory plant protection (quarantine) must be viewed as one aspect of the larger realm of integrated plant pest management (Rohwer 1991).

Regulations are intended to modify human behavior with the intention of eliminating or lessening to acceptable levels the risks of pest distribution, while at the same time minimizing trade disruption and infringement on personal liberties. As one might expect, any attempts at modifying human behavior, particularly when those attempts interfere with economic affairs or privacy, can be controversial and require careful drafting with the majority consent and endorsement of the affected parties. As fewer and fewer persons are directly involved in the foundational production aspects of agriculture, an automatic awareness by the affected parties (i.e., all persons who use plant materials for food, fiber and construction material) of food security issues can no longer be assumed. In other words, many in the "affected parties" category are largely unaware of that status. They have forgotten their dependence upon healthy plants. Creating a general public awareness of the wisdom behind plant pest regulations demands a full-time, intensive public relations program that maintains some positive impressions among all the other awareness campaigns that simultaneously clamor for public attention.

HISTORY

Two major influences inspired the introduction of many plants to our continent and specifically to the citrus production regions of North America: 1) The relative scarcity of native North American plant material useful for crop production in the warmer climates, and 2) the human propensity to bring plant materials along on migrations. These influences prevailed largely unchecked prior to the recognition of the serious risks involved in the uninformed movement of plant materials.

By the start of the previous century, the catastrophic results of many introduced pests were apparent around the world (Mathys and Baker 1980). These introductions were the direct result of the increasingly popular practice of long distance movement of vegetative plant propagation material with no regard for hitchhiking pests. In fact, the idea that microbes *caused* disease (the new germ theory of disease for which de Bary and Pasteur provided the basis in the 1860s with their studies on late blight of potato and fermentation respectively) instead of *being the result of* plant sickness (the declining autogenic model of plant disease) and the parallel concept that disease-causing pathogens could be transported on healthy appearing plant materials were only beginning to take root and bear fruit, so to speak, in the minds of plant scientists. Only a minority of scientists were willing to admit that plant propagative material might outwardly appear healthy but still harbor harmful pests.

Economic and social upheaval resulted from the introduction of the chromistan pathogen *Phytophthora infestans* into the potato fields of Europe in the 1840s. The grape industry in France was nearly destroyed due to the successive and inadvertent introductions of *Uncinula necator* (powdery mildew of grape, 1840s) *Viteus vitifolae* (Fitch) (grape Phylloxera, 1860s)), *Plasmopara viticola* (grape downy mildew fungus, 1875), and *Guignardia bidwellii* (black rot fungus, 1885) on propagative material from the New World. Elsewhere, the introduction of coffee rust fungus, *Hemilia vastatrix*, into Ceylon (Sri Lanka) around 1869 caused the demise of the coffee industry there. Here in the United States, white pine blister rust (*Cronartium ribicola*) was introduced to five-needled pines in the western hemisphere around the turn of the last century on nursery stock from Europe, where the disease had gained a foothold from Asia some time in the 18th century on susceptible exotic American white pines widely planted there (Maloy 2001). A second domestic example in modern times is the discovery in Arizona in March 1996 of Karnal bunt of wheat (*Tilletia indica*) in seed intended for planting (Marshall *et al.* 2003). The pathogen had been known in Mexico for almost 25 years, and had presumably made the original trip to the Western Hemisphere from the pathogen's point of origin in India by way of contaminated seed.

Not all introductions take place as a result of introducing contaminated, infected or infested plant propagative material. The gypsy moth (*Lymantria dispar* L.) was introduced to the U.S. in 1869 from Europe by a French experimenter hoping to breed a hardier silkworm. Accidentally released caterpillars eventually spread into the New England forests and orchards (McCubbin 1954; Elkinton and Liebhold 1990). A current program is still attempting to limit the spread of this destructive pest. The American chestnut tree was devastated throughout its North American range by the fungus *Cryphonectria parasitica*, which was introduced to the New York area from the Orient around 1910 (Anagnostakis 2000), not on propagation material, but on unprocessed logs, an important distinction. Dutch elm disease caused by the fungus *Ophiostoma ulmi* arrived in the New World several times around 1930 in similar fashion, on unprocessed logs, and happened to find a suitable efficient vector already here, the native elm bark beetle *Hylurgopinus rufipes* (Eichoff), plus another exotic vector, the imported elm bark beetle *Scolytus multistriatus* (Marsham).

Among the earliest of plant pest legislative acts on the world scene in response to these multiple devastating introductions were the following (Mathys and Baker 1980):

- an act in Germany in 1873 to prohibit the importation from the United States of plants and plant products that might harbor the Colorado potato beetle, *Leptinotarsa decemlineata* (Say);
- the Destructive Insects Act in the United Kingdom in 1877 to prevent the introduction of the Colorado potato beetle and to limit the spread of coffee rust from Ceylon to Indonesia;
- legislation by the State of California in 1903 to provide general protection to the state's agriculture;

- legislation enacted by Australia in 1909 to establish a federal quarantine service;
- the Federal Plant Quarantine Act passed by the United States Congress in 1912;
- legislation to protect the state's agriculture enacted by the State of Florida in 1914 in response to the citrus canker epidemic (Stall and Seymour 1983).

A thorough coverage of the history of the development of plant health regulations in response to significant outbreaks of exotic pests is available (Foster 1991). Suffice it to say that many mistakes in plant pest regulations (almost all of them oversights and omissions) are apparent in hindsight, and we would do well to review those mistakes often in order to avoid repeating them.

Xanthomonas axonopodis pv. *citri*, the cause of bacterial citrus canker, warrants more detailed attention for three reasons: 1) because of its role as a serious citrus fruit pathogen; 2) because of the widespread perception that there is a substantial risk of transmitting the pathogen successfully on fresh fruit, and 3) because citrus canker, along with the contemporaneous gift of infested flowering cherry trees to the U.S. from Japan and the arrival of chestnut blight, played a foundational role in early U.S. plant pest regulations at both the federal and state levels mentioned above. Canker was first introduced into the Gulf region of the United States from Japan on infected citrus rootstocks in the early years of the twentieth century, probably around 1910 (Dopson 1964; Loucks 1934). Citrus canker caused severe losses in the Gulf Coast states before this first introduction was eventually eradicated. Further details of the history and biology of citrus canker follow later.

The learning and implementation processes in plant health regulation are not as fast and efficient as one might hope. Lest the reader get the impression that the parade of introduced pests into the United States has been largely curtailed by better regulations and enforcement, some modern examples of recent exotic plant pest introductions are:

- Peanut stripe virus discovered on peanuts in Florida in 1982 (Schoulties 1984);
- Sweet potato whitefly and silverleaf whitefly plus a host of Begomoviruses transmitted by them (Jones 2003; http://www.apsnet.org/pd/PDFS/1997/1028-01F.PDF;
- A second introduction of citrus canker into west central Florida found in 1986 (Schubert *et al.* 2001);
- Asian citrus leaf miner (*Phyllocnistis citrella* Stainton) discovered in Homestead, FL area in 1993 (Heppner 1993);
- A third introduction of citrus canker into the Miami, FL area discovered in 1995 (Schubert *et al.* 2001; Gottwald *et al.* 2002);

- A fourth introduction of a strain of citrus canker with a restricted host range in the West Palm Beach, FL area discovered in 2000 (Sun *et al.* 2004);
- A fifth introduction of another restricted host range strain of citrus canker found in the Orlando area in 2003 (Sun, personal communication)
- Daylily rust (*Puccinia hemerocallidis*) into the southeastern U.S. in 2001 (Williams-Woodward *et al.* 2001; Hernandez *et al.* 2002);
- Emerald ash borer (*Agrilus planipennis* Fairmaire) in 2002 (Haack *et al.* 2002; McCollough and Roberts 2002);
- Brown citrus aphid [(*Toxoptera citricida* (Kirkaldy)], the most efficient vector of citrus tristeza virus first found in North America in the Miami and Ft. Lauderdale, FL area in 1995 and now present throughout peninsular Florida (Halbert *et al.* 1998);
- Citrus psyllid *Diaphorina citri* (Kuwayama), the vector of citrus greening disease, found in 1998 in the Delray Beach, FL and surrounding areas, and now spread as far west as Texas (Halbert and Manjunath 2004);
- Sudden oak death pathogen *Phytophthora ramorum*, discovered on the West Coast of the United States and in Europe in the mid 1990s. (California Oak Mortality Task Force 2006; http://apsnet.org/online/SOD/Papers/APS/0115-01R.pdf);
- Huanglongbing, or citrus greening disease caused by *Candidatus* Liberibacter asiaticus discovered in Miami-Dade County in late 2005, and now present in 12 counties of South Florida as of this writing (http://www.doacs.state.fl.us/pi/chrp/greening/citrusgreening.html);
- *Phytophthora hedraiandra* on rhododendrons in MN (NAPPO 2006A);
- *Phytophthora tropicalis* on *Epipremnum aureum* cuttings in FL and rhododendrons in VA (NAPPO 2006B);
- Gladiolus rust, caused by *Uromyces transversalis*, discovered in April, 2006 on gladiolus being grown for cut flowers in West central Florida (NAPPO 2006C).

Exotic pest appearances are notoriously difficult to trace back to their origins, but in many cases where some trail of evidence persists, the clues point to probable introduction either by private citizens or those involved in the increasingly widespread marketing of a plant or plant product, not the community engaged in commercial plant propagation. These and other catastrophic pest introductions have prompted a long series of progressively stricter limitations on the movement of agricultural goods in a good faith effort to minimize the movement of plant pests culminating in the current phytosanitary regulations contained in the Federal Plant Protection Act of 2000 (http://www.aphis.usda.gov/ppq/weeds/PPAText.PDF). On the worldwide front, McGregor (1978) in his study of emigrant pests reported that by the early 1970s only 11 of 171 countries had no form of plant pest regulation on trade or travelers.

Though not the first, citrus was among the earliest commodities to benefit from specific regulations. California led the way in drafting the first plant protection legislation in the U.S. in 1885 by authorizing the inspection of both interstate and international shipments of fruit plants and trees. The legislation was prompted primarily by grape phylloxera (*Viteus vitifolae*) scares. Citrus trees in California were being fumigated to eliminate scale insects under this regulatory authorization in 1886. Florida followed shortly after in 1889 with a regulation making it unlawful to "knowingly sell or give away any diseased nursery stock or seeds in the State of Florida", however authorizing legislation to actually enforce this law did not come about until 1911 (Rosenberg 1989). The most recent version of plant protection legislation in the United States is the Plant Protection Act of 2000 (http://nahln.aphis.usda.gov/ppq/Ppa.pdf; http://www.aphis.usda.gov/lpa/pubs/fsheet_faq_notice/fs_phproact.html)

As an example of how difficult it can be to enact, enforce and adapt reasonable and intelligent plant pest regulations even in the modern era, consider the disease first called nursery strain citrus canker, now known as citrus bacterial spot. A canker-like disease first called nursery strain or E-strain citrus canker emerged in central Florida during the summer of 1984. The disease appeared in a commercial citrus nursery, the worst possible circumstances in terms of having any chance at preventing pathogen spread. The disease was causing considerable damage to the foliage and stems of the succulent nursery stock, and significantly reducing the success of budding operations. The disease had all the characteristics of a new strain of citrus canker, the only difference being the relative flatness of the lesions, whereas typical canker lesions are raised and corky. Thorough accounts of the events of the evolution of knowledge and attempts to regulate this new disease are available (Schoulties *et al.* 1987; Schubert 1991; Schubert *et al.* 2001). The episode affords a good example of the struggle to balance the biological risks of trying to contain a new pathogen possessing obvious damage and spread capabilities with the desperate need for comprehensive information on the full potential for damage by the pathogen previously unknown to science. The most modern taxonomic tools were brought to bear, the stability of citrus markets was considered, and a consensus of scientists familiar with citrus diseases was sought. After about two years of study under very strict containment conditions, scientists concluded the disease was of minor consequence outside the nurseries, and the pathogen was gradually deregulated. But before that could take place, considerable amounts of citrus stock in nurseries, commercial plantings and dooryards were sacrificed in what is now reckoned in hindsight as an overly cautious regulatory response. Unavoidable and inevitable legal complications during the period added additional costs, delays, and confusion. The citrus bacterial spot episode highlights the vital importance of adapting regulations to new information. Subsequent regulatory programs in Florida directed at eradication of typical citrus canker (a known disease with predictable and significant spread and damage potential) in 1986 and 1995 have had to undergo extreme scrutiny and delays which have only permitted further disease spread and prolonged the necessary actions for successful eradication (Gottwald *et al.* 2002; Schubert *et al.* 2001). Eventually, in January of 2006 the goal of canker eradication in Florida was deemed unachievable (http://www.doacs.state.fl.us/press/2006/01112006_2.html), in large part because of legal delays that frequently invoked the misinterpretations of the 1984-87 citrus bacterial spot episode.

In the United States where California was the first to enact plant pest legislation at the state level, the individual states retained broad powers to regulate plants and plant products from other states and overseas, even after passage of federal legislation. Today, the regulatory powers are centralized under the federal government. The federal government through the U.S. Department of Agriculture (USDA)—Animal and Plant Health Inspection Service (APHIS) regulates the movement of plants and plant products in foreign commerce and interstate commerce, and maintains cooperative agreements with the states. The state governments through their state departments of agriculture regulate intrastate commerce and commerce into the state not specifically regulated by the federal government. States may not impose regulations on foreign commerce or require more stringent interstate regulations than are imposed by the federal government. However, states can impose regulations if federal regulations are lacking. A proposed rule was recently published for comment that would allow for states or smaller political subdivisions to regulate over and above federal regulations under special needs circumstances, criteria for which are not yet established (Federal Register 2006). State regulatory control over foreign commerce of plants and plant products cannot be exercised under present regulations until the item has reached the designated state location. Generally, the federal government is cooperative in these matters and will advise both the prospective importer as to specific state regulations and the state regulatory officials as to entry of shipments of interest.

In spite of the more stringent restrictions on plant and plant product movement, it is apparent that introductions of exotic pests continue to occur, and with alarming frequency. The appropriate balance in the struggle between free trade and ecosystem protection from exotic pests is no more easily achieved today than it was a century ago. Costs to derive the benefits of regulatory programs are borne by the consuming public, either in the form of taxes or fees to provide the revenue to support the regulatory agencies, or in the form of higher prices for the commodity. (http://www.whitehouse.gov/omb/circulars/a094/a094.pdf) In most cases where an exotic introduction is traceable to its origin, illegal movement by private individuals of prohibited plant propagative material, illegal movement of plant products, or overly liberal plant pest regulations geared more to un-impeded international and interstate commerce than regional plant protection have been responsible.

PRINCIPLES

Each country is responsible for developing its own regulations concerning the introduction of threatening exotic pests on or within plant materials. What is considered a threat by one country may be of no concern to another country. Countries that have these threatening pests of limited distribution and that wish to export plant materials must meet or negotiate the regulations with the importing country. The International Plant Protection Congress (http://www.ippc.int/IPP/En/default.jsp) (http://www.fao.org/Legal/treaties/004t-e.htm) and the World Trade Organization Sanitary and Phytosanitary Agreement (WTO-STS Agreement) (http://www.wto.org) (http://edis.ifas.ufl.edu/FE492) are the agencies/policies dealing with these matters. Trading partners engaged in disputes relative to phytosanitary issues can bring their case to the WTO for a negotiated settlement (Hedley 1999).

The development of plant pest regulations best derives from certain principles. According to J. R. Morchel (cited by Mathys and Baker 1980), plant pest regulations:
1. should be based upon sound biological principles;
2. should not be used to artificially restrict free trade;
3. must derive from adequate law and authority;
4. should be modified as conditions change and new facts emerge;
5. should be economically feasible to achieve;
6. require cooperation on an international scale and from the public (informed voluntary cooperation; this is an honor system for the most part);
7. can be effective only if those responsible for them are well informed; and
8. are only one facet of domestic pest management programs.

In effect, by enacting and enforcing plant pest regulations, a balance must be obtained between the biological realities of host, pest (and possibly vector) and the achievement of reasonable level of agricultural protection with minimum inconvenience to trade, tourism, or scientific progress. The unavoidable inherent subjectivity of these deliberations sometimes makes for lengthy and frustrating negotiations. The temptation and long history of domestic trade protection under the guise of plant health regulations adds a level of skepticism to these negotiations (Powell 2002).

Living plants or plant parts usually represent the most dangerous carriers of insect pests and pathogens (McGregor 1978; Rosenberg *et al.* 1978).

Thus, when only certain plant parts are attacked, other parts may be moved safely in commerce. For example, citrus blackfly *(Aleurocanthus woglumi)* is not found on fruit but only on leaves; therefore, fruit from an infested area can be safely moved to an uninfested area, if the commodity is free of leaves. On the other hand, Mediterranean fruit fly [*Ceratitis capitata* (Wiedemann)] infests fruit; accordingly, budsticks from an infested area can be moved safely into an uninfested area, assuming other indexing requirements of the propagation material are met. However, soil or roots should not be moved because *C. capitata* pupates in the soil (Rosenberg *et al.* 1978). Another example: All known strains of the citrus canker bacterium *(Xanthomonas axonopodis* pv. *citri)* infect fruit, leaves, petioles, and stems; thus, it would be unwise to move any plants or plant parts (propagative material or fruit) from an infested area to an uninfested area without taking special precautions. This would be true even if the various plant tissues were not exhibiting symptoms, because the fruit or other tissue may be infested (contaminated) or infected but may not display overt symptoms until a sufficient incubation period elapses and/or symptoms exceed that subjective threshold such that common methods of visual detection can succeed. Sanitation of symptomless yet possibly contaminated commodity is a reasonable requirement under such circumstances.

The huge volumes of containerized commodities make the visual inspection process exceedingly difficult. There are few published examples of a plant disease being transmitted on contaminated plant product (some examples being Dutch elm disease and chestnut blight), but there are several examples of insect transmission (most notably fruit flies) over long distances via plant products that pass the "apparently free of infestation" standard that prevails in most phytosanitary regulations.

In the formulation of plant pest regulations, an intimate knowledge of insect, pathogen, and host biology is fundamental if pest spread is to be prevented or mitigated (Rosenberg *et al.* 1978). Ideally, this biological knowledge is the sole basis of plant pest regulations. However, the plant pest specialist must recognize that the scientific considerations in regulatory decision-making are only part of the driving forces, albeit they should be a large part. Other factors outside the immediate expertise and authority of the biological scientist must also carry some weight (logistics, economics, legal issues, political issues, public education issues, etc.). Much of the controversy over plant health regulations lies within this context: are the plant protection regulations actually based on sound biological principles, or are they a smokescreen for protectionism of local agriculture and/or ecosystems? Are local production subsidies and protections ever legitimate reasons to ensure a reliable, safe domestic food supply and perhaps a robust local economy and community? If a subsidy or a protection is based more on economic factors than biological ones (or any factors other than biology), it should be clearly identified as such and defended on that basis. Production costs must reflect all costs (some of which may be largely intangible, i.e., community integrity, environmental health, cultural heritage, food security, aesthetics, etc.). In the end, all considerations must be holistically fashioned into reasonable and transparent regulations that have a good chance at successfully preventing pest dissemination, while still balancing the biological realities with the economic, political, and logistical necessities of moving goods and people most efficiently.

Though regulatory plant protection is criticized by some as outdated, regulations actually provide growers in the regulated area with one of the most cost effective means of managing plant diseases and pests known. By starting with clean, pest- and disease-free plants, one can eliminate or reduce the need for other management techniques that are costly in terms of human resources, supplies, and negative environmental impact. Furthermore, the process actually provides some protection to other potential hosts in the area. Starting with clean propagation material is valuable for both fast-cycling annual crops and especially to perennial crops. For annual crops, the protection may not need to endure through the entire growing season in order to result in a profitable crop. With perennial crops such as citrus, the need to start clean and remain relatively pest-free as long as possible is imperative.

The element of *acceptable* risk lies at the heart of the claim of a biological basis for regulations that keep products out of certain markets. Nowhere is that subjective and relative level of acceptable risk specifically prescribed in guidelines or regulations. One must recognize that the elimination of all risk is an impossibility, and cannot serve as the basis for prohibitive regulations. Standardization and harmonization of plant health regulations at the international level is a primary goal of the FAO (http://www.wto.org/english/docs_e/legal_e/17-tbt.pdf).

The level of skill and technology brought to bear on this question of pest and pathogen distribution differs from place to place. Also, the incentive for careful inspection of one's own production areas and products for pests and diseases initially is not great if it might result in restricted market access. This flawed reasoning and deficient technical approach to the problem can be completely reversed to effectively *promote* agricultural products from an area if the prospective customers are certain that a credible job is being done to detect pest invasions and outbreaks early, thereby preventing pest dispersal with the commodity. It is important to remember that good diagnostic services must be coupled with thorough commodity and timely production area surveys by trained plant health inspectors to be able to contribute meaningful information for interstate and international trade policies. One is no good without the other; both require considerable investment. The question arises: What level of investment and expertise sets the minimum standard for plant health surveillance, thereby permitting full participation in interstate and international trade in plants and plant products?

To summarize, the purposes and goals of regulatory plant protection are to:

1) Manage plant pests and diseases in advance and by design using uniform regulations/laws;
2) Prevent introduction and dispersal of non-indigenous pests and pathogens;
3) Modify human behavior relative to plant and plant product handling and movement;
4) Satisfy a general societal demand for plant health regulation balanced with free trade;
5) Require a shared ethic from all participants—"transparency". All parties must commit to a reasonable effort to determine what pests and pathogens occur in their production areas, and be willing to disclose that information freely;
6) Furnish the regulations with a minimal reasonable network of compliance checks—phytosanitary certification, standardized survey procedures, and penalties for violations;
7) Strive for this standard: "apparently free of pests and diseases" unless a more stringent standard is specified. This assumes that quick identification of pests and pathogens by visual means or by using swift and reliable alternative test methods is possible. Time is a real concern, because perishable commodities can spoil while deliberations are in progress. Pre-clearance is advisable;
8) Encourage and expect voluntary compliance through enlightened self-interest. An entire police force to enforce regulations would make the process too costly and insufferable;

For a more complete discussion of all aspects of regulatory plant pest management, see Rohwer 1991.

NATURAL BARRIERS TO SPREAD OF PESTS

Although plant pest regulations have kept many pests from having a wider distribution, natural barriers to the spread of pests are extremely important. The two most notorious citrus fruit pests, citrus canker and the Mediterranean fruit fly (Medfly), would have become well established earlier in the United States had not serious and expensive regulatory eradication programs been successful. Moreover, interception statistics indicate that these two pests are encountered continuously at U.S. ports. According to USDA Port Interception Network data over the last twenty years, citrus canker has been intercepted at ports of entry an average of over 500 times per year, while Medfly has been intercepted and average of over 120 times per year. Fortunately, many of the interceptions take place at ports of entry located in an inhospitable environment for the two pests to establish.

The first of the natural obstacles to outward expansion of the pest habitat is host restriction (McCubbin 1954). Comparatively few pests have a wide host range. The citrus canker bacterium naturally infects only certain members of the citrus family. To the canker bacterium, territorial expansion is meaningless beyond the area occupied by those hosts. On the other hand, a few pests, such as some of the fruit flies, infest more than a hundred different hosts including citrus. Thus, fruit flies would have considerably more host and geographical expansion opportunities than the canker bacterium, more in line with their overall climate tolerance.

For some pests, it is climate presenting the most formidable obstacle to further distribution (McCubbin 1954). Because of climatic limitation, certain pests cannot follow their hosts and establish themselves in a new environment. For example, the citrus canker bacterium was formerly unable to establish in warm-dry (Mediterranean) climatic areas but established quite readily in many warm-humid climatic areas. The recent spread of the foliage-wounding Asian citrus leaf miner, *Phyllocnistis citrella*, into new territories has made some establishment of canker in drier climates such as Yemen possible. The inoculum efficiency-boosting effects of the Asian citrus leaf miner (Sohi and Sanhu 1968; Cook 1998; Gottwald *et al.* 1997) have also been one of several contributing biological factors in the abandonment of the most recent canker eradication effort in Florida. A recent attempt to introduce illegal citrus budwood into California resulted in the confiscation of canker-infected budsticks, resulting in the first conviction under the new Plant Protection Act of 2000 (http://www.cbp.gov/xp/cgov/newsroom/news_releases/archives/2005_press_releases/0092005/09092005_3.xml). A similar incident apparently linked to illegal budwood in Emerald, Australia has caused enormous damage, though the eradication of the disease is now nearing success (http://www.agnic.org/agnic/pmp/2005/cca021105.HTML). The Medfly, on the other hand, can establish itself in both warm-dry and warm-humid areas but not in cooler temperate areas because preferred hosts are not present year-round. No one would be so bold as to claim that all the Medfly-infested and canker-infested plant materials are intercepted. Why have there not been more outbreaks? Nature, in fact, plays a profound role in preventing pest establishment, especially in terms of climatic barriers.

Vectored pathogens such as *Candidatus* L. *asiaticus* will spread only by propagation if a vector is not present. In all probability, plant material infected with the Huanglongbing pathogen has been introduced into Florida several times without any serious consequences. Now that the vector *D. citri* is present, stopping disease spread is essentially impossible.

While host restrictions and climatic requirements tend to be absolute, physical barriers to the spread of pests tend to be more conditional. Mountains, deserts, and oceans are formidable barriers to cross autonomously or accidentally. Most pests require the assistance of man to overcome these barriers. Modern methods of travel and commodity movement certainly facilitate the spread of plant pests.

A pest having overcome all other absolute and conditional barriers may meet a formidable predator, parasite, antagonist, or competitor in its new location and be annihilated. Further, if the pest is a nongravid or nonparthenogenic arthropod, it must eventually find a suitable mate to perpetuate its kind before it dies. Such biological barriers work against the dispersal of plant pests.

Because exotic pest threats are largely conceptual and somewhat speculative prior to their actual manifestation (Schoulties *et al.* 1983), threat magnitude perception differs from place to place and person to person. Our biological knowledge and experience with a pest includes its destructiveness, host range, climatic requirements, reproductive capabilities, movement and dispersal capabilities, and control methods, all coupled with regulatory repercussions. These factors serve to increase or diminish on a continuum the perceived threat of a given pest in a given locale. There are so many considerations, interactions, and unknowns in assessing threats that no one can predict with certainty what a destructive pest will do when introduced into a noninfested area. Nor can anyone predict with certainty what a relatively nondestructive pest in a given area will do in a previously noninfested area. Often, if a nondestructive pest is moved without its natural antagonists, it may become a very prolific and destructive pest in its new environment. This lack of certainty makes it challenging to formulate reasonable and effective pest regulations.

CITRUS FRUIT PESTS

In this section, we focus on citrus fruit pests that have the following characteristics: (1) they can directly infest or infect fruit; (2) they can move with commercially packed fruit; and (3) they are perceived to be threats in noninfested regions of citriculture. Relevant also to this main concern are those citrus fruit pests that may accompany noncitrus produce, tourist-carried citrus produce, and citrus plant propagative parts. The movement of all of these various plant materials could lead to further distribution of threatening pests and to a widening application of citrus fruit regulations. Little or no consideration will be given to those important citrus pests that do not infest or infect fruit, even though many may indirectly affect fruit quality or quantity. Recent discoveries of the potential for seed transmission of some viral and procaryotic citrus pathogens, albeit at low levels, may reinvigorate the discussions pertaining to the risks of fresh citrus fruit commerce in the spread of some of these diseases. This topic is covered later in this chapter.

ARTHROPODS

Fruit Flies

Many insects classified under the family Tephritidae are serious pests of citrus and other fruits and vegetables. Fruit fly larvae feed upon the pulp of host fruits, sometimes tunneling through them and eventually reducing the fruit to a decaying inedible mass (Weems 1981 B). Fruit flies are of major concern in fruit transport because egg and larval stages infesting the fruit may go undetected throughout picking, grading, and packing. Consequently, many of these fruit flies have been distributed to distant parts of the tropical and subtropical areas of the world. California and Arizona are the only major areas of citriculture that do not have an established population of citrus-infesting fruit flies. A constant worldwide effort is being waged to prevent further movement of fruit flies in citrus fruit. Fruit flies are the major regulated arthropods that affect the movement of citrus fruit, and their presence is ample reason for quarantine restrictions.

The fruit fly genera *Anastrepha, Bactrocera, Ceratitis,* and *Dacus* are all important for their citrus-infesting species. At least 36 different species of fruit flies are known to attack citrus. Many of these species are highly polyphagous, thus any one of a large variety of fruits or vegetables may serve as a vehicle for introduction of these damaging pests into citrus production areas. These fruit flies are tropical or subtropical in native distribution, and they reproduce prolifically over multiple generations per year.

South American Fruit Fly

Anastrepha fraterculus (Wiedemann) is widespread in South and Central America and extends north into Mexico. It is part of a group of very similar species that are not well defined taxonomically or biologically (Steck 1999), some of which are citrus pests, and others not. For example, *A. fraterculus* is a major pest of citrus in Brazil (Enkerlin *et al.* 1989), but in Mexico it has never been reported from citrus and indeed seems incapable of developing in citrus (Aluja *et al.* 2003).

Mexican Fruit Fly

Anastrepha ludens (Loew) occurs from middle central America north into Mexico and frequently breeches the U.S. border in southern Texas and southern California. It is thought that *A. ludens* originated in northeastern

Mexico and spread to other areas in historical times (Baker *et al.* 1944). One of its native host plants in Mexico is *Sargentia greggii*, also a member of the citrus plant family, thus the fly is pre-adapted to commercial citrus. One of its most preferred hosts is grapefruit, *Citrus × paradisi.*

West Indian Fruit Fly

Anastrepha obliqua (Macquart) is the most widely distributed species of *Anastrepha* in the New World, occurring throughout South America (except Chile and southern Argentina), Central America, Mexico, the Greater Antilles, and many islands of the Lesser Antilles. Occasionally it invades Texas and California, and it was present for an unknown duration of time in southern Florida prior to 1936, though not presently (Steck 2001). Its preferred hosts are members of plant families such as Anacardiaceae (e.g., *Mangifera* and *Spondias* spp.) and Myrtaceae (e.g., *Psidium*), but it may infest citrus as well.

Caribbean Fruit Fly

Anastrepha suspense (Loew) is indigenous to the Greater Antilles. It was present at low levels in Florida for an unknown duration of time prior to 1936, at which time it apparently vanished, probably due to an eradication program conducted against it and other *Anastrepha* species during 1933-1936. It reappeared in 1965 and successfully colonized southern and central Florida where it continues to thrive (Clark *et al.* 1996). Its favored hosts in Florida include fruits such as guava, Surinam cherry and loquat (Swanson and Baranowski 1972). Citrus is attacked only when it becomes overly ripe.

Mediterranean Fruit Fly

Ceratitis capitata (Plate 25) is native to sub-Saharan Africa from which it began its relentless spread to other parts of the world as early as 1824. During the succeeding decades of the 19th century, it spread widely in the circum-Mediterranean countries. By the 1890s and early 1900s it had further spread to southern Africa, South America (Brazil), Australia, and Hawaii. The countries of Central America and Mexico were successively colonized between 1955 and 1977. Its first appearance in North America was in Florida in 1929. The ensuing first-ever eradication program in Florida was exceedingly costly, but a remarkable accomplishment that paved the way for the development of area-wide early detection systems for not only Medfly but numerous other pest fruit fly introductions and their many subsequent eradications. Mediterranean fruit fly remains the most feared of pest fruit flies (http://creatures.ifas.ufl.edu/fruit/mediterranean_fruit_fly.htm).

Natal Fruit Fly

Ceratitis rosa Karsch is an important fruit pest in its indigenous home-lands of East, Central, and southern Africa. After its accidental introduction into Mauritius, it displaced the Mediterranean fruit fly as the major pest within 4 years (Hancock 1984). It has a broad host range that includes several species of *Citrus*.

Oriental Fruit Fly

Bactrocera dorsalis (Handel) is one of the most serious of all fruit fly pests, comparable in many ways to Mediterranean fruit fly, which it may out-compete in some environments. It is native to a broad swath of area from India east to southern China, Taiwan, and southeast Asia. It has become established in some Pacific islands, including the Hawaiian Islands since about 1945, and Guam since 1947. *B. dorsalis* is a member of a large and taxonomically complex group of species. Several species of this complex are difficult or impossible to identify, especially when only a limited sample of males is examined. (Typically, only males are captured in early detection trapping systems.) An identification may be more or less certain when the exact origin of the specimen is known, as these species do not all overlap in their geographic distributions. However, in the case of adults that appear from unknown origins in detection traps in Florida or California, for example, they are typically assigned to the Oriental fruit fly complex without further distinction. These are highly polyphagous fruit and vegetable pests wherever they occur. In the Hawaiian Islands, *B. dorsalis* has been recorded from well over 100 hosts (see White and Hancock 1997). In the case of an introduced population whose exact identity and origin is unknown, it is not safe to exclude nearly any commercial fruit as a potential host.

Queensland Fruit Fly

Bactrocera tryoni (Froggatt) is the most serious insect pest of fruit and vegetable crops in its native Australia. There it infests nearly all commercial fruit crops including citrus, and also has a large number of wild hosts which serve as reservoirs to maintain populations. It has also spread to other islands in the south Pacific (White and Elson-Harris 1992).

Japanese Orange Fly

Bactrocera tsuneonis (Miyake) is one of the most important pests of citrus in parts of Japan and China (Weems 1967). Sweet oranges, mandarin oranges, and grapefruit are known hosts. Commercial citrus production for export from Japan continues under careful regulation for this pest.

Scale Insects

The armored and soft scales of the family Diaspididae and Coccidae respectively constitute the predominant citrus-infesting fauna in the majority of the important citrus-growing regions of the world. The presence of a specific scale in the growing area may be of significant regulatory importance. Scales may hitchhike on fruit as adults or in the immature crawler stage. The crawlers may be found under the calyx around the stem as well as in the stem scars. It is not practical to list the many scales that are of regulatory significance. In general, receiving countries restrict fruit from any other area of the world that is infested with a scale not found in the receiving country. For example, Japan requires that fruit shipments from Florida be certified to contain less than 1% Florida red scale (*Chrysomphalus aonidum* L.) dead or alive. Florida fruit entering Japan is fumigated for surface pests, particularly scale insects and the Caribbean fruit fly. Both the U.S. and Australia use high pressure fruit washing techniques to rid fruit of scale insects (http://www.sardi.sa.gov.au/pdfserve/supply/postharvest_hort/citruspacker_news/pdf/packnews67.pdf).

Mealybugs

Mealybugs are in the scale family Pseudococcidae. They cause citrus damage similar to that caused by other scales. Some species may damage roots as well as foliage. Mealybugs feed on the plant sap, reducing plant vitality and thus reducing production. Like the scale insects, whiteflies, and aphids, mealybugs produce "honey-dew", which is a food source for sooty mold fungi. Mealybugs are a regulatory problem because eggs and crawlers may be transported on fruit under the calyx and in the stem scars. Certain mealybugs, such as the highly polyphagous pink hibiscus mealybug (*Maconellicocus hirsutus*) is considered a quarantine pest. Additionally, some mealybugs are vectors of such citrus pathogens as citrus yellow mosaic virus by *Planococcus citri* (Risso) (Timmer *et al.* 2000).

White Flies (Including Citrus Blackfly)

As is true of scale insects, most countries regulate fruit shipments for whiteflies and particularly citrus blackfly (*Aleurocanthus woglumi* Ashby). These pests are transported on the leaves, stems, and debris accompanying the shipment but probably not on the fruit. If care is taken to remove all leaves, stems, and debris, no other regulatory restrictions for these pests must be met. Some citrus fruits (e.g., kumquats) are normally shipped with foliage attached. Consequently, with the advent of the citrus blackfly in Florida, shipments of such fruits are regulated when destined for California.

Aphids

Aphids, family Aphididae, are often problematic on citrus but are not transported on fruit without leaves. The brown citrus aphid *(Toxoptera citricida)* is of serious concern because it is a very efficient vector of the tristeza virus; it is established in South America, central and southern Africa, southern Asia, and Indonesia as well as Australia and many Pacific islands including Hawaii, and peninsular Florida (CAB International 2005). Where threatening aphids such as the brown citrus aphid occur, removal of leaves is required before fruit is eligible for movement to many noninfested countries.

Mites

Mites, order Acarina, family Tenuipalpidae, are of major concern in the production of citrus. Mite damage to the foliage reduces chlorophyll resulting in loss of production, and damage to the skin of the fruit reduces its market value. Mites may be transmitted by fruit shipments. On waxed and polished fruit, mites may hide under the calyx around the stem and in the stem scars. Assuring the absence of mites is difficult without chemical treatment. Two species not known to occur in the United States but of serious concern are *Eutetranychus orientalis* (Klein) (oriental spider mite) and *Eutetranychus yumensis* (McGregor) (Yuma spider mite). *Brevipalpus* spp. that transmit the citrus leprosis virus are widespread in most if not all citrus production areas of the world, but the pathogen has been reported and reconfirmed in modern times only in the Western Hemisphere (CAB International 2005). Many species of citrus-feeding mites are geographically widespread, due most probably to their wide host range and the increased transport on fruit and other plant materials.

Psyllids

Citrus psyllids are potentially important pests of citrus. They cause direct damage to new growth by their feeding activities, and cause indirect damage as a result of transmission of the huanglongbing pathogen. The disease complex is found in Asia east of Iran, Africa south of the Sahara Desert, the Saudi Arabian peninsula, several islands in the Indian Ocean, and most recently in Brazil and the U.S. Asian citrus psyllids *(D. citri)* may travel on unprocessed citrus fruit (Halbert and Manjunath 2004). Additional information on the vector and pathogen is found under the Huanglongbing (Citrus Greening) heading later.

Moths and Butterflies

The order Lepidoptera includes the moths and butterflies. The larval stages of Lepidoptera are commonly referred to as borers, leaf miners, worms, caterpillars, cutworms, loopers, etc. Lepidoptera are not usually transported by citrus shipments. Some Lepidoptera that may be found infesting fruit are *Citripestis sagittiferella* Moore (moth borer) and *Prays endocarpa* Meyrick (citrus rind borer) (Ebeling 1959). In Brazil, the 'bicho furão' (*Ecdytolopha aurantiana* Lima) adult males are trapped using a pheromone, thus interfering with the reproductive cycle of this fruit-boring pest (CAB International 2005).

Thrips

Several species of thrips, family Thripidae, are damaging to citrus. Thrips attack the foliage, the young fruit, and particularly the flowers, causing serious bloom drop. *Asprothrips nigricornis* causes silver russeting on citrus fruit similar to damage caused by citrus rust mite. It is native to Australia, and has become established in California and Hawaii (Edwards 1995). Occasional Florida greenhouse populations may have been eradicated. Other than these examples, thrips are not generally transported in fruit shipments if foliage, stems, and flowers are absent.

Beetles and Weevils

Beetles and weevils of the order Coleoptera are some of the most damaging citrus pests. Coleoptera adults feed on the foliage and sometimes the fruit. The larvae, sometimes referred to as grubs, feed on roots, bore into trunks and branches, and may feed on leaves and fruit. The damage to root systems by borers may so injure the tree as to render it unproductive or kill it. Generally, fruit damage by Coleoptera is easily detected, therefore beetles and weevils are not of major regulatory concern in shipment of fruit. Care must be taken to assure freedom from leaves and stems because eggs may be deposited on the foliage. Also of regulatory concern is the possibility that adult weevils and beetles may be attracted to light and crawl or fall into containers, ships, railcars, or trucks at the packing or loading point. The existence of numerous species of weevils and beetles and their ability to change host association make it impractical to list all species of economic significance. Among the genera that contain known citrus-feeding species are *Diaprepes, Exophthalmus, Lachnopus, Pachnaeus, Pantomorus, Prepodes, Macrodactylus, Phyllophaga, Agrilus, Melanauster,* and *Throscoryssa.*

MOLLUSCA

Snails and Slugs

Snails and slugs, phylum Mollusca, feed on the foliage and fruit of many species of plants including citrus. Snails and slugs are of concern to fruit shippers because many are nocturnal and may seek shelter in or on the exterior of containers, railcars, trucks, or pallets used to transport the fruit. It is sometimes difficult to kill hibernating snails even by methyl bromide fumigation.

PLANT PATHOGENS

Procaryotes

There are several bacteria and phytoplasmas that affect citrus fruits in quantity and quality (Timmer *et al.* 2000). All of them occur in limited geographical areas but not worldwide and can be very destructive to citrus fruit production once introduced and established in a new area.

Two major bacterial pathogens infect citrus fruit (Klotz 1978). *Pseudomonas syringae* pv. *syringae* causes black pit of fruit and blast of twigs and leaves. Black pit and blast do not occur in many citrus-growing areas where it is hot and humid such as Florida and Brazil. Florida has regulations against importation of citrus fruit with black pit to prevent introduction of possible exotic strains of *P. syringae* pv. *syringae* that are more adaptable to Florida's climate and could cause a problem. *Xanthomonas axonopodis* pv. *citri*, the causal agent of citrus canker, is considered one of the world's most destructive citrus pathogens and is widespread in Asian citrus productions areas, parts of Africa, South America, Mexico, and recently Florida. However, due to its localized disease expression, unique pathogen dispersal pattern and its limited distribution worldwide, citrus canker is notoriously the most regulated of all citrus fruit pathogens. Canker has been eradicated from South Africa, Australia, The Fiji Islands, Mozambique, New Zealand, and the United States. Citrus canker was detected in Florida several times since 1910 and was eradicated in 1933 and again in 1994 (Schubert *et al.* 2001). The pathogen was found in 1995 near the Miami International Airport. Following two consecutive summers in 2004 and 2005 with many tropical storm systems in the state, the citrus canker eradication effort was abandoned in favor of a detailed and dynamic management plan (http://www.aphis.usda.gov/ppq/ pdmp/citrushealth/). In some citrus-producing regions that have limited canker infestations, regulations specify the destruction of infected trees along exposed citrus within a certain distance around the infection sites (http://www.fundecitrus.com.br/english/dtproced_us.html#canker).

Bacterial leaf spot, caused by *Xanthomonas axonopodis* pv. *citrumelo* (previously E-strain or nursery strain citrus canker) was discovered in central Florida 1984 on citrus nursery stock (Schubert *et al.* 2001). Lesions are flat, not raised. The disease diminishes and eventually disappears after infected trees are moved out of the nursery environment. Eradication was attempted due to uncertain etiology of the causal bacterium at the time when the pathogen was first detected. The program destroyed about twenty million citrus plants, almost all small nursery plants, with a total program cost and plant loss value of about $94 million. Research during eradication revealed that pathogen was quite variable, widely distributed in state, and less virulent than the citrus canker pathogen (*X. axonopodis* pv. *citri*), The origin of the citrus bacterial spot pathogen is unknown, and it is still found only in Florida to this day.

Black Pit

Black pit refers to the lesions on fruit caused by *P. syringae* pv. *syringae*. Lesions are small pits, specks, or sunken spots measuring 6-12 mm in diameter and affecting the flavedo and albedo of the fruit (Klotz 1978). The opportunistic pathogen is a normal inhabitant of citrus leaves and is usually not aggressive or virulent; infections start only in injuries and then may enlarge during fruit transit and storage. Lemons are most susceptible to the disease. Since the pathogen is cosmopolitan, specific regulation targeting this disease is largely unwarranted.

Citrus Canker

Asian strain of the canker bacterium (Plate 26) attacks all young developing parts of citrus. Natural hosts are all in the citrus family Rutaceae, most in the subfamily Rutoidae. The lesions start as yellow-white, pinhead-sized eruptions and eventually enlarge and turn tan-brown (Klotz 1978). The margins become water-soaked and have a greasy appearance and are greenish to yellow-brown in color, producing a halo effect. Raised, crater-like lesions on leaves and fruit attain a size of 3-5 mm and are formed with most strains. Sometimes hundreds of lesions form on a single fruit, a condition that often leads to premature fruit drop. Lesions may deform the fruit if infections occur early in fruit development. Fruit lesions do not penetrate the albedo, so juice quality is not affected as long as fruit remain on the tree until ripe. However, postharvest fruit-rotting fungi may enter through large and coalesced canker lesions.

Several distinct groups of the canker causing bacteria have been reported although their appropriate taxonomic placement within the genus *Xanthomonas* is still somewhat controversial. Cancrosis B, or false canker (formerly known as B-strain canker), was discovered on lemon [*Citrus limon* (L.) Burm.f.] in Argentina in 1923 (Brenner *et al.* 2001). The disease occurred primarily on *C. limon* and *C. aurantiifolia*, but also affected *C. aurantium*. Mexican lime cancrosis (formerly known as C-strain canker) was reported in Brazil on Mexican lime (*C. aurantiifolia*) in 1963. Both causal bacteria of the latter diseases produce a very similar canker syndrome on their limited range of citrus hosts and are therefore referred to as *Xanthomo-*

*nas axonopod*is pv. *aurantifolii* (Gabriel *et al.* 1988; Gabriel *et al.* 1989). Vernière *et al.* (1998) designated some strains of the citrus canker bacterium as A* based on their host range restricted naturally to Mexican lime, their physiological and genetic similarities, and their serological difference in comparison with the ACC bacterium. An A strain variant (A^w) was recently discovered in Palm Beach Co., Florida. It is capable of inducing canker symptoms on a restricted range of citrus hosts including Mexican lime and alemow (*C. macrophylla*) (Sun *et al.* 2000; Sun *et al.* 2004).

Safe fresh fruit shipments from areas of endemic citrus canker may be possible if certain precautions are taken. This would include regular surveys and employment of best management practices for disease suppression in the orchard coupled with packinghouse inspection of fruit to insure that no lesioned fruit enter the fresh fruit product stream. Postharvest sanitizing of the symptomless fruits serves as a back-up measure. USDA-APHIS-PPQ recently published a Pest Risk Assessment concluding that safe shipment of fresh citrus fruit from canker endemic areas is achievable (USDA-APHIS 2006).

Several systemic citrus diseases caused by prokaryotes have been identified recently, including Australian Citrus Dieback, Huanglongbing (citrus greening), Stubborn, Citrus Variegated Chlorosis (CVC), and Witches'-Broom. All impact fruit production once introduced to a new area. These diseases are usually transmitted through grafting or via insect vectors and cause symptoms similar to those induced by viruses or nutritional deficiencies. Since the very poor quality fruit on trees infected with these pathogens do not enter the fresh fruit market, there is little concern for pathogen dissemination by this route.

Huanglongbing (Citrus Greening)

Huanglongbing, caused by a phloem-limited, fastidious bacterium, "*Candidatus* Liberibacter spp.," is a highly destructive disease of most citrus cultivars, species, and hybrids, and some citrus relatives. It seriously affects production on the Indian subcontinent and in Asia, Southeast Asia, the Arabian Peninsula, and Africa. The Asian form of the pathogen along with the new American form were recently detected in Brazil (2004), and the Asian form appeared in South Florida in the late summer of 2005 (http://www.pestalert.org/viewArchNewsStory.cfm?nid=353). Young trees infected with the huanglongbing agent die prematurely and infected mature trees soon become nonproductive. Most sweet oranges, mandarins, and mandarin hybrids are severely affected. In general, the characteristic symptoms of trees infected by Asian or African greening bacterium are leaf mottling (normal-green patches on a pale green to yellow background), shoot yellowing, tree stunting, twig dieback with fruit small, poorly colored, and/or lopsided with brownish and aborted seeds. Varieties, tree maturity, time of infection, stage of disease, and other abiotic or biotic agents that affect the tree at the same time can alter this syndrome to some degree. Root systems of diseased trees are poorly developed with relatively few fibrous roots, possibly because of root starvation and phloem degeneration. Where huanglongbing disease is endemic, citrus commonly survives only 6-8 years, and most never bear commercial quantities of fruit (Roistacher 1996).

Three forms of huanglongbing, *Candidatus* Liberobacter *asiaticus* (Asian form). *Candidatus* L. *africanus* (African form), and *Candidatus* L. *americanus* (American form) have been reported and described. Leaf and fruit symptoms caused by the three forms are almost identical, although the Asian and American forms are more severe and devastating, and develop more rapidly in the field. African greening is restricted to cooler climates, and its associated vector (*Trioza erytrea*) does not tolerate very hot temperatures. With African greening, the symptom is very mild under warm conditions (in excess of 1,500 degree hours above 30°C) or may disappear where high summer temperatures prevail. The symptoms of the Asian and American forms are pronounced at both temperatures.

Illegally imported vegetative citrus propagative material is the most likely source of huanglongbing inoculum, however, the disease could theoretically be introduced by way of infected psyllid vectores. Two psyllid species are implicated in the transmission of huanglongbing—*Diaphorina citri* (associated with Asian huanglongbing) and *Trioza erytreae* (associated with African huanglongbing). Both vectors can transmit both strains of the pathogen. In addition to these species, there are a dozen or so obscure species of psyllids associated with citrus (Halbert and Manjunath 2004). None of these obscure species have been implicated in transmission of huanglongbing, but it is doubtful that any have been specifically tested. *D. citri* has been intercepted in significant numbers in unprocessed citrus fruit shipped for processing to Ft. Pierce, FL from the Bahamas (Halbert and Manjunath 2004). Minimal processing such as washing and bagging would be expected to eliminate the risk of transporting psyllids on fresh fruit.

The remote possibility of seed transmission of the greening pathogen (Tirtawijaja 1981) may require some regulations on fresh fruit shipments such that the risk of long distance movement of the huanglongbing pathogen(s) is removed. The study cited was done in Indonesia at a time when modern diagnostic methods for huanglongbing were unavailable, so conclusions are difficult to draw. Seeds usually abort in fruit from huanglongbing-infected trees. Furthermore, the likelihood that infected fruit would enter the fresh fruit product stream is so remote that, combined with the extremely low chance that the pathogen could be seed transmitted, regulation of fruit movement on account of huanglongbing is unwarranted based on currently available information. This topic is discussed further in the section entitled "What To Do About Seed-Transmitted Citrus Pathogens?"

Australian Citrus Dieback

Australian citrus dieback, possibly caused by phytoplasma-like organisms, has so far only been reported in eastern Australia. The causal agent induces symptoms similar to those of huanglongbing. Affected young leaves appear to be chlorotic first, suggestive of zinc or iron deficiency and then develop to irregular blotches with occasional small round spots. Leaf and vein yellowing remain prominent. Fruit of affected grapefruit is small but not distorted, bitter or lopsided as with as with huanglongbing. Fruit size is less affected in sweet orange cultivars. Dieback symptoms have been reported in the field on grapefruit, citron, mandarins, bergamot, sour orange, yuzu, and trifoliate orange. Infected trees remain in a state of chronic and severe decline due to continuous foliage loss, resulting in reduction of fruit production.

The causal agent has not been characterized and attempts to transmit the disease with various potential vectors have been inconclusive. It has been postulated that the vectors are psyllids or planthoppers associated with native Australian flora. These insects are suspected of feeding on irrigated citrus during dry times, thereby transmitting the uncharacterized pathogen from their natural hosts (Broadbent 2000; Broadbent *et al.* 1976) With no direct evidence of fruit or seed transmission, no regulations targeting fresh fruit are warranted.

Stubborn

Stubborn, caused by a helical mollicute *Spiroplasma citri* transmitted by various leafhoppers, is a serious disease primarily of young citrus trees of most citrus species and cultivars as well as a wide range of noncitrus plants. The disease is a serious problem in several hot and dry climates such as California, most of North Africa, the eastern Mediterranean Basin, and the Middle East. Stubborn causes a reduction in the quality and quantity of the yield. In California, USA, the main economic hosts are orange, grapefruit and tangelo, of which 5-10% of trees are estimated to be affected. In the Mediterranean area, stubborn is very serious in some countries, especially in Syria where the leafhopper vector *Neoaliturus haematoceps* is common. In Syria, introduced healthy budwood was rapidly reinfected (Bové 1986). Although *S. citri* naturally infects many other hosts including some crop plants, it is not presently reported to have any economic impact on these. Their main significance would be as reservoirs of *S. citri* for infection of citrus. Though initially quite damaging, horseradish brittle root caused by *S. citri* is now of largely anecdotal interest (Fletcher *et al.* 1981). Many citrus-producing areas in the rest of world (i.e., most of sub-Saharan Africa, Australia, most of South America and eastern Asia) are free from stubborn and from its vectors (although other local leafhoppers possibly could become vectors). *S. citri* should certainly be considered as a quarantine pest for those areas.

Affected trees are more or less stunted. Some susceptible species or cultivars such as orange, grapefruit, mandarin, can be severely stunted. Foliage is dense and abnormally upright. Leaves may be cupped and abnormally thick, and they frequently show variable chlorotic patterns that may resemble those of a nutritional deficiency. A mottled appearance and associated chlorosis of the leaf veins may also be observed. Under very hot conditions, leaves on some shoots may have misshaped, blunted or heart-shaped yellow tips (an important diagnostic character). Shortened shoots, off-season flowering and crop heterogeneity may occur on infected trees. Infected trees produce less and smaller fruit that often are lopsided or acorn-shaped with thickened peel near the stem end and aborted seeds inside. Drastic fruit quality reduction is enough to keep stubborn infected fruit out of the fresh fruit arena, and vectors do not travel with the commercially packed fresh fruit, so specific regulations regarding fresh fruit are unnecessary.

Citrus Variegated Chlorosis (CVC)

Citrus variegated chlorosis, caused by a fastidious, xylem-limited bacterium *Xyllela fastidiosa*, was first noticed and described in 1987 in Brazil and has spread from São Paulo and Minas Gerais to north-eastern Brazil by 1996 (Laranjeira *et al.* 1998), becoming a serious problem in sweet orange production in that area. To date the disease has been reported from Argentina and Paraguay (Timmer *et al.* 2000) and recently from Costa Rica (http://www.agnic.org/agnic/pmp/2005/cvc081505.HTML). The disease affects mostly sweet oranges.

The causal bacterium affects citrus at various ages although young infected trees develop more severe symptoms than mature trees. Affected trees show foliar chlorosis resembling zinc deficiency with interveinal chlorosis. The chlorosis occurring on young leaves persists into maturity. Sectoring of symptoms in the tree canopy can be observed on newly affected trees, whereas a general syndrome of variegated chlorosis usually appears on the trees infected for more than one season. As the leaves mature, small, light-brown to dark-brown, slightly raised gummy lesions appear on the underside of the affected leaves. Affected trees are stunted. Twigs and branches of an infected tree die back and the canopy thins. Affected branches show abnormal flowering and fruit setting. Affected fruit are much smaller than healthy ones, have hard rinds and often are sunburned.

Specific strains of *Xylella fastidiosa* are associated with diseases in many economically important plants, including Pierce's disease of grapevine, plum leaf scald, phony disease of peach, and leaf scorch in oak, almond, sycamore and coffee. On citrus, the variegated chlorosis disease appears to spread from tree to tree within citrus groves. The 9-12 month incubation period before symptoms appear facilitates the spread of infected nursery trees and probably explains the seemingly rapid progress of the disease across Brazil within a decade. The vectors of citrus strains appear to have the same vector group specificity as grapevine strains (suctorial xylem feeders), but transmission trials indicate that vector transmission is much less efficient in citrus compared with grape (Roberto *et al.* 1996).

Citrus-growing countries similarly should prohibit or severely restrict importation of citrus planting material from South America. Peach and other *Prunus* material from a country where the peach or plum strain occurs should come from a reliable certification scheme, with particular emphasis on preventing re-infection of healthy material via the vectors.

Recent reports have shown the possibility of seed transmission of the strain of *Xylella fastidiosa* that causes CVC (Li *et al.* 2003). Historically, citrus seed has been considered the safest means of acquiring pathogen-free citrus propagative material. This may still be the case, but it is certainly not as safe as previously thought. Further discussion of this topic is found in the section entitled "What To Do About Seed-transmitted Citrus Pathogens?"

Fungi

Fungi are the most common pathogens of citrus fruit. However, only four fungal fruit diseases are perceived as risky in fruit commerce because of their limited distribution and destructiveness. They are: 1) the scab complex *(Elsinoe fawcettii*—common scab, *E. australis*—sweet orange scab, and *Sphaceloma fawcettii* var. *scabiosa*—Tyrone's scab); 2) the Alternaria complex; 3) black spot (*Guignardia citricarpa*); and 4) post bloom fruit drop (PBFD) caused by a particular strain of *Colletotrichum acutatum*. Recent research studies, in part instigated because of the regulatory importance of these diseases relative to the commerce in fresh citrus fruit, have helped to clarify the understanding of all four. There is no solid evidence that any of these fungal pathogens have successfully established in a new area having arrived there in or on fresh fruit.

The species of *Phytophthora* that cause brown rot of citrus fruit, as well as citrus root and trunk diseases, are considered to be of worldwide distribution. Hence, brown rot of citrus fruit is generally not specifically regulated in the commerce of citrus fruit. Greasy spot caused by *Mycosphaerella citri* occurs in hot-humid citrus-growing areas and may be subject to some regulatory sanctions by citrus-growing areas that do not have the disease, in spite of the fact that the pathogen does not sporulate on the fruit (Mondal and Timmer 2002). However, the absence of greasy spot on fruit in certain areas is probably due more to poor environmental conditions for disease development than plant exclusionary practices. Melanose, caused by *Diaporthe citri*, occurs in nearly all citrus-growing areas of the world, is most serious in areas where there is plentiful moisture during the formative stages of fruit and leaf development, and is the prime factor in lowering the grade of fruit in Florida (Klotz 1978). Despite the pathogen's effect on the fruit, it is not generally regulated with quarantine rigor because of its worldwide distribution. Moreover, melanose lesions on the fruit do not readily yield the fungus upon culturing in the laboratory nor are they a source of inoculum for further fruit or foliage infections (Knorr 1973). Lime anthracnose is a bud-blasting, fruit-spotting, shoot-killing disease of Mexican (Key) lime caused by *Colletotrichum acutatum* (*Gloeosporium limetticola*). In the U.S., this pathogen, along with cold weather, limits where Mexican limes can be commercially productive. The pathogen is probably widely distributed, has a limited host range, and is generally not regulated.

Sooty molds, while unsightly and a problem in citrus packing plants, are ubiquitous and are usually not damaging; but they do indicate the presence of insects. Many fungi that cause postharvest decay of fruit such as *Penicillium digitatum*, *P. italicum*, *Geotrichum candidum*, *Phomopsis citri*, and *Diplodia natalensis*, while potentially destructive to fruit in transit and storage, are widely distributed and are not regulated as quarantine pests.

Citrus Scab Diseases

Elsinoe australis and *E. fawcetti* cause scablike lesions on citrus fruit, leaves, and stems. Four pathotypes of *E. fawcettii* are now recognized based on host range: Florida Broad Host Range, Florida Narrow Host Range, Tyron's, and Lemon (Timmer *et al.* 1996; Tan *et al.* 1996).

Sour orange scab, a.k.a. common scab, is widely distributed in Asia, South Africa, the South Pacific, the Gulf Coast states of the United States, the West Indies, and South America. Common scab pathotypes do not seem to establish well in Mediterranean climates or in hot, dry climates; disease development is apparently favored in hot-humid climates. The diseases are most severe on sour orange (*C. aurantium*), lemon (*C. limon*), Temple orange (*C. reticulata* hybrid), calamondin (× *Citrofortunella mitis*), and tangelo (*C. reticulata* × *C.* × *paradisi);* it is less severe on grapefruit, Tahiti lime, and mandarin varieties *(C. reticulata).* It occurs only rarely on some sweet oranges and does not occur on citron (*C. medica*) and most kumquats (*Fortunella* spp.). The Tyron's scab pathotype of common scab occurs on lemons, satsumas (*C. reticulata*), tangerines (*C. reticulata*), and sweet and sour oranges (Klotz 1978) in Australia, New Zealand, New Caledonia, New Guinea, Sri Lanka, Zimbabwe, South Africa, and Argentina (Knorr 1973).

Sweet orange scab caused by *Elsinoe australis* is limited to South America and Sicily, and is most severe on sweet oranges and mandarins. In Sicily, it occurs on lemon fruit growing in shaded areas. Florida does not yet have sweet orange scab, and embargoes are enforced to maintain this status. Introduction and establishment of this pathogen in Florida might lead to a loss in fruit quality, plant quality, and fresh fruit market.

The lesions of Tyron's scab pathotype of common scab and sweet orange scab on citrus fruit are more rounded and less spongy than those of typical common orange scab and can become so numerous as to cover the fruit surface with a corky layer of buff-to-black eruptions. Fortunately, all pathotypes of scab can be controlled by timely applications of fungicides (Klotz 1978).

The *Alternaria* Complex

Apparently several species of *Alternaria* (not yet formally named with consensus) are capable of causing blemishes on the peel of citrus fruit, thus posing some theoretical regulatory concerns for fresh fruit in the channels of commerce. The diseases are especially troublesome on mandarins and their hybrids and on lemons, fruits that are usually marketed and consumed fresh. Recent research into the genetic differences of the various Alternaria pathogens from the United States, South Africa, Australia, Israel, Turkey and Columbia have concluded that: 1) based on phylogenetic analysis of protein-coding genes, there are perhaps three distinct species now included in *Alternaria alternata* (*A. citri*) isolates; 2) that there can be much variability even within single orchards in the pathogenic *Alternaria* spp. found there; 3) that virulence does not necessarily coincide with the distinct clades possibly representing the three separate species; and 4) that toxin production appears to be linked with virulence (Peever *et al.* 2002). Though the lesions are unsightly and generally disqualify fruit for the fresh market, *Alternaria*-induce peel blemishes do not warrant fresh fruit regulatory measures because sporulation of the pathogen does not occur from these lesions (Timmer *et al.* 2000).

Black Spot

Guignardia citricarpa Kiely is a fungal pathogen of great importance in South Africa, Australia, Taiwan, China (Klotz 1978) New Zealand, and South America (Timmer *et al.* 2000). Losses exceeding 80% of the orange crop have been reported in Australia. Black spot is not known to occur in citrus groves in the Mediterranean basin or in North America (Klotz 1978). Embargoes have limited its spread to citrus in noninfested areas. Unfavorable weather conditions during the period of fruit susceptibility may have also limited its spread into all citrus areas (Klotz 1978). All commercial varieties of citrus are susceptible.

Citrus black spot is a fruit disease that affects the rind of citrus fruit but does not cause internal decay. Heavy infection near the pedicel of the developing fruit may lead to premature fruit drop. Losses may be substantial because affected fruits are no longer suited for the fresh fruit market, and yield losses and costs for chemical control can be significant. The pathogen is subject to phytosanitary legislation in the Europe Union and the United States.

There are four types of fruit spots in the black spot syndrome (Klotz 1978): 1) the 'speckled blotch', type, which has lesions that are gummy and raised and which may appear on immature fruit if high temperatures prevail for 5-6 months after blossoming; 2) the common black-edged 'hard spots' which may appear on maturing oranges and young lemons; 3) the small reddish-brown 'freckle spots', which develop on mature fruit; and 4) the 'virulent spots', which are not delimited and may cover much of the fruit surface on harvested fruit and occasionally on mature fruit on the tree if temperatures are high. The fungus infects only young tissues and remains dormant until temperatures reach about 21°C. It is for this reason that symptoms often develop only after harvest; their sudden appearance during transit or at the market can cause considerable loss.

The formerly confusing *Guignardia* picture on citrus in which a "non-pathogenic form" of *Guignardia citricarpa* frequently held up shipments of fresh fruit was recently resolved using molecular diagnostic techniques. The non-pathogenic form is now properly recognized as *Guignardia mangiferae*, a weak pathogen that occasionally inhabits citrus tissues but has no regulatory significance (Baayen *et al.* 2002; Bonants *et al.* 2003).

Post Bloom Fruit Drop (PBFD)

This fungal disease (PBFD) caused by a particular strain of *Colletotrichum acutatum* is a relative newcomer, first appearing in Belize in 1979, and now present throughout the humid citrus production areas of the Americas (Timmer *et al.* 1994). Recall that this is the same genus and species of the Key lime anthracnose pathogen. The pathogen has caused locally severe outbreaks three times in Florida (1988, 1993, and 1998), and remains at a low level in some areas. The fungus is active in blighting the flowers during wet weather bloom periods. Infection interferes with fruit set, after which time the pathogen goes dormant for the remainder of the growing season. However, it is possible to have quiescent appressoria of the pathogen formed on fruits that do successfully form in spite of the substantial yield losses due to the flower blight phase of the disease. It is these dormant appressoria that can be stimulated back to sporulation by exposure to petal extracts that, at least theoretically, present a regulatory problem for fresh fruit movement (Timmer *et al.* 1998). Negotiations between Florida (where PBFD is established in certain areas) and Australia (which has *Colletotrichum acutatum* but not the specific PBFD strain) are proceeding with mitigation efforts directed at harvesting fruit in areas where PBFD is not active based on surveys, and sending fruit through proper packinghouse procedures to minimize the risk of viable appressoria remaining on the fruit. This disease emphasizes again the need for taxonomic skills at the subspecific level in order to correctly identify the pathogen.

Viruses and Virus-Like Agents

Viruses and virus-like agents cause or are suspected of causing more than 30 diseases of citrus (Wallace 1978). Economic losses in citrus production attributable directly to these agents are difficult to establish because they frequently do not kill the tree but can cause the following effects: decline, reduced growth, reduced yield, and reduced fruit size, weight, and quality. In addition to these effects, infected trees are weakened and made more susceptible to stresses from weather, soil conditions, insects, and other pathogens. The most devastating loss of citrus directly attributable to a viral cause occurred in Brazil following World War II. Salibe (1973) estimated that over 12 million citrus trees that were budded on sour orange rootstock succumbed to tristeza virus (CTV) that was introduced into Brazil on infected nursery stock from other countries. Valiela (1959) estimated 10 million citrus trees were killed in neighboring Argentina at about the same time. A similar outbreak called citrus sudden death is taking place now in South American citrus. Although the exact etiology is unknown, some believe a new strain of CTV is responsible that can cause serious problems on the Rangpur lime and rough lemon rootstocks that were widely used in the wake of the post-WW II era (Bassanezi *et al.* 2003; Roman *et al.* 2004). Others (Maccheroni *et al.* 2005) have reported a new *Marafivirus* associated with the syndrome.

Even though infectious viruses can be recovered from fruit having certain virus or virus-like diseases, such as psorosis (Bridges *et al.* 1965) and stubborn (a phytoplasma) (Wallace 1978), the movement of fresh citrus fruit is not believed to be associated with the spread of these pathogens. This is especially true if stems and leaves are removed from the fruit and if the fruit have been graded for commercial export markets (i.e., are essentially blemish-free). Therefore, commercial fruit movement is usually not regulated even though viruses or virus-like agents may be present in fruit tissues. Citrus yellow mosaic virus could move on fruit infested with the mealybug vector (*Plancoccus citri*) (Baranwal *et al.* 2005), though the vector status of the mealybug is now in question http://www.eppo.org/QUARANTINE/virus/Citrus_mosaic_virus/CIMV00_ds.pdf). On the other hand, as was stated earlier in other contexts, the movement of citrus plants and citrus bud wood is very strictly regulated because these are the principal means by which citrus viruses, virus-like agents and other pathogens are spread. Regulators need more research on the possible fruit or seed transmission of these disease agents. Our assumptions on non-transmission need to be replaced by solid research data. Guerri *et al.* (2004) recently reported seed transmission of Citrus leaf blotch virus (CLBV) at levels around 2.5% in citrange, kumquat and sour orange seedlings, prompting reconsideration of seed importation regulations for citrus rootstock production. Further discussion of this topic is given in the section entitled "What To Do About Seed-transmitted Citrus Pathogens?"

CERTIFICATION PROCEDURES FOR CITRUS FRUITS

Much of the world's citrus is shipped in spite of the occasional pest that may accompany otherwise healthy-appearing fruit. No threat is apparently perceived. What difference would a few canker-infested fruits make in a market in Norway? Probably none. But if the place of introduction was canker-free Orange County, California, the reaction would be much different because citrus is grown there, even though the climate may be quite inhospitable to establishment of the disease. If a citrus fruit pest occurs somewhere and a threat is perceived, an embargo on citrus fruit and other produce may be the result. To be sure, embargoes limit trade, but in the process they also effectively protect any threatened crops. Fortunately, regulatory procedures less stringent than embargoes often can satisfy the objective of assuring freedom from pests without greatly impeding trade. Systems approaches with several pest-reducing measures taken collectively are becoming increasingly useful.

The official document indicating that plant materials are pest-free is called a phytosanitary certificate. Certification implies that certain regulatory procedures were followed that assure reasonable and specified pest freedom. Thus, the objective of an embargo has been accomplished, and the fruit consignment can be moved. Certification is the written, legal endpoint of a pre-arranged agreement between governments of exporting and importing countries or states. In essence, representatives of the noninfested, threatened importing country require safeguards; authorized agricultural representatives at the place of origin agree to meet those certification requirements.

Preclearance

Phytosanitary Certification can be based upon the apparent absence of a pest in a geographic area during citrus production and/or packing. Information gained by preclearance methods may periodically change certification requirements.

Ground Surveys. Systematic and repeated ground surveys of commercial, nursery-based, and dooryard citrus can be used to determine the occurrence and distribution of pests in a production area. Survey crews should be well-trained in recognizing any departure from normal citrus appearance during inspection, and specifically trained in the syndromes and life cycles of citrus pests. Accomplished surveyors accompanied by competent diagnostic laboratory personnel, both significant investments, are absolutely essential to successful regulatory programs, regardless of the agricultural commodity.

Trapping. Various insect traps are placed throughout areas of citriculture and are periodically monitored for target pests. Many types of traps are in common usage to lure and trap citrus fruit insects. Traps are baited with sexual attractants, chemical attractants, food, insect-attractive colors, and insect-attractive lights combined with sticky, trapping substances. Some lures are more successful than others for certain insects. For example, the oriental fruit fly (*B. dorsalis*) is effectively lured to a sex attractant, but such an efficient sex attractant for the Caribbean fruit fly (*A. suspensa*) is not presently available. A very successful protocol to insure fresh fruit is free of Caribbean fruit fly has been used for many years in Florida (Simpson 1993).

Growing Practices. The planting of resistant varieties, the absence of alternate hosts, and the use of buffer (citrus-free) zones may significantly diminish pest populations and become part of the certification requirements.

Packinghouse Requirements and Inspections. The removal of stems and foliage during the packing procedure may fully or partially meet certain certification requirements for many pests. Inspections for specific pests can also occur in the packinghouse.

Product Treatment

Phytosanitary Certification can be based upon the apparent absence of the pest after various treatments to eliminate the pest. These treatments can occur before, during, or after fruit movement.

Chemical. At present, the most common method to certify large shipments of citrus fruit from an insect-infested area is to treat with a chemical. Shipments of citrus fruit from Florida to Japan must be certified free from the Caribbean fruit fly. In 1971, this requirement was met primarily by fumigating fruit with ethylene dibromide (EDB); some 6 million boxes per year were treated. However, recommendations by the Environmental Protection Agency limited the use of EDB for produce fumigation after September I, 1984. Other major chemicals used for fumigation are methyl bromide and hydrogen cyanide (HCN). Ethylene dibromide is effective for pests within the fruit, such as egg and larval stages; methyl bromide is effective for both surface and internal pests; but HCN is effective against surface pests only. Sodium hypochlorite and sodium orthophenylphenate (SOPP) are used to effectively eliminate the citrus canker bacterium from the surface of symptomless fruits (Brown and Schubert, 1987). However, there presently is no known effective chemical *eradicant* for canker, or any other citrus fruit pathogen, once the disease has become established in its host.

Controlled Environment. Both heating and cooling of fruit can be used to eliminate some insect pests. Careful temperature control is vital for such treatments to be both efficacious and not harmful to the produce. For example, Caribbean fruit fly can be eliminated from many citrus fruits by maintaining pulp temperatures of 1°C for 14 days. However, grapefruit are subject to cold injury at 4°C or below and may require a period of preconditioning at 13°-15°C prior to treatment. The larvae of Mediterranean fruit fly (*Ceratitis capitata*) and South American fruit fly (*Anastrepha fraterculus*) can be eliminated from citrus fruit by cold treatment at 2 ± 0.5°C and 90% RH for 16 and 10 days respectively, providing the basis for a quarantine treatment (http://www.aphis.usda.gov/ppq/manuals/port/Treatment_Chapters.htm) Heat treatments (both dry and wet) are often used alone and in combination with chemical treatments. Such controlled environmental procedures will become more commonplace as chemical treatments become unavailable. At present, their cost makes them prohibitive.

Other Methods. Gamma radiation, sound waves, and microwaves are currently being tested for their effectiveness in eliminating pests from citrus fruit. Practical applications are not yet available. Some consumers perceive gamma radiation as an undesirable method of fruit treatment. Other radiation sources perhaps would be more acceptable to the consuming public.

Entry Requirements and Inspection

Phytosanitary certification can be based upon fulfilling certain requirements before the fruit enter an area for further distribution.

Because ports are high-risk areas for pest introduction, certification often requires that citrus fruit consignments arrive at ports far removed from citriculture or other areas where the pest might become established. Further, fruit consignments may be allowed to move only to certain areas of a country where the pest is not likely to become established. Requirements concerning ports of entry and produce distribution are established cooperatively between the areas of export and import.

At or near the port of entry, consignments can be inspected to verify the completion of certification procedures for pests, and various product treatments can be applied to destroy any pest infestations.

Certification Examples

Regulatory procedures for certification range from simple to complex. A summary of USDA approved phytosanitary commodity treatments is available at http://ecfr.gpoaccess.gov/cgi/t/text/text-idx?c=ecfr&sid=15cc fdef133249d6b2269160c1c98b43&tpl=/ecfrbrowse/Title07/7cfr305_main_02.tpl. A product treatment procedure, ethylene dibromide fumigation, was previously used to eliminate egg and larval stages of fruit flies and other insect pests from fruit. This product treatment exemplified a widely used, simple, one-step certification procedure that is no longer acceptable due to environmental and toxicity concerns. However, the certification requirements for other citrus fruit pests often involve the integration of many procedures, as the following two examples illustrate.

http://www.aphis.usda.gov/ppq/manuals/port/pdf_files/20Fruits_and_Vegetables.pdf

1. In order for Japanese shippers to certify that their U.S. consignments of Unshiu orange (*C. unshiu*) are free of citrus pests, a number of steps including pre-clearance inspections, fumigation, limited distribution in the U.S. are utilized (http://www.aphis.usda.gov/ppq/enviro_docs/pdf_files/unshuea.pdf).

2. With the detection of citrus canker in Florida and the abandonment of the eradication effort in early 2006, an Emergency Action Notification Attachment specifying where harvesting could take place in relation to known canker outbreaks was used to make certain citrus fruit are canker-free (http://www.doacs.state.fl.us/onestop/forms/08359.pdf and http://www.doacs.state.fl.us/pi/canker/schedules.html).

USDA recently unveiled for comment a Pest Risk Assessment to allow surface sanitized, symptomless citrus fruit to enter the fresh fruit market without destination restrictions (http://www.aphis.usda.gov/about_aphis/printable_version/06-045-1_PRA_032006.pdf). Provisions devised to safen the movement of fresh fruit from canker endemic areas of the U.S. in interstate and international commerce will also apply to foreign citrus producers desiring access to the U.S. market.

WHAT TO DO ABOUT SEED-TRANSMITTED CITRUS PATHOGENS?

As mentioned in some previous sections, new information is emerging to indicate that several serious citrus diseases of limited geographic distribution are capable of seed transmission. Among those are citrus greening (huanglongbing) (Tirtawidjaja 1981), citrus variegated chlorosis (Li *et al.* 2003), and citrus leaf blotch virus (Guerri *et al.* 2004). Whereas the risks of seed transmission historically have been regarded as too small to be a factor in fresh fruit import-export matters, the stakes are gradually getting higher and higher. Of course the greatest concerns lie within the context of acquiring pathogen-free propagation material. It is no longer possible to assume automatically that citrus propagative material in seed form is pathogen-free. But seed necessarily travel with imported citrus fruit marketed for fresh consumption, too. Granted, export quality fruit is not as likely to be infected, and most of that seed never has the opportunity for germination. Still, with increasing emphasis on composting (usually minimal) and recycling of kitchen food wastes at the household or at the community level, the possibility of infected volunteer citrus seedlings presents a small unquantified danger. Many commercial citrus production areas now prohibit any propagation of citrus other than that which is done under the auspices of the state and/or federal plant health regulatory agency. No easy solution to this new problem is obvious. Two suggested methods of safening the importation of fresh citrus from areas where these seed-transmitted diseases are established might be restricting shipments to fruit from surveyed and apparently disease-free areas, or perhaps restricting export to only "seedless" citrus varieties.

SUMMARY

Governmental regulations placed upon citrus produce that harbors or may harbor potential citrus pests are intended to limit further distribution of these pests. It is evident that non-citrus produce will also be subject to regulation should this produce harbor potential citrus pests. Obviously, the most effective method of limiting pest distribution is to limit the distribution of produce. However, because embargoes infringe upon trade, other procedures (specified by certification requirements) have been developed that meet the pest freedom objectives of the regulations.

A challenging task facing regulatory agencies is the development of alternatives to pesticide fumigation treatments. Where applicable, cold treatment of citrus fruit will probably become more commonplace. In Florida, establishment of Caribbean fruit fly-free areas by the use of intensive, high-density insect trapping procedures and freedom from preferred hosts has proven very effective and workable (http://www.doacs.state.fl.us/onestop/plt/cfffprotocol.html and http://www.doacs.state.fl.us/pi/plantinsp/docs/cff-pestmanagement.pdf).

Another set of challenges that face regulatory agencies in their quest to keep commerce safe are: 1) the ability to reliably and quickly detect introduced pests early in their establishment period; 2) the ability to implement certification procedures to ensure pest freedom on the commodity while taking regulatory action against the pest; 3) and the eradication of pests if possible. Mandatory budwood indexing programs in Florida and California insure that new citrus plantings get a clean start and discourage illegal movement of propagation materials. A joint federal-state perpetual citrus surveillance program has been implemented in Florida in the wake of the latest citrus canker introduction into Florida, the third successful establishment in the past century (http://www.doacs.state.fl.us/pi/chrp/index.html and http://www.aphis.usda.gov/ppq/pdmp/citrushealth/). The program targets citrus health in general, not just citrus canker. A Citrus Sentinel Program that targets well-distributed and accessible sentinel citrus trees in residential areas recognizes the increasing likelihood that well-traveled citizens will occasionally arrive home with unintended companions. The sentinel program coupled with annual statewide citrus surveys in commercial areas are reasonable steps to insure that all citrus areas are examined for all pests and diseases routinely. Further assessments of aerial surveillance technology with hyperspectral imaging in concert with robotic or human ground surveys using animal or mechanical "sniffers" for unique volatile signals are underway and may soon become reality. Eradication and management techniques can be fine-tuned based on more precise knowledge of pest whereabouts and population levels.

Identification methods supporting regulatory actions must be capable of adapting to the drastic conceptual changes that are taking place in systematics. Likewise, regulations must be flexible enough to quickly accommodate new information on pest biology and pest systematics and still remain legally enforceable. The time has already come to regulate not just diseases and infestations, but the causal agents before they begin to cause damage. This will require the technology to discern dead from live pests. Even more progressive is the idea that certain gene sequences may require regulation, regardless of the genetic context or organism in which they reside. Though expensive, gene/DNA array technology and other similar molecular methods are emerging as the methods of choice to accomplish these goals rapidly and accurately.

Regardless of methods used, continuous monitoring and study of exotic plant pests is still essential, perhaps even more important in modern times of unprecedented emphasis on free trade zones and world trade in agricultural commodities. Improved capabilities in pest and disease detection all the way from propagation to production, from harvesting through packing, all the way to the destination are certainly welcome. As in all other scientific arenas, it seems that greater knowledge of the biology of plant pests and their detection in the environment only spawn ever more detailed and complex questions in our attempts to regulate intelligently the movement of plant products while minimizing the risk of pest dispersal.

Finally, it should be recognized that some regulated pests cause very little or no damage to citrus where they occur, but they legitimately may be perceived as threats elsewhere. Regulatory costs sometimes exceed actual pest damage in their native locale; initially, such costs must be borne by the producers. However, with most pests, there are both economic and regulatory consequences to having the infestation.

REFERENCES

ALUJA, M., PEREZ-STAPLES, D., MACIAS-ORDONEZ, R., PINERO, J., McPHERON, B. and HERNANDEZ-ORTIZ, V. 2003. Nonhost status of *Citrus sinensis* cv. Valencia and *C. paradisi* (sic) cv, Ruby Red to Mexican *Anastrepha fraterculus* (Diptera: Tephritidae). J. Economic Entomology 96, 1693-1703.

ANAGNOSTAKIS, S. L. 2000. Revitalization of the majestic chestnut: Chestnut blight disease. APSNet feature article, http://www.apsnet.org/online/feature/chestnut/

BAAYEN, R. P., BONANTS, P. J. M., VERKLEY, G., CARROLL, G. C., VAN DER AA, H. A., DE WEERDT, M., VAN BROUWERSHAVEN, I. R., SCHUTTE, G. C., MACCHERONI, W., JR., GLIENKE DE BLANCO, C. and AZEVEDO, J. L. 2002. Nonpathogenic isolates of the citrus black spot fungus, *Guignardia citricarpa*, identified as a cosmopolitan endophyte of woody plants, *G. mangiferae* (*Phyllosticta capitalensis*). Phytopathology 92, 464-477.

BAKER, A. C., W. E. STONE, C. C. PLUMMER, and M. McPHAIL. 1944. A review of studies on the Mexican fruitfly and related Mexican species. U.S. Dept. Agric. Misc. Publ. 531.

BARANWAL, V. K., SINGH, J., AHLAWAT, Y. S., GOPAL, K. and CHARAYA, M. U. 2005. Citrus yellow mosaic virus is associated with mosaic disease in Rangpur lime rootstock of citrus. Current Science 89, 1596-1599.

BASSANEZI, R. B., BERGAMIN FILHO, A., AMORIM, L., GIMENES-FERNANDES, N., GOTTWALD, T. R. and BOVÉ, J. M. 2003. Spatial and temporal analyses of Citrus Sudden Death as a tool to generate hypotheses concerning its etiology. Phytopathology 93, 502-512.

BONANTS, P. J. M., CARROLL, G. C., DE WEERDT, M., VAN BROUWERSHAVEN, I. R. and BAAYEN, R. R. 2003. Development and validation of a fast PCR-based detection method for pathogenic isolates of the citrus black spot pathogen, *Guignardia citricarpa*. European Journal of Plant Pathology 109, 503-513.

BOVÉ, J. M. 1986. Stubborn and its natural transmission in the Mediterranean area and in the Near East. FAO Plant Protection Bulletin 34, 15-23.

BRENNER, D. J., STALEY, J. T. and KRIEG, N. R. 2001. Classification of procaryotic organisms and the concept of bacterial speciation. *In* Bergey's Manual of Systematic Bacteriology, Vol. 1, 2nd Ed., D. R. Boone, and R. W. Castenholz (Editors); G. M. Garrity (Editor-in-Chief). Springer, New York, Berlin, and Heidelberg.

BRIDGES, G. D., YOUTSEY, C. O. and NIXON, R. R. 1965. Observations indicating psorosis transmissions by seed of Carrizo citrange. Proc. Fla. State Hort. Soc. 78, 48-50.

BROADBENT, P. FRASER, L. R. and McGECHAN, J. 1976. Australian citrus dieback. pp. 141-146. *In* Proc. 7th Conf. Int. Organization Citrus Virologists (IOCV), E. C. Calavan (Editor). University of California, Riverside.

BROADBENT, P. 2000. Australian citrus dieback. *In* Compendium of Citrus Diseases, second edition, L. W. Timmer, S. M. Garnsey, and J. H. Graham (Editors). APS Press, St. Paul, MN.

BROWN, G. E. and SCHUBERT, T. S. 1987. Use of *Xanthomonas campestris* pv. *vesicatoria* to evaluate surface disinfectants for canker quarantine treatment of citrus fruits. Plant Disease 71, 319-323.

CAB INTERNATIONAL. 2005. Crop Protection Compendium, 2005 Edition.Wallingford, UK. CAB International. www.cabicompendium.org/cpc

CALIFORNIA OAK MORTALITY TASK FORCE. 2006. http://nature.berkeley.edu/comtf/html/p__ramorum_overview.html

CLARK, R. A., STECK, G. J. and WEEMS, H. V., JR. 1996. Detection, quarantine, and eradication of fruit flies in Florida. *In* Pest Management in the Subtropics: Integrated Pest Management—A Florida Perspective, D. Rosen, F. D. Bennett, and J. L. Capinera (Editors). Intercept Ltd., Andover, UK.

COOK, A. A. 1988. Association of citrus canker pustules with leaf miner tunnels in North Yemen. Plant Disease 73, 546.

DOPSON, R. N. 1964. The eradication of citrus canker. Plant Dis. Rep. 48, 30-31.

EBELING, W. 1959. Subtropical fruit pests. Division of Plant Sciences, University of California, Berkeley.

EDWARDS, G. B. 1995. Thrips (Thysanoptera) new to Florida: II Thripidae: Thripinae (*Psydrothrips, Asprothrips*). Fla. Dept. Agr. Consumer Serv., Div. Plant Ind. Entomology Circ. 371.

ELKINTON, J. and LIEBHOLD, A. 1990. Population dynamics of gypsy moth in North America. Ann. Rev. Entomology 35, 571-596.

ENKERLIN, D., L. GARCIA R. and F. LOPEZ M. 1989. Taxonomy and zoogeography. Chapter 2.7 Mexico, Central and South America. pp. 83-90 *In* Robinson, A. S. & G. Hooper. 1989. Fruit flies. Their biology, natural enemies, and control. W. Helle (Editor). World crop pests, Vol. 3(A), xii + 372 p., and Vol. 3(B), xv + 447 p. Elsevier, Amsterdam.

FEDERAL REGISTER 2006. Proposed Rules: Special needs requests under the Plant Protection Act. 7 CFR Part 301. Docket No. APHIS-2005-0103, RIN 0579-AB98. Federal Register 71, 16711-16716 (Tuesday, April 4, 2006).

FLETCHER, J., SCHULTZ, G. A., DAVIS, R. E., EASTMAN, C. E., and GOODMAN, R. M. 1981. Brittle root disease of horseradish: evidence for and etiological role of *Spiroplasma citri*. Phytopathology 71, 1073-1080.

FOSTER, J. A. 1991. Exclusion of plant pests by inspections, certifications and quarantines. pp. 311-338. *In* CRC Handbook of Pest Management in Agriculture, 2nd Edition. D. Pimentel (Editor). CRC Press, Inc., Boca Raton, FL.

GABRIEL, D. W., HUNTER, J. E., KINGSLEY, M. T., MILLER, J. W. and LAZO, G. R. 1988. Clonal population structure of *Xanthomonas campestris* and genetic diversity among citrus canker strains. Mol. Plant-Microbe Interact. 1, 59-65.

GABRIEL, D. W., KINGSLEY, M. T., HUNTER, J. E., and GOTTWALD, T. R. 1989. Reinstatement of *Xanthomonas citri* (ex Hasse) and *X. phaseoli* (ex Smith) to species, and reclassification of all *X. campestris* pv. *citri* strains. Int. J. Systematic Bacteriology 39, 14-22.

GOTTWALD, T. R., GRAHAM, J. H. and SCHUBERT, T. S. 1997. An epidemiological analysis of the spread of citrus canker in urban Miami, Florida, and synergistic interaction with the Asian citrus leaf miner. Fruits 52, 371-378.

GOTTWALD, T. R., GRAHAM, J. H. and SCHUBERT, T. S. 2002. Citrus canker: The pathogen and its impact. On line http://www.apsnet.org/online/feature/citruscanker/

GUERRI, J., PINA, J. A., VIVES, M. C., NAVARRO, L., and MORENO, P. 2004. Seed transmission of Citrus leaf blotch virus: Implications in quarantine and certification programs. Plant Disease 88, 906.

HAACK, R. A., JENDEK, E., LIU, H-P., MARCHANT, K. R., PETRICE, T. R., POLAND, T. M., and YE, H. 2002. The emerald ash borer: a new exotic pest in North America. Newsletter of the Michigan Entomological Soc. 47(3-4), 1-5.

HALBERT, S. E., EVANS, G. A., and CLINTON, D. C. 1998. Establishment of *Toxoptera citricida* in Florida. *In* Aphids in Natural and Managed Ecosystems. J. M. Nieto Nafria and A. F. G. Dixon (Editors). Universidad de Leon (Secretariado de Publicaciones). Leon, Spain.

HALBERT, S. E. and MANJUNATH, K. L. 2004. Asian citrus psyllids (Sternorrhyncha: Psyllidae) and greening disease of citrus: a literature review and assessment of risk in Florida. Fla. Entomologist 8, 330-353.

HANCOCK, D. L. 1984. Ceratitinae (Diptera: Tephritidae) from the Malagasy subregion. J. Ent. Soc. Southern Africa 47, 277-301.

HEDLEY, J. 1999. Procedures for the settlement of disputes concerning phytosanitary measures. OEPP/EPPO Bulletin 29, 11-21.

HEPPNER, J. P. 1993. Citrus leafminer, *Phyllocnistis citrella*, in Florida. Tropical Lepidoptera 4, 49-64.

HERNÁNDEZ, J. R., PALM, M. E., and CASTLEBURY, L. A. 2002. *Puccinia hemerocallidis*, cause of daylily rust, a newly introduced disease in the Americas. Plant Dis. 86, 1194-1198.

JONES, D. R. 2003. Plant viruses transmitted by whiteflies. European Journal of Plant Pathology 109, 195-219.

KLOTZ, L. J. 1978. Fungal, bacterial, and nonparasitic diseases and injuries originating in the seedbed, nursery, and orchard. *In* The Citrus Industry, Volume IV. W. Reuther, E. C. Calavan, and G. E. Carman (Editors). University of California, Berkeley.

KNORR, L. C. 1973. Citrus diseases and disorders. University of Florida Presses, Gainesville.

LARANJEIRA, F. F., BERGAMIN FILHO, A., and AMORIM, L. 1998. Dynamics and structure of citrus variegated chlorosis (CVC) foci. Fitopatologia Brasileira 23, 36-41.

LI, W.-B, PRIA, JR., W. D., LACAVA, P. M., QIN, X., and HARTUNG, J. S. 2003. Presence of *Xylella fastidiosa* in sweet orange fruit and seeds and its transmission to seedlings. Phytopathology 93, 953-958.

LOUCKS, K. W. 1934. Citrus Canker and its Eradication in Florida. Archives Fla. Dept. Agr. Consumer Serv., Div. Plant Ind. Gainesville.

MACCHERONI, W., ALEGRIA, M. C., GREGGIO, C. C., PIAZZA, J. P., KAMLA, R. F., ZACHARIAS, P. R. A., BAR-JOSEPH, M., KITAJIMA, E. W., ASSUMPCÃO, L. C., CAMAROTTE, G., CARDOZA, J., CASAGRANDE, E. C., FERRARI, F., FRANCO, S. F., GIACHETTO, P. F., GIRASOL, A., JORDÃO, JR., H., SILVA, V. H. A., SOUZA, L. C. A., AGUILAR-VILDOSO, C. I., ZANCA, A. S., ARRUDA, P., KITAJAMA, J. P., REINACH, F. C., FERRO, J. A. and DA SILVA, A. C. R. 2005. Indentification and genomic characterization of a new virus (*Tymoviridae* Family) associated with citrus sudden death disease. Journal of Virology 79, 3028-3037. http://jvi.asm.org/cgi/reprint/79/5/3028

MALOY, O. C. 2001. White pine blister rust. Online. Plant Health Progress doi:10.1094/PHP-2001-0924-01-HM.

MARSHALL, D., WORK, T. T., and CAVEY, J. F. 2003. Invasion pathways of Karnal bunt of wheat into the United States. Plant Disease 87, 999-1003.

MATHYS, G. and BAKER, E. A. 1980. An appraisal of the effectiveness of quarantines. Annual Review of Phytopathology 18, 85-101.

McCUBBIN, W. A. 1954. The plant quarantine problem. Ann. Cryptogam. Phytopathology, Vol. XI.

McCULLOUGH, D. G., and D. L. ROBERTS. 2002. Emerald ash borer. Pest Alert, USDA Forest Serv. State and Private Forestry Northeastern Area. NA-PR-07-02.

McGREGOR, R. C. 1978. People-placed pathogens: the emigrant pests. *In* Plant Disease: An Advanced Treatise, Vol. II. J. G. Horsfall and E. B. Cowling (Editors). Academic Press, New York.

MONDAL, S. N. and TIMMER, L. W. 2002. Environmental factors affecting pseudothecial development and ascospore production of *Mycosphaerella citri*, the cause of citrus greasy spot. Phytopathology 92, 1267-1275.

NAPPO PHYTOSANITARY ALERT SYSTEM. 2006A. *Phytophthora hedraiandra*. http://www.pestalert.org/viewNewsAlert.cfm?naid=4

NAPPO PHYTOSANITARY ALERT SYSTEM. 2006B. *Phytophthora tropicalis*. http://www.pestalert.org/viewNewsAlert.cfm?naid=14

NAPPO PHYTOSANITARY ALERT SYSTEM. 2006C. USDA confirms gladiolus rust, *Uromyces transversalis*, in Florida. http://www.pestalert.org/oprDetail.cfm?oprID=198

PEEVER, T. L., IBAÑEZ, A., AKIMITSU, K., and TIMMER, L. W. 2002. Worldwide phylogeography of the citrus brown spot pathogen, *Alternaria alternata*. Phytopathology 92, 794-802.

POWELL, M. R. 2002. A model for probabilistic assessment of phytosanitary risk reduction measures. Plant Disease 86, 552-557.

ROBERTO, S. R., LIMA, J. E. D., MIRANDA, V. S., COUTINHO, A., and CARLOS, E. F. 1996. Transmissio de *Xylella fastidiosa* pelas cigarrinhas *Acrogonia terminalis, Dilobopterus costalamai*, e *Oncometopia facialis* (Hemiptera: Cicadellidae) en citros. Fitopatologia Brasiliera 21, 517-518.

ROHWER, G. G. 1991. Regulatory plant pest management, pp. 285-310. *In* CRC Handbook of Pest Management in Agriculture, 2nd edition. Vol. 1. D. Pimentel (Editor). CRC Press, Boca Raton, FL.

ROISTACHER, C. N. 1996. The economics of living with citrus diseases: Huanglongbing (greening) in Thailand. *In* Int. Organization Citrus Virologists (IOCV). University of California, Riverside.

ROMAN, M. P., CAMBRA, M., JUAREZ, J., MORENO, P., DURAN-VILA, N., TANAKA, F. A. O., ALVES, E., KITAJIMA, E. W., YAMAMOTAT, P. T., BASSANEZI, R. B., TEIXEIRA, D. C., JUSUS, JR., W. C., AYRES, A. J., GIMENES-FERNANDES, F., GIROTTO, L. F., and BOVÉ, J. M. 2004. Sudden death of citrus in Brazil: a graft-transmissible bud union disease. Plant Disease 88, 453-467.

ROSENBERG, D. Y., McEACHERN, E. H., BLANC, F. L., ROBINSON, D. W., and FOOTE, H. L. 1978. Regulatory measures for pest and disease control. In The Citrus Industry, Vol. IV. W. Reuther, E. C. Calavan, and G. E. Carman (Editors). Div. Agr. Science, University of California, Berkeley.

ROSENBERG, D. Y. 1989. The interaction of state and federal quarantines in the US. In Plant Protection and Quarantine, Vol. III. R. P. Kahn (Editor). CRC Press, Boca Raton, FL.

SALIBE, A. A. 1973. The Brazilian citrus industry. Proc. First Int. Citrus Short Course: Citrus Rootstocks. 1:44-60. L. K Jackson, A. H. Krezdorn and J. Soule (Editors). Fruit Crops Dept., University of Florida, Gainesville.

SCHOULTIES, C. L., SEYMOUR, C. P., and MILLER, J. W. 1983. Where are the exotic disease threats? In Exotic Plant Pests in North American Agriculture. C. L. Wilson and C. L. Graham (Editors). Academic Press, New York.

SCHOULTIES, C. L. 1984. Peanut stripe virus. Fla. Dept. Agr. Consumer Serv., Div. Plant Ind., Plant Pathology Circ. #261. http://www.doacs.state.fl.us/pi/enpp/pathology/pathcirc/pp261.pdf

SCHOULTIES, C. L., CIVEROLO, E. L., MILLER, J. W., STALL, R. E., KRASS, C. J., POE, S. R., and DUCHARME, E. P. 1987. Citrus canker in Florida. Plant Disease 71, 388-395.

SCHUBERT, T. S. 1991. Recent history of the citrus canker eradication programs in Florida. Newsletter Fla. Phytopathological Soc. 2, 1-6.

SCHUBERT, T. S., RIZVI, S. A., SUN, X., GOTTWALD, T. R., GRAHAM, J. H., and DIXON, W. N. 2001. Meeting the challenge of eradicating citrus canker in Florida—again. Plant Disease 85, 340-356.

SIMPSON, S. E. 1993. Caribbean fruit fly-free zone certification protocol in Florida (Diptera: Tephritidae). Fla. Entomologist 76, 228-233.

SOHI, G. S. and SANDHU, M. S. 1968. Relationship between citrus leafminer (Phyllocnistis citrella Stainton) injury and citrus canker [(Xanthomonas citri (Hasse) Dowson] incidence on citrus leaves. J. Res. Punjab Agr. University of (Ludhiana) 5, 66-69.

STALL, R. E. and SEYMOUR, C. P. 1983. Canker, a threat to citrus in the Gulf-Coast states. Plant Disease 67, 581-585.

STECK, G.J. 1999. Taxonomic status of Anastrepha fraterculus. In The South American fruit fly, Anastrepha fraterculus (Wied.); advances in artificial rearing, taxonomic status and biological studies, IAEA-TECDOC-1064, International Atomic Energy Agency, Vienna.

STECK, G. J. 2001. Concerning the occurrence of the West Indian fruit fly in Florida. Fla. Entomologist 84, 320-321.

SUN, X., STALL, R. E., CUBERO, J., GOTTWALD, T. R., GRAHAM, J. H., DIXON, W. D., SCHUBERT, T. S., PEACOCK, M. E., DICKSTEIN, E. R., and CHALOUX, P. H. 2000. Detection of a unique isolate of citrus canker bacterium from Key lime in Wellington and Lake Worth, Florida. Proc. Int. Citrus Canker Res. Workshop, Ft. Pierce, FL, June 20-22, 2000 (Abstr.). www.doacs.state.fl.us/pi/canker/workshop/abstracts.pdf

SUN, X., STALL, R. E., CUBERO, J., GOTTWALD, T. R., GRAHAM, J. H., DIXON, W. D., SCHUBERT, T. S., CHALOUX, P. H., STROMBERG, V. K., LACY, G. H., and SUTTON, B. D. 2004. Detection and characterization of a new strain of citrus canker bacteria from Key/Mexican lime and alemow in South Florida. Plant Dis. 88, 1179-1188.

SWANSON, R. W., and BARANOWSKI, R. M. 1972. Host range and infestation by the Caribbean fruit fly, Anastrepha suspensa (Diptera: Tephritidae), in South Florida. Fla. State Hort. Soc. 85, 271-274.

TAN, M. K., TIMMER, L. W., BROADBENT, P., PRIEST, M., and CAIN, P. 1996. Differentiation by molecular analysis of *Elsinoe* spp. causing scab diseases of citrus and its epidemiological implications. Phytopathology 86, 1039-1044.

TIMMER, L. W., AGOSTINI, J. P., ZITKO, S. E., and ZULFIQAR, M. 1994. Postbloom fruit drop, an increasingly prevalent disease of citrus in the Americas. Plant Disease 78, 329-334.

TIMMER, L. W., BROWN, G. E., and ZITKO, S. E. 1998. The role of *Colletotrichum* spp. in postharvest anthracnose of citrus and survival of *C. acutatum* on fruit. Plant Disease 82, 415-418.

TIMMER, L. W., GARNSEY, S. M., and GRAHAM, J. H. (Editors). 2000. Compendium of Citrus Diseases. APS Press. 2nd edition. 92 pp.

TIMMER, L. W., PRIEST, M., BROADBENT, P. and TAN, M-K. 1996. Morphological and pathological characterization of species of *Elsinoe* causing scab diseases of citrus. Phytopathology 86, 1032-1038.

TIRTAWIDJAJA, S. 1981. Insect, dodder, and seed transmissions of citrus vein phloem degeneration (CVPD). Proc. Int. Soc. Citriculture 1981, Vol. 1, 469-471.

USDA-APHIS-PPQ. 2006. Evaluation of asymptomatic citrus fruit (*Citrus* spp.) as a pathway for the introduction of citrus canker disease (*Xanthomonas axonopodis* pv. *citri*). Plant Epidemiology and Risk Analysis Laboratory, Center for Plant Health Science and Technology, Plant Protection and Quarantine. Raleigh, NC. 22 pp. http://www.aphis.usda.gov/about_aphis/printable_version/06-045-1_PRA_032006.pdf

VALIELA, M. V. F. 1959. The present state of tristeza in Argentina. *In* Citrus Virus Diseases - Proc. Conf. Citrus Virus Diseases. J. M. Wallace (Editor). University of California, Riverside.

VERNIERE, C., HARTUNG, J. S., PRUVOST, O. P., CIVEROLO, E. L., ALVAREZ, A. M., MAESTRI, P. and LUISETTI, J. 1998. Characterization of phenotypically distinct strains of *Xanthomonas axonopodis* pv. *citri* from Southwest Asia. Eur. J. Plant Pathology 104, 477-487.

WALLACE, A. R. 1978. Virus and viruslike diseases. *In* The Citrus Industry, Vol. IV. W. Reuther, E. C. Calavan, and G. E. Carman (Editors). University of California, Berkeley.

WEEMS, H. V. 1967. Japanese orange fly (*Dacus tsuneonis* Miyake) (Diptera: Tephritidae). Entomology Circ. No. 51. Fla. Dept. Agr. Consumer Serv., Div. Plant Ind.

WEEMS, H. V. 1981. Mediterranean fruit fly, *Ceratitis capitata* (Wiedemann). Entomology Circ. No. 230 Fla. Dept. Agr. Consumer Serv., Div. Plant Ind.

WHITE, I. M. and ELSON-HARRIS, M. M. 1992. Fruit flies of economic significance: their identification and bionomics. CAB International, Wallingford, Oxon, UK and The Australian Center for Agr. Res., Canberra, Australia.

WHITE, I. M. and HANCOCK, D. L. 1997. Indo-Australasian Dacini fruit flies (Computer Aided Biological Identification Key). Int. Inst. Entomology, London.

WILLIAMS-WOODWARD, J. L., HENNEN, J. F., PARDA, K. W., and FOWLER, J. M. 2001. First report of daylily rust in the United States. Plant Dis. 85, 1121.

18

Pesticide Tolerances

Teung F. Chin, John Reilly, and David J. Hall

Handlers of fresh citrus fruits do not generally concern themselves with pesticide residues or tolerances. They generally leave those concerns to the packer, who, in turn often rely upon their pesticide product suppliers to provide them with appropriate and legal pesticide applications. Even so, the packer is ultimately responsible for the fruit he ships. With this in mind, the packer needs to have a basic understanding of pesticide tolerances and what constitutes a legal application.

In the United States (US) all pesticide uses are governed by the regulations of the Environmental Protection Agency (EPA) at the federal level. State regulations may also apply. Federal regulations are published in Title 40 of the Code of Federal Regulations (40 CFR). These promulgate the rules stating which pesticides may be used, how they may be applied and what residues are allowed. Most other countries have regulations but can be more or less restrictive than those of the US. While many countries have parallel authority and rules, within their jurisdiction the specific requirements will differ greatly.

The basic authority of the US EPA to regulate pesticides is set out in the Federal Insecticide, Fungicide and Rodenticide Act (FIFRA 2004). In that law a pesticide is defined thus:

"(u) Pesticide.—The term "pesticide" means (1) any substance or mixture of substances intended for preventing, destroying, repelling, or mitigating any pest, (2) any substance or mixture of substances intended for use as a plant regulator, defoliant, or desiccant, and (3) any nitrogen stabilizer, except E (exceptions apply to human health applications)."

The EPA sets limits on the amount of pesticides that may remain in or on foods. These limits are called tolerances. A tolerance is the maximum amount of a pesticide residue that may lawfully remain on a food commodity that has been treated with a pesticide. The federal standards for tolerances are set forth in the Federal Food, Drug and Cosmetic Act (FFDCA 1996) and the Food Quality Protection Act (FQPA 1996). Tolerances may also be referred to as maximum residue limits (MRLs) in other countries and the Codex Alimentarius Commission, an international standards setting body.

FIFRA provides several sets of conditions under which a pesticide may be used in the US. These conditions are set out in various sections of the statute and that section number usually refers to the type of use. The principal sections are:

Full registration. The label, formulation, application and safety data have been reviewed and approved by the EPA for a Section 3 registration or authorized on the condition that when additional data is required it will be supplied.

Experimental use permit (EUP). EUPs are approved under Section 5 of FIFRA and issued to any applicant for the purpose of gathering data for a Section 3 registration. These permits usually apply to growing crops. Once the EPA determines that such use will not adversely affect the environment or endanger the public the permit is issued. The permit limits the amount to be used and how the treated product may be disposed. If appropriate, a temporary tolerance may be issued to allow the treated product to enter commercial channels, otherwise destruction of treated materials is required. EUPs may be issued by individual states as well as the US EPA. State issued permits require the approval of the EPA.

Under certain emergency conditions government agencies may receive an exemption from the requirements of registration in order to deal with a short-term emergency under section 18 of the Federal Insecticide, Fungicides and Rodenticides Act (FIFRA).

A state may issue a special local need registration in order to use a pesticide within that state in a manner not specified on any label, such as using a product at a level higher than the label specifies or using a pesticide on a site or against a pest not covered on the label of any registered product. Such application does not allow for exceeding established tolerances (MRL) unless approved by the EPA. These are permitted under section 24(c) of FIFRA.

Known as Section 25(b) chemicals, certain chemicals and naturally occurring substances have been determined to be of a character that their use as pesticides does not pose a threat to the environment or a hazard to humans. These do not require EPA registration, however many states do require that section 25(b) pesticides be registered for use within their boundaries. The EPA has issued a list of these and a list of the other (inert) ingredients that may be used with them. In many countries these chemicals are not considered pesticides and therefore are not regulated.

When pesticide products are used under the conditions of an EUP, Emergency Exemption, or Special Local Need, the supplier is obligated to provide the packer with the documentation required and full knowledge of what is required for him to use the product.

In order to use a pesticide product in the US the product applied must meet two conditions. It must either be registered with the EPA or be exempt from the requirements of registration. And, it must also either have an established tolerance (MRL), or be exempt from the requirements of a tolerance. In any case the product must bear a label specifying, the site of application, the pests to be controlled, the maximum amount to be applied. The label must also bear either an EPA registration number or a statement of exemption if it is a 25(b) product.

Every pesticide product used in the U.S. must bear a label displaying, the product name, percent active ingredients, the name and address of the seller, EPA specified warnings and precautionary statements, directions for use, and except in the case of Section 25(b) registrations, the EPA Registration Number and Manufacturing Establish Number (EPA 2003).

Products registered by the EPA under Section 3 are issued a unique registration number. This number appears as two components separated by a dash in the format "EPA Reg. No. 1234-56". The first part of the number is the registrant identifier and the second is the individual product identifier. Registrants may sub register their products to one or more third parties; these are called "Distributor Products". In that case the registration number will consist of three components in the format "EPA Reg. No. 1234-56-7890". The last component is the EPA's identification number for the Distributor, and it is their name that appears on the label. A Distributor product must be identical to the basic product. But it may have a different brand name and the sellers name must be qualified by the term "Sold by", "Distributed by" or "Manufactured for".

A basic registrant may also split their own label using different brand names and selected sites. For example the fungicide thiabendazole (TBZ) is effective against postharvest diseases of potatoes, apples and citrus. By splitting the label and marketing three different brand names, the registrant may concentrate on different markets, offer differing levels of service and price their product accordingly.

Products issued an Experimental Use Permit will bear a number composed of three elements in the form "EPA Reg. No. 1234-EUP-56. Products registered as a Special Local Needs are also termed as "Section 24(c)s", will adopt the format, "EPA SLN No. NC950034". Of this number the first letters are the two-letter abbreviation for the state issuing (in the example NC = North Carolina). The next two numbers are the last two digits of the year of issue (95 = 1995) and the last four digits represent the order of acceptance. In the example 0034 would indicate that it is the 34th permit issued by the state of North Carolina in the year 1995.

The Establishment number identifies the place where a product was manufactured. This appears in the form "EPA Est. No. 1234-CA-1" indicating that company number 1234 produced this product at the establishment in California registered with the EPA as their number 1. A single company may have several establishments in one state or in many different states. Some or all of these numbers may appear on the label, but the establishment that produced the product bearing the label must clearly indicate the producing establishment in some manner, an arrow, check mark, circling, etc.

The label must also specify the site where the pesticide is to be applied (e.g., citrus, grapefruit), the pest to be controlled (e.g., Sour Rot, *Geotrichum candidum*), and the rate and method of application (e.g., 1000 ppm as a drench for 3 minutes).

Using the example of an imaginary product registered to control blue mold on stored lemons, applied by drenching at the rate of 500 ppm in water for 3 minutes. The packer may use less than 500 ppm and/or may drench for less than 3 minutes. This packer cannot use more than 500 ppm in any solvent or exceed the 3 minutes exposure, nor may he use it on any other citrus not on the label. This holds true, even if similar products allow such uses. In the US, the label on the container is the controlling factor.

Pesticide residues are the result of preharvest or postharvest applications. The packer and handler usually have control over postharvest application, which are considered here. Postharvest residues result from one of two actions, either due to direct application as in the case of decay control fungicides and quarantine treatments, or, from incidental contact due to pest control procedures.

Specific Tolerances

The packer of fresh citrus is normally only concerned with those pesticide products that are applied postharvest. US regulations prohibit the postharvest application of any pesticide unless it has a specific tolerance or an exemption from the requirements for a tolerance for postharvest application. This specific tolerance may be for combined pre- and postharvest applications.

How Are Tolerances Established and Managed Internationally

Maximum residue levels (MRLs) or tolerances established by the U.S. Environmental Protection Agency (EPA) apply to pesticide residues found in or on foods that are produced and consumed in the United States, as well as to foods that are imported into the United States from other countries. Foods produced in the United States for export must meet the MRL standards and other related entry requirements established by the country receiving the shipment.

A number of countries establish the MRLs based on conducting their own risk assessments and other evaluations. The most widely recognized bodies that establish national MRLs include regulatory authorities in Australia, Canada, the European Union member nations, Japan, New Zealand, and the United States.

The underlying criteria used in establishing MRLs vary from one country to the next for a variety of economic, political and other reasons. For example, for non-public health pesticides, EPA generally does not require that the pesticide manufacturer submit efficacy data, that is, data to demonstrate that the MRL requested results from use of the least amount of pesticide that would be effective. Another country may have a lower MRL if they have this requirement. Dietary consumption patterns, which are a factor in determining MRLs may differ from country to country. Residue levels are also affected by variables such as climate conditions, pest threats and other factors as to what is necessary under good agricultural practices (GAPs).

A number of other countries choose to adopt the MRLs established by the international standard-setting body, Codex Alimentarius (Codex). In some cases this is because the country lacks the resources or technical expertise to conduct comprehensive science-based risk assessments for pesticides. However, Codex has only established MRLs for a limited number of pesticide\commodity combinations at this time. There is a continuing effort to harmonize pesticide residues (MRLs) on food through the Codex Alimentarius Commission.

One result of these developments is that there are numerous pesticides approved in the United States for use on specific commodities without corresponding approval in the countries that import these commodities from the U.S. or alternatively, the MRLs established in those other countries differ from the level set in the United States.

Enforcement of Tolerances by Other Countries

Countries vary in their approach to enforcing MRLs. Some countries, in the absence of establishing an MRL for a particular pesticide\commodity combination, will defer to the Codex standard, if available. Other countries will apply a uniform limit or default level to apply to situations where it has not established an applicable MRL for that particular pesticide\commodity combination. In other cases, a country may choose to defer to the MRL that has been established in the exporting country for that particular combination. Some countries have a process where exporters can apply for an import tolerance in the absence of an existing MRL standard in that country. Finally, there are countries such as the United States where a shipment could potentially be rejected if a residue is found for which a tolerance has not been established.

MRLs set by Codex are advisory and not statutory. They are used as guidance of acceptable levels when there are no other MRLs in place. National governments can choose whether or not to accept and use the Codex MRL recommendations as national standards. Many developing countries depend upon Codex MRLs to set acceptable pesticide residue levels in their own countries. Industrialized countries with long-established regulatory programs review the Codex MRL recommendations and usually accept them when they are consistent with their national standards. While not obligatory, Codex food safety standards, including established MRLs, are officially recognized by WTO under the Sanitary and Phytosanitary (SPS) Agreement. Therefore, Codex MRLs may be used by the WTO for purposes of settling trade disputes brought under the SPS Agreement.

Most countries, including the United States, test only a small percentage of imported foods for pesticide residues. What inspectors decide to check is based on a number of considerations. Typically, countries will have conducted sampling programs to develop a risk profile as to what they should be focusing their limited inspection resources on.

Further Information Relating to Establishment and Enforcement of MRLs

U.S. Government Sources

EPA: To access general information on pesticide issues, you can go to EPA's website at http://www.epa.gov and click on pesticides. More specific information on current EPA MRLs and tolerances can be found at **http://www.epa.gov/pesticides/food/viewtols.htm**. You can also access this information by going to the U.S. Code of Federal Regulations (CFR) directly at **http://www.access.gpo.gov/nara/cfr/waisidx_04/40cfr180_04.html**. EPA MRLs and tolerances are located in title 40, part 180 of the CFR. For information on international pesticide issues, go to: **http://www.epa.gov/oppfead1/international/**.

FDA general site on Pesticides, Metals, Chemical Contaminants & Natural Toxins: **http://www.cfsan.fda.gov/~lrd/pestadd.html** [this site includes information on pesticide monitoring at time of inspection, etc.].

FDA site on import requirements: **http://www.fda.gov/ora/inspect_ref/iom/contents/ch6_toc.html**.

International MRL Database for U.S. specialty crops (Unofficial Site): **http://www.mrldatabase.com/** [or **http://www.croplifeamerica.org/learn_**

more/mrl.htm or http://www.fas.usda.gov/htp/MRL.htm]. You can search for specific country and Codex MRLs for a number of pesticide\crop combinations. You can also learn more about the policies and procedures of a particular country in the establishment and enforcement of pesticide tolerances. At this time, the MRL information focuses on minor crops.

Regulatory Authorities of Other Countries Involved in Establishing and Enforcing Pesticide MRLs

Other than the United States, the most widely recognized bodies that establish national MRLs include the regulatory authorities in Australia, Canada, the European Commission, Japan, and New Zealand.

Australia (Australian Pesticides & Veterinary Medicines Authority): http://www.apvma.gov.au/residues/subpage_residues.shtml

Canada (Health Canada, Pest Management Regulatory Agency): http://www.pmra-arla.gc.ca/english/legis/maxres-e.html

European Commission (DG Health and Consumer Protection): http://europa.eu.int/comm/food/plant/protection/pesticides/index_en.htm. Additional information on EC tolerances can be accessed by through the web sites of member nations. For example, see the United Kingdom's Pesticides Safety Directorate (PSD) at https://secure.pesticides.gov.uk/MRLs/. PSD's MRL database can be found at: https://secure.pesticides.gov.uk/MRLs/main.asp

Japan (Ministry of Health, Labor, and Welfare): http://www.mhlw. go.jp/english/index.html. See also Japan Ministry of Agriculture, Forestry, and Fisheries: http://www.maff.go.jp/eindex.html. See also http://www. ffcr.or.jp/zaidan/FFCRHOME.nsf/pages/e-lists [compiled by The Japan Food Chemical Research Foundation]

New Zealand (New Zealand Food Safety Authority): http://www. nzfsa.govt.nz/policy-law/legislation/food-standards/index.htm#mrl. See also http://www.nzfsa.govt.nz/plant/subject/horticulture/ residues/index.htm, with a number of links to other country web sites

Codex MRL Information

Codex MRLs can be viewed at the following site: http://faostat.fao.org/ faostat/pestdes/jsp/pest_q-e.jsp. The web address for Codex Alimentarius is http://www.codexalimentarius.net/web/index_en.jsp. From the home page, you can access information about past and current activities of the Codex Committee of Pesticide Residues, as well as the Joint FAO\WHO

Meetings on Pesticide Residues (JMPR), which perform risk assessments and other evaluations for CCPR.

A number of countries also have their own national web sites covering Codex activities, which includes the work of the Codex Committee of Pesticide Residues. Examples of several such sites follow:

Australia: **http://www.affa.gov.au/content/output.cfm?ObjectID= A521 EE9F-AB34-4BB0-B03143AD22807649**

Canada: **http://www.hc-sc.gc.ca/fn-an/intactivit/codex/index_ e.html**

New Zealand: **http://www.nzfsa.govt.nz/policy-law/codex/.**

United States: **http://www.fsis.usda.gov/regulations_&_policies/ Codex_Alimentarius/index.asp**

Other Sites Covering Pesticides

There are numerous web sites on the Internet that provide a wide spectrum of information and data on pesticides. Some examples include the following:

EPA "What the Pesticide Residue Limits are on Food" (Index Page): **http://www.epa.gov/pesticides/food/viewtols.html**

Extoxnet (University of California): **http://extoxnet.orst.edu/ ghindex.html**

International MRL Database, **http://www.mrldatabase.com/**

Tolerance Matrices prepared by the California Quality Citrus Council, **http://www.citrusresearch.com/ccqc/frameset.html**

International Portal on Food Safety, Animal & Plant Health: **http://www.ipfsaph.org/En/default.jsp**. A general clearinghouse on food safety issues and standards, including pesticides

The IR-4 Project: **http://www.ir4.rutgers.edu/index.html**

National Pesticide Information Retrieval System (NPIRS): **http:// ppis.ceris.purdue.edu/**

PAN Pesticides Database: **http://www.pesticideinfo.org/Index. html**. Provides current toxicity and regulatory information for pesticides

Pesticide Product Label System (U.S. Label Images): **http:// www.epa.gov/pesticides/pestlabels/index.htm** or **http://oaspub. epa.gov/pestlabl/ppls.home**

University of Florida, IFAS Extension, Postharvest Program & Information: **http://postharvest.ifas.ufl.edu**

Washington State Pesticide Notification Network: **http://ext.wsu.edu/pnn/user/blank.php**

Comparison of U.S. vs. International Tolerances for Selected Postharvest Fungicides Used with Citrus

(1) The Tables 18.1 through 18.8 list those countries\governments that have established specific MRLs or tolerances for certain post-harvest fungicides used with citrus fruit crops. The list of selected fungicides is not exclusive, but does represent some of the more commonly used fungicides used in post-harvest applications. With the exception of guazatine, all of these fungicides are approved for use in the United States.

(2) The tolerance information that appears below was obtained from the International MRL Database [**http://www.mrldatabase.com/**], as well as other official and unofficial sources. We make no representations, guarantees, or warranties as to the total accuracy or completeness of the information provided. Since tolerances are established or revised or revoked on an ongoing basis, one should refer to more current official government sources, or regularly updated compilations such as the International MRL Database, to confirm the latest tolerances in effect.

(3) In some cases, countries may not establish specific MRLs for a particular pesticide/commodity combination, but instead, follow a policy of deferring to the existing MRL established in the exporting country, or alternatively relying on the tolerance established by Codex, if applicable. The International MRL Database indicates that Albania, Antigua and Barbuda, Bermuda, Cayman Islands, Haiti, Jamaica, Nevis, Sri Lanka, and St. Lucia currently follow a policy of deferring to the tolerance established in the exporting country in the absence of establishing their own MRL. The International MRL Database also indicates that the following governments will generally adopt the existing Codex standard in the absence of having set their own MRL: Algeria, Angola, Bahamas, Bangladesh, Barbados, Columbia, Costa Rica, Dominican Republic, Ecuador, El Salvador, Guatemala, Honduras, Hong Kong, Jordan, Lebanon, Nicaragua, Pakistan, Panama, Peru, Philippines, Thailand, Trinidad and Tobago, Tunisia, and Venezuela. There may be other situations where countries will follow these policies of deferring to the tolerance of Codex or the exporting country on a more selective basis. A few countries, in the absence of having established their own tolerance or deferring to a tolerance set elsewhere, may apply a uniform limit or default tolerance under certain conditions. For example, where no specific tolerance has been established, Canada has a default tolerance of 0.10 ppm (which is

currently under review). Similarly, Japan has just implemented a uniform limit of 0.01 ppm. Additional information on this subject can be found in the country profile section of the International MRL database.

(4) The tolerance information in the tables herein was obtained from, Internet sources referenced elsewhere in this chapter. Individual Member States of the EU are not listed unless the country MRL differs from the EU standard. Norway and Switzerland are not members of the EU, so MRLs established by these two countries are listed in addition to the EU standard.

(5) Japan differs from most countries and Codex in how it regulates the use of fungicides. Essentially, Japan regulates the pre-harvest use of fungicides as a pesticide, and post-harvest applications as a food additive. Consequently, registrants must seek separate approval for use of the fungicide in post-harvest situations even if the fungicide has been approved and has established tolerances covering its use in pre-harvest situations as a pesticide. So in listing MRLs for Japan, we indicate when the tolerance has been approved for pre-harvest applications as a pesticide, or post-harvest applications as a food additive, or both. If there is no reference to post-harvest, then assume that Japan has not approved the use of the particular agricultural chemical with citrus in post-harvest situations as a food additive.

(6) The MRL or tolerance values are expressed in parts per million (PPM) and apply to the crop or crop group in its raw agricultural state unless otherwise noted.

Tables 18.1 through 18.8 the designation "Fruit, Citrus" means all citrus unless otherwise specified. In the US the EPA defines citrus as "Crop Group 10". This is defined as: Citrus Fruits (*Citrus* spp., *Fortunella* spp.). Citrus which are included in Group 10: Calamondin (*Citrus mitis* × *Citrofortunella mitis*); Citrus citron (*Citrus medica*); Citrus hybrids (*Citrus* spp.) (includes chironja, tangelo, tangor); Grapefruit (*Citrus paradisi*); Kumquat (*Fortunella* spp.); Lemon (*Citrus jambhiri*, Citrus limon); Lime (*Citrus aurantiifolia*); Mandarin (tangerine) (*Citrus reticulata*); Orange, sour (*Citrus aurantium*); Orange, sweet (*Citrus sinensis*); Pummelo (Citrus grandis, *Citrus maxima*); Satsuma mandarin (*Citrus unshiu*).

The European Union defines citrus to include grapefruit, lemon, lime, mandarin, oranges, pomelo, and citrus fruit—other. The EU lists kumquat separately under the Miscellaneous Fruit category.

The number of pesticides acceptable for postharvest use in international commerce is limited. The U.S. postharvest registration of the fungicide Benomyl (Table 18.1) was canceled in 1991 (Hall 2003). but a tolerance for imported fruit and use of existing stocks is in effect until January of 2008. The fungicide Guazatine (Table 18.2) has widespread use, but is not currently allowed in the U.S.

The fungicide Imazalil (Table 18.3). the insecticide/fumigant Methyl Bromide (Table 18.4), the fungicide *o*-Phenylphenol (Table 18.5) and the

TABLE 18.1. Benomyl (Tolerance Parts per Million)

Commodity	U.S. tolerance[a,b]	Codex MRL	Representative countries[c]
Fruit, Citrus	10.0 (postharvest, expires 1/1/08) 50.0 (dried pulp, postharvest, expires 1/1/08)	No codex MRLs for citrus group or individual citrus crops	Argentian: 2.0; Brazil: 5.0; Canada: 10.0; China: 0.5; EU: 5.0; French Pacific Islands: 5.0; French West Indies; 5.0; India: 5.0; Indonesia: 10.0; Japan (pre-harvest only)[d] 3.0; Kenya: 5.0; Korea: 7.0; Malaysia: 10.0; Mexico: 10.0; New Zealand: 5.0; Norway: 5.0; Singapore: 10.0; South Africa: 5.0; Switzerland: 5.0; Taiwan: 3.0
Grapefruit	10.0	None	Japan (pre-harvest): 7.0
Lemon	10.0	None	Japan (pre-harvest): 7.0

[a]40 CFR 180.294.

[b]Benomyl is no longer manufactured for sale in the U.S. tolerances are for existing stocks in the hands of users. The U.S. tolerance will expire on January 1, 2008.

[c]Note: The MRLs for the EU and Japan appear under the pesticide carbendazim (not benomyl). For example, the Japan tolerance definition is expressed as carbendazim, which is a "total of carbendazim, benomyl, and thiophanate-methyl."

[d]Note: Japan's MRL for carbendazim wit6h grapefruit and lemon is 7.0. For all other citrus, the MRL is 3.0. Japan has only approved the use of carbendazim with citrus in pre-harvest applications.

TABLE 18.2. Guazatine (Tolerance Parts per Million)

Commodity	U.S. tolerance	Codex MRL	Representative countries[a]
Fruit, Citrus	Not registered in the U.S.	5.0[b]	Australia: 5.0, New Zealand: 5.0; South Africa: 5.0; Spain: 5.0

[a]Note: According to the PAN Pesticide database (**http://www.pesticideinfo.org/Index.html**), guazatine is also registered in the following countries: Germany, Hungary, India, Netherlands, and the United Kingdom.

[b]Note: Codex guideline level, not yet implemented.

TABLE 18.3. Imazalil (Tolerance Parts per Million)

Comodity	U.S. tolerance[a]	Codex MRL	Representative countries
Fruit, Citrus	10.0 (post-harvest) 25.0 (dried pulp) 25.0 (oil)	5.0	Argentina: 5.0; Australia: 10.0; Brazil: 5.0; Canada: 5.0; Chile: 5.0; China: 5.0; EU: 5.0; French Pacific Islands: 5.0, French West Indies: 5.0; Iceland: 5.0; Indonesia: 5.0; Israel: 5.0; Japan: 5.0 (pre-harvest and post-harvest);[b] Kenya: 5.0; Korea: 5.0; Mexico: 10.0; Netherlands Antilles: 5.0; New Zealand: 5.0; Norway: 5.0; Singapore: 5.0; South Africa: 5.0; Spain: 0.02; Switzerland: 5.0; Taiwan: 2.0 (post-harvest)

[a]40 CFR 180.413.

[b]Note: For Japan, the pre-harvest pesticide tolerance of 5.0 applies to all citrus fruits except Unshu orange, which has no pre-harvest tolerance. The post-harvest food additive tolerance of 5.0 applies to all citrus fruits.

TABLE 18.4. Methyl Bromide (Tolerance Parts per Million)

Commodity	U.S. tolerance[a]	Codex MRL	Representative countries
Fruit, Citrus		No MRLs for citrus group or individual citrus crops	Australia: 30.0; EU: 0.05; India: 30.0; Japan: 30.0 (pre-harvest);[b] New Zealand: 50.0
Citron, Citrus	30.0 (post-harvest)		
Grapefruit	30.0 (post-harvest)		Korea: 30.0
Kumquat	30.0 (post-harvest)		
Lemon	30.0 (post-harvest)		Korea: 30.0
Lime	30.0 (post-harvest)		
Orange	30.0 (post-harvest)		Korea: 30.0
Tangerine	30.0 (post-harvest)		

[a]40 CFR 180.123.
[b]Note: Japan's MRL of 30.0 just applies to pre-harvest applications. Japan has not approved post-harvest uses of methyl bromide with citrus.

TABLE 18.5. o-Phenylphenol (Tolerance Parts per Million)

Commodity	U.S. tolerance[a]	Codex MRL	Representative countries
Fruit, Citrus	10.0	10.0	Australia: 10.0; Canada: 10.0; France: 12.0; Israel: 10.0; Japan: 10.0 (pre-harvest and post-harvest); Korea: 10.0; Malaysia: 10.0; Spain: 12.0; Sweden: 12.0; Switzerland: 12.0

[a]40 CFR 180.129.

TABLE 18.6. Thiabendazole (Tolerance Parts per Million)

Commodity	U.S. tolerance[a]	Codex MRL	Representative countries
Fruit, Citrus	10.0 (post-harvest) 35.0 (dried pulp, post-harvest)	10.0	Argentina: 10.0; Australia: 10.0; Brazil: 10.0; Canada: 10.0; Chile: 10.0; EU: 5.0; French Pacific Islands: 5.0; French West Indies: 0.05; Indonesia: 10.0; Israel: 10.0; Japan: 10.0 (post-harvest); Kenya: 5.0; Korea: 10.0; Malaysia: 10.0; Mexico: 10.0; New Zealand: 3.0; Norway: 5.0; Singapore: 10.0; South Africa: 6.0; Switzerland: 5.0; Taiwan: 10.0
Grapefruit			France: 6.0; French Pacific Islands: 6.0; French West Indies: 6.0
Kumquat			EU: 0.05; French Pacific Islands: 0.05; French West Indies: 0.05; Kenya: 0.05; Netherlands Antilles: 0.05; Norway: 0.05
Lime			France: 6.0; French Pacific Islands: 6.0; French West Indies: 6.0.
Orange			France: 6.0; French Pacific Islands: 6.0; French West Indies: 6.0.
Pummelo			France: 6.0; French Pacific Islands: 6.0; French West Indies: 6.0.
Tangerine			France: 6.0; French Pacific Islands: 6.0; French West Indies: 6.0

[a]40 CFR 180.242.

TABLE 18.7. Pyrimethanil (4,6-Dimethyl-N-phenyl-2-pyridinamine) (Tolerance Parts per Million)

Commodity	U.S. tolerance[a]	Codex MRL	Representative countries
Fruit, Citrus	10.0 (post-harvest only)	No Codex MRLs for citrus group or individual citrus crops	Japan: 15.0 (pre-harvest)[b]; Netherlands: 0.05; Spain: 0.02

[a]40 CFR 180.518.
[b]Note: Japan's MRL of 15.0 just applies to pre-harvest applications for lemon, orange, grapefruit, lime, and other citrus fruits. Japan provides separate tolerances of 0.5 and 10.0 for Unshu orange and Natsudaidai respectively. Japan has not approved the post-harvest use of pyrimethanil with citrus.

TABLE 18.8. Fludioxonil

Commodity	U.S. tolerance[a]	Codex MRL	Representative countries
Fruit, Citrus	10.0	No Codex MRLs for citrus group or individual citrus crops	Japan: 1.0 (pre-harvest)[b]; Germany: 0.05; Netherlands: 0.05; Spain: 0.05
Grapefruit oil	500.0	None	None
Spanish lime	1.0	None	None

[a]40 CFR 180.516.
[b]Note: Japan's MRL of 1.0 just applies to pre-harvest applications for lemon, orange, grapefruit, lime, and other citrus fruits. However, the tolerance for Unshu orange is 0.1. Japan has not approved the post-harvest use of fludioxonil with citrus.

fungicide Thiabendazole (Table 18.6) have been in use for many years and have widespread acceptance.

The newest postharvest fungicides Pyrmethanil (Table 18.7) and Fludioxonil (Table 18.8) have limited acceptance and are still under review by several countries.

REFERENCES

EPA. 2003. Label Review Manual 3rd Edition. U.S. Environmental Protection Agency Washington, DC.

FIFRA. 2004. Federal Insecticide, Fungicide and Rodenticide Act. As amended through P. L.108-199. January 23, 2004.

FFDCA. 1996. Federal Food, Drug and Cosmetic Act. As amended through P. L. 104-170. August 3, 1996.

FQPA. 1996. Food Quality Protection Act. P. L. 104-170. August 3, 1996

HALL, D. J. 2003. Twentieth century developments in handling Florida's fresh citrus fruit—an overview. Proc. Fla. State Hort. Soc. 116, 369-374.

19

Packing Organic Fresh Citrus

David J. Hall

The packer of fresh organic citrus faces many challenges in order to deliver sound fruit with an acceptable appearance to his customers. When the market is nearby and the time between picking and sale is short, there are usually few difficulties. However, when the shipper is attempting to serve distant markets and there is considerable time between harvest and sale, many obstacles have to be overcome in order to deliver acceptable fruit to the customer. While the standards of the USDA's National Organic Program (NOP) have placed severe restrictions on what is acceptable in handling organic citrus, they have also eliminated the confusing mix of interpretations encountered before they became law.

There is a great body of scientific research aimed at reducing postharvest loss in fruits and vegetables, however most of this has focused on conventional methods using synthetic chemical pesticides. The packer of organic produce, however, is faced with the lack of research devoted strictly to the problems of organic packers. Several factors are involved. The first of these is the fact that while there are hundreds or even thousands of producers of a specific crop, there are relatively few packers and only a handful of businesses serving those packers. Research costs money, time and material, commercial enterprises are usually not willing to invest in research that will not show an eventual profit. Not for profit (University, Government) research dollars are limited and usually spent on projects for which there is the greatest public interest. In conventional agriculture the growers speak much louder that the packers and the same is true of organic agriculture.

Another factor limiting the amount of research done by commercial interests is the lack of exclusivity. Once a technique has been developed, there is little likelihood that it can be protected with patents or other methods. This means that the one developing the method has little chance of recovering the expense, let alone make a profit.

The Loss Triangle

The packer of organic citrus has several options available in ensuring the arrival of sound, acceptable fruit. What is involved is the conscientious application of some basic principles. Figure 19.1 illustrates what is sometimes called the loss triangle. Just as a triangle requires all three legs to maintain its stability, so too the three legs of host, pathogen and environment must be present for decay to occur. The principles of the triangle can be applied to any form of agricultural or horticulture loss, but the focus herein will be on fresh citrus.

The first leg of the triangle is the host, the citrus fruit. Included in this is the condition of the host as to it acceptability to the pathogen. Some postharvest diseases of citrus are caused by what are referred to as wound pathogens. These organisms require a wound in order to infect the fruit. The organisms that cause green mold, blue mold and sour rot are among these. Of course, once established, the growing infection produces toxins that kill or weaken adjoining healthy tissue allowing for the disease to spread. In some cases fruit contacting the infected fruit become infected. This is called nesting and is often seen with sour rot (*Geotrichum candidum*) and blue mold (*Penicillium italicum*). Another type of decay is caused by quiescent infections. These organisms infect the fruit in the grove but do not become manifest until conditions become right for their growth. The major quiescent infection organisms are the cause of Phomopsis and Diplodia stem-end rot, Anthracnose and brown rot.

Protecting the fruit from injury is the first line of defense of the host. This principle was noted early in the twentieth century when it was reported that gentle handling resulted in less decay. In one report (Ramsey 1912) gentle picking and handling reduced decay from 14% to less than 2% when compared to the then standard of commercial picking and handling. More recently it has been demonstrated that gentle handling throughout the entire process from harvest to packing is an important factor in reducing loss due to decay (MacRill 1971).

The next leg of the triangle is the pathogen. If one can keep the pathogen, generally its spores, from contacting the host no decay can occur. Of course, since citrus fruit is subject to many different pathogens and modes of infection, this is not always possible. However, keeping the packinghouse and all handling equipment as clean as possible is a major step toward reducing loss due to decay (Hall 2003). The major pathogens affecting citrus differ with growing area. In the Mediterranean climate of California, with its hot dry summers and cool wet winters, has one set of problem diseases, while Florida, with its semi-tropical climate of hot wet summers and cool dry winters has another. Table 19.1 lists the major, and significant minor diseases of citrus encountered in the United States.

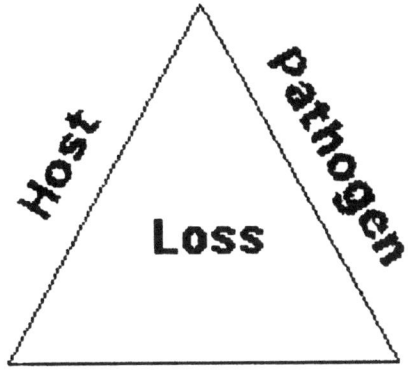

Fig. 19.1. Loss triangle.

The third leg is environment. Outside of their ideal conditions of temperature, humidity, and atmospheric gases many pathogens have greatly retarded growth or even total inhibition. For example green mold will grow well on California oranges while they are held under degreening conditions there, yet green mold is seldom seen on the same variety of Florida oranges degreened under Florida's conditions. The reason for this is that Florida packers normally degreen their fruit at a temperature that inhibits green mold. Unfortunately, Florida's degreening conditions are ideal for the growth of the stem-end rots and Anthracnose while California citrus will not degreen properly at the temperatures used in Florida.

"Chem-Free"

A relatively recent development in domestic and international trade is the demand for fruit packed without the use of synthetic pesticides or "Chem-Free" fruit. There is currently no generally accepted definition of "Chem-Free", each buyer sets his own standards. In general, the fruit may be produced by conventional methods, using synthetic pesticides, fertilizers, etc., but no synthetic pesticides may be applied post-harvest. The packer may use synthetic detergents for cleaning and coatings containing ingredient than are not allowed under the NOP may also be used (Hall 1981).

With these differences in mind, the packer of "Chem-Free" fruit should apply the same standards and principles for packing organic fruit.

PREVENTION

There are many steps the packer of organic citrus may take that will help to break the legs of the triangle. Some of these have been proven by long

TABLE 19.1. Principal US Regional Decay Organisms

Disease	Organism	Region as Major	Region as Minor
Green Mold	*Penicillium digitatum*	California/Arizona	Florida
Blue Mold	*Penicillium italicum*	California/Arizona[a]	
Diplodia Stem End Rot	*Diplodia natalensis*	Florida/Texas	
Phomopsis Stem End Rot	*Phomopsi citri*		Florida[c]
Sour Rot	*Geotrichum candidum*	California/Arizona[a] Florida[b]	
Brown Rot	*Phytophthora citrophthora*	California	Florida/Texas
Anthracnose	*Colletotricum gleosporioides*		Florida

[a]Principally affecting stored lemons.
[b]Principally affecting Grapefruit, Tangerines and hybrids.
[c]Principally affecting late season degreened oranges.

practice and others have only been reported relatively recently as a result of research. Many of these will not see application in non-organic packing-houses because conventional methods and chemicals are cheaper and more effective.

When considering the host it is important to remember that citrus is a non-climacteric fruit and that its maturity stops at harvest. This means that whatever susceptibilities or resistances develop naturally during the growth and maturation cycle have stopped. And that any process, or environments, that involve these are essentially stopped.

An example of this is the changing susceptibility of Florida citrus to An-thracnose infection, The Anthracnose spore becomes attached to the fruit long before maturity but remains dormant until ethylene stimulates its growth. If the fruit were not to be harvested it would eventually reach senes-cence and fall from the tree. Naturally produced ethylene at this time would stimulate Anthracnose. By the time the citrus reaches the stage of maturity, in the industry referred to as a "strong color break" it has developed a resis-tance to Anthracnose infection that lasts until the fruit has passed peak maturity, this resistance then begins to fade.

One Florida packer experienced problems with this in a very real way. Amber Sweet oranges harvested from a grove near the southwestern coast of Florida had passed the test for brix, acid and juice content but had only a weak color break. When degreened this lot of fruit experienced a greater than 80% loss to Anthracnose. Fruit from the same grove harvested just 7 days later had less than 5% loss to Anthracnose.

Another consideration as to the host is its availability to the infectious agent. Those decays that are most commonly encountered in the packing-house can only enter through wounds in the fruit. Hence they are referred to as wound pathogens. The wound does not have to be very large, in fact, wounds too small to be noticed are the usual culprits in an infection. There are steps that the packinghouse management should take to minimize injuries on the process line.

One of these is to periodically have an experienced technician run a dye injury test. In this test, fruit taken from various places along the packingline are immersed in a solution of 2,3,5-triphenyl-2H-tetrazolium chloride or TTC. This compound reacts with the agents released when a cell is ruptured by precipitating a bright red compound (Ismail and Wardowski 1990; Roistacher *et al.* 1956). Since the compound reacts more strongly on fresh injuries than on older injuries, an experienced worker can determine which area of the packline is the source of the injury.

The other method is a visual and hands on inspection. A old proverb states that if a farmer says "good morning" to his land each day, it will reply "good year" to him. The thought being that *daily* attention is needed for success. The same applies to packing fresh fruit. The operator should do a daily inspection of the process line, this includes literally running their hands over all surfaces that a fruit may contact. They should feel smooth with no rough edges. Transfer points, especially when a change in direction or rotation is involved are especially important.

PRINCIPLE ORGANISMS

In general the climate of the growing area has a major impact upon which decay organisms are economically important. California with its hot dry summers and cool wet winters is representative of one type of growing area. By contrast Florida winters are warmer relatively dry and the summers are hot and wet. These conditions not only affect which decay organisms are important but also have an effect on other aspects of postharvest handling such as degreening and storage.

In order to control decay it is necessary to identify the organism(s) involved and to understand which environmental conditions favor their development. The principle decay organisms are summarized below, for more detailed information refer to Chapter 13.

Wound Pathogens

Of the two types of decay organisms causing postharvest loss the wound pathogens are the easiest to control. For citrus these are;

Citrus Green Mold (*Penicillium digitatum*) and **Blue Mold** (*Penicillium italicum*). These organisms infect the fruit through a wound in the peel. Under the right conditions a single spore has the potential of producing a colony that will produce billions of spores. Due to the natural resistance of citrus several spores need to enter a single wound in order to establish an infection. The infection first enters the tissue of the peel producing a water soaked area, then a mass of white mycelia will begin to spread over the surface of the fruit, finally green spores will develop. These spores become airborn and can infect other fruit. The ideal conditions for the growth of these organisms is a humid environment with a temperature between 68° and 77° F (Snowden 1990). Temperatures higher or lower than these slow and the growth of the mold. At lower temperatures, below 40°F, the growth of blue mold is favored over the green.

Sour Rot (*Geotrichum candidum*). This organism is commonly found in the soil and during wet or windy weather is blown or splashed on the fruit. Infected areas develop a water soaked appearance which, when the infection site is small, is easily overlooked. Once the infection has become well established, white mycelia appear on the surface and the fruit begins to break down. In packed fruit spore-laden juices can then cause the infection to spread to healthy uninjured fruit. The ideal temperature for growth is between 77° and 86°F, while at temperatures below 50°F, the rate of growth is greatly slowed.

Under some conditions, sour rot infected fruit will be overgrown by blue or green mold. When this happens, the fruit will disintegrate more slowly, but both diseases will eventually spread to healthy fruit.

Along with green mold (*Penicillium digitatum*) sour rot is one of the most significant causes of postharvest losses in fruit grown in California. In Florida, sour rot is significant on grapefruit, tangerines and hybrids thereof, while the Penicilliums are of lesser significance.

Quiescent Infection Organisms

The quiescent infections are more difficult to control, but methods have been developed to reduce loses from these. The most commercially significant of these organisms are:

Stem-end Rots (*Phomopsis citri* and *Diplodia natelensis*). The organisms causing these two decays are known by several names. The Phomopsis stem-end rot organism is also referred to in the literature as *Diaporthe citri* and Diplodia is also known as *Physalopora rhodinia*, or *Botryodiplodia therbromae* (Ainsworth 1971). In the United States the stem end rots are uncommon in the arid growing areas of Arizona and California while they are significant decays of fruit of Texas and Florida (Snowden 1990).

Both of these organisms get their start in the dead wood of the citrus tree where a sac-like structure produces spores that are then washed down to lodge under the button. Immature fruit are immune to infection, therefore decay does not usually become manifest until after harvest. After harvest exposure to ethylene will stimulate the growth of the organisms. Exposing the fruit to ethylene concentrations higher or for longer times than absolutely necessary will greatly increase the rate of decay (Brown 1986).

If grove management is under the packers control, some benefit in controlling stem-end rots is obtained by removing the dead wood from the trees (Ismail and Zhang 2004).

Anthracnose (*Colletotrichum gloeosporioides*). While the fruit is growing on the trees Anthracnose spores become embedded in the waxy cuticle of the fruit. When the fruit is exposed to ethylene the spores are stimulated and will infect fruit that is not fully mature. This is especially common in warmer growing areas where early season fruit will attain the juice and sugar levels to signal maturity, but the peel has not yet developed a good color. Once the fruit has achieved a good color-break, is essentially resistant to this organism (Snowdon 1990)

Brown Rot (*Phytophthora citrophthora* and other *P.* sp.). This decay organism is caused by a common fungi found in the soil. During rainy weather low hanging fruit may become infected by splashing. Once infection starts it can readily spread to adjacent fruits. This organism survives best in soil with a high organic content and poorly in light sandy soils. It is also more prevalent in California's coastal and inland valley growing areas than elsewhere in the United States. Once established, holding the fruit at a temperature below 40°F will greatly retard the growth and spread of brown rot. Once fruit are infected, disease will readily spread by contact, "nesting" (Klotz and DeWolfe 1961A).

As with the stem-end rots removing dead wood, from the trees and pruning lower branches the tree, to be out of the splash zone is also beneficial (Ismail and Zhang 2004).

Peel Disorders

While not the result of any pathogenic organism, losses due to various peel disorders need to also be considered. Among these are various types of pitting and breakdowns due to oleocellosis, chilling injury, stem-end rind breakdown (SERB), blossom end clearing, and others. Some of these may become entry points for decay and many of these are preventable by some of the practices that prevent decay (See Chapter 14).

REGULATORY CONCERNS

The United States packer of organic citrus has the regulations of three Federal agencies to consider as well as their state equivalents. The Department of Agriculture (USDA), through the National Organic Program (NOP), defines what qualifies as organic and regulates certifying agencies. The Food and Drug Administration (FDA) regulates additives for food use. The Environmental Protection Agency (EPA) regulates the use of pesticides. This latter includes sanitizers, natural pesticides and biologicals, as well as conventional chemical products. References to the appropriate regulations may be found in Table 19.2. In most other countries similar provisions are in effect.

In order to market citrus as organic the process must be certified by one accredited by the USDA/NOP. A list of certifying agents currently accredited by the USDA is posted on their web site (Table 19.3).

PACKINGLINE DESIGN

Ideally a packingline for organic citrus would be designed to incorporate the latest advances in gentle handling such as bin tippers and powered turns (Hall 2003) In such a design, many of the principles developed for handling fresh market apples should be incorporated. Unfortunately, economics often forces the packer of organic citrus into using equipment that has been designed and constructed for packing conventional citrus. Such packing lines focus on high volume and are often somewhat rough on the fruit, and rely on the application postharvest chemicals to prevent decay.

Often minor modifications of existing equipment can be implemented which will greatly reduce the number and severity of injuries on the packingline. Careful attention to brush type and condition, strategic padding, adjustment of deliveries, installation of self cleaning shears, and operating the packingline at the design capacity are all among the things that the operator can do to minimize injury. One excellent source of information on this subject is a publication from the University of Florida (Miller *et al.* 2001, Chapter 12).

There are several points of potential problems for the packer of organic citrus. Among these are:

1. Each time the fruit changes direction, there is a potential for injury.

2. Brushes become worn and can injure fruit.

3. Brushes can harbor decay organisms, especially sour rot, and should be easily cleanable.

4. Water elimination donuts can catch twigs, etc. and be a source of injury to the fruit.

5. Water elimination donuts can harbor decay organisms.

BREAKING THE TRIANGLE

There are several places where the packer of organic citrus can take steps to reduce the risk of decay or breakdown. While most of these will not be as effective as conventional methods, their cumulative effect will improve the overall result.

TABLE 19.2. US Regulations Involving Citrus

Agency	Description	Code of Federal Regulations	Section[a]
USDA	National Organic Program	Title 7	Subchapter M, Part 205
FDA	Food and Drug Administration	Title 21	Subchapter B, Parts 170-190
EPA	Pesticide Programs	Title 40	Subchapter E, Part 150-189

[a]Not all regulations except those under the USDA's National Organic Program apply to Organic Citrus.

The Grove. If the organic packer has control of the grove, this is the place to start. By removing dead wood from the trees before spores of the stem-end rots can be produced, infection of the fruit can be reduced. Pruning is more effective against *Diplodia* than *Phomopsis* but even then is only about 50% effective (Fulton 1925). Keeping the grove free of weeds and dropped fruit will further reduce the spore load of blue and green mold (*Penicillium*) as well as sour rot. Herbicides based upon organic sources of eugenol have been demonstrated to be useful in weed control (Chase *et al.* 2004). Lime-sulfur and peroxide-based fungicides can also contribute to the reduction of pathogen spores.

In areas where brown rot is a factor, keeping the tree skirt trimmed up high enough to avoid splashing from the ground (at least 24 inches) can help reduce this decay. Other treatments include spraying the ground under the trees and the lower outside areas of the trees with organically approved copper based sprays such as bordeaux or zinc sulfate-copper sul-

TABLE 19.3. Useful Web Sites

Site name	Address
National Organic Program Main	http://www.ams.usda.gov/nop/indexIE.htm
NOP Accredited Certifiers	http://www.ams.usda.gov/nop/CertifyingAgents/Accredited.html
National Organic Standards Board (NSOB)	http://www.ams.usda.gov/nosb/index.htm
Code of Federal Regulations National Organic Program 7CFR	http://www.access.gpo.gov/nara/cfr/cfr-table-search.html (Follow links to current Title 7 Part 205)
OMRI Organic Materials Review Institute	http://www.omri.org
Washington State Organic Program	http://agr.wa.gov/FoodAnimal/Organic/default.htm
Organic (LTD)[a]	http://organic.com.au/certify
Organic Europe	http://www.organic-europe.net
The New Farm	http://www.newfarm.org

[a]International listing of organic organizations, by country.

fate-hydrated lime mixtures where copper toxicity is not a problem (Ohr and Menge 2004).

Harvesting. In areas where the stem-end rots are a problem, since the organism is harbored in the dead tissue of the button, harvesting to leave the button behind will contribute to reduction of this decay. Unfortunately when some varieties are pulled to leave the button, plugging may result. This wound will increase the chance of Penicilluim molds or sour rot.

Other procedures can help reduce loss. Testing for rind oil rupture pressure before harvesting will help prevent oleocellosis (Oberbacher 1965; Wardowski *et al.* 1997). Prompt transportation to the packinghouse after harvesting will reduce the build-up of field heat. Above all, the advantages of gentle handling cannot be over stressed (MacRill 1971, Ismail 2004).

At the Packinghouse. Upon receipt of the fruit at the packinghouse the fruit should be processed with minimal delay. Moving the fruit into high humidity will reduce the development of SERB in susceptible varieties and help promote lignification of minor wounds.

If the fruit is to be degreened, carefully control the temperature, humidity and ethylene content of the degreening rooms (Chapter 10). One factor often overlooked by packers is that the exhaust from internal combustion engines (propane, gasoline, diesel) contains gasses that can have the same deleterious effects that are caused by ethylene. For this reason least one packer has changed to electrically powered fork lifts for in all fruit handling areas.

Degreening. The degreening conditions used by various packers will vary according to the variety and especially with the growing area (Chapter 10). In all cases, high humidity should be maintained. This is beneficial in promoting the healing of minor wounds that do not penetrate to the albedo (Brown *et al.* 1978). If harvested fruit are placed into conditions of high humidity without delay, wound pathogens have a reduced chance of becoming established and some peel disorders are prevented (McCornack and Grierson 1965; Davis *et al.* 1963).

Special care needs to be taken when fruit from growing areas where the stem-end rots are endemic. Ethylene concentrations should be kept to a minimum, as ethylene tends to stimulate the organisms while reducing the fruit's natural resistance to decay (Zhang 2004), while the temperatures used for degreening this fruit are ideal for pathogen growth.

Since ethylene both stimulates many pathogens and reduces the resistance of the fruit to decay (Brown 1986), it is important that degreening conditions be carefully controlled, and that the amount of ethylene be kept to a minimum. Using the lowest effective levels of ethylene 0.1 to 1.0 ppm (Reid 2002) is strongly advised for the packer of organic citrus.

Some varieties of fruit have been found to respond favorably, and with less decay, when lower temperatures and shortened degreening times are used. In Florida the normal degreening conditions used are 5 ppm ethylene, 85°F (29°C), 92-96% RH, for up to 96 hours. Tests with the tangerine hybrid Fallglo have shown that a reduced temperature of 65-70°F (18-21°C) and degreening times of 8-12 hours resulted in less decay without sacrificing color development (Dou *et al.* 2004).

The Packline. Operating the packline with the precautions noted below will help ensure the greatest chance of having sound, decay free fruit at arrival. When packing do not over fill the cartons, the "bulge pack" favored by many conventional packers, will injure the fruit, thus making it susceptible to decay.

DECAY CONTROL TECHNIQUES—CURRENT AND FUTURE

Current Treatments

Some treatments and processes are already available to the packer of organic citrus. These meet the requirements of the NOP, and where appropriate, the requirements of the EPA and FDA. Formulated products and, in some cases, single chemical products require approval by one or more of the agencies concerned.

Biological Control Agents

These may be divided into two main groups, microorganisms and biological products. In the United States there are currently two microorganism based products available for postharvest decay control in citrus. The product sold under the trade name Aspire® is based on the yeast *Candida oleophila* and the product sold under the trade name BioSave® is based on the bacterium *Pseudomonas syringae*. Both Aspire® and BioSave® have US EPA registrations.

The microorganism-based products have shown some efficacy, but only under very limited circumstances. Since their mode of action is to compete with plant pathogens for nutrients and space, the timing of their application is critical. Once a wound pathogen has established itself in the tissue of the citrus, its eradication is most difficult.

A factor to be considered when using microorganism based products, is that they cannot be used as simple substitutes for conventional fungicides. They have a limited spectrum of efficacy when compared to conventional products (Butt and Copping 2000). They are not as effective as the synthetic fungicides and have a limited effective life (Narciso 2004). Another consideration is that both Aspire® and BioSave® are living organisms and that their action is a function of their continued growth, therefore, they must be stored and used under conditions that will keep them alive. In addition to that the user must avoid treatments that will impair their usefulness.

Biological products would also include plant extracts including volatile or essential oils. Since many of these oils contain large amounts of natural compounds that have bactericidal and fungicidal properties, there is a potential for formulating products that could function as postharvest fungicides for citrus (Hall and Fernandez 2004). A limited number of these products have reached the marketplace but their utility is yet unproven.

Sanitizers

Sanitizers destroy microorganisms on the surface they contact. This could be equipment, fruit or process waters. In the case of organic processes the available sanitizers have no residual effect beyond immediate contact. Their main contribution is in providing pathogen free water for washing, rinsing, floating, etc. Using clean pathogen free water will provide a measure of decay control, especially in the case of wound pathogens. Before synthetic pesticides were introduced, Florida packers using clean water were successful in reducing the incidence of decay in shipped fruit (Hall 2003).

Ozone. Ozone is a normal oxygen molecule (O_2) with an extra atom of oxygen forming O_3. This is a powerful oxidizer and will vigorously attack microorganisms. While it is more selective than chlorine, attacking living organisms in preference to nonliving organic material, it will oxidize any organic matter on contact (Kelley 2004).

As a postharvest treatment of citrus, experimental work has demonstrated that ozone in the storage room air will suppress sporulation of *P. digitatum* in fruit stored at 50°F (10°C) or less, however the concentrations required far exceed safe levels for worker exposure (Smilanick 2003; Ritenour *et al.* 2001).

In water ozone will act as a sanitizer, in effect providing biologically clean water for fruit washing. The use of fresh clean water, as opposed to recirculated and potentially contaminated water, for fruit washing was one of the earliest decay reduction techniques used by Florida packers (Hall 2003).

Currently, ozone must be generated on site and the equipment required is expensive and complex. This and ozone's high corrosiveness an human health hazards has prevented it's extensive use.

Chlorine. The hypochlorites (chlorine) are extremely effective biocides. They are inexpensive and relatively simple to use. Their use in organic processing is strictly controlled but the United States regulations are ambiguous as to the amount that can be used. One interpretation of current regulation is that any amount may be used on the fruit as long as the waste stream does not exceed drinking water standards. Another interpretation limits their use to the lower drinking water standard throughout (USDA 2004). The State of Washington limits the use of chlorine to 50 ppm in contact with produce and in much of Europe, the postharvest use of chlorine is prohibited (McEvoy 2001, 2003).

In use, chlorine, most commonly in the form of sodium hypochlorite, is added to the process water. To be effective, an acid needs to be added to bring the pH to about 6.5. At this pH the chlorine has a high level of activity coupled with a lowered level of corrosiveness. Even so the level of chlorine must be in the range of 25-50 ppm to be of any practical use as a sanitizer. In the United States the use of chlorine compounds in agricultural applications is subject to restrictions by the US EPA. When using chlorine compounds at a level greater than 25 ppm, products specifically registered for that use must be used.

The disadvantages of using a sodium hypochlorite form of chlorine are due to the fact that the active form, the hypochlorite ion, is a nonselective oxidizer. It will attack any organic matter, not just microorganisms. When used at low levels in tank and flume systems, chlorine has been seen to cause an increase of available decay organisms due to their having been released from the biofilm (Kelley 2004).

Other concerns are the possibility of forming trihalomethanes (THCs) (Katz 1980) and finally, when sodium hypochlorite is the source, there can be a build-up of salt in the process water.

Chlorine Dioxide. Second only to ozone as a disinfectant in water chlorine dioxide (ClO_2) is also listed as a specifically approved material under the US NOP (USDA 2004). It is subject to the same limitations as the hypochlorites. ClO_2 is favored by some because it does not form THCs.

ClO_2 is usually generated on site by reacting sodium chlorite, sodium hypochlorite and an acid. In the case of organic production, an approved acid such as citric or acetic would be used. One note of caution in this regard is that if the balance between the three ingredients is not strictly controlled, the possibility of producing undesirable by-products is increased (Katz 1980).

Beside the possibility of producing THCs in an out of balance system, there is also the possibility of releasing chlorine dioxide into the atmosphere of the packinghouse. In the United States the established threshold limit value for chlorine dioxide is 0.1 ppm and it is classified as being "Highly Toxic" (Plunkett 1976).

Peroxide. Hydrogen peroxide (H_2O_2) is a powerful oxidizing agent and therefore acts as a strong disinfectant. It will destroy bacteria, yeasts, and mold spores on contact. It is used as a spray or wash for both equipment and produce. Its greatest advantage is that as it dries, it breaks down into oxygen and water leaving no residue of any kind.

When used to sanitize equipment, a concentration of 2500-3000 ppm is used. Since this compound is quite corrosive at this concentration, treatment should be followed by a potable water rinse.

For fresh citrus typical treatments of 250-300 ppm are applied as a spray or drench. Hydrogen peroxide may be applied immediately after the dump, and/or incorporated into the post washing rinse. Since there is no residue after the product has dried, it should not interfere with any subsequent treatment such as waxing or labeling. However, some formulations may contain ingredients not approved for organic use and should be checked before use.

Fungicides

Soda Ash. The use of heated sodium carbonate solutions as a decay control measure has a long history of use in the citrus industry. Typically the fruit are immersed in a 1 ¼-3% solution at 110-120°F for 3 minutes, followed by brushing and a fresh water rinse. This method of decay control dates back al least to the mid 1920s and is reported to be effective against the Penicillium molds and brown rot (Fulton and Bowman 1925; Fawcett 1936). In recent times some packers have substituted sodium bicarbonate with equally effective results (Smilanick *et al.* 1999; Zhang and Swingle 2003).

The United States regulatory status of this treatment is unclear. There is also a problem with disposing of spent solutions due to their high sodium content. Packers using the carbonates have extended the useful life of the solutions by filtering and heating the dirty solutions to 160°F (71°C) for half an hour. The concentration is usually maintained by the use of specific gravity hydrometer. Table 19.4 provides the specific gravity of fresh solutions of sodium carbonate and sodium bicarbonate (Weast and Astle 1981).

Lime Sulfur. One promising postharvest treatment is the use of lime sulfur (calcium polysulfide). In tests conducted in California, immersion in a 3% solution of lime sulfur for 3 minutes at 110°F, significantly reduced green mold and sour rot in lemons and oranges without significant phytotoxicity (Smilanick and Sorenson 1999). Tests against other postharvest decay organisms have not been reported.

The advantages of this treatment is that a formulation is currently available that has been approved by the US EPA and it conforms the NOP. Lime-sulfur is also approved as an organic fungicide/insecticide for preharvest use, therefore the disposal of spent solutions may not be a significant problem.

A major disadvantage is the odor of hydrogen sulfide (rotten eggs) given off by heated solutions which could be a nuisance to workers. There is also the possibility that the concentration of hydrogen sulfide could exceed the established Threshold Limit (TLV) of 10 ppm in unventilated areas, therefore some regulatory agencies require that when used indoors, a closed system be used.

TABLE 19.4. Specific Gravity of Carbonate Solutions at 20°C

Concentration	Sodium carbonate	Sodium bicarbonate
1.0%	1.0104	1.0072
1.5%	1.0156	1.0107
2.0%	1.0208	1.0143
2.5%	1.0260	1.0178
3.0%	1.0312	1.0214

Physical Methods

There are a number of practices that the packer of organic citrus may implement with minimal change in his operation. Many of these merely involve careful attention to the details of current practices.

Recent research aimed at increasing the natural resistance of citrus to decay has focused on two different approaches. Each is aimed at slightly stressing the fruit which stimulates the production of antifungal compounds in the peel (Ben-Yehosha 2003; Rodov et al. 1994).

Heat—With/without Soda Ash. Decay control by immersing citrus in hot water has been practiced for many years. By immersing California lemons for 4 minutes in 115-120°F (46-49°C), with or without other chemicals, brown rot is significantly reduced. The effectiveness of this method, and the possibility of peel injury depends upon, the turgidity of the fruit, its temperature at the time of treatment and the length of time since infection. Slightly wilted fruit, at room temperature and within 60 hours of infection had the best results (Klotz and DeWolfe 1961B). No significant control of either green mold or sour rot has been noted by this method. However the incorporation of soda ash in the hot water treatment has been effective against these other two organisms.

Lanza et al. (2000) demonstrated that green mold could be controlled in organic lemons with a hot water dip of 144°F (62°C) for 60 seconds, but notes that rind injury can occur if the fruit are cold and turgid at the time of treatment.

In tests where citrus fruit were brushed vigorously for 20-30 seconds with water heated to 145°F (63°C) control of green mold in inoculated fruit was equal to that attained by synthetic fungicides (Porat et al. 2000).

UV-C. Ultraviolet light at 254 will kill green mold and sour rot (Fernandez and Hall 2004) and also stimulates the development of development of resistance to decay in citrus fruits. This effect does not manifest itself for 2 to 10 days after exposure, and. the exposures required are very high (Rodov et al. 1994). UV-C dose not, at present, have usefulness as a decay control measure.

Tissue Wraps. A very old method of packing citrus is the use of tissue wraps (Hall 2003). Each piece of fruit was wrapped in a tissue that, among other things, isolated a decaying fruit from adjacent pieces. Subsequently, these wraps were impregnated with oil or wax, which helped reduce shrinkage. Modern waxes and fungicides later obviated their use.

Some packers of premium gift fruit have used tissue wrapped fruit as a top layer. These wraps are more for appearance and advertising. With recipes and reordering information printed on the wrap, they are considered useful for advertising. Modern organic packers could use this as a useful replacement or an addition to waxing and as an adjunct to their decay control program.

Pressure Wash. As a decay control method pressure washing (See Chapter 15) has limited usefulness. Recirculated water can become a source of infection unless kept clean with an approved sanitizer. Since a pressure washer will help remove buttons, a source of stem end rot infection, it may help in areas where these diseases are endemic. Pressure washing can help improve packout by removing sooty mold residue. However excessive pressure in such a system can cause physical injury to the fruit (Petracek *et al.* 1998).

Temperature. Maintaining citrus at the proper temperature during all phases of the packing operation is crucial for optimum results. Once the fruit is packed it should be quickly cooled to the lowest safe temperature for the variety, growing area and season, in order to avoid chilling injury, etc. (Kader and Arpaia 2002). A thorough discussion of these appear in Chapters 13, 14 and 20.

The Future

There are many procedures under development that have potential usefulness for the packer of organic citrus. Most have passed the laboratory stage but have yet to be proven practical. A few have been tried with varying results, even receiving enthusiastic support from those trying them, however trials under controlled conditions and with variable factors are lacking.

The use of an organic abscission agent to loosen the fruit before harvest can help reduce plugging (Burns and Beader 2003). Where stem-end rot is problem, this could also help as most spores would have been left behind with the button.

Essential Oil Fungicides

The essential oil of clove is high in the compound eugenol with the natural oil distilled from the leaves of this plant containing as much as 88% (Lawless 1995). Products containing either synthetic or natural eugenol are available in the United States and Europe. Preliminary tests in the United States have not been entirely successful. Treatments that controlled green mold, also resulted in peel damage in some trials (Smilanick 2004).

Certification. Packers of organic citrus in the United States must be certified by an Accredited Certifying Agent who will inspect the operation and the chemicals used. Under NOP regulations the decision of a USDA certified agent is binding on all other agents. Many certifying agents rely of the certification of others when approving process materials. At least two organizations, the privately run Organic Materials Review Institute (OMRI) and the state administered Washington State Organic Food Program publish lists of approved materials on the internet (Table 19.3).

However if a packer is to export organic citrus it must comply with the regulations of the receiving country. At this time this Organic (Ltd.) lists 363 organic organizations in 55 countries from Albania to Zimbabwe (Table 19.3). Information regarding regulatory factors is continually changing. Table 19.3 also lists useful web sites to keep the packer of organic citrus apprised of the changes that are taking place.

The challenges facing the packer of fresh organic citrus are not insurmountable. By carefully observing the following, one can greatly improve their product. Each of these points is aimed at one or more of the legs of the loss triangle.

1. Harvest only fruit that do not require excessive degreening time (Host, Environment).

2. Pressure test the fruit before harvest (Host).

3. Transport the fruit to the packinghouse as quickly as possible and protect the fruit from over heating by direct sun (Environment).

4. Process the fruit (degreening or packing) with minimal delay (Host).

5. Keep the fruit in the optimum environment for the variety at all stages under the packers control (Environment).

6. Protect the fruit from injury (Host, Pathogen).

7. Keep the packinghouse as clean of decaying fruit as possible and do not allow spores from decaying fruit to drift onto sound fruit (Pathogen).

8. Keep the process line clean (Pathogen).

9. Regularly inspect the packing line for places that might cause injury (Host).

10. Do not overfill cartons (Host).

11. Cool packed fruit to the proper temperature for the variety as quickly as possible after packing (Host, Pathogen, Environment).

By applying these simple rules, the packer of fresh organic citrus can offer their customers an attractive product with the minimum of problems.

REFERENCES

AINSWORTH, G. C. 1971. Dictionary of the Fungi. Commonwealth Mycological Institute. Kew, Surry, England.

BEN-YEHOSHUA, S. 2003. Effects of postharvest heat and UV applications on decay, chilling injury and resistance against pathogens of citrus and other fruits and vegetables. Acta Hort. 599, 159-173.

BROWN, G. E. 1986. Diplodia stem-end rot, a decay of citrus fruit increased by ethylene degreening treatment and its control. Proc. Fla. State Hort. Soc. 99, 105-186.

BROWN, G. E., ISMAIL, M. A. and BARMORE, C. R. 1978. Lignification of injuries to citrus fruit and susceptibility to green mold. Proc. Fla. State Hort. Soc. 91, 124-126.

BURNS, J. K. and BEADER, C. 2003 Coronatine as an Abcission Agent. U.S. Patent No. 6,511,939.

BUTT, TARIQ M. and COPPING, L. G. 2000. Fungal biological control agents. Pest. Outlook 11, 186-191.

CHASE, C. A., SCHOLENBERG, J. M. and MacDONALD, G. E. 2004. Preliminary evaluation of nonsynthetic herbicides for weed management in organic orange production. Proc. Fla. State Hort. Soc. 117, 135-138.

DAVIS, P. L., HARDING, P. L. and SUNDAY, M. B. 1963. Factors affecting rind breakdown of citrus fruits. U.S. Dept. Agr. MRR No. 596.

DOU, H., JONES, S., LEE, J-Y. and RITENOUR, M. 2004. Alternative degreening of "Fallglo" tangerines. Proc. Fla. State Hort. Soc. 117, 392-295.

FAWCETT, HOWARD S. 1936. Citrus Diseases and Their Control. McGraw-Hill Book Company, Inc., New York.

FERNANDEZ, Y. J. and HALL, D. J. 2004. In vitro response of *Penicillium digitatum* and *Geotrichum candidum* to ultraviolet (UV-C) exposure. Proc. Fla. State Hort. Soc. 117, 380-381.

FULTON, H. R. 1925. The Borax treatment for prevention of decay. Proc. Fla. State Hort. Soc. 38, 117-123.

FULTON, H. R. and BOWMAN, J. J. 1925. Process for prevention of decay of citrus fruits. U.S. Patent No. 1,560,558.

HALL, D. J. 1981. Innovations in citrus waxing—an overview. Proc. Fla. State Hort. Soc. 94, 258-263.

HALL, D. J. 2003. Twentieth century developments in handling Florida's fresh citrus fruit - an overview. Proc. Fla. State Hort. Soc. 116, 369-374.

HALL, D. J. and FERNANDEZ, Y. J. 2004. In vitro evaluation of selected essential oils as fungicides against *Penicillium digitatum* Sacc. Proc. Fla. State Hort. Soc. 117, 377-379.

ISMAIL, M. A., 2004. Handle with care. Florida Grower. 97(10), 12,14.

ISMAIL, M. A. and W. F. WARDOWSKI, W. F. 1990. Quality Control for a Florida Citrus Packinghouse. Quality Control Assessment Methodology. Short Course Proceedings. Lake Alfred, CREC. 92-99

ISMAIL, M. A. and ZHANG, J. X. 2004. Post-harvest citrus disease control. Outlooks Pest Manag. 15, 29-35.

KADER, A. A. and ARPAIA, M. L. 2002. Postharvest Handling Systems: Subtropical Fruits. *In* Postharvest Technology of Horticultural Crops. Adel A. Kader (Technical Editor). University of California. Publication 3311.

KATZ, J. 1980. Ozone and Chlorine Dioxide Technology for Disinfection of Drinking Water. Noyes Data Corporation, Park Ridge, NJ.

KELLEY, D. 2004. Using chlorine effectively and ORP technology. Wash. State Hort. Assoc. Tree Fruit Postharvest Conf., Yakima, WA.

KLOTZ L. J. and DeWOLFE, T. A. 1961A. Brown rot contact infection of citrus fruits prior to hot water treatment. Plant. Disease Reptr. 45, 268-271.

KLOTZ L. J. and DeWOLFE, T. A. 1961B. Limitations of the hot water immersion treatment for the control of Phytophthora Brown Rot of lemons. Plant. Disease Reptr. 45, 264-267.

LANZA, G., ALEPPO, E. di MARTINO, STRANO, M. C. and RECUPEREO, G. R. 2000. Evaluation of hot water treatments to control postharvest green mold in organic lemon fruit. Proc. Int. Soc. Citricult, IX Congr. 1167-1168.

LAWLESS, J. 1995. The Illustrated Encyclopedia of Essential Oils. Harper/Collins. Hammersmith, London.

MacRILL, J. R. 1971. Valencia orange treatment and storage system. U.S. Pat. No. 3,592,665.

McEVOY, M. 2001. Organic regulations for Washington and the United States. Proc. Wash. State. Hort. Assoc. Tree Fruit Postharvest Conf.

McEVOY, M. 2003. Organic certification in the United States and Europe. Proc. Wash. State. Hort. Assoc. Tree Fruit Postharvest Conf.

McCORNACK, A. A. and GRIERSON. W. 1965. Practical measures for control of rind breakdown of oranges. Agric. Ext. Serv. University of Florida, Circular 286.

MILLER, W. M., WARDOWSKI, W. F. and GRIERSON, W. 2001. Packingline machinery for Florida citrus packinghouses. Fla. Coop. Ext. Svc. Bul. 239. April 2001. University of Florida, Lake Alfred.

NARCISO, J. A. 2004. Pseudomonas biological control agents: Do they have a role in citrus packinghouses? Packinghouse Newsletter No. 200. University of Florida, IFAS, Lake Alfred.

OBERBACHER, M. F. 1965. A method to predict the post-harvest incidence of oleocellosis on lemons. Proc Fla. State Hort. Soc. 78, 237-240

OHR, H. D. and MENGE, J. A. 2004. Brown Rot. UC IPM Pest Management Guidelines: Citrus. UC ANR Publication 3441. University of California, Riverside.

PETRACEK, P. D., KELSEY, D. F. and DAVIS, C. 1998. Response of citrus fruit to high-pressure washing. J. Amer. Hort. Soc. 123(4), 661-667.

PLUNKETT, E. R. 1976. Handbook of Industrial Toxicology. Chemical Publishing Co. New York, NY.

PORAT, R., DAUS, A., WEISS, B, COHEN, L., FALLIK, E. and DROBY, S. 2000. Reduction of postharvest decay in organic citrus fruit by a short hot water brushing treatment. Postharvest Biol. Technol. 18(2), 151-157.

RAMSEY, H. J. 1912. The relation of handling to decay of Florida oranges in transit and on the market. Proc. Fla. State Hort. Soc. 25, 28-42.

REID, M. S. 2002. Ethylene in Postharvest Technology. In Postharvest Technology of Horticultural Crops, Adel A. Kader (Technical Editor). University of California. Publication 3311.

RITENOUR, M. A., SARGENT, STEVEN A. and BRECHT, J. K. 2001. Sanitizers for citrus packinghouse recirculated water systems. Packinghouse Newsletter No. 193. University of Florida, IFAS, Fort Pierce.

RODOV, V., BEN-YEHOSHUA, S., FANG, D., D'HALLEWIN, G. and CASTIA, T. 1994. Accumulation of Phytoalexins scoparone and scopoletin in citrus fruits subjected to various postharvest treatments. Acta Hort. 381, 517-523.

ROISTACHER, C. N., KLOTZ, L. J. and EAKS, I. L. 1956. Detecting surface injuries to fruit. Citrograph 41, 239-242.

SMILANICK, J. L. 2003. Postharvest use of ozone on citrus fruit. Packinghouse Newsletter No. 199. University of Florida, IFAS. Fort Pierce.

SMILANICK, J. L. 2004. Personal communication. USDA, Parlier, CA.

SMILANICK, J. L. and SORENSON, D. 1999. Use of Lime-Sulfur solutions for the control of postharvest mold of citrus fruit. Subtropical Fruit News 7(1), 18-22.

SMILANICK, J. L., MARGOSAN, D. A., MILKOTA, F., USALL, J. and MICHAEL, I. F. 1999. Control of citrus green mold by carbonate and bicarbonate salts and he influence of commercial postharvest practices on their efficacy. Plant Dis. 83, 139-145.

SNOWDEN, A. L. 1990. A Color Atlas of Post-Harvest Diseases of Fruits and Vegetables. Vol. 1: General Introduction and Fruits. CRC Press, Boca Raton, FL.

USDA. 2004. Subchapter M—Organic Foods Production Act Provisions. Code of Federal Regulations. Title 7. U.S. Dept. Agr. Washington, DC.

WARDOWSKI, W. F., PETRACEK, P. D. and Grierson, W. 1997. Oil Spotting (Oleocellosis) of Citrus Fruit. University of Florida, Coop. Ext. Serv. Circular 410.

WEAST, R. C. and ASTLE, M. J. 1981. Handbook of Chemistry and Physics. CRC Press, Inc., Boca Raton, FL.

ZHANG, J. X. 2004. Effect of ethylene on natural resistance of citrus fruit to stem-end rot caused by *Diplodia natalensis* and its relation to postharvest control of this decay. Proc. Fla. State Hort. Soc. 117, 364-367.

ZHANG, J. X. and SWINGLE, P. 2003. Control of green mold on Florida citrus fruit using bicarbonate salts. Proc. Fla. State Hort. Soc. 116, 375-378.

Storage of Citrus Fruits

William Grierson and William M. Miller

Storage *per se* cannot be considered by itself. Successful storage of citrus fruits is conditional on correct procedures being followed prior to storage. These are touched upon briefly here, but dealt with in detail in several previous chapters, which should be studied carefully before undertaking a storage program. These are dealt with in Chapter 2 (Maturity), Chapter 7 (Harvesting), Chapter 8 (Transportation to the Packinghouse). Of particular importance for citrus fruits are fungicides (Chapter 13) and packaging (Chapter 16). Without careful attention to such prior considerations, storage of citrus fruits can be an expensive waste of product and of money.

One of the advantages of citrus, as opposed to deciduous fruits, is that most cultivars have good keeping qualities, both on and off the tree. Many of these fruits may be stored for long periods on the tree without loss of flavor and with minimum spoilage. It is common practice to extend the harvest period of many citrus cultivars after they have reached maturity in order to optimize factors such as profitability, orderly marketing, weather, and available manpower. However, *for storage the fruit must be picked well before termination of the normal tree storage period* (Grierson 1995). Postbloom storage on the tree can severely limit the potential for postharvest cold storage and also reduce the next year's yield. Unlike almost all other fruits, tree storage competes economically with postharvest storage.

IDENTIFYING THE MAJOR HAZARDS

Successful storage of any living product depends on prior accurate evaluation of whatever is the major hazard liable to end successful storage life. The commercial life span of harvested citrus fruit may be reduced or terminated because of several processes: (1) decay, (2) weight loss and resulting shrinkage, (3) overmaturity resulting in off-flavor and/or undesirable color changes, (4) softening, (5) physiological disorders in general, and (6) chilling injury (CI) in cold storage. Citrus fruits have no respiratory climacteric;

their respiration declines gradually after harvest (Biale 1961). The fruit achieves maturity and reaches its full flavor on the tree. Subsequent physiological and chemical changes on and off the tree are slow, and nutritional value and flavor are maintained over a long period.

Citrus fruit generally become unmarketable either because of the development of decay or peel shrinkage, even though the juice vesicles are still turgid and the fruit possesses normal flavor. The relative importance of decay and shrinkage varies in different regions. In warm, humid climates, such as Florida, Brazil, or southeastern Asia, decay is more important than in arid regions, such as California or Israel, where postharvest shrinkage and softening play larger roles. Problems in postharvest storage are often related to the time of picking fruit within the season. Early in the season, citrus fruit are more sensitive to oleocellosis and other harvest-induced blemishes but are more resistant to decay. As the season progresses and the fruit senesce, they also become more susceptible to decay and granulation (Burns and Albrigo 1997). Other preharvest factors (e.g., rootstock and scion selection, tree condition, cultural practices, weather prior to time of picking, and grove treatments) also influence the keeping quality of citrus fruits (see Chapter 3).

Successful postharvest storage of citrus depends to a large extent on minimizing losses from fungal decay, shrinkage, and softening; the latter leads to fruit deformation that adversely affects marketability. Postharvest life depends on complicated interactions between the physiology of the fruit and of its pathogens; these interactions need to be manipulated by various storage techniques to prolong the life span of stored fruit.

Before going into the details of storage, preharvest factors that influence the keeping quality of fruit and into the details of storage techniques, several of the processes leading to the deterioration of citrus fruit should be considered.

Maturity

As noted above, citrus fruits that have expended their storage potential during tree storage *must not be placed in storage nor shipped to distant markets.* Seeking to do so can be very expensive. Internal quality determinations, which are virtually automatic for Florida citrus (Wardowski et al. 1995), should be heeded scrupulously (Grierson 1995).

A large, usually very well run, packinghouse stored Valencia oranges for late summer sale. The State inspectors routinely took juice samples from every incoming load, to which, unfortunately, no heed was paid. After one storage was filled (A samples in Figs. 20.1 and 20.2), there was a 10-day delay before filling the second storage (B samples in Figs. 20.1 and 20.2). In that period, juice acid declined sharply with consequent dramatic increase in solids:acid ratio, a clear indication of over maturity. Three hundred thou-

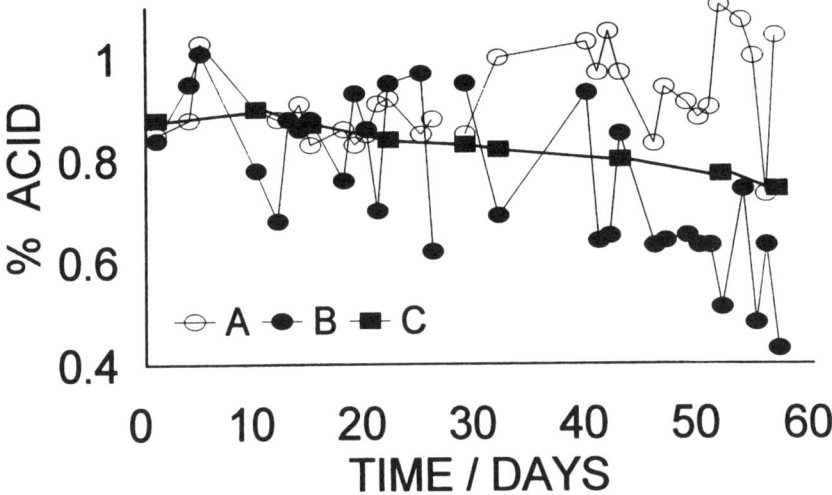

Fig. 20.1. Percentage acid of Valencia oranges going into (A) the home storage and (B) the contract storage. State averages (from fruit received at the canneries) are shown for comparison (C). *From Grierson (1995).*

sand dollars worth of fruit put into the second (delayed) storage proved to be totally unmarketable after storage. *They had been stored with virtually no potential storage life left* (Grierson 1995).

Decay

There are two types of infection of citrus that lead to postharvest diseases: (1) quiescent infections of the fruit initiated during the growing season (e.g., stem-end rots) that become active after picking (Brooks 1942), and (2) fungi (mainly *Penicillium* spp.) that develop from airborne spores infecting lesions (injuries) incurred during harvesting and packinghouse handling. The etiology and modes of infection of these various fungi are discussed in Chapter 13.

Sour rot (*Geotrichum candidum*) and black rot or stem-end rot (*Alternaria citri*) vary unpredictably. Not only can it be problematical when to store a given variety, but storage conditions may need to be varied with the time of picking (Chace *et al.* 1966; Grierson 1974; Khalifah and Kuykendall 1965). Greater amounts of all decays developed in Florida Valencia oranges harvested in May and stored for 16 weeks than in fruit harvested from the same trees in April (Smoot 1969).

Such controllable variables complicate the selection of optimal storage conditions for a given situation, but they are minor compared with the ex-

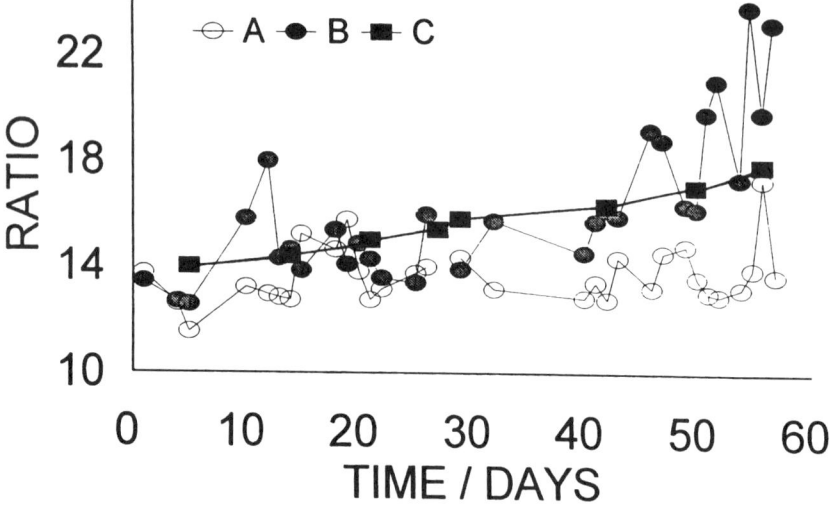

Fig. 20.2. Ratio of Valencia oranges going into (A) the home storage and (B) the contract storage. State averages, from fruit received at the canneries, are given for comparison (C).
From Grierson (1995).

traordinary amount of unexplained variability. Year-to-year variation is not as surprising (Chase 1969) as the day-to-day variation found, for example, in the response of Pineapple oranges picked from the same trees at approximately weekly intervals (Grierson 1962) or the diurnal variation between early morning and late afternoon picking (Grierson, unpublished data).

Water Loss

Weight loss during storage is a major factor in the postharvest deterioration of citrus fruit. Transpiration is the major process leading to weight loss and other aspects of physiological deterioration of citrus fruits. Not only does transpiration cause desiccation, shrivelling, accelerated softening, and loss of the attractive (saleable) appearance of fruit, but the resultant water stress also accelerates senescence (Ben-Yehoshua 1969; Ben-Yehoshua and Shapiro 1981). Weight loss as low as 5% renders oranges unsalable, and shrinkage becomes visible at half this value, i.e., 50% of the commercially tolerable weight loss is invisible (Kaufmann *et al.* 1956; Grierson and Wardowski 1978). The loss of weight involves mainly the peel, not the pulp of the fruit. Thus, after 2 months' storage at 20°C at 50-75% relative humidity (RH), the peel of Valencia oranges lost 9.5% of its weight, whereas the pulp lost only 2.1% (Ben-Yehoshua 1969). The peel changes its water status much more rapidly than the pulp; indeed, the diurnal fruit moisture loss while fruit are still on the tree comes primarily from the peel (Kaufmann 1970). Since the peel is a critical marketing feature, peel appearance is just as economically important, if not more so, than the flavor of the pulp.

Most of the water vapor, and other gases moving through detached citrus fruit, flow freely throughout the spongy parenchyma of the mesocarp (albedo) and the central axis, diffuses through the exocarp and the colored portion of the rind (flavedo), and evaporates on the surface (Kaufmann 1970). This gas exchange may be described by a modified form of Fick's Law (Burg and Burg 1965). The flavedo portion of the rind seems to be the primary site of resistance (Ben-Yehoshua 1969). Loss of water vapor from fruits is a passive process whose driving force is provided by the vapor pressure gradient between the peel and the air around the fruit (Grierson 1969; Grierson and Wardowski 1978). The effects of vapor pressure deficit (VPD) are illustrated in simulated transit experiments by Grierson (1969), who concluded that relative humidity (RH), considered alone, can be meaningless; rather, storage (or transit) effects on the fruit must be evaluated in terms of vapor pressure deficit (see also Gaffney 1978).

Anatomically, the fruits of some citrus cultivars are well suited for long postharvest life *if undamaged and picked at prime maturity.* But, unlike most other fruits, preharvest on tree storage of citrus competes economically with postharvest cold storage. The edible pulp, containing the juice vesicles and sacs is sealed off from the ambient atmosphere by the peel (flavedo and albedo). Within the flesh (endocarp), the surfaces of the juice vesicle, stalk, and sac have waxy cuticles (Shomer and Fahn 1976). Because of this, water vapor movement occurs primarily along the vesicle stalks and not between the vesicles. The vesicles, in addition to being relatively impermeable, also possess high osmotic pressure, so the pulp retains its turgidity and juices long after the peel has become brittle and dry. The edibility of such fruit is meaningless since they are no longer saleable.

The pulp of Shamouti oranges dries out much faster than that of grapefruit; Valencia oranges retain their juice the longest of any tested orange cultivar (Schiffmann-Nadel 1977). The peculiarities relating to the susceptibility of citrus fruits to desiccation are largely related to peel anatomy (see Chapter 1). Fruit size also affects water loss; transpiration rate is greater in smaller fruits, apparently due to their larger surface area per unit weight or volume in oranges (Haas 1927), but this effect does not show in grapefruit (McCornack 1975). The change in location of osmotically active substances within the fruit, with accompanying changes in osmotic and turgor pressures, plays a part in determining from which part of the fruit water loss will occur most readily (Haas and Klotz 1935). Limes kept in storage showed increases in amounts of juice, soluble solids, and ascorbic acid relative to the original fresh weight, even while there was a decrease in total fresh weight

(Eaks and Mosias 1965). However, because they have minimal cuticle, limes are subject to excessive water loss (Lincoln 1949).

Control of humidity and temperature is of critical importance in reducing the weight loss of citrus fruit that leads to shrinkage, softening, and susceptibility to decay. Good control of RH should include the prevention of water condensation on the surface of fruits (Grierson 1969), since the presence of free water at relatively high temperatures provides an ideal medium for the development of decay organisms (Eckert 1978).

Weight loss and shrinkage are directly related to vapor pressure deficit (VPD) but less to RH (Grierson and Wardowski 1978; Wells 1962). In an extensive study that included lemons, oranges, and grapefruit, weight loss at constant temperature increased about 50% with a twofold increase in VPD (Wells 1962).

The relative humidity in storage should be as high as possible, to prevent commercially unacceptable weight loss, without causing damage to the container (Kawada and Hale 1980). The rate of water loss during the first few days after harvest, when the peel of the citrus fruit is fully turgid and before the fruit reaches storage temperature, is much higher than during the rest of the storage period. Even small changes in RH significantly affect the rate of weight loss during the pull down period, which should be as rapid as possible to minimize this desiccating period.

In Marsh grapefruit stored for 20 weeks at 12°C, weight loss was 6.8% when the RH was 90% but increased to 12.4% when the RH was 80% (Schiffmann-Nadel *et al.* 1980). Very high humidity conditions at low temperatures (10°C) can be obtained with the Filacell® method (refrigeration and wetting of the air by passing it through wetted filaments), which leads to very low rates of weight loss. However, when the Filacell method is used, fibreboard storage cartons may collapse more frequently (Meredith 1973).

Physiological Disorders

Most physiological disorders that affect citrus fruit storage tend to be related to water loss or to chilling injury. An interesting finding, not yet exploited commercially, is that some of these disorders can be ameliorated by the use of preharvest antitranspirant sprays (Albrigo 1977). See Chapter 14 for a full discussion of physiological disorders.

Changes in Fruit Composition

Fruit color, flavor, firmness, and juice content may all undergo changes during storage, depending on cultivar, storage conditions (e.g., temperature or RH), packinghouse treatments (e.g., degreening), and even orchard (grove) conditions and treatments.

During storage of oranges, softening and subsequent deformation of the peel are accompanied by a concomitant increase in soluble pectins and in pectinates at the expense of insoluble protopectin (Sinclair and Jolliffe 1958); increases in malonic, succinic, and malic acids, although malic acid decreases in the juice (Sasson and Monselise 1977); increase in electrical conductivity (Monselise and Sasson 1977); decrease in uronic acid (the main component of pectins); and an increase in relative amounts of cellulose and sugars, especially galactose, arabinose, and rhamnose (Ben-Gad et al. 1981).

The chemical composition of grapefruit (acid and sugars in particular) is maintained without significant changes during a rather long period of storage, up to 6 weeks. During even more prolonged storage (16 weeks at 14°C), the concentration of acids decreased from 2 to 1.5% and total soluble solids decreased from 11.8 to 10%; thus, the sugar:acid ratio increased (Schiffman-Nadel et al. 1980). Ethanol concentration in the juice increased during prolonged storage (Davis 1974), resulting in a deterioration in the flavor of the fruit. Ethanol can be used as an indicator for fruit quality in storage (Davis and Hoffman 1973).

PREHARVEST FACTORS

Postharvest performance of citrus fruits is affected by the origin of the young tree (rootstock and scion selection), cultural or production methods, weather up to time of picking, and postharvest practices (see Chapter 3).

Rootstock

Keeping quality of a given variety is strongly influenced by rootstock (McDonald and Wutscher 1974; Grierson, unpublished data), much more so than with deciduous fruits. Rootstocks, however, are commonly selected not for the keeping quality of the resultant fruit, but for yield and their adaptation to the soil, groundwater, and perhaps climate. It is axiomatic among Florida citrus packers that high-solids fruit (those with high soluble solids, largely sugar) store and ship best. All other factors being equal (which they seldom are), fruit on sour orange rootstock will have higher solids than those on rough lemon (Harding and Fisher 1945; Harding et al. 1940). Unfortunately, sour orange rootstock is having to be widely discontinued due to calamitous losses from the Tristeza virus.

Grove Treatments

In selecting citrus for storage, grove treatments should be taken into account. Gibberellin sprays, though of recent use in Florida (Ismail and Wilhite 1992), are regularly used in California to extend storage life of lemons and limes (Coggins 1965). Composite sprays of gibberellin (20 ppm) and 2,4-D (16 ppm), applied to grapefruit trees in Israel during December and January, increased fruit viability and reduced rate of softening and decay (Monselise 1973A,B). Gibberellic acid sprays resulted in firmer late-season grapefruit (Ali-Dinar and Krezdorn 1976; Gilfillan *et al.* 1973; Chapter 4). Storage of Florida navels is not usual, being a very early crop. But if this is likely to be necessary, storage quality was improved by an October gibberellin spray (Ismail and Wilhite 1992). Preharvest gibberellin sprays preserved peel condition of Florida grapefruit cold-sterilized for 19 days at 1°C, but had no affect on decay (Miller and McDonald 1992).

The reported effects of fertilizer treatments on storage quality are highly inconsistent (Chapter 3). However, high nitrogen levels decrease storage potential (deFossard and Lenz 1967), whereas addition of GA_3, 2-4-D, urea phosphate and potassium sulphate increase it in Israel (Monselise 1981).

HARVESTING

The single most critical factor in fruit storage is careful harvesting. Although this indisputable fact was clearly established in a landmark study of 40 harvesting operations in California and Florida 90 years ago (Ramsey 1902, Grierson 1987), it is still very generally ignored. Fruit that has been abused during harvesting will have very poor storage potential in addition to decay losses. Harvesting abuses make fruit susceptible to subsequent distortion in transit and storage that leads to internal damage (Rivero *et al.* 1979).

The high cost and shortage of harvesting labor have resulted in the unfortunate practice of dropping picked fruit to the ground for harvest. Fruit harvested in this manner is subject to injury from thorny branches and is likely to be infected with sour or brown rot from ground contact. Such fruit should *never* be shipped as fresh fruit nor stored due to the high risk of decay. Florida Indian River Marsh grapefruit that were dropped when picked suffered severe internal bruising, as evidenced by the symptom designated as blossom-end clearing (McCornack 1966; Smoot and Melvin 1975; Chapter 14).

Many have thought that pulling oranges and grapefruit, rather than clipping them, is harmful, but when properly done, this is not so (Hopkins and McCornack 1960; Cohen *et al.* 1970). However, tangerines usually cannot be pulled because the peel is torn by pulling. It has long been known that decays such as mold and, to a lesser degree, sour rot, are directly related to rind injury (Smoot *et al.* 1971). The incidence of *Penicillium* mold has been shown to be related to the type and severity of the injury (Smoot and Melvin 1961). Rough handling by commercial pickers more than doubled the decay of grapefruit over those handled carefully. Many rind injuries not readily observable at the grading belt can act as avenues of infection (Smoot and Melvin 1975). *Roughly harvested fruit are not suited to commercial storage.*

Light ladders, picking bags of modest size (ca. 20 kg) with rigid framing, and rigid containers into which the fruit is placed should be used (see Chapter 7).

Optimal Harvest Time for Prolonged Storage

For long storage, fruit must be picked when it still has considerable vitality; however, determining the optimal harvest time is a matter of judgment, since there is no well-defined physiological indication such as is usual with deciduous fruits. In Israel, much work has been carried out on the effect of time of harvest on storage potential of Marsh grapefruit. Schiffmann-Nadel *et al.* (1980) found that the overall harvest season may be subdivided into three periods according to response to prolonged storage. Fruit harvested during the first period, November to the beginning of February, exhibit the highest rate of decay (especially of stem-end rot) during prolonged storage until August. These fruit, especially those harvested in January until mid-February, store well until the beginning of June, and the level of decay increases only in July and August. Fruit from the second harvest period, February and March, develop relatively less decay and the shorter the storage period the less the incidence of stem-end rot. Fruit from the third harvest period, which includes April and May, should remain in storage for no more than 3-4 months and are characterized by somewhat increased, but still low levels of decay, particularly those caused by molds, and a very low level of stem-end rot and internal breakdown rot in contrast to fruit harvested earlier. The color and firmness of grapefruit at the end of storage is better in fruit harvested in February and afterwards than in those harvested earlier. In order to store Israeli grapefruit until mid-August, grapefruit may be picked in April and sometimes as late as the end of May, thus saving on the costs of cold storage.

Year-to-year changes in maturity, and hence storage potential, are probably influenced primarily by climatic factors. Earlier maturity requires earlier harvests by 2-4 weeks, and *vice versa* for late maturity. The storage potential of grapefruit for prolonged periods is also influenced by the location of groves (Monselise 1981). In Israel, fruit from more humid coastal areas, where light soils predominate, tend to develop more decay, especially molds and stem-end rots, than fruit from the central parts of the country where the groves are planted in heavy soils, as they are in the south and the Galilee. In both Israel and Florida, black rot caused by *Alternaria* and *Fusarium* has been appearing more frequently, especially during prolonged storage of fruit harvested early in the season (Schiffmann-Nadel *et al.* 1981; Brown and McCornack 1972).

The optimal period for picking for storage in Israel, after all these factors have been taken into account, is mid-February until the end of May. The best time for picking for prolonged storage potential is from mid-March to mid-April (Schiffmann-Nadel *et al.* 1980).

POSTHARVEST PRESTORAGE TREATMENTS

It was once common practice in most citrus areas to "cure" fruit before shipping or storing it. Any curing involving drying is very harmful to oranges (Hopkins and McCornack 1960), although treatment at ca. 30°C and high humidity can reduce subsequent losses from penicillium mold (Hopkins and Loucks 1948). This had originally been attributed solely to attenuation of *Penicillium*. Later research shows that at such temperatures (28°-29°C) and very high (ca. 95%) RH, healing of minor wounds in the flavedo takes place by lignification (Brown and Wilson 1968; Ismail and Brown 1975). In lignification, a two to threefold increase in phenolic compounds occurs, catalyzed by the enzyme phenylalanine ammonia-lyase (PAL) (Ismail and Brown 1979). Care must be taken that no water vapor condenses on the fruit, which often occurs at high RH and fluctuating temperatures (Grierson 1969; Meredith 1973), because condensation favors the development of decay.

Prestorage curing has been reported to be advantageous for chilling susceptible species such as grapefruit. Curing periods at 15.5°C (Hatton and Cubbedge 1975), 21°C (Hatton *et al.* 1975), and 29°C (Grierson 1974) have all been reported as mitigating susceptibility to CI in subsequent storage. South African grapefruit are shipped in nonrefrigerated railcars in hot weather for 4 or more days before reaching dockside refrigeration facilities. L. Ginsburg (1972) attributes their subsequent resistance to CI as much to the low humidities during this period as to the high temperatures. Grierson (1974) reporting on 10 successive pickings of Marsh grapefruit throughout a single season stated that the effect on subsequent CI of high-temperature, high-humidity curing varied considerably with the time of the year when the grapefruit were picked. Such curing is only recommended when fruit are to be stored or shipped at temperatures that would otherwise cause chilling injury, for example, low-temperature sterilization for fruit fly disinfestation (Hatton and Cubbedge 1982).

Citrus fruits are sometimes stored grove run, that is, as they come from the tree often in the original harvesting containers, usually pallet boxes. This procedure has the advantage that such fruit are exposed to minimal postharvest handling damage and all rots can be graded out after storage when the fruit are dumped, washed, waxed, graded, etc. However, this approach has the disadvantage that expensive cold storage is used for blemished fruit that do not meet fresh fruit standards and so have to be later graded out for the cannery or other disposal. For grove run fruit, about the only practical prestorage treatment is a fungicidal drench (see Chapter 13), perhaps incorporating a growth regulator, as discussed later in this section.

It is more usual to run the fruit through the packingline before storage. Control of decay and desiccation are then of critical importance, especially if such fruit are packed before storage. Washing, waxing, decay control, grading, etc., are covered in Chapters 12, 13, and 15. Here we deal only with those aspects that relate to citrus fruit storage. Of these, preventive measures against molds are paramount. Packinghouses that consistently ship fruit within a few days after harvest are unlikely to be seriously troubled by entrenched strains of molds resistant to the usual fungicides. But wherever fruit are held for long periods after a fungicidal treatment, the hazard from entrenched resistant molds can become very great, even to the point of forcing the shutdown of the packinghouse and/or storage. Eckert (1978) and Gutter *et al.* (1981) advise the following precautions to cope with such resistance: (1) the premises should be disinfected with formaldehyde as often as necessary; (2) the buildup of fungicide-resistant strains should be monitored and the fungicide program altered when the resistant strains reach a predetermined level; (3) fruit should be treated after storage with a fungicide that is structurally (chemically) unrelated to the fungicide applied before storage; and (4) repacking within the same packinghouse of stored fruit that have received a terminal fungicide treatment should be discouraged to avoid contamination of the packinghouse with fungicide-resistant pathogens. The color add process used in Florida on mature, but poorly colored, oranges provides some control of *Penicillium* mold in storage due to the heated solution used (Smoot 1977; Chapter 15).

A special case occurs when lemons crop in cool weather and are to be held for many months until the hot-weather market, as in the coastal areas of California and Israel. Such lemons are picked with adequate size as the sole criterion; at harvest they are hard and green. They are washed, treated with a fungicide and with about 500 ppm of 2,4-D, and waxed with a storage wax (Chapter 15). These treatments greatly delay the change in color from green to yellow. As such lemons color in storage, the yield of extractable juice increases markedly (Cohen and Schiffmann-Nadel 1978). However, resistant molds are very likely to build up during such prolonged storage.

Degreening

Because it stimulates metabolism, degreening is not usually advisable before storage. Sunburst, a mandarin hybrid, was stored for four weeks at 40°F (4.4°C) without decay *unless degreened* (Hatton *et al.* 1986). However, Florida Ambersweet tangerine hybrid stored well for two weeks although degreened (Hearn 1990). See Chapter 10 for degreening procedures and conditions.

Growth Regulator Treatments

Growth regulator treatments (Chapter 4) afford a particularly interesting form of decay protection in storage since their action is not on the pathogen but on the host, e.g. an aqueous solution of 2,4-D is applied postharvest on California lemons to keep the calyx tissue green and healthy, thereby preventing stem-end rot. As with fungicides and waxes, any growth regulators so used must be approved for the markets where the fruit is to be sold. In the California lemon industry, stem-end rot commonly refers to alternaria rot; elsewhere it usually refers to diplodia or phomopsis rots (Chapter 13). Even when *Alternaria is* not a major hazard, 2,4-D can afford surprising resistance to decay, though in the concentrations used it is not fungicidal (Erickson *et al.* 1958). In a series of 70 experiments with seven types of citrus over 3 years, decay in storage was reduced 30% by the use of a postharvest 2,4-D treatment (McCornack 1979). The addition of 2,4-D (500 ppm) to the wax also helps to preserve the viability of the green calyx during prolonged storage, thereby decreasing the incidence of stem-end rot.

Addition of gibberellin (500 ppm) to wax was somewhat less effective than 2,4-D for the preservation of calyx vitality but did prevent overripe coloration, thus reducing decay and improving marketability (Ben-Yehoshua 1978). Gibberellin has been used successfully on winter-harvested California lemons to delay color change until the summer market (Coggins 1965).

Postharvest application of growth regulators mitigated CI of grapefruit, but response from preharvest applications was unpredictable (Ismail and Grierson 1977). An effect curiously similar to that of growth regulators is the mitigation of CI (Schiffman-Nadel *et al.* 1975) and fumigation injury (Chalutz *et al.* 1973) by the fungicide thiabendazole. Using diphenyl (biphenyl), a vaporphase fungistat, increased susceptibility of grapefruit to chilling injury (McCornack 1976).

Waxing

The natural wax coating of citrus fruits is deposited in lightly attached irregular platelets and is largely removed in washing or, most particularly, in the highly alkaline SOPP (Dowicide, Dow-hex) fungicidal treatment. Therefore, it is necessary to replace the missing natural wax with an artificial coating, a process usually referred to as waxing. Although various resins are also commonly used (see Chapter 15), only those aspects of waxing that are particularly related to fruit storage are discussed here.

The effectiveness of coating applications in the packinghouse can be greatly increased by utilizing a scale (weight loss rate of a ten-fruit sample) that makes possible rapid evaluation of the adequacy of the coating procedure. Moreover, the data can be gathered during the same week the coating is applied, whereas direct measurement of the effects of coating on storage life would require more than 1 month (Giladi 1969). The optimal rate of loss of weight provides a basis for computing proper coating application. It has been reported that some such coatings can affect the physiology of citrus fruit (Ben-Yehoshua 1967).

In anything but ultrahigh-humidity storage, peels of unwaxed, washed citrus fruit tend to dry to a thin, hard, unsightly shell, thereby making the fruit unmarketable. Therefore, for usual storage conditions (<90% RH), prior waxing is considered essential. However, Chace (1969) and Chace *et al.* (1967) reported that in a very high-humidity atmosphere, storage decay was less in unwaxed fruit. In Israel polyethylene wax was found to exacerbate the development of latent stem-end rot such as *Alternaria* in various citrus cultivars (Waks 1981).

The effects of waxing are particularly contradictory for chilling-susceptible species. Waxing decreases susceptibility to chilling in grapefruit (Davis and Harding 1960; Grierson 1971; Pantastico *et al.* 1968) and Temple, a reputed tangor (Chace 1969), but increases susceptibility to chilling in limes (Hatton and Reeder 1968; Pantastico *et al.* 1968).

Seal-Packaging of Individual Fruit

Use of plastic bags, carton liners, etc., for storage or prolonged shipment has often resulted in unacceptable increases in decay even when the films were heavily perforated. This was attributable to condensation between the film and the fruit under conditions of changing temperature (Grierson 1969). Stahl and coworkers (Stahl and Fifield 1936; Stahl and Vaughan 1942) reported sealing fruit in various films. They advocated use of Pliofilm (rubber hydrochloride), but this material was not adopted commercially, probably because the Florida industry was at that time concentrating on development of frozen concentrated orange juice. In Japan, because of the risks of a hard winter, industrious growers often harvest citrus crops early and hold them in a nonrefrigerated family common storage. The fruit is sorted weekly in order to remove rotten fruit. Kitagawa (1980) explained that under these circumstances wrapping (not sealing) in polyethylene is very helpful in reducing weight loss and decay. Such individually wrapped fruit is unwrapped and handled conventionally when marketed. The Chinese follow a similar procedure and have reused individual film wraps (Wardowski and Bonnell 1973).

Development of both better plastic films and suitable machinery to apply the film to individual fruit provide the basis for new interest in seal-packaging. Ben-Yehoshua *et al.* (1979) found that sealing harvested fruit in plastic film reduced weight loss to one-tenth that in fruit treated with the best waxing formulation available. Seal-packaging of individual Israel-grown citrus fruits (lemons, grapefruit, oranges, and tangerines) has been demonstrated to drastically inhibit shrinkage and weight loss, without deleterious effect on flavor; to double and at times treble the life of the fruit as measured by appearance, firmness, shrinkage, weight loss, and other keeping qualities; to reduce the incidence of blemishes of sensitive fruit; and to enhance the healing of fruit damage and reduce spoilage. Seal-packaging delays physiological deterioration.

In studies in Israel, sealed fruit at 20°C lost less weight, shrank less, and were firmer than nonsealed fruit at optimal low temperature (Ben-Ye-hoshua 1978; Ben-Yehoshua and Shapiro 1981; Ben-Yehoshua and Nahir 1980; Ben-Yehoshua *et al.* 1979, 1981A, B). Seal-packaging also reduced CI in various citrus cultivars (Ben-Yehoshua *et al.* 1981B); thus, it could be combined with cooling to maximize the life of fruit. Cooling reduces decay and together with seal-packaging delays deterioration of fruit, incurring much less CI. Another important effect of sealing fruit was the considerable delay in the development of the undesirable orange color in Marsh grapefruit and lemons that is popularly associated with over maturity. But degreening of stored lemons was accelerated by incorporating an ethylene-releasing agent in the film (Ben-Yehoshua *et al.* 1982).

Seal-packaging affected decay in different, contradictory ways. Importantly, it completely prevented secondary infection and spoilage of fruit. Seal packaging also affected the distribution of pathogens: Sealed fruit had more stem-end rots generally, especially those caused by *Alternaria*, and less molds *(Penicillium* spp.). Fortunately, the alternaria rots enhanced by sealing developed only 8-10 weeks after harvest; by this time the fruit could have been marketed and consumed. Effective decay control methods before film packaging (both in terms of careful fruit handling and of optimum use of fungicides) are essential, as conditions within sealed fruit are beneficial for pathogenic fungi. In Israel, this technique has been applied to lemons in a specially built packinghouse with six automatic sealing machines.

Working in Florida, Kawada and Albrigo (1979), Kawada and Hale (1980) and Kawada *et al.* (1981) successfully film-sealed grapefruit in low-density polyethylene, a process they called Unipack. This technique combines the Japanese experience with unsealed low-density polyethylene wraps with the Israeli shrink-film approach. Film wrapped Florida tangelos stored well (Miller and McDonald 1989).

In Australia, the seal-packaging technique was introduced in the cooperative in Waikeri, South Australia. Tugwell and Gillespie (1981) reported that by sealing citrus in high-density polyethylene (HDPE) they could keep the fruit at near ambient temperatures for several months for out-of-season marketing. Fungicide treatment with Panoctine and Benlate provided adequate control of wastage due to blue and green mold and sour rot but wastage due to *Alternaria* was a problem, especially with overmature or late-stored Ellendale mandarins and Valencia oranges. However, because sealed Ellendale mandarins could be shipped at higher temperatures than previously utilized for nonsealed fruit, the fruit maintained better flavor, had less CI, and was better accepted in overseas markets.

In research on seal-packaging, the following films have given good results: high-density polyethylene, low-density polyethylene, and a mixture of 9:1 polypropylene and polyethylene. However, at high temperatures, off-flavors may occur with films inadequately permeable to oxygen and carbon dioxide.

The advantages of film wrapping include extended storage life, reduced need for refrigeration, much less water loss, and reduced CI. However, due to the expense involved, most citrus fruit is (and will continue to be) waxed, not seal-packaged, and further discussion in this chapter will assume that waxed (not sealed) fruit are involved.

STORAGE CONDITIONS

Temperature

Although storage temperature is obviously of prime importance, the response of citrus fruits to temperature is much less dramatic than that of climacteric fruit such as apples or bananas (Biale 1961). The rate of postharvest respiration of citrus fruit is low and, unlike the response of deciduous fruits, is directly proportional to temperature in the range of 10°-35°C. Lemons have the lowest respiration rate and tangerines the highest (Vines *et al.* 1968). Too high a temperature during storage favors fungal decay, rapid water loss, increased softening, and an enhanced decrease in ascorbic acid (vitamin C) content; too low temperature leads to CI (see Chapter 14). Optimal temperatures must be carefully chosen with respect to these factors. Any treatment, such as precooling, waxing, or film wrapping, that eliminates the need for expensive refrigeration is of obvious economic value.

There is no single criterion for determining optimal storage and shipping temperatures for different citrus cultivars from various areas. Among the various factors that must be taken into account are susceptibility to CI, storage period required, development of decay at higher temperatures, effect of waxing or seal-packaging, preharvest treatments, time of harvest, prestorage cooling, and cold sterilization for fruit fly eradication. Any recommendation is at best an approximation and recommendations for a given growing area do not necessarily apply to other growing areas. e.g., The U.S. Dept. of Agriculture recommended refrigerated transit temperatures for California and Arizona oranges is 3°-9°C (37°-48°F) but for Florida and Texas it is 0°-1°C (32°-34°F) (McGregor 1987).

In Florida, grapefruit exhibit varying susceptibilities to CI throughout the harvest season. Hence, the recommendation (Chace *et al.* 1966) to use a storage temperature of 15.5°C in early fall and decrease it to 10°C later in the season is questionable, particularly for spring pickings. Since late-season fruit are more sensitive to decay, temperatures higher than 10°C cannot be generally recommended.

In Israel, Marsh grapefruit may be stored at 2°C for 2 weeks, but suffer from CI during longer storage periods (Schiffmann-Nadel *et al.* 1980). At 4°-6°C, CI symptoms appear even earlier, and about 5% of the fruit spoiled after 4 weeks. Storage at 11°C did not bring about CI, even during long storage periods, and is the recommended Israeli temperature for prolonged storage (Shiffmann-Nadel *et al.* 1980). Although CI does not occur at higher temperatures (14°-17°C), the incidence of sour rot and stem-end rots increases, accompanied by increased weight loss and shrinkage, especially during prolonged storage. Fruit storage at gradually decreasing temperatures from 17°-6°C over a 2-week period (which simulates the conditions prevailing on nonrefrigerated, ventilated ships from Israel to northern Europe) significantly decreased the postvoyage incidence of CI that developed during prolonged storage at 4°-6°C, compared with CI in fruit continuously stored at these lower temperatures. Hence, it is possible to store Israeli fruits in Europe at temperatures lower than 10°C (i.e., 9°C) following ventilated shipment. The same approach was the basis for a successful recommendation for shipping Florida grapefruit to Japan in a season when persistent diplodia stem-end rot was proving a major hazard. Development of *Diplodia natalensis* is arrested below 10°C, but lower temperatures invite injury from CI. Several shiploads successfully made the 3-week voyage starting at 10°C and lowering the temperature 1°C each week, arriving in Tokyo at 7°C with no CI (Grierson, unpublished data).

Waxing the fruit, especially with a formulation containing TBZ, decreases the susceptibility of Marsh grapefruit to CI and permits the lowering of the optimal storage temperature by 2°C (Pantastico *et al.* 1968; Schiffmann-Nadel *et al.* 1980). Intermittent warming can reduce CI to a great extent (Davis and Hoffman 1973). However, use of this apparently simple way of controlling CI is limited by the additional cost of either labor to move fruit in and out of storage or by the energy cost of warming, then again cooling, the whole room full of fruit.

In general, Florida and Texas oranges are less susceptible to CI and so can be held at 0°C, whereas California and Arizona oranges store best at 5°-6°C (McGregor 1987). However, Khalifah and Kuykendall (1965) reported that Arizona Valencia oranges stored best at 9°C when picked in March, but at 3°C when harvested in June. The sensitivity of Marsh grapefruit to CI in Israel decreases with the advance of the picking season and with the stage of ripening from the beginning of the season until January, after which sensitivity increases, especially from March until the end of the picking season (Schiffmann-Nadel *et al.* 1980). In addition, differences from year to year are apparent and apparently arise from climatic conditions affecting growth regulator status of the fruit (Grierson 1999A).

Rapid cooling of fruit before packing, from field temperature down to 10°C, decreased weight loss by about 50% and somewhat decreased the incidence of decay that developed during storage, without causing injury to the fruit (Chalutz *et al.* 1973). Contrary to traditional beliefs, drying conditions at the packinghouse accelerates weight loss and increases the incidence of stem-end rot during subsequent storage. Hopkins and McCornack (1960) reported a study in which leaving oranges for 24 hr on the packing floor increased subsequent decay by 300% and leaving them outdoors for 48 hr increased decay by 1200%. Trials with Valencia oranges and Marsh grapefruit in cooling installations and ripening rooms (18°C and 80% RH) showed that it was possible to decrease economic damage by keeping the fruit at high humidity and cool temperatures before packing (Waks *et al.* 1979). Precooling the fruit, which helps maintain firmness and resistance to decay during and even after storage, is recommended for warm days in low-humidity areas, especially toward the end of the season (Chalutz *et al.* 1973).

In growing districts with endemic fruit fly infestations, even chilling susceptible citrus such as grapefruit (unless fumigated) must sometimes be cold-sterilized for fruit fly eradication (Miller and McDonald 1992; Ismail *et al.* 1986; Chapter17). This treatment did not cause much injury (less than 2%) to Israeli grapefruit subjected to a subsequent period of 14 days at 11°C. Keeping the fruit for as little as 4 extra days in sterilization conditions significantly increased CI (Schiffmann-Nadel *et al.* 1980). This effect was reduced either by using TBZ as the fungicide or by retaining the fruit at an intermediate temperature of 17°C for several days before the sterilization treatment (Hatton and Cubbedge 1982).

Lutz and Hardenburg (1968) list recommended storage temperatures for citrus fruits from various U.S. growing districts. These districts have humid subtropical (Florida), arid desert (Arizona), and Mediterranean (California) climates; and so give an indication of the considerable effect of climate on storage requirements of any given cultivar. McGregor (1987) reiterates these geographical differences in the U.S. Dept. Agriculture recommendations for transit temperatures. Nevertheless, fruit handlers in each district need to check the requirements for their specific cultivars. Typical storage conditions for various citrus are listed in Table 20.1.

Humidity

Although humidity control is considerably more difficult to achieve than temperature control, recommendations are much simpler. Water should never precipitate on the fruit either due to inefficient humidifiers or to temperature fluctuations at very high humidity. In reasonably moisture-proof containers (e.g., wooden pallet boxes or plastic crates), humidity should be as high as possible. In nonmoisture-proof containers (e.g., unwaxed car-

TABLE 20.1. Typical Storage Conditions for Citrus Fruits

Temperature Type of fruit	(°F)	(°C)	Relative humidity (%)	Est. storage life[a] (weeks)	Chilling injury symptoms if held too cold[b]	Typical storage diseases
Oranges						
Calif. & Arizona	40-44	4.4-6.7	85-90	6	Rind staining and pitting	Stem-end rot, Penicillium molds, stem-end rind breakdown
Florida & Texas	32-34	0-1	85-90	8	Light surface pitting	
Grapefruit						
Early	60	15.5	90-95	5	Severe peel pitting, oil gland darkening	Stem-end rot
Midseason	55	12.8	90-95	7		Penicillium molds
Late[c]	50	10.8	90-95	8		Stem-end rot and Penicillium molds
Tangerines						
Temples						
Tangelos (most U.S. varieties)	38-40	3.3-4.4	85-90	2	Off flavors, rind staining	Stem-end rot, Penicillium molds, sour rot, anthracnose rot
Coorg mandarins	42-45	6-7	85-90	8	Shriveling	Penicillium molds
Japanese satsumas	34-36	1-2	85-90	16	Rind puffing[d]	Penicillium molds
Limes	50	10.0	90-95	4	Severe peel pitting	Yellowing, peel collapse
Lemons						
Green	58-60	14.4-15.5	85-90	20	Peel pitting (peteca), membranous staining, albedo browning	Penicillium molds, stem-end rot, sour rot
Yellow	38-40	3.3-4.4	85-90	4		

Source: Adapted from Grierson (1976).
[a]Any estimate of storage life is very approximate and varies greatly with variety, district, care in harvesting, use of fungicides, etc. These estimates are conservative.
[b]For illustrations of these disorders see Smoot et al. (1971).
[c]Very late grapefruit picked after the next bloom can become as susceptible to chilling as early fruit.
[d]Rind puffing of satsumas is accentuated by very high humidities.

tons), humidity should be as high as the containers can stand, provided no precipitation occurs. Very high humidity *per se* does NOT cause decay.

Ventilation and Air Purification

Long experience has shown that ventilation of stored citrus is necessary (Baier 1945; Hinds 1970), and some remarkable decreases in decay losses have been attributed to adequate ventilation (Tanaka *et al.* 1957). Traditionally, the beneficial effect of ventilation was regarded as being due to elimination of carbon dioxide, but recent studies tend to attribute such benefits to reduction or elimination of various volatiles (Norman and Houck 1977; Waks *et al.* 1981). Although oranges were previously reported not to produce ethylene (Biale 1961), more sensitive techniques demonstrate that citrus fruits can produce physiological amounts of ethylene. In fact, ethylene is by far the most potent volatile in storage rooms (Biale 1961; Davis 1974; McGlasson and Eaks 1972; Wild *et al.* 1977). In addition to ventilation, the types and proportions of volatiles present can be affected by cultivars; decays, particularly those caused by *Penicillium* (Biale and Young 1947); and even the type of refrigeration system (Grierson-Jackson 1952).

In general, enough ventilation is required to keep the ethylene level at 0.1–1.0 ppm. The usual practice is to periodically monitor the ethylene level and adjust the ventilation system as required. A more precise control method, proposed by Waks *et al.* (1981), involves monitoring the internal atmosphere of the fruit. In warm climates, excessive ventilation can greatly increase energy costs, even when confined to nighttime hours.

An alternative to ventilation is to use some form of air purification (Smock 1979). Activated carbon will absorb most volatiles other than ethylene, which can be chemically scrubbed with potassium permanganate absorbed into a suitable medium (e.g., Purafil® pellets). Wild *et al.* (1977) reported remarkable extension of the storage life of lemons using a shielded ultraviolet (UV) radiation source to destroy ethylene and other volatiles. Such a method is particularly desirable when nonfruit products (particularly of dairy origin), which might pick up off-flavors are held in the same storage area.

When organic volatiles are not controlled, Lipton and Harvey (1972) advise grouping compatible products on the basis of both temperature and volatile substances emitted.

Controlled-Atmosphere Storage (Modified Atmospheres)

Lipton's comment (1975) that "Fruits that are fully ripe at harvest . . . are not good candidates for controlled-atmosphere (CA) storage . . . when there is no vital process to be slowed down" applies precisely to citrus fruits. Controlled atmosphere research based on efforts to duplicate successes with climacteric fruits are therefore ill-advised in citrus (Smock 1979). Since there are no intensive ripening changes to suppress in citrus fruits, CA storage of citrus must achieve other objectives to be justified (Grierson 1970). Decay control is not a practical goal, there being no evidence that modified atmospheres control fungal decay in citrus. However, because storage and shipment of grapefruit, lemons, and limes are severely limited by the cooling they can withstand, possible control of the CI syndrome by a CA is one logical goal. Indeed, carbon dioxide, applied either as a pretreatment at very high dosage (Brooks and McCulloch 1937; Hatton *et al.* 1972, 1975; Schiffmann-Nadel *et al.* 1980) or at lower concentrations throughout storage (Chace *et al.* 1967; Vakis *et al.* 1970; Wardowski *et al.* 1973), has been found to ameliorate CI of grapefruit. A particularly disconcerting report was that naturally accumulated levels of carbon dioxide of up to 20% almost completely arrested CI at 4.4°C in Marsh grapefruit harvested early and midseason, but provided almost no control of CI in grapefruit from the same plots picked late (postbloom) (Wardowski *et al.* 1975).

Early treatment by carbon dioxide decreases the incidence of peel injuries in Marsh grapefruit caused by fumigation of fruit with EDB (Schiffmann-Nadel *et al.* 1980). High concentrations of carbon dioxide during CA storage also reduced the incidence of pitting in lemons (Brooks and McCulloch 1937).

Another obvious goal of CA storage of citrus is prevention of color change when that is beneficial, or even essential, for successful marketing. Persian (Tahiti) limes must be green to be sold as U.S. No. 1 grade. CA storage can delay yellowing, but at a risk of increased penicillium mold (Grierson unpublished data), and decrease CI of unwaxed limes (Wardowski *et al.* 1973). Hypobaric (low-pressure) storage has been more successful for limes (Pantastico *et al.* 1968; Spalding and Reeder 1976). When lemons are picked in winter and stored for summer sale, it is essential to delay color change. This is a common situation with California lemons, in which color changes can be delayed by CA storage at 0-6% oxygen and zero carbon dioxide (Grierson *et al.* 1966). With CA storage, removal of ethylene is critical for lemons (Wild *et al.* 1977) and oranges (McGlasson and Eaks 1972).

Preservation of flavor is another possible goal and some success has been reported with Temples and Valencias (Chace 1969) and with Red Marsh grapefruit (Chace *et al.* 1967). But this is hard to exploit commercially.

CRITERIA FOR JUDGING STORAGE LIFE

No two lots of fruit are exactly alike and it is not possible to forecast just how long a given crop can be stored. Therefore, if an extended storage period is contemplated, provision should be made for several samplings as the possible end of storage life approaches. Extra fruit should be stored for these samplings, *from each size, each planting, and each day's picking.* In general, trouble shows up first in the smallest and largest sizes, so these should be well represented. As soon as trouble can be reasonably expected, sampling should be done at least once a week.

At each sampling two lots are withdrawn. The first is placed at room temperature and observed for poststorage breakdown. For most purposes, it is necessary that the fruit should have at least 1 week of poststorage shelf-life, often much longer. The second sample is examined for the following:

Externally Visible Decay

In almost any area, losses due to green and blue molds *(Penicillium digitatum* and *P. italicum)* can be expected. In some areas, stem-end rot is common and in its incipient stage is detected by thumb pressure on the button (calyx).

Internal Decay

Black rot caused by *Alternaria citri,* and other pathogens is ubiquitous but curiously intermittent, being a major factor in some years and almost absent in others. It is purely internal and cannot be detected without cutting the fruit, preferably longitudinally. It develops very slowly, seldom becoming a problem in less than 8 weeks at usual storage temperatures. In the incipient stages, black rot appears as grayish threads in the center core of the fruit. Fruit infected with *Alternaria* are often particularly highly colored due to the ethylene evolved by this fungus.

Peel Injuries

Fruit should be removed when peel injuries (CI, stem-end rind breakdown, etc.) are barely detectable in storage. This is because they are apt to darken and turn into sunken lesions during the marketing period if held any longer in storage.

Granulation

Granulation takes various forms from a simple drying out of the juice vesicles at the stem-end to a gelling of the contents of the juice vesicles (Chapter 14), typically at the stem end of Valencia oranges or down the central axis of navel oranges. When this is detected, storage should be terminated as soon as possible. Burns and Albrigo (1997, 1998) report that granulation of stored grapefruit is affected by both time of harvest and by storage conditions.

POSTSTORAGE HANDLING

Fruit from storage is handled very much as fruit that has not been stored, but it should be treated with particular care.

Some decay is inevitable, and molds from storage offer a particular hazard because there is a constant tendency for fungicide-resistant strains to develop. This became such a problem for California lemon packers (who store huge amounts of fruit) that they now take special precautions to limit the spread of *Penicillium* mold spores from poststorage fruit. It is common to have a hood over the dumper that evacuates air from the dumping area to the outside. It is also customary for workers who pick out the moldy fruit to use a vacuum attachment that sucks up the fruit and its spores. Packinghouses anywhere are well advised to take similar precautions when handling fruit from cold storage.

After being examined, poststorage fruit should be washed, treated with fungicide, waxed, and packed just as any other citrus fruit. Particular care should be taken not to pack storage fruit too tightly. After any considerable amount of handling, the fruit has lost much of its resilience and is very easily deformed (Rivero *et al.* 1979).

MANDARIN-TYPE VARIETIES

Unless otherwise specified, the preceding discussion applies generally to oranges, grapefruit, and lemons for which postharvest storage (or equivalent long-distance transit conditions) is commonly used for one reason or another. Because of their extreme frailty, mandarin-type varieties merit special consideration. These might be defined as table fruits that, though sometimes described as mandarin oranges in the literature, are definitely not *Citrus sinensis* (L.) Osbeck. They include varieties that are usually classified as *Citrus reticulata* Blanco in occidental citrus areas, together with its many hybrids. In oriental citrus-growing areas, mandarin-type oranges include many subspecies in the Tanaka system of classification of which the Ponkan, Tankan, and Unshu-mikan are typical. Traditionally, such varieties have predominated in the Orient largely because of their adaptation to the habitat as well as to their comparative immunity to preharvest diseases (Cooper 1982). Such partial immunity very definitely does not apply to their susceptibility to postharvest diseases, although some are stored far more successfully than most types of citrus.

Dancy, the traditional tangerine of Florida, was widely grown until recently. It is seldom stored except to last over brief periods of market glut. Akamine (1967) after an extensive storage study of this variety in Hawaii reported that very careful harvesting and handling was essential; curing, waxing, fumigation, and irradiation did not reduce decay; the fungicides then available [e.g., dehydroacetic acid (DHA) and sodium o-phenylphenate (SOPP)] did more to reduce poststorage decay than to reduce decay while in cold storage; temperatures below 5°C induced off-flavors; and humidities had to be high to prevent unacceptable shriveling. Storage at 4.5°-7.3°C and 93% RH was recommended, providing commercial storage for up to 4 weeks. This very closely approximates Florida experience with Dancy and presumed tangors such as Temple and Honey tangerine (formerly Murcott). Hatton (1980) reported on storage trials extending over several years with Florida-grown mandarin hybrids, including Nova (marketed as a tangelo) and Robinson (marketed as a tangerine). The optimum storage temperature was 4°C. Even though standard fungicides (thiabendazole or benomyl) were used, poststorage decay was unacceptable when Robinson was stored for longer than 1 week or Nova for longer than 2 weeks. Chiang *et al.* (1963) in Taiwan working with Ponkan (*C. reticulata*) and Tankan (*C. tankan* Hayata) reported similar frailty, particularly with regard to handling damage; they also stated that picking in wet weather "fills the garbage cans rather than the markets."

Such high spoilage draws attention to the problem of separating climate from varietal effects, since Hawaii, Florida, and Taiwan all have moist, monsoon-type climates. However, an arid climate does not seem to assure storability for mandarin-type varieties. For example, Bassily *et al.* (1961), working in a desert climate, reported on the effects of many pre- and postharvest factors on storage of Egyptian-grown Baladi mandarins but did not attempt to store them beyond 2 weeks. The Coorg mandarin of India reportedly has better storage potential. Srivastava and Mathur (1954) reported on an interesting and meticulous storage study in which Coorg mandarins were picked with great care, placed in boxes presterilized with Lysol, and sorted in a room previously disinfected with formaldehyde. Under these conditions, decay losses were 4-10% after 60 days at 5.6°-7.2°C; when a marketing period extended this to 62-84 days from original storage, losses were still only 7.2-15.6% and these mandarins were sold at a profit after accounting for all normal storage and marketing costs. All postharvest studies should be so meticulous. Any comparisons of keeping quality among mandarin varieties from various climates is greatly confounded by the great number of varieties involved, e.g., Dancy in the United States, Michal in Israel, Baladi in Egypt, Coorg in India, Imperial in Australia. Even when reports are available on the same variety grown in different climates, cultural and handling methods can be very different.

But it is in Japan that mandarin-type varieties are most widely grown and where they are most successfully stored. In an extensive series of studies on storage metabolism of Satsumas (*C. unshiu* Marc.), Japanese workers (e.g., Murata 1977) routinely held these fruit in storage for 3 months pending analysis. Manago *et al.* (1978) reported successful storage of Satsumas for 6-

7 months, but with meticulously controlled conditions, both before and during storage. Even without such elaborately controlled storage conditions, Japanese growers routinely store Satsumas for 4 months, even in air-cooled common storage, by placing each fruit in an unsealed plastic bag and storing them in trays one fruit deep (Kitagawa 1980). In general, Japanese authorities favor only moderately high humidities (ca. 85-90% RH), believing that extremely high humidities contribute to puffing of Satsumas in storage (Kuraoka 1962; Manago and Ogaki 1976; Ogaki and Manago 1977).

Harvesting

Climate and varietal characteristics are of prime importance, but meticulously careful handling is the third indispensable condition for successful storage of these varieties. A brochure on the Japanese citrus industry describes their citrus fruits as being "picked politely," a phrase that very well expresses the attitude that makes such successes possible. Such care often starts with spot (selective) picking for size and color and even for position on the tree and, most particularly, for optimum maturity for storage [e.g., Manago and Ogaki (1976) reporting on Japanese Satsumas or El-Zeftawi (1982) describing successful storage of Australian Early Imperial mandarins]. Similar care at every stage is crucial for successful storage of these frail varieties.

These mandarin-type varieties should be picked (usually by clipping, being careful to leave no protruding stems) with scrupulous care into rigid-framed picking bags of not over 20-kg capacity. Fruit should not be picked when the trees are wet *or within a week of a severe drought stress having been relieved by rain or irrigation* (Grierson *et al.* 1965; Grierson 1981). Pick only at optimum maturity and, if necessary, spot pick for size and color.

Packingline Handling

Dips of any kind can be hazardous, as they rapidly become cultures for fungi, many resistant to fungicides. Fruit should be carefully dumped dry, washed and rinsed with clean water. Rinses, fungicides, and waxes should be applied as nonrecovery sprays (Miller *et al.* 2001). Never polish; this is a particularly harmful practice, especially after ethylene degreening (Grierson and Newhall 1960). Apply 2,4-D, separately or in the wax emulsion to improve the storage condition (Chiang *et al.* 1964; McCornack 1979).

Storage Conditions

If specific local and varietal requirements are not known (Table 20.1), mandarin-type fruit should initially be stored at 5°C and 90% RH and with ventilation adequate to keep ethylene in the storage atmosphere below 1 ppm. Samples should be withdrawn for checking and poststorage observation at least once per week.

COOLING AND COLD STORAGE FACILITIES

The various mechanical systems for cooling and storing fruit are not properly within the purview of this text. Attention is drawn, however, to the excellent coverage of such aspects in Kader (1992).

Design of a Cold Storage

Design of a cold storage is properly the province of architects and engineers and so not covered in detail here. However, managers contracting for construction of a cold storage need to know certain fundamental principles in order to evaluate proposals from would-be contractors and suppliers.

Building Construction. Walls, ceilings and floors should be well insulated and should include a properly positioned vapor barrier. Skimping on insulation or misplacing vapor barriers greatly increases operating costs and are exceedingly expensive faults to correct.

Floors. A 25-30 cm layer of *well-drained* coarse gravel usually provides adequate subfloor insulation.

Walls and ceiling. The vapor barrier *must be outside the insulation*, otherwise moisture will condense within the insulation. Covering foam insulation with plywood can constitute a considerable fire hazard, even when supposedly fire resistant polyurethane foam is used.

Compressor. The heart of all refrigeration systems is the compressor that compresses refrigerant vapor sufficiently that it can be condensed to liquid. Contractors seeking to offer the low bid when only room temperature or total refrigeration tonnage is specified may offer a too small compressor that runs very fast with a wide difference between incoming (suction) and outgoing (head) pressures (Grierson 1972). Though initially inexpensive, such a unit can be very expensive to run and maintain. A larger compressor with a much narrower pressure differential costs more initially, but has a much longer potential working life and is much less expensive to run.

The cooling capacity of a refrigeration system is expressed in tons, originally defined as the amount of refrigeration supplied by the melting of one ton of ice. Fig. 20.3 shows how narrowing the head pressure/suction pressure differential from 180/10 (A) to 80/30 (B) more than doubles the tons of refrigeration delivered per horsepower (HP), i.e., from 0.6 tons/HP to 1.4 tons/HP. Fig. 20.4 expresses this another way. At 180/10 (A) two HP is needed to produce one ton of refrigeration. At 80/30 (B) only 0.75 HP is needed to produce that ton of refrigeration. This is a very considerable difference in operating expense and in the use of increasingly expensive electricity.

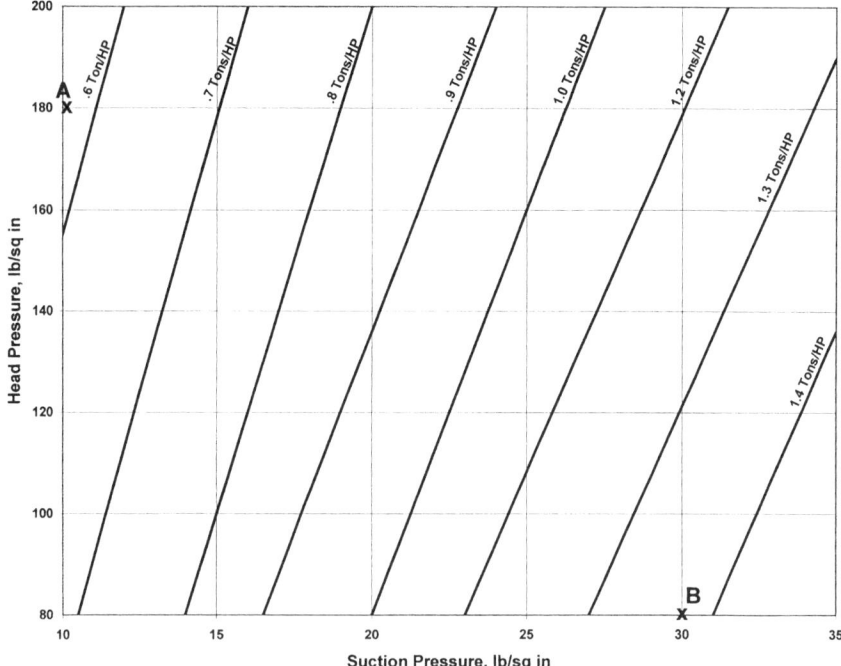

Fig. 20.3. Suction pressure/head pressure differential as related to tons of refrigeration per horsepower expended. Conversions: 1 hp = 0.75 kW, 1 Ton (refrigeration) = 3.52 kW, 1 psi = 6.895 kPa.
From Grierson (1972).

Condenser. In this, the refrigerant vapor is condensed to liquid by removing heat with either air or water. The more easily this is done, the less the cost of running the system. A very common error is to locate an air condenser in an unnecessarily hot place (usually on the roof) or to supply a water-cooled condenser with warmer than necessary water due to the water supply piping being unnecessarily exposed to the sun.

Fan-coil units. Inside the cold storage, a fan draws air through an evaporator coil within which evaporation of condensed refrigerant absorbs heat from the air, thus cooling the room. Two expensive pitfalls should be avoided.

Initially inexpensive installations commonly use a small evaporator coil with a wide temperature differential (delta t) between incoming and outgoing air. This drastically reduces humidity within the storage. (The larger the coil, the lower the delta t and the higher the equilibrium humidity within the storage.) Attempts to correct this with humidifiers are largely futile due to consequent icing on the coils necessitating added expense for defrosting measures.

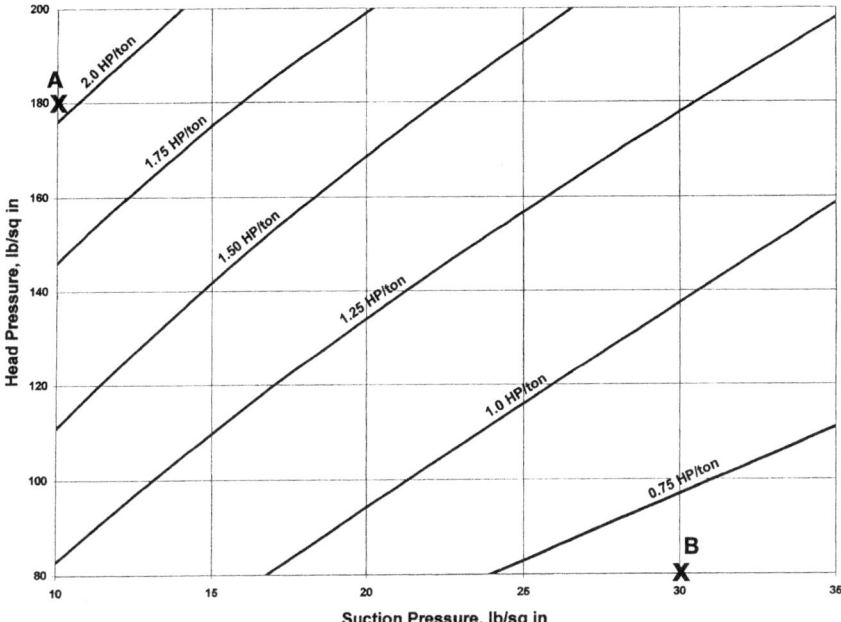

Fig. 20.4. Suction pressure/head pressure differential as related to horsepower used to produce one ton of refrigeration. Conversions: 1 hp = 0.75 kW, 1 Ton (refrigeration) = 3.52 kW, 1 psi = 6.895 kPa.
From Grierson (1972).

Fan/coil configuration is critical to inexpensive operation (Grierson 1999B). *Fans should always pull air through the coil, not push it through*, thus involving totally unnecessary excess use of electricity. This effect is particularly marked with axial flow (propeller type) fans as contrasted with centrifugal (squirrel cage) fans. In various tests in storages, reefer (refrigerated) trucks, and degreening rooms (Grierson, unpublished data) air delivery was reduced by a curiously consistent *ca.* 25% with a push through (rather than a pull through) fan/coil configuration. Any attempt to overcome this effect by increasing horsepower is prohibitively expensive due to air pressure buildup against the coil.

A NOTE ON THERMODYNAMICS

Occasionally it is necessary for engineers designing storages or scientists conducting experiments to know something of the thermodynamic properties of the fruit. Such data can be curiously hard to find, being scattered throughout diverse journals, often with wide discrepancies between various reports. Such differences are not surprising since the values of thermodynamic properties may vary with variety, maturity, district, and even within the lifetime of a single fruit. A hard, green, thick-skinned California lemon picked in February will have different thermodynamic values than the same fruit sold in July as a smaller, bright yellow, juicy lemon after 5 months of curing. Nevertheless, calculations for storage capacities, cooling rates, etc., require knowledge of the values for parameters such as specific gravity, specific heat, thermal diffusivity, and heat of respiration. Representative values are therefore given in Table 20.2.

As mentioned in Chapter 1, the rate of respiration of citrus fruits is (under constant conditions) rather constant and typically low, more comparable with that of root vegetables than with that of climacteric-type fruits such as apples or pears. Nevertheless, heat of respiration increases approximately tenfold between 0° and 29°C. This is why a van-container equipped with refrigeration to hold frozen produce below -18°C cannot necessarily cool down a load of citrus that has been transferred from a hot packinghouse to a refrigerated truck. To keep frozen produce below -18°C, the refrigeration unit only has to remove the ambient heat leaking in through the truck's insulation. To cool down a load of citrus, it also has to remove the field heat (referred to by engineers as the sensible heat load) from approximately 20 tons of citrus fruit while also removing the heat of respiration, a very much greater load on the refrigeration unit. For a more detailed discussion of such factors, see Grierson 1976.

TABLE 20.2. Thermodynamic Data for Citrus Fruits[a]

Parameter	Oranges	Grapefruit	Lemons
Specific gravity	0.98	0.88	0.95
Specific heat Btu/lb °F	0.86	0.88	0.89
Thermal diffusivity ft²/hr	0.0049	0.0047	0.0049
Thermal conductivity:			
BTU/hr/ftz/°F/in.	2.95	3.00	2.85
kcal/sec/cm=/°C/cm	1.1	0.78	1.05
Heat of respiration (BTU/ton/day) at:			
32°F 0°C	900	500	580
40 4.5	1400	1100	800
50 10.0	1300	1500	2300
60 15.5	5000	2800	3000
70 21.0	6200	3500	4100
80 27.5	8000	4200	6200
90 32.0	9900	6000	8000

Source: Grierson (1976).
[a]Values listed as means of data from various sources. Values will vary with horticultural variety (cultivar), district, maturity, size of fruit, etc.

REFERENCES

AKAMINE, E. K. 1967. Tangerine storage. Hawaii Agr. Expt. Stn. Bull. 142.

ALBRIGO, L. G. 1977. Comparison of some antitranspirants on orange trees and fruit. J. Am. Soc. Hort. Sci. 102, 270-273.

ALI-DINAR, H. M. and KREZDORN, A. H. 1976. Extending the grapefruit harvesting season with growth regulators. Proc. Fla. State Hort. Soc. 89, 4-6.

BAIER, W. E. 1945. How the citrus industry measures it: IV. Lemon storage ventilation. Calif. Citrogr. 30, 306-318.

BASSILY, S., EL-MAHMOUDI, L. and ABDEL-RAHMAN, L. 1961. Effect of the application of P and K to mandarin trees in sandy soils on the maturity stage and keeping quality of fruits. Agr. Res. Rev. (Egypt) 39, 201-218.

BEN-GAD, D. Y., GOLDSCHMIDT, E. E. and MONSELISE, S. P. 1981. Changes in cell wall components of Shamouti (*Citrus sinensis* (L.) Osbeck) orange peel during maturation and senescence. Israel J. Bot. 30, 48 (Abstr.).

BEN-YEHOSHUA, S. 1967. Some physiological effects of various skin coatings on orange fruit. Israel J. Agr. Res. 17, 17-27.

BEN-YEHOSHUA, S. 1969. Gas exchange, transpiration and the commercial deterioration of orange fruit in storage. J. Am. Soc. Hort. Sci. 94, 524-526.

BEN-YEHOSHUA, S. 1978. Delaying deterioration of individual citrus fruit by seal-packaging in film of high density polyethylene. I. General effects. Proc. Int. Soc. Citriculture 110-115.

BEN-YEHOSHUA, S. and NAHIR, D. 1980. Seal-packaging of individual fruit in film. HortScience 15, 11.

BEN-YEHOSHUA, S. and SHAPIRO, B. 1981. Effects of pre- and postharvest applications of ethylene-releasing agents and auxins and individual seal-packaging with high-density polyethylene film on coloration of citrus fruit and its quality. Proc. Int. Soc. Citriculture Vol. 1, 226-229.

BEN-YEHOSHUA, S., KOBILER, L. and SHAPIRO, B. 1979. Some physiological effects of delaying deterioration of citrus fruits by individual seal-packaging in high density polyethylene film. J. Am. Soc. Hort. Sci. 104, 868-872.

BEN-YEHOSHUA, S., APELBAUM, A. and COHEN, E. 1981A. Decay control of fungicide residues in citrus fruits seal-packed in high density polyethylene film. Pestic. Sci. 12, 485-490.

BEN-YEHOSHUA, S., KOBILER, I. and SHAPIRO, B. 1981B. Effects of cooling versus sealpackaging with high density polyethylene on keeping qualities of various citrus cultivars. J. Am. Soc. Hort. Sci. 106, 536-540.

BEN-YEHOSHUA, S., SHAPIRO, B. and KOBILER, L. 1982. New method of degreening lemons by a combined treatment of ethylene-releasing agents and seal-packaging in highdensity polyethylene film. J. Am. Soc. Hort. Sci. 107, 365-368.

BIALE, J. B. 1961. Postharvest physiology and chemistry. *In* The Orange Fruit. W. B. Sinclair (Editor). University of California Press, Berkeley.

BIALE, J. B. and YOUNG, R. E. 1947. Critical oxygen concentrations for the respiration of lemons. Am. J. Bot. 34, 301-309.

BROOKS, C. 1942. Prevention of stem-end rot. Proc. Fla. State Hort. Soc. 55, 61-69.

BROOKS, C. and McCULLOCH, L. P. 1937. Some effects of storage conditions on certain diseases of lemons. J. Agr. Res. 55, 795-810.

BROWN, G. E. and McCORNACK, A. A. 1972. Decay caused by *Alternaria citri* in Florida citrus fruits. Plant Dis. Rep. 56, 909.

BROWN, G. E. and WILSON, W. C. 1968. Mode of entry of *Diplodia natalensis* and *Phomopsis citri* into Florida oranges. Phytopathology 58, 736-739.

BURNS, J. K. and ALBRIGO, L. G. 1997. Granulation in grapefruit. Proc. Fla. State Hort. Soc. 110, 204-208.

BURNS, J. K. and ALBRIGO, L. G. 1998. Time of harvest and method of storage affect granulation in grapefruit. HortScience 33(4), 728-730.

BURG, S. P. and BURG, E. A. 1965. Gas exchange in fruits. Physiol. Plant 18, 870-884.

CHACE, W. G. 1969. Controlled atmosphere storage of Florida citrus fruits. Proc. Int. Soc. Citriculture Vol. 3, 1365-1373

CHACE, W. G., HARDING, P. L., SMOOT, J. J. and CUBBEDGE, R.H. 1966. Factors affecting the quality of grapefruit exported from Florida. USDA Marketing Res. Rept. 739.

CHACE, W. G., DAVIS, P. L. and SMOOT, J. J. 1967. Response of citrus fruits to controlled atmosphere storage. Proc. XII Int. Congr. Refrigeration. Vol. III, 383-391.

CHALUTZ, E., BIRON, S. and ALUMOT, E. 1973. Reduction of ethylene dibromide peel injury in citrus fruits by thiabendazole. Int. Inst. Refrig. Comm. C2, Jerusalem, 205-209.

CHIANG, M-N., LEE, N., CHEN, C-H. and YEH, C-H. 1963. The effects of postharvest treatments on decay in loose-skin oranges. Nat. Taiwan Univ., Coll. Agr. Spec. Publ. 17.

CHIANG, M-N., LEE, N., CHEN, C-H. and YEH, C-H. 1964. The effect of 2,4-D, sodium o-phenylphenate, diphenyl and waxes on decay of loose-skinned oranges. Nat. Taiwan Univ., Coll. Agr. Spec. Publ. 17 (Chinese with English summary).

COGGINS, C. W. 1965. Gibberellin research on citrus. Calif. Citrogr. 50, 457-458.

COHEN, E. and SCHIFFMANN-NADEL, M. 1978. Storage capability at different temperatures of lemons grown in Israel. Sci. Hort. 9, 251-257.

COHEN, E., WAKS, J., SARIG, Y. and NADLER, A. 1970. Picking Shamouti oranges by hand-pulling (1969/70). Rep. 677. Volcani Inst. Agr. Res., Bet Dagan, Israel. (Hebrew.)

COOPER, W. C. 1982. In Search of the Golden Apple. Vantage Press, New York.

DAVIS, P. L. 1974. Biochemical changes in grapefruit stored in air containing ethylene. Proc. Fla. State Hort. Soc. 87, 222-227.

DAVIS, P. L. and HARDING, P. L. 1960. The reduction of rind breakdown of 'Marsh' grapefruit by polyethylene emulsion treatments. Proc. Am. Soc. Hort. Sci. 75, 271-274.

DAVIS, P. L. and HOFFMAN, R.C. 1973. Reduction of chilling injury of citrus fruits in cold storage by intermittent warming. J. Food Sci. 38, 871-873.

deFOSSARD, R. A. and LENZ, F. H. 1967. Influence of nitrogen fertilization on quality, respiration and storage life of 'Washington' navel oranges. Qual. Plant. Mater. Veg. 14, 289-304.

EAKS, L. L. and MOSIAS, E. 1965. Chemical and physiological changes in lime fruits during and after storage. J. Food Sci. 30, 509-515.

ECKERT, J. W. 1978. Postharvest diseases of citrus fruits. Outlook Agr. 9, 225-232.

EL-ZEFTAWI, B. M. 1982. Response of 'Early Imperial' mandarins to selective harvesting. J. Hort. Sci. 57, 243-246.

ERICKSON, L. C., DeWOLFE, T. A. and BRANNAMAN, B. L. 1958. Growth of some citrus fruit pathogens as affected by 2,4-D and 2,4,5-T. Bot. Gaz. 120, 31-36.

GAFFNEY, J. J. 1978. Humidity: Basic principles and measurement techniques. HortScience 13, 551-555.

GILADI, J. 1969. Performance and control of treatment of citrus fruits in packinghouses. Proc. Int. Citrus Symposium. University of California, Riverside Vol. 3, 1361-1364.

GILFILLAN, I. M., KOEKEMPER, W. and STEVENSON, J. 1973. Extension of the grapefruit harvest season with gibberellic acid. Proc. Int. Soc. Citriculture Vol. 3, 335-341.

GINSBURG, L. 1972. Personal communication. Stellenbosch, Republic of South Africa.

GRIERSON, W. 1962. Are there "weak" and "strong" crops? Prod. Mktg. 5, 31,32,34.

GRIERSON, W. 1969. Consumer packaging of citrus fruits. Int. Soc. Citriculture Vol. 3, 1389-1401.

GRIERSON, W. 1970. Prospects for controlled atmosphere storage in Florida. Sunshine State Agr. Res. Rep. 15, 8-10.

GRIERSON, W. 1971. Chilling injury in tropical and subtropical fruits. IV. The role of packaging and waxing in minimizing chilling injury of grapefruit. Proc. Trop. Reg., Am. Soc. Hort. Sci. 15, 76-88.

GRIERSON, W. 1972. Refrigeration capacity and power requirement. University of Florida IFAS, Packinghouse Newsletter 49, 2.

GRIERSON, W. 1974. Chilling injury in tropical and subtropical fruit. V. Effect of harvest date, degreening, delayed storage and peel color on chilling injury of grapefruit. Proc. Trop. Reg., Am. Soc. Hort. Sci. 18, 66-73.

GRIERSON, W. 1976. Preservation of citrus fruits. Service Application Manual, Section 7. Refrig. Serv. Engrs. Soc., Des Plaines, IL.

GRIERSON, W. 1981. Physiological disorders of citrus fruits. Proc. Int. Soc. Citriculture Vol. 2, 764-767.

GRIERSON, W. 1987. Relation of handling to decay of Florida oranges in transit and on the market. Univ. Fla. IFAS Packinghouse Newsletter No. 150.

GRIERSON, W. 1995. Late season storage & export: How to make some money or lose a bundle. Citrus Industry Mag. 76(12), 34-38.

GRIERSON, W. 1999A. Beneficial aspects of stress on plants. Chap. 56, pp. 1194-1195. In M. Pessarakli (Editor), Handbook of Plant and Crop Stress. Marcel Dekker, New York and Basel.

GRIERSON, W. 1999B. How to pour money down the drain. Citrus Industry Mag. 89, 49, August.

GRIERSON, W. and NEWHALL, W. F. 1960. Degreening of Florida citrus fruits. Fla. Agr. Exp. Stn. Bull. 620.

GRIERSON, W. and WARDOWSKI, W. F. 1978. Relative humidity effects on the postharvest life of fruits and vegetables. HortScience 13, 22-28.

GRIERSON, W., McCORNACK, A. A. and HAYWARD, F. W. 1965. Tangerine handling. Fla. Agr. Ext. Circ. 285.

GRIERSON, W., VINES, H. M., OBERBACHER, M. F., TING, S. V. and EDWARDS, G. F. 1966. Controlled atmosphere storage of Florida and California lemons. Proc. Am. Soc. Hort. Sci. 88, 311-318.

GRIERSON-JACKSON, W. R. F. (W. GRIERSON). 1952. Cooling methods affect volatile content in storage atmosphere. Refrig. Eng. 60, 147-152.

GUTTER, Y., SHACHNAI, A., SCHIFFMANN-NADEL, M. and DINOOR, A. 1981. Chemical control in citrus of green and blue molds resistant to benzimidazoles. Phytopath. Z. 102, 127-138.

HAAS, A. R. C. 1927. Relation between fruit size and abscission of young orange fruits. Bot. Gaz. 83, 307-313.

HAAS, A. R. C. and KLOTZ, L. T. 1935. Physiological gradients in citrus fruits. Hilgardia 9, 179-217.

HARDING, P. L. and FISHER, D. F. 1945. Seasonal changes in Florida grapefruit. USDA Tech. Bull. 886.

HARDING, P. L., WINSTON, J. R. and FISHER, D. F. 1940. Seasonal changes in Florida oranges. USDA Tech. Bull. 753.

HATTON, T. T. 1980. Storage requirements of the 'Nova,' 'Page,' and 'Robinson' citrus cultivars. Proc. Fla. State Hort. Soc. 93, 309-310.

HATTON, T. T. and CUBBEDGE, R. H. 1975. Curing grapefruit prior to low temperature storage. HortScience 10, 334 (Abstr.).

HATTON, T. T. and CUBBEDGE, R. H. 1982. Reducing chilling injury in grapefruit by prestorage conditioning. USDA/ARS Advances in Agricultural Technology AAT-S-25, June.

HATTON, T. T., HEARN, J. and SMOOT, J. J. 1986. Degreening and storage of Sunburst citrus hybrid fruit. Proc. Fla. State Hort. Soc. 99, 127-128.

HATTON, T. T. and REEDER, W. F. 1968. Quality of 'Persian' limes after different packinghouse treatments and storage in various controlled atmospheres. Proc. Trop. Reg., Am. Soc. Hort. Sci. 11, 23-32.

HATTON, T. T., SMOOT, J. J. and CUBBEDGE, R. H. 1972. Influence of carbon dioxide exposure on stored mid- and late-season 'Marsh' grapefruit. Proc. Trop. Reg., Am. Soc. Hort. Sci. 16, 49-58.

HATTON, T. T., CUBBEDGE, R. H. and GRIERSON, W. 1975. Effects of prestorage carbon dioxide treatments and delayed storage on chilling injury of 'Marsh' grapefruit. Proc. Fla. State Hort. Soc. 88, 335-338.

HEARN, C. J. 1990. Degreening, color-add, and storage of Ambersweet orange fruit. Proc. Fla. State Hort. Soc. 103, 259-260.

HINDS, R. H., JR. 1970. Transporting fresh fruits and vegetables overseas. USDA Agr. Res. Serv. 52-39.

HOPKINS, E. F. and LOUCKS, K. W. 1948. A curing procedure for the reduction of mold decay in citrus fruits. Fla. Agr. Exp. Stn. Bull. 450.

HOPKINS, E. F. and McCORNACK, A. A. 1960. Effect of delayed handling and other factors on rind breakdown and decay in oranges. Proc. Fla. State Hort. Soc. 73, 263-269.

ISMAIL, M. A. and BROWN, G. E. 1975. Phenolic content during healing of 'Valencia' orange peel under high humidity. J. Am. Soc. Hort. Sci. 100, 249-251.

ISMAIL, M. A. and BROWN, G. E. 1979. Postharvest wound healing in citrus fruit: induction of phenylalanine ammonia-lyase in injured 'Valencia' orange flavedo. J. Am. Soc. Hort. Sci. 104, 126-129.

ISMAIL, M. A. and GRIERSON, W. 1977. Chilling injury of grapefruit: Modification by pre- and postharvest application of growth regulators. HortScience 12, 118-120.

ISMAIL, M. A., HATTON, T. T., DEZMAN, D. J. and MILLER, W. R. 1986. In transit cold treatment of Florida grapefruit shipped to Japan in refrigerated van containers: problems and recommendations. Proc. Fla. State Hort. Soc. 99, 117-121.

ISMAIL, M. A. and WILHITE, D. L. 1992. Effect of gibberellic acid and postharvest storage on quality of Florida navel oranges. Proc. Fla. State Hort. Soc. 105, 168-173.

KADER, A. A. (Editor). 1992. Postharvest Technology of Horticultural Crops, 2nd Edition. University of California Div. Agr. and Nat. Sci., Special Pub. 3311.

KAUFMANN, M. R. 1970. Water potential components in growing citrus fruits. Plant Physiol. 46, 145-149.

KAUFMANN, J., HARDENBURG, R. E. and LUTZ, J. M. 1956. Weight losses and decay of Florida and California oranges in mesh and perforated consumer bags. Proc. Am. Soc. Hort. Sci. 67, 244-250.

KAWADA, K. and ALBRIGO, L. G. 1979. Effects of film packaging, in-carton air filters, and storage temperatures on the keeping quality of Florida grapefruit. Proc. Fla. State Hort. Soc. 92, 200-212.

KAWADA, K. and HALE, P. W. 1980. Effect of individual film wrapping and relative humidity on quality of Florida grapefruit and condition of fiberboard boxes in simulated export tests. Proc. Fla. State Hort. Soc. 93, 314-323.

KAWADA, K., WARDOWSKI, W. F., GRIERSON, W., ALBRIGO, L. G. and HALE, P. W. 1981. "Unipack" individually wrapped storage of citrus fruit. Proc. Int. Soc. Citriculture Vol. 2, 175.

KHALIFAH, R. A. and KUYKENDALL, J. R. 1965. Effect of maturity, storage, temperature, and prestorage treatment on storage quality of 'Valencia' oranges. Proc. Am. Soc. Hort. Sci. 86, 288-296.

KITAGAWA, H. 1980. Personal communication. Kagawa, Japan.

KURAOKA, T. 1962. Histological studies on the development of the Satsuma orange with special reference to peel-puffing. Memoirs, Ehime Univ. Sect. VI 8, 106-154.

LINCOLN, F. 1949. Investigation of the proper maturity of Tahiti limes for marketing. Proc. Fla. State Hort. Soc. 62, 232.

LIPTON, W. J. 1975. Controlled atmospheres for fresh vegetables and fruits: Why and when. In Postharvest Biology and Handling of Fruits and Vegetables, N. F. Haard and D. K. Salunkhe (Editors). AVI Publishing Co., Westport, CT.

LIPTON, W. J. and HARVEY, J. M. 1972. Compatibility of fruits and vegetables during transport in mixed loads. USDA Marketing Res. Rept. SI-48.

LUTZ, J. M. and HARDENBURG, R. E. 1968. The commercial storage of fruits, vegetables and florist and nursery stocks. USDA Agr. Handb. 66.

MANAGO, M. and OGAKI, C. 1976. Studies on the pretreatments of *Citrus unshiu*: IV. Fruit characteristics and effect of pretreatment. Kanagawa Hort. Exp. Stn. Bull. 23 [Japanese, cited from Hort. Abstr. (1978) 48, 1796].

MANAGO, M., USHIYAMA, K., YUKAWA, L., WATANABE, T. and OGAKI, C. 1978. Studies on the cold storage of satsumas by the purified air circulating system: I. Standard storage conditions and practical use of the system. Kanagawa Hort. Exp. Stn. Bull. 25 [Japanese, cited from Hort. Abstr. (1980) 50, 1465].

McCORNACK, A. A. 1966. Blossom-end clearing of grapefruit. Proc. Fla. State Hort. Soc. 79, 258-264.

McCORNACK, A. A. 1975. Postharvest weight loss of Florida citrus fruits. Proc. Fla. State Hort. Soc. 88, 33-35.

McCORNACK, A. A. 1976. Chilling injury of 'Marsh' grapefruit as influenced by diphenyl pads. Proc. Fla. State Hort. Soc. 89, 200-202.

McCORNACK, A. A. 1979. Personal communication. Lake Alfred, FL.

McDONALD, R. E. and WUTSCHER, H. K. 1974. Rootstocks affect postharvest decay of grapefruit. HortScience 9, 455-456.

McGLASSON, W. B. and EAKS, L. L. 1972. A role of ethylene in the development of wastage and off-flavors in stored 'Valencia' oranges. HortScience 7, 80-81.

McGREGOR, B. M. 1987. Tropical Products Transport Handbook. U.S. Dept. Agr. Handbook No. 668.

MEREDITH, D. 1973. The Humi-fresh system. Design and operating experience. Symposium on Relative Humidity and the Storage of Fresh Fruits and Vegetables: Recent Research and Developments, Am. Soc. Heat., Refrig., Air Cond. Engrs. 29-34.

MILLER, W. R. and McDONALD, R. E. 1989. Condition of waxed or film-wrapped Minneola tangerines after storage. Proc. Fla. State Hort. Soc. 102, 190-192.

MILLER, W. R. and McDONALD, R. E. 1992. Condition of preharvest GA-treated grapefruit after cold treatment and storage. Proc. Fla. State Hort. Soc. 105, 116-119.

MILLER, W. M., WARDOWSKI, W. F. and GRIERSON, W. 2001. Packingline machinery for Florida citrus packinghouses. Ext. Bull. 239.

MONSELISE, S. P. 1973A. Growth regulators used to extend picking season of grapefruits. Proc. Int. Soc. Citriculture Vol. 2, 393-398.

MONSELISE, S. P. 1973B. Fruit quality in citrus and the effect of growth regulators. Acta Hort. 34, 457-1168.

MONSELISE, S. P. 1981. Effects of climatic districts, orchard treatments and seal packaging on citrus fruit quality and storage ability. Proc. Int. Soc. Citriculture Vol. 2, 705-709.

MONSELISE, S. P. and SASSON, A. 1977. Effects of orchard treatments on orange fruit quality and storage ability. Proc. Int. Soc. Citriculture Vol. 1, 232-237.

MURATA, T. 1977. Studies on the postharvest physiology and storage of citrus fruit: VII. Acid metabolism in satsuma fruit during storage. J. Japan Soc. Hort. Sci. 46, 283-287.

NORMAN, S. M. and HOUCK, L. 1977. The role of volatiles in storage of citrus fruits. Proc. Int. Soc. Citriculture, Vol. 1, 238-242.

OGAKI, C. and MANAGO, M. 1977. Studies on the controlled atmosphere storage of 'Satsuma' mandarin (*Citrus unshiu* Marc.). Proc. Int. Soc. Citriculture Vol. 3, 1127-1133.

PANTASTICO, E. G., SOULE, J. and GRIERSON, W. 1968. Chilling injury in tropical and subtropical fruits. II. Limes and grapefruit. Proc. Trop. Reg., Am. Soc. Hort. Sci. 12, 171-183.

RAMSEY, H. J. 1902. Relation of handling to decay of Florida oranges in transit and on the market. Proc. Fla. State Hort. Soc. 25, 28-42. 1912.

RIVERO, L. G., GRIERSON, W. and SOULE, J. 1979. Resistance of 'Marsh' grapefruit to deformation as affected by picking and handling methods. J. Am. Soc. Hort. Sci. 104, 551-554.

SASSON, A. and MONSELISE, S. P. 1977. Organic acid composition of 'Shamouti' oranges at harvest and during prolonged storage. J. Am. Soc. Hort. Sci. 102, 331-336.

SCHIFFMANN-NADEL, M. 1977. Chemical and physiological changes in citrus fruits during storage and their relation to fungal infection. Proc. Int. Soc. Citriculture Vol. 1, 311-317.

SCHIFFMANN-NADEL, M., CHALUTZ, E., WAKS, J. and DAGAN, M. 1975. Reduction of chilling injury in grapefruit by thiabendazole and benomyl during tong-term storage. J. Am. Soc. Hort. Sci. 100, 270-272.

SCHIFFMANN-NADEL, M., CHALUTZ, E. and WAKS, J. 1980. Postharvest grapefruit: Its treatment and storage. Fruit and Vegetable Storage Dept., Volcani Agr. Res. Orgn. Bet Dagan, Israel (Hebrew).

SCHIFFMANN-NADEL, M., WAKS, J., GUTTER, Y. and CHALUTZ, E. 1981. *Alternaria* rot of citrus fruit. Proc. Int. Soc. Citriculture Vol. 2, 791-793.

SHOMER, I. and FAHN, A. 1976. Structure and development of juice sacs in citrus fruits Proc. VI European Cong. on Electron Microscopy. Jerusalem. 470-471.

SINCLAIR, W. B. and JOLLIFFE, V. A. 1958. Free galacturonic acid in citrus fruits. Bot. Gaz. 120, 117-121.

SMOCK, R. M. 1979. Controlled atmosphere storage of fruit. Hort. Rev. 1, 301-336.

SMOOT, J. J. 1969. Decay of Florida citrus fruits stored in controlled atmosphere and in air. Proc. First Int. Citrus Symp. Vol. 3, 1285-1293.

SMOOT, L. J. 1977. Factors affecting market diseases of Florida citrus fruits. Proc. Int. Soc. Citriculture Vol. 1, 250-254.

SMOOT, J.J. and MELVIN, C.F. 1961. Effect of injury and fruit maturity on susceptibility of Florida citrus fruit to green mold. Proc. Fla. State Hort. Soc. 74, 285-287.

SMOOT, J. J. and MELVIN, C. F. 1975. Market quality of citrus fruits dropped to the ground for harvesting. Proc. Fla. State Hort. Soc. 88, 276-280.

SMOOT, J. J., HOUCK, L. G. and JOHNSON, H. B. 1971. Market diseases of citrus and other subtropical fruits. USDA Agr. Handb. 398.

SPALDING, D. H. and REEDER, W. F. 1976. Low pressure (hypobaric) storage of limes. J. Am. Soc. Hort. Sci. 101, 367-370.

SRIVASTAVA, H. C. and MATHUR, P. B. 1954. Semi-commercial trial on the cold storage of Coorg oranges. Bull. Cent. Food Technol. Res. Inst. (Mysore, India) 3, 248-249.

STAHL, A. L. and FIFIELD, W. M. 1936. Cold storage studies of Florida citrus fruits. II. Effects of various wrappers and temperatures on the preservation of citrus fruits in storage. University of Florida Agr. Exp. Stn. Bull. 304.

STAHL, A. L. and VAUGHAN, P. J. 1942. Pliofilm in the preservation of Florida fruits and vegetables. Univ. Fla. Agr. Exp. Stn. Bull. 369.

TANAKA, S. H., KITAJIMA, H., YAMADA, S., KISHI, K. and KAKAJIMA, S. 1957. Studies on the control of citrus fruit decay in storage. V. Survey of fruit decay of Satsuma orange in storage. (2). Hort. Div. Nat. Tokai-Kinki Agr. Exp. Stn. Bull. (Japanese with English summary).

TUGWELL, B. L. and GILLESPIE, K. 1981. Australian experience with citrus fruits wrapped in high density polyethylene film. Proc. Int. Soc. Citriculture Vol. 2, 710-714.

VAKIS, N., GRIERSON, W. and SOULE, J. 1970. Chilling injury in tropical and subtropical fruits. III. The role of CO_2 in suppressing chilling injury of grapefruit and avocados. Proc. Trop. Reg., Am. Soc. Hort. Sci. 14, 89-100.

VINES, H. M., GRIERSON, W. and EDWARDS, G. J. 1968. Respiration, internal atmosphere and ethylene evolution of citrus fruits. Proc. Am. Soc. Hort. Sci. 92, 227-234.

WAKS, J. 1981. Personal communication. Bet Dagan, Israel.

WAKS, J., CHALUTZ, E. and FELZENSTEIN, G. 1979. Evaporative cooling of citrus fruit prior to packing. Hassadeh 59, 1169-1172 (Hebrew).

WAKS, J., GISSER, A. and CHALUTZ, E. 1981. Ventilation of grapefruit under prolonged storage. Volcani Inst. for Agr. Res. Orgn., Bet Dagan, Israel (Hebrew).

WARDOWSKI, W. F. and BONNELL, J. M. 1973. Observations on citrus in China. Proc. Fla. State Hort. Soc. 96, 361-366.

WARDOWSKI, W. F., GRIERSON, W. and EDWARDS, G. J. 1973. Chilling injury of stored limes and grapefruit as affected by differentially permeable packaging films. HortScience 8, 173-175.

WARDOWSKI, W. F., ALBRIGO, L. G., GRIERSON, W., BARMORE, C. R. and WHEATON, T. A. 1975. Chilling injury and decay of grapefruit as affected by thiabendazole, benomyl and CO_2. HortScience 10, 381-383.

WARDOWSKI, W. F., WHIGHAM, J., GRIERSON, W. and SOULE, J. 1995. Quality tests for Florida citrus. University of Florida IFAS SP 99.

WELLS, A. W. 1962. Effects of storage temperature and humidity on loss of weight by fruit. USDA, Agr. Marketing Serv. Manual Res. Rept. 539.

WILD, B. L., McGLASSON, W. B. and LEE, T. H. 1977. Ethylene in CA long term lemon storage. Proc. Int. Soc. Citriculture Vol. 1, 259-263.

Energy in Citrus Packing

William M. Miller and R. Paul Singh

The increased productivity of United States agriculture has been coupled with a high dependence on fossil fuel energy, especially energy from natural gas and petroleum. This dependence also has evolved in postharvest handling, packaging, storage, and transportation of fruits and vegetables. In fact, demands for year-round uniform produce have escalated energy requirements in long distance transportation and long-term storage. Estimates for the amount of energy used in the food production and delivery system range from 12 to 17% of the total U.S. energy use (Hirst 1974; FEA 1976). Such estimates vary depending on inclusion or exclusion of off-site energy utilization for operating and capital items. Over one-half of the energy was required beyond the farm gate for marketing, processing, and distribution (Van Arsdall 1976).

ENERGY USAGE IN PRODUCING CITRUS FOR FRESH MARKET

Reitz (1980) quantified production and harvesting energy for irrigated Florida grapefruit managed for fresh market. He found that total energy for irrigated fresh citrus was 1.68 times that for nonirrigated processing grapefruit. Additionally, labor requirements for irrigated, fresh market production were 225 hr/ha compared with 183 hr/ha for processing fruit. Grove heating was not included in the analysis, but energy use during one cold night exceeds the combined production and harvesting energy utilization for an entire year.

Griffiths (1976) collected data on picking and hauling citrus to both packing and processing plants. Average consumption of diesel fuel was 0.0036 liter/kg fruit for pick and roadside hauling plus 0.0096 liter/kg fruit for over-the-road hauling. A liter of diesel fuel has a heat energy content of approximately 37,900 kJ.

Beyond the packinghouse, the principal energy inputs are for storage and transportation. Although rail transport may return to favor, the predominant mode for U.S. fresh fruit and vegetable transportation is refrigerated truck. Barton (1980) found that trucks accounted for 72% of fruit and vegetable transportation expressed as ton-miles. He further estimated diesel fuel consumption at 0.36 liter/km for an unloaded tractor-trailer and 0.59 liter/km for loaded conditions. Additionally, fuel consumption for a refrigerated trailer averages 2.1-2.8 liter/day (Miller *et al.* 1982). In the winter season, comparable quantities of fuel are consumed in preventing the freezing of fresh commodities.

Energy data with regard to wholesale/retail marketing and home consumer are very sparse for citrus or other fresh fruits and vegetables. Zhang and Groll (2000) have addressed design parameters to lower electrical costs in refrigerated warehouses. Faramarzi (1999) performed a thermal analyses of open refrigerated display cases noting infiltration as the principal factor. Such figures reflect indirect energy, e.g., construction of supermarkets and refrigerators, plus the direct energy required for materials handling and food shopping via automobile. The FEA (1976) estimates that transportation related to in-home food preparation accounts for about 4% of the food system energy consumption, or 0.7% of total U.S. energy use. Consumers and government agencies have become cognizant of the interrelationship of food quality and safety with optimal refrigerated storage. For example, food display case temperatures are regulated through FDA's food code (Faramarzi and Woodworth 1997).

ENERGY SURVEY FOR CITRUS PACKING

Packinghouses link the movement of fresh citrus fruit from grove to consumer. At the packinghouse, grading and government inspection are performed to meet quality standards; discarded fruit, ultimately used for juice and by-products, is stored for transport to processing plants. Acceptable fruit undergoes washing, waxing, fungicide treatment, and containerization. Following the general escalation in fuel prices, concerns about energy use in packing fruit have increased. Citrus packers must compete with processors for a grower's fruit. Since higher energy inputs and costs are generally associated with growing citrus for the fresh fruit market, a grower expects a higher return to maintain an equivalent profit margin. Also, it is more difficult to pass along higher operating costs because the bulk of fresh citrus is marketed immediately upon packing, thus eliminating the economic advantage associated with storing produce for anticipated higher prices. Vulnerability to interruptions of fuel supplies, either on- or off-site, constitutes another major concern. Thompson (2001) has addressed various design elements to plan for electrical interruptions.

Since commercial citrus production in the United States is limited to Arizona, California, Florida, and Texas, transportation of citrus to consumers throughout the United States and to international markets requires significant amounts of energy. Hence, the trend must be toward more efficient delivery systems as opposed to a nationwide diffuse production scenario.

Baseline energy utilization data for citrus packing have been obtained in Florida by mail surveys of individual packers (Wardowski and Miller 1979; Miller *et al.* 1982) and in California through questionnaires (Mayou and Singh 1980) and unit operation energy estimates (Naughton *et al.* 1979). Some unit operations vary significantly between California and Florida. For example, California coloring and storage recommendations are 14°-15°C for lemons and 21°-22°C for degreening oranges. These temperatures make refrigerated storage a significant energy consideration. In contrast, Florida degreening of citrus requires space heating, with some fruit undergoing a red dye color process in a heated bath (Grierson *et al.* 1978). Recommended temperature for Florida degreening is 29.5°C and maximum color-add temperatures are set at 46°-49°C.

Secondary energy inputs were not calculated for either the California or Florida studies. Therefore, the energy associated with operating materials (cartons, fungicides, waxes) or capital items (buildings, machinery) was not included. Although the energy related to such items may be significant, such estimates are difficult to obtain and they do not follow the general accounting classification of packinghouse management.

California Studies

Three citrus districts were identified in the California survey. The three districts had in excess of 134,000 ha in bearing and nonbearing groves and produced over 2.6×109 kg of citrus fruit during the 1976-1977 crop year.

In late 1977, a questionnaire was mailed to 21 citrus packing plants in California, and 17 plants responded. The total production of these plants accounted for 24% of the total citrus production in California during the 1976-1977 crop year. In all plants surveyed, the largest percentage of dollars spent on utilities was for electric consumption. All but one plant used natural gas for heating air and water. Heated air is used to remove surface moisture from the fruit, and heated water is used to clean the fruit. Only low-grade heat is required, since water and air temperatures do not exceed 40° and 70°C, respectively.

The data collected for energy use and production were used to calculate energy intensities for the different plants in each district. To account for the inefficiency of electrical power generation, a conversion factor of 11.08 MJ/kWh (10,500 Btu/kWh) was used. Average energy intensities for plants surveyed by district and plant type are given in Table 21.1. Electrical power intensities varied from 163.3 kJ/kg to 583.8 kJ/kg and natural gas unit consumption levels from 53.9 kJ/kg to 159.8 kJ/kg.

The average energy intensities of orange packing indicate that energy consumption was higher in central California than in southern California. Because the harvest time for Valencia oranges is in May-November, degreening and precooling costs in central California, where ambient temperatures are quite high

TABLE 21.1. Average Energy Intensities for California Citrus Packing, 1976-1977

District/fruit	Electrical power (kJ/kg)	Natural gas (kJ/kg)
Central California		
Oranges-grapefruit	480.9	159.8
Southern California		
Oranges-grapefruit	163.3	53.9
Lemons	515.6	135.9
Oranges-grapefruit-lemons	583.8	135.9
Arizona-California desert		
Oranges-grapefruit-lemons	297.6	107.2

Source: Mayou and Singh (1980).

during summer, are greater than in southern California; in addition, the refrigerated holding costs are higher for the central valley during summer. Similar to electric consumption, the natural gas consumption in central California is higher than that in southern California. Navel oranges harvested during November-June require more heat for surface moisture removal in foggy winter days in the central valley. The energy requirements for lemon packing were almost twice those of orange packing. Lemon packing requires storage for up to 4 months in comparison to a short holding period of 2 to 3 weeks for orange packing. These trends were identified in all plants studied.

Florida Studies

In a 1981 survey (Miller *et al.* 1982), a questionnaire was sent to the 85 members of the Florida Citrus Packers who collectively ship 95% of Florida's fresh citrus. Sixty-nine percent of the citrus packinghouses handling large volumes of fruit ($\geq 22.5 \times 10^6$ kg) responded to the questionnaire. The largest packinghouse reporting for the 2-year study packed an average of 48.8×10^6 kg fruit for the two seasons. However, 60% of the firms packed between 0.6×10^6 and 15.1×10^6 kg. The average fruit mass packed for all respondents was 16.1×10^6 kg. Actual incoming fruit throughputs were substantially higher than volume packed because the average pack-out was 66.9% for the seasons included in this study (Hooks and Kilmer 1980). Typically, the packing season extends from September to May with 1200-1400 hr of operation per year.

Three principal energy categories were identified: electricity, boiler fuel (either fuel oil or natural gas), and refined fuels (either gasoline or LP gas). Electricity is used primarily for lighting and packingline machinery, whereas forklift trucks consume gasoline or LP gas in handling both incoming fruit and pallet loads of carton-packed fruit. Some packers used both fuel oil and natural gas for boilers with fuel oil as a reserve for interruptible natural gas service. Only one packer used both gasoline and LP gas for forklift trucks. The breakdown between on-site fossil fuel consumption and purchased electricity showed greater on-site energy use. It should be noted that for equivalency to fossil fuels, electrical energy values incorporated a 32.5% generation-transmission factor. On this basis, on-site fossil fuels constituted 56.1% of the total energy in packing citrus; the gasoline and LP gas fraction of this on-site fossil fuel use was 11.4% (Table 21.2).

Florida results are more comparable to California orange packing than lemon packing due to the minimal refrigeration employed for oranges. Boiler-related energy consumption was significantly higher in Florida. This can be traced to the additional color-add and degreening processes, plus higher humidity levels that retard surface drying. ASHRAE (1997) winter design dry bulb and mean coincident wet-bulb conditions for Ontario, California, and Orlando, Florida, result in drying potentials expressed as humidity ratio differences of 0.0074 and 0.0042 kg/kg, respectively. Greater efficiency with larger operations has usually been considered to exist for many industries. However, a significant linear regression relationship existed only for fuel oil plus natural gas versus packinghouse throughput in this study. Certain large packers had switched from oil to natural gas boilers to take advantage of the price disparity between these fuel sources. Hence, upgraded boiler facilities, affordable to larger packers, may be an attributable factor to the boiler fuel-packinghouse volume relationship.

Change in the volume of fruit packed between the two seasons resulted in a highly significant change in unit energy consumption (Fig. 21.1). This relationship indicated the potential for reduced unit energy consumption through maximum productivity and optimum scheduling. Seasonal factors affecting fruit maturity and market prices would also have to be considered. However, some cooperatives must run below maximum capacity because of limited fruit supply from cooperative members.

ENERGY AUDITING

Standard methodology for conducting energy audits is currently evolving. Whitehead and Shupe (1980) presented a review on electrical energy audits, and a detailed discussion on electrical motor efficiency was prepared by the DOE (1980). Efficiencies of boiler combustion and steam generation were considered by Troeger (1977) while Singh (1980) cited various steam flow measurement techniques. An overall approach to energy auditing in industrial plants with emphasis on critical factors dependent on the audit goals has been developed (Anon. 1981). Pre-cooling facilities have been introduced to immediately cool citrus to mitigate peel disorders and reduce weight loss. Gaffney and Baird (1991) have estimated the costs of an optimal installation at 0.4 to 0.64/kg of product cooled assuming power costs at $0.10/kw hour.

Jarrett and Tugwell (1975) have outlined principles relevant to fresh citrus packing. Grierson et al. (1978) developed procedures for determining

TABLE 21.2. Average Energy Source Utilization in Florida Citrus Packing, 1978-1980

Source	Energy use (kJ/kg)
Electricity	321.3[a]
Fuel oil and/or natural gas	313.3
LP gas and/or gasoline	40.1
Total energy	630.2[b]

Source: Miller *et al.* (1982).
[a]Incorporates a 32.5% electrical generation-transmission efficiency.
[b]Total is not equivalent to summation of individual energy sources due to incomplete reporting of some packers.

packingline capacity and discussed equipment design considerations. They note that energy utilization can be markedly improved by discarding both fruit to be processed and unwholesome fruit before the majority of packinghouse unit operations.

Specific Study

Singh (1978) proposed standard procedures to identify and quantify energy and mass flow in food processing operations. This approach was undertaken for two California packinghouses: one for oranges and the second for lemons.

Orange packing consisted of seven primary operations: unload/dump, degreening, wash/wax, sort/size, pack/seal, holding, and the juice system. Using energy accounting symbols presented by Singh (1978), an energy and mass flow diagram (Fig. 21.2) was constructed for an individual packinghouse denoted Plant A. Electrical energy and natural gas consumptions were assigned to each functional unit. On an annual basis, degreening/precooling was the most energy-consuming operation in Plant A since it had a greater proportion of motors and operated twice as many hours as the other plants. It should be noted that in packing plants where precooling is not done, this operation will be less energy consuming.

Lemon packing consists of ten primary operations: unload/dump I, wash/wax/ dry I, sort/size I, storage, unload/dump II, wash/wax/dry II, sort/size II, pack/seal, juice system, and maintenance system. The basic material and energy flow structure within a lemon packing plant (Plant C) is shown in Fig. 21.3. Outstanding energy-consuming operations include both wash/wax/dry units along with the storage area.

Available Energy Analysis

Both first and second law efficiencies of citrus packinghouse operations are summarized in Table 21.3. Efficiency levels for electric motors are biased upward as optimal conditions were assumed, i.e., 100% load with

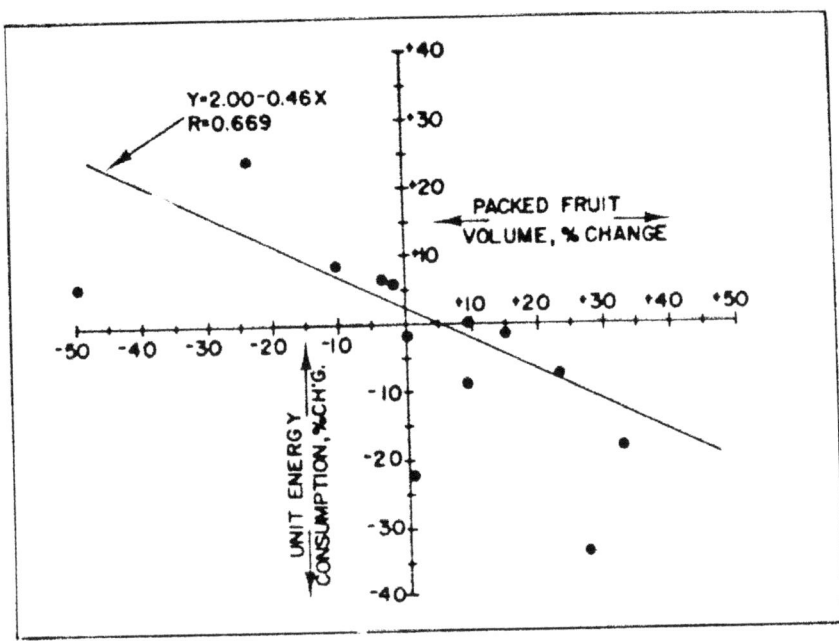

Fig. 21.1. Relationship of unit energy consumption and packinghouse production.
From Miller et al. *(1982).*

proper lubrication and maintenance. Boiler operations were considered separately. To estimate the overall efficiency for an in-plant steam process, the product of the unit operation and boiler efficiencies is computed. For example, surface drying citrus combined with a boiler source at 690 kPa has a resultant second law efficiency of 0.01 (0.26 × 0.04). Subsystem efficiencies, such as that for heat transfer in heating air or water, were not calculated. Shinskey (1978) has made second law determinations for both isothermal and nonisothermal heat transfer.

The very low second law efficiencies for all thermal processes indicates the potential for better energy utilization within packing plants. Energy conservation techniques such as air recycling and proper insulation require optimization and implementation. Further heat extraction from steam is possible by using steam condensate for low-temperature color-add and degreening room heating. The low efficiencies for drying, liquid heating, and space heating are commonplace. Berg (1974) cites values <0.25 for kiln operations, <0.10 for water heating, and <0.07 for residential space heating.

This availability analysis disregards process options that might be developed. In fruit drying, water can be removed mechanically (Miller 1978 1986) with appreciably less energy. Also, utilization of high-solids wax emul-

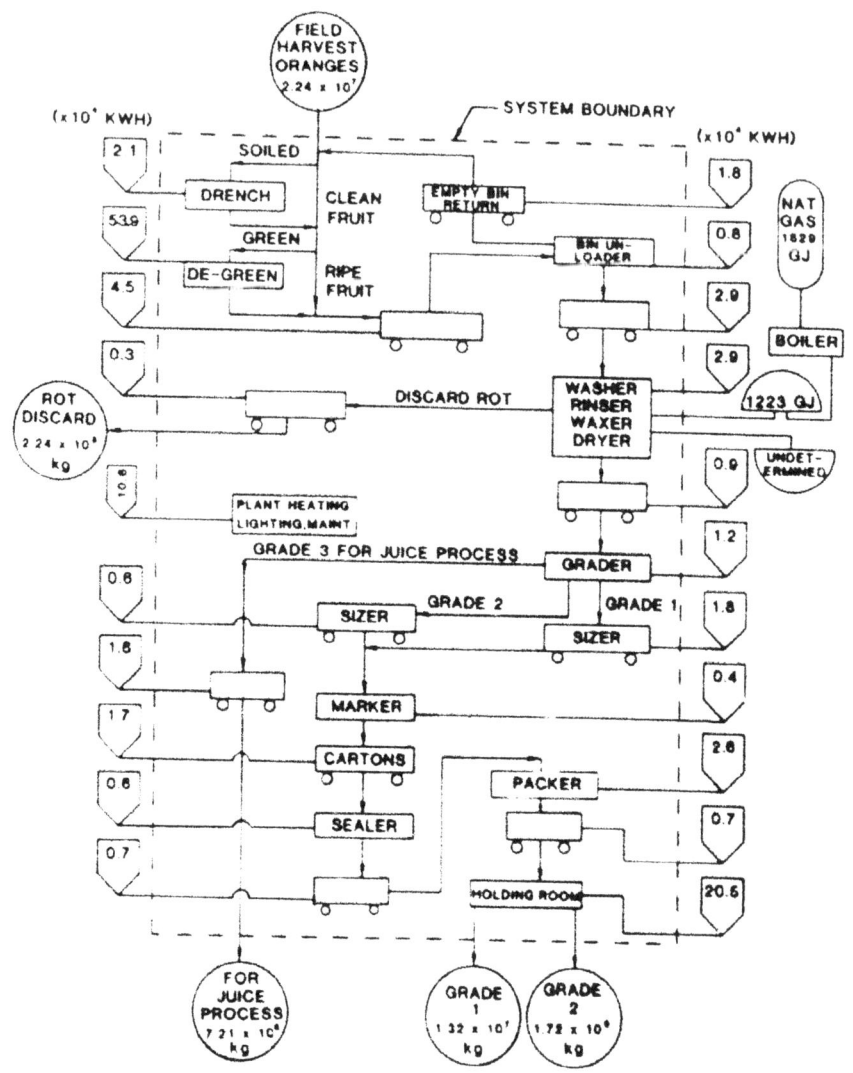

Fig. 21.2. Material and energy flow chart for California orange packing. *From Naughton et al. (1979).*

sions may reduce the water vaporization load. Potential for gravity fruit flow and passive solar technology should be considered with new packinghouse installations. Active solar has advantages when only low-grade process energy is required (Miller *et al.* 1977; Kreith and Kreider 1978).

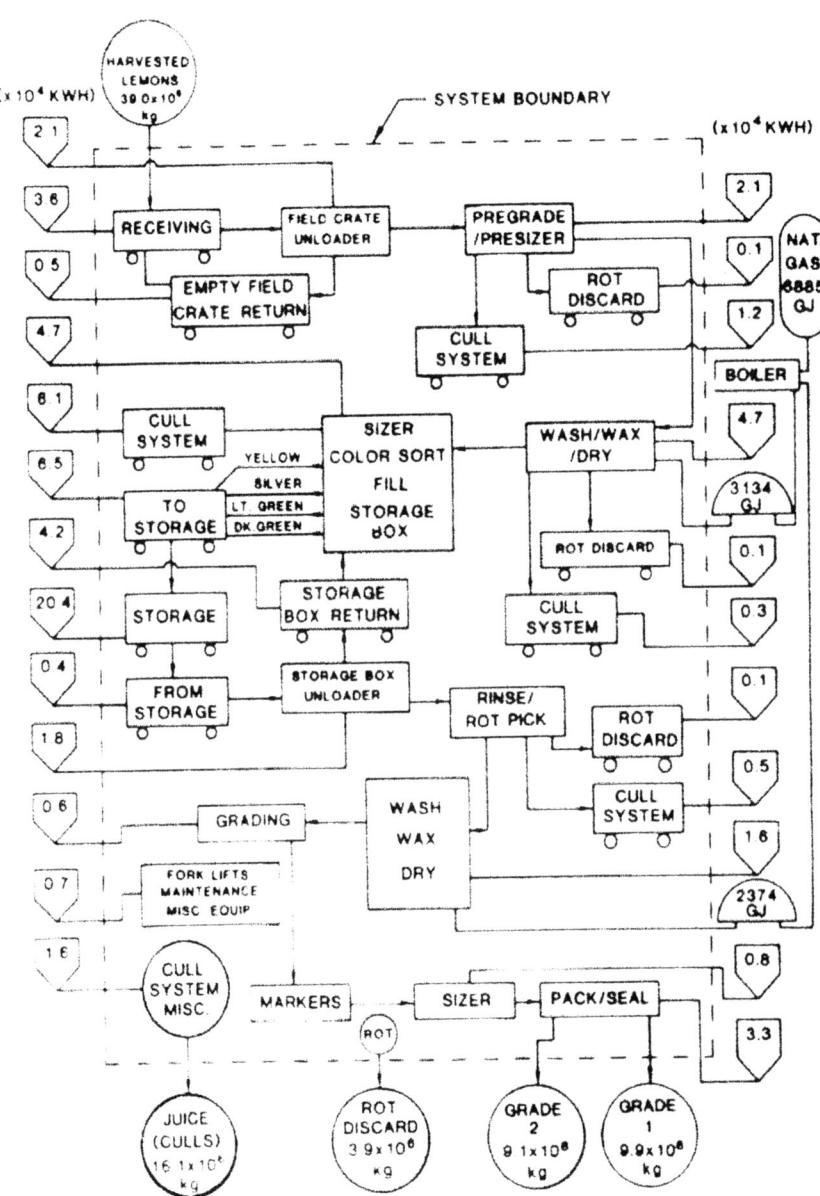

Fig. 21.3. Material and energy flow chart for California lemon packing.
From Naughton et al. *(1979).*

TABLE 21.3. First and Second Law Thermodynamic Efficiencies for Citrus Packing-house Operations

Component	First law efficiency	Second law efficiency[a]
Boiler at 690 kPa	0.88[b]	0.26
Surface drying	0.42[c]	0.04
Color-add operation	0.09[d]	0.01
Degreening space heating	0.70[b]	0.03
Lighting[e]		
Incandescent	0.05	0.05 (0.02)
Mercury vapor	0.15	0.14 (0.04)
Fluorescent	0.21	0.20 (0.06)
Metal halide	0.22	0.21 (0.06)
High-pressure sodium	0.32	0.30 (0.09)
Electric motor		
Small (<3.7 kW)	0.80	0.80 (0.25)
Large (>3.7 kW)	0.90	0.90 (0.28)
Forklift, gasoline powered	0.25	0.25

[a]Numbers in parentheses incorporate 32.5% electrical generation-transmission efficiency.
[b]Reistad (1980).
[c]Based on Miller (1978).
[d]Based on 10% in-service factor and 0.5 g emulsion uptake/fruit at 48°C.
[e]Based on lumen output/wattage from Grainger (1980) and Summers (1971).

Heat pump and refrigeration cycles could be integrated to provide both heating and cooling needs. For example in California, hot water is required in citrus packing to wash the fruit prior to waxing. Large open tanks are maintained at 38°C by the use of steam-heat exchangers. The energy required to heat water can be supplied through the use of heat presently dissipated at the condenser of the refrigeration system (Mayou and Singh 1980). Energy available exceeds that which is necessary to maintain the wash tank water temperature. Additional energy could be used to preheat incoming air to the dryers or provide hot water for general plant cleanup. The recoverable heat that is not used either for heating water or air would be dissipated in the condenser of the present system. However, parasitic energy for pumping heated water must he considered and condenser location becomes critical.

Overall, packinghouse steam process operations have a large potential for improved energy utilization. A second law analysis tends to direct energy utilization improvement toward the packinghouse as opposed to electrical generation facilities. Fruit drying, which accounts for substantially more operating hours per year than degreening or color-add operations, merits primary attention. Unless unit operations are altered, efficiencies of mechanical drive tasks and lighting are limited by the electrical generation

TABLE 21.4. Energy Input for Harvesting, Handling, Packing, and Transporting Florida Fresh Citrus

Operation	Estimated energy input (kJ/kg)
Field production	402.7[a]
Field-to-packinghouse transport	507.5[b]
Packing	630.2
Transport to market	1705.1[c]
Temperature control	310.7[c]

[a]Reitz (1980), direct energy only.
[b]Griffiths (1976).
[c]Based on 1600-km, 54-hr trip.

efficiency and required capital expenditures for high-efficiency motors and more effective lighting.

OVERALL ENERGY PROJECTIONS

Direct energy inputs for various sectors in handling fresh citrus are compiled in Table 21.4. Estimates were based on Florida studies and energy input values were not included for distribution to retailers and consumer transportation. An average 1600-km, 54-hr trip was assumed for domestic shipments. This transportation sector was the major element in energy consumption with packing energy second.

Economic implications are usually cited as the driving force in altering energy consumption patterns both in the United States and worldwide. However, the direct energy in citrus packing constituted less than 6% of the cost incurred in packing Florida citrus. Incorporating field production and tree-to-packinghouse energy costs, direct energy costs for a packed carton constituted 3.2% of the commodity price.

Because energy costs represent a relatively small portion of the total costs of packed citrus, major changes in packing operations based on energy economics are not anticipated. Major impetus will probably arise from schedule interruptions due to fuel unavailability, as such interruptions directly affect all packing operations and could result in severe marketing losses.

REFERENCES

ANON. 1981. Guide to plant energy auditing. Plant Eng. 35, 137-159.
ASHRAE. 1997. Fundamentals. Am. Soc. Heating, Refrigerating and Air Conditioning Engr. New York.
BARTON, J. A. 1980. Transportation fuel requirements in the food and fiber system. USDA Agric. Econ. Rept. 444. Washington, DC.
BERG, C. A. 1974. A technical basis for energy conservation. Mech. Engr. 96, 30-42.
DOE. 1980. Energy efficient electric motors. DOE/CS-0163. U.S. Dept. of Energy, Oak Ridge, TN.

FARAMARZI, R. and WOODWORTH, M. 1997. Colder temperatures in display cases. ASHRAE Journal 39(12), 35-39.

FARAMARZI, P. E. 1999. Efficient display case refrigeration. Practical Guide. November 46-54.

FEA. 1976. Energy use in the food system. Federal Energy Admin., Office of Industrial Programs, Washington, DC.

GAFFNEY, J. J. and BAIRD, C. D. 1991. Factors affecting the costs of forced-air cooling of fruits and vegetables. ASHRAE Journal 33(1), 40-49.

GRAINGER. 1980. Grainger Motorbook Catalog. W. W. Grainger, Inc., Chicago, IL.

GRIERSON, W., MILLER, W. M. and WARDOWSKI, W. F. 1978. Packingline machinery for Florida citrus packinghouses. Univ. Fla. Agric. Exp. Stn. Bull 803.

GRIFFITHS, J. T. 1976. Calculating fuel requirements. Citrus Ind. 57, 26-38.

HIRST, E. 1974. Food-related energy requirements. Science 184, 134-138.

HOOKS, R. C. and KILMER, R. L. 1980. Estimated costs of packing and selling fresh Florida citrus. 1978-79. IFAS, University of Florida Econ. Inf. Rep-133.

JARRETT, L. D. and TUGWELL. B. L. 1975. Post-harvest handling of citrus fruit. Spec. Bull. 11.75. Dept. of Agriculture and Fisheries, South Australia.

KREITH, F. and KREIDER, J. F. 1978. Principles of Solar Energy. McGraw-Hill, New York.

MAYOU, L. P. and SINGH, R. P. 1980. Energy use profiles in citrus packing plants in California. Trans. ASAE 23, 234.

MILLER, W. M. 1978. Surface moisture drying analysis of citrus fruit. Trans. ASAE 21, 1237.

MILLER, W. M. 1986. Mechanical dewatering techniques for fresh citrus. Energy in Agriculture 5, 225-238.

MILLER, W. M., WARDOWSKI. W. F. and BAIRD, C. D. 1977. Solar energy utilization in citrus packinghouse operations. Proc. Int. Soc. Citriculture Vol. 1, 304-308.

MILLER. W. M., WARDOWSKI, W. F. and NAGY. S. 1982. Trends in energy use of Florida citrus packinghouses. Food Technol. 36(5), 227-230.

NAUGHTON, M., SINGH, R. P., HARDT, P. and RUMSEY. T. R. 1979. Energy use in citrus packing plants. Trans. ASAE 22, 441.

REISTAD, G. M. 1980. Availability-energy utilization in the U.S. *In* Thermodynamics: Second Law Analysis, R. A. Gaggioli (Editor). ACS Symp. Series 122. Washington, DC.

REITZ, H. J. 1980. Energy use in U.S. citrus production and harvesting. *In* Handbook of Energy Utilization in Agriculture, D. Pimentel (Editor), CRC Press, Boca Raton, FL.

SHINSKEY, F. G. 1978. *Energy Conservation Through Control.* Academic Press, New York.

SINGH, R. P. 1978. Energy accounting in food process operations. Food Technol. 32, 40-46.

SINGH, R. P. 1980. Methods for determining steam utilization in food processing plants. Pap. No. 80-6552 Am. Soc. Agric. Eng., St. Joseph, MI.

SUMMERS, C. M. 1971. The conversion of energy. Sci. Am. 224(3), 149-160.

THOMPSON, J. 2001. Planning for a blackout. Perishable Handling Quarterly Issue No. 105, 6-7.

TROEGER, W. A. 1977. Electrical power and energy measurement. *In* Energy Technology Handbook, D. M. Conoidine (Editor). McGraw-Hill, New York.

VAN ARSDALL, R. T. 1976. Energy requirements in the U.S. food system. Agric. Outlook 8 (March) 18-21.

WARDOWSKI, W. F. and MILLER. W. M. 1979. Survey of energy consumption in Florida citrus packinghouses. Proc. Fla. State Hortic. Soc. 92, 175-177.

WHITEHEAD, W. K. and SHUPE, W. L. 1980. Electric energy audits in food processing facilities-A review. Pap. No. 80-6521. Amer. Soc. Agric. Eng., St. Joseph, MI.

ZHANG, J. and GROLL, E. A. 2000. Saving energy in refrigerated warehouses. ASHRAE Journal 42(8), 35-39.

Index